BCh-3rded.

LIFESTYLES *AND*
CONSUMER
BEHAVIOR OF
OLDER AMERICANS

LIFESTYLES AND CONSUMER BEHAVIOR OF OLDER AMERICANS

Howard G. Schutz
Pamela C. Baird
Glenn R. Hawkes

PRAEGER

PRAEGER SPECIAL STUDIES • PRAEGER SCIENTIFIC

Library of Congress Cataloging in Publication Data

Schutz, Howard G
   Lifestyles and consumer behavior of older
Americans.

   Bibliography: p.
   Includes index.
   1. Aged 25 consumers--United States.
2. Aged--United States. I. Baird, Pamela
C., joint author. II. Hawkes, Glenn Rogers,
1919-   joint author. III. Title.
HC110. C6S33   658.8'34   79-13212
ISBN 0-03-049821-X

The authors wish to acknowledge Elizabeth B. Hurlock,
Developmental Psychology, 4th edition, 1975:353, New York:
McGraw-Hill, appearing in Fred D. Reynolds and William D.
Wells, Consumer Behavior, McGraw-Hill Series in Marketing,
1977, Figure 7-5, p. 187.

Published in 1979 by Praeger Publishers
A Division of Holt, Rinehart and Winston/CBS, Inc.
383 Madison Avenue, New York, New York 10017 U.S.A.

© by Howard G. Schutz

9 038 987654321

Printed in the United States of America

PREFACE

It has often been pointed out in the literature that the elderly, as consumers, have until very recently been forgotten by researchers, educators, and practitioners in the fields of gerontology, consumer affairs, marketing, psychology, business, and government policy making. Because of a lack of reliable data, confusion exists as to just who the elderly are. Many take the viewpoint that those over 65 are a distinct group with its own attitudes, needs, and problems. Social workers, researchers, and government policy makers have isolated those over 65 for the purposes of study and assistance. The tendency of marketers has been to regard the elderly as a single market segment, distinguishable from other segments on the basis of age and homogeneous as a subpopulation. However, this isolation may be culturally artificial. It has been suggested by numerous authors that the older population in many ways exhibits a greater variety of lifestyles and personalities than any other category in society (Atchley 1972; Botwinick 1973; Riley, Foner, and associates 1968).

The perspective that one adopts has profound implications for the direction of public policy, the design of consumer education and protection programs for the elderly, and the efforts of marketers to meet the needs of older persons.

The purpose of this study was to define lifestyle patterns existing among older Americans empirically and to relate lifestyle quantitatively to consumer behavior in the following areas: consumer problems, buying style, store choice, income management, health care, food and nutrition, transportation, housing, and clothing. Lifestyle was conceptualized as a configuration of attitudes, activities, interests, and opinions. Consumer behavior was defined as the acts of individuals involved in obtaining and using economic and social goods and services, including the decision processes that precede and determine these acts.

The objectives were congruous with the research and development issues and goals outlined by the Administration on Aging: the need for knowledge about the characteristics, attitudes, and behaviors of older persons, including low-income, minority, and other subpopulations, which will require consideration in relation to existing and future policies and program designs; the need for knowledge of social, economic, and environmental forces that impinge on the ability of the elderly to secure and maintain "freedom, independence free exercise of individual initiative in planning and managing their own lives" (Title I, sec. 101, of the Older Americans Act); and the need for knowledge necessary for the development, organization, delivery, and coordination of service delivery systems.

Objectives for the research were formulated on the following rationale, based on a review of the literature and the investigators' previous work:

- There is a need for comprehensive, current, empirical, respondent-generated data on lifestyles among the aging. In the literature of social gerontology, one constantly finds the terms "the aged" or "older people" used as if they identified a single homogeneous category of people. In reality, however, the older population in many ways exhibits a greater variety of lifestyles, personalities, and opportunities than any other group in society. Past studies that have attempted to delineate lifestyles among the aging are very few in number, and those that do exist are dated and exhibit serious shortcomings in scope, sample selection, methodology, and generalizability.
- The consumer behavior of aging persons is poorly documented. Especially in need of attention is consumer behavior in areas crucial to the well-being of the individual.
- Research findings indicate that lifestyle variables are largely responsible for differences in economic behavior.

This study has produced empirical, respondent-generated descriptions of lifestyles and consumer behavior among aging individuals and among specific age groups, and an understanding of the critical relationship between lifestyle and consumer behavior of the aging population. It has been demonstrated that the well-being of the individual depends to a large extent on the utilization of certain social and economic goods and services, which in turn is determined by lifestyle. A better understanding of the lifestyle differences among aging individuals and among specific age groups provides implications for an improved utilization of goods and services—and, thus, an improvement in the well-being of the individual.

Information gained from the research provides knowledge for planning, policy decisions, and program design that affect the elderly. The vulnerable subpopulation groups that lack opportunity for fulfillment of the objectives of Title I have been described in order to provide greater knowledge of the social and environmental conditions that increase the vulnerability of the elderly and to assess important consumer needs of older persons by allowing for actual input from them.

This study will be of interest to government agencies: departments of consumer affairs, transportation, commerce, education, food and agriculture, health, housing development, and insurance, and offices on aging. Private-sector consumer advocacy groups, senior citizen groups, educational institutions, and providers of goods and services for the elderly should find it useful in meeting their responsibilities more effectively.

ACKNOWLEDGMENTS

We wish to express our deep gratitude to Fernne Schnitzer, who so ably assisted in the development of the lifestyle instruments used in this study; to Shirley Cramer, who compiled the review of the literature; and to Barbara McCormack, who helped in the analysis of the data. Joie B. Hubbert and the Field Research Corporation provided their expertise and time in developing the sampling procedure, training the interviewers, and gathering the data on which our findings are based.

The discussants in Sacramento who told us how they felt about aging and consumerism were essential to the orderly progression of the study. The anonymous respondents from the San Francisco Bay area were gracious in giving us their time and cooperation.

Gala Rinaldi provided invaluable editorial assistance, Hal Grade served with great skill as our computer consultant, and Joan Learned labored with great tolerance as manuscript typist.

This research was supported by Administration on Aging grant #90-A-645 and the California Agricultural Experiment Station at the University of California at Davis.

CONTENTS

LIST OF TABLES AND FIGURE

LIFESTYLES AND CONSUMER BEHAVIOR OF OLDER AMERICANS

PART I:
INTRODUCTION

1

REVIEW OF THE LITERATURE

DEFINITION, MEASUREMENT, AND SIGNIFICANCE OF LIFESTYLE

The concept of lifestyle has been recognized by behavioral scientists as an important determinant of human behavior. In 1927 the psychologist Alfred Adler coined the term "style of life" to refer to the goals a person shaped for himself or herself and the methods employed to achieve them. More recently sociologists have viewed it as a criterion for social stratification (Mayer 1955; Kahl 1965).

Approaches to the measurement of lifestyle are diverse. Subjective evaluations of intensive individual interviews were used by Richard Williams and Claudine Wirth (1965). These investigators developed the concept of "social systems" of individuals, which they defined as all the transactions of an individual in his or her social life space. The social system of an individual in his or her behavior directed toward ends, goals, and values, which in turn can be communicated to, and usually shared by, others. Both structural properties (social position, orientation to interaction, type of social relations) and functional properties (degrees of anomie, alienation, isolation, and coping) were considered. In arriving at a definition of lifestyle, each of the two authors read the same case studies and made judgments concerning the relevant variables in each case.

Value judgments were also used by Bernice Neugarten, Robert Havighurst, and Sheldon Tobin (1968) in defining a concept closely related to lifestyle that they called "patterns of aging." This concept represents a synthesis of three other concepts: social life space, life satisfaction, and personality type, based on an ego–psychology model.

Using the observational methods of field anthropology, Margaret Clark, Barbara Anderson, and associates (1967, p. vii) described the lifestyles of a group of aging individuals within the American

3

cultural context. They noted that the anthropologist gathers "information on a wide range of data—styles of dress, details of religious rituals, the implicit contractual understandings underlying trade or monetary credit, and the particular form that the symptoms of hysteria take in the society he is studying. He comes, in time, to see the functional interrelationships among these disparate elements of culture."

An empirically grounded technique of lifestyle measurement has been developed by specialists in the discipline of marketing. Joseph Plummer (1974) defines the marketing approach to lifestyle thus: "The new construct combines the virtues of demographics with the richness and dimensionality of psychological characteristics and depth research. It deals with everyday, behaviorally oriented facets of people as well as their feelings, attitudes and opinions." William Wells and Douglas Tigert (1971) have traced the development of the "Activities-Interests-Opinions" (AIO) questionnaire used by marketers in defining lifestyles. However, Jerry Wind (1971) notes that the proper use of AIO or any other measure of lifestyle is based on the assumption that the set of attributes being measured is fairly exhaustive. He notes that an examination of the currently used AIOs reveals that they are not based on an explicit theoretical model for determining the appropriate dimensions of lifestyle.

In spite of the past difficulties involved in the measurement of lifestyle, social scientists agree that it is closely related to economic decisions and well-being in the total marketplace of goods and services (Thal and Guthrie 1967). Research findings have confirmed the hypothesis that it is such noneconomic variables as attitudes and expectations that must be held largely responsible for differences in the economic behavior of people (Katona, Strumpel, and Zahn 1971).

In short, lifestyle is the orientation to self, others, and society that each individual develops and follows. Such an orientation reflects the values and cognitive style of the individual. This orientation is derived from personal beliefs based on cultural context and the psychosocial milieu related to the stages of the individual's life. These elements shape the preference system that guides the individual in the formation of goals and in the exercise of choice. Thus the behavior of the individual involved in obtaining and using economic and social goods and services, including the decision processes that precede and determine these acts, are not random, but rest upon a limited number of distinct values that give meaning and direction to his or her life and influence choices among alternatives.

LIFESTYLES OF THE AGING

A great deal of work has been done in areas that have implications for the understanding of lifestyles among the aging. An exhaustive review of literature on the personalities and social roles of the aging has been compiled by Matilda Riley, Anne Foner, and associates (1968). Douglas Kimmel (1974) and Neugarten (1968) also present comprehensive syntheses of psychological and sociological data on the aging.

Several authors have attempted to divide the life course into phases or stages: from the standpoint of the family life cycle (Lansing and Kish 1957), individual psychosocial development (Erikson 1950), the "dominant concerns" of each decade (Havighurst 1960), and meaning in life (Young 1974). Related to these is Milton Rokeach's study of values in American society (1973).

With regard to lifestyle per se, evidence is quite limited. The most significant data have come out of the Kansas City Study of Adult Life. Williams and Wirth (1965) subjectively identified six lifestyles among their aging subjects: the world of work, familism, living alone, couplehood, easing through life with minimal involvement, and living fully. However, in addition to the limitations of their methodology, which have already been discussed, these authors point out that their subjects were a relatively homogeneous group of white working-class and middle-class individuals, mostly from the Midwest. Blacks and the very important lower class were excluded. These limitations require caution in generalizing from their findings. Moreover, the study, conducted in 1956-62, is dated.

Also on the basis of the Kansas City study, Neugarten and associates (1964) defined eight patterns of aging, using personality as the pivotal dimension: reorganizers (active, competent individuals), focused (middle level of activity), disengaged (calm, withdrawn, and contented), holding on, constricted, "succorance-seeking," apathetic, and disorganized. Methodological limitations of this study have been mentioned.

Clark, Anderson, and associates (1967) describe individual case histories in detail and in relation to the American culture, but make no attempt to group individuals.

Other authors have identified styles of disengagement (Cumming 1964), patterns in family lives of older people (Cuber and Harroff 1965; Kerckhoff 1966), patterns of friendship (Rosow 1967), patterns of leisure (Havighurst and Feigenbaum 1959), and activity types (Lemmon, Bengston, and Peterson 1972).

Life satisfaction has been examined in relation to such lifestyle variables as degree of activity (Lemmon, Bengston, and Peterson 1972), availability of personal transportation and residential location

(Cutler 1972), constraint (Smith and Lipman 1972), and economic
level and achievement of goals (Bortner and Hultsch 1970).

CONSUMER BEHAVIOR OF OLDER AMERICANS

Numerous studies have been conducted that attempt to describe
various aspects of the consumer behavior of the elderly considered
as a single subpopulation. The most comprehensive review of this
literature to date is to be found in Frederick Waddell's The Elderly
Consumer (1976). This impressive anthology of pertinent articles
covers demographic characteristics, income and expenditure patterns, retirement, market characteristics, consumer problems,
decision making, and implications for program development, as well
as a survey of related doctoral dissertations and master's theses in
the areas of consumer needs and problems, clothing, housing, nutrition and food practices, retirement income, and financial management.
Fred Reynolds and William Wells (1977) have profiled attitudes,
interests, and opinions by age and sex across the categories of optimism and happiness, modern-traditional ideas, travel, mobility,
anxiety, personal adornment, and views on income, personal equity,
spending, staying home, spouse and children, durable goods, housekeeping, cooking, grocery shopping, and health and nutrition.
However, as has been pointed out, age needs to be supplemented
by other characteristics in order to have a better understanding of the
market behavior of older persons. Little work has been done to segment the elderly consumer group. In the only study of its kind,
Jeffrey Towle and Claude R. Martin, Jr. (1976), used cluster analysis to define six buying-style segments and associated psychographic
characteristics of a sample of elderly consumers selected from the
1973 National Target Group Index Study (see Table 1.1). However,
the authors present methodological cautions in interpretation of data.
Observers have noted a paucity of research into the consumption
behavior of older persons ("Forgotten Generation" 1969; Waddell
1975; White House Conference on Aging 1971). Most of the available
research has focused on senior citizens' share of aggregate expenditures and the types of foods and services purchased by them, often
without regard to income level or the presence or absence of retirement (Chu 1972; Crockett 1963; Fleming 1971; "Forgotten Generation"
1969; Goldstein 1965, 1966; "Don't Write Off the Senior Citizen Markets" 1973; Reinecke 1964). The concept of the family life cycle has
often been used as a basis for analyzing the purchasing patterns of
older consumers (Engel, Kollat, and Blackwell 1973; Reynolds and
Wells 1977).

TABLE 1.1

Buying-Style Segments and Psychographic Descriptions
of Elderly Market

Segment	Psychographic Description	Share of Elderly Market (percent)
Saver/planner (buys unknown brands)	frank candid self-assured confident	25.1
Brand loyalist (does not buy for approval of friends)	brave courageous reserved conventional insecure not stubborn	8.4
Information seeker (persuasible)	kind sincere	10.1
Economy shopper (not brand-loyal)	not brave not dominating not egocentric not frank candid funny witty	10.6
Laggard (not persuasible)	not witty not kind not reserved liberal	11.2
Conspicuous consumer	stubborn egotistical dominating	34.6

Source: Jefferey G. Towle and Claude R. Martin Jr., "The Elderly Consumer: One Segment or Many?", Beverlee Anderson, ed., Advances in Consumer Research, 1976, pp. 463-68, Table-Figure 5, Buying Style Segments--Psychographic Descriptions. Reprinted with permission.

It has been found that older persons generally buy the same kinds of things most other adults do and tend to retain most of their living habits (Atchley 1972), but some of their purchases tend to be skewed toward the relief of age-related physical difficulties: medical care, medical appliances, products that aid health, sleep, and digestion. They may sell their homes and move to smaller ones or to apartments or condominiums (Reynolds and Wells 1977). While vacationing is not as frequent among older Americans as for the 45-54 age group, older consumers are above average in foreign travel, air travel, and possession of passports, airline and auto rental credit cards, and traveler's checks (Grey Advertising 1973). Another set of items that shows a steady increase with age but peaks during the 55-64 age period consists primarily of luxuries or near luxuries, such as fur coats and stoles, men's jewelry and watches, blenders, whiskey (bourbon, scotch, rye), manicures, massages, slenderizing treatments, gifts and contributions, laundry and dry cleaning sent out, and repairs by contractors (Reinecke 1964; Wells and Gubar 1966).

Very little research has been conducted on consumer behavior patterns of older persons. Studies have been made of the expenditures, leisure activities, and media habits of middle-class and upper-middle-class members of a senior citizens' center (Samli and Palubinskas 1972); the shopping behavior, distance traveled, and sources of information used by elderly residents of a public housing project (Mason and Smith 1973); and the perceived risk, importance of informal sources of information, and social interactions involved in the purchase decision for a salt substitute (Schiffman 1971; 1972a; 1972b).

Kenneth Bernhardt and Thomas Kinnear (1976) criticized the limitations of the populations surveyed and the sample sizes of these studies, and profiled the store choice, credit behavior, media habits, and leisure activities of a large probability sample of older persons from a major metropolitan area. They found that persons over 65 are more likely to shop at traditional department stores and are willing to travel to downtown shopping districts and pay higher prices for department store merchandise. Only one in six of the senior citizens surveyed possessed a department store credit card, however, compared with one in three among the rest of the population. They found that the elderly read selectively and prefer to get their news from newspapers and broadcast media. Patterns of leisure activity were found to be similar to those of other age groups, but the activity level was lower. As a group the elderly spend their time reading books, sewing, gardening, attending church activities, and going out to eat. They are heavy users of the telephone (long-distance calls), taxis, mass transit, and laundromats. The authors concluded that the senior market is large and economically important, and has specific shopping, credit, and media habits.

MARKET RESEARCH

Tables 1.2 and 1.3 profile attitudes by age and sex across the categories of optimism and happiness, modern-traditional ideas, travel, mobility, anxiety, personal adornment, views on income, personal equity, spending, staying at home, husband and children, durable goods, housekeeping and cooking, grocery shopping, and health and nutrition. Age and sex categories were found to vary by only a few percentage points in most instances (Reynolds and Wells 1977).

Table 1.2 reveals that women 55 and older, in contrast with younger women, tend to feel their greatest achievements are behind them, to dread the future more, and to feel slightly less happy. They have much more trouble relaxing and sleeping than do younger women. Their perception of themselves as old-fashioned is only slightly more than that of younger women, yet they more strongly espouse traditional ideas regarding youth, marriage, and women's roles. Furthermore, they like to feel attractive to members of the opposite sex, yet, more so than younger women, feel there is too much emphasis on sex today.

They say their days follow a definite routine; they perceive themselves as homebodies, not swingers, and express less interest in travel and changing residences than do younger women. In spite of anticipating no future increases in income, they express more satisfaction with their financial circumstances than younger women do, have fewer debts, and are more careful shoppers and spenders. They are more relaxed about housekeeping than younger women, and tend to look for comfort in furnishings and dependability in appliances.

Table 1.3 shows that men over 55 display a pattern similar to that of older women in terms of agreement with traditional values, a stable, home-oriented lifestyle, desire for comfort and dependability in durable goods, satisfaction with financial circumstances, and conservative monetary and shopping behavior. Like older women, they feel their greatest achievements are behind them and are less happy than when younger, but they dread the future less than older women do and express less anxiety. They are fussier about housekeeping than younger men (as opposed to women, who become more relaxed about housekeeping as they grow older).

Men and women also differ in two important areas related to husband and children. Men are more likely to say that a wife's first obligation is to her husband, not her children, and to feel more

TABLE 1.2

Female Interests and Opinions
(percent agreeing, by age group)

Statement	Sample Total	Under 25	25–34	35–44	45–54	55 and Older
			Age Group			
Optimism and Happiness						
My greatest achievements are still ahead of me	64	92	84	73	52	28
I dread the future	23	20	18	17	24	30
I am much happier now than I ever was before	79	85	82	80	74	74
Modern–Traditional Ideas						
I have somewhat old-fashioned tastes and habits	86	78	84	87	88	89
There is too much emphasis on sex today	87	70	74	90	89	93
I like to think I am a bit of a swinger	26	43	34	26	19	15
A woman's place is in the home	46	39	39	44	49	60
The working world is no place for a woman	17	15	11	14	19	28
Young people have too many privileges	76	57	74	77	76	83
The U.S. would be better off if there were no hippies	55	32	37	46	54	82
My days seem to follow a definite routine—eating meals at the same time each day, etc.	67	59	62	61	67	75

10

Travel

I would like to take a trip around the world	67	78	83	73	65	51
I would like to spend a year in London or Paris	34	38	40	34	34	25
I would feel lost if I were alone in a foreign country	68	66	66	64	68	76
I like to visit places that are totally different from my home	85	85	83	86	82	88

Mobility

We will probably move at least once in the next five years	38	71	53	27	28	23
Our family has moved more often than most of our neighbors have	24	36	32	26	18	17

Anxiety

I have trouble getting to sleep	33	29	24	26	33	49
I wish I knew how to relax	52	51	49	49	51	59

Personal Adornment

Dressing well is an important part of my life	81	84	80	78	79	83
I like to feel attractive to members of the opposite sex	85	93	91	77	82	72
I want to look a little different from others	69	71	78	70	63	72
I often wear expensive cologne	28	19	24	28	27	33
I have more stylish clothes than most of my friends	30	31	34	27	29	27

(continued)

TABLE 1.2 (continued)

Views on Income, Personal Equity, and Spending

Statement	Sample Total	Age Group				
		Under 25	25-34	35-44	45-54	55 and Older
I will probably have more money to spend next year than I have now	45	71	70	58	53	30
Five years from now our family income will probably be a lot higher than it is now	65	87	85	75	61	26
Our family income is high enough to satisfy nearly all our important desires	74	59	66	78	78	80
No matter how fast our income goes up, we never seem to get ahead	53	62	65	61	47	32
Investing in the stock market is too risky for most families	86	79	83	82	85	87
Our family is too heavily in debt today	27	36	33	37	23	11
I like to pay cash for everything I buy	77	83	79	74	71	77
I pretty much spend for today and let tomorrow bring what it will	22	33	21	22	25	18

Views on Staying at Home

I would rather spend a quiet evening at home than go out to a party	65	50	66	64	68	78
I am a homebody	69	59	65	64	72	79
I stay home most evenings	83	81	95	80	83	83

Views on Husband and Children

A wife's first obligation is to her husband, not her children	69	53	65	74	74	76
When children are ill in bed, parents should drop everything else to see to their comfort	74	61	71	73	80	83
Children are the most important thing in a marriage	52	42	44	49	56	64
When making important family decisions, consideration of the children should come first	54	69	58	44	48	56
A wife should have a great deal of information about her husband's work	82	83	84	75	88	85

Views on Durable Goods

Our home is furnished for comfort, not for style	90	83	88	88	94	94
If I must choose, I buy stylish rather than practical furniture	17	19	31	13	15	15
When buying appliances I am more concerned with dependability than price	90	85	89	89	89	94
A subcompact car can meet my transportation needs	66	85	74	60	61	57

(continued)

13

TABLE 1.2 (continued)

Statement	Sample Total	Age Group				
		Under 25	25-34	35-44	45-54	55 and Older
Views on Housekeeping and Cooking						
When I see a full ashtray or wastebasket, I want it emptied immediately	71	77	70	72	64	64
I am uncomfortable when the house is not completely clean	67	76	67	70	61	68
The kind of dirt you can't see is worse than the kind you can see	77	77	72	73	79	85
I am a good cook	91	93	92	88	90	91
I like to cook	87	91	88	84	85	87
I like to bake	40	43	43	42	39	38
Meal preparation should take as little time as possible	42	42	41	40	41	44
Views on Grocery Shopping						
Shopping is no fun anymore	54	49	43	58	55	51
Before going shopping, I sit down and prepare a complete shopping list	72	68	73	71	69	74
I try to stick to well-known brands	74	58	67	71	82	86

14

I find myself checking prices even on small items	90	89	93	92	89	86
I like to save and redeem trading stamps	75	72	70	70	75	83
I pay a lot more attention to food prices now than I ever did before	90	92	91	88	88	87
I am an impulse buyer	38	39	40	37	42	27
I shop a lot for specials	84	85	86	83	84	81

Views on Health and Nutrition

I am very concerned about nutrition	87	87	89	87	82	89
I am concerned about how much salt I eat	56	52	55	56	50	66
I am careful what I eat in order to keep my weight under control	57	63	57	58	62	68
I try to avoid foods that are high in cholesterol	62	37	53	60	65	79
I try to avoid foods that have additives in them	56	45	52	57	53	62
I get more headaches than most people	28	30	31	28	27	22
I eat more than I should	70	68	70	75	73	69

Source: Needham, Harper, and Steers. 1975. "Life Style Surveys" appearing in Fred D. Reynolds and William D. Wells, Consumer Behavior, McGraw-Hill Series in Marketing, 1977, pp. 173–78, "Female Interests and Opinions and Male Interests and Opinions", Tables 7–4 through 7–5. Reprinted with permission.

TABLE 1.3

Male Interests and Opinions
(percent agreeing, by age group)

Statement	Sample Total	Under 25	25–34	35–44	45–54	55 and Older
				Age Group		
Optimism and Happiness						
My greatest achievements are still ahead of me	64	98	93	76	55	25
I dread the future	20	21	15	19	23	23
I am much happier now than I ever was before	78	87	92	97	76	74
Modern–Traditional Ideas						
I have somewhat old-fashioned tastes and habits	85	73	78	84	92	89
There is too much emphasis on sex today	66	56	65	74	81	93
I like to think I am a bit of a swinger	31	51	43	29	26	15
A woman's place is in the home	54	45	52	53	52	62
The working world is no place for a woman	27	24	20	25	26	37
Young people have too many privileges	75	60	63	77	74	88
The U.S. would be better off if there were no hippies	59	33	38	57	67	81

My days seem to follow a definite routine—eating meals at the same time each day, etc.	63	50	53	59	67	76
All men should be clean shaven every day	67	47	55	66	75	85

Travel

I would like to take a trip around the world	67	74	73	77	68	53
I would like to spend a year in London or Paris	34	38	39	40	32	23
I would feel lost if I were alone in a foreign country	52	59	46	47	44	67
I like to visit places that are totally different from my home	72	80	73	75	73	67

Mobility

We will probably move at least once in the next five years	37	75	52	28	23	20
Our family has moved more often than most of the neighbors have	22	27	30	23	18	17

Anxiety

I have trouble getting to sleep	24	20	20	23	25	30
I wish I knew how to relax	47	40	48	51	44	50

Personal Adornment

Dressing well is an important part of my life	72	70	73	72	72	67
I like to feel attractive to members of the opposite sex	81	87	87	87	66	74
I want to look a little different from others	55	74	62	55	49	42

(continued)

TABLE 1.3 (continued)

Statement	Sample Total	Age Group				
		Under 25	25-34	35-44	45-54	55 and Older
I often wear expensive cologne	14	16	14	12	15	13
I have more stylish clothes than most of my friends	25	24	26	28	24	22
Views on Income, Personal Equity, and Spending						
I will probably have more money to spend next year than I have now	56	74	65	64	58	29
Five years from now our family income will probably be a lot higher than it is now	68	87	85	79	69	28
Our family income is high enough to satisfy nearly all our important desires	75	63	72	78	78	79
No matter how fast our income goes up, we never seem to get ahead	58	60	68	56	52	39
Investing in the stock market is too risky for most families	83	86	82	81	87	86
Our family is too heavily in debt today	28	41	42	28	25	11
I like to pay cash for everything I buy	75	79	74	70	69	81
I pretty much spend for today and let tomorrow bring what it will	26	31	29	23	23	26

Views on Staying at Home

Statement						
I would rather spend a quiet evening at home than go out to a party	73	65	67	73	75	79
I am a homebody	72	55	67	73	79	82
I stay home most evenings	80	70	77	79	78	89

Views on Husband and Children

Statement						
A wife's first obligation is to her husband, not her children	57	43	52	54	64	66
When children are ill in bed, parents should drop everything else to see to their comfort	70	66	68	66	73	78
Children are the most important thing in a marriage	53	37	44	50	57	78
When making important family decisions, consideration of the children should come first	53	63	54	48	49	53
A wife should have a great deal of information about her husband's work	77	74	75	73	80	82
Our family is a close-knit group	87	86	94	89	83	88

Views on Durable Goods

Statement						
Our home is furnished for comfort, not for style	93	89	92	94	95	94
If I must choose, I buy stylish rather than practical furniture	15	18	20	14	15	9
When buying appliances I am more concerned with dependability than price	93	91	93	90	94	95
When buying appliances the brand name is more important than the reputation of the store	56	56	53	49	55	64

(continued)

TABLE 1.3 (continued)

Statement	Sample Total	Under 25	25–34	35–44	45–54	55 and Older
A subcompact car can meet my transportation needs	59	71	57	56	58	57

Views on Housekeeping and Cooking

Statement	Sample Total	Under 25	25–34	35–44	45–54	55 and Older
When I see a full ashtray or wastebasket, I want it emptied immediately	56	56	46	54	60	63
I am uncomfortable when the house is not completely clean	51	57	48	53	49	52
The kind of dirt you can't see is worse than the kind you can see	77	68	74	73	79	86
I am a good cook	51	63	57	50	48	41
I like to cook	50	60	58	48	48	41
I like to bake	30	34	35	27	26	30
Meal preparation should take as little time as possible	42	42	41	38	40	46

Views on Grocery Shopping

Statement	Sample Total	Under 25	25–34	35–44	45–54	55 and Older
Shopping is no fun anymore	59	54	55	55	63	64

Before going shopping, I sit down and prepare a complete shopping list	44	35	42	38	56
I try to stick to well-known brands	79	71	79	76	86
I find myself checking prices even on small items	79	78	74	75	84
I like to save and redeem trading stamps	43	43	31	35	58
I pay a lot more attention to food prices now than I ever did before	81	81	79	81	84
I am an impulse buyer	38	46	47	40	30
I shop a lot for specials	60	61	59	63	61

Views on Health and Nutrition

I am very concerned about nutrition	61	66	65	60	63
I am concerned about how much salt I eat	40	28	32	32	54
I am careful what I eat in order to keep my weight under control	51	38	43	44	64
I try to avoid foods that are high in cholesterol	49	31	42	41	63
I try to avoid foods that have additives in them	44	36	35	39	56
I get more headaches than most people	17	18	17	19	12
I eat more than I should	66	57	67	68	64

Source: Needham, Harper, and Steers . 1975. "Life Style Surveys" appearing in Fred D. Reynolds and William D. Wells, Consumer Behavior, McGraw-Hill Series in Marketing, 1977, pp. 173-78, "Female Interests and Opinions and Male Interests and Opinions", Tables 7-4 through 7-5. Reprinted with permission.

strongly than women that a wife should have a great deal of information about her husband's work. Like women, men want to feel attractive to the opposite sex. There is almost no difference among age groups in enjoyment of visiting places totally different from home.

This survey demonstrates that the attitudes and opinions of the elderly vary only a little from those of the younger people except in their having more traditional values. Old and young alike should be taught that the elderly are valuable as economic resources through their marketing behavior and, in addition, are valuable as human resources because of the life experiences they have had over time.

CONSUMER PROBLEMS AND FRAUD

Much attention has been directed to the specific consumer problems that older persons face (White House Conference on Aging 1971). In 1972 a group of older Americans listed the needs most crucial to their well-being as medical care, housing, income, public transportation, protection from fraud, legal advice, insurance, assistance in preparing for old age, and activities and associations in which they feel needed (Clark and Cochran 1972). The areas of need for older persons outlined by the Administration on Aging included sound nutrition, economic food purchasing, careful use of credit, avoidance of quackery, avoidance of fraudulent products and practices, safe and effective use of drugs, management of retirement income, Medicare and supplemental health insurance, and care of clothing and household equipment (Atchley 1972). Specific studies have been conducted in many of these areas (Alfin-Slater 1975; Boone and Bonno 1971; Committee on Research and Development Goals in Social Gerontology 1969; Hamovitch and Peterson 1969; Lawton and Cohen 1974; Sherman and Brittan 1973; Snyder 1971; Waddell 1975, 1976; Watkin 1975), and multitudinous suggestions for social policy and service programs for the elderly have been produced.

It has been repeatedly pointed out that a critical consumer problem of older people is fraud and quackery (U.S. Senate 1963, 1965; Atchley 1972; Schutz and Bump 1974; Waddell 1975, 1976; Perloff and McCaskey 1978; Valle and Koeski 1978). Older persons are commonly believed to be vulnerable for myriad social and psychological reasons: low income, lack of education, desire for security and stability, helplessness, loneliness, grief, lack of feedback from trusted information sources, suggestibility, and desire for health and avoidance of pain. Fraudulent moneymaking schemes, real estate deals, and preneed burial plans, for example, have defrauded many

TABLE 1.4

The Older Consumer Population, 1970-85
(million persons)

		Age Group			
		55-64		65 and Older	
Year	Total Population	N	Percent	N	Percent
1970	204.8	18.6	9.0	20.2	9.9
1975	216.6	19.8	9.1	21.9	10.1
1980	230.9	21.2	9.1	23.7	10.3
1985	246.3	21.4	8.7	25.5	10.4

Note: These are series D (moderate-low series) projections; data include armed forces overseas, and are as of July 1.
Source: Department of Commerce 1971a.

older people. Comprehensive consumer education programs for the elderly have been outlined as a possible solution (Waddell 1976; Burton and Hennon 1978).

THE GROWTH OF THE OLDER AMERICAN POPULATION

In recent years there has been a great deal of discussion in the marketing literature regarding the growth of the senior citizen market (Fleming 1971; "The Forgotten Generation" 1969; Goldstein 1968; Samli and Palubinskas 1972). Persons 65 and older are expected to increase by 4 million in 1975-85, a faster-than-average rate compared with the rest of the population. Table 1.4 gives a distribution of the older persons by aggregate number and by percent, with expected changes, through 1985. Persons aged 55-64 are expected to increase slightly in aggregate number during this period.

On the basis of a review of the literature on the lifestyles and consumer behavior of older Americans, we began our approach to the study.

2

APPROACH TO THE STUDY

THEORETICAL BACKGROUND

Our use here of the concept of lifestyle is similar to the concept proposed by Alfred Adler (1927), in that our focus is on the individual and his or her interaction with the social systems. We accept the basic assumption of the unity and uniqueness of the individual, who is conceived as a self-consistent, self-directed person whose central theme is reflected in all actions and determined by values, attitudes, and goals, and interaction with the environment. Like that of Richard Williams and Claudine Wirth (1965), our conceptual frame for lifestyle reflects Talcott Parsons and Edward Shils's (1962) theory of action, for behavior is viewed both as meaningfully oriented to the individual and as a reflection of his or her central life theme(s).

Like the work of Robert Havighurst (1971), Bernice Neugarten (1968), and George Maddox (1970), our exploration of individual behavior is based on the individual's use of time through involvement in seven social roles: worker, homemaker,* spouse, parent, user of leisure time, friend, and community member. In contrast with Lowenthal et al. (1975), in which five of the seven social roles investigated were oriented toward the family, the individual's action within and outside this primary group is pursued equally.

Within our concept of use of time or action through investment in a role, three major dimensions are explored to permit the articulation of specific, rather than crude, lifestyle patterns. Our goal is to derive a clear, unified view of the individual's unique and creative style of living, including attitudes toward life.

---

*"Homemaker" refers to all activities related to the management of the home, irrespective of gender.

24

Lifestyle is an eclectic concept, and while approaches to its measurement are diverse, most are based on qualitative judgments rather than on empirical data. It was felt that empirical measures could be superior to qualitative judgments in reliability and validity. However, current quantitative approaches, as has been noted, are not based on explicit theoretical models. Therefore, it was initially necessary to develop an operational definition of the components of lifestyle. The following was arrived at: The psychological nature includes self-concept and ego ideals, cognitive style, values and goals, traits and types, self-rated health, life satisfaction, and demographic component. Role-related behavior embraces primary relationships, reference groups, group affiliation, work-leisure-consumption, education, and the demographic component. The cultural environment consists of the material, the normative, and the psychological.

THE MODEL

With these components in mind, a framework for the measurement of lifestyle was developed that was based on the use of time through role involvement. Lifestyle as reflected in the use of time was categorized into seven roles: worker, homemaker, parent, spouse, friend, community worker, and leisure-time user. Within this concept three major dimensions were considered (see Table 2.1).

The first dimension, quantity of time invested in these roles, is similar to Havighurst's pattern of role performance, and permits the development of a hierarchy or configuration of the characteristic way in which the individual fills and combines various social roles. The portion of energy expended in a specific role pattern—the degree of involvement—is identified. This dimension provides a crude view of the individual's actions, a view that is expanded by the other two dimensions.

The affective domain is explored in the second dimension, which considers the emotional investment and energy expenditure in the individual's action. The individual's perception of his or her behavior in the roles, his or her wishes in regard to goals and aims within the roles, the satisfaction with these behaviors, and the attitude and value orientation are pursued.

Last, similar to Francis Carp's (1975) component of lifestyle that emphasizes social network and space, and reinforcing Adler's concern with the individual's interaction with the environment, the third dimension explores the interactive aspect of the individual's behavior in the seven roles investigated. This exploration reflects the individual's style of interaction and its integration into his or

TABLE 2.1

Lifestyle Model

Quantity of time in roles
  Hierarchy of roles
  Configuration of roles
Affective aspect of roles
  How individual perceives roles
  How individual would like to spend time in roles
  How satisfied individual is with time spent in roles
  Value of roles
Interactive aspect of roles
  Solitary or group orientation in roles
  Informal or formal orientation in roles
  Provincial or cosmopolitan orientation in roles
  Reference group

Source: Compiled by the authors.

her action, whether that be a formal or informal, provincial or cosmopolitan, solitary or group orientation, and includes reference-group orientation.

CONSUMER BEHAVIOR

The Engel-Kollat-Blackwell model of consumer behavior (1973), recognized as the most comprehensive in the field, was selected as the theoretical framework for the investigation of consumer behavior. The model is given in Figure 2.1.

The following basic assumptions serve as a foundation for a definition of the consumer behavior model:

1. Consumers are influenced by a wide variety of stimuli or sources of information.
2. Consumers actively and purposefully engage in many different kinds of decisions and resulting activities.
3. Consumers engage in decisions and activities in many different settings or situations.
4. Consumers differ greatly in many ways, and these differences mediate the effects of stimuli from various situations upon decisions and behavior.

FIGURE 2.1

Model of Consumer Motivation and Behavior:
Outcomes of a Buying Decision

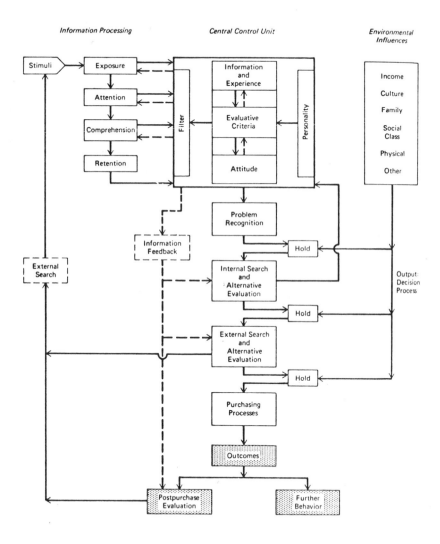

Source: Engel, Kollat, and Blackwell 1973.

5. Not only do consumers differ, but these differences change over time.

Consumer behavior, to summarize, consists of the various behaviors of persons over time as they acquire, process, and utilize information from various sources and settings in purchasing, consuming, and communicating about brands, products, and clusters of products.

METHODOLOGICAL PROBLEMS
IN SOCIAL GERONTOLOGY

It has been customary to assume that old age begins somewhere in the seventh decade of life, and until recently much of the research and the majority of action programs have focused on the period beginning at 65. It is now recognized, however, that the real turning point comes much earlier (Vedder 1965). On the basis of present knowledge, it seems possible to identify three stages of advanced adulthood: middle age (roughly the forties and fifties), later maturity (approximately the sixties and seventies), and old age (Tibbetts 1960). While a systematic or developmental approach in defining the stages of later life is preferable to a chronological approach, we are forced to use chronological age as the operational definition of these stages because no one has developed a satisfactory method of systematically identifying older people (Atchley 1972).

Three age groups of adults were arbitrarily defined for study in recognition of the differences in psychosocial development, dominant concerns, and social roles that exist in a broad age range of adults. Forty-five was selected as the starting point because of the consensus among gerontologists that changes in middle age greatly affect the quality of life of the individual in later years. Seventy-five was selected as the cutoff point in order to account for as many age differences in lifestyle as possible, while minimizing difficulties involved in studying individuals who may be frail or disabled due to advanced age. For the same reason it was decided not to sample institutionalized adults.

With regard to research design, three basic approaches have been employed in the study of older persons: cross-sectional, longitudinal, and cohort-sequence. Most of these studies have been cross-sectional. The cross-section approach yields data essential to the understanding of the age structure of the society. However, there is danger of fallaciously interpreting this type of data and inferring that differences among age categories in the society are due to the aging process of individuals. Longitudinal studies have been conducted that attempt to define the aging process by tracing changes in attitude and experience of the same individuals over time. Changes in attitude and experience may not be due to the aging process itself, but may reflect changes in society. In recognition of this, cohort-sequence studies have been undertaken to isolate the effects of aging from the effects of social change (Riley, Foner, and associates 1968). Both longitudinal and cohort-sequence studies are inhibited by problems of time, financing, attrition rates, and the difficulty of following the same people over a period of years (Atchley 1972).

The cross-sectional approach was selected in order to obtain data essential to the understanding of the age structure of the society in the 1970s and to minimize the problems of time, money, attrition rates, and the difficulty of observing the same individuals over a period of years. In addition, such a methodology facilitates potential future sequential cross-sectional studies, provided consistent measuring tools and sampling techniques are used.

In the interpretation of age studies there is the ever-present problem of separating the results that are truly age-specific from those related to changes in the environment over time. Although cross-sectional studies such as the one proposed are susceptible to this problem, longitudinal studies also share in this confounding. There is no way to eliminate culture changes, but in the interpretation of the data one can be cognizant of the problem and use what knowledge is available concerning the environment to help clarify what might be pure age effects.

In addition, the use of a probability sample helps insure that at least at one point in time, the cross section represents groups that are not biased on any other variable, such as education and income.

Probability sample selection also maximizes reliability, validity, and generalizability of the data, and facilitates potential future sequential cross-sectional studies.

Last, there is often criticism regarding the reliability of data gathered from personal interviews of the elderly. It is frequently stated that the interviewee will be too embarrassed to tell the truth, for instance, in regard to consumer problems and questions of fraud, or will simply give any answer in order to hurry through the interview. To measure this potential problem, interviewer observation analyses were incorporated into the survey, in which the interviewers would record their observations of the apparent emotional, physical, and mental state of the respondent at the time of the interview.

HYPOTHESES

With this rationale in mind, the following hypotheses were developed for testing:

- Lifestyle pattern is a valid concept, and can be quantitatively defined with empirical techniques.
- Differences in lifestyle among age groups of older Americans and among individuals within the same age group can be identified and quantitatively defined.
- Differences in consumer behavior among age groups of older Americans and among individuals within the same age group can be quantitatively identified and defined.
- Lifestyle as defined is significantly and quantitatively related to important aspects of the consumer behavior of older Americans.

PART II:
THE SURVEY

3

PRELIMINARY STUDY

FOCUSED GROUP INTERVIEWS

Focused group interviews were held in Sacramento, California, with three age categories of individuals (45-54, 55-64, and 65-75) in order to obtain qualitative data on subjects' lifestyle and consumer behavior. Black, Anglo, Mexican, and Japanese ethnic groups were represented. Most were from middle-class and lower-middle-class backgrounds. Five men and five women were present at each discussion. Questions, presented for open discussion, centered on individuals' dominant concerns and activities over the years, external influences on attitudes and behavior, and inner feelings and experiences.

The younger subjects were preoccupied with responsibilities of rearing children and earning a living. Both men and women were counting the days until they could "pull the plug," and felt that their obligation to society had been met by raising their children to self-sufficiency. Even though children were gone, ties were maintained, especially with those needing money. Older subjects, relieved of the responsibility for children, expressed enjoyment of other children as grandparents and baby-sitters. All groups were concerned that family unity was being undermined by working mothers, who "dump" their children with baby-sitters and share decision making with their husbands. However, many of the women present were or had been employed.

Men in all groups had rarely found their work rewarding, and talked of being "in a rut." Retirement was, however, viewed apprehensively by younger men. Loss of income was a concern, especially in view of inflation. Subjects aged 55-64, on the other hand, were optimistic about retirement and were looking forward to the opportunity to do what they wanted to do after many years of doing what others had expected of them. Subjects aged 65-75 were generally happy about being retired, and felt relieved that they were finished with their responsibilities. All felt that times had been hard, but now were looking up.

With regard to happenings in the outside world, all groups mentioned the attitudes and lifestyle of the younger generation, who were perceived as freer, more intelligent, and living by truer values than the older generation. Other areas of concern mentioned were political corruption, inflation, ethnic militancy, student demonstrations, and government "handouts."

The two younger groups had few answers for questions dealing with their inner feelings and experiences. It may be because introspection and open expression of emotion are relatively new popular phenomena, or because these age groups have been so burdened with family and job responsibilities that they have had no time for contemplation. Subjects aged 45-54 felt that happiness had to do with having a real goal and seeing it to completion. Subjects aged 55-64 had adopted a compromising attitude and were content to have attained some success, although not what they had originally wanted. Subjects aged 65-75 felt these were their best years. They had no troubles nor burdens. Some mentioned the growing importance of religion in their lives and an ecumenical attitude.

Consumer behavior questions centered on subjects' recognition of consumer problems, their sources of information, the role of the family in the decision structure, evaluation of alternatives, the purchase process, and postpurchase behavior. Repeatedly among all groups the importance of personal influence was mentioned. Friends' recommendations, personal experience with a product or brand, independent judgment, and directing the complaint were emphasized. Established, reliable name brands and stores were generally favored. Repair services, medical care costs, health insurance, and inflation were most frequently brought up as consumer problems.

DESIGN, SAMPLING, INTERVIEWING, AND EVALUATION

The services of Field Research Corporation of San Francisco were utilized for design consultation, sampling, and interviewing for the pilot test. A comprehensive lifestyle and consumer behavior questionnaire was developed on the basis of theoretical models already discussed, the review of literature, and results of the focused group interviews.

Questions on lifestyle were developed to help create role constructs according to the model shown in Table 2.1.

To measure the "time element," such variables as "Do you work?" were followed by "Do you work regularly?" and "How often do you bring work home?" Responses ranged from "always" to "never." Similar questions, some agree-disagree statements, were asked regarding each of the seven roles (worker, homemaker, parent, spouse, friend, community member, and leisure-time user) to ascertain the actual time spent in performing these roles and the degree of involvement that the respondent maintained. The "affective dimension" was designed to be measured by a five-point scale, using a satisfaction variable for each role that was phrased "How satisfied are you with work, parenting, and so on?"

The questionnaire was then planned to measure an individual's "interactive aspect" by variables such as "How often do you chat or visit with others while at work?" measured in terms of time and ranging from responses of "once or more a week" to "never." In addition, the creation of a composite interaction variable, which would combine interactive aspects of all seven roles, was planned.

Consumer behavior based on the model presented in Figure 1.1 was covered by questions on food, housing, health care, money matters, transportation, clothing, and major appliances. Also, questions were included concerning shopping attitudes and behavior and perceived consumer problems with providers and servicers of the above goods and services.

A group of personal value questions was collected that appeared to have predictive ability with regard to consumer behavior. These were agree-disagree statements that relate to personal values rather than roles, such as "In most situations it is clear to me that there is a right and wrong way" and "Young people have too many privileges and not enough responsibilities."

Finally, a set of demographic questions was collected on age, sex, income, education, occupation, marital status, employment status, home ownership, residence in youth, as well as political orientation, self-rated social status, and health (see Appendix B).

Because many more questionnaire items were developed than could be included in a one-hour interview, the most critical questions were framed for in-person interviewing (about 2/3) and a self-administered instrument was constructed for the remaining material (about 1/3). This was left with the respondents, to be returned by mail.

A preliminary form of each of the two questionnaires (in-person and mailback) was pretested among a small number of persons in the specified age groups, and revisions were made.

The survey area was defined as the five counties comprising the San Francisco-Oakland Standard Metropolitan Statistical Area: San Francisco, Alameda, Contra Costa, San Mateo, and Marin. The survey universe was defined as all adults 45 years of age or older who reside in noninstitutional dwelling units in those five counties.

The latest telephone directories covering the survey area were assembled. This constituted the sampling frame from which households were drawn at random, using a systematic random sampling technique (use of random numbers to designate page, column, and line listing for each household). The households selected in this manner were the "key address" households, which determined the starting point for each cluster of dwellings called on to provide the face-to-face interviews for the pilot test. The number of "key addresses" drawn from each of the five counties was in proportion to that county's share of the total five-county household population.

Interviewers started their assignments at the household next door to the "key address." (The "key address" household was not used, so as to reduce the bias toward households having telephones in the sample.) The interviewer then called on households along a predetermined route in order to complete four in-home interviews per cluster location, two interviews with men and two with women. No callbacks were made to households where no one was home. (The age quotas were rotated from cluster to cluster.)

Interviewers introduced themselves by saying: "Hello. I'm . . . from Field Research survey group. We're doing a study on several different community issues of concern to people. For this particular interview, I have to talk to persons 45 years of age or older. Do you, or does anyone in your household who is at home now, happen to qualify?" The interviewer then consulted a quota assignment sheet to fit a potential respondent into the age and sex categories needed to complete that cluster. If no one in the household who qualified was at home, the interview was terminated.

Full-time Field Research staff personally briefed all interviewers, closely supervised their work, and evaluated their performance. The in-home interviewing was done between June 26 and July 10, 1976. The cutoff date for the mailback questionnaires was July 26. A total of 48 face-to-face interviews was completed in the homes of the respondents, 16 in each of three age groups: 45-54, 55-64, and 65 or older. Within each age group half of the respondents were men and half were women. One respondent per household was interviewed. The face-to-face interview took an average of one and one-quarter hours to administer.

The completed face-to-face interviews were checked and edited for completeness and consistency. Any data inadvertently omitted by the interviewers in the field was retrieved by telephone calls to respondents.

Self-administered questionnaires were mailed back by 43 of the original sample of 48, for a mailback completion rate of 90 percent. Those who completed and returned the questionnaires were sent a check for $5 for their participation.

According to standard Field Research practice, respondents' names, addresses, and telephone numbers were removed from the face-to-face interview questionnaires before they were turned over to the principal investigator. They had also been removed from the mailback questionnaires, which were linked to the face-to-face interviews by a simple numbering procedure.

RESULTS OF INTERVIEW ATTEMPTS

In order to complete a total of 48 face-to-face interviews, it was necessary to make attempts at 913 households. It should be kept in mind that the relatively high number of "attempts made" and "interviews not completed" is due in part to the fact that interviewers were screening for particular age groups and that no callbacks were made.

At the completion of each face-to-face interview, the interviewer filled out a form giving impressions of the respondent's reaction, attitude, and general appearance during the interview.

Interviewer Observation Analysis

Responses to two key questions were tabulated:

"Did the respondent have any difficulty understanding the questions?"
    Yes, great difficulty— 0%
    Yes, some difficulty—18.8%
    No, none at all   —81.2%
"What was the respondent's attitude during the interview?"
    Friendly and eager, volunteered information—62.5%
    Cooperative but not particularly eager   —27.1%
    Indifferent or bored   — 8.3%
    Often irritated or hostile—seemed anxious   — 2.1%
        to get interview over with

It was concluded that the vast majority of respondents understood the questions, were open to the interview, and appeared to have a good rapport with interviewers.

For every respondent all questions were examined for evidence of problems in understanding.

In order to test for sensitivity, selected questions were tabulated to ascertain whether a range of responses was obtained. Also, key questions were cross-tabulated by age group in order to obtain data on the meaningfulness of our age-group selection. For all the agree-disagree questions, a frequency analysis and a cross-tabulation by age group were performed. This was to determine the distribution of responses and potential differentiation by age group. Some interpretations of the results are given, but they were made more to determine the usefulness of the questionnaire than to portray generalizable information.

Lifestyle Analysis

The two major objectives of the lifestyle portion of the study were to explore the variety and diversity of lifestyle patterns among three age groups of older adults, and to explore the differences in lifestyle patterns of individuals within each group.

A tabulation of important variables revealed a diversity of role involvement both across age groups and between individuals in each group. As would be expected, those 45-54 years old invested more time and energy—physical and psychological—in work and family/child rearing. All respondents in this group were full-time workers and/or homemakers with children at home. Unlike those aged 45-54, individuals over 65 indicated less involvement with work and family/child rearing. The latter indicated life changes requiring their time and energy to be invested in different activities. While those over 65 and 45-54 were either strongly involved or not involved in the world of work and family, those 55-64 indicated more diversity in these two areas. Fifty-five percent were full-time workers, 11 percent were retired, and 11 percent were disabled and not working. Sixty percent had no children living at home, while 28 percent had children living at home. Like those over 65, changes requiring lifestyle alterations have occurred in the lives of those in the younger groups.

Our pilot study findings indicated that the original hypothesis of differences in lifestyle patterns between and within age groups is valid. On the basis of our complete examination of the questionnaires and the discussion above, it was decided to pursue the exploration of lifestyles among the three age groups in the large-scale study, with particular attention to differences between lifestyles of the sexes.

Consumer Behavior Analysis

The two major purposes of the consumer behavior portion of the study were to explore areas of need that are considered crucial to the well-being of the older consumer (housing, transportation, food and nutrition, health care, and income management), and to investigate the buyer behavior of the older consumer. Age-correlated differences in needs and behavior were hypothesized to exist.

A tabulation of important variables revealed that across all age groups the high cost of living was the most critical consumer problem. Problems with housing generally centered on environment. Crime and traffic were the most frequently mentioned problems of the people who indicated a desire to move, many saying they want a less expensive place, and one that provides more privacy and outdoor space.

Specific problems with health care generally had to do with costs of professional services and insurance premiums, and waiting time for appointments. Twenty-five percent reported problems communicating with and being responded to by medical personnel. The costs of automobile purchase and upkeep, the cost of insurance, and the quality of auto repair were most frequently mentioned under the category of transportation. Public transportation was not an issue with the sample, perhaps because of the comprehensive bus and rapid-transit system found in the Bay area. The cost of food was another major concern. Twenty-two percent across all age groups indicated a need to know more about nutrition.

Expectations that the elderly would experience higher rates of consumer fraud and quackery were not borne out by the study. The highest rate of consumer dissatisfaction (47 percent) was found among those 45-54. Thirty-seven percent of those 55-64 and 20 percent of those over 65 indicated some type of particularly disappointing and frustrating experiences as a consumer.

Disappointments with health care providers, automobiles and automobile dealers, and insurance companies were predominant among the complaints of all age groups. Individuals reporting these experiences often had more than one type of complaint and form of redress at the same place.

Frequency of shopping for clothing was found to differ by age: The percentages shopping for clothing several times a year were 45-54, 93 percent; 55-64, 63 percent; over 65, 73 percent. These data tend to support findings by Claude R. Martin, Jr. (1976), that "the elderly woman is a viable market segment for the fashion apparel industry."

Such findings indicated that the original hypothesis of age-correlated differences in consumer behavior was valid. It was decided to pursue the exploration of the differences among the three age groups in the large-scale study.

Personal Value Statements, Agree-Disagree Analysis

Age-related trends were also noted in the analysis of the agree-disagree items. The pattern of relationships among the age groups was not consistent, however, In some instances attitudes were found in common between the oldest and youngest groups, with the middle group deviating. In other instances attitudes of the middle and oldest group were found to be similar, with the youngest group deviating, and so on. There was evidence of a distribution of responses for all items.

Revision of the Questionnaire

For ease of administration and to ensure that critical information was collected from all respondents, certain questions were redistributed from the mailback questionnaire to the face-to-face interview schedule. Questions that appeared insensitive to age, sex, or individual differences were deleted. Questions related to family involvement were modified for further accommodation of individual differences within and among age groups. Certain questions were added to the consumer behavior portion of the questionnaire in order to cover areas that were missed. Additional response categories suggested by the face-to-face interviews were incorporated into the revision. Last, instructions were improved for ease of administration

Field Research reported that all of the other survey procedures worked smoothly and satisfactorily in the pilot test, and no specific changes to improve the survey design were recommended. Despite the fairly long face-to-face interview, the interviewers did not experience an unusual amount of respondent resistance. In fact, the 7 percent refusal rate was lower than is generally encountered in surveys of the general public in California.

4

THE LARGE-SCALE STUDY

SAMPLE DESIGN

In October 1976, the revised in-person and mailback questionnaires were administered by the Field Research Corporation using the same survey area, survey universe, sampling techniques, and interview procedures that were used in the pilot test.* The in-home interviewing was done between October 5 and 27, 1976. The cut-off date for the mailback questionnaires was November 30.

A total of 309 face-to-face interviews was completed in the homes of respondents, with roughly 100 interviews in each of the three age groups: 45-54, 55-64, and 65 or older. Within each age group half of the respondents were men and half were women. One respondent per household was interviewed. Self-administered questionnaires were mailed back by 271 of the original sample of 309, for a completion rate of 88 percent.

SURVEY AREA

The distribution of the sample by county is shown in Table 4.1. As in the pilot study, the survey area was defined as the five counties comprising the San Francisco-Oakland Standard Metropolitan Statistical Area: San Francisco, Alameda, Contra Costa, San Mateo, and Marin.

---

*The survey instrument may be obtained by contacting the author: Dr. Howard Schutz, Center for Consumer Research, University of California, Davis 95616.

41

TABLE 4.1

Large-Scale Survey Area Data

County	12/31/75* Population (1,000)		Cluster of Four Assigned		Expected Interviews		Completed Interviews	
	N	Percent of Total	N	Percent of Total	N	Percent of Total	N	Percent of Total
San Francisco	660.2	21	16	21	65	21	64	21
Alameda	1,108.3	35	27	35	108	35	106	34
Contra Costa	602.4	19	15	19	60	19	60	19
San Mateo	573.5	18	14	18	56	18	56	18
Marin	214.1	7	6	8	24	8	23	7
Total	3,158.5	100	78	100	312	100	309	100

*Estimate from Sales Management (Factbook).
Note: See Appendix A for results of field interviewing.
Source: Compiled by the authors.

The sample plan called for the assignment of 78 clusters of 4 interviews each, or 312 interviews. The number of "key addresses" drawn from each of the five counties was in proportion to that county's share of the total five-county household population.

DESCRIPTION OF THE SAMPLE

As can be seen in Table 4.2, most of our sample was either currently married (63 percent) or had been married (31 percent). The average income was perhaps low for two persons, but in the absence of children it would not be at the poverty level. The sample also included large numbers of retired persons. The mean education was 12.4 years, a higher level of schooling than is sometimes attributed to the elderly. This is due in part to the inclusion of persons aged 45-54 and 55-64, as is the fact that 32 percent had children still living at home.

Most of the respondents identified themselves with the middle class (53 percent) or working class (25 percent), although 17 percent identified with the upper-middle class. Occupational status included clerical and sales (29 percent), skilled (22 percent), unskilled (14 percent), and smaller percentages of managers or officials, and professionals.

The ethnic distribution was predominantly Anglo (88 percent), with the four other classifications accounting for 10 percent of the sample population. Most of the sample from these urban districts had resided in either a suburb, a small city or a large city in their youth (85 percent); 15 percent grew up on a farm.

A description of the political affiliation of the sample covers a moderate range: 33 percent conservative, 36 percent middle, and 23 percent liberal in their views. Only 4 percent described themselves as either strongly conservative or radical.

The religious backgrounds of our sample included 48 percent Protestant, 32 percent Catholic, and 4 percent Jewish.

APPROACH TO STATISTICAL ANALYSIS

The data were edited, cleaned, coded, keypunched, and then transferred to magnetic tape and subsequent analyses were all performed utilizing the Statistical Package for the Social Sciences of N. H. Nie et al. (1975).

Frequency distributions for all variables for the entire sample were obtained. In order to reduce redundancy and to uncover the basic dimensions underlying the data, lifestyle and consumer behavior

TABLE 4.2

Description of the Large-Scale Survey Sample
(N = 309)

Characteristic	Percent
Marital status	
Married	63
Divorced	12
Separated	3
Never married	5
Widowed	16
Average income: $10,500	
Years of schooling completed (mean): 12.4	
Children living at home	
Yes	32
Class identification	
Upper-middle	17
Middle	53
Working	25
Own home	
Yes	66
Occupational status	
Sales-clerical	29
Skilled laborer	22
Unskilled laborer	14
Manager/official/self-employed	13
Professional	11
Race/ethnic background	
Anglo	88
Black	5
Mexican-American	2
Spanish-American	2
Asian	1
Residence in youth	
Farm	15
Small city	35
Suburb	8
Large city	42
Political orientation	
Strong conservative	4
Conservative	33
Middle	36
Liberal	23
Radical	4
Religion	
Catholic	32
Protestant	48
Jewish	4

Notes: Occupational status includes both current working status and former occupations of retirees.

    See Appendix B for details of the major demographic variables.

    Source: Compiled by the authors.

variables were reduced by scale construction and factor analysis. The variables identified in the factor analysis were cross-tabulated by age group, controlling for sex of respondent. Stepwise linear multiple regression was used to predict consumer behavior factor scores with lifestyle scales, agree-disagree value statements, and demographics.

Method for Examining Lifestyle

For each of the seven roles studied (worker, homemaker, parent, spouse, friend, community worker, leisure-time user), questions were asked relating to three components: quantity of time in the role; affective aspect of the role; interactive aspect of the role. From this set of questions, five role-related composite-scale variables were created across all seven roles. The five variables were interaction, composed of 18 questions involving the respondents' talking, being with, or doing things with other people; satisfaction, made up of a single question on satisfaction for each role; role change, consisting of one question, for each role, on interest in changing the activity; near involvement, composed of 30 questions on frequency of activities conducted around the home; far involvement, consisting of 32 questions on frequency of participation in activities away from home. For each respondent an average was computed for each composite variable over the questions in that variable. (The composite variables and their components are listed in Appendix C.3.)

In order to simplify the nonrole lifestyle variables, a set of 57 variables representing personal value statements was factor analyzed. Nie et al. principal factoring with iteration, varimax rotation, pairwise deletion, and an eigen value cutoff point of 1.0000 were utilized. These lifestyle variables were ones that dealt primarily with personal values, and were not specifically identified with roles.

The results of the factor analysis were not satisfactory, in that the 20 variables extracted accounted for only 64 percent of the variance, and 8 variables did not weight .40 or higher on any of the factors. Therefore, in order to reduce the 57 variables, the highest weighting variable in each factor (20) and 8 variables that were not weighted on any factor were selected, resulting in a total of 28 lifestyle variables. These variables are listed in Appendix C-1 and can be identified as the agree-disagree statements.

The item tapping the variable "Do you live with another adult?" was chosen to represent interdependent living status, taking into consideration the variety of existing lifestyles in today's society.

"Do you work for pay?" was used to represent employment status.
Both were answered by "yes" or "no."

Method for Examining Consumer Behavior

In order to uncover the basic dimensions of consumer behavior
underlying the data and to reduce redundancy, seven individual factor
analyses were performed on a total of 222 consumer behavior variables, which were assigned to appropriate categories. The factor
analysis technique was the same as described for the lifestyle variables. Factor scores were computed for each respondent for each
factor.

The following areas were selected as a framework for the
analyses: buying style, which included frequency of actual shopping,
brand loyalty, credit use, venturesomeness, planning, impulsiveness,
price orientation, information sources, and degree of family involvement in purchase decisions; store relations, or types of stores
shopped at and mode of transportation; budget allocations; inventory;
alienation; attribute importance; and store choice. (See Tables 4.3-
4.9.)[*]

Selected elements of Richard Williams and Claudine Wirth's
lifestyle model (1965) and James Engel, David Kollat, and Roger
Blackwell's consumer behavior model (1973) were incorporated into
the theoretical framework used for the factor analyses. Williams
and Wirth divide lifestyle into psychological nature (values, goals,
life satisfaction, and self-rated health) and role-related behavior
(type of relationships, social position, orientation to interaction).
The Engel, Kollat, and Blackwell model includes the elements of
environmental influences (cultural, socioeconomic), the "central
control unit" (personality, attitudes, evaluative criteria, learning),
and the decision process (problem recognition, search and alternative
evaluation, store choice, and postpurchase process).

Tables 4.3-4.9 present the factors extracted from these
analyses. Names were chosen to highlight the variables weighted
0.40 or more, and are given for each factor. When the factor consisted primarily of negatively loaded variables, names were chosen
to reflect the positive dimensions.

---

[*]The consumer behavior factors correspond with Tables 4.3-
4.9. The factors were categorized by consumer behavior (buying
style, store relations, and so on), not by topic areas (income management, health, food and nutrition, and others).

TABLE 4.3

Factors and Factor Weights for Buying Style

Factor	Weight
Factor A: bank credit card use	9.3%
Use bank credit card for household items	.74
Use bank credit card for small appliances	.73
Use bank credit card for personal care items	.67
Use bank credit card for furniture	.67
Use bank credit card for clothing	.66
Use bank credit card for services	.63
Use bank credit card for recreation	.57
Use bank credit card for large appliances	.56
Frequently use bank credit card	.54
Use bank credit card for education, reading	.52
"I buy many things with a credit card"	.47
Factor B: solitary decision making	5.8%
Other person makes household purchase decisions	-.83
Respondent shops for small appliances	.61
Respondent makes own purchase decisions	.54
Factor C: brand switching	5.0%
"I often try new brands before my friends and neighbors do."	.87
"I often like to switch brands just for the sake of variety."	.59
Factor D: warranty more important than price or service	4.4%
Local dealer's reputation for service more important than price and warranty	-.95
Manufacturer's reputation and warranty more important than price or local dealer's service	.88
Factor E: planned purchases	3.8%
"Usually I shop with a list of specific things to buy and stick closely to that list."	.74
"I plan my purchases in advance."	.71
Factor F: price-value comparison	3.5%
Stay with familiar brand of packaged goods	-.71
Compare prices of packaged goods	.65
Compare weights and volumes of packaged goods	.48
Factor G: total interest more important than size of payment	3.3%
Total interest most important in obtaining a loan	.81
Size of monthly payment most important in obtaining a loan	-.79

(continued)

TABLE 4.3 (continued)

Factor	Weight
Factor H: joint decision making	3.2%
Respondent makes purchase decisions jointly with other person	.90
Respondent makes own purchase decisions	-.80
Factor I: auto repair in a shop	2.9%
Shop auto repair	.76
Personal auto repair	-.73
Factor J: price more important than warranty or service	2.8%
Price more important than manufacturer's warranty or local dealer's service	.92
Manufacturer's reputation and warranty more important than price or local service	-.43
Factor K: bargain hunting	2.6%
Frequently compare prescription drug prices	.79
"I shop around for sales and bargains."	.40
Factor L: reliance on printed sources of information	2.5%
Reliance on printed sources of information	.67
Reliance on own past experience or personal judgment	-.62
Factor M: other-directed decision making	2.4%
"When I shop, I like to talk to salespeople."	.56
"Before I buy something, I like to make sure my family and friends will like it too."	.46
Factor N: frequency of shopping	2.3%
Frequently shop for household items	.75
Frequently shop for personal care items	.70
Frequently shop for clothing	.55
Factor O: inner-directed decision making	2.2%
Reliance on family, friends, and salespeople for consumer information	-.71
Reliance on own past experience and personal judgment	.43
Factor P: quality consciousness	2.1%
"Quality is what I look for."	.58
"When I have questions about a product, I seek more information about it."	.50
Factor Q: belief that credit is unwise	2.0%
"To buy anything other than a house or car on credit is unwise."	.40
Factor R: do not use bank credit card for convenience	2.0%
Use bank credit for convenience	-.88

(continued)

TABLE 4.3 (continued)

Factor	Weight
Factor S: brand loyalty	1.9%
Compare ingredient labels of packaged goods	-.52
"I stick only to certain brands."	.41
Stay with familiar brands of packaged goods	.39
Factor T: impulse shopping	1.8%
"Often I purchase things on the spur of the moment, just because they have attracted my attention."	.42
"I often become confused if I have to consider a lot of information about a product I am thinking about buying."	.41
"My friends and neighbors usually give me pretty good advice about what brands to buy in the grocery store."	.40
Factor U: tv as information source	1.7%
Television as a source of product information	.41

Notes: 67.5 percent of total variance was accounted for by 21 factors.

Underlined numbers indicate percent of variance accounted for by each factor.

Source: Compiled by the authors.

49

TABLE 4.4

Factors and Factor Weights for Store Relations

Factor	Weight
Factor A: HMO (Kaiser) member	9.4%
Have Kaiser Health Plan	.96
Have Blue Cross insurance	−.90
Factor B: purchased auto by personal transaction	7.2%
Purchased vehicle by personal transaction	.96
Purchased vehicle from new-car dealer	−.75
Factor C: shop by public transportation	6.9%
Frequently shop by public transportation	.67
Frequently shop by foot	.63
Factor D: prefer department store over discount store	6.0%
Purchase small appliances at major department store	.83
Purchase small appliances at discount store	−.62
Purchase clothing at discount store	−.43
Factor E: chain drugstore shopping	5.7%
Shop for personal care items at large chain drugstore	.98
Shop for household items at large chain drugstore	.41
Factor F: chain supermarket shopping	5.2%
Shop for household items at large chain supermarket	.72
Shop for household items at small neighborhood store	−.62
Shop for personal care items at large chain supermarket	.41
Factor G: specialty store shopping	5.1%
Shop for clothing in specialty store	.68
"I like to shop in specialty stores."	.53
Factor H: discount drugstore shopping	5.0%
Shop for personal care items at discount drugstore	.78
Shop for household items at discount drugstore	.58
Factor I: prefer department store over specialty store for tires	4.6%
Shop for tires at major department store	.75
Shop for tires at specialty tire store	−.69
Factor J: used-car dealer shopping	4.3%
Purchased vehicle from used-car dealer	.96
Purchased vehicle from new-car dealer	−.60
Factor K: appliance store shopping	4.0%
Shop for small appliances at appliance store	.85

(continued)

TABLE 4.4 (continued)

Factor	Weight
Factor L: high-trust health insurance company	3.5%
Purchased health insurance through employer or major insurance company office	.69
Purchased health insurance by mail order, telephone, door-to-door sales, or other	-.50
Factor M: nondriver	3.2%
Other person drives respondent to shop	.66
Respondent drives self to shop	-.66
Factor N: catalog shopping	3.1%
Clothing shop from catalog	.73
"I often shop from the Wards or Sears catalog."	.49

Notes: 73.2 percent of total variance was accounted for by 14 factors.

Underlined numbers indicate percent of variance accounted for by each factor.

Source: Compiled by the authors.

51

TABLE 4.5

Factors and Factor Weights for Budget

Factor	Weight
Factor A: medical-furnishings-clothing-personal budget	<u>30.3%</u>
Monthly medical-dental expense	.62
Monthly home furnishings, appliances, and equipment expense	.47
Monthly clothing expense	.46
Monthly personal care expense	.42
Factor B: food-transportation budget	<u>12.2%</u>
Monthly food expense	.66
Monthly transportation expense	.47
Factor C: housing-recreation-savings budget	<u>12.0%</u>
Monthly housing expense	.52
Monthly reading, recreation, and education expense	.43
Monthly savings	.42

Notes: 54.5 percent of total variance was accounted for by three factors.
      Underlined numbers indicate percent of variance accounted for by each factor.
     Source: Compiled by the authors.

TABLE 4.6

Factors and Factor Weights for Inventory

Factor	Weight
Factor A: nonreal estate investments (stocks)	19.1%
Have investments	.91
Own common stocks	.58
Factor B: covered by Medicare	10.3%
Covered by Medicare	.62
Own or lease a motor vehicle	-.46
Frequently take prescription drugs	.41
Factor C: home ownership	9.7%
Own housing	.52
Credit union account	.49
Factor D: real estate investments	7.3%
Have investment in real estate	.66
Factor E: have health insurance policy	6.9%
Have health insurance policy	.41

Notes: 53.3 percent of total variance was accounted for by five factors.

Underlined numbers indicate percent of variance accounted for by each factor.

Source: Compiled by the authors.

TABLE 4.7

Factors and Factor Weights for Alienation

Factor	Weight
Factor A: problems with food, money, housing, transportation	29.0%
Problems with food, nutrition	.66
Problems with finances	.62
Problems with housing	.59
Problems with transportation	.56
Factor B: dissatisfied with health care services	13.6%
Dissatisfied with Medicare	.81
Problems with health care services	.58
Factor C: poor health	10.9%
Self-rated health status	.68
Self-rated disabilities	.47
Interviewer-rated disabilities	.40
Factor D: disappointing consumer experiences	8.9%
Number of disappointing experiences as a consumer in the past year	.46

Notes: 62.4 percent of total variance was accounted for by four factors.

Underlined numbers indicate percent of variance accounted for by each factor.

Source: Compiled by the authors.

TABLE 4.8

Factors and Factor Weights for Attribute Importance

Factor	Weight
Factor A: clothing fashionableness	14.5%
Clothing cut	.81
Clothing fashionableness	.62
Clothing color	.54
Factor B: hedonic food characteristics	9.7%
Food taste	.77
Food enjoyment	.70
Food appearance	.54
Food brand	.46
Factor C: price	8.5%
Clothing price	.77
Food price	.71
Auto purchase price	.46
Factor D: auto longevity	5.8%
Auto lifespan	.79
Auto safety features	.47
Auto handling	.43
Factor E: clothing durability	5.4%
Clothing durability	.71
Clothing washability	.51
Clothing alterability	.48
Factor F: auto design	4.9%
Auto make	.64
Auto styling	.59
Factor G: auto self-image	4.5%
Importance of self-concept derived when driving auto	.66
Factor H: brand	4.2%
Clothing brand	.70
Food brand	.45
Factor I: rational-pragmatic food characteristics	3.8%
Food preferences of family members	.61
Nutritional value of food	.55
Factor J: auto operating expense	3.7%
Auto operating expenses	.51

Notes: 65.0 percent of total variance was accounted for by ten factors.

Underlined numbers indicate percent of variance accounted for by each factor.

Source: Compiled by the authors.

TABLE 4.9

Factors and Factor Weights for Store Choice

Factor	Weight
Factor A: friendly personnel	13.9%
Household store for friendly personnel	.84
Personal care store for friendly personnel	.82
Small appliance store for friendly personnel	.67
Clothing store for friendly personnel	.55
Grocery store for friendly personnel	.48
Tire store for friendly personnel	.41
Factor B: easy to get to	7.3%
Personal care store because easy to get to	.74
Small appliance store because easy to get to	.70
Household store because easy to get to	.70
Clothing store because easy to get to	.62
Grocery store because easy to get to	.57
Factor C: convenient hours	6.0%
Personal care store because hours	.89
Household store because hours	.86
Grocery store because hours	.72
Small appliance store because hours	.68
Clothing store because hours	.64
Factor D: parking ease	4.7%
Personal care store for parking	.91
Household store for parking	.86
Small appliance store for parking	.75
Grocery store for parking	.72
Clothing store for parking	.62
Tire store for parking	.41
Factor E: low prices	4.4%
Household store for low prices	.69
Personal care store for low prices	.69
Tire store for low prices	.65
Small appliance store for low prices	.63
Clothing store for low prices	.54
Factor F: merchandise quality	3.8%
Personal care store for merchandise quality	.81
Small appliance store for merchandise quality	.70
Household store for merchandise quality	.54
Tire store for merchandise quality	.44

(continued)

TABLE 4.9 (continued)

Factor	Weight

Factor G: sales promotion activity	3.4%
Small appliance store for sales promotion	.75
Personal care store for sales promotion	.69
Household store for sales promotion	.65
Factor H: credit availability	3.1%
Small appliance store for credit	.73
Tire store for credit	.70
Clothing store for credit	.64
Factor I: atmosphere	2.8%
Household store for appearance of store and clientele	.81
Grocery store for appearance of store and clientele	.67
Personal care store for appearance of store and clientele	.61
Clothing store for appearance of store and clientele	.48
Factor J: tire, appliance, and personal care product assortment	2.7%
Tire store for product assortment	.68
Small appliance store for product assortment	.52
Personal care store for product assortment	.50
Factor K: household and grocery product assortment	2.6%
Household store for product assortment	.70
Grocery store for product assortment	.56
Factor L: specialty products available	2.4%
Grocery store for specialty products	.64
Personal care store for specialty products	.59
Factor M: trustworthy tire sales personnel	2.4%
Tire store for trustworthy personnel	-.45
Factor N: tire merchandise quality	2.1%
Tire store for merchandise quality	.61
Factor O: tire store convenient location	2.0%
Tire store because easy to get to	.68
Tire store because close by	.60
Tire store for parking	.50
Factor P: good grocery specials	2.0%
Grocery store for good specials	.59
Factor Q: convenient small appliance store location	1.8%
Small appliance store because close by	.45
Factor R: clothing store for friendly personnel	1.6%
Clothing store for friendly personnel	.39

TABLE 4.9 (continued)

Factor	Weight
Factor S: convenient location	1.6%
Household store because close by	.81
Personal care store because close by	.74
Grocery store because close by	.51
Small appliance store because close by	.44
Factor T: in-home convenience	1.6%
Clothing catalog for in-home convenience	.56

Notes: 72.2 percent of total variance was accounted for by 20 factors.

Underlined numbers indicate percent of variance accounted for by each factor.

Source: Compiled by the authors.

Examination of Tables 4.3-4.9 reveals that the seven factor analyses were successful in reducing the 222 consumer behavior variables to 77. The representativeness and inclusiveness of these factors is indicated by the variance accounted for, which ranges from 53 to 73 percent.

Prediction of Consumer Behavior Variables by Lifestyle and Demographic Variables

In order to relate the lifestyle and demographic variables to our consumer behavior factors, a series of 77 stepwise multiple-regression analyses were conducted (Nie et al. 1975). This analysis allows the determination of the "best" set of predictors of consumer behavior from among the total of lifestyle and demographic independent variables.

Since this type of regression is linear and additive, curvilinear and interaction relationships are not accounted for. Examination of the zero-order scattergrams between the dependent and independent variables revealed no strong nonlinear trends, so this should not be a factor in our analyses. The possible contribution of interactions was not investigated. In conducting the analyses the program options were as follows:

1. F-value for inclusion in a prediction equation was about 3.8 at the .05 level of significance.
2. Pairwise deletion was utilized, which would allow maximum use of the data; since missing data were few, there is a low distortion of the regression results.
3. The N for calculating the degrees of freedom was 300, which was determined by averaging 100 randomly selected N's from the zero-order correlation matrix.

The 54 independent variables are listed in Appendix C.2 with their coded values. The 77 dependent variables were the factor scores for each respondent on the factors shown in Tables 4.3-4.9. The values for the factor scores vary from low to high, with a high score meaning that an individual weights high on that factor. Multicollinearity was minimized by the fact that a majority of the variables were chosen on the basis of factor analyses and by the utilization of a stepwise-regression program. The results of the 77 regressions, organized by the seven consumer behavior areas used for the factor analyses, are given in appendixes E through M. These give a summary of the results, showing the statistically significant variables in the regression equation (.05 or less), the sign of the beta (standardized regression coefficient), rank by size of beta (a measure of importance), the multiple-correlation coefficient (R), and the amount of variance accounted for in the dependent variables by the independent variables (R^2).

Interviewer Observation Analysis

In addressing the problem of the reliability of data gathered from personal interviews of the elderly, part of the questionnaire included interviewer observations. These were collected along with the survey and analyzed, with the following results: interviewers reported that 75 percent of the respondents reacted "fairly normally" to "normal," in relation to their level of activity and speed of response, in answering the questionnaire, and 85 percent were confident and assured, as opposed to anxious, about the interview.

The respondents' emotional reactions were quite good, with 88 percent fairly sociable or sociable, 86 percent fairly comfortable or comfortable, and 87 percent fairly calm or calm during the interview. Moreover, in 83 percent of the cases emotional involvement did not change throughout the interview.

As far as attitude is concerned, 88 percent of the respondents were interested in the interview and 93 percent were eager to be interviewed. There was no difficulty with hearing (86 percent), read-ing (79 percent), or understanding (77 percent).

These findings, as reported by the interviewers, lend confidence to the validity of the survey as a likely representation of the attitudes and opinions of our sample of older Americans.

GENERALIZABILITY OF THE SURVEY

The results of this study on lifestyle and consumer behavior of older Americans may be generalized to the population of any area of California or elsewhere in terms of ordinal categories, descrip-tions of roles in lifestyle, some age-related characteristics, con-sumer behavior patterns, and the relationship between lifestyles and consumer behavior.

Although the California counties surveyed have a relatively high standard of living, income, and cultural mix compared with other areas, these data identify recognizable categories with which to view the habits and behavior of older Americans as members of and contributors to the consumer marketplace anywhere. The differ-ences that may occur in trying to replicate the same kind of infor-mation in another location will be a question of differences in absolute numbers in each category; the rank order of categories should remain the same.

PART III:
SURVEY RESULTS

5
LIFESTYLES

THE ROLE OF OLDER AMERICANS

How do the elderly see themselves? How do lifestyles influence their attitudes and opinions? Older Americans reflect different experiences as individuals, related to their passages through life (Sheehy 1976), and how they get through one stage affects the next. They also experience similar role-related societal pressures linked to cultural determinants of life satisfaction, such as the change in emphasis on the family as a source of support and interdependency. For instance, homemaking is no longer the most valued career option for women, and the high value placed on economic well-being and the strong formalized work ethic has separated men from their families and contributed to the mobility of men and women alike in their pursuit of individual careers. Social legislation emphasizing individual rights, mobility, more mothers working, and the problems connected with raising children have distorted the roles and relationships within the family unit. Both economic and sociological factors have to be considered in determining life satisfaction of the aged.

Some of the questions related to lifestyle roles are given in Table 5.1, with the survey results for those questions. Most of the questions related to the work role are listed. Selected questions relating to satisfaction with the other roles are also given.

Of the 56.6 percent who answered "no" to the work-for-pay question, almost two-thirds of those persons not working are either retired or classify themselves as retired because they are out of the job market. Another 30 percent who are not working for pay consider themselves homemakers. A full 8 percent of those persons who are not working would like to have a job, as indicated by the category "unemployed." The implication here is that some of those who are not working consider themselves to be capable, and desire work, which is not available, possibly for the income they would

TABLE 5.1

Roles of Older Americans

Question	Cases	Responses (percent)	
Do you work for pay, either full-time or part-time?	309	yes	43.4
		no	56.6
If no (56.6%), ask:	184	yes	91.8
Have you worked for pay in the past?		no	8.2
(Answer all that apply)			
Are you: unemployed	178	yes	8.4
		no	91.6
retired	178	yes	60.7
		no	39.3
student	178	yes	0.6
		no	99.4
homemaker	177	yes	30.5
		no	69.5
other	177	yes	3.4
		no	96.6
If yes (43.4%), ask:	129	yes	90.7
Do you work regularly?		no	9.3
Do you work full-time or part-time?	127	full	72.4
		part	27.6
Do you socialize (once or more a week) at work?	132	yes	84.1

(continued)

receive. A survey by Harris and Associates (1976) indicated that people in their late fifties and early sixties have trouble finding jobs. They suggest that by 65, people probably stop calling themselves "unemployed" and call themselves "retired."

Of the respondents who answered that they work for pay, 90 percent indicated that they work regularly. Almost three-fourths work full-time and a little over one-fourth work part-time. Interestingly, over half of the respondents who are working are very satisfied with their work and 33 percent are at least satisfied. This may indicate that those who are not working retire because they are forced to, are not satisfied with working, or do not need the money,

TABLE 5.1 (continued)

Question	Cases	Very Satisfied	Satisfied	Neither Satisfied nor Dissatisfied	Dissatisfied	Very Dissatisfied
		Responses (percent)				
How satisfied are you with work?	131	54.2	32.8	13.0	7.6	4.6
The following were asked of all respondents:						
How satisfied are you with homemaking activities?	308	33.1	53.6	8.4	4.5	0.3
How satisfied are you with your partner?	230	64.3	27.0	4.8	3.0	0.9
How satisfied are you with parenthood?	246	45.5	45.1	5.3	2.8	1.2
How satisfied are you with community activities?	250	33.2	46.8	12.8	4.4	2.8
How satisfied are you with leisure activities?	309	28.5	49.5	11.0	8.1	2.9

Source: Compiled by the authors.

whereas those who continue working do so because their work is satisfying either their monetary or their worker-producer needs.

SATISFACTION WITH ROLES

A study surveying factors influencing life satisfaction of the aged indicated that there was lower life satisfaction among the recently retired, resulting from the loss of income and not of the worker-producer role. Further, greater life satisfaction resulted when the aged lived in a family setting. This, it was suggested, resulted from the higher income available to the household as a result of this arrangement (Chatfield 1977).

According to our sample, all but 8 percent of the respondents either work for pay now or have worked for pay in the past, indicating a strong relationship between economic value and work. It may be assumed that most of those never having worked for pay are home-makers. Further, 84 percent indicated they socialize at work at least once a week, suggesting a strong social value related to work.

Looking at satisfaction with other roles, we find that almost 87 percent of all respondents are satisfied with homemaking activities, perhaps because older men become more interested in household tasks, and women worry less about homemaking chores, as they grow older.

Of the married respondents, 91.3 percent are satisfied with their partners. It may be surmised that those who remain married become more satisfied over time, and those who were unhappily married have found new, more compatible partners by this time in their lives. Nonetheless, 8.7 percent are neither satisfied nor dissatisfied, dissatisfied, or very dissatisfied.

A large number of respondents (91 percent) have indicated they are satisfied with parenthood, while 90 percent are either dissatisfied or neither satisfied nor dissatisfied. We may conclude that pressures inherent in raising children are increased among single-parent families, and that single-parent status and low income may account for some of the dissatisfaction.

There was a satisfaction rate of 80 percent among respondents related to community activities, indicating that at least 20 percent were either dissatisfied or neither satisfied nor dissatisfied. The implication is that in the absence of worker roles among the retired homemakers, other kinds of organizations are necessary to meet the social needs of the elderly. Church groups and associations and senior citizen affiliations that provide outlets for the creative pursuits and social networks of older Americans are indicated.

Additionally, as far as life satisfaction and well-being are concerned, Reed Larson, reviewing 30 years of research on the subjective well-being of older Americans, found that one study (Edwards and Klemack 1973) indicated that differences were apparent in relation to formal activity of older Americans between urban and nonurban samples. In nonurban samples organizational participation and church-related activity is consistently associated with well-being.

In the area of leisure activities, 78 percent are satisfied or very satisfied, while another 22 percent are either dissatisfied or neither satisfied nor dissatisfied. Perhaps they cannot afford leisure activity or, more likely, have not developed an interest in pursuing leisure activities because of the present emphasis on economic value and a strong, formalized work ethic leaving little time for other pursuits. Further, the value of leisure time increases with education (Harris and Associates 1976).

There is growing evidence that health, social activity, income, and education are influential in the prediction of individual satisfaction; there is less evidence as to the importance of other background factors in a person's satisfaction level.

Role-related variables were used to measure satisfaction with seven roles, defined as worker, homemaker, partner, parent, community worker, friend, leisure-time user (see Appendix C.3 for satisfaction variables). A number of demographic variables—including income, sex, age, ethnic background, religion, education—as well as selected interactions from the seven roles that included marital status and employment were used as the independent variables and measures of satisfaction for the seven roles of worker, homemaker, partner, parent, community worker, friend, and leisure-time user as dependent variables in multiple regression analyses (see Table 2.1).

The interaction variables represent combinations of demographic variables the interaction of which the researchers believed might be related to life satisfaction.

These combinations of variables centered on age, income, and Anglo. One of the major purposes of this portion of the study was to ascertain whether different patterns of behavior exist among the three age groups chosen for analysis. Therefore, some of the two-way interactions consisted of age and gender in combination with other variables. The first set of interactions dealt with age and gender: age by living alone, age by income, age by education, age by gender, age by employment status, Catholic by age, Protestant by age, and gender by living alone.

The individual at 45 is different from the person of 65 in relation to the roles played. He or she is primarily coping with middle age at age 45: parenting, spousal relationships, careers, and homemaking responsibilities, all at the same time. At 65 he or she is coping with the problems of old age, including the death of friends and changing careers or retirement, and is less involved with parenting, for instance (Atchley 1972; Rose and Peterson 1965).

During those 20 years changes generally take place in a person's employment status: the 45-year-old works; the 65-year-old is often retired. By age 65, 50 percent of women and 20 percent of men are widowed and/or living alone (Atchley 1972).

In addition, the investigators wished to know if age, in combination with education level or ethnic background, affected satisfaction with life among the three age groups under study. Variables used included Anglo by age, Anglo by income, and Anglo by education. In a journal article on the well-being of older Americans by Reed Larso (1978), the point is made that there are limitations on interpretation of measurements of well-being. Larson questions whether instruments measure the same thing in different populations, such as goals and life assessment, by class and age. He states that the relationship between ethnic background and well-being is more a matter of socioeconomic status, and well-being contains several factors: income, occupational status, and education.

A third set of two-way variables was concerned with income and whether educational level, employment status, and being male or female had to do with an individual's role satisfaction. These variables were income by employment status, income by gender, and income by education.

Several three-way interactions were also used to ascertain whether a third variable provided a more significant interaction level. The three-way variables were set up as follows, using a number of the same variables used for the two-way set. They included age by income by gender, age by income by education, and age by living alone by gender.

Our intention was to explore the effect of the various demographic and situational factors as they relate to lifestyle roles in order to determine life satisfaction and, thus, well-being.

REGRESSION ANALYSIS AND RESULTS

The independent variables (demographics) were entered into seven stepwise multiple regressions, one for each of the seven roles, with the satisfaction variable for that particular role used as the dependent variable. The analyses were computed using the stepwise program of Nie et al. (1975). Only those variables that contributed to the regression at least at the .05 level of significance were included in the final equation.

The results of the analyses showed that for the seven roles, there was a low but significant relationship (p = .05) with the independent variables (demographic interactions). (See Appendix D.)[*]

---

*A summary of standardized regression weights for the significant variables, and the $\underline{R}$ and $\underline{R}^2$ for each role, are presented in Appendix D. In choosing significant variables, the significant $\underline{F}$-value (.05) was used as a point of reference. Variables were not considered significant when, upon the inclusion of new variables, the $\underline{F}$-value no longer remained significant.

While these results were significant, the multiple $\underline{R}$'s are small and life satisfaction is not completely accounted for with the use of roles and demographic variables. Associations found were as follows:

1. "Worker role"—Anglo by income. The highest percentage of those satisfied with work were Anglos in the $12,000-$14,000 income group. This group made up 38 percent of all Anglos. If we add the $15,000-$19,000 group who were satisfied, the total increases to 53 percent of all Anglos in the sample. With Anglos in general, as income increased, so did satisfaction levels up to $20,000. Above $20,000 the numbers who were satisfied were at about the same level of satisfaction as those whose incomes ranged below $20,000. With non-Anglos the results show similar patterns with the highest percentage of those satisfied with work in the $12,000-$14,000 income group. The level of satisfaction for Anglos is generally higher, on the average, than that of other minority groups. Sixty percent of Mexican-Americans 65 and over, and 35 percent of those 45-64, have incomes below $3,000 a year, compared with 55 and 15 percent for blacks and 50 and 5 percent for whites, respectively (Kimmel 1974).

2. "Homemaker role"—gender. This result showed that males were more satisfied with homemaking than females were. There is some evidence (Atchley 1972) that older males take more interest in the home as their work role lessens and they spend more time in the home.

3. "Partner role"—gender by education. Males with less education were the most satisfied with their partners. Such men may base their expectations on very traditional styles of marriage learned from their parents, and thus are not involved in conflicts often associated with woman's changing role in the home.

4. "Parenthood role"—Anglo by education. Minorities (24 percent) and Anglos (33 percent) with a high school education were by far the most satisfied with parenthood.

5. "Community role"—Non-Catholics were the most satisfied with community activities.

6. "Friends role"—Protestants were more satisfied with friends than members of other denominations were.

7. "Leisure time user"—age by income. Group 3 (65+) members who earned $11,000-$12,000 appeared the most satisfied with leisure. There is evidence (Atchley 1972; Rose and Peterson 1965) that as they age, both males and females spend more time on leisure pursuits and are more satisfied with them, but generally only those above minimum incomes have the freedom to pursue leisure.

Although the above results do point out a number of interacting situational-demographic variables as contributing to the prediction of life satisfaction in the roles examined in this study, these results do not adequately explain satisfaction. As was stated earlier, current research efforts (including Tornstom 1975; Medley 1976) have suggested that there is need for a multidimensional approach to the prediction of life satisfaction that would include not only demographic variables but also such endogenous variables as "self-perceived health status" and exogenous variables that portray social interaction and social activity levels of respondents (within the seven roles), as suggested in the lifestyle model presented here. How much time an individual spends in the roles, the degree of involvement, and whether there is a desire to change the roles may influence satisfaction as well, and are not accounted for with the inclusion of demographic variables alone.

Gerontological researchers have so far identified a number of the cogent correlates of life satisfaction. Reed Larson (1978) found that life satisfaction was the most strongly related to health, followed by socioeconomic factors and degree of social interaction, after age 60. Marital status and living arrangements have also been conclusively related to well-being. In his research Larson finds that among all the studies conducted, age, sex, race, and employment did not show consistent, independent relation to well-being. Rather, problems relating to poor health and low income were found to create a vulnerability to the effect of other negative conditions.

CROSS-TABULATIONS OF SELECTED LIFESTYLE VARIABLES BY AGE AND SEX

This analysis included the 44 variables made up of a number of demographic variables, including age, occupational status, and gender. Also present were the 34 variables represented in the factor analysis and the scales created to measure satisfaction, social interaction, and role change within the seven roles. (The role scales were grouped into low, moderate, and high categories by dividing each scale into thirds.)

Fifteen variables emerged in which the chi square was significant at the .05 level or less, some of them significant for both males and females, others for only one sex. A number of occupational status variables were significant. These included the "retirement" variable. For both males and females, as expected, the percentage of retirees increased dramatically from the first to the third age group. In the males the percentage doubled between age 55-64 and 65+, whereas in the females the percentage increase from the second to the third age group was four times greater. Perhaps females do not identify so strongly with the work role, and thus are willing to retire earlier because they are generally homemakers as well. Women may also retire more often because of poor health, since they have, or complain of, poor health more often than males (Rose and Peterson 1965).

The "work for pay" variable also was significant for both males and females, and follows the same pattern as the "retirement" variable, in that the majority of individuals working for pay appeared in the 45-54 age group for both males and females, while the smallest percentage working occurred in the 65+ group. The actual numbers in the "retirement" variable versus the "work for pay" variable differed slightly, and perhaps this difference may be attributed to the fact that some individuals continued to "work" although it may not have been for pay.

Two other occupational variables were significant. These were the variable "unskilled" for males (are you unskilled?)· and "homemaker" (are you a homemaker?) for females. In the former the female counterpart did not reach significance, since there are probably few jobs for females in our primarily urban sample that would fall into the unskilled classification. It may have been significant for males because of the large number of individuals in the 55-64 age group. The fact that many of the 65+ group are retired perhaps accounts for the dropoff in that age group. A plausible explanation for the low number of respondents in the 45-54 age group might be that the younger group is better educated, because education became more widespread in the United States after World War II (Rose and Peterson 1965). And as more individuals attended high school and/or college, fewer went into unskilled jobs.

The "homemaker" variable appeared only for females; males generally do not consider themselves homemakers even if they work in the home. The percentage in the 65+ group was half the figure in the first and second groups, which may indicate that women no longer consider themselves homemakers if they are not caring for children and/or a husband. By age 65+, children generally have left home permanently and women often are widowed.

"Far involvement," the variable created for the purpose of measuring involvement outside the home, including community, friendship, and (out-of-the-home) leisure roles, proved more significant for females than for males. Perhaps it proved significant because all respondents in the two younger age groups had some degree of involvement. The oldest group had less involvement, but a large percentage was involved. This finding might be explained by the fact that as respondents age, they begin to shed their work, parenting, and community activity roles, for which they often substitute social interactions. Margaret Clark and Barbara Anderson (Atchley 1972) suggest that this reevaluation of roles is one of the adaptive tasks necessary to successful aging, and state: "Certain roles and activities must be relinquished and there must follow a reconstitution of social relationships." And, according to Richard Williams and Claudine Wirth (1965), the individual who is aging successfully remains autonomous, which means preserving a balance between what is taken from and what is given to the social system. The fact that a similar level of activity was maintained by all three age groups in this study would lend support to this theory. In addition these findings also support the activity theory of aging that stresses the maintenance of a large number of roles and remaining very active in them (Atchley 1972).

In addition to the variables already discussed, several of the value-statement variables extracted from the factor analysis appeare significant. These variables were set up on a five-point agree-disagree scale. The only variable appearing significant for both males and females was "daily activities limited by health." The percentage of "agrees" rose sharply in the 65+ female group, whereas in the male group, although the number of "agrees" increased at age 65, the percentage of "disagrees" was higher than the "agrees." Literature supports the fact that although older women may not have more health problems, they more often have those of a chronic nature. Men more often die from heart attacks and strokes at this age. In addition, women complain of health problems more and see doctors more often (Rose and Peterson 1965; Atchley 1972).

Examination of other significant variables revealed that males in the oldest age group most often had fewer friends than those in the two younger groups and preferred people their own age. Females tended not to introduce themselves to strangers very often. Literatur that supports these findings suggests that the elderly constrict their social space after age 60-65 at which time some disengagement occurs (Kimmel 1974; Atchley 1972). Surprisingly, the 45-54 age group believed more strongly that older people were poorly treated. Males in the 55-64 age group were more venturesome than those in the other two groups, liking to "go alone to strange places." All three groups of males "dislike set schedules," but this may be wishful thinking, since generally the oldest group is the only retired group that may be without a set schedule. The two older groups of males felt "marriage was a problem if the wife brings home money," which may be indicative of change in attitudes in the 45-54 group toward women working outside the home. Finally, the two younger male groups felt children were the primary considerations in their decisions, which is logical, since children are usually out of the home by the time the parents are 65 and the older person turns inward to a greater degree, focusing upon himself or herself (Bischoff 1976; Kimmel 1974).

6

THE CONSUMER BEHAVIOR PROCESS

On what basis do we relate lifestyles and satisfaction to consumer decision making? Through the choice of stores, shopping frequency, kind of transportation used for shopping, family role behavior, sources of consumer information, purchase information, brand behavior, and the kinds of consumer problems and bad experiences confirmed by the elderly, we can trace patterns of behavior that delineate both the attitudes and the opinions of older Americans, as determined by their lifestyles.

STORE CHOICE

Store choice is the process by which the consumer compares the characteristics of stores by means of personal evaluative criteria and then makes a decision as to which one to shop in. Types of stores and products considered in this study include those listed below.

Stores	Products
Large chain supermarkets	groceries
Neighborhood grocery stores	household items
Large chain drugstores	personal care items
Neighborhood drugstores	small appliances
Discount department stores	clothing
Specialty stores (including appliance stores)	
Catalog/mail order	
PX	

Evaluative criteria that were used to determine attitudes and opinions toward store choice include the following:

merchandise quality	specialty products
product assortment	sales promotion
proximity of store	personnel
accessibility	special services
parking facilities	hours
prices	appearance of store and clientele
credit availability	loyalty to owner
in-home convenience	

Older persons shopped at a variety of stores across the product classes for which we tested (see Table 6.1). Three dichotomies appeared in the store-relations factor analysis: department store-discount store; large chain supermarket-small neighborhood grocery store; and department store-specialty store (in the case of tires only). Specialty stores, discount drugstores, large chain drugstores, appliance stores, and catalog shopping appeared as independent factors, which indicates that these types of stores are unrelated in the cognitive structure of the older persons in the study.

Table 6.2 presents the percentages of older persons in the study who use these criteria to select the stores tested for. When averaged, these percentages indicate that product assortment, prices, and location (accessibility and proximity) are most important across all classes of stores, with special services, loyalty to owner, and in-home convenience the least important. Parking facilities, merchandise quality, sales promotion, availability of special products, personnel, appearance of store and clientele, and credit availability were intermediate.

In most instances these dimensions of evaluative criteria were clear-cut when factor analyzed (see Tables 6.2 and 4.9). There are apparently, general store-choice sets existing across most store and product classes rather than varying selection criteria for specific stores and products. Exceptions to this included separate factors for grocery store sales promotion, appliance store location, tire and clothing store personnel, tire store location and merchandise quality, grocery store and household item store product assortment, and tire, appliance, and personal care item store product assortment.

In the regression analysis store choice was primarily a function of attitude toward homemaking, marriage, and family, and social class and employment status. Age figured in the regression equation for only one factor: tire, appliance, and personal care store choice based on product assortment. "Retired" had a negative relationship to personal care, appliance, household item, and tire store choice based on merchandise quality. (A complete summary of consumer behavior factors and lifestyle predictor variables is in Appendix E. A complete summary of the regression equation for store choice is

TABLE 6.1

Store Choice by Products

Type of Store	Percent (N) of Older Persons in Study Purchasing Specified Commodity at Store Type Listed	
Large chain supermarket		
Groceries	79.9	(247)
Household items	50.5	(156)
Personal care items	15.9	(49)
Department store		
Clothing	62.1	(192)
Small appliances	34.6	(107)
Tires	14.9	(46)
Large chain drugstores		
Personal care items	34.0	(105)
Household items	13.9	(43)
Discount department store		
Small appliances	30.7	(95)
Clothing	12.6	(39)
Tires	6.5	(20)
Personal care items	5.5	(17)
Household items	3.9	(12)
Specialty stores		
Tires	28.5	(88)
Small appliances	16.5	(51)
Clothing	12.6	(39)
Neighborhood drugstore		
Personal care items	16.5	(51)
Discount drugstore		
Personal care items	19.7	(61)
Household items	12.9	(40)
Neighborhood grocery store		
Household items	12.9	(40)
Groceries	7.1	(22)
Personal care items	2.9	(9)
Catalog/mail order		
Clothing	12.6	(39)
Small appliances	7.1	(22)
Tires	1.3	(4)

(continued)

ype of Store	Percent (N) of Older Persons in Study Purchasing Specified Commodity at Store Type Listed	
ther store		
Tires	8.4	(26)
Household items	6.9	(21)
Groceries	5.8	(18)
Small appliances	2.3	(7)
Clothing	1.3	(4)
Personal care items	1.3	(4)
X		
Small appliances	1.3	(4)
Personal care items	1.3	(4)
Household items	1.0	(3)
Groceries	0.6	(2)

Source: Compiled by the authors.

TABLE 6.2

Factor Analysis of Store Choice by Evaluative Criteria

Criteria (in order of stated importance)	Percent (N) of Older Persons in Study Selecting Stores by Criteria Listed		Me
Product assortment			
Clothing store	58.9	(182)	
Grocery store	55.3	(171)	
Small appliances store	54.4	(168)	
Personal care items store	53.7	(166)	50
Household items store	51.8	(160)	
Tire store	27.8	(86)	
Prices			
Personal care items store	46.9	(145)	
Small appliances store	43.4	(134)	
Household items store	41.4	(127)	
Grocery store	30.1	(93)	36
Tire store	30.1	(93)	
Clothing store	28.8	(89)	
Accessibility			
Household items store	42.1	(130)	
Personal care items store	41.7	(129)	
Small appliances store	35.6	(110)	
Grocery store	34.3	(106)	34
Clothing store	32.0	(99)	
Tire store	19.7	(61)	
Proximity			
Grocery store	43.0	(133)	
Personal care items store	40.1	(124)	
Household items store	39.5	(122)	
Small appliances store	28.8	(89)	32.
Clothing store	23.9	(74)	
Tire store	18.8	(58)	
Parking facilities			
Personal care items store	35.9	(111)	
Household items store	35.3	(109)	
Grocery store	33.7	(104)	
Small appliances store	32.7	(101)	31.
Clothing store	30.7	(95)	
Tire store	20.1	(62)	

(continued)

78

TABLE 6.2 (continued)

Criteria (in order of stated importance)	Percent (N) of Older Persons in Study Selecting Stores by Criteria Listed		Mean
Merchandise quality			
Clothing store	44.3	(137)	
Grocery store	36.9	(114)	
Small appliances store	31.4	(97)	30.3
Household items store	26.9	(83)	
Tire store	22.7	(70)	
Personal care items store	19.4	(60)	
Sales promotion			
Clothing store	30.4	(94)	
Grocery store	29.1	(90)	
Household items store	22.3	(69)	24.4
Personal care items store	22.3	(69)	
Small appliances store	18.1	(56)	
Availability of special products			
Clothing store	23.9	(74)	
Personal care items store	20.7	(64)	20.1
Grocery store	15.9	(49)	
Personnel			
Grocery store	29.1	(90)	
Clothing store	18.8	(58)	
Household items store	18.4	(57)	18.1
Personal care items store	17.5	(54)	
Tire store	12.6	(39)	
Small appliances store	12.3	(38)	
Hours			
Grocery store	19.7	(61)	
Personal care items store	18.1	(56)	
Household items store	17.8	(55)	15.8
Clothing store	15.9	(49)	
Small appliances store	14.2	(44)	
Tire store	9.1	(28)	
Appearance of store and clientele			
Grocery store	17.8	(55)	
Clothing store	13.6	(42)	
Household items store	9.7	(30)	10.3
Personal care items store	9.7	(30)	
Small appliances store	7.4	(23)	
Tire store	3.6	(11)	

TABLE 6.2 (continued)

Criteria (in order of stated importance)	Percent (N) of Older Persons in Study Selecting Stores by Criteria Listed		Mean
Credit availability			
Clothing store	24.3	(75)	
Small appliances store	11.3	(35)	
Tire store	9.4	(29)	9.1
Household items store	4.9	(15)	
Grocery store	2.6	(8)	
Personal care items store	2.6	(8)	
Special services			
Tire store	15.2	(47)	
Clothing store	8.1	(25)	
Small appliances store	5.2	(16)	6.3
Household items store	3.9	(12)	
Grocery store	3.6	(11)	
Personal care items store	2.3	(7)	
Other			
Tire store	4.5	(14)	
Grocery store	4.2	(13)	
Clothing store	2.6	(8)	3.0
Personal care items store	2.6	(8)	
Small appliances store	2.3	(7)	
Household items store	1.9	(6)	
Loyalty to owner			
Tire store	5.2	(16)	
Grocery store	3.2	(10)	
Personal care items store	3.2	(10)	2.8
Small appliances store	1.9	(6)	
Clothing store	1.9	(6)	
Household items store	1.6	(5)	
In-home convenience			
Clothing store	7.4	(23)	1.4
Household items store	1.3	(4)	

Source: Compiled by the authors.

TABLE 6.3

Summary of Lifestyle Correlates of Store Relations and Store Choice

Frequency of Appearance in Regression Equations	Lifestyle Correlate
	Homemaking, Marriage, and Family
6	"Homemaking is a lonely life."
5	"Older people are poorly treated in America."
4	"I worry my children will not turn out right."
3	Married
3	Homeowner
3	"I'm a homebody."
3	"A marriage has problems when the wife brings home money."
3	"When making important decisions, a primary consideration is my children."
2	"I wish I were single."
2	"A woman's most important interests and activities tend to be ones in which her husband cannot participate."
1	"Children don't spend enough time with their parents."
37	
	Occupation and Social Class
13	Occupation and employment status
4	Self-rated social class
3	Education
2	Income
22	
	Local-Cosmopolitan Orientation and Attitude Toward Change and New Experience
4	Far involvement
3	"Belonging to a local club would be more rewarding than belonging to a state or national organization."
3	Role change
3	"I'm a little leery of trying new things, so my free time activities don't change very much."

TABLE 6.3 (continued)

Frequency of Appearance in Regression Equations	Lifestyle Correlate
2	"I am more interested in news about national and international events than things that happen in this community."
2	"I dislike following a set schedule."
1	"Change and new experiences are important in the life of every person."
$\frac{1}{19}$	"I have never felt I was too old to take up new ways."

Inner-Directedness

4	"I am a better listener than conversationalist."
2	Religiosity
1	Satisfaction
1	"In most situations it is clear to me there is a right way and a wrong way."
$\frac{1}{9}$	"I should take some time each day to look into my mind and feelings."

Social Interaction

1	Interaction
1	"I would feel lost without my friends."
$\frac{1}{3}$	"I seem to have fewer friends now than in the past."

Age and Sex

4	Gender
$\frac{1}{5}$	Age

Source: Compiled by the authors.

in Appendix F.) Table 6.3 provides a summary of the contributions of the various lifestyle variables to store choice, organized into seven groups.

These results do not lend themselves to neat theorizing, although individual lifestyle correlates can be interpreted in light of the Gregory Stone and P. Ronald Stephenson-Ronald Willett shopper typologies (Engel, Kollat, and Blackwell 1973). Gregory Stone identified the economic shopper, the personalizing shopper, the ethical shopper, and the apathetic shopper, and found that they were related to lifestyle factors of social position, community identification, length of residence in the community, and level of aspiration and success. P. Ronald Stephenson and Ronald Willett named their shopper types store-loyal, compulsive and recreational, convenience, and price and bargain-conscious. At any rate, age appears to be irrelevant as a predictor of store relations and store choice. Shoppers of all ages in the study apparently select stores that provide them with the products and services they need, and do so in a rational manner.

SHOPPING FREQUENCY

Food is the most frequently shopped-for commodity among older persons (Table 6.4). Seventy-five percent of all older persons shop for groceries at least weekly. Shopping for household items, such as light bulbs, detergent, and paper products, peaks at weekly and at monthly intervals. The largest proportion of older persons shops for personal care items once a month. Most of them shop for clothing several times a year.

Frequency of shopping was predicted by general level of involvement in life, both in the home and in the community, by marriage, by higher levels of social interaction, and by the feeling that homemaking is a lonely life. (See Appendix G.11.)

TRANSPORTATION TO SHOPPING

Self-driven automobile is the most frequently utilized mode of transportation to shopping areas; nearly two-thirds of the older persons in the survey used this mode always or often (see Table 6.5). Walking (24 percent always or often), being driven by someone else (18 percent always or often), and public transportation (12 percent always or often) were other means of reaching stores.

TABLE 6.4

Shopping Frequency

Commodity	Several Times/Week		Weekly		Bimonthly		Monthly		Several Times/Year		Once a Year or Less		Never	
	%	N	%	N	%	N	%	N	%	N	%	N	%	N
Food	29.8	92	45.0	139	6.5	20	6.8	21	4.2	13	0.6	2	7.1	22
Household items	5.2	16	26.3	81	16.2	50	29.5	91	10.0	31	2.6	8	10.0	31
Personal care items	2.6	8	16.2	50	16.2	50	38.3	118	16.6	51	3.9	12	6.2	19
Clothing	—	1	1.0	3	3.2	10	18.8	58	58.9	182	15.2	47	2.9	9

Source: Compiled by the authors.

TABLE 6.5

Transportation to Shopping

Mode	Always		Often		Sometimes		Hardly Ever		Never	
	%	N	%	N	%	N	%	N	%	N
Self-driven auto	53.7	166	9.1	28	2.9	9	1.6	5	25.6	79
Walk	9.1	28	15.2	47	19.4	60	12.3	38	41.7	129
Other-driven auto	8.7	27	9.1	28	17.8	55	15.2	47	45.6	141
Public transport	2.9	9	8.4	26	14.6	45	11.3	35	59.9	185
Bicycle	—	—	0.3	1	2.9	9	2.3	7	88.0	272

Source: Compiled by the authors.

TABLE 6.6

Family Role Behavior

Commodity	Solitary		Spouse		With Spouse		With Other Person		Other Person	
	%	N	%	N	%	N	%	N	%	N
Solitary vs. Joint Shopping										
Food	56.9	175	24.0	74	11.0	34	3.6	11	4.5	14
Household items	56.6	175	14.9	46	22.3	69	2.0	6	4.2	13
Personal care items	77.3	239	12.0	37	7.8	24	1.0	3	1.9	6
Clothing	73.5	227	9.7	30	14.9	46	0.6	2	1.3	4
Small appliances	70.9	219	—	—	—	—	—	—	—	—
Tires	48.5	150	—	—	—	—	—	—	—	—
Solitary vs. Joint Decision Making										
Carpet	37.7	114	13.9	42	39.4	119	6.3	19	2.7	8
Refrigerator	36.5	110	9.3	28	47.5	143	4.7	14	2.0	6
Life insurance policy	37.8	104	11.3	31	43.6	120	5.5	15	1.8	5
Automobile tires	58.5	158	23.0	62	10.7	29	3.7	10	4.1	11
Bathroom fixtures	39.0	117	10.3	31	41.7	125	5.0	15	4.0	12
Bill paying	62.1	192	24.0	74	10.7	33	1.6	5	1.6	5

Source: Compiled by the authors.

FAMILY ROLE BEHAVIOR

Three-quarters of older persons shop for clothing and personal care items by themselves, and half shop for food and household items on their own. Grocery shopping is the type of shopping most likely to be left up to the spouse, and procuring household supplies is most likely to be a joint effort. Decisions on the purchase of carpet, refrigerators, bathroom fixtures, and life insurance are almost equally likely to be a solitary or a joint effort, with a few more people reporting joint. Automobile tires and bill paying are most likely to be taken care of independently or left to the spouse (see Table 6.6).

Joint decision making was, logically, predicted by variables that reflect strong family ties, certain conservative values, and the ability to make rational decisions: marriage, relative lack of appreciation for female autonomy, worry about children, positive attitude toward the treatment of older people, cosmopolitan orientation toward group membership, the feeling that clubs are enjoyable but not really important, reluctance to take up new ways, and self-employment/managerial/official and nonhomemaker employment status (see Appendix G.6).

On the other hand, persons who shop and make purchase decisions on their own are characterized by an independent lifestyle. They tend to be younger and unmarried, to take much responsibility for homemaking, to feel open to change, and to be employed as other than a skilled worker (see Appendix G.1).

SOURCES OF CONSUMER INFORMATION

Personal judgment and experience and the advice of family and friends, in that order, were by far the most frequently relied-on sources of consumer information among older people (see Table 6.7). Printed sources, including consumer publications, package labels, newspapers, magazines, books, and Yellow Pages were a distant third.

Reliance on personal judgment and experience appeared in the factor analysis in dichotomous relationships to advice from family, friends, and sales personnel and to information from printed sources. Persons who use personal judgment and experience rather than interpersonal sources tend to be employed in occupations requiring rational decision making or independent judgment: self-employed/ manager/official or skilled worker. They also tend to be talkers rather than listeners, and not to be homebodies (see Appendix G.12). Conversely, then, older persons who rely on family, friends, and

TABLE 6.7

Sources of Consumer Information

	Personal Judgment and Experience		Family and Friends		Consumer Publications		Professional Directories and Referral Services		Displays, Samples		Package Labels		Sales Personnel	
	%	N	%	N	%	N	%	N	%	N	%	N	%	N
Make of new car	54.8	159	22.0	64	15.8	46	0.7	2	1.0	3	—	—	2.7	8
New-car dealer	50.1	144	37.2	107	3.1	9	1.4	4	0.7	2	—	—	2.8	8
Investments for retirement income	38.0	107	26.3	71	9.6	27	21.4	60	—	—	—	—	2.1	6
Insurance policy	47.7	136	31.9	91	5.3	15	9.8	28	—	—	—	—	3.9	11
Frozen vegetables	52.3	154	11.4	34	3.8	11	0.7	2	6.3	19	20.5	61	0.7	2
Plumber	24.7	72	37.0	108	0.3	1	7.2	21	—	—	—	—	—	—
Doctor or dentist	35.4	108	41.6	127	—	—	18.4	56	—	—	—	—	—	—
Television set	47.7	145	21.7	66	18.1	55	1.0	3	1.6	5	—	—	4.9	15
Total N		1,025		668		164		176		29		61		50

	Television		Radio		Newspaper		Magazines		Books		Adult Education Class		Yellow Pages	
	%	N	%	N	%	N	%	N	%	N	%	N	%	N
Make of new car	0.7	2	—	—	1.3	3	0.7	2	—	—	—	—	0.3	1
New-car dealer	1.0	3	0.3	1	1.4	4	—	—	0.3	1	—	—	1.7	5
Investments for retirement income	—	—	—	—	0.7	2	—	—	0.7	2	1.1	3	1.1	3
Insurance policy	—	—	—	—	0.4	1	—	—	—	—	—	—	1.0	3
Frozen vegetables	2.9	8	—	—	1.2	3	0.3	1	—	—	—	—	—	—
Plumber	—	—	—	—	1.4	4	—	—	—	—	0.3	1	29.1	85
Doctor or dentist	—	—	—	—	0.3	1	—	—	—	—	—	—	4.3	13
Television set	1.6	5	—	—	2.0	6	—	—	—	—	—	—	1.3	4
Total N		18		1		24		3		3		4		127

Source: Compiled by the authors.

sales personnel tend to be "homebodies" and listeners, and possibly possess poorly developed powers of rational decision making. Persons who like to discuss their purchases with sales personnel and who need the approval of family and friends before they buy anything score high on the social interaction scale, are higher in income, open to trying new things, child-centered, homebodies, Anglo, and in poor health, and wish they were single (see Appendix G.10).

Older persons who rely on printed sources rather than personal judgment tend to be homemakers, say they would feel lost without their friends, are not widowed, and are not skilled workers (see Appendix G.9). Are these older Americans targets for fraud? One suggestion to avoid such a situation is to teach rational decision making in youth and adult classes.

Television as a source of product information was predicted by a group of variables that suggest sociability combined with anxiety: talker, not listener; no desire to be single; feeling that marriage has problems when the wife brings home money; worry about how children will turn out; would be lost without friends; wish to be famous; dislike a set schedule; good health; higher self-rated social class; female; and not employed in a clerical or sales position (see Appendix G.16).

Motivation to seek further information about a product when there are questions about it was related to the search for quality in the factor analysis and, in the regression analysis, to variables that indicate introspection, social independence, good health, openness to change, no opposition to a set routine, more involvement around the home than in the community, local rather than national ties, tolerance of female economic independence, and Anglo ethnic identity (see Appendix G.13). Conversely, the older consumer least likely to seek information before buying tends to be nonintrospective, nonwhite, more involved away from home than in the home, and beset by restlessness and fears, including fear of change, fear of female economic independence, and fear of being alone.

Therefore, those needing consumer protection are characterized by psychographic traits that make them vulnerable. Age, sex, and income are less relevant.

Personal judgment and experience and consumer publications were the sources of information most likely to be used by older persons when purchasing durables such as automobiles or television sets. Family and friends were most often turned to when choosing service providers, such as car dealers, doctors, dentists, and plumbers. Older persons used professional directories and referral services when evaluating investment possibilities or choosing a doctor or dentist. Samples and package labels were consulted for frozen vegetables; sales personnel, for insurance policies and television sets; television, for frozen vegetables and television sets; radio, for a new-car dealer; newspapers, for car dealers, television sets, and frozen vegetables; magazines, for a make of new car and frozen vegetables; books and adult education classes, for investments; and the Yellow Pages, for plumbers.

A summary of multiple-regression results for consumer buying behavior variables is given in Appendix H.

PURCHASE INFORMATION

Older shoppers who plan their purchases in advance and shop with a list tend to be homebodies who want to be famous (see Appendix G.4). Impulsive shopping was related to confusion over too much information and the acceptance of advice from friends and neighbors in the factor analysis, and was predicted in the regression analysis by variables that imply passivity, a high degree of involvement around the home, dissatisfaction with the married role, and undeveloped powers of rational decision making (see Appendix G.15).

Bargain hunting was related to cosmopolitan attitudes, an active lifestyle, and an openness to strange and new places. Older persons who shop in this style also tend to be professionals who are dissatisfied with the married role (see Appendix G.8).

BRAND BEHAVIOR

Both brand loyalty and brand switching/early adoption of new brands among older persons were related to a positive attitude toward change and new experience coupled with lack of desire for actual change in their own lives. Perhaps this ambivalence is suppressed in brand loyalty and sublimated in brand switching. Characteristics of brand loyalists include greater involvement away from home than in the home, a desire to be single, a feeling that homemaking is a lonely life, being a homemaker, and not being widowed (see Appendix G.14). Brand switchers, on the other hand, tend to be higher-income persons, to be dissatisfied with the course of their lives, to claim many friends, and to be in poor health (see Appendix G.2).

Persons who make purchase decisions about packaged goods on the basis of rational characteristics of price, weight, and volume comparison rather than brand are, more often than not, employed in occupations that require rational decision making (self-employed/ manager/official), are satisfied with the married role, prefer working with others to working alone, and are not widowed (see Appendix G.5).

With regard to the relative importance of food and clothing price and brand, again it is the self-employed/managers/officials, as well as skilled workers, who tend to devalue the importance of brand. Older persons who feel food and clothing brand are more important than price may be fearful of expansion; they tend to prefer the company of people their own age, to be leery of trying new things, to prefer local clubs to national organizations, to dislike set schedules, and to feel free about introducing themselves to strangers (see Appendix M.13).

Older persons who look more at food, clothing, and automobile price than at brand tend to be females in good health, to be homeowners, to feel that homemaking is a lonely life, and to be hesitant to meet strangers or go alone to strange and new places (see Appendix M.12).

Manufacturer's reputation and warranty were regarded by the majority of older persons as more important than price or the local dealer's reputation for service. However, 25 percent said service is most important and 12 percent emphasized price. The lifestyle variables "I am a better listener than conversationalist" and "I prefer to work alone than with others" correlated with the manufacturer's reputation and warranty factor and with the price factor. In addition, the preference for manufacturer's reputation and warranty over price and local dealer's reputation for service was predicted by respect for female autonomy and higher self-rated social class (Appendix G.3). Persons who emphasize the importance of price over warranty and local service tend not to mind a set schedule, not to be female, and to have no desire to be famous, and are not self-employed/managers/officials (see Appendix G.7).

CONSUMER PROBLEMS

The greatest general problem areas reported in our survey had to do with the high cost of living, the quality of goods and services, the quality of the environment (crime, traffic), and the availability of health care—not different from the set of problems any other age group faces (see Table 6.8).

The picture of the frustrated consumer that emerges is of someone struggling with the high cost of living, finding available goods and services below expectations, yet feeling competent to attempt to solve problems alone.

Transportation and finances headed the list of bad experiences, followed by health service providers, mail order, and appliances. Fewer problems were reported with department and discount stores, utilities, government agencies, housing, and door-to-door sales (see

TABLE 6.8

Consumer Problems Reported: Summary

Problem Area	Percent Describing Problem as Moderate or Serious (N = 309)
Finances	
Maintaining standard of living during inflation	31.0
Drop in income after retirement	24.6
Cost of legal services	20.1
Cost of life insurance	13.2
Living within budget	12.3
Keeping credit in line	9.0
Obtaining life insurance	9.0
Finding an attorney	7.1
Making a will	6.8
Meeting credit obligations	3.3
Obtaining credit	2.3
Transportation	
Purchase price of automobiles	27.2
Cost of automobile upkeep	25.6
Quality of automobile repair	24.6
Cost of automobile insurance	23.3
Possibility of accidents	10.6
Qualifying for automobile insurance	6.5
Physical handicaps that interfere with driving	6.1
Availability of public transportation	4.2
Cost of public transportation	
Health care	
Cost of medical care	23.6
Cost of health insurance	20.0
Cost of prescription drugs	18.5
Waiting time for appointment with doctor	17.1
Health insurance red tape	16.5
Communication with doctors	8.1
Health insurance coverage	7.5
Inadequate health insurance reimbursement	7.1
Competence of doctors	6.8
Obtaining information on prescription drugs	3.1

(continued)

TABLE 6.8 (continued)

Problem Area	Percent Describing Problem as Moderate or Serious (N = 309)
Food	
Cost of food	42.7
Quality of food available where shop	13.5
Determining nutritional value of food	12.8
Inadequate kitchen facilities	5.5
Selecting food for a special diet	3.2
Meal preparation	2.2
Housing	
Property taxes	26.3
Traffic in the neighborhood	24.0
Crime in the neighborhood	18.8
Obtaining reliable home repairs	13.9
Cost of housing	5.5
Quality of housing construction	5.5
Distance from public transportation	5.2
Landlord	5.1
Distance from shopping	4.2
Restrictive leases	0.6

Note: See Appendix L—Alienation Factor.
Source: Compiled by the authors.

TABLE 6.9

Areas of Bad Experiences

Area	Percent of Sample Reporting Bad Experience Within Past Year
Automobiles	
Automobile	5.5
Automobile dealer	5.5
Automobile repair shop	8.1
Total	19.1
Financial institutions	
Bank	3.9
Insurance company	3.6
Credit card company	3.2
Investment company	1.6
Total	12.3
Sales outlets	
Department store	5.5
Door-to-door sales company	3.2
Discount store	0.3
Total	9.0
Health care	
Doctor, dentist, or other health practitioner	7.8
Nursing home	0.6
Hearing aid company	—
Total	8.4
Appliances	
Appliance manufacturer	2.9
Appliance repair shop	4.5
Total	7.4
Mail order company	7.1
Housing	
Real estate company	2.6
Contractor	1.9
Landlord	1.6
Mobile home	—
Total	5.1
Utility company	4.2
Government agency	3.6
Other	1.9

Source: Compiled by the authors.

TABLE 6.10

Nature of Bad Experience

	Frequency Mentioned
	N
Performance	
Product or service did not meet expectations	82
Service	
Faulty repairs	29
Charge for services not rendered	20
Total	49
Financial transaction	
Billing	18
Unsatisfactory refund or return	9
Interest rate	7
Refused credit	4
Security deposit problems	2
Total	40
Advertising	
Deceptive advertising	23
Offensive advertising	14
Total	37
Delivery	
Failure to deliver/wrong product delivered/other delivery	21
Guarantee/warranty/contract	
Deceptive or failure to honor	17

Source: Compiled by the authors.

TABLE 6.11

Response to Bad Experience

	Frequency Mentioned
	N
Active responses	
Complained to the store or salesman in person	74
Wrote a letter	36
Telephoned	36
Contacted a consumer protection agency, hot line, Better Business Bureau, professional examining board, or police	17
Sued	5
Total	168
Passive responses	
Did nothing	28
Refused to do further business	56
Total	84
Other (unspecified)	13

Source: Compiled by the authors.

Table 6.9). Disappointments were most likely to arise from faulty performance, repair and service problems, financial transactions, and advertising. Fewer experiences had to do with delivery problems or guarantee problems (see Table 6.10). The data reveal that older persons took the active response to these experiences and complained in person, by telephone, or by letter, contacted a consumer protection agency, or sued twice as often as they did nothing or simply refused to do business any further (see Table 6.11).

Specific problem areas seem to involve highly complex machines (automobiles, appliances, the human body) that, when they malfunction, require the services of trained specialists with superior technical knowledge, or the intricacies of the computer-based financial system. Perhaps more consumer education is one solution to the problems . . . or else a simplification of the world.

SUMMARY OF REGRESSION RELATIONSHIPS
OF AGE AND SEX TO CONSUMER BEHAVIOR FACTORS

The data in this study do not support the popular view of the
elderly as more frequent victims of fraud and deception. Age actually
had a negative relationship to the factor "disappointing consumer
experieces" and no relationship to "consumer problems." (See
Appendix L, Alienation factor for disappointing consumer experiences
Widowhood also correlated negatively with each of these factors.
Besides being younger and not widowed, persons in the survey report
ing specific disappointing consumer experiences in the past year were
more likely to be independent, introspective, active in the world, and
employed in a capacity that requires rational decision making and
independent judgment (see Appendix I.1). Perhaps higher levels of
activity in the outside world simply place these people in a greater
number of circumstances and increase the odds that they will have a
disappointing experience. Also, being thinkers, they are perhaps
more sensitive to events and circumstances, and more likely to
observe and report disappointing incidents. This does not mean that
persons with other personal characteristics do not encounter the
same types of experiences. However, one must ask the question, "If
the tree falls in the forest and no one hears it, has it made a sound?"
Older persons reporting general consumer problems, as
opposed to specific disappointing incidents, tend to be not widowed,
active in the world, and to desire changes in social roles (see Appendix G.17). Perhaps the general restlessness and dissatisfaction that
is felt is reflected in dissatisfaction as a consumer.

CROSS-TABULATIONS OF SELECTED CONSUMER
BEHAVIOR VARIABLES BY AGE AND SEX

In addition to looking at the relationship of age and sex to consumer behavior in terms of the regression analyses, for the 77 consumer behavior factors we selected the variable weighted highest on
each factor for a cross-tabulation analysis by age group, controlling
for sex of the respondent (see Tables 4.3-4.9). Only those factors
significant at the .05 level will be discussed.
In general, age with or without the consideration of sex was not
highly related to consumer behavior. Slightly greater relationships
were found to exist between consumer behavior and age in women
than in men, and most differences occurred in the 65+ group (see
Table 6.12).
Compared with women 45-54 and 55-64, women over 65 tend
to own their own homes and automobiles less frequently, to make

TABLE 6.12

Summary of Regression: Relationships of
Age and Sex to Consumer Behavior Factors

Age
+ Belief that credit is unwise   - solitary decision making
+ Covered by Medicare   - food-transportation budget
+ Tire, appliance, and personal   - disappointing consumer expe-
   care product assortment   riences
                                    - total interest more important
                                      than size of monthly payment
                    Observations
   Conservative attitudes toward income management (credit)
   Less reported consumer dissatisfaction
   Logically varying pattern of expenditures
   Tendency to consult with others before making decisions
Sex (female)
+ TV as information source   - price more important than
+ Price (attribute importance)   warranty or service
+ Prefer department store over   - impulsive shopping
   specialty store for tires   - friendly personnel (as store
+ Nondriver   choice criterion)
+ Covered by Medicare   - shop by catalog for in-home
                                      convenience
                                    - importance of self-image pro-
                                      vided by automobile
                                    - appliance store shopping
                                    - real estate investments
         Observations (older women compared with older men)
   May be more careful shoppers, more "rational" shoppers,
     but perhaps more persuasible (through electronic media)
   Wary of slick sales personnel
   Enjoy going out to shop
   Less automobile-conscious, less likely to drive
   Less confident in making investments

Note: "+" indicates a positive relationship and "-" indicates a
negative relationship.
   Source: Compiled by the authors.

fewer joint purchase decisions, to have more auto repair work done by friends and relatives than by repair shops, to feel that the expected lifespan of an auto is a relatively unimportant purchase criterion, to believe that the use of credit is unwise, to shop for bargains more often, and to shop from mail order catalogs less often. Monthly food expenditures and reported bad experiences decline with age among women.

Men over 65 also report fewer bad consumer experiences than did men in the two younger groups. The older men are less likely to be concerned with maintaining their standard of living than are men 45-54 and 55-64. The two younger groups feel that automobile upkeep costs are a problem, while those over 65 report that the purchase price of autos is a greater problem. Men 45-54 feel that family and friends must like what they buy to a greater degree than do those over 65. The oldest group was most positive in its evaluation of the competence of doctors. Men of all ages do not like to shop for clothing at home.

In a study of consumers over 65, Kenneth Bernhardt and Thomas Kinnear (1976) report that senior citizens are more likely to prefer department stores to discount stores and to own fewer credit cards than younger consumers do. Jeffrey Towle and Claude Marin, Jr. (1976), found that elderly women, compared with women 40-59 and women 18-30, tend to shop alone more frequently, to consult more often with sales personnel in making decisions, and to formulate preferences before shopping. Data on comparable variables from this study were not significant at the .05 level, with the possible exception of a relationship between the tendency of elderly women to shop alone and to make fewer joint purchase decisions.

The lack of major significance of age (controlling for sex) in relation to consumer behavior may indicate that lifestyle factors affect consumer behavior in ways that transcend age and sex differences.

It might be hypothesized that widowhood, and not specifically age, accounts for the differences in consumer behavior observed in women over 65 in this study, and that the presence or absence of pressures to support a family account for some of the differences among men.

7

INCOME MANAGEMENT

INCOME OF THE ELDERLY

Table 7.1 presents the number of U.S. households and their incomes, broken down by age group. In 1980 and 1985 the over-65 group will account for 20 percent of households but only 11 percent of household income, an obvious effect of retirement. Half of the households of persons over 65 will have incomes of less than $5,000. However, it has been noted that while income is low for the elderly, persons over 65 have larger tax exemptions, Social Security is tax-free income, pension benefits up to $1,200 are not taxed, and indebtedness among this group is less (Reynolds and Wells 1977). Aggregate expenditures of senior citizens are estimated to be far larger than the billions spent by the youth market (Chen 1971; Fleming 1971).

In contrast, the 55-64 age group will become somewhat less important by 1985. While the number of households, like the number of individuals, will increase slightly, the growth will be below average and income less than among the 45-54 age group. However, obligations of older persons are often less than those of younger ones. In many cases children are financially independent, the house is paid for, and there is an adequate inventory of durable goods, leaving household income for basic necessities and luxury goods and services (Reynolds and Wells 1977).

AUTONOMY OR POSSESSIONS?

It has been noted that the older consumers' interest in money is oriented more toward preserving independence than toward acquiring possessions. They generally express a realistic view of their financial situation and shift their expenditures accordingly. While income may be less, they usually feel it is high enough to satisfy

101

TABLE 7.1

Older Consumer Households, by Age of Head and Income Class: 1972, 1980, and 1985 (all figures in 1972 dollars)

| | All Households | Age of Household Head | | | | | |
		Under 25	25-34	35-44	45-54	55-64	65 and Over
			1972				
Households							
Million dollars	68.3	5.5	13.6	11.7	12.8	11.2	13.5
Distribution (%)	100.0	8.0	20.0	17.0	19.0	16.5	19.5
Spending power							
Total (%)	100.0	5.5	20.5	21.5	24.5	17.0	11.0
Discretionary (%)	100.0	1.5	14.5	25.0	33.0	19.5	6.5
Household income distribution (%)	100.0	100.0	100.0	100.0	100.0	100.0	100.0
Under $3,000	14.0	15.5	6.0	5.0	6.5	13.5	35.5
$ 3,000- 5,000	11.0	16.5	7.5	6.0	6.5	10.0	23.0
$ 5,000- 7,000	10.5	17.5	10.0	8.0	7.5	10.5	13.5
$ 7,000-10,000	16.0	24.0	20.0	15.5	14.0	16.0	12.0
$10,000-15,000	23.0	19.5	32.5	28.0	25.0	23.0	8.5
$15,000-25,000	19.5	6.5	20.5	29.0	29.0	19.0	5.5
$25,000 and over	6.0	0.5	3.5	8.5	11.5	8.0	2.0

1980

Households						
Million dollars	77.3	6.0	18.3	13.1	11.8	12.4	15.6
Distribution (%)	100.0	8.0	23.5	17.0	15.5	16.0	20.0
Spending power						
Total (%)	100.0	5.5	25.0	21.5	20.0	17.0	11.0
Discretionary (%)	100.0	1.5	19.5	26.5	27.5	18.5	6.5
Household income distribution (%)	100.0	100.0	100.0	100.0	100.0	100.0	100.0
Under $3,000	12.0	13.0	5.0	4.0	5.5	12.0	31.0
$ 3,000– 5,000	10.5	14.5	6.5	5.5	6.0	9.0	23.0
$ 5,000– 7,000	10.0	17.0	8.5	7.0	6.5	10.0	14.5
$ 7,000–10,000	14.5	23.0	17.0	13.0	12.0	14.0	12.0
$10,000–15,000	23.0	22.5	32.5	25.5	22.5	23.0	10.0
$15,000–25,000	22.0	9.0	25.0	32.0	32.0	22.5	6.5
$25,000 and over	8.0	1.0	5.5	13.0	15.5	9.5	3.0

(continued)

TABLE 7.1 (continued)

	All Households	Age of Household Head					
		Under 25	25–34	35–44	45–54	55–64	65 and Over
				1985			
Households							
Million dollars	84.2	6.0	20.5	16.3	11.7	12.7	17.1
Distribution (%)	100.0	7.0	24.5	19.5	14.0	15.0	20.0
Spending power							
Total (%)	100.0	5.0	26.0	24.5	18.0	15.5	11.0
Discretionary (%)	100.0	1.5	20.5	29.5	25.0	17.0	6.5
Household income distribution (%)	100.0	100.0	100.0	100.0	100.0	100.0	100.0
Under $3,000	11.0	12.0	5.0	4.0	5.5	11.0	28.5
$ 3,000– 5,000	10.0	13.5	5.5	5.0	5.5	8.5	23.0
$ 5,000– 7,000	9.0	14.5	8.0	6.0	6.0	9.0	14.0
$ 7,000–10,000	14.0	23.0	15.5	11.5	10.5	14.0	13.5
$10,000–15,000	22.0	23.5	29.5	24.0	21.0	22.0	11.0
$15,000–25,000	25.0	12.5	30.5	35.5	33.5	24.5	7.0
$25,000 and over	9.0	1.0	6.0	14.0	18.0	11.0	3.0

Source: Fabian Linden, "Reshuffling the Age-Income Mix", The Conference Board Record, March 1974.

104

their basic needs. They tend to have fewer debts than younger people (Reynolds and Wells 1977). The conservative use of credit has been commented upon (Bernhardt and Kinnear 1976).

Older persons in our study appear able to manage their incomes competently. Problems reported with finances were primarily due to the cost of living, and not to difficulties with budgeting or indebtedness. Reported financial problems fell into the same factor as problems with food and nutrition, housing, and transportation, indicating that problems in one area are frequently experienced as problems in others. This factor was predicted not be age, income, or widowhood but by expressed desire for change in the roles of worker, spouse, parent, friend, community worker, leisure-time user, and homemaker, by higher degree of involvement in activities away from home, and by not being widowed (see Appendix G. 17). If the lonely, lower-income aged experience problems, they did not report them.

One-fifth of older persons surveyed budget all expenses, and one-half said they do not budget at all (see Table 7.2). Monthly household expenditures clustered in three factors. Housing and recreation expense and savings logically increased with income, higher self-rated social class, and aggressive conversation behavior (see Appendix I. 11). Food and transportation expenses declined with age and a homebody self-image, and increased with marriage (see Appendix I. 10). Medical-dental expenses fell together with dollars spent for home furnishings, appliances, clothing, and personal care, which suggests a common element of personal adornment and self-gratification in these kinds of expenditures (see Appendix I. 9).

SAVINGS AND CREDIT

Almost half of the older persons in our survey save regularly, mostly at commercial banks, although sizable proportions keep their money in savings and loan institutions and credit union accounts. (Appendix J shows regression results for store relations and inventory of spending behavior.) Half have other investments, primarily stocks and real estate. Stock investments were related to income, respect for female autonomy, relative lack of importance of children in decision making, self-rated poor health, and retirement (see Appendix I. 6). Investment income is obviously needed if wage earnings are threatened by poor health or retirement. Older persons possessing investment real estate are more likely to be male, to rate the state of their health lower, to own their own homes, to be socially introverted yet desire to be famous, to be more interested in national and international events than local happenings, to be employed in an occupation requiring rational decision making, and to have relatively

TABLE 7.2

Financial Behavior of Older Persons

	Percent	N
Income budgeting behavior		
Budget all expenses	20.4	63
Budget some expenses	21.4	66
Budget no expenses	55.3	171
Saving behavior		
Never save	29.1	90
Hardly ever save	8.1	25
Sometimes save	14.2	44
Often save	11.7	36
Always save	36.7	104
Save at commercial bank	56.3	174
Save at savings and loan	36.2	112
Save at credit union	19.7	61
Buy U.S. savings bonds	17.2	53
Investment behavior		
Have investments	50.5	156
Common stocks	27.8	86
Investment real estate	19.7	61
Mutual funds	11.0	34
Reasons given for not investing		
Don't have money	15.5	48
Not familiar with possibilities	3.6	11
Risk too great	2.3	7
Not interested	1.6	5
Too much investment required	1.6	5
Don't believe in investing	0.6	2
Bank credit card use		
Have bank credit card	50.8	157
Frequency of use		
Several times a week	5.8	18
Once a week	5.8	18
More than monthly, less than weekly	10.4	32
Once a month	10.0	31
Few times a year	16.2	50
Once a year or less	3.3	10
Reasons for use		
Convenience	40.8	126
Stretching payments	3.9	12
Convenience and stretching payments	3.9	12

(continued)

TABLE 7.2 (continued)

	Percent	N
Items purchased		
Recreation	32.0	99
Clothing	28.8	89
Services	20.7	64
Small appliances	17.8	55
Personal care items	15.2	47
Large appliances	14.6	45
Furniture	12.3	38
Education, reading	7.8	24
Medical bills	4.9	15
Taxes	4.9	15
Other	4.9	15
Loan considerations		
Total interest paid most important	40.1	124
Size of monthly payments most important	35.6	110
Size of down payment most important	6.8	21
Other consideration most important	9.7	30
Feel credit union charges lowest interest	37.2	115
Feel bank charges lowest interest	13.9	43
Feel finance company charges lowest interest	0.3	1
Feel all charge the same	—	—
Information sources for investments and insurance		
Investments		
Personal judgment and experience	38.2	118
Family and friends	26.6	82
Professional directories and referral services	23.3	69
Consumer publications	10.0	31
Sales personnel	2.2	7
Newspapers, magazines, books	1.5	5
Adult education	1.0	3
Yellow Pages	1.0	3
Insurance		
Personal judgment and experience	49.5	153
Family and friends	32.3	100
Professional directories and referral services	11.0	34
Sales personnel	4.6	14
Yellow Pages	1.0	3
Newspapers	0.6	2

Source: Compiled by the authors

TABLE 7.3

Reported Financial Problems

	No Problem		Slight Problem		Moderate Problem		Serious Problem	
	%	N	%	N	%	N	%	N
Maintaining standard of living during inflation	42.1	130	25.6	79	15.5	48	15.5	48
Drop in income after retirement	34.3	106	12.6	39	8.4	26	16.2	50
Cost of legal services	57.9	179	3.6	11	9.4	29	10.7	33
Cost of life insurance	58.3	180	7.8	24	5.8	18	8.4	26
Making a budget and living within it	58.9	182	10.4	32	5.8	18	6.5	20
Controlling the use of credit	68.9	213	8.4	26	4.5	14	4.5	14
Obtaining life insurance	70.2	217	2.3	7	1.6	5	7.4	23
Making a will	75.1	232	6.5	20	4.2	13	2.6	8
Finding an attorney	77.7	240	5.5	17	3.2	10	4.2	13
Obtaining credit	83.8	259	3.2	10	1.0	3	1.3	4
Meeting credit obligations	77.7	240	3.9	12	2.3	7	1.0	3

Note: The percentage total of a problem may exceed 100 because multiple responses were given.
Source: Compiled by the authors.

less respect for female autonomy (see Appendix I.8). Most persons who said they did not have investments gave lack of money as the reason. It could be concluded that older persons of lower income are least able to take action to improve their financial circumstances.

The majority of older Americans rely on personal judgment and the advice of family and friends in making decisions regarding investments; one-third mentioned the use of professional referral services and consumer publications. With regard to insurance, the proportion was weighted more heavily toward personal judgment and advice of family and friends.

The belief that the use of credit is unwise was related to age and also what might be interpreted as ambivalence toward risk taking. Older persons who feel the use of credit is unwise are more likely to say they are better talkers than listeners, want to be famous, dislike following a set schedule, prefer a national club to a local one, and tend to be relatively noninvolved around the home. They say they are not homebodies, yet do not like going alone to strange and new places and do not often introduce themselves to strangers at social gatherings (see Appendix I.2).

With regard to loan considerations, older persons are almost equally divided in their feelings about the relative importance of total interest paid versus the size of monthly payments. Persons feeling total interest was most important were more likely to be younger, professional, socially active yet emotionally independent, to dislike following a set schedule, and to be satisfied with the married role. A good proportion appear to be informed about credit sources (see Appendix I.4). None felt that banks, credit unions, and finance companies charge equal interest; the majority felt credit unions charge the lowest.

Half of older persons possess a bank credit card (see Table 7.2). Most use it primarily for convenience anywhere from a few times a year to a few times a month. Recreation, clothing, and services are items most frequently purchased with it. Use was related to higher income, openness to trying new things, desire for a change in social roles played, and relative lack of importance of children in decision making (see Appendix I.3). This is consistent with results of studies of bank credit card use among the general population, which have found users of all ages characterized by higher income and education, professional occupational status, middle age, rejection of conservative, traditional concepts (such as that financial transactions should be made in cash), risk orientation, service organization affiliation, an active urban-suburban lifestyle, many outside interests, achievement orientation, and the perception of credit as a cash substitute (Plummer 1974).

TABLE 7.4

Disappointing Consumer Experiences with Financial Institutions

	Percent	Number
Source of disappointing experience		
Bank	3.9	12
Insurance company	3.6	11
Credit card company	3.2	10
Investment company	1.6	5
Type of problem		
Bank		
Charge for services not rendered	0.6	2
Refused credit	0.6	2
Billing	0.6	2
Unsatisfactory performance	0.3	1
Security deposit	0.3	1
Unsatisfactory refund	0.3	1
Insurance company		
Unsatisfactory performance	1.3	4
Guarantee or contract not honored	1.0	3
Charge for services not rendered	0.6	2
Billing	0.6	2
Deceptive advertising	0.3	1
Interest rate	0.3	1
Credit card company		
Offensive advertising	1.0	3
Refused credit	0.6	2
Interest rate	0.6	2
Deceptive advertising	0.3	1
Unsatisfactory performance	0.3	1
Charge for services not rendered	0.3	1
Billing	0.3	1
Investment company		
Unsatisfactory performance	0.6	2
Unsatisfactory refund	0.3	1
Interest rate	0.3	1
Billing	0.3	1
Action taken		
Bank		
Complained in person	1.5	5
Refused to do further business	1.3	4

(continued)

TABLE 7.4 (continued)

	Percent	Number
Telephoned or wrote letter	0.6	2
Contacted consumer protection agency	0.3	1
Insurance company		
Did nothing	0.6	2
Telephoned or wrote letter	0.6	2
Complained in person	0.3	1
Refused to do further business	0.3	1
Contacted consumer protection agency	0.3	1
Sued	0.3	1
Credit card company		
Telephoned or wrote letter	1.8	6
Refused to do further business	0.6	2
Contacted consumer protection agency	0.3	1
Other	0.3	1
Investment company		
Complained in person	0.6	2
Refused to do further business	0.6	2
Telephoned or wrote letter	0.6	2

Source: Compiled by the authors.

FINANCIAL PROBLEMS

The most serious financial problems reported by older persons was maintaining their desired standard of living during inflation. Nearly one-third of the sample reported this to be either a moderate or a serious problem. One-quarter found drop in income after retirement to be either a moderate or a serious problem. The problem appears to be chiefly one of the cost of living (problems with the costs of food, medical care, transportation, legal services, life insurance, and taxes were reported by large numbers of the sample) and not of individual approaches to income management. Twelve percent reported trouble making a budget and living within it and 9 percent, controlling the use of credit. Obtaining life insurance, finding an attorney, and making a will were lesser problems. Obtaining credit and meeting credit obligations were almost negligible (Table 7.3).

An average of 3 percent of the sample reported specific disappointing experiences in the past year with banks, utilities, credit cards, and investment and real estate companies (see Table 7.4). The largest numbers of these complaints fell into the categories of unsatisfactory performance, billing, charges for services not rendered, and excessive interest. Smaller numbers of complaints were recorded for denial of credit, failure to honor guarantee, offensive advertising, deceptive advertising, and problems with refunds and security deposits.

8

HEALTH CARE

Since health is the primary concern among the elderly as compared with younger persons (Harris and Associates 1976) and health repeatedly has been related to well-being (Palmore and Luikart 1972; Chatfield 1977), the following results translate consumer behavior into a framework for policy discussion.

Studies of consumer attitudes toward medical care that have included the elderly as a subgroup of the population studied have found that people are generally satisfied with health care services and express favorable attitudes toward the leadership, professional competency, and personal qualities of health professionals. They have found greater concern for economic, time-related, convenience, and psychosociological factors of health care than for the technological "quality of care" or where to go for health care. Little support was found for national health insurance. Greatest dissatisfaction with health care services in general was found among women, blacks, and Medicaid recipients. Greatest concern for cost was found among the elderly with Medicare coverage only, persons of low income and low social class, those without insurance, those with self-rated poor health, and blacks. The elderly, persons with less than a high school education, and those with low income felt that the medical profession, and not the consumer, should have the greater role in planning and control of health care services (Hilka et al. 1975; Stratman et al. 1975).

RELATIONSHIP OF AGE TO HEALTH CARE BEHAVIOR

Age, with or without the consideration of sex, was not highly related to consumer health behavior in the cross-tabulation analyses. The only relationship significant at the .05 level was the positive evaluation of the competence of doctors by men over 65. In the

TABLE 8.1

Self-Rated Health Status

Status	Percent	Number
Excellent	24.8	76
Good	45.3	139
Fair	23.5	71
Poor	6.5	20

Source: Compiled by the authors.

TABLE 8.2

Self-Rated Disabilities

Disability	Percent	Number
Chronic vision disability	23.6	73
Chronic hearing disability	11.0	34
Chronic speech disability	0.3	1
Chronic paralysis	2.3	7
Loss of limb	1.3	4
Other disability	20.1	62

Source: Compiled by the authors.

TABLE 8.3

Use of Alternative Health Care Services

Alternative Service	Percent	Number
Public health clinic	5.8	18
Private clinic*	4.2	14
Veterans' hospital	2.6	8
Visiting nurse service	2.3	7
Home health aide service	1.3	4
Spiritual healer	0.3	1

*Other than Kaiser-Permanente.
Source: Compiled by the authors.

TABLE 8.4

Information Sources on Health Practitioners

Source	Percent	Number
Family and friends	41.1	127
Personal experience and judgment	35.0	108
Professional directories and referral services	18.1	56
Yellow Pages	3.9	12
Newspapers	0.3	1

Source: Compiled by the authors.

TABLE 8.5

Problems with Health Care Services

Problem	Degree of Problem							
	None		Slight		Moderate		Serious	
	%	N	%	N	%	N	%	N
Cost of medical care	59.9	185	14.9	46	11.3	35	12.3	38
Cost of health insurance	61.5	190	12.0	37	11.3	35	8.7	27
Health insurance red tape	61.8	191	11.3	35	9.1	28	7.4	23
Health insurance coverage	73.1	226	8.1	25	3.9	12	3.6	11
Adequacy of insurance payments	71.2	220	7.8	24	2.6	8	4.5	14
Cost of prescription drugs	61.2	189	13.6	42	12.0	37	6.5	20
Obtaining prescription drug information	81.2	251	5.2	16	0.6	2	2.3	7
Waiting time for appointment	79.3	245	12.0	37	2.6	8	5.5	17
Competence of doctors	82.5	255	8.4	26	3.2	10	3.6	11
Communication with doctors	79.3	245	12.0	37	2.6	8	5.5	17

Source: Compiled by the authors.

regression analyses age was a major predictor of only one health care behavior factor, which was composed of the variables covered by Medicare and frequency of prescription drug use. Also included in the regression equation for this factor were female, "My daily activities are limited by health," widowed, lack of identification with the homemaker role, low near-involvement score, higher self-rated social class, and not self-employed/manager/official (see Appendix K. 5).

HEALTH STATUS

No relationship was found between age and self-rated health status (Table 8.1). As concluded by E. Shanas et al. (1968), "Old age and illness are not synonymous." Poor health appears, from these data, to be related to fear of trying new things, low income, and lack of involvement in the home (see Appendix K. 11). It would, of course, be difficult to determine which came first, this particular lifestyle or poor health. Over two-thirds of the sample rated their health as "good" or "excellent" (see Table 8.1), yet problems with vision, hearing, and other disabilities were reported by half of the sample (see Table 8.2).

SOURCES OF HEALTH CARE DELIVERY AND INFORMATION

The great majority of older persons apparently rely on conventional modes of health care delivery, although 16.5 percent reported the use of alternative modes, including public and private clinics, veterans' hospitals, visiting nurse service, and home health aide service. One person reported consulting a spiritual healer (Table 8.3). Most people (76 percent) said they rely on family, friends, and personal judgment for information regarding health practitioners. Of the rest 18 percent consulted professional directories and referral services, and 4 percent the Yellow Pages (see Table 8.4).

THE COST OF MEDICAL CARE

Cost was the most frequently reported problem with health care services (Table 8.5). Costs of medical care, health insurance, and prescription drugs were rated as a slight, moderate, or serious problem by approximately one-third of those questioned. Monthly medical-dental expense appeared in the factor that also included monthly expense for home furnishings and equipment, clothing, and

TABLE 8.6

Health Insurance Behavior

	Percent	Number
Have health insurance	83.2	257
Kaiser-Permanente member	25.2	78
Fee-reimbursement insurance	56.3	174
Obtained insurance through employer	57.6	178
Obtained insurance from major insurance company office	9.4	29
Obtained insurance by mail order, door-to-door, or telephone sales	2.3	7

Source: Compiled by the authors.

personal care items, and was predicted not by health status, income, or age but by married status, education, degree of religiosity, importance of children in decision making, the desire to be a famous person, the belief that "a marriage has problems when the wife brings home money," and a sense of moral ambiguity (see Appendix I.9).

HEALTH INSURANCE

Of the sample, 83.2 percent were covered by health insurance (see Table 8.6). These people tended to be homeowners, higher-income, married, and extroverted. Conversely, it was the lower-income, renters, unmarried, and the socially isolated who tended not to be covered (see Appendix K.6). The two-thirds of the sample who obtained their insurance through their employers or from a major insurance company office were more likely to be higher-income, nonhousewives, generally dissatisfied with life, and concerned with children in decision making (see Appendix K.3). Purchase of health insurance by mail order, telephone, or door-to-door sales was related to lower income, housewife, satisfaction with life, and lack of importance of children in decision making. Twenty-eight percent of the sample reported problems with health insurance red tape,

15 percent with breadth of insurance coverage, and 15 percent with adequacy of insurance payments (see Table 8.5). One-quarter of the sample were members of the Kaiser-Permanente Health Plan, the largest American health maintenance organization, while slightly over half possessed a Blue Cross or similar fee-reimbursement policy. Membership in Kaiser-Permanente was related to lifestyle variables that suggest receptivity to change—dissatisfaction with life, decrease in religiosity, "I've never felt I was too old to take up new ways"—and to "A marriage has problems when the wife brings home money." (See Appendix K.1 and for complete regression results, see Appendix L.)

PRESCRIPTION DRUG USE

Frequency of prescription drug use and its relationship to Medicare eligibility, age, female, restricted activity, widowed, social class, and occupation have already been discussed. While 58 percent of the sample said they take prescription drugs sometimes, often, or always, and one-third claimed the cost of prescription drugs to be some degree of a problem, only 13 percent said they compare drug prices when shopping (Tables 8.7 and 8.8). Comparison shopping for prescription drugs was included in the factor with "I shop around for sales and bargains," and was related to interest in national and international events, openness to strange and new places, involvement in community and leisure activities away from home, other than professional employment status, and to the desire to be single (see Appendix K.9). It would appear that those in poor health who must take prescription drugs regularly may be least willing or able to lead the active life associated with comparison shopping. Fifty-nine percent of the sample were aware of the differences between generic and brand-name drugs but only 16 percent said they had ever asked the doctor for the cheapest drug.

PROBLEMS WITH HEALTH CARE SERVICES

Waiting time for appointments was cited as some degree of problem by 20 percent of the sample, competence of doctors by 15 percent, and communication with doctors by 20 percent (Table 8.5). Men over 65 had the highest opinion of the competence of doctors. Of the sample, 7.8 percent reported specific disappointing consumer experiences with health care providers in the past year (see Table 8.10). This percentage was exceeded only by the 8.1 percent who reported complaints about auto repair shops. A 1975 NTRA/AARP

TABLE 8.7

Frequency of Prescription Drug Use

	Percent	Number
Never	21.7	67
Hardly ever	19.8	61
Sometimes	19.5	60
Often	4.9	15
Always	34.1	105

Source: Compiled by the authors.

TABLE 8.8

Frequency of Prescription Drug Price
Comparison Shopping

	Percent	Number
Never	41.1	127
Hardly ever	7.8	24
Sometimes	3.6	11
Often	3.2	10
Always	6.5	20

Source: Compiled by the authors.

TABLE 8.9

Generic Drug Use

	Percent	Number
Aware of difference between generic and brand-name drugs	58.6	181
Have used generic drugs	18.4	57
Have used brand-name drugs	17.2	53
Have used both	31.4	97
Don't know which have used	17.2	53
Have asked doctor for the cheapest drug	15.9	49

Source: Compiled by the authors.

TABLE 8.10

Disappointing Consumer Experiences with Health Care

	Percent	Number
Source of disappointing experience		
Doctor, dentist or other health practitioner	7.8	24
Nursing home	0.6	2
Hearing aid company	—	—
Type of problem		
Doctor, dentist, or other health practitioner		
Unsatisfactory performance or		
"faulty repairs"	6.1	17
Billing	1.3	4
Nursing home		
Unsatisfactory performance	0.6	2
Action taken		
Doctor, dentist, or other health practitioner		
Refused to do further business	4.1	13
Did nothing	1.3	4
Telephoned	0.6	2
Complained in person	0.6	2
Contacted consumer protection agency	0.3	1
Nursing home		
Telephoned or wrote letter	0.6	2
Refused to do further business	0.3	1

Source: Compiled by the authors.

TABLE 8.11

Satisfaction with Medicare

	Percent	Number
Covered by Medicare	35.6	110
Of those covered by Medicare		
Very satisfied with Medicare	22.8	21
Satisfied with Medicare	47.9	44
Neither satisfied nor dissatisfied	8.7	8
Dissatisfied with Medicare	13.0	12
Very dissatified with Medicare	7.6	7

Source: Compiled by the authors.

TABLE 8.12

Satisfaction with Medi-Cal

	Percent	Number
Currently receiving Medi-Cal benefits	7.4	23
Of those currently receiving Medi-Cal benefits		
Very satisfied with Medi-Cal	8.3	2
Satisfied with Medi-Cal	12.5	3
Neither satisfied nor dissatisfied	—	—
Dissatisfied with Medi-Cal	33.3	8
Very dissatisfied with Medi-Cal	45.8	11

Source: Compiled by the authors.

survey of consumer complaints received from older persons found only 3 percent of the sample reporting medical-dental complaints. Perhaps consumer expectations have grown since that time and people are more aware of medical care that does not satisfy their needs. Complaints regarding health practitioners were primarily the precoded categories of "faulty performance—product or service did not meet expectations," "faulty repairs," and "billing." In response to these complaints most individuals did nothing or refused to do further business. Only two persons reported a disappointing experience with a nursing home, and none with a hearing aid company (Table 8.10). Of the one-third of the sample covered by Medicare, 70 percent claimed to be satisfied with it, while 79 percent of the 23 persons currently receiving Medi-Cal (California Medicaid) were dissatisfied (Tables 8.11 and 8.12). Medicaid appears not to be the solution to satisfactory care for the low-income. This has been confirmed in other studies of consumer satisfaction. The consumer behavior factor that included "dissatisfied with Medicare" and a composite variable, problems with health care services, was predicted by "I would feel lost without my friends," low involvement in the home, and self-rated poor health (see Appendix K.10), which suggests that those in poor health and needing a support system of friends find the medical care system least responsive to their needs.

9

FOOD AND NUTRITION

NUTRITION AND FOOD PURCHASING

Concern for the food behavior of the elderly has been focused primarily on specific nutritional needs and on problems with food purchase among low-income elderly that are attributable to high prices and difficulties with mobility and transportation. Recommendations have been made for changes in the design and distribution of technical and social services to the elderly, including transportation systems, homemaker services, food stamp awareness and utilization, and alternative living and eating arrangements (Sherman and Brittan 1973). However, it has been pointed out that even though low-income elderly may pay more for food purchases if they shop at small neighborhood stores, they are aware of the consequences of their actions and balance higher prices against the benefits of convenience, personal friendships, and credit service (Boone and Bonno 1971). It has been concluded that "Their actions reflect not those of uneducated consumers some writers describe but rather those of purchasers who have deliberately chosen to patronize stores providing them with products and services they desire" (Boone and Bonno 1971).

Women over 65 have been found to be more relaxed about cooking than younger women are, a probable effect of reduced demands by family members, and to be slightly more concerned about nutrition than younger women are, most likely a result of age-related health concerns. Men over 65 have also been found to be less interested in cooking than younger men are and, while not so concerned about nutrition as older women, are more concerned than younger men about salt, cholesterol, and weight control (Reynolds and Wells 1977). The role of informal sources of information, social interaction patterns, and perceived risk involved in the purchase decision for a new salt substitute by the elderly residents of a single building has been studied (Schiffman 1971, 1972a, 1972b), but no comprehensive studies of the consumer food behavior of a large probability sample of the population of a major metropolitan area have been conducted.

Older persons exhibit various consumer food behaviors. They are not homogeneous. With the exception of monthly food expenditure, no behavior measured was related to increasing age or to income but, rather, to various lifestyle factors.

GENERAL GROCERY SHOPPING BEHAVIOR

Tables 9.1-9.5 present data on general grocery shopping behavior. Almost three-fourths (72 percent) of older persons are directly involved in shopping for their own food, while 24 percent leave the shopping to their spouses. Among those older persons who do shop, the vast majority make at least one trip to the store weekly, with 85 percent shopping in a large chain supermarket, a cooperative, or a PX. One-quarter of the older persons studied rely on modes of transportation other than automobiles when doing their grocery shopping. The most frequently mentioned reasons for store choice included product assortment, proximity to home, merchandise quality, store accessibility, parking facilities, and low prices. Seven percent of older persons queried reported shopping regularly at small neighborhood stores. It may be this 7 percent who listed loyalty to store owner and credit availability as criteria for grocery store selection. Small neighborhood store shoppers in this analysis tended to be single or widowed, to believe that homemaking is a lonely life, and to have uncertain feelings about standards of right and wrong. (See Appendix K.2.) Age and income are unrelated to neighborhood store shopping in this analysis.

IN-STORE SHOPPING BEHAVIOR

Table 9.6 presents data on in-store shopping behavior. Almost half of older persons shop for grocery specials at least once a month. The older person who selects a grocery store for its specials and promotional activities tends to be employed, blue-collar, socially independent, and nonintrospective, and to believe that "Change and new experiences are important in the life of every person" (see Appendix K.2). Over half compare prices, weights, volumes, or ingredients when selecting packaged goods. Those who do so are more likely to be self-employed/managers/officials, not to be widowed, and to enjoy being married and working with others (see Appendix K.8). However, one-third of the sample reported that they

TABLE 9.1

Who Does the Grocery Shopping

	Percent	Number
Respondent	56.6	175
Spouse	23.9	74
Respondent and spouse	11.0	34
Respondent and other person	3.6	11
Other person	4.5	14

Source: Compiled by the authors.

TABLE 9.2

Frequency of Grocery Shopping

	Percent	Number
Several times a week	29.8	92
Once a week	45.0	139
Less often than weekly, more than monthly	6.5	20
Once a month	6.8	21
Less than monthly	4.8	15

Source: Compiled by the authors.

TABLE 9.3

Types of Grocery Stores Shopped

	Percent	Number
Large chain supermarket	79.9	247
Small neighborhood store	7.1	22
Cooperative	3.9	12
PX	0.6	2
Health food store	0.3	1
Other	1.6	5

Source: Compiled by the authors.

TABLE 9.4

Reasons for Grocery Store Choice

	Percent	Number
Product assortment	55.3	171
Proximity to home	43.0	133
Merchandise quality	36.9	114
Accessibility	34.3	106
Parking facilities	33.7	104
Low prices	30.1	93
Specials, promotions	29.1	90
Friendly checkers	29.1	90
Store hours	19.7	61
Appearance of store and clientele	17.8	55
Carries specialty food items	15.9	49
Special services (e.g., home delivery)	3.6	11
Loyalty to owner	3.2	10
Credit availability	2.6	8
Other	4.2	13

Source: Compiled by the authors.

TABLE 9.5

Modes of Transportation to Grocery Store

	Percent	Number
Drive	43.0	133
Other person drives	13.3	41
Walk	15.2	47
Bicycle	0.3	1
Bus	4.9	15
Other	3.6	11

Source: Compiled by the authors.

TABLE 9.6

In-Store Grocery Shopping Behavior

	Percent	Number
Shop for specials almost every week	29.8	92
Shop for specials at least monthly	13.9	43
Shop for specials rarely	18.9	58
Shop for specials never	6.8	21
Believe national brands superior to house brands	27.5	85
Believe house brands superior to national brands	4.5	14
Believe house brands and national brands equal	39.2	121
Compare weights and volumes of packaged goods	17.5	54
Compare prices of packaged goods	22.7	70
Compare ingredient labels of packaged goods	14.9	46
Stay with familiar brands of packaged goods	33.7	104

Source: Compiled by the authors.

TABLE 9.7

Information Sources for Brand of Frozen Vegetables

	Percent	Number
Personal judgment and experience	49.8	166
Labels	18.0	60
Family and friends	12.9	43
Consumer publications	3.6	11

Source: Compiled by the authors.

TABLE 9.8

Evaluative Criteria for Food

	Very Important		Somewhat Important		Not at All Important	
	%	N	%	N	%	N
Taste	50.5	156	6.8	21	3.6	11
Enjoyment	46.3	143	10.4	32	3.2	10
Nutritional value	44.7	138	13.6	42	3.2	10
Price	35.3	109	25.6	79	2.6	8
Family preferences	30.7	95	18.1	56	7.8	24
Appearance	27.8	86	27.2	84	4.9	15
Preparation ease	15.5	48	31.1	96	12.3	38
Brand	14.9	46	37.9	137	9.4	29

Source: Compiled by the authors.

stick with familiar brands when selecting packaged goods. Most older persons say they rely on personal sources of information when choosing a brand of frozen vegetables, but nearly one-quarter read labels and consult consumer publications (Table 9.7).

EVALUATIVE CRITERIA FOR FOOD SELECTION

Table 9.8 lists evaluative criteria for food selection. Taste and enjoyment headed the list of very important criteria for food selection among older persons, and appearance made a strong showing. However, 45 percent reported nutritional value as very important and another 14 percent as somewhat important. Nutrition consciousness was related to positive feelings toward the homemaker role, to the importance of family preferences in selecting food, and to self-rated poor health (see Appendix K.12). The solitary elderly may lose some of their motivation to prepare nutritious meals when they have no one else to prepare them for. Sixty percent reported price as either very important or somewhat important. Brand and preparation ease were rated as somewhat important by about one-third.

PROBLEMS WITH FOOD

Table 9.9 presents problems with food. Cost was by far the greatest problem with food reported by older persons. Two-thirds rated cost as a slight, moderate, or serious problem. Quality of food available and the determination of nutritional value were secondary problems, while adequacy of kitchen facilities and problems with meal preparation were generally slight. Monthly food expenditure appeared in the same factor as monthly transportation expenditure, and was the only consumer food behavior variable related to age. Food (and transportation) expenditure tends to decline with age, to be higher among the married, and to be lower among the homebodies (see Appendix I.10). Five percent of the sample reported applying for food stamps in the past year, and 3 percent received them (see Table 9.10). Nearly one-quarter of the older persons sampled reported being on some kind of special diet and a nearly equal proportion were overweight, in the opinion of the interviewer (see Table 9.11). Reported problems with food selection, purchase, preparation, and nutrition appeared in the same factor as problems with income sufficiency and management, housing, and transportation, which suggests the interrelatedness of nearly all consumer problems. Yet these reported problems were related not to increasing

TABLE 9.9

Reported Problems with Food

	No Problem		Slight Problem		Moderate Problem		Serious Problem	
	%	N	%	N	%	N	%	N
Cost of food	32.4	100	24.6	76	22.7	70	19.7	61
Quality of food available where respondent shops	64.1	198	21.0	65	7.8	24	5.5	17
Determining nutritional value of foods	69.3	214	14.6	45	7.1	22	5.2	16
Adequacy of kitchen facilities	88.7	274	4.9	15	4.2	13	1.3	4
Meal preparation	82.5	255	7.1	22	1.9	6	1.0	3

Source: Compiled by the authors.

TABLE 9.10

Food Stamp Use

	Percent	Number
Applied for food stamps in past year	4.9	15
Received food stamps	2.9	9
Appealed food stamp case if denied	0.3	1
Had communication problem with food stamp eligibility worker	1.0	3

Source: Compiled by the author.

TABLE 9.11

Special Diet Behavior

	Percent	Number
Follow a special diet	22.7	70
Low-calorie	5.5	17
Bland	3.6	11
Low-fat	3.2	10
Diabetic	2.6	8
Other	7.8	26
Interviewer perceived overweight	23.9	74

Source: Compiled by the authors.

133

age or lower income, but to desire for change in social roles played, to involvement in leisure and community activities away from home, and to not being widowed (see Appendix G.17). Perhaps the active and restless older person is more inclined to perceive and report situations as presenting problems than is the quiescent and satisfied.

Older persons exhibit various consumer food behaviors. With the exception of monthly food expenditure, no behavior measured was related to increasing age or to income but, rather, to lifestyle factors. Three-quarters of older persons are directly involved in shopping for their own food. They have definite reasons for grocery store choice. Over half shop regularly for specials, and compare prices, weights, volumes, and ingredients when purchasing packaged goods. Yet one-third reported staying with familiar brands. Most older persons say they rely on personal sources of information when choosing a brand of frozen vegetables (Table 9.7), but nearly one-quarter read labels and consult consumer publications. Taste and enjoyment headed the list of very important criteria for food selection among older persons, but 45 percent reported nutritional value as very important.

10

TRANSPORTATION, HOUSING, AND CLOTHING

TRANSPORTATION

Automobile Ownership

The importance of transportation for the elderly has often been pointed out (Clark and Cochran 1972; Cutler 1972; White House Conference 1971). Three-quarters of older persons in the survey own or lease a motor vehicle; slightly less than one-third own two or more vehicles. Most vehicles are low-to-medium-price domestic models, and 16.8 percent are compact imports. Sedans are by far the most popular body type, with hardtops and station wagons second and third. Three years was the midpoint for length of ownership. Approximately half of the persons surveyed purchased their first vehicle from a new-car dealer; the remainder were divided almost equally between used-car dealers and personal transactions. Older consumers purchasing from a used-car dealer, as opposed to a new-car dealer, tend to be less educated and to disagree with the statement that older people are poorly treated in America (see Appendix M.4). Those preferring a personal transaction to a new-car dealer tend to rate themselves in a lower social class and say they would feel lost without their friends (see Appendix M.2). Information sources for both a make of new car and a new-car dealer are predominantly personal judgment and experience and the advice of family and friends (see Table 10.3).

The most important features of an automobile, in descending order, were repair record, handling, anticipated lifespan, purchase price, safety features, and operating expense. In other words, older consumers desire their automobiles to be reliable, easy to handle, long-lasting, inexpensive, and safe (see Table 10.2). One-quarter of older persons felt the "image" of their automobile is very important, but make and styling were of lesser importance. These evaluative criteria clustered in four separate factors: reliability, make

TABLE 10.1

Automobile Ownership

	Percent	Number
Own or lease a motor vehicle	74.1	229
Make of automobile owned (1st car)		
Low-price domestic	30.1	93
Medium-price domestic	16.5	51
Compact import	10.7	33
Luxury domestic	2.9	9
Luxury import	2.9	9
Compact domestic	1.3	4
Model of automobile owned (1st car)		
Sedan	38.1	118
Hardtop	10.4	32
Truck	4.8	15
Bus, van, camper	2.9	9
Wagon	1.6	5
Sports	0.3	1
Make of automobile owned (2nd car)		
Low-price domestic	12.9	40
Compact import	6.8	21
Medium-price domestic	5.5	17
Luxury domestic	1.6	5
Compact domestic	1.0	3
Luxury import	0.3	1
Model of automobile owned (2nd car)		
Sedan	10.0	31
Truck	3.9	12
Hardtop	2.9	9
Wagon	2.9	9
Sports	2.3	7
Bus, van, camper	1.9	6
Source of purchase (1st car)		
New-car dealer	49.2	152
Personal transaction	14.2	44
Used-car dealer	12.3	38
Length of ownership (1st car; years)		
1	15.5	48
2	8.1	25
3	14.2	44
4	5.8	18
5	4.9	15
6	5.5	17
7	6.1	19
8	3.9	12
9+	10.4	32

Source: Compiled by the authors.

TABLE 10.2

Evaluative Criteria for the Purchase of an Automobile

	Very Important		Somewhat Important		Not at All Important	
	%	N	%	N	%	N
Repair record	50.8	157	10.0	31	1.6	5
Handling	48.9	151	13.3	41	0.6	2
Anticipated lifespan	47.2	146	13.9	43	1.6	5
Purchase price	45.0	139	19.4	60	0.6	2
Safety features	44.3	137	17.2	53	2.3	7
Operating expense	42.4	131	20.1	62	1.3	4
"Image"	24.3	75	20.7	64	14.6	45
Make	17.8	55	35.0	108	9.4	29
Styling	12.0	37	34.3	106	15.2	47
Other	5.2	16	0.3	1	2.6	8

Source: Compiled by the authors.

and styling, operating expense, and image. Emphasis on reliability and longevity was predicted by clerical and sales occupation, higher income, and lack of worry about children (see Appendix M.7); make and styling, by lack of involvement in activities away from home, renting, fear of new ways and strange places, and not retired (see Appendix M.9). Operating expense logically appears to be most important to those who do a lot of driving—those who are involved in many activities away from home, who prefer working with others, who feel homemaking is a lonely way of life, and who are confident of the difference between right and wrong. Older persons to whom image is important tend to be men, in good health, desirous of role change, dissatisfied with life, and confident of the difference between right and wrong (see Appendix M.10).

Automobile Insurance

Of those older persons who own automobiles, only 2.3 percent carry no auto insurance (see Table 10.4). Of those who do carry insurance, most (93 percent) obtained it from a major insurance

TABLE 10.3

Sources of Information for Automobile Purchase

	Percent	Number
Selecting a make of new car		
Personal judgment and experience	58.3	180
Family and friends	23.9	74
Consumer publications	19.4	60
Sales personnel	2.9	9
Newspapers	1.6	5
Displays, samples	1.3	4
Television	0.6	2
Magazines	0.6	2
Yellow Pages	0.3	1
Selecting a new-car dealer		
Personal judgment and experience	53.4	165
Family and friends	37.8	117
Newspapers	3.6	11
Consumer publications	2.9	9
Sales personnel	2.9	9
Yellow Pages	1.9	6
Television	1.6	5
Professional directories and referral services	1.3	4
Displays, samples	1.0	3
Radio	0.3	1
Books	0.3	1

Source: Compiled by the authors.

company office or an independent agent, or through their employers. While no regression was performed on source of auto insurance, the analysis on source of health insurance revealed that consumers who purchase from relatively low-trust sources tend to be low-income, white, and satisfied with life (see Appendix K.3).

Automobile Repair

Approximately 55 percent of those surveyed who own cars have repair done by an auto repair shop, a dealer, or a gas station (see

TABLE 10.4

Automobile Insurance

	Percent[*]	Number
Have automobile insurance	96.7	203
Have no automobile insurance		
(of respondents who own automobiles)	3.3	7
Source of automobile insurance		
Major insurance company office	50.5	106
Independent agent	35.7	75
Employer	3.8	8
Mail order	2.4	5
Elsewhere	3.8	11

*Based on 210 who own automobiles.
Source: Compiled by the authors.

TABLE 10.5

Sources of Automobile Repair

	Percent	Number
Automobile repair shop	28.5	88
Automobile dealer	14.9	46
Gas station	10.7	33
Do-it-yourself	9.4	29
Spouse	6.8	21
Friend, relative	5.5	17
Other	1.0	3

Source: Compiled by the authors.

TABLE 10.6

Disappointing Consumer Experiences in Transportation

	Percent	Number
Source of disappointing experience		
Automobile	5.5	17
Automobile dealer	5.5	17
Automobile repair shop	8.1	25
Type of problem		
Automobile		
Unsatisfactory performance	3.2	10
Faulty repairs	1.6	5
Charge for services not rendered	0.6	2
Guarantee not honored	0.6	2
Deceptive advertising	0.3	1
Automobile dealer		
Faulty repairs	2.7	9
Deceptive advertising	1.3	4
Unsatisfactory performance	1.0	3
Guarantee not honored	1.0	3
Offensive advertising	0.3	1
Automobile repair shop		
Faulty repairs	5.5	17
Unsatisfactory performance	2.6	8
Guarantee not honored	0.3	1
Charge for services not rendered	0.3	1
Deceptive advertising	0.3	1
Offensive advertising	0.3	1
Action taken		
Automobile		
Complained in person	2.6	8
Refused to do further business	1.0	3
Wrote letter or telephoned	0.6	2
Other	0.6	2
Automobile dealer		
Complained in person	2.6	8
Refused to do further business	1.9	6
Wrote letter or telephoned	1.2	4
Automobile repair shop		
Complained in person	3.8	12
Refused to do further business	2.1	7
Telephoned	1.0	3
Did nothing	0.6	2
Contacted consumer protection agency,		
Better Business Bureau, other	0.6	2

Source: Compiled by the authors.

140

TABLE 10.7

Problems with Transportation

	Serious Problem		Moderate Problem		Slight Problem		No Problem	
	%	N	%	N	%	N	%	N
Cost of automobile insurance	16.8	52	16.5	51	14.6	45	35.3	109
Automobile purchase price	13.9	43	13.3	41	12.3	38	44.3	137
Cost of upkeep	11.0	34	14.6	45	16.2	50	42.7	132
Quality of automobile repair	13.3	41	11.3	35	9.7	30	46.6	144
Possibility of accidents	4.5	14	6.1	19	12.3	38	68.6	212
Availability of public transportation	3.6	11	5.5	17	4.2	13	82.5	255
Qualifying for automobile insurance	4.5	14	1.9	6	3.2	10	71.8	222
Physical driving handicaps	5.5	17	0.6	2	2.6	8	71.5	221
Cost of public transportation	1.0	3	3.2	10	4.5	14	83.8	259

Source: Compiled by the authors.

141

Table 10.5). The remainder chose to do it themselves or have a spouse, friend, or relative do it. Shop auto repair was predicted by high social interaction and health restrictions. Those choosing personal sources of repair tended to be less sociable and unrestricted by health problems (see Appendix M.1). Auto repair was the area that received the most mention of specific disappointing consumer experiences with transportation in the recent past. However, more older persons took an active role rather than a passive role in response to these problems and complained in person, telephoned, or wrote letters.

Problems in Transportation

With regard to general transportation problems, cost (of insurance, purchase price, and upkeep) and the quality of repair headed the list (see Table 10.7). The cost and availability of public transportation, physical handicaps that interfere with driving, and trouble qualifying for auto insurance were problems for fewer persons. Reported problems with transportation clustered with those for food, income sufficiency and management, and housing, and were predicted by role change, far involvement, and not widowed (see Appendix G.17).

Dependence on public transportation is predicted by renter, unmarried, and low-income (see Appendix M.3). Nondrivers tend to be women with lower education but higher self-rated social class and a desire for fame. They have a conservative attitude toward women's roles. They may be lonely and dependent on others for many things. They say they have fewer friends now, and would feel lost without the ones they do have. See Appendix L for a summary of "attribute," "budget," and "alienation" variables for auto as a means of transportation; Appendix M.5; and Table 9.5 for a summary of the modes of transportation used by older persons to shop.

HOUSING

Housing Status

Housing needs and satisfactions of older persons have been widely discussed in the literature (Hamovitch and Peterson 1969; Snyder 1971; Lawton and Cohen 1974).

Table 10.8 reveals the housing status of older consumers relative to younger consumers. The data show a steadily increasing percentage of families owning their homes until age 65 or older,

TABLE 10.8

Housing Status of the Elderly, 1970
(percentage distribution of nonfarm families)

	Housing Status		
Age or Life-Cycle Stage	Own	Rent	Other*
Age of family head			
18-24	12	77	11
25-34	48	45	7
35-44	72	24	4
45-54	74	22	4
55-64	77	18	5
65 or older	71	22	7
Age 45 or older			
Married, has children	79	16	5
Married, no children, head in labor force	81	15	4
Married, no children, head retired	82	14	4
Unmarried, no children, head in labor force	58	35	7
Unmarried, no children, head retired	62	28	10

*Includes trailer owners and families who neither own nor rent.
Source: George Katona, Lewis Mandell, and Jay Schmiedeskamp, 1970 Survey of Consumer Attitudes. Ann Arbor, Michigan: Survey Research Center, Institute for Social Research, The University of Michigan. Reprinted with permission.

after which there is increased rental and less ownership. These data suggest that there is much mobility in old age, and there is: changed economic conditions upon retirement, too much space, failing health, loneliness, and a change in marital status all contribute to mobility among older consumers. Probably the greatest of these mobility contributors is widowhood. There is also a big increase in "other" living arrangements during widowhood. Mobile homes are popular because they are inexpensive, easy to maintain, and modern.

Mobility, while precipitated by one or more of the factors mentioned above, is not necessarily unwanted by older consumers. Their housing needs and wants vary greatly, and not all of them will find the same living arrangements suitable. Whatever the dwelling style, however, almost all older consumers have certain physical

TABLE 10.9

Home Ownership and Mobility Statistics

	Percent	Number
Home Ownership		
Own	64.4	199
Rent	35.6	110
Length of Residence at Present Address (years)		
1- 2	20.1	62
3- 5	11.7	36
6-10	13.6	42
11-20	25.2	78
More than 20	24.9	77
Propensity to Move		
Might move	20.7	64
Probably will move	6.1	19
Definitely will move	11.3	35
Type of Housing Desired by Those Planning to Move		
House	15.5	48
Apartment	9.4	29
Mobile home	6.1	19
Condominium	2.9	9
Hotel	1.0	3
Farm	0.6	2
Retirement community	0.3	1
Boardinghouse	0.3	1
Other	2.6	8
Reasons for Moving		
Less outdoor upkeep desired	7.1	22
Less expense	6.8	21
More privacy	6.5	20
Safer neighborhood	5.5	17
More attractive neighborhood	3.9	12
A yard	3.9	12
People own age	3.2	10
Special architectural features	2.3	7
Planned recreation	1.9	6
Climate change	1.9	6
Better construction	1.3	4
Freedom from housekeeping	1.0	3
Other	15.9	49

Source: Compiled by the authors.

144

and psychological needs that must be met within their dwelling quarters (Reynolds and Wells 1977).

Living Arrangements

The physical needs in the living arrangements of the elderly include moderate temperatures, with even distribution of heat from floor to ceiling to prevent chilling, because circulation generally grows poorer with age. Large windows that admit plenty of light are similarly encouraged, because of the gradual impairment of vision.

Safety needs include unwaxed floors and few steps. Living quarters should be on one floor. It is advisable to provide indoor and outdoor recreation space.

Noise should be controlled, especially during the night. This may be accomplished by locating the elderly person's sleeping quarters in a quiet part of the house.

Labor-saving devices are advisable for cooking and cleaning.

Psychological Needs

Privacy is important for the elderly person, who needs a room of his or her own. The living arrangements should include space for sedentary recreations, such as reading and watching television. There should be provisions for storage of cherished possessions.

The elderly person should live close to stores and community organizations, in order to be independent in his or her activities, and should also be near relatives and friends, so that frequent contacts are possible (Hurlock 1975). These needs are similar to those of the general population.

Home Ownership

Slightly less than two-thirds (64.4 percent) of older persons own their own home. Home ownership correlated with marriage, higher income, regard for female autonomy, and "better talker than listener" (see Appendix I.7). One-quarter of those surveyed had been at the same residence for 11 to 20 years, and another quarter for more than 20 years. However, one-fifth had recently moved and another 17 percent said they probably or definitely would move. Most who were planning to move said they wanted a house or apartment, but significant numbers of those planning a move opted for a

TABLE 10.10

Reported Housing Problems

	Serious Problem		Moderate Problem		Slight Problem		No Problem	
	%	N	%	N	%	N	%	N
Property taxes	14.6	45	11.7	36	10.7	33	36.6	113
Neighborhood traffic	11.7	36	12.3	38	23.6	73	52.1	161
Neighborhood crime	6.5	20	13.3	41	27.8	86	51.8	160
Obtaining reliable repairs	5.2	16	8.7	27	9.4	29	65.7	203
Meeting monthly housing cost	3.2	10	2.3	7	6.8	21	79.9	247
Landlord repairs	3.2	10	1.9	6	3.9	12	32.4	100*
Quality of housing construction	1.9	6	3.6	11	12.0	37	80.9	250
Distance from public transport	1.3	4	3.9	12	3.6	11	87.7	271
Distance from shopping	1.3	4	2.9	9	7.8	24	86.7	268
Restrictive lease	0.3	1	0.3	1	1.0	3	33.7	104*

*Large amounts of data missing.
Source: Compiled by the authors.

mobile home, and only half as many desired a condominium. Most frequently given reasons for moving included the desire to have less outdoor upkeep, the need for a cheaper place, and desire for privacy and safety. Special architectural features were mentioned by only seven persons (2.3 percent).

Reported Housing Problems

Property taxes (before Proposition 13 in California), traffic, crime, and obtaining reliable home repairs headed the list of reported housing problems. Problems with housing appeared in the same factor as problems with food, income sufficiency and management, and transportation, and was predicted by role change, far involvement, and not widowed (see Appendix G.17). Some specific disappointing experiences with real estate companies, contractors, and landlords were reported: unsatisfactory performance, faulty repairs, and guarantee not honored (Table 10.10). Various active responses to these complaints were undertaken. Renters apparently are more likely than homeowners to be passive in the face of disappointing experiences.

CLOTHING

In a study of intergenerational differences in fashion behavior, women over 60 were found to perceive themselves as fashion-conscious, and a high proportion said they enjoy shopping for clothes. However, this study found major differences among generations with regard to alternatives considered, predispositions formed prior to shopping, and reliance on sales personnel and newspapers (Martin 1976). Another study found that women over 55 are even more concerned than younger women about dressing well, and express more desire to look "different" than do all groups except 25-34, but feel less motivated to be attractive to the opposite sex. Men over 65, by contrast, were found to be less concerned about their clothing and personal appearance than older women or younger men, but to express a greater need to feel sexually attractive than men 45-54 (Reynolds and Wells 1977).

Who Shops for Clothing?

Three-quarters of older persons shop for clothing on their own, 15 percent with spouse, and 10 percent leave the responsibility to

TABLE 10.11

Clothing Shopping: Who Shops, Frequency, and Transportation

	Percent	Number
Who Shops		
Respondent	73.5	227
Respondent and spouse	14.9	46
Spouse	9.7	30
Other person	1.3	4
Respondent and other person	0.6	2
Frequency		
Once a week	1.0	3
Less than weekly, more than monthly	3.2	10
Once a month	18.8	58
Few times a year	58.9	182
Once a year	10.0	31
Less than once a year	5.2	16
Transportation		
Drive	48.2	149
Public transportation	15.5	48
Someone else drives	13.9	43
Walk	5.8	18
Other	3.6	11

Source: Compiled by the authors.

the spouse alone. Apparently very few shop with friends (Table 10.11).
Most shop a few times a year, but one-quarter shop once a month or
more often. Less than half drive themselves to clothing shopping;
approximately one-seventh are driven by someone else, and another
seventh use public transportation. Six percent walk.

Store Preference

By far the most frequently given reason for selection of a
particular clothing store was product assortment, with merchandise
quality second. Accessibility, parking, sales promotion, and prices
were each mentioned by approximately 30 percent of the sample.

TABLE 10.12

Sources of Clothing and Reason for Store Selection

	Percent	Number
Source		
Major department store	62.1	192
Specialty store	12.6	39
Catalog/mail order	12.6	39
Discount store	12.3	38
In-home shopping	1.3	4
Reason for Store Selection		
Product assortment	58.9	182
Merchandise quality	44.3	137
Accessibility	32.0	99
Parking	30.7	95
Sales promotion	30.4	94
Prices	28.8	89
Credit availability	24.3	75
Proximity	23.9	74
Special sizes or styles	23.9	74
Friendly personnel	18.8	58
Hours	15.9	49
Appearance of store and clientele	13.6	42
Special services	8.1	25
In-home convenience	7.4	23
Loyalty to owner	1.9	6
Other	2.6	8

Source: Compiled by the authors.

Credit availability, proximity, and availability of special sizes and styles were mentioned by approximately one-quarter. Of less importance were friendly personnel, appearance of store and clientele, and special services. Loyalty to owner was negligible (see Table 10.12).

Preference for department or discount stores for clothing purchase, and selection of individual stores on the basis of accessibility, hours, parking facilities, low prices, credit, and appearance of store and clientele were part of a general store-choice set

TABLE 10.13

Evaluative Criteria for Clothing

	Very Important		Somewhat Important		Not at All Important	
	%	N	%	N	%	N
Fit	59.5	184	11.3	35	1.3	4
Durability	51.5	159	16.5	51	2.3	7
Washability	48.2	149	20.7	64	2.3	7
Price	47.2	146	25.6	79	2.3	7
Cut	38.5	119	23.0	71	3.6	11
Color	35.0	108	29.4	91	5.2	16
Fashionableness	24.6	76	30.4	94	12.6	39
Alterability	21.7	67	24.6	76	16.5	51
Brand	11.7	36	33.7	104	22.7	70
Other	1.0	3	0.6	2	2.9	9

Source: Compiled by the authors.

existing across product categories and not confined exclusively to clothing store selection. Fit was the most important characteristic of clothing among older persons, followed by the practical concerns of durability and washability. Price was fourth on the list. Aesthetic considerations of cut, color and fashionableness were of lesser importance. One-fifth of the sample reported alterability to be very important. Brand was rated the least important (see Table 10.13).

Consumer Behavior Variables for Clothing

The factor analysis of these evaluative criteria indicate separate dimensions for practical and aesthetic considerations. Importance of the practical was predicted by lower education, lack of introspection, lack of religiosity, preference for working with others versus working alone, preference for persons of one's own age, value placed on children's companionship, and near involvement (see Appendix M.8). Aesthetic considerations were related to desire to be single, desire for role change, lack of importance of children in decision making, and clerical or sales occupation (see

Appendix M.6). Clothing specialty store shoppers tend to feel that homemaking is a lonely life, to worry their children won't turn out right, and to be more interested in national and international events than in things that happen in their own community, which may indicate they are anxious, personalizing, and somewhat cosmopolitan (see Appendix E.21). Catalog shoppers tend to be married, less well educated, and interested in role change (see Appendix E.25). Those who base their choice on personality characteristics of store personnel rate themselves in a lower socioeconomic class (see Appendix M.14). The desire for in-home clothing shopping convenience was related to preference for state and national organizations over local ones, lack of desire for role change, male gender, "better talker than listener," acceptance of working wives, and lack of religiosity (see Appendix M.15).

11

SUMMARY AND IMPLICATIONS

Visible aging begins with middle age (roughly the forties and fifties) and continues through later maturity (around the sixties and seventies) and older age (75, 80, or more). The aging process is related to physical and mental changes that occur throughout life. After conception we grow and age simultaneously until life ends. The quality of life is a more important determinant of old age, however, than chronological years. Moreover, it is the quality of environment—perhaps more important, our adaptation to it—that determines satisfaction.

Older Americans are not a subcultural population with separate needs and a homogeneous identity distinguishable from younger persons. Garson Kanin, in his book It Takes a Long Time to Become Young, states his case for age, speaking of older Americans:

> Our strength lies in our differences, in our diversity of
> interests, and talents. We age differently, and even the
> causes can be diverse: physical, mental, emotional,
> occupational or geographical. The species has repro-
> duced itself billions and billions of times, yet there
> have never been two human beings exactly alike. We
> grow at varying speeds, reaching various heights. We
> are fat, thin, too fat, too thin, astigmatic, bald,
> mechanically inclined, or all thumbs, coordinated or
> clumsy, quick to learn or slow; in short, we are indi-
> viduals. We age differently, the process being controlled
> by several factors; genes, heredity, environment,
> nutrition, climate, occupation, temperament (Kanin
> 1978, p. 30).

Lifestyles, including attitudes and expectations for the roles we play, may have more of an effect than age in predicting the quality of our lives. The roles we experience and create correspond somewhat with various life stages, such as child rearing and spousal relationships, retirement, changing responsibilities in household management, community involvement, and leisure activities. How well we pass through one stage has an effect on how successfully we grow into the next (Sheehy 1976).

The older we grow, the more our lives are touched by the loss of loved ones and friends. We experience role changes and a lessening of income. These are the challenges of maturity (U.S. DHEW 1978). By examining these roles and their concomitant behaviors, we have looked at the value of older Americans as individuals who uniquely express their experiences. In looking at lifestyle factors, clustered in groups of psychosocial roles and relationships (marriage, family and homemaking, socioeconomic status, cosmopolitanism-venturesomeness, social interaction, and introspectiveness-personal vitality), the implication for human development theory is the need for continuing opportunities in role development, for social interaction, and for social activities among the elderly.

In employment, leisure and social activities, marital roles and relationships, and personal habits and health, older Americans' needs are not different from those of their younger counterparts. The differences that do appear are related to lifestyle, or how the elderly person copes with the unique set of circumstances he or she experiences and creates, and not to age. When the myths and stereotypes are removed and when older Americans are viewed as individuals, in lifestyle and in the marketplace, a range of differences becomes apparent similar to the distribution among younger age groups (Harris and Associates 1976).

The image of the elderly as human resources has been indicated by their value as persons. Furthermore, the image of the elderly as economic resources has been clearly demonstrated in our survey analyzing consumer behavior in the marketplace.

There are, further, gaps to be filled between the public's image of the problems of the elderly and their actual experiences. Overall, fears attributable to older Americans do not include lack of money, loneliness, lack of friends or education, and not being needed, contrary to the perceptions of younger persons (Harris and Associates 1976).

The popular press should be aware that a realistic image of the elderly would represent them as active, diverse in temperament and personality, and unique in their life experiences, while being mindful of their value as individual human and economic resources.

FINANCIAL SITUATION AND OPPORTUNITIES

Older Americans are better off financially than is generally believed. Even though they anticipate no future increases in income, they express more satisfaction with their financial circumstances than do younger persons, have fewer debts, and are more careful shoppers and spenders. They generally express a realistic view of their financial situation and shift expenditures accordingly (Reynolds and Wells 1977). Pension and security plans remain important sources of income in this regard. The public, according to Harris, fully supports Social Security benefits and feels that cost-of-living increases would be appropriate (Harris and Associates 1976).

The elderly have much confidence in themselves. They feel they are entitled to rewards they have earned, and are willing to work or provide services to fulfill their needs. They are also more resourceful and independent than previously imagined, yet many are retired against their will. There is reason to believe, from our survey and others (Harris and Associates 1976), that many of those who claim they are too old or too sick to work do so because of public expectation. There is, therefore, an untapped source of manpower among the elderly. Career options, such as consultantships for those who want to work, or the opportunity for voluntary or other creative experiences for those who do not need the income, are suggested by the data. Since career variety and new experiences are important for change and growth, either full-time or part-time work may fill the gaps. Likewise, house-managing activities are interchangeable for both men and women, for a broader range of role experiences. Organizational activity is also strongly suggested for older Americans as a means of social interaction.

The emphasis here is on the social support that is gained from involvement with others, whether through employment, social and organizational groups for peer support, or social or political action.

SUPPORT NETWORKS

Maggie Kuhn, 73, founder in 1970 of the Gray Panthers and leading advocate of the philosophy of the aged as not "useless" or "sexless," has demonstrated the effectiveness of support networks in attaining socially desirable goals. "Using senior centers and other organizational facilities as forums for social problems," she states, "provides the opportunity for the older American to utilize his talents and skills and to share information with his peers" (Kuhn 1978).

The variance in activities and interests among the elderly is the same as for any other age group. Those with poor health have fewer interests and those in higher socioeconomic strata have more interests. The implication is that support networks can provide outlets that help the elderly to achieve new relationships and experiences that will allow them to improve their status and conditions, when necessary.

The Unexpected Community, an account of a group of widows who are living at or below the poverty level in a lower-class housing project in a marginal neighborhood of San Francisco, points out the effectiveness of a social network in meeting the needs of these individuals "as a mutual aid society, as a source of jobs, as an audience, as a pool of models for growing old, as a sanctuary and as a subculture with its own customs, gossip, and humor" (Hochschild 1973). The implication of this account reinforces the findings in our survey that age, sex, and income are not accurate indicators of vulnerability or helplessness among the population. The use of age alone as a criterion for making policy regarding the needs of various segments of the population is unwarranted.

The public, it seems, feels guilty about the elderly, and would support efforts to improve their status and conditions. "Free handouts and paying lip service to respect for their wisdom will not substantially improve the status or conditions of people over 65, however" (Harris and Associates 1976). Rather, support networks of peers, family, and friends of all ages, and recognition of individual talents, skills, and abilities through increased opportunities for self-expression offer the most lasting means for improving the status and conditions of older Americans.

TWO FEARS OF THE ELDERLY:
POOR HEALTH AND CRIME

There are two fears that may be accurately attributed to the elderly: poor health and crime, although they are not necessarily experiencing either. (See Tables 8.1-8.12 and discussion of consumer problems, Table 6.8.) Health and mobility are concerns of the elderly, especially men. Women report more chronic health problems than men do. Men, on the other hand, are more anxious about health.

Programs for the handicapped person (including technical and social services, transportation, homemaker services, and alternative living and eating arrangements) have been described in many texts. Older Americans should not be considered handicapped only as a result of their age, however.

The multivariate analysis of lifestyle and consumer behavior of our sample of 309 persons over 45 revealed almost no significant relationships between increasing age and consumer health care attitudes and behavior. Among this sample, low income and social isolation were the most frequent correlates of poor health and alienation from the medical care system. Age was a major predictor of only one health-care behavior factor, which included the variables covered by Medicare and frequency of prescription drug use. No relationship was found between increasing age and self-rated health status, monthly expenditures for health care, possession of health insurance, type of policy, source of policy, or reported problems with health care services. Low self-rated health status was predicted by low income, low activity level, low involvement around the home, and fear of trying new things. The low-income and the socially isolated tended not to possess health insurance, or to obtain it from unreliable sources. Monthly health care expenditure was related to marriage, religiosity, education, and several conservative value statements, and not to health status, age, or income. Persons eligible for Medicare were generally satisfied with the health care system, while those receiving Medi-Cal (the California Medicaid) were generally dissatisfied. Persons in poor health and needing a support system of friends were most likely to report problems with health care services.

In other words, those with perhaps the greatest need report that the system is least responsive to them. In order to serve those with the greatest need, the health care system must consider the social, emotional, and financial characteristics of persons, regardless of age. Medi-Cal is not the answer, and little support has been found for national health insurance (Hilka et al. 1975; Stratman et al. 1975). Numerous models for comprehensive, humanized health care systems have been presented in the literature (Blum 1976), and the success of such care among the low-income has been demonstrated (Robertson 1974). The challenge ahead is the expanded implementation of this type of care.

As for violent crime or theft, Michael Hindelang of the State University of New York's School of Criminal Justice suggested that except for the widespread fear of crime among the elderly, they are not more victimized than younger persons. Hindelang, a member of the National Crime Panel, reviewed data gathered from surveys interviewing about 2 million Americans in major cities during 1974 and 1975. This was reported in the American Psychological Association Monitor (Foltz 1978).

In cities or neighborhoods where there is a high incidence of crime, volunteer efforts can be effective. The old and the young can live side by side, as pointed out by Garson Kanin in retelling the story of Michael Mirakian, coordinator of student affairs at Robert Taft High School in the Bronx. Mirakian, who became concerned over a number of assaults on and harassments of older people in his neighborhood, organized over 200 of his students into a volunteer force to escort and protect them on shopping trips, walks, and visits to doctors and dentists. Crimes against older people became virtually nonexistent. This kind of voluntary effort is an indication of the kind of humanity that should be experienced in a civilized society (Kanin 1978).

The view of the elderly as suffering, vulnerable, and incompetent does them a disservice. The only thing older Americans are actually lacking in substantial amounts is respect. Programs and services that separate the elderly from other age groups are unnecessary, unless they are sponsored by the elderly themselves as peer supports. For instance, discount rates on goods and services and early retirement, irrespective of individual needs and abilities, waste monetary and human resources. Programs that provide opportunities for individual expression of needs and abilities, such as senior centers that are run and operated by older Americans and employment opportunities and organizational participation where knowledge and skills may be utilized, are indicated by our survey.

Older persons appear, in general, to be competent consumers, and more often than not are active complainers when they feel something is wrong. Their problems appear to be similar to those of persons in any other age group. Therefore, programs and policies that benefit consumers of all ages (anti-inflationary, fiscal, and monetary policies; product quality and standards; education programs; environmental control; crime education; comprehensive health care) will have positive effects for older persons too. Consumer educators should be particularly aware of this implication as it applies to the public generally, rather than direct programs and information to the elderly as a subpopulation.

MARKETING

Older Americans are generally wise, careful shoppers, and their expenditures have a logically varying pattern. They expect reliability and quality when making their purchases, and shop accordingly, as indicated in our survey.

As for buying style and store choice of the elderly, it is apparent that they are willing to pay more for quality merchandise and for variety in product choice. They like department stores for product variety in one location, and neighborhood stores for convenience in daily and weekly shopping, such as for groceries. As far as food and nutrition are concerned, taste and enjoyment rated above price and family preferences as criteria in choice.

Older Americans are, for the most part, rational rather than impulsive in their shopping habits. They rely on family and friends as sources of information, then media, followed by consumer publications when they feel unsure of a purchase decision. For the most part they are as rational and independent as the rest of the population and rely on their own judgment.

The portrayal of the elderly as a separate market segment, based on mythic stereotyping that characterizes them as having physiological impairments, is unfounded; they are actually part of the larger, general market. They do not represent a separate market in society for laxatives, special foods, pep pills, and tranquilizers. According to Maggie Kuhn, who is fighting against the use of drugs among both young and old, she is especially concerned with the practice of sedating old people into vegetables (Kuhn 1978). Older Americans demand integrity in advertising, and rely on media such as television for some product information; thus, accuracy in representing product benefits and services is suggested by the data.

There is an interest in tires, appliances, and personal product assortment indicated by our survey that contributes to feelings of autonomy among the elderly. Men and women share shopping responsibilities and experience the effects of inflation as much as younger adults do.

Women are less interested than men in house management as they grow older, and both are likely to sell large homes and rent or buy smaller units. Men are more ego-involved with automobiles, perhaps because of the mobility it provides them, while older women tend to rely on others for their transportation needs. They like the freedom to travel without the responsibility of home maintenance and upkeep, since family and friends may be many miles away. Therefore, improved transportation systems that provide convenient, dependable service are implied for men and women alike, as an alternative to the automobile. "Greyhound has been able to interest oldsters in travel with T.V. commercials showing older people (as well as young) travelling by bus" (Reynolds and Wells 1977).

The fact that credit card use is not widely valued among the elderly is practical in terms of having more available income than responsibilities (in contrast with previous years) and in not wanting to create unnecessary bills. Further, they appear to be adequately insured. There is nonetheless a suggested need for younger adults to plan for the future through wise money management and investment and through various educational, social, and employment experiences, and to adopt values that will establish respect for individuals of all ages, thus allowing the continued opportunity for self-expression to occur among the aged.

CONSUMER BEHAVIOR THEORY

An average of only 11 percent of the variance in the consumer behavior factor was accounted for by 57 independent lifestyle variables. Some aspects of consumer behavior were predicted at a slightly better-than-average percent: a few buying-style variables (frequency of shopping, decision-making style [joint, solitary, other-directed], attitude toward credit, television as an information source, quality-consciousness, impulsive shopping, brand loyalty); disappointing consumer experiences, consumer problems; type of investments possessed, home ownership, health insurance behavior; nondriver; and food and transportation budget. Store choice, store relations, and attribute importance were in general predicted at a less-than-average percent. The percent of variance accounted for never exceeded 25 percent, except for "covered by Medicare" (40 percent), an obvious function of age in this sample composed of persons 45 and older.

The implication for consumer behavior theory is that consumer behavior is dependent upon individual needs and psychosocial relationships that contribute to personal buying styles. The styles consist of the way an individual views himself or herself and how he or she interacts with others, including near involvement, far involvement, the desire to change roles, and life satisfaction. The combination of lifestyles (role behavior) and buying styles (consumer behavior) has provided us with categories for determining life satisfaction and well-being among the elderly. One conclusion is that consumer behavior, per se, is one of the most stable conditions in the lives of older Americans, and that lifestyles or role experiences, relationships, level of activities, and involvement in or away from home have more of an effect on the elderly than age, sex, or income.

APPENDIXES

APPENDIX A: RESULTS OF FIELD INTERVIEWING

APPENDIX A

Results of Field Interviewing

	#N	%
Total attempts	6,696	100
No contact	3,241	48
No one home	2,974	44
Inaccessible residence	138	2
Illness in household	30	–
Communication barrier	87	1
Other, not specified	12	–
Contact made	3,455	52
Interview not completed	3,146	47
No eligible respondent	2,167	32
Refused	531	8
Quota filled	448	7
Interview completed	309	5

Source: Compiled by the authors.

APPENDIX B

Demographics

Owner Homeowner
    yes,   no

Working for pay
yes, no

Age
    45–54
    55–64
    65+

Unemployed
yes, no

Retired
yes, no

Homemaker
yes, no

Class
    lower
    working
    middle
    upper-middle
    upper

Change in religiosity in last 5 years
  much more religious
  somewhat more religious
  stayed about the same
  somewhat less religious
  much less religious

What was the income of your family last year before taxes?

None or loss
Less than $2,000
$2,000 to $2,999
$3,000 to $3,999
$4,000 to $4,999
$5,000 to $5,999
$6,000 to $6,999
$7,000 to $7,999
$8,000 to $8,999
$9,000 to $9,999

$10,000 to $10,999
$11,000 to $11,999
$12,000 to $14,999
$15,000 to $19,999
$20,000 to $24,999
$25,000 to $29,999
$30,000 or over

Don't know
No answer

What is your marital status?

Married
Widowed
Divorced
Separated
Never been married

Self-rated health status
  poor
  fair
  good
  excellent
Highest grade completed in school
1 through 17+

Interviewer Observations

Sex of respondent	male	female	
Age group	45–54	55–64	65+

164

Observed ethnic background	Occupation[a]
White or Anglo	Unskilled worker
Mexican-American	Skilled worker
Other Spanish-American	Clerical and Sales
Black	Self-employed, manager, official
Chinese, Japanese, Korean	Professional
Other	Other[b] (Reference)

[a]Occupation was an open ended question that was categorized using standard U. S. Bureau of Labor Statistics definition.

[b]Other category includes unemployed, retired, student, and housewife.

Source: Compiled by the author.

165

APPENDIX C: LIFESTYLE VARIABLES

APPENDIX C. 1

Agree-Disagree Personal Value Statements

Daily activities limited by health
Young people have too many privileges
Personal religion
Join local "action" group
Clear right and wrong
Better listener than conversationalist
Prefer people my own age
Should continue education
Older people poorly treated
Change is important
People should work harder
Prefer large parties
Separate vacations
National over local news
Have fewer friends now
Well-established family over newcomer
Rarely introduce self to strangers
Enjoy showing foreigner around
Like going alone to strange places
Local club over national
Should spend time with younger people
Happy with life so far
Personal relationships over work
Sex should not be regulated by law
Should look into mind and feelings
Accept public authority unquestioningly
Children not enough time with parents
Housekeeping once over lightly
Man should rule money matters
Working staves off old age
Clubs not important
Dislike set schedule
Too old to run around
Children primary consideration in decisions
Feel lost without friends
Homemaking is a lonely life
Wish I were single
Rather be brilliant than steady

Leery of new things.
Understand Young people less.
Never too old to take up new ways.
Worry children won't turn out right.
Harder to make new friends as get older.
Express my creativity in the home.
Woman's most important activities and interests tend to be ones in
  which her husband cannot participate.
Do better work now than ever before.
Wish I had more contact with people.
Most of my friends live in the neighborhood.
Changes are too much for me.
Parents insufficient time with children.
People are an important part of my life.
Marriage problems if wife brings home money.
Prefer to work alone.
Playing cards a waste of time.
I'm a homebody.
Children grow up too fast.
I want to be a famous person.

Source: Compiled by the authors.

APPENDIX C. 2

Independent Variables

Working for pay
  2 = yes, 1 = no

Unemployed
  2 = yes, 1 = no

Retired
  2 = yes, 1 = no

Homemaker
  2 = yes, 1 = no

Married
  2 = yes, 1 = no

Widowed
  2 = yes, 1 = no

Divorced
  2 = yes, 1 = no

Change in religiosity in last 5 years
  5 = much more religious
  4 = somewhat more religious
  3 = stayed about the same
  2 = somewhat less religious
  1 = much less religious

Self-rated health status
  1 = poor
  2 = fair
  3 = good
  4 = excellent

Highest grade completed in school
  1 through 17+

Owner Homeowner
  2 = yes, 1 = no

Income
  01 = none or loss
  02 = less than $2,000
  03 = $2,000-$2,999
  04 = $3,000-$3,999
  05 = $4,000-$4,999
  06 = $5,000-$5,999
  07 = $6,000-$6,999
  08 = $7,000-$7,999
  09 = $8,000-$8,999
  10 = $9,000-$9,999
  11 = $10,000-$10,999
  12 = $11,000-$11,999
  13 = $12,000-$14,999
  14 = $15,000-$19,999
  15 = $20,000-$24,999
  16 = $25,000-$29,999
  17 = $30,000+

Agree-Disagree Statements

"My daily activities are limited by
  health."
"In most situations, it is clear to me
  there is a right way and a wrong way."
"I am a better listener than conversationalist."

5 = strongly agree
4 = agree
3 = neither agree nor disagree
2 = disagree
1 = disagree strongly

"I prefer to spend time around people my own age."
"Older people are poorly treated in America."
"Change and new experiences are important in the life
  of every person."
"I am more interested in news about national and
  international events than in things that happen
  in this community."
"I seem to have fewer friends now than in the past."
"I rarely introduce myself to strangers at social gatherings."
"I like going alone to strange and new places."
"Belonging to a local club would be more rewarding than
  belonging to a state or national organization."
"I am happy with the way my life has gone so far."
"I should take some time every day to look into my mind
  and feelings."
"Children don't spend enough time with their parents."
"While I enjoy clubs, they are not really important."
"I dislike following a set schedule."
"When making important decisions, a primary consideration
  is my children."
"I would feel lost without my friends."
"Homemaking is a lone life."
"I wish I were single."
"I'm a little leery of trying new things, so my free-time
  activities don't change very much."
"I have never felt I was too old to take up new ways."
"I worry my children will not turn out right."
"A woman's most important activities and interests tend
  to be ones in which her husband cannot participate."
"A marriage has problems when the woman brings home money."
"I prefer to work alone than with others."
"I'm a homebody."
"I want to be a famous person."

Age
  1 = 45-54
  2 = 55-64
  3 = 65+

APPENDIX C-2 (continued)

Class
  1 = lower
  2 = working
  3 = middle
  4 = upper-middle
  5 = upper

Gender
  2 = female
  1 = male

Interaction	ascending
Satisfaction	ascending
Role change	ascending
Near involvement	ascending
Far involvement	ascending

Anglo
  2 = yes
  1 = no

Unskilled worker	2 = yes, 1 = no
Skilled worker	2 = yes, 1 = no
Clerical and sales	2 = yes, 1 = no
Self-employed, manager, official	2 = yes, 1 = no
Professional	2 = yes, 1 = no
Other (Reference)	2 = yes, 1 = no

Source: Compiled by the authors.

APPENDIX C. 3

Composite of Role Related Variables

Interaction   How often do you chat or visit with others while at work?
When you're home during the day, how often do you chat
or visit with other people?
How much companionship do you and your husband/wife/
friend have? How often do you do things just with each
other?
How often do you go places or do things with children or
grandchildren who live at home with you?
How often do you watch TV or listen to music with
children or grandchildren who live at home with you?
How often do you talk things over with children or grandchildren who live at home with you?
How often do you go places and do things with children
or grandchildren who live near but not at home?
How often do you watch TV or listen to music with
children or grandchildren who live near but not at home?
How often do you talk things over with children or grand-
children who live near but not at home?
How often do you write or telephone children or grand-
children who do not live near you?
How often do children or grandchildren who do not live
near visit you?
How often do you visit children or grandchildren who do
not live near you?
How often do you go places and do things with children or
grandchildren who do not live near you?
How often do you watch TV or listen to music with children
or grandchildren who do not live near you?
How often do you talk things over with children or grand-
children who do not live near you?
How often do you chat or visit with friends while at club
and community meetings and functions?
How much companionship do you and your friends have?
How often do you and your friends participate in social
and leisure activities together?

Satisfaction   How satisfied are you with your work?
How satisfied are you with your homemaking?
How satisfied are you with your partner?
How satisfied are you with your parenthood?
How satisfied are you with your community activities?
How satisfied are you with your friendship activities?
How satisfied are you with your leisure activities?

171

APPENDIX C. 3 (continued)

Role Change	Would you like to change your work activities?
	Would you like to change your home activities?
	Would you like to change things with your partner?
	Would you like to change your family activities?
	Would you like to change your community activities?
	Would you like to change your friendship activities?
	Would you like to change your leisure activities?
Near Involve- ment	How often do you do laundry?
	How often do you paint?
	How often do you wash windows?
	How often do you decorate?
	How often do you take care of bills?
	How often do you make beds?
	How often do you clean the bathroom?
	How often do you clean other rooms?
	How often do you dust, sweep, vacuum?
	How often do you straighten, put things away?
	How often do you clean and repair the car?
	How often do you clean outside?
	How often do you grocery shop?
	How often do you go to the bank or the post office?
	How often do you do other shopping?
	How often do you prepare breakfast?
	How often do you prepare lunch?
	How often do you prepare dinner?
	How often do you clean up after breakfast?
	How often do you clean up after lunch?
	How often do you clean up after dinner?
	How often do you watch TV?
	How often do you listen to radio or music?
	How often do you work around the house?
	How often do you garden?
	How often do you read?
	How often do you write letters?
	How often do you sit and think?
	How often do you sleep?
	How often do you care for older or younger family members?
Far Involve- ment	How involved are you with church/synagogue?
	How involved are you with church groups?
	How involved are you with labor unions?
	How involved are you with fraternal, lodge, or veterans' organizations?

How involved are you with business or civic groups?
How involved are you with professional groups?
How involved are you with the Parent-Teacher Association?
How involved are you with youth groups?
How involved are you with community centers?
How involved are you with neighborhood improvement associations?
How involved are you with social or card-playing groups?
How involved are you with sports teams?
How involved are you with a country club?
How involved are you with political organizations?
How involved are you with action groups?
How involved are you with charity organizations?
How involved are you with other?
How often do you participate in group singing?
How often do you participate in socializing with friends?
How often do you participate in church group activities?
How often do you participate in organizations and clubs?
How often do you participate in shopping?
How often do you participate in attending theater, movie, lecture, sports events?
How often do you participate in hobbies?
How often do you participate in fishing or hunting?
How often do you participate in nightclubs and bars?
How often do you participate in sports?
How often do you participate in travel?
How often do you participate in classes?
How often do you participate in gambling?
How often do you participate in going for walks?
How often do you participate in doing volunteer work?

Source: Compiled by the authors.

APPENDIX D: REGRESSION WEIGHTS FOR PREDICTING ROLE SATISFACTION WITH DEMOGRAPHIC VARIABLES

APPENDIX D

Regression Weights for Predicting Role Satisfaction with Demographic Variables

	Work Satis.	Homemaking Satis.	Partner Satis.	Parenthood Satis.	Community Satis.	Friend Satis.	Leisure Satis.
Age							
Income				-.812			
Gender		-.111	-.173				
Education			.111				
Employment status				-.913			
Living alone							
Catholic							
Protestant					-.129		
Anglo						.122	
Age x live alone							
Age x income							
Age x education							
Age x gender							
Age x empl. status							
Anglo x age							
Anglo x income	.183						

174

Anglo x education							-.151
Age x income x gender				-.143			
Age x income x ed.							
Income x emp. status				1.48			
Income x gender							
Income x education							
Gender x live alone				.151			
Catholic x age							
Protestant x age							
Age x live alone x gen.							
R	.183	.111	.211	.333	.129	.122	.151
R^2	.033	.012	.045	.111	.017	.015	.023

Source: Compiled by the authors.

APPENDIX E: CONSUMER BEHAVIOR PROCESS FACTORS—STORE CHOICE AND STORE RELATIONS

APPENDIX E.1

Friendly Personnel (store choice factor A)

Consumer Behavior Variables	Factor Loading
Household store for friendly personnel	.84
Personal care store for friendly personnel	.82
Small appliances store for friendly personnel	.67
Clothing store for friendly personnel	.55
Grocery store for friendly personnel	.48
Tire store for friendly personnel	.41

Standardized Slope Coefficient (B)	Zero-Order Correlation Coefficient	Lifestyle Predictor Variables
-.22	-.12	female
.15	.11	far involvement
-.15	-.12	working for pay
.15	.15	Anglo
-.14	-.14	"I worry my children won't turn out right."
.12	.13	unskilled $R^2 = .12$

Notes: The consumer behavior factors that appear are the ones with the highest weighted factor loadings for the lifestyle predictors. Only those variables with a weight of .40 or higher are listed.

The consumer behavior factors corresponmd to Tables 4.3–4.9.

APPENDIX E. 2

Easy to Get to (store choice factor B)

Consumer Behavior Variables	Factor Loading
Personal care store because easy to get to	.74
Small appliances store because easy to get to	.70
Household store because easy to get to	.70
Clothing store because easy to get to	.62
Grocery store because easy to get to	.57

Standardized Slope Coefficient (B)	Zero-Order Correlation Coefficient	Lifestyle Predictor Variables
.21	.21	"I'm a homebody."
-.14	-.15	self-rated social class
-.13	-.10	skilled
		$R^2 = .08$

Note: The consumer behavior factors that appear are the ones with the highest weighted factor loadings for the lifestyle predictors. Only those variables with a weight of .40 or higher are listed.

Source: Compiled by the authors.

177

Convenient Hours (store choice factor C)

Consumer Behavior Variables	Factor Loading
Personal care store because hours are convenient	.89
Household store because hours are convenient	.86
Grocery store because hours are convenient	.72
Small appliances store because hours are convenient	.68
Clothing store because hours are convenient	.64

Standardized Slope Coefficient (B)	Zero-Order Correlation Coefficient	Lifestyle Predictor Variables
.18	.13	"I wish I were single." far involvement
-.14	-.12	"A marriage has problems when the wife brings home money."
-.13	-.07	
.13	.13	"I should take some time each day to look into my mind and feelings."
-.13	-.10	"I am a better listener than conversationalist."
-.12	-.08	"Homemaking is a lonely life."
.12	.09	"I'm a homebody."
.11	.12	clerical, sales

$R^2 = .11$

Note: The consumer behavior factors that appear are the ones with the highest weighted factor loadings for the lifestyle predictors. Only those variables with a weight of .40 or higher are listed.

APPENDIX E.4

Parking Ease (store choice factor D)

Consumer Behavior Variables	Factor Loading
Personal care store for parking ease	.91
Household store for parking ease	.86
Small appliances store for parking ease	.75
Grocery store for parking ease	.72
Clothing store for parking ease	.62
Tire store for parking ease	.41

Standardized Slope Coefficient (B)	Zero-Order Correlation Coefficient	Lifestyle Predictor Variables
.14	.15	married
-.14	-.11	working for pay
-.13	-.14	"I'm a little leery of trying new things, so my free-time activities don't change much."
		$R^2 = .05$

Note: The consumer behavior factors that appear are the ones with the highest weighted factor loadings for the lifestyle predictors. Only those variables with a weight of .40 or higher are listed.

Source: Compiled by the authors.

179

APPENDIX E. 5

Low Prices (store choice factor E)

Consumer Behavior Variables	Factor Loading
Household store for low prices	.69
Personal care store for low prices	.69
Tire store for low prices	.65
Small appliances store for low prices	.63
Clothing store for low prices	.54

Lifestyle Predictor Variable	Zero-Order Correlation Coefficient	Standardized Slope Coefficient (B)	
near involvement	-.16	-.16	$R^2 = .02$

Note: The consumer behavior factors that appear are the ones with the highest weighted factor loadings for the lifestyle predictors. Only those variables with a weight of .40 or higher are listed.

Source: Compiled by the authors.

APPENDIX E.6

Merchandise Quality (store choice factor F)

Consumer Behavior Variables	Factor Loading
Personal store for merchandise quality	.81
Small appliances store for merchandise quality	.70
Household store for merchandise quality	.54
Tire store for merchandise quality	.44

Standardized Slope Coefficient (B)	Zero-Order Correlation Coefficient	Lifestyle Predictor Variable
-.12	-.12	retired

$R^2 = .12$

Note: The consumer behavior factors that appear are the ones with the highest weighted factor loadings for the lifestyle predictors. Only those variables with a weight of .40 or higher are listed.

Source: Compiled by the authors.

181

APPENDIX E.7

Sales Promotion Activity (store choice factor G)

Consumer Behavior Variables	Factor Loading
Small appliances store for sales promotion	.75
Personal care store for sales promotion	.69
Household store for sales promotion	.65

Standardized Slope Coefficient (B)	Zero-Order Correlation Coefficient	Lifestyle Predictor Variables
-.13	-.13	"I dislike following a set schedule."
-.12	-.12	homeowner
		$R^2 = .03$

Note: The consumer behavior factors that appear are the ones with the highest weighted factor loadings for the lifestyle predictors. Only those variables with a weight of .40 or higher are listed.

Source: Compiled by the authors.

APPENDIX E. 8

Credit Availability (store choice factor H)

Consumer Behavior Variables	Factor Loading
Small appliances store for credit	.73
Tire store for credit	.70
Clothing store for credit	.64

Lifestyle Predictor Variables	Zero-Order Correlation Coefficient	Standardized Slope Coefficient (B)
role change	.23	.23
far involvement	.11	.12

$R^2 = .06$

Note: The consumer behavior factors that appear are the ones with the highest weighted factor loadings for the lifestyle predictors. Only those variables with a weight of .40 or higher are listed.
Source: Compiled by the authors.

183

APPENDIX E. 9

Atmosphere (store choice factor I)

Consumer Behavior Variables	Factor Loading
Household store for appearance of store and clientele	.81
Grocery store for appearance of store and clientele	.67
Personal care store for appearance of store and clientele	.61
Clothing store for appearance of store and clientele	.48

Standardized Slope Coefficient (B)	Zero-Order Correlation Coefficient	Lifestyle Predictor Variables
-.15	-.15	far involvement
-.12	-.12	homeowner
.12	.11	"Belonging to a local club would be more rewarding than belonging to a state or national organization."

$$R^2 = .03$$

Note: The consumer behavior factors that appear are the ones with the highest weighted factor loadings for the lifestyle predictors. Only those variables with a weight of .40 or higher are listed.

Source: Compiled by the authors.

Tire, Appliance, and Personal Care Product Assortment (store choice factor J)

Consumer Behavior Variables	Factor Loading
Tire store for product assortment	.68
Small appliances store for product assortment	.52
Personal care store for product assortment	.50

Lifestyle Predictor Variables	Standardized Slope Coefficient (B)	Zero-Order Correlation Coefficient
income	.20	.04
education	-.16	-.11
"I wish I were single."	.14	.10
age	.13	.11
"I am more interested in news about national and international events than in things that happen in this community."	.12	.10
"I worry my children won't turn out right."	-.12	-.09

$R^2 = .08$

Note: The consumer behavior factors that appear are the ones with the highest weighted factor loadings for the lifestyle predictors. Only those variables with a weight of .40 or higher are listed.

Source: Compiled by the authors.

APPENDIX E.11

Household and Grocery Product Assortment (store choice factor K)

Consumer Behavior Variables	Factor Loading
Household store for product assortment	.70
Grocery store for product assortment	.56

Standardized Slope Coefficient (B)	Zero-Order Correlation Coefficient	Lifestyle Predictor Variables
-.14	-.17	"I am a better listener than conversationalist." interaction
.13	.16	
.11	.14	"Older people are poorly treated in America."
		$R^2 = .06$

Note: The consumer behavior factors that appear are the ones with the highest weighted factor loadings for the lifestyle predictors. Only those variables with a weight of .40 or higher are listed.

Source: Compiled by the authors.

APPENDIX E. 12

Special Products Available (store choice factor L)

Consumer Behavior Variables	Standardized Slope Coefficient (B)	Zero-Order Correlation Coefficient	Lifestyle Predictor Variables	Factor Loading
Grocery store for special products	.22	.23		.64
Personal care store for special products	.13	.12		.59
	.12	.15		
			Anglo	
			"Homemaking is a lonely life."	
			degree of religiosity	
		$R^2 = .08$		

Note: The consumer behavior factors that appear are the ones with the highest weighted factor loadings for the lifestyle predictors. Only those variables with a weight of .40 or higher are listed.

Source: Compiled by the authors.

APPENDIX E. 13

Trustworthy Tire Sales Personnel (store choice factor M)

Consumer Behavior Variable	Factor Loading
Tire store for trustworthy personnel	-.45

Lifestyle Predictor Variables	Standardized Slope Coefficient (B)	Zero-Order Correlation Coefficient
"When making important decisions, a primary consideration is my children."	-.16	-.15
"I dislike following a set schedule."	.14	.11
skilled	.13	.14
"Homemaking is a lonely life."	-.12	-.11
homemaker	.12	.10
	$R^2 = .08$	

Note: The consumer behavior factor that appears is the one with the highest weighted factor loading for the life-style predictors. Only those variables with a weight of .40 or higher are listed.

Source: Compiled by the authors.

APPENDIX E.14

Tire Merchandise Quality (store choice factor N)

Consumer Behavior Variable		Factor Loading
Tire store for merchandise quality		.61

Standardized Slope Coefficient (B)	Zero-Order Correlation Coefficient	Lifestyle Predictor Variable
-.13	-.13	unskilled
	$R^2 = .02$	

Note: The consumer behavior factor that appears is the one with the highest weighted factor loading for the life-style predictor. Only those variables with a weight of .40 or higher are listed.
Source: Compiled by the authors.

APPENDIX E. 15

Tire Store Convenient Location (store choice factor O)

Consumer Behavior Variables	Factor Loading
Tire store because easy to get to	.68
Tire store because close by	.60
Tire store for parking	.50

Standardized Slope Coefficient (B)	Zero-Order Correlation Coefficient	Lifestyle Predictor Variables
.17	.17	"I'm a little leery of trying new things, so my free-time activities don't change very much."
-.13	-.14	"A woman's most important interests and activities tend to be ones in which her husband cannot participate."
		$R^2 = .05$

Note: The consumer behavior factors that appear are the ones with the highest weighted factor loadings for the lifestyle predictors. Only those variables with a weight of .40 or higher are listed.

Source: Compiled by the authors.

190

APPENDIX E.16

Convenient Small Appliances Store for Location (store choice factor Q)

Consumer Behavior Variable			Factor Loading
Small appliance store because close by			.45

Standardized Slope Coefficient (B)	Zero-Order Correlation Coefficient	Lifestyle Predictor Variables
.14	.14	"Older people are poorly treated in America."
-.13	-.13	unemployed
.12	.14	"When making important decisions, a primary consideration is my children."
.12	.15	"I worry my children won't turn out right."
	$R^2 = .07$	

Note: The consumer behavior factor that appears is the one with the highest weighted factor loading for the life-style predictors. Only those variables with a weight of .40 or higher are listed.

Source: Compiled by the authors.

191

APPENDIX E.17

Convenient Location (store choice factor S)

Consumer Behavior Variables		Factor Loading
Household store because close by		.81
Personal care store because close by		.74
Grocery store because close by		.51
Small appliances store because close by		.44

Standardized Slope Coefficient (B)	Zero-Order Correlation Coefficient	Lifestyle Predictor Variables
.29	.21	self-rated social class
-.18	-.12	"I seem to have fewer friends now than in the past."
-.17	-.10	income
-.16	-.08	satisfaction
-.15	-.08	homemaker
-.14	-.13	"When making important decisions, a primary consideration is my children."
.12	.14	clerical, sales
.11	.09	"A marriage has problems when the wife brings home money."
-.10	-.13	"Older people are poorly treated in America."

$$R^2 = .18$$

Note: The consumer behavior factors that appear are the ones with the highest weighted factor loadings for the lifestyle predictors. Only those variables with a weight of .40 or higher are listed.

192

APPENDIX E.18

Prefer Department Store to Discount Store (store relations factor D)

Consumer Behavior Variables	Zero-Order Correlation Coefficient	Factor Loading
Purchase small appliances at major department store		.83
Purchase small appliances at discount store		-.62
Purchase clothing at discount store		-.43

Lifestyle Predictor Variables	Zero-Order Correlation Coefficient	Standardized Slope Coefficient (B)
"Children don't spend enough time with their parents."	-.14	-.16
self-rated social class	-.11	-.13
"Change and new experiences are important in the life of every person."	.10	.12
		$R^2 = .05$

Note: The consumer behavior factors that appear are the ones with the highest weighted factor loadings for the lifestyle predictors. Only those variables with a weight of .40 or higher are listed.

Source: Compiled by the authors.

APPENDIX E.19

Chain Drugstore Shopping (store relations factor E)

Consumer Behavior Variables	Factor Loading
Shop for personal care items at large chain drugstore	.98
Shop for household items at large chain drugstore	.41

Standardized Slope Coefficient (B)	Zero-Order Correlation Coefficient	Lifestyle Predictor Variables
-.18	-.18	"Homemaking is a lonely life."
-.16	-.16	clerical, sales
.13	.08	"Belonging to a local club would be more rewarding than belonging to a state or national organization."
-.11	-.08	homeowner
	$R^2 = .08$	

Note: The consumer behavior factors that appear are the ones with the highest weighted factor loadings for the lifestyle predictors. Only those variables with a weight of .40 or higher are listed.

Source: Compiled by the authors.

APPENDIX E. 20

Chain Supermarket Shopping (store relations factor F)

Consumer Behavior Variables	Factor Loading
Shop for household items at large chain supermarket	.98
Shop for household items at small neighborhood store	-.62
Shop for personal care items at large chain supermarket	.41

Standardized Slope Coefficient (B)	Zero-Order Correlation Coefficient	Lifestyle Predictor Variables
.14	.17	"In most situations it is clear to me there is a right way and a wrong way."
.13	.14	married
-.12	-.15	"Homemaking is a lonely life."
		$R^2 = .06$

Note: The consumer behavior factors that appear are the ones with the highest weighted factor loadings for the lifestyle predictors. Only those variables with a weight of .40 or higher are listed.

Source: Compiled by the authors.

APPENDIX E.21

Specialty Store Shopping (store relations factor G)

Consumer Behavior Variables	Factor Loading
Shop for clothing in specialty store	.68
"I like to shop in specialty store"	.53

Standardized Slope Coefficient (B)	Zero-Order Correlation Coefficient	Lifestyle Predictor Variables
.17	.18	"Homemaking is a lonely life."
-.15	.14	"I worry my children won't turn out right."
.14	.16	"I am more interested in news about national and international events than in things that happen in this community."

$$R^2 = .07$$

Note: The consumer behavior factors that appear are the ones with the highest weighted factor loadings for the lifestyle predictors. Only those variables with a weight of .40 or higher are listed.

Source: Compiled by the authors.

APPENDIX E. 22

Discount Drugstore Shopping (store relations factor H)

Consumer Behavior Variables	Factor Loading
Shop for personal care items at discount drugstore	.78
Shop for household items at discount drugstore	.58

Standardized Slope Coefficient (B)	Zero-Order Correlation Coefficient	Lifestyle Predictor Variables
-.19	-.18	"I have never felt I was too old to take up new ways."
.12	.11	"I worry my children won't turn out right."
.12	.12	"Older people are poorly treated in America."
$R^2 = .06$		

Note: The consumer behavior factors that appear are the ones with the highest weighted factor loadings for the lifestyle predictors. Only those variables with a weight of .40 or higher are listed.

Source: Compiled by the authors.

197

APPENDIX E. 23

Prefer Department Store over Specialty Store for Tires (store relations factor I)

Consumer Behavior Variables	Factor Loading
Shop for tires at major department store	.75
Shop for tires at specialty store	-.69

Standardized Slope Coefficient (B)	Zero-Order Correlation Coefficient	Lifestyle Predictor Variables
.16	.12	skilled
.12	.06	female
		$R^2 = .03$

Note: The consumer behavior factors that appear are the ones with the highest weighted factor loadings for the lifestyle predictors. Only those variables with a weight of .40 or higher are listed.
Source: Compiled by the authors.

198

APPENDIX E.24

Appliance Store Shopping (store relations factor K)

Consumer Behavior Variable	Factor Loading
Shop for small appliances at appliance store	.85

Standardized Slope Coefficient (B)	Zero-Order Correlation Coefficient	Lifestyle Predictor Variables
-.18	-.14	female
.16	.15	"I am a better listener than conversationalist."
-.14	-.07	"A woman's most important activities tend to be ones in which her husband cannot participate."
-.14	-.11	self-employed/manager/official
.13	.14	"I'm a little leery of trying new things, so my free-time activities don't change very much."

$R^2 = .09$

Note: The consumer behavior factor that appears is the one with the highest weighted factor loading for the life-style predictors. Only those variables with a weight of .40 or higher are listed.

Source: Compiled by the authors.

199

APPENDIX E. 25

Catalog Shopping (store relations factor N)

Consumer Behavior Variables			Factor Loading
Clothing shop from catalog			.73
"I often shop from the Wards or Sears catalog."			.49

Standardized Slope Coefficient (B)	Zero-Order Correlation Coefficient	Lifestyle Predictor Variables
.13	.12	married
.11	.07	role change
-.10	-.09	education
		$R^2 = .04$

Note: The consumer behavior factors that appear are the ones with the highest weighted factor loadings for the lifestyle predictors. Only those variables with a weight of .40 or higher are listed.

Source: Compiled by the authors.

APPENDIX F: SUMMARY OF MULTIPLE-REGRESSION RESULTS FOR STORE CHOICE VARIABLES

APPENDIX F

Summary of Multiple-Regression Results for Store Choice Consumer Behavior Variables

Dependent Variables

Independent Variables	Friendly Personnel	Easy to Get to	Convenient Hours	Parking Ease	Low Prices	Merchandise Quality	Sales Promotion Activity	Credit Availability	Atmosphere	Tire, Appliance, and Personal Care Prod. Asst.	Household and Grocery Product Assortment	Special Products Available	Trustworthy Tire Sales Personnel	Tire Merchandise Quality	Tire Store Convenient Location	Good Grocery Specials	Convenient Sm. Appliances Store Location	Clothing Store for Friendly Personnel	Convenient Location	In-home Convenience
Working for pay	−3				−2											−5	−2		−5	
Unemployed																				
Retired							−1													
Homemaker				+1	+1								+5							+6
Married												+3								
Widowed																				
Divorced																				
How religious are you ?																			−3	
Self-rated health status																				
Highest grade completed in school																				
Income										−2										
Daily activities limited by health										+1										
Clear right and wrong																				
Better listener than conversationalist			−5								−1									+2
Prefer people my own age											+3						+1		−9	
Older people poorly treated										+5										
Change is important																+4				
National over local news																			−2	
Have fewer friends now																				
Rarely introduce self to strangers																				
Like going alone to strange places																				
Local club over national																				
Happy with life so far			+4						+3							−2				−1
Should look into mind and feelings																−2				
Children not enough time with parents																				
Clubs not important																				
Dislike set schedule													+2	+3						
Children primary consideration in decisions													−1						−6	

201

Dependent Variables

Independent Variables	Friendly Personnel	Easy to Get to	Convenient Hours	Parking Ease	Low Prices	Merchandise Quality	Sales Promotion Activity	Credit Availability	Atmosphere	Tire, Appliance, and Personal Care Prod. Asst.	Household and Grocery Product Assortment	Special Products Available	Trustworthy Tire Sales Personnel	Tire Merchandise Quality	Tire Store Convenient Location	Good Grocery Specials	Convenient Sm. Appliances Store Location	Clothing Store for Friendly Personnel	Convenient Location	In-home Convenience
Feel lost without friends																				
Homemaking is a lonely life			-6							+3	-6		+2	-4		-3				
Wish I were single		+1													+1			+1		
Leery of new things					-3															
Never too old to take up new ways	-5																+4			
Worry children won't turn out right			-3														-2			
Woman's most imp. acts, husband no part																				
Marriage prob. if wife brings home money	+1	+7																	+8	-5
Prefer to work alone																				
I'm a homebody																				
I want to be a famous person																				
Age									+4											
Class	-2																	-1 +1	-3	
Gender	-1																			
Interaction												+2								
Satisfaction																		-4		
Role change							+1													-4
Near involvement		-2		-1			+2	-1												
Far involvement	+2										+1									
Anglo	+4											+3								
Unskilled	+6																			
Skilled	-3	+8											-1		+1					
Clerical																				
Self-employed/manager/official																		+7		
Professional																				
Owner																				
R	.34	.28	.34	.22	.16	.12	.25	.17	.19	.28	.25	.29	.29	.13	.22	.26	.27	.18	.43	.30
R^2	.12	.08	.11	.05	.03	.01	.03	.07	.04	.08	.06	.09	.08	.02	.05	.07	.03		.18	.09

Notes: Regressions are organized by consumer behavior areas rather than by areas of consumer consumption.

The numbers in the columns represent the size of the beta coefficient and are measures of the relative importance in the stepwise equations in terms of beta values. The numbers are the statistically significant ones from the stepwise equations, and the direction of the relationship is given by + or -.

Source: Compiled by the authors.

APPENDIX G: CONSUMER BEHAVIOR PROCESS FACTORS— BUYING STYLE AND ALIENATION

APPENDIX G.1

Solitary Decision Making (buying style factor B)

Consumer Behavior Variables	Factor Loading
Other person makes household purchase decisions	-.83
Respondent shops for small appliances	.61
Respondent makes own purchase decisions	.54

Standardized Slope Coefficient (B)	Zero-Order Correlation Coefficient	Lifestyle Predictor Variables
-.30	-.33	married
.25	.36	near involvement
-.17	-.15	age
-.15	-.08	"Change and new experiences are important in the life of every person."
-.14	-.09	"I'm a little leery of trying new things, so my free-time activities don't change much."
-.10	-.17	skilled $R^2 = .25$

Note: The consumer behavior factors that appear are the ones with the highest weighted factor loadings for the lifestyle predictors. Only those variables with a weight of .40 or higher are listed.

Source: Compiled by the authors.

APPENDIX G. 2

Brand Switching (buying style factor C)

Consumer Behavior Variables	Factor Loading
"I often try new brands before my friends and neighbors do."	.87
"I often like to switch brands just for the sake of variety."	.59

Standardized Slope Coefficient (B)	Zero-Order Correlation Coefficient	Lifestyle Predictor Variables
-.20	-.12	"I am happy with the way my life has gone so far."
-.17	-.15	"I seem to have fewer friends now than in the past."
.15	.15	income
.14	.06	"My daily activities are limited by health."
-.13	-.04	role change
.13	.13	"Change and new experiences are important in the life of every person."
.12	.10	"While I enjoy clubs, they are not important."
		$R^2 = .11$

Note: The consumer behavior factors that appear are the ones with the highest weighted factor loadings for the lifestyle predictors. Only those variables with a weight of .40 or higher are listed.

APPENDIX G. 3

Warranty More Important than Price or Service (buying style factor D)

Consumer Behavior Variables			Factor Loading
Local dealer's reputation for service more important than price and warranty			-.95
Manufacturer's reputation and warranty more important than price or local dealer's service			.88

Standardized Slope Coefficient (B)	Zero-Order Correlation Coefficient	Lifestyle Predictor Variables
.19	.18	"I am a better listener than conversationalist."
-.15	.12	"A woman's most important activities tend to be ones in which her husband cannot participate."
.12	.13	self-rated social class
.12	.11	"I prefer to work alone than with others."
		$R^2 = .08$

Note: The consumer behavior factors that appear are the ones with the highest weighted factor loadings for the lifestyle predictors. Only those variables with a weight of .40 or higher are listed.

Source: Compiled by the authors.

APPENDIX G. 4

Planned Purchases (buying style factor E)

Consumer Behavior Variables		Factor Loading
"Usually I shop with a list of specific things to buy and stick closely to that list."		.74
"I plan my purchases in advance."		.71

Lifestyle Predictor Variables	Zero-Order Correlation Coefficient	Standardized Slope Coefficient (B)
"I'm a homebody."	.19	.19
"I want to be a famous person."	.14	-.14
		$R^2 = .05$

Note: The consumer behavior factors that appear are the ones with the highest weighted factor loadings for the lifestyle predictors. Only those variables with a weight of .40 or higher are listed.

Source: Compiled by the authors.

206

APPENDIX G. 5

Price–Value Comparison (buying style factor F)

Consumer Behavior Variables	Factor Loading
Stay with familiar brands of packaged goods	-.71
Compare prices of packaged goods	.65
Compare weights and volumes of packaged goods	.48

Lifestyle Predictor Variables	Standardized Slope Coefficient (B)	Zero-Order Correlation Coefficient
"I prefer to work alone than with others."	-.14	-.14
"I wish I were single."	-.12	-.13
self-employed/manager/official	.12	.11
widowed	-.12	-.14

$R^2 = .07$

Note: The consumer behavior factors that appear are the ones with the highest weighted factor loadings for the lifestyle predictors. Only those variables with a weight of .40 or higher are listed.
Source: Compiled by the authors.

APPENDIX G. 6

Joint Decision Making (buying style factor H)

Consumer Behavior Variables	Factor Loading
Respondent makes purchase decisions jointly with other person	-.90
Respondent makes own purchase decisions	-.80

Standardized Slope Coefficient (B)	Zero-Order Correlation Coefficient	Lifestyle Predictor Variables
.51	.50	married
-.16	-.18	"A woman's most important activities tend to be ones in which her husband cannot participate."
-.13	-.10	"Belonging to a local club would be more rewarding than belonging to a state or national organization."
.12	.11	"I worry my children won't turn out right."
.12	.10	self-employed/manager/official
-.11	-.06	"Older people are poorly treated in America."
-.11	-.02	homemaker
-.10	-.09	"While I enjoy clubs, they are not important."
-.10	-.09	"I have never felt I was too old to take up new ways."

$R^2 = .35$

Note: The consumer behavior factors that appear are the ones with the highest weighted factor loadings for the lifestyle predictors. Only those variables with a weight of .40 or higher are listed.

Source: Compiled by the authors.

APPENDIX G. 7

Price More Important than Warranty or Service (buying style factor J)

Consumer Behavior Variables	Factor Loading
Price more important than manufacturer's warranty or local dealer's service	.92
Manufacturer's reputation and warranty more important than price or local service	-.43

Standardized Slope Coefficient (B)	Zero-Order Correlation Coefficient	Lifestyle Predictor Variables
.17	.16	"I am a better listener than conversationalist."
-.17	-.12	"I dislike following a set schedule."
.16	.11	"I wish I were single."
-.15	-.07	female
.13	.12	"I prefer to work alone than with others."
-.12	-.05	"I want to be a famous person."
-.11	-.12	self-employed/manager/official

$R^2 = .11$

Note: The consumer behavior factors that appear are the ones with the highest weighted factor loadings for the lifestyle predictors. Only those variables with a weight of .40 or higher are listed.

Source: Compiled by the authors.

APPENDIX G. 8

Bargain Hunting (buying style factor K)

Consumer Behavior Variables		Factor Loading
Frequently compare prescription drug prices		.79
"I shop around for sales and bargains."		.40

Standardized Slope Coefficient (B)	Zero-Order Correlation Coefficient	Lifestyle Predictor Variables
.15	.14	"I am more interested in news about national and international events than in things that happen in this community."
.15	.10	"I like to go alone to strange and new places."
.14	.10	far involvement
.13	.11	professional occupation
.11	.09	"I wish I were single." $R^2 = .08$

Note: The consumer behavior factors that appear are the ones with the highest weighted factor loadings for the lifestyle predictors. Only those variables with a weight of .40 or higher are listed.

Source: Compiled by the authors.

APPENDIX G.9

Reliance on Printed Sources of Information (buying style factor L)

Consumer Behavior Variables	Factor Loading
Reliance on printed sources of information	.67
Reliance on own past experience or personal judgment	-.62

Standardized Slope Coefficient (B)	Zero-Order Correlation Coefficient	Lifestyle Predictor Variables
-.17	-.16	widowed
-.15	-.17	skilled
.13	.15	homemaker
.11	.09	"I would feel lost without my friends."

$R^2 = .08$

Note: The consumer behavior factors that appear are the ones with the highest weighted factor loadings for the lifestyle predictors. Only those variables with a weight of .40 or higher are listed.

Source: Compiled by the authors.

APPENDIX G.10

Other–Directed Decision Making (buying style factor M)

Consumer Behavior Variables	Factor Loading
"When I shop, I like to talk to sales people."	.56
"Before I buy something, I like to make sure my family and friends will like it too."	.46

Standardized Slope Coefficient (B)	Zero–Order Correlation Coefficient	Lifestyle Predictor Variables
.24	.16	self–rated poor health
.19	.20	interaction
.18	.01	"My daily activities are limited by health."
.15	.17	income
.14	.09	"When making important decisions, a primary consideration is my children."
−.14	.19	"I'm a homebody."
.11	.05	"I wish I were single."
.11	.14	"I have never felt I was too old to take up new ways."
.11	.06	Anglo
		$R^2 = .17$

Note: The consumer behavior factors that appear are the ones with the highest weighted factor loadings for the lifestyle predictors. Only those variables with a weight of .40 or higher are listed.

Source: Compiled by the authors.

Frequency of Shopping (buying style factor N)

Consumer Behavior Variables	Factor Loading
Frequently shop for household items	.75
Frequently shop for personal care items	.70
Frequently shop for clothing	.55

Standardized Slope Coefficient (B)	Zero-Order Correlation Coefficient	Lifestyle Predictor Variables
.33	.37	near involvement
.20	.10	married
.15	.33	far involvement
.12	.15	interaction
.11	.11	"While I enjoy clubs, they are not really important."
.10	.07	"Homemaking is a lonely life."
		$R^2 = .23$

Note: The consumer behavior factors that appear are the ones with the highest weighted factor loadings for the lifestyle predictors. Only those variables with a weight of .40 or higher are listed.

Source: Compiled by the authors.

APPENDIX G. 12

Inner–Directed Decision Making (buying style factor O)

Consumer Behavior Variables	Factor Loading
Reliance on family, friends and sales personnel for consumer information	-.71
Reliance on own past experience and personal judgment	.43

Standardized Slope Coefficient (B)	Zero–Order Correlation Coefficient	Lifestyle Predictor Variables
.16	.16	self-employed/manager/official
-.15	-.17	"I am a better listener than conversationalist."
.12	.06	skilled
-.11	-.15	"I'm a homebody."
		$R^2 = .08$

Note: The consumer behavior factors that appear are the ones with the highest weighted factor loadings for the lifestyle predictors. Only those variables with a weight of .40 or higher are listed.
    Source: Compiled by the authors.

Quality–Consciousness (buying style factor P)

Consumer Behavior Variables			Factor Loading
"Quality is what I look for."			.58
"When I have questions about a product, I seek more information about it."			.50

Standardized Slope Coefficient (B)	Zero–Order Correlation Coefficient	Lifestyle Predictor Variables	
.24	.26	"I should take some time each day to look into my mind and feelings."	
.15	.10	near involvement	
-.15	-.09	"My daily activities are limited by health."	
-.13	-.07	working for pay	
-.13	.01	far involvement	
.12	.07	Anglo	
.12	.12	"Belonging to a local club would be more rewarding than belonging to a state or national organization."	
.12	.16	"Change and new experiences are important in the life of every person."	
-.12	-.08	"I would feel lost without my friends."	
-.12	-.06	"A marriage has problems when the wife brings home money."	
-.11	-.06	"I dislike following a set schedule."	
		$R^2 = .16$	

Note: The consumer behavior factors that appear are the ones with the highest weighted factor loadings for the lifestyle predictors. Only those variables with a weight of .40 or higher are listed.

Source: Compiled by the authors.

APPENDIX G. 14

Brand Loyalty (buying style factor S)

Consumer Behavior Variables			Factor Loading
Compare ingredient labels of packaged goods			-.52
"I stick only to certain brands."			.41
Stay with familiar brands of packaged goods			.39

Standardized Slope Coefficient (B)	Zero-Order Correlation Coefficient	Lifestyle Predictor Variables
-.25	-.14	near involvement
.16	.03	far involvement
-.15	-.12	role change
.14	.17	"I wish I were single."
.13	.10	"Homemaking is a lonely life."
-.13	-.15	widowed
.12	.08	homemaker
.12	.15	Anglo
.11	.05	"Change and new experiences are im-
		portant in the life of every person."
		$R^2 = .11$

Note: The consumer behavior factors that appear are the ones with the highest weighted factor loadings for the lifestyle predictors. Only those variables with a weight of .40 or higher are listed.

Source: Compiled by the authors.

APPENDIX G.15

Impulsive Shopping (buying style factor T)

Consumer Behavior Variables	Factor Loading
"Often I purchase things on the spur of the moment, just because they have attracted my attention."	.42
"I often become confused if I have to consider a lot of information about a product I am thinking about buying."	.41
"My friends and neighbors usually give me pretty good advice about what brands to buy in the grocery store."	.40

Standardized Slope Coefficient (B)	Zero-Order Correlation Coefficient	Lifestyle Predictor Variables
.21	.17	near involvement
.20	.21	"I wish I were single."
-.18	-.01	female
.17	.19	"I am a better listener than conversationalist."
-.14	-.13	self-employed/manager/official
.11	.14	"I prefer to spend time around people my own age."
.11	.16	"My daily activities are limited by health."

$R^2 = .16$

Note: The consumer behavior factors that appear are the ones with the highest weighted factor loadings for the lifestyle predictors. Only those variables with a weight of .40 or higher are listed.

Source: Compiled by the authors.

217

TV as Information Source (buying style factor U)

Consumer Behavior Variable		Factor Loading
Television as a source of product information		.41

Standardized Slope Coefficient (B)	Zero-Order Correlation Coefficient	Lifestyle Predictor Variables
-.22	-.16	"I am a better listener than conversationalist."
-.21	-.12	clerical, sales
.18	.05	female
.16	.11	"A marriage has problems when the wife brings home money."
.15	.08	"I dislike following a set schedule."
-.15	-.06	"I wish I were single."
.14	.09	"I want to be a famous person."
-.18	-.09	self-rated poor health
.11	.12	self-rated social class
.11	.08	"I would feel lost without my friends."
.11	.13	"I worry my children will not turn out right."

$R^2 = .23$

Note: The consumer behavior factor that appears is the one with the highest weighted factor loading for the lifestyle predictors. Only those variables with a weight of .40 or higher are listed.

Source: Compiled by the authors.

APPENDIX G. 17

Problems with Food, Money, Housing, Transportation (alienation factor A)

Consumer Behavior Variables	Factor Loading
Reported problems with food selection, purchase, preparation, and nutrition	.66
Reported problems with income sufficiency and income management	.62
Reported problems with housing	.59
Reported problems with transportation	.58

Lifestyle Predictor Variables	Zero-Order Correlation Coefficient	Standardized Slope Coefficient (B)
role change	.23	.22
widowed	-.17	-.14
far involvement	.13	.14

$R^2 = .09$

Note: The consumer behavior factors that appear are the ones with the highest weighted factor loadings for the lifestyle predictors. Only those variables with a weight of .40 or higher are listed.

Source: Compiled by the authors.

219

APPENDIX H: SUMMARY OF MULTIPLE-REGRESSION RESULTS FOR CONSUMER BUYING VARIABLES

APPENDIX H

Summary of Multiple-Regression Results for Buying Style Consumer Buying Behavior Variables

Independent Variables	Bank Credit Card Usage	Solitary Decision Making	Brand Switching	Warr. More Imp. Than Price or Service	Planned Purchases	Price-Value Comparison	Tot. Int. More Imp. Than Size of Payment	Joint Decision Making	Auto Repair in a Shop	Price More Imp. Than Warr. or Service	Bargain Hunting	Reliance on Printed Sources of Info.	Other-Directed Decision Making	Frequency of Shopping	Inner-Directed Decision Making	Quality-Consciousness	Belief That Credit is Unwise	Not Use Bank Credit Card for Convenience	Brand Loyalty	Impulsive Shopping	TV as an Information Source
Working for pay							-1														
Unemployed																					
Retired																					
Homemaker		-1						-7				+3				-4			+6		
Married								+1						+2							
Widowed						-4						-1							-5		
Divorced																					
How religious are you?																					
Self-rated health status	+1		+3										+1								
Highest grade completed in school			+4																		
Income													+4		-2	-3					-8
Daily activities limited by health																					
Clear right and wrong								-1					+3								
Better listener than conversationalist				+1						+1											
Prefer people my own age																	-4		+4	+4	-1
Older people poorly treated								-6								+8			+8	+7	
Change is important										+1										+6	
National over local news		-4	+6																+4		
Have fewer friends now			-2																		

Table organized by consumer behavior areas (beta coefficients, stepwise regressions):

	.33	.46	.33	.23	.23	.25	.37	.50	.20	.33	.27	.26	.41	.46	.27	.41	.41	.14	.37	.40	.41
Rarely introduce self to strangers																			+5		
Like going alone to strange places																			−3		
Local club over national																+7			−7		
Happy with life so far		−1														+1					
Should look into mind and feelings						−3															
Children not enough time with parents																					
Clubs not important		+7																			
Dislike set schedule				+4		−8		−2		+5				−11	+6				+5		
Children primary consideration in decision	−4																				
Feel lost without friends				−8						+4					−9				+10		
Homemaking is a lonely life												+6							+4	+2	−6
Wish I were single	−2	−5		−5				+3	−5		+7					+2					
Leery of new things											+6										
Never too old to take up new ways						−9				+5									+11		
Worry children won't turn out right						+4															
Woman's most imp. acts. Husband no part			−2			−2															
Marriage prob. if wife brings home money										+8											
Prefer to work alone														−10					+4		
I'm a homebody			+3	−1				+5													
I want to be a famous person			+1					−6		−6				−8	+2	+1			+7		
Age			−2											+2	+1						
Class		−3		−3				−4					−4							−3	+3
Gender			+4																+9		
Interaction	+3			+6						+2	+4										
Satisfaction																					
Role change		−5												+2	−9			−3			
Near involvement		+2								+1	+1			−5				−1	+1		
Far involvement										+3	+3			+6				+2			
Anglo								+3										+7			
Unskilled				−7																	
Skilled		−6							−2				+3								
Clerical														+1							
Self-employed/manager/official			+3	+2		+5		−7												−2	
Professional								−4												−5	
Owner																					
R	.33	.46	.33	.23	.23	.25	.37	.50	.20	.33	.27	.26	.41	.46	.27	.41	.41	.14	.37	.40	.41
R²	.11	.22	.11	.09	.05	.06	.14	.25	.04	.11	.08	.07	.17	.21	.08	.16	.17	.02	.04	.16	.17

Notes: Regressions are organized by consumer behavior areas rather than by areas of consumer consumption.

The numbers in the columns represent the size of the beta coefficient and are measures of the relative importance in the stepwise equations in terms of beta values. The numbers that appear are the statistically significant ones from the stepwise equations, and the direction of relationship is given by + or -.

Source: Compiled by the authors.

221

APPENDIX I: CONSUMER INCOME MANAGEMENT

APPENDIX I. 1

Disappointing Consumer Experiences (alienation factor D)

Consumer Behavior Variable			Factor Loading
Number of disappointing experiences as a consumer in the past year			.46

Standardized Slope Coefficient	Zero-Order Correlation Coefficient	Lifestyle Predictor Variables
.23	.22	self-employed/manager/official
-.16	-.25	age
.15	.21	self-rated poor health
-.14	-.22	widowed
.14	.17	far involvement
.14	.06	skilled
.13	.13	"I prefer to work alone than with others."
.10	.08	"I should take some time each day to look into my mind and feelings."
		$R^2 = .21$

Note: The consumer behavior factor that appears is the one with the highest weighted factor loading for the lifestyle predictors. Only those variables with a weight of .40 or higher are listed.

Source: Compiled by the authors.

APPENDIX I. 2

Belief That Credit Is Unwise (buying style factor Q)

Consumer Behavior Variable			Factor Loading
"To buy anything other than a house or car on credit is unwise."			.40
Standardized Slope Coefficient (B)	Zero-Order Correlation Coefficient	Lifestyle Predictor Variables	
.19	.16	age	
.18	.13	"I want to be a famous person."	
-.16	-.12	"I like going alone to strange and new places."	
-.16	-.08	"I am a better listener than conversationalist."	
.16	.14	"I rarely introduce myself to strangers at social gatherings."	
.15	.14	"I dislike following a set schedule."	
-.13	-.11	"Belonging to a local club would be more rewarding than a national one."	
-.12	-.09	"I'm a homebody."	
-.11	-.11	near involvement	$R^2 = .16$

Note: The consumer behavior factor that appears is the one with the highest weighted factor loading for the lifestyle predictors. Only those variables with a weight of .40 or higher are listed.

Source: Compiled by the authors.

223

APPENDIX I. 3

Bank Credit Card Use (buying style factor A)

Consumer Behavior Variables			Factor Loading
Use bank credit card for household items			.74
Use bank credit card for small appliances			.73
Use bank credit card for personal care items			.67
Use bank credit card for furniture			.67
Use bank credit card for clothing			.66
Use bank credit card for services			.63
Use bank credit card for recreation			.57
Use bank credit card for large appliances			.56
Frequently use bank credit card			.54
Use bank credit card for education, reading			.52
"I buy many things with a credit card"			.47

Lifestyle Predictor Variables	Standardized Slope Coefficient (B)	Zero-Order Correlation Coefficient
Income	.20	.23
"I'm a little leery of trying new things, so my free-time activities don't change much."	-.16	-.19
role change	.14	.13
"When making important decisions, a primary consideration is my children."	-.12	-.13
		$R^2 = .11$

Note: The consumer behavior factors that appear are the ones with the highest weighted factor loadings for the lifestyle predictors. Only those variables with a weight of .40 or higher are listed.

Source: Compiled by the authors.

224

APPENDIX I.4

Total Interest More Important Than Size of Payment (buying style factor G)

Consumer Behavior Variables	Factor Loading
Total interest more important in obtaining a loan	.81
Size of monthly payment most important in obtaining a loan	-.79

Standardized Slope Coefficient (B)	Zero-Order Correlation Coefficient	Lifestyle Predictor Variables
-.21	-.08	working for pay
.19	.16	professional
-.15	-.07	age
.14	.12	"I dislike following a set schedule."
-.13	-.13	"I wish I were single."
.13	.11	interaction
-.13	-.15	unskilled
-.13	-.12	"I would feel lost without my friends."
		$R^2 = .13$

Note: The consumer behavior factors that appear are the ones with the highest weighted factor loadings for the lifestyle predictors. Only those variables with a weight of .40 or higher are listed.

Source: Compiled by the authors.

APPENDIX I.5

Do not Use Bank Credit Card for Convenience (buying style factor R)

Consumer Behavior Variable	Factor Loading
Use bank credit card for convenience	-.88

Standardized Slope Coefficient (B)	Zero-Order Correlation Coefficient	Lifestyle Predictor Variable
.14	.14	"I want to be a famous person."

$$R^2 = .02$$

Note: The consumer behavior factor that appears is the one with the highest weighted factor loading for the lifestyle predictor. Only those variables with a weight of .40 or higher are listed.

Source: Compiled by the authors.

APPENDIX I.6

Nonreal Estate Investments (Stocks) (inventory factor A)

Consumer Behavior Variables	Standardized Slope Coefficient (B)	Zero-Order Correlation Coefficient	Lifestyle Predictor Variables	Factor Loading
Have investments				.91
Own common stocks				.58
	.36	.34	income	
	.15	.12	"A woman's most important activities tend to be ones in which her husband cannot participate."	
	.14	.24	self-rated poor health	
	.14	-.03	retired	
	.11	.08	clerical, sales	
	-.11	-.07	"I have never felt I was too old to take up new ways."	
	-.10	-.13	"When making important decisions, a primary consideration is my children."	
				$R^2 = .20$

Note: The consumer behavior factors that appear are the ones with the highest weighted factor loadings for the lifestyle predictors. Only those variables with a weight of .40 or higher are listed.

Source: Compiled by the authors.

APPENDIX I.7

Home Ownership (inventory factor C)

Consumer Behavior Variables	Factor Loading
Own housing	.52
Credit union account	.49

Standardized Slope Coefficient (B)	Zero-Order Correlation Coefficient	Lifestyle Predictor Variables
.26	.32	income
.23	.32	married
.16	.11	"A woman's most important activities tend to be ones in which her husband cannot participate."
-.13	-.01	self-rated poor health
-.13	-.13	"I am more interested in news about national and international events than in things that happen in this community."
-.12	.03	female
-.11	-.10	"I am a better listener than conversationalist."
.11	.11	"I am happy with the way my life has gone so far."

$R^2 = .21$

Note: The consumer behavior factors that appear are the ones with the highest weighted factor loadings for the lifestyle predictors. Only those variables with a weight of .40 or higher are listed.

Source: Compiled by the authors.

APPENDIX I.8

Real Estate Investments (inventory factor D)

Consumer Behavior Variable			Factor Loading
Have real estate investments			.66

Standardized Slope Coefficient (B)	Zero-Order Correlation Coefficient	Lifestyle Predictor Variables
.28	.27	homeowner
.19	.19	self-rated poor health
-.15	-.11	"A woman's most important activities tend to be ones in which her husband cannot participate."
.13	.12	"I want to be a famous person."
.12	.07	"I rarely introduce myself to strangers at social gatherings."
.12	.08	"I am more interested in national and international events than in things that happen in this community."
.11	.14	self-employed/manager/official
-.10	-.13	female

$R^2 = .19$

Note: The consumer behavior factor that appears is the one with the highest weighted factor loading for the lifestyle predictors. Only those variables with a weight of .40 or higher are listed.

Source: Compiled by the authors.

Medical–Furnishings–Clothing–Personal Budget (budget factor A)

Consumer Behavior Variables	Factor Loading
Monthly medical-dental expense	.62
Monthly home furnishings, appliances, and equipment expense	.47
Monthly clothing expense	.46
Monthly personal care expense	.42

Standardized Slope Coefficient (B)	Zero-Order Correlation Coefficient	Lifestyle Predictor Variables
.16	-.15	"In most situations it is clear to me there is a right way and a wrong way."
.15	.09	"A marriage has problems when the wife brings home money."
.14	.11	married
.13	.12	degree of religiosity
.13	.11	"When making important decisions, a primary consideration is my children."
.12	.10	"I want to be a famous person."
.11	.09	education
		$R^2 = .06$

Note: The consumer behavior factors that appear are the ones with the highest weighted factor loadings for the lifestyle predictors. Only those variables with a weight of .40 or higher are listed.

Source: Compiled by the authors.

APPENDIX I. 10

Food and Transportation Budget (budget factor B)

Consumer Behavior Variables			Factor Loading
Monthly food expense			.66
Monthly transportation expense			.47

Standardized Slope Coefficient (B)	Zero-Order Correlation Coefficient	Lifestyle Predictor Variables
-.30	-.35	age
.21	.25	married
-.10	-.13	"I'm a homebody."

$R^2 = .17$

Note: The consumer behavior factors that appear are the ones with the highest weighted factor loadings for the lifestyle predictors. Only those variables with a weight of .40 or higher are listed.

Source: Compiled by the authors.

231

Housing–Recreation–Savings Budget (budget factor C)

Consumer Behavior Variables	Factor Loading
Monthly housing expense	.52
Monthly reading, recreation, and education expense	.43
Monthly savings	.42

Standardized Slope Coefficient (B)	Zero–Order Correlation Coefficient	Lifestyle Predictor Variables
.24	.29	income
-.16	-.19	"I am a better listener than conversationalist."
.11	.18	self-rated social class

$R^2 = .12$

Note: The consumer behavior factors that appear are the ones with the highest weighted factor loadings for the lifestyle predictors. Only those variables with a weight of .40 or higher are listed.

Source: Compiled by the authors.

APPENDIX J: SUMMARY OF MULTIPLE-REGRESSION RESULTS FOR STORE RELATIONS AND INVENTORY

APPENDIX J

Summary of Multiple-Regression Results for Store Relations and Inventory Consumer Behavior

Independent Variables	Store Relations													Inventory					
	HMO (Kaiser) Member	Purchased Auto by Personal Transaction	Shop by Public Transportation	Dept. Store over Discount Store	Chain Drugstore Shopping	Chain Supermarket Shopping	Specialty Store Shopping	Discount Drugstore Shopping	Dept. Store over Specialty Store for Tires	Used Car Purchase	Appliance Store Shopping	High-Trust Health Insurance Co.	Nondriver	Catalog Shopping	Nonreal Estate Investments (stocks)	Covered by Medicare	Home Ownership	Real Estate Investments	Have Health Insurance Policy
Working for pay																			
Unemployed																			
Retired																			
Homemaker			-2			+2						-5							
Married															+4	-5	+2		+3
Widowed														+1		+4			+5
Divorced	-2																		
How religious are you?																			
Self-rated health status																			
Highest grade completed in school													-2		+3		-4	+2	
Income			-3							-2		+1			+1		+1		+2
Daily activities limited by health																			
Clear right and wrong						+1										+3			
Better listener than conversationalist											+2								
Prefer people my own age										-1							-7		
Older people poorly treated					+3														
Change is important				+3				+3											
National Over local news													+3						
Have fewer friends now							+3										-5	+6	
Barely introduce self to strangers																		+5	
Like going alone to strange places																			
Local club over national																	+8		
Happy with life so far																			
Should look into mind and feelings																			
Children not enough time with parents				-1											-7				
Clubs not important																			
Dislike set schedule																			
Children primary consideration in decisions												+4							
Feel lost without friends														-3					
Homemaking is a lonely life					-1	-3	+1												-6

233

APPENDIX J, (continued)

	Store Relations														Inventory				
Independent variables	HMO (Kaiser) Member	Purchased Auto by Personal Transaction	Shop by Public Transportation	Dept. Store over Discount Store	Chain Drugstore Shopping	Chain Supermarket Shopping	Specialty Store Shopping	Discount Drugstore Shopping	Dept. Store over Specialty Store for Tires	Used Car Purchase	Appliance Store Shopping	High-Trust Health Insurance Co.	Nondriver	Catalog Shopping	Nonreal Estate Investments (stocks)	Covered by Medicare	Home Ownership	Real Estate Investments	Have Health Insurance Policy
Wish I were single	+3																		
Leery of new things																			
Never too old to take up new ways								-1			+5				-6				
Worry children won't turn out right								+2											
Woman's most imp. acts, husband no part	+4																		
Marriage prob. if wife brings home money							-2					+7			+2		+3	-3	
Prefer to work alone											-3								
I'm a homebody													+5						
I want to be a famous person																			-7
Age		-2											+4			+1		+4	
Class				-2												+8			
Gender									+2		-1		+1			+2	+6	-8	
Interaction																			
Satisfaction												-3							+4
Role change														+2					
Near involvement																-6			
Far involvement												-2							
Anglo																			
Unskilled									+1										
Skilled																			
Clerical					-2										+5	-7			
Self-employed/manager/official					-4						-4							+7	
Professional																			
Owner	-1																	+1	+1
R	.31	.21	.31	.22	.28	.26	.27	.25	.16	.20	.31	.41	.40	.22	.45	.64	.38	.37	.50
R²	.09	.04	.10	.05	.08	.07	.07	.06	.03	.04	.09	.16	.16	.05	.20	.40	.15	.14	.25

Notes: Regressions are organized by consumer behavior areas rather than by areas of consumer consumption.

The numbers in the columns represent the size of the beta coefficient and are measures of the relative importance in the stepwise equations in terms of beta values. The numbers that appear are the statistically significant ones from the stepwise equations, and the direction of relationship is given by + or -.

Source: Compiled by the authors.

234

APPENDIX K.1

HMO (Kaiser) Member (store relations factor A)

Consumer Behavior Variables	Factor Loading
Kaiser–Permanente Health Plan member	.96
Possess fee–reimbursement health insurance	-.90

Standardized Slope Coefficient (B)	Zero–Order Correlation Coefficient	Lifestyle Predictor Variables
.13	-.18	satisfaction
-.16	-.17	degree of religiosity
.13	.16	"I've never felt I was too old to take up new ways."
.10	.11	"A marriage has problems when the wife brings home money."

$R^2 = .09$

Note: The consumer behavior factors that appear are the ones with the highest weighted factor loadings for the lifestyle predictors. Only those variables with a weight of .40 or higher are listed.

Source: Compiled by the authors.

Chain Supermarket Shopping (store relations factor F)

Consumer Behavior Variables	Factor Loading
Shop at large chain supermarket	.72
Shop at small neighborhood store	-.62

Standardized Slope Coefficient (B)	Zero-Order Correlation Coefficient	Lifestyle Predictor Variables
.15	.17	"In most situations it is clear to me there is a right way and a wrong way."
.13	.14	married
-.12	-.15	"Homemaking is a lonely life."
		$R^2 = .05$

Note: The consumer behavior factors that appear are the ones with the highest weighted factor loadings for the lifestyle predictors. Only those variables with a weight of .40 or higher are listed.

Source: Compiled by the authors.

APPENDIX K.3

High-Trust Health Insurance Company (store relations factor L)

Consumer Behavior Variables	Factor Loading
Purchased health insurance through employer, spouse's employer, or major insurance company office	.69
Purchased health insurance by mail order, door-to-door sales, or telephone	-.50

Standardized Slope Coefficient (B)	Zero-Order Correlation Coefficient	Lifestyle Predictor Variables
.28	.28	income
-.22	-.24	Anglo
-.13	-.10	satisfaction
.12	.08	"When making important decisions, a primary consideration is my children."
-.12	-.08	homemaker
		$R^2 = .16$

Note: The consumer behavior factors that appear are the ones with the highest weighted factor loadings for the lifestyle predictors. Only those variables with a weight of .40 or higher are listed.
Source: Compiled by the authors.

237

APPENDIX K. 4

Good Grocery Specials (store choice factor P)

Consumer Behavior Variable			Factor Loading
Select grocery store for specials and promotional activities			.59

Standardized Slope Coefficient (B)	Zero–Order Correlation Coefficient	Lifestyle Predictor Variables
.15	.13	unskilled worker
-.14	-.11	"I should take some time every day to look into my mind and feelings."
-.13	-.12	"I would feel lost without my friends."
.12	.06	"Change and new experiences are important in the life of every person."
-.11	-.10	unemployed
		$R^2 = .06$

Note: The consumer behavior factor that appears is the one with the highest weighted factor loading for the lifestyle predictors. Only those variables with a weight of .40 or higher are listed.

Source: Compiled by the authors.

Covered by Medicare (inventory factor B)

Consumer Behavior Variables	Factor Loading
Covered by Medicare	.62
Frequency of prescription drug use	.41

Standardized Slope Coefficient (B)	Zero-Order Correlation Coefficient	Lifestyle Predictor Variables
.30	.51	age
.22	.18	female
.20	.37	"My daily activities are limited by health."
.16	.37	widowed
-.15	-.11	homemaker
-.12	-.03	near involvement
-.11	-.14	self-employed/manager/official
.09	.09	self-rated social class
		$R^2 = .40$

Note: The consumer behavior factors that appear are the ones with the highest weighted factor loadings for the lifestyle predictors. Only those variables with a weight of .40 or higher are listed.

Source: Compiled by the authors.

APPENDIX K. 6

Have Health Insurance Policy (inventory factor E)

Consumer Behavior Variable	Factor Loading
Covered by health insurance	.41

Standardized Slope Coefficient (B)	Zero-Order Correlation Coefficient	Lifestyle Predictor Variables
.32	.44	homeowner
.23	.35	income
.18	-.00	retired
.14	.25	interaction
.13	.35	married
-.12	-.20	"I rarely introduce myself to strangers at social gatherings."
-.09	-.14	"I'm a homebody."

$R^2 = .34$

Note: The consumer behavior factor that appears is the one with the highest weighted factor loading for the lifestyle predictors. Only those variables with a weight of .40 or higher are listed.

Source: Compiled by the authors.

APPENDIX K. 7

Medical–Furnishings–Clothing–Personal Budget (budget factor A)

Consumer Behavior Variables		Factor Loading
Monthly medical-dental expenditure		.62
Monthly home furnishings, appliances, and equipment expenditure		.47
Monthly clothing expenditure		.46
Monthly personal care expenditure		.42

Standardized Slope Coefficient (B)	Zero-Order Correlation Coefficient	Lifestyle Predictor Variables
-.16	-.15	"In most situations it is clear to me there is a right way and a wrong way."
.15	.09	"A marriage has problems when the wife brings home money."
.14	.11	married
.13	.12	degree of religiosity
.13	.11	"When making important decisions, a primary consideration is my children."
.12	.10	"I want to be a famous person."
.11	.09	education

$R^2 = .06$

Note: The consumer behavior factors that appear are the ones with the highest weighted factor loadings for the lifestyle predictors. Only those variables with a weight of .40 or higher are listed.

Source: Compiled by the authors.

241

APPENDIX K.8

Price (buying style factor F)

Consumer Behavior Variables	Factor Loading
Stay with familiar brands of packaged goods	-.71
Compare prices of packaged goods	.65
Compare weights and volumes of packaged goods	.48

Standardized Slope Coefficient (B)	Zero-Order Correlation Coefficient	Lifestyle Predictor Variables
-.14	-.14	"I prefer to work alone than with others."
-.12	-.13	"I wish I were single."
.12	.11	self-employed/manager/official
-.12	-.14	widowed

$R^2 = .07$

Note: The consumer behavior factors that appear are the ones with the highest weighted factor loadings for the lifestyle predictors. Only those variables with a weight of .40 or higher are listed.

Source: Compiled by the authors.

APPENDIX K. 9

Bargain Hunting (buying style factor K)

Consumer Behavior Variables		Factor Loading
Frequency of prescription drug comparison price shopping		.79
"I shop around for sales and bargains."		.40

Standardized Slope Coefficient (B)	Zero-Order Correlation Coefficient	Lifestyle Predictor Variables
.15	.14	"I am more interested in news about national and international events than in things that happen in this community."
.15	.10	"I like to go alone to strange and new places."
.14	.10	far involvement
-.13	.11	professional occupation
-.11	.09	"I wish I were single."
		$R^2 = .08$

Note: The consumer behavior factors that appear are the ones with the highest weighted factor loadings for the lifestyle predictors. Only those variables with a weight of .40 or higher are listed.

Source: Compiled by the authors.

APPENDIX K. 10

Dissatisfied with Health Care Services (alienation factor B)

Consumer Behavior Variables	Factor Loading
Dissatisfied with Medicare	.81
Reported problems with health care services	.58

Standardized Slope Coefficient (B)	Zero-Order Correlation Coefficient	Lifestyle Predictor Variables
.20	.18	"I would feel lost without my friends."
-.20	-.21	self-rated poor health
-.14	-.14	near involvement

$$R^2 = .10$$

Note: The consumer behavior factors that appear are the ones with the highest weighted factor loadings for the lifestyle predictors. Only those variables with a weight of .40 or higher are listed.
Source: Compiled by the authors.

244

APPENDIX K. 11

Poor Health (alienation factor C)

Consumer Behavior Variables	Factor Loading
Self-rated poor health	.68
Self-rated disabilities	.47
Interviewer-rated disabilities	.40

Standardized Slope Coefficient (B)	Zero-Order Correlation Coefficient	Lifestyle Predictor Variables
.16	.52	"My daily activities are limited by health problems."
.14	.31	"I'm a little leery of trying new things, so my free-time activities don't change very much."
.09	-.15	income
-.09	-.18	near involvement
		$R^2 = .11$

Note: The consumer behavior factors that appear are the ones with the highest weighted factor loadings for the lifestyle predictors. Only those variables with a weight of .40 or higher are listed.

Source: Compiled by the authors.

APPENDIX K. 12

Rational, Pragmatic Food Characteristics (attribute factor I)

Consumer Behavior Variables	Factor Loading
Importance of family preferences in selecting foods	.61
Importance of nutritional value in selecting foods	.55

Standardized Slope Coefficient (B)	Zero-Order Correlation Coefficient	Lifestyle Predictor Variables
-.21	-.19	"Homemaking is a lonely life."
.19	.18	self-rated poor health
.15	.12	"A woman's most important activities tend to be ones in which her husband cannot participate."
.11	.07	clerical or sales occupation

$$R^2 = .10$$

Note: The consumer behavior factors that appear are the ones with the highest weighted factor loadings for the lifestyle predictors. Only those variables with a weight of .40 or higher are listed.

Source: Compiled by the authors.

APPENDIX L.

Summary of Multiple-Regression Results for Attribute, Budget, and Alienation Consumer Behavior Variables

Independent Variables	Attribute										Budget			Alienation			
	Clothing Fashionableness	Hedonic Food Characteristics	Price	Auto Longevity	Clothing Durability	Auto Design	Auto Self-Image	Brand	Rational-Pragmatic Food Characteristics	Auto Operating Expenses	Med.-Furn.-Clothing-Personal Budget	Food-Transportation Budget	Housing-Recreation-Savings Budget	Prob. with Food, Money, Housing, Transportation	Dissatisfied with Medicare	Poor Health	Disappointing Consumer Experience
Working for pay																	
Unemployed																	
Retired																	
Homemaker																	
Married																	
Widowed						-5						+2		-2			
Divorced																	-4
How religious are you?																	
Self-rated health status			-2		-6		-4				+3				-2	-1	+3
Highest grade completed in school					-1				+2		+4					+4	
Income				+2							+7		+1			+2	
Daily activities limited by health																	
Clear right and wrong																	
Better listener than conversationalist							+3			+2	+1		-2				
Prefer people my own age					+9			+3									
Older people poorly treated																	
Change is important																	
National over local news																	
Have fewer friends now																	
Rarely introduce self to strangers			+5					-5									
Like going alone to strange places			-6			-3											
Local club over national																	
Happy with life so far								+7									
Should look into mind and feelings					-3												
Children not enough time with parents					+2			+6									
Clubs not important																	
Dislike set schedule											+5						
Children primary consideration in decision	-1																
Feel lost without friends			+3												+1		+8
Homemaking is a lonely life									-1	+4							

Independent Variables	Clothing Fashionableness	Hedonic Food Characteristics	Price	Auto Longevity	Clothing Durability	Auto Design	Auto Self-Image	Brand	Rational-Pragmatic Food Characteristics	Auto Operating Expenses	Med.-Furn.-Clothing-Personal Budget	Food-Transportation Budget	Housing-Recreation-Savings Budget	Prob. with Food, Money, Housing, Transportation	Dissatisfied with Medicare	Poor Health	Disappointing Consumer Experience
	Attribute										**Budget**			**Alienation**			
Wish I were single	+2																
Leery of new things																+3	
Never too old to take up new ways				-3	+7	-4		+4									
Worry children won't turn out right																	
Woman's most imp. acts, husband no part									+3								+7
Marriage prob. if wife brings home money					-4					-3	+2						
Prefer to work alone												-3					
I'm a homebody		-1									+6	-1					-2
I want to be a famous person																	
Age													+3				
Class			+1				-2										
Gender																	
Interaction																	
Satisfaction							+5										
Role change	+3				+8		+1							+1			
Near involvement						-1									-3	-5	
Far involvement										+1				+3			+5
Anglo																	
Unskilled																	
Skilled								-1	+4								
Clerical	+4			+1												+6	
Self-employed/manager/official								-2						+1			+1
Professional					+5	-2											
Owner			+4														
R	.28	.13	.35	.22	.34	.21	.34	.31	.32	.29	.25	.41	.35	.42	.32	.77	.48
R²	.08	.02	.12	.05	.12	.04	.11	.10	.10	.09	.06	.17	.12	.18	.10	.59	.23

Notes: Regressions are organized by consumer behavior areas rather than by areas of consumer consumption.

The consumer behavior factors that appear are the ones with the highest weighted factor loadings for the lifestyle predictors. Only those variables with a weight of .40 or higher are listed.

Source: Compiled by the authors.

248

APPENDIX M: CONSUMER TRANSPORTATION AND CLOTHING FACTORS

APPENDIX M.1

Auto Repair in a Shop (buying style factor I)

Consumer Behavior Variables	Factor Loading
Shop auto repair	.76
Personal auto repair	-.73

Standardized Slope Coefficient (B)	Zero–Order Correlation Coefficient	Lifestyle Predictor Variables
-.14	.16	"My daily activities are limited by health."
.12	.14	interaction
		$R^2 = .04$

Note: The consumer behavior factors that appear are the ones with the highest weighted factor loadings for the lifestyle predictors. Only those variables with a weight of .40 or higher are listed.
Source: Compiled by the authors.

249

APPENDIX M. 2

Purchased Auto by Personal Transaction (store relations factor B)

Consumer Behavior Variables			Factor Loading
Purchased vehicle by personal transaction			.96
Purchased vehicle from new-car dealer			-.75

Standardized Slope Coefficient (B)	Zero-Order Correlation Coefficient	Lifestyle Predictor Variables	
.15	.15	"I would feel lost without my friends."	
-.14	-.15	self-rated social class	

$R^2 = .04$

Note: The consumer behavior factors that appear are the ones with the highest weighted factor loadings for the lifestyle predictors. Only those variables with a weight of .40 or higher are listed.
Source: Compiled by the authors.

250

APPENDIX M. 3

Shop by Public Transportation (store relations factor C)

Consumer Behavior Variables	Factor Loading
Frequently go shopping by public transportation	.67
Frequently go shopping by foot	.63

Standardized Slope Coefficient (B)	Zero-Order Correlation Coefficient	Lifestyle Predictor Variables
-.15	-.24	homeowner
-.13	-.24	married
-.12	-.22	income

$R^2 = .09$

Note: The consumer behavior factors that appear are the ones with the highest weighted factor loadings for the lifestyle predictors. Only those variables with a weight of .40 or higher are listed.

Source: Compiled by the authors.

251

APPENDIX M. 4

Used-Car-Dealer Shopping (store relations factor J)

Consumer Behavior Variables			Factor Loading
Purchased vehicle from used-car dealer			.96
Purchased vehicle from new-car dealer			-.60
Standardized Slope Coefficient (B)	Zero-Order Correlation Coefficient	Lifestyle Predictor Variables	
-.16	-.15	"Older people are poorly treated in America."	
-.13	-.12	education	
			$R^2 = .04$

Note: The consumer behavior factors that appear are the ones with the highest weighted factor loadings for the lifestyle predictors. Only those variables with a weight of .40 or higher are listed.

Source: Compiled by the authors.

APPENDIX M. 5

Nondriver (store relations factor M)

Consumer Behavior Variables	Factor Loading
Other person drives respondent to shop	.66
Respondent drives self to shop	-.66

Standardized Slope Coefficient (B)	Zero–Order Correlation Coefficient	Lifestyle Predictor Variables
.22	.24	female
-.17	-.20	education
.14	.15	"I seem to have fewer friends now than in the past."
.13	.11	self-rated social class
.12	.12	"I want to be a famous person."
.11	.09	"I would feel lost without my friends."
.10	.14	"A marriage has problems when the wife brings home money."
		$R^2 = .16$

Note: The consumer behavior factors that appear are the ones with the highest weighted factor loadings for the lifestyle predictors. Only those variables with a weight of .40 or higher are listed.

Source: Compiled by the authors.

APPENDIX M.6

Clothing Fashionableness (attribute importance factor A)

Consumer Behavior Variables	Factor Loading
Importance of clothing cut	.81
Importance of clothing fashionableness	.62
Importance of clothing color	.54

Standardized Slope Coefficient (B)	Zero-Order Correlation Coefficient	Lifestyle Predictor Variables
-.15	-.16	"When making important decisions, a primary consideration is my children."
.14	.18	"I wish I were single."
.12	.15	role change (composite variable indicating desire for change in 7 roles: worker, house manager, parent, spouse, friend, community member, and leisure-time user)
.11	.13	clerical

$R^2 = .08$

Note: The consumer behavior factors that appear are the ones with the highest weighted factor loadings for the lifestyle predictors. Only those variables with a weight of .40 or higher are listed.

Source: Compiled by the authors.

APPENDIX M.7

Auto Longevity (attribute importance factor D)

Consumer Behavior Variables	Factor Loading
Importance of auto lifespan	.79
Importance of auto safety features	.47
Importance of auto handling	.43

Standardized Slope Coefficient (B)	Zero-Order Correlation Coefficient	Lifestyle Predictor Variables
.15	.14	clerical, sales
.14	.11	income
-.12	-.09	"I worry my children won't turn out right."

$R^2 = .05$

Note: The consumer behavior factors that appear are the ones with the highest weighted factor loadings for the lifestyle predictors. Only those variables with a weight of .40 or higher are listed.

Source: Compiled by the authors.

APPENDIX M.8

Clothing Durability (attribute importance factor E)

Consumer Behavior Variables		Factor Loading
Importance of clothing durability		.71
Importance of clothing washability		.51
Importance of clothing alterability		.48

Standardized Slope Coefficient (B)	Zero-Order Correlation Coefficient	Lifestyle Predictor Variables
-.16	-.10	education
.16	.12	"Children don't spend enough time with their parents."
-.15	-.12	"I should take some time each day to look into my mind and feelings."
-.15	-.12	"I prefer to work alone than with others."
.12	.03	professional
-.12	-.10	degree of religiosity
.11	.05	"I have never felt I was too old to take up new ways."
.11	.09	near involvement (activities around the home)
.11	.10	"I prefer to spend time around people my own age."
		$R^2 = .11$

<u>Note</u>: The consumer behavior factors that appear are the ones with the highest weighted factor loadings for the lifestyle predictors. Only those variables with a weight of .40 or higher are listed.

<u>Source</u>: Compiled by the authors.

APPENDIX M. 9

Auto Design (attribute importance factor F)

Consumer Behavior Variables			Factor Loading
Importance of auto make			.64
Importance of auto styling			.59

Standardized Slope Coefficient (B)	Zero-Order Correlation Coefficient	Lifestyle Predictor Variables
-.20	-.16	far involvement
-.16	-.13	homeowner
-.12	-.10	"I like going alone to strange and new places."
-.12	-.11	"I have never felt I was too old to take up new ways."
-.12	-.10	retired

$R^2 = .09$

Note: The consumer behavior factors that appear are the ones with the highest weighted factor loadings for the lifestyle predictors. Only those variables with a weight of .40 or higher are listed.
Source: Compiled by the authors.

APPENDIX M.10

Auto Self-Image (attribute importance factor G)

Consumer Behavior Variable		Factor Loading
Importance of self-concept derived from driving automobile		.66

Standardized Slope Coefficient (B)	Zero-Order Correlation Coefficient	Lifestyle Predictor Variables
.22	.12	role change
-.18	-.17	gender
.17	.18	"In most situations it is clear to me there is a right way and a wrong way."
-.16	-.17	self-rated poor health
.15	-.01	satisfaction

$R^2 = .12$

Note: The consumer behavior factor that appears is the one with the highest weighted factor loading for the lifestyle predictors. Only those variables with a weight of .40 or higher are listed.

Source: Compiled by the authors.

258

Auto Operating Expense (attribute importance factor J)

Consumer Behavior Variable	Factor Loading	Standardized Slope Coefficient (B)	Zero-Order Correlation Coefficient	Lifestyle Predictor Variables
Auto operating expense	.51			far involvement
		.22	.21	far involvement
		.15	.11	"In most situations it is clear to me there is a right way and a wrong way."
		-.11	-.12	"I prefer to work alone than with others."
		.11	.08	"Homemaking is a lonely life."
				$R^2 = .09$

Note: The consumer behavior factor that appears is the one with the highest weighted factor loading for the lifestyle predictors. Only those variables with a weight of .40 or higher are listed.

Source: Compiled by the authors.

Price (attribute importance factor C)

Consumer Behavior Variables	Factor Loading
Clothing price	.77
Food price	.71
Auto purchase price	.46

Standardized Slope Coefficient (B)	Zero-Order Correlation Coefficient	Lifestyle Predictor Variables
.17	.19	female
-.16	-.18	self-rated poor health
.15	.10	"Homemaking is a lonely life."
.12	.09	homeowner
.12	.15	"I rarely introduce myself to strangers at social gatherings."
-.12	-.15	"I like going alone to strange and new places."

$R^2 = .12$

Note: The consumer behavior factors that appear are the ones with the highest weighted factor loadings for the lifestyle predictors. Only those variables with a weight of .40 or higher are listed.
Source: Compiled by the authors.

APPENDIX M.13

Brand (attribute importance factor H)

Consumer Behavior Variables	Factor Loading
Clothing brand	.70
Food brand	.45

Standardized Slope Coefficient (B)	Zero-Order Correlation Coefficient	Lifestyle Predictor Variables
-.16	-.10	skilled
-.14	-.10	self-employed/manager/official
.13	.13	"I prefer to spend time around people my own age."
.13	.15	"I'm a little leery of trying new things, so my free-time activities don't change very much."
-.13	-.07	"I rarely introduce myself to strangers at social gatherings."
.11	.11	"I dislike following a set schedule."
.11	.11	"Belonging to a local club would be more rewarding than belonging to a state or national organization."

$R^2 = .10$

Note: The consumer behavior factors that appear are the ones with the highest weighted factor loadings for the lifestyle predictors. Only those variables with a weight of .40 or higher are listed.

Source: Compiled by the authors.

APPENDIX M. 14

Clothing Store for Friendly Personnel (store choice factor R)

Consumer Behavior Variable			Factor Loading
Select clothing store for friendly personnel			.40

Standardized Slope Coefficient (B)	Zero-Order Correlation Coefficient	Lifestyle Predictor Variable	
-.18	-.18	self-rated social class	

$$R^2 = .03$$

Notes: See also Appendix E. 21. The consumer behavior factor that appears is the one with the highest weighted factor loading for the lifestyle predictor. Only those variables with a weight of .40 or higher are listed.

Source: Compiled by the authors.

262

APPENDIX M. 15

In-Home Convenience (store choice factor T)

Consumer Behavior Variable		Factor Loading
Clothing catalog for in-home convenience		.56

Standardized Slope Coefficient (B)	Zero-Order Correlation Coefficient	Lifestyle Predictor Variables
-.13	-.13	"Belonging to a local club would be more rewarding than belonging to a state or national organization."
.13	.11	"I am a better listener than conversationalist."
-.12	-.11	female
-.12	-.13	role change
-.12	-.12	"A marriage has problems when the wife brings home money."
.12	.10	degree of religiosity
		$R^2 = .09$

Note: The consumer behavior factor that appears is the one with the highest weighted factor loading for the lifestyle predictors. Only those variables with a weight of .40 or higher are listed.
Source: Compiled by the authors.

263

BIBLIOGRAPHY

Adler, Alfred. 1927. Understanding Human Nature. New York: Greenburg.

Alfin-Slater, Roslyn B. 1975. "Nutritional Problems in the Aging." Nutrition and the M. D. 1, no. 10: 1 (Aug.).

American Sociological Association. 1977. "Issues in Promoting Health." Committee Reports of the Medical Sociology Section of the American Sociological Association. Medical Care 15, supp. (May).

Atchley, Robert C. 1972. The Social Forces in Later Life, an Introduction to Social Gerontology. Belmont, Calif. : Wadsworth.

Bernhardt, Kenneth L. , and Thomas C. Kinnear. 1976. "Profiling the Senior Citizen Market." In Advances in Consumer Research, Vol. III, ed. Beverlee B. Anderson. Chicago: Association for Consumer Research, pp. 449-52.

Bischoff, Ledford J. 1976. Adult Psychology. New York: Harper and Row.

Blum, H. L. 1976. Expanding Health Care Horizons from a General Systems Concept of Health to a National Health Policy. Oakland, Calif. : Third Party Associates.

Boone, Louis E. , and John A. Bonno. 1971. "Food Buying Habits of the Urban Poor." Journal of Retailing 47, no. 3: 78-84 (Fall).

Bortner, Rayman, and David J. Hultsch. 1970. "A Multivariate Analysis of Correlates of Life Satisfaction in Adulthood." Journal of Gerontology 25, no. 1: 41-47.

Botwinick, Jack. 1973. Aging and Behavior. A Comprehensive Integration of Research Findings. New York: Springer.

Burton, John, and Charles Hennon. 1978. "Consumer Education Programs for the Elderly." American Council on Consumer Interests Proceedings, pp. 154-58. Chicago, Apr. 21.

Carp, Francis. 1975. "Lifestyle and Location Within the City." The Gerontologist 32, no. 1, pt. 1: 68-72 (Feb.).

Chatfield, Walter F. 1977. "Economic and Sociological Factors Influencing Life Satisfaction of the Aged." Journal of Gerontology 32, no. 5: 593-99.

Chen, Yung-ping. 1971. "Income Background." Background and Issues series: White House Conference on Aging. Washington, D. C.: U. S. Government Printing Office.

Chu, Kwang-wen. 1972. "Consumption Patterns Among Different Age Groups—an Econometric Study of Family Budgets." Ph. D. dissertation, University of California at Los Angeles. Microfilm copy available from University Microfilms, Ann Arbor, Mich.

Clark, Lincoln H., ed. 1955. Consumer Behavior: The Life Cycle and Consumer Behavior. New York: New York University Press.

Clark, Lorraine H., and Samuel Cochran. 1972. "Needs of Older Americans Assessed by Delphi Procedures." Journal of Gerontology 27, no. 2: 275-78.

Clark, Margaret, Barbara G. Anderson, and associates. 1967. Culture and Aging: An Anthropological Study of Older Americans. Springfield, Ill.: Charles C. Thomas.

Committee on Research and Development Goals in Social Gerontology. 1969. "Summary of Research in Applied Social Gerontology." The Gerontologist 9, no. 4, pt. II: 4-90 (Winter).

Crockett, Jean A. 1973. "Older People as Consumers." In Aging and the Economy, ed. Harold L. Orbach and Clark Tibbetts. Ann Arbor: University of Michigan Press.

Cumming, Elaine. 1964. "New Thoughts on the Theory of Disengagement." In New Thoughts on Old Age, ed. Robert Kastenbaum. New York: Springer.

Cuber, John, and Peggy Harroff. 1965. The Significant Americans. New York: Appleton, Century, Crofts.

Cutler, Stephen J. 1972. "The Availability of Personal Transportation, Residential Location and Life Satisfaction Among the Aged." Journal of Gerontology 27, no. 3: 383-89.

Department of Commerce. 1971a. Current Population Reports. Series D projections.

___. 1971b. Current Population Reports. Series P-25, no. 470 (Nov.).

"Don't Write off the Senior Citizen Markets. " 1973. Media Decisions July: 64-67, 112-16.

Edwards, John N. and David L. Klemack. 1973. "Correlates of Life Satisfaction: A Reexamination. " Journal of Gerontology 28, no. 4: 497-502.

Engel, James F. , David T. Kollat, and Roger D. Blackwell. 1973. Consumer Behavior. 2nd ed. New York: Holt, Rinehart and Winston.

Erikson, Erik. 1950. "Eight Stages of Man. " In Childhood and Society, ed. Erik Erikson, pp. 219-34. New York: Norton.

Fleming, Arthur S. 1971. "The Power of the Aging in the Marketplace. " In Business Week; Nov. 20, pp. 52-58.

Foltz, Don. 1978. "Crime Against the Old. " APA (American Psychological Association) Monitor 9, no. 3: 1 (Mar.).

"The Forgotten Generation. " 1969. In Forbes; Jan. 15, pp. 22-29.

French, Warren, and Melvin Crask. 1978. "The Credibility of Media Advertising for the Elderly. " Unpublished paper, University of Georgia.

Friedman, Monroe P. , and Ira M. Wasserman. 1978. "A Community Survey of Purchase Experiences of Older Consumers. " American Council on Consumer Interests Proceedings, pp. 159-61. Chicago: American Council on Consumer Interests.

Goldstein, Sidney. 1965. "Changing Income and Consumption Patterns of the Aged 1950-1960. " Journal of Gerontology 20, no. 4: 453-61.

___. 1966. "The Effect of Income Level on the Consumer Behavior of the Aged. " In proceedings of the 7th International Congress of Gerontology. Vol. 7, pp. 1-5. Vienna: International Association of Gerontology.

___. 1968. "The Aged Segment of the Market. " Journal of Marketing 32: 62-68 (Apr.).

Grey Advertising, Inc. 1973. Grey Matter. New York.

Gustafson, William A. , William Bearden, and J. Barry Mason. 1978. "Consumer Alienation and Food Shopping: An Exploratory Analysis of the Behavior of the Elderly. " Paper presented at the American Council on Consumer Interests Conference. Chicago, Apr. 2.

Hamovitch, Maurice B. , and James E. Peterson. 1969. "Housing Needs and Satisfactions of the Elderly. " The Gerontologist 9: 30-32.

Hamrin, Janice G. 1974. "Life Style and Purchasing Pattern of Adolescents. " Unpublished master's thesis, University of California, Davis.

Harris, Louis, and Associates. 1975. The Myth and Reality of Aging in America. Washington, D. C. : National Council on Aging, Inc.

Havighurst, Robert J. 1960. Sociological Backgrounds of Adult Education. Notes and Essays no. 41, Center for Study of Liberal Education for Adults, pp. 25-36. Boston: Boston University.

___. 1971. "Social Class Perspectives on the Life Cycle. " Human Development 14, no. 2: 110-24.

___, and Kenneth Feigenbaum. 1968. "Leisure and Life Style. " In Middle Age and Aging: A Reader in Social Psychology, ed. Bernice L. Neugarten. Chicago: University of Chicago Press.

Hilka, B. S. , et al. 1975. "Correlates of Satisfaction and Dissatisfaction with Medical Care. " Medical Care 13: 648-58 (Aug.).

Hochschild, Russell. 1973. The Unexpected Community. Englewood Cliffs, N. J. : Prentice-Hall.

Hurlock, Elizabeth B. 1975. Developmental Psychology. 4th ed. New York: McGraw-Hill.

Kahl, J. A. 1965. The American Class Structure. New York: Holt, Rinehart and Winston.

Kanin, Garson. 1978. It Takes a Long Time to Become Young. Garden City, N. Y. : Doubleday.

Katona, George, Lewis Mandell, and Jay Schmiedeskamp. 1970. Survey of Consumer Attitudes. Ann Arbor: Michigan Survey Research Center, Institute for Social Research, University of Michigan.

___, Burkhard Strumpel, and Ernest Zahn. 1971. Aspirations and Affluence. New York: McGraw-Hill.

Kerckhoff, Alan C. 1966. "Norm Value Clusters and the Strain Toward Consistency Among Older Married Couples." In Social Aspects of Aging, ed. Ida H. Simpson and John C. McKinney, pp. 138-59. Durham, N. C.: Duke University Press.

Kimmel, Douglas C. 1974. Adulthood and Aging: An Interdisciplinary, Developmental View. New York: John Wiley.

Knapp, Martin R. J. 1976. "Predicting the Dimensions of Life Satisfaction." Journal of Gerontology 31, no. 5: 595-604.

Kuhn, Maggie. 1978. "Insights on Aging." Journal of Home Economics 70, no. 4: 18-20 (Fall).

Lansing, John B. , and Leslie Kish. 1957. "Family Life Cycle as an Independent Variable." American Sociology Review 22, no. 5: 512-19.

Larson, Reed. 1978. "Thirty Years of Research on the Subjective Well-Being of Older Americans." Journal of Gerontology 33, no. 1: 109-25.

Lawton, M. Powell, and Jacob Cohen. 1974. "The Generality of Housing Impact on the Well-Being of Older People." Journal of Gerontology 29, no. 2: 194-204.

Lemmon, Bruce W. , Vern Bengston, and James Peterson. 1972. "An Exploration of the Activity Theory of Aging: Activity Types and Life Satisfaction Among In-Movers to a Retirement Community." Journal of Gerontology 27, no. 4: 511-23.

Linden, Fabian. 1974. "Reshuffling the Age-Income Mix." The Conference Board Record 11, no. 3: 58-60 (Mar.).

Lowenthal, Majorie Fish, et al. 1975. Four Stages of Life. San Francisco: Josey-Bass.

Maddox, George L. 1966. "Persistence of Lifestyle Among the Elderly: A Longitudinal Study of Patterns of Social Activity in Relation to Life Satisfaction." In Proceedings of the 7th International Congress of Gerontology, vol. 6.

Martin, Claude R., Jr. 1976. "A Transgenerational Comparison—the Elderly Fashion Consumer." In Advances in Consumer Research, vol. III of Chicago: Association for Consumer Research, ed. Beverlee B. Anderson, pp. 453-56.

Mason, Joseph Barry, and Brooks E. Smith. 1973. "An Exploratory Note on the Shopping Behavior of the Low Income Senior Citizen." Journal of Consumer Affairs 7, no. 1: 204-10 (Summer).

Mayer, K. B. 1955. Class and Society. New York: Random House.

McConnell, John W. 1960. "Aging and the Economy." In Handbook of Social Gerontology, ed. Clark Tibbetts, pp. 489-520. Chicago: University of Chicago Press.

Medley, Morris. 1976. "Satisfaction with Life Among Persons Sixty-Five and Older." Journal of Gerontology 31, no. 4: 448-55.

Needham, Harper and Steers Advertising Inc. 1975. Lifestyle Surveys. Los Angeles.

Neugarten, Bernice L. 1968. Middle Age and Aging: A Reader in Social Psychology. Chicago: University of Chicago Press.

___, and associates. 1964. Personality in Middle and Later Life. New York: Atherton.

___, Robert Havighurst, and Sheldon S. Tobin. 1968. "Personality and Patterns of Aging." In Middle Age and Aging: A Reader in Social Psychology, ed. Bernice L. Neugarten. Chicago: University of Chicago Press.

Nie, N. H., et al. 1975. Statistical Package for the Social Sciences. 2nd ed. New York: McGraw-Hill.

NRTA/AARP. 1975. Proceedings of the First National Forum on the Consumer Concerns of Older Americans. Washington, D. C.: NRTA/AARP Consumer Office.

Palmore, Erdman, and Vera Kivett. 1977. "Changes in Life Satisfaction: A Longitudinal Study of Persons Aged 46-70." Journal of Gerontology 32, no. 3: 311-16.

___, and C. Luikart. 1972. "Health and Social Factors Related to Life Satisfaction." Journal of Health and Social Behavior 13, no. 1: 68-80.

Parsons, Talcott, and Edward Shils. 1962. Toward a General Theory of Action. Reprint. New York: Harper and Row.

Perloff, Robert, and Patrick McCaskey. 1978. "Non-monetary Costs Associated with Consumer Fraud and Dissatisfaction of the Elderly. Paper presented at the American Council on Consumer Interests Conference. Chicago, Apr. 21.

Plummer, Joseph T. 1974. "The Concept and Application of Life Style Segmentation." Journal of Marketing 38, no. 1: 33-37.

Reinecke, John. 1964. "The Older Market—Fact or Fiction?" Journal of Marketing 28, no. 1: 60-64.

Reynolds, Fred D., and William D. Wells. 1977. Consumer Behavior. New York: McGraw-Hill.

Riley, Matilda White, Anne Foner, and associates. 1968. Aging and Society, Vol. 1, An Inventory of Research Findings. New York: Russell Sage Foundation.

Robertson, L. S. 1974. Changing the Medical Care System: A Controlled Experiment in Comprehensive Care. New York: Praeger.

Rokeach, Milton. 1973. Nature of Human Values. New York: Free Press.

Rose, Arnold M., and Warren A. Peterson. 1965. Older People and Their Social World. Philadelphia: F. A. Davis.

Rosow, Irving. 1967. Social Integration of the Aged. New York: Free Press.

Samli, A. Coskun, and Feliksas Palubinskas. 1972. "Some Lesser Known Aspects of the Senior Citizen Market—a California Study." Akron Business and Economic Review 3, no. 4: 47-55 (Winter).

Schiffman, Leon. 1971. "Sources of Information for the Elderly." Journal of Advertising Research 11: 33-37 (Oct.).

___. 1972a. "Perceived Risk in New Product Trial by Elderly Consumers." Journal of Marketing Research 9: 106-08 (Feb.).

___. 1972b. "Social Interaction Patterns of the Elderly Consumer." Proceedings of the American Marketing Association. Series no.

34, ed. Boris Becker and Helmut Becker, pp. 445-51. Chicago: AMA.

Schutz, Howard G. , and Jeri Bump. 1974. "The Evaluation of Consumer Complaint Mediation of the California Department of Consumer Affairs." Unpublished report, University of California, Davis.

___, Margaret H. Rucker, and Gerald Russell. 1979. "Food Use Classification Systems." Food Technology.

___, Glenn R. Hawkes, et al. 1977. Final Report on Administration on Aging Grant, Lifestyle and Consumer Behavior of the Aging. Grant #90-A-645102. University of California, Davis.

Shanas, E. , et al. 1968. Old People in Three Industrial Societies. New York: Atherton.

Sheehy, Gail. 1976. Passages. New York: Dutton.

Sherman, Edith M. , and Margaret R. Brittan. 1973. "Contemporary Food Gatherers." The Gerontologist 13: 358-64 (Fall).

Smith, Kenneth J. , and Aaron Lipman. 1972. "Constraint and Life Satisfaction." Journal of Gerontology 27, no. 1: 77-82.

Snyder, Lorraine H. 1971. "The Environmental Challenge and the Aging Individual." Council of Planning Librarians Exchange Bibliography no. 254.

Stratman, W. C. , et al. 1975. "A Study of Consumer Attitudes Towards Health Care: The Control, Cost and Financing of Health Services." Medical Care 13: 659-68 (Aug.).

Streib, Gordon F. , and Clement J. Schneider. 1971. Retirement in American Society. Ithaca, N. Y. : Cornell University Press.

The Survey of Buying Power Data Service. 1976. New York: Sales and Marketing Magazine.

Thal, Helen M. , and Lois J. Guthrie. 1967. "Dynamics of Teaching." Journal of Home Economics 61, no. 10: 762-67.

Tibbetts, Clark. 1960. Handbook of Social Gerontology. Chicago: University of Chicago Press.

Tornstom, Lars. 1975. "Health and Self-Perception." The Gerontologist 15, no. 3: 264-70 (June).

Towle, Jeffrey G., and Claude R. Martin, Jr. 1976. "The Elderly
Consumer: One Segment or Many?" In Advances in Consumer Research, vol. III, ed. Beverlee B. Anderson. Chicago: Association
for Consumer Research, pp. 463-68.

Tubesing, D. A., et al. 1977. "The Wholistic Health Center Project."
Medical Care 15, no. 3: 217-27 (Mar.).

U. S. Department of Health, Education and Welfare, Public Health
Service, National Institute of Health. 1978. Changes: Research on
Aging and the Aged. DHEW Publication no. NIH 78-85. Washing-
ton, D. C.: U. S. Government Printing Office.

U. S. Senate. 1963. Hearings Before the Subcommittee on Aging,
Frauds, and Quackery Affecting Older Citizens. Pt. I. Washington,
D. C.: U. S. Government Printing Office.

___. 1965. Report of the Subcommittee on Frauds and Misrepresenta-
tions Affecting the Elderly: Frauds and Deception Affecting the
Elderly. Washington, D. C.: U. S. Government Printing Office.

___. 1967. Hearings Before the Subcommittee on Consumer Interests
of the Elderly of the Senate Special Committee on Aging. Pt. II.
Washington, D. C.: U. S. Government Printing Office.

___. 1973. Hearings Before the Subcommittee on Aging, Frauds, and
Quackery Affecting Older Citizens. Pt. II. Washington, D. C.: U. S.
Government Printing Office.

Valle, Valeria, and Randi Koeski. 1978. "Elderly Consumer Problems." Unpublished paper, University of Pittsburgh, Graduate
School of Business.

Vedder, Clyde B., ed. 1965. Problems of the Middle Aged. Springfield, Ill.: Charles C. Thomas.

Waddell, Frederick E. 1975. "Consumer Research and Programs
for the Elderly—the Forgotten Dimension." Journal of Consumer
Affairs 9: 164-75 (Winter).

___, ed. 1976. The Elderly Consumer. Columbia, Md.: Human
Ecology Center, Antioch College.

Watkin, Donald M. 1975. "The Nutrition Program for Older Americans." Nutrition and the M. D. 1, no. 10: 2-3 (Aug.).

Wells, William D. , and George Gubar. 1966. "Life Cycle Concept in Marketing Research. " Journal of Marketing Research 3: 355-63 (Nov.).

___, and Douglas J. Tigert. 1971. "Activities, Interests, and Opinions." Journal of Advertising Research 11, no. 4: 27-35.

White House Conference on Aging. 1971. "The Elderly Consumer." In Reports of the Special Concern Sessions on the Elderly Consumer. Washington, D. C. : U. S. Government Printing Office.

Williams, Richard H. , and Claudine G. Wirth. 1965. Lives Through the Years: Styles of Life and Successful Aging. New York: Atherton.

Wind, Jerry. 1971. "Life Style Analysis: A New Approach." Proceedings of American Marketing Association. Series no. 33, ed. Fred C. Allvine. Chicago: A. M. A.

Wolk, Stephen, and Sharon Telleen. 1976. "Psychological and Social Correlates of Life Satisfaction as a Function of Residential Constraint. " Journal of Gerontology 31, no. 1: 89-98.

Young, Diana. 1974. "A Three Generation Study of Meaning in Life." Unpublished master's thesis, University of California, Davis.

INDEX

AIO questionnaire, 4
activity theory of aging, 71-72
Administration on Aging, 22
age, chronological: old age
 identified by, 28
aging: activity theory of, 71-72;
 definition of, 29; patterns of,
 3, 5; process of, 152; Administration on Aging, 22; White
 House Conference on Aging,
 6, 22
automobile: consumer problems,
 92, 97; costs, 100; insurance, 137-38; mobility,
 158-59

brand choice, 91, 131, 134
budgeting, 105

central control unit, 46
consumer behavior: decisions,
 26, 28, 46, 74, 75, 83-84,
 87, 90, 157-58; information
 sources, 87-91; model, 26,
 28, 46; variables, 46, 58,
 98, 150, 151, 159
consumer fraud (see fraud,
 consumer)
consumer problems, 92, 97,
 100, 131
cost of living, 92, 100, 105,
 111, 131; increases, 154
credit, 100, 105-09, 111-12,
 158-59

decision-making: process, 26,
 28, 46, 74, 75, 91; joint,
 87; planned/impulsive
 purchases, 90-91, 158

drugs, 119, 158

employment, 64, 157 (see also,
 work, retirement)
Engel-Kollat-Blackwell model of
 consumer behavior, 26, 28,
 46

family: changes, 63; shopping,
 role in, 83, 87
fraud, consumer: incidence
 among the elderly, 98; vulnerability of elderly to, 22

health: activities limited by, 72;
 insurance, 118, 156; and lifestyle, 117 (see also medical
 care)
housing: mobility, 143, 147;
 problems, 147

insurance: automobile, 137-38,
 142; health, 118, 156; National
 Health Insurance, 113, 156
investments, 105-06

Kansas City Study of Adult Life,
 5

leisure activity: patterns of, 8
lifestyle: components of, 25;
 definition of, 4-5; and health,
 117; hypotheses, 30; origin
 of term, 3; model, 25, 26, 46;
 patterns of, 24, 38; variables,
 43, 45, 46, 58

market, senior citizen: growth
 of, 23

275

ABOUT THE AUTHORS

HOWARD G. SCHUTZ is professor of consumer science and research psychologist in the Agricultural Experiment Station at the University of California at Davis. Before his academic career he worked as a research psychologist in government and a nonprofit organization, and in industry as a research and marketing administrator. He has done research and written articles in a wide variety of consumer behavior areas, including food preferences, energy conservation, complaints, and community satisfaction.

Dr. Schutz received his advanced degrees in psychology at the Illinois Institute of Technology. He has published articles in Journal of Consumer Affairs, Social Indicators Research, Journal of the American Dietetic Association, and Journal of Food Science.

PAMELA C. BAIRD is staff research associate at the University of California at Davis. She has conducted research on the relationship of food attitudes to nutritional status in addition to her work on consumer behavior of the elderly. For her work on cognitive structure of food attitudes of four ethnic groups she received the American Council on Consumer Interests Research Award.

Ms. Baird graduated from the University of California with a degree in sociology and an advanced degree in consumer science. She has published articles in Journal of Nutrition Education and Journal of the American Dietetic Association.

GLENN R. HAWKES is professor of human development and research psychologist in the Agricultural Experiment Station at the University of California at Davis. He is also associate dean for applied economic and behavioral sciences. In addition to his work on lifestyles, of which this volume is a part, he has done research on quality of life. Dr. Hawkes has written extensively on the social needs of diverse age and ethnic groups in this and other societies. His most recent work (written with Joe L. Frost) is The Disadvantaged Child.

Dr. Hawkes received his advanced degrees in psychology at Cornell University. He has published articles in Growth and Development, Family Life Coordinator, Journal of Marriage and Family, and Journal of Counseling Psychology.

Physical Anthropology

an introduction

To my wife, Mary,
and to my children, Colette and William

Physical Anthropology

Second Edition

Anthropology

an introduction

A. J. KELSO

UNIVERSITY OF COLORADO

J. B. LIPPINCOTT COMPANY

PHILADELPHIA   NEW YORK   TORONTO

ISBN-0-397-47296-X

Library of Congress Catalog Card Number 73-17175

Printed in the United States of America

1 3 5 7 9 10 8 6 4 2

Library of Congress Cataloging in Publication Data

Kelso, Alec John, 1930-
    Physical anthropology.

    Includes bibliographies.
    1. Somatology. I. Title.
GN60.K4 1974   573   73-17175
ISBN 0-397-47296-X

ACKNOWLEDGMENTS

A NEW EDITION of any book owes much to preceding editions, therefore I wish to acknowledge with sincere thanks those who assisted me with the first edition of this work.

This edition also benefited from the assistance of students—graduate and under-graduate—at the University of Colorado. Special thanks are due to Dr. Kenneth Beals, of Oregon State University, Dr. Gerald Broce, Lake Erie College, and Dr. James Tinsman, Kutztown State College.

While the manuscript was reviewed in whole or in part by several of my associates, three were particularly thoughtful and helpful: Dr. Christopher Meiklejohn, University of Winnipeg, Dr. Milford Wolpoff, University of Michigan, and Dr. Francis Johnston, University of Pennsylvania.

In more ways than they can know, my family has been helpful in bringing this effort to a successful conclusion. Their contribution is deeply appreciated.

CONTENTS

ILLUSTRATIONS

TABLES

PREFACE TO THE SECOND EDITION

WHEN I WAS A GRADUATE STUDENT, I was asked to write an evaluation of the differences between two editions of a physical anthropology textbook. The editions were written six years apart, and, on first reading, the differences appeared to be enormous. As I examined them more carefully, however, I realized that the second differed from the first only in the large number of pieces of new information it contained. The apparent differences were simply more of the same thing. Thus one might conclude from a comparison of the texts that the discipline of physical anthropology had remained basically the same for six years except for a quantitative increase.

I don't know how a student might see the differences between this book and the first edition, but I am certain he would not find that these consisted solely of the addition of new pieces of information. To be sure, some of the changes are additions, particularly the reports of new discoveries, some of which carry vast implications for interpretations. Most of these are contained in Chapters 5 and 6.

But the main effort in preparing this revision has been directed toward clarifying content so that students can grasp more easily the elements of physical anthropology. I have been helped considerably in conversations and correspondence with students and faculty who have used the first edition. In response to their thoughtful suggestions I have made several major changes in the text as follows:

1. *Revision of the sequence in which the material in Chapter 6 is presented.* In the first edition the fossil evidence for recent hominid forms was considered first, and this was followed by discussions of geologically older forms. This caused unnecessary confusion, and in this edition the sequence begins with the oldest fossil forms and proceeds to the most recent.

2. *Addition of a concluding chapter.* The final chapter in this edition speculates on the future of physical anthropology. I put myself out on a limb with this discussion, for the passage of time will prove me right or wrong.

3. *Inclusion of brief summary statements itemizing the important points contained in each chapter.* These are at the end of each chapter, but the reader may wish to refer to them before and after completing the chapter.

In addition to these changes in the text, the subject matter has been clarified and amplified by the careful and painstaking effort of the artist and illustrator, Mr. James Snow. I wish to express my appreciation to him and to acknowledge his special talent in being able to translate my vague descriptions into clear and helpful illustrations.

A. J. KELSO

Boulder, Colorado
September, 1973

PART I   BACKGROUND
TO PHYSICAL
ANTHROPOLOGY

ANTHROPOLOGY IS A SCIENCE.   Its subject matter is man, and its major objective is to provide an understanding of human variability. However, since there are endless ways in which human beings differ, anthropology must by necessity focus its attention on particular kinds of variation. Thus, anthropology deals with two major ways in which human beings differ: culturally and biologically.

Culture is the basic unifying concept of anthropology. To study man without a consideration of culture is analogous to studying fishes without an understanding of the properties of water. Culture is the medium in which man resides. It presents simultaneously its own adaptive challenges and also the primary means by which the human species meets these challenges and others provided by the environment. Yet, in spite of its obvious importance, anthropologists disagree on the correct definition of culture. For example, A. L. Kroeber and Clyde Kluckhohn (1952) compiled 161 definitions of culture from the writings of anthropologists and other scientists over the eighty-year period from 1871 to 1951. That was twenty years ago, but the situation remains the same today. In four widely used introductory textbooks, all published since 1970, we may find culture defined variously as "a system of logically related ideas and values . . ." (Peacock and Kirsch, 1970), as "the basic adaptive technique of man" (CRM, 1971), as "the learned patterns of thought and behavior characteristic of a population or society" (Harris, 1971), or as "man's learned behavior, acquired by experience, as opposed to inborn genetically determined behavior" (Barnouw, 1971).

Why is it that anthropologists are unable to define culture with sufficient "accuracy"? Because defining culture is not a problem of accuracy or precision. It is a matter of convenience and usefulness. How, then, does one decide upon the most useful definition? This depends on the problem at hand.

To the physical anthropologist, it is practical to use the term *culture* to designate that which man employs in adapting to the requirements of his environment. Like other animals, man is readily able to adapt to a restricted range of environmental conditions by drawing upon nothing more than his biological resources. But unlike other animals, only man is able to use an enormously diverse range of things over and above his limited biological resources. He makes tools, builds houses, wears clothing,

1

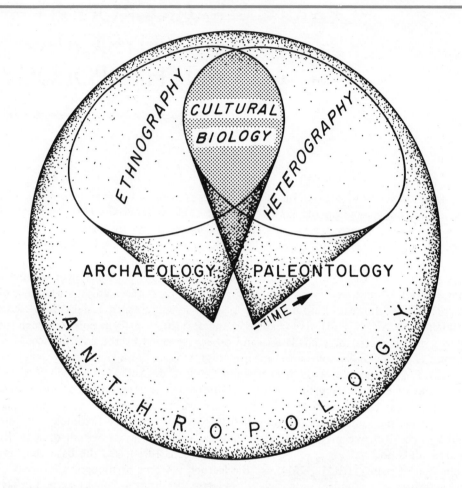

Figure 1. Anthropology and its subdivisions.

As this figure shows, cultural and biological anthropology (we will call it *physical anthropology* in recognition of a long tradition in the United States) have very similar basic structures. Their subject matters, emphases, and vocabularies are, however, clearly different and perhaps growing more so all the time. Thus cultural biology, as an area of overlap and integration, is not only in its earliest infancy; there is reason to believe it may die in the cradle. We hope not and try to show why in Chapter 11.

lives in socially organized groups, joins churches, forms corporations, establishes armies, devises legal codes, and believes in a life after death. These and many other conditions and events have enabled human beings to adjust to a wide variety of environmental circumstances. Collectively they are the conditions and events referred to by the term *culture*, and they constitute the primary subject matter of cultural anthropology.*

Since culture is man's primary means of adjusting to his environment, one might anticipate that within anthropology the most interesting and fully developed sector of the field would be the part that integrates the cultural and biological spheres. However, such is not the case; anthropology lacks the theory needed to join together these two realms. That cultural evolution has had a profound effect on man's biological evolution is basic anthropological doctrine, but precisely how this occurs remains vague and uncertain. Thus, even though it is clear that both cultural and biological factors are significant to the anthropologist, it continues to be necessary to discuss them separately. In the last chapter of this book we make an effort to formulate some integrating theories. That such formulations are so rare is almost certainly due to the very different directions that physical and cultural anthropology have taken. In doing so, each has diversified and specialized, which is but another way of saying that their interests have grown further apart. Even so, their structures have remained very similar, as may be seen in Figure 1.

Physical anthropology investigates man's biological variability, but the structure of the field is not as clearly defined and agreed upon as is the structure of cultural anthropology. Students in an introductory course are likely to get the impression that physical anthropology is either hopelessly complex or distressingly disorganized. Often in one semester they move through mammalian-primate-human morphology, fossil ancestors of man and the primates, evolutionary mechanisms, genetics, contemporary human biological variation, the classification of human variations, the measurement of man, growth, physiological adaptation, constitution, and applied physical anthropology. The only feature common to all of these is the fact that each is concerned, at least in part, with man. Beyond this the field is structurally undifferentiated.

There are several useful ways to order physical anthropology, but the one used in this book divides the field along the same dimensions (i.e., time and space) that provide the basis for the subdivisions of cultural anthropology (see Figure 1). *Human paleontology* investigates variability among man's ancestors; hence its primary data are obtained from fossils. This material is discussed in Part II. *Human heterography* investigates biological variation among living populations. It would be in some ways more logical to refer to this part of physical anthropology as human biography, but because of the already well-established use of the word *biography*, *heterography* will be used here. This subject is considered in Part III.

Before dealing with human paleontology and heterography, some essential preliminary topics must be considered. These constitute Part I, and they are: 1) a history of physical anthropology, 2) man's place in nature, and 3) some background in genetics.

---

* *Archaeology* investigates the forms of cultural variability along the dimension of time; *ethnography* investigates them among contemporary peoples, and thus primarily along the dimension of space.

REFERENCES AND SUGGESTIONS FOR ADDITIONAL READING

BARNOUW, V.
  1971 *An introduction to anthropology: Ethnology.* Homewood, Ill.: Dorsey.
Communications Research Machines (CRM), Inc.
  1971 *Anthropology today.* Del Mar, Calif.: CRM.
HARRIS, M.
  1971 *Culture, man, and nature.* New York: Thomas Y. Crowell.
KELSO, A. J.
  1966 The subdivisions of physical anthropology. *Current Anthropology* 7:315–319.
KROEBER, A. L., AND CLYDE KLUCKHOHN
  1952 Culture: A critical review of concepts and definitions. *Papers of the Peabody Museum of American Archaeology and Ethnology* 47.
PEACOCK, J. L., AND A. THOMAS KIRSCH
  1970 *The human direction.* New York: Appleton-Century-Crofts.
SPUHLER, J. N.
  1959 Somatic paths to culture. *Human Biology* 31:1–13.
WASHBURN, S. L.
  1953 The strategy of physical anthropology. In *Anthropology today: An encyclopedic inventory*, ed. A. L. Kroeber, pp. 714–727. Chicago: University of Chicago Press.

1 History of Physical Anthropology

INTRODUCTION

The history of physical anthropology is the history of man's concern with problems of human evolution and human variation. Insofar as these general problems indicate an interest in man's origin and development, they are problems that have interested man from his beginning. The following is directed at the development of our present attitudes about the problems of human evolution and human variation within the general context of scientific inquiry.

ORIGINS (1600–1859)

Before the publication of *The Origin of Species* in 1859, physical anthropology had not yet emerged as a separate, self-conscious, independent discipline. There was, however, a great deal of concern with the problems that were ultimately to form the central questions of the field, and many attitudes toward these problems were firmly held. These attitudes were based on the following: the Old Testament story of Creation, the presumption that the living animals always were and always will continue to be as they are, the belief that "life" had a special spiritual or unknowable quality, the reckoning of the earth's antiquity in terms of a few thousand years, and an all-pervasive conceptualization of the real world in terms of the Platonic ideal types (Mayr, 1959).

There were, of course, many other elements of the ideology of the times preceding Darwin that influenced the emergence and acceptability of an evolutionary theory. An evaluation of those listed above, however, is helpful in indicating the ideological context of the period from 1600 to 1850. While in many ways these attitudes seem to dominate this period, there were many discoveries made and new understandings reached during this same time that ultimately placed the dominant attitudes in a position of secondary importance. Perhaps the most far-reaching of the new understandings in terms of influence on modern science was the emergence of empiricism over a purely rationalistic approach to the understanding of problems arising out of our experience with the real world.

5

Rationalism and Empiricism

The rationalistic approach characterized the writing and thinking of many of the classical Graeco-Roman scholars and continued to exert much influence on thoughtful men throughout the seventeenth century. The movement was based particularly on the writings of Aristotle and is best represented in the work of Abelard, Thomas Aquinas, the scholastics of the thirteenth and fourteenth centuries, and later by Leibnitz and Descartes. The essential feature of the position taken by rationalists is that truths about the problems of man's experience can be reached by the power of reasoning alone. Thus, if one begins with self-evident premises, he might be able to string together a complete philosophical system of true propositions by correctly applying the rules of logic. Therefore, the rationalists regarded the checking of their conclusions against naturalistic observation as unnecessary.

As long as theological considerations remained the dominant concern, rationalists could draw upon the self-evident truths of revelation to arrive at proofs of theological dogma. In the thirteenth century, however, there began to appear elements which slowly brought about the decline of rationalism. Scholasticism, an extreme form of the rationalist approach that flourished in the thirteenth century, generated a revival of interest in the writings of the classical Greek and Roman scholars and directed attention to the problem of harmonizing the events of this world with those of the next.

A growing interest in the affairs of this world, the development of mathematics, and the secularization of scholarship within a growing middle class are among the most important factors that led to empiricism. The empiricist is not fundamentally opposed to the rationalist, but rather insists on adding to correct reasoning the provision of empirical observation, or, in short, the testing of the correctness of the reasoning process by recourse to sense experience. This empirical approach was exemplified in the work of Galileo, Boyle, Bacon, and, most notably, Newton. It can be recognized as the basis of exploration in modern science.

Thus, the emergence of the empiricist approach provided a new means by which man could come to understand nature and his part in it. However, even more significant than this was the realization that the empirical approach actually worked, that is, that it did in fact make it possible to predict with great precision the occurrence of events over which man exerted no direct control and which were previously thought to be capricious and undetermined. Such striking results, originally made in astronomy and later in physics, stimulated similar inquiries in other aspects of our experience with the real world. One area affected by this stimulus was the study of life—the science of biology.

Linnaeus and the Classification of the Varieties of Life

There are several landmarks in the history of biology during the seventeenth and eighteenth centuries that represent the products of herculean effort. One of the most notable of these serves as a reasonable beginning point in a discussion of the history of physical anthropology, and that is the work of Carolus Linnaeus (1707–1778), who set out to achieve no less than a classification of all living things. The importance of this work on the history of biology would be difficult to overemphasize; it is to biology what the periodic chart of elements is to physics and chemistry. Now having asserted that Linnaeus's work was of fundamental importance, how did it affect the development of biology? On one level his influence is obvious: he set forth rules for classifying the forms of life that remain the basic rules of taxonomy today. Moreover, he applied the rules to obtain a comprehensive classification which he believed reflected the rational plan of creation, and this had a more subtle, though perhaps more significant, effect. Thus in a sense Linnaeus was a theologian. He believed that the varieties of life were created by God, that they are now what they have always been, and therefore that a classification of the varieties would lead to a better knowledge of the Creator's plan.

In viewing the array of life forms as the fixed and immutable products of creation, Linnaeus established the antithesis that led eventually to the evolutionary synthesis. Once the rigid structure of the classification was established, some peculiar and unexpected patterns made it difficult to discern the anticipated rational order. For example, at some points in the classification there were many kinds of organisms that differed only slightly from one another, whereas at other points there were groups of organisms separated by wide gaps from any others in the classification. Moreover, remains had been found in the earth's strata of organisms that had no living representatives. How could these inconsistencies be explained? One answer is God, but if so, then it appears that God created some forms of life and then obliterated them, and the anticipated reflection of the Creator's plan was not at all obvious from the classification. In this way, Linnaeus's work raised issues that gradually were formulated into questions to which answers were eventually offered. One such answer was evolution, which stated that groups of organisms are similar because they have descended from a common ancestor. This helped to clarify how varieties alive today could be different from those that lived in the past. However, the evolutionary "answer" could be thought of only as speculative, for no one was able to explain satisfactorily how such differences could have come about. This is the problem Darwin attacked, and it will be considered in detail later on in this chapter.

Selecting Linnaeus's work to begin a history of physical anthropology is largely a matter of convenience, for in the history of biology, he represents but one manifestation of the increasing interest and the rapid growth that can be detected clearly from the beginning of the seventeenth century. Between 1600 and the publication of *The Origin of Species* in 1859, an understanding of life was abetted by the rapid accumulation of data, its systematization into classifications, the development of laboratory instruments, and the validation of basic theories. To be more specific, consider the following important events: William Harvey (1578–1657) presented evidence that the blood circulates; John Ray (1627–1705) completed a monumental series of detailed descriptions of the various forms of life; Georges Louis Leclerc, Comte de Buffon (1707–1788), published his forty-four-volume *Natural History;*

Figure 1–1. Carolus Linnaeus (1707–1778). (Courtesy of the American Museum of Natural History)

Figure 1–2. Johann Friedrich Blumenbach (1752–1840). (Courtesy of the New York Academy of Medicine)

and the microscope was applied to the investigation of microanatomy, which led to an improved understanding of tissues and eventually to the cell theory.

Blumenbach and the Classification of the Varieties of Man

These and many other developments have had a lasting effect on biology. Likewise, one may see one specific consequence of the growing interest in description and classification that had a particularly important bearing on physical anthropology: the classification of man's biological variation. The problem of racial classification of man may be seen partly as the by-product of this interest in classification and partly as the by-product of a controversy over the origin of the varieties of man. One side of this controversy consisted of the view that all men share a common origin (*monogenesis*); opposed to this was the belief that the varieties of man had separate origins (*polygenesis*).

To Europeans the controversy was particularly vexing since it was not possible to take either stand without approaching or committing heresy. If one accepted monogenesis, a single act of creation, then how are the different races of men to be regarded? If one holds to polygenesis, then what is to be made of the clear account of creation as told in the Bible? Perhaps a proper classification would resolve the difficulty. The most notable and lasting of the early attempts to classify man was made by Johann F. Blumenbach (1752–1840), who classified man's variations into five groups: negroid (Ethiopian) or black, mongoloid or yellow, caucasoid or white, American Indian or red, and Malayan or brown. Then, as now, the classification appeared reasonably to represent the distribution of variation in the human species.

To be sure, there were those who disagreed with Blumenbach, but their differences were not fundamental. Everyone agreed that mankind was divisible into types, that the types were real, though variable, and that identifying them properly was of great importance. Where differences existed, they were based merely on the accuracy of Blumenbach's classification. For example, Anders Retzius (1796–1860) of Sweden indicated that Blumenbach's classification was inadequate, for within the races there was far too much variability, particularly in head form, which, he claimed, should not be ignored. He invented the cephalic index as a way of expressing head form numerically (see Chapter 7). Likewise, as Darwin (1871) pointed out, "There is the greatest possible diversity among capable judges whether [man] should be classed as a single species or race, or as two (Virey), as three (Jacquinot), as four (Kant), five (Blumenbach), six (Buffon), seven (Hunter), eight (Agassiz), eleven (Pickering), fifteen (Bory St. Vincent), sixteen (Desmoulins), twenty-two (Morton), sixty (Crawfurd), or as sixty-three, according to Burke."* But in most important respects these differences are trivial in comparison with the broad area of agreement on the subject of race. One should keep clearly in mind that Blumenbach and the others were, like Linnaeus, attempting to reflect a natural order; moreover, they were trying to do this long before an understanding of evolution, and thus the classifications consisted of groupings of mankind that: 1) were presumed largely to be fixed, unchanging, and eternal, 2) were based on the assumption that one race differs from another by the possession of a particular cluster of identifying attributes, 3) implied that the individual members of a race, while imperfect representations of the racial type, could be recognized as belonging to one or another by the possession of these attributes, and 4) drew the attention of early anthropologists to the problems of ascertaining and describing these races in as complete a manner as possible.

Possessing these implications, racial classifications are irreconcilable with an evolutionary approach. We might expect, then, that the approach would have been abandoned soon after Darwin published *The Origin of Species*. However, the old traditional view of race is still common among modern anthropologists, reconciled apparently by compartmentalization; when on the subject of race, they lapse into typological thinking (see Mayr, 1959, 1963), but on the subject of genetics and evolution they think in terms of processes, mechanisms, and the dynamics of population changes. Oddly, the only sign of progress is a growing confusion over some basic issues (Kelso, 1969). We will return to the subject presently, but first we will need to understand some of the implications of natural selection and genetics.

Other Advances in Science

Substantial refinements in science outside of biology were also paving the way for imminent advances in areas of central importance to physical anthropology. Among

---

* From Charles Darwin, *The Descent of Man* (1871), quoted in Earl W. Count, ed., *This Is Race: An Anthology Selected from the International Literature on the Races of Man* (New York: Henry Schuman, 1950), p. 138.

the most significant of the new discoveries were those being made by early geologists, paleontologists, and archaeologists. Geologists were beginning to find convincing evidence that the antiquity of the earth was not to be measured in a few thousands of years, but rather that the earth must have taken millions of years to form. That is, by observing the rate at which geological phenomena were going on at the present time and assuming that present rates are the same as those in the past (*uniformitarianism*), a geologist could conclude that it must have taken millions of years for the earth's crust to accumulate and form its present structure.

Early paleontologists were discovering fossil bones of animals very different from the ones living in the same zones today. Evidence of marine life and strange-looking large mammals and reptiles was found in fossilized form in Europe. In addition, the fauna of one layer of rocks was often quite different from that in adjacent layers. At the same time, archaeologists were finding evidence that Europe was once occupied by people whose way of life differed distinctively from that of modern man.

The evidence obtained in the times before Darwin from geology, paleontology, and archaeology can be seen to have made two major contributions: 1) the demonstration of the fact of great antiquity for the earth and for the life that occupies it, and 2) the presentation of conclusive evidence for earlier faunal and cultural variants that differed not only from modern forms in the same area, but also from forms known anywhere else in the world.

Taken as a totality, these advances can be seen as steps that made possible the formulation of new questions. Why are there so many species of one kind in Linnaeus's classification, whereas other genera have so few? Why do living forms seem to cluster in their similarities at some points in the classification, yet show sharp discontinuities at other points? How did the variation observed within modern species come about? More particularly, how and when did racial variation arise in the human species? What are the relationships between the fossil forms and modern fauna? Long before Darwin, there were many proposed answers which attempted to shed light on one or more of these questions. There were, of course, obvious theological answers; any of these questions can be answered by claiming God's will. There were also many proposals suggesting that modern species are a consequence of evolution. That is, many authors long before Darwin saw the possibility of explaining many of these problems by calling upon an evolutionary explanation that claimed that today's fauna comprises the descendants of the fossil forms, and thus is the product of a long line of modifications. The deficiency of these early explanations was their inability to explain how it was that the modern forms differed from the evolutionary antecedents. What caused them to evolve? Anthropologists were particularly interested in the question as it pertained to human races. Darwin's work provided an answer.

DARWIN AND THE ORIGIN OF SPECIES

Consider for a moment that you have just been asked the question: How do species originate? What would your answer be, and how would you formulate it? One way to begin is to determine just exactly what the question means. It could mean, for example, that the questioner wishes to know how the first species came into existence; this is unlikely, however, for, if he were concerned with that, he would be more likely to ask about the origin of life. Thus, the question must mean something else—there are thousands of species in existence today and thousands more that existed in the past. What processes have been in operation that have, by their action, caused these species to appear? This is essentially the question which Darwin attempted to answer.

The Apparent Paradox

Darwin arrived at an answer to this question only after confronting a seemingly paradoxical situation which came to his attention through many years of careful study and observation. On the one hand, Darwin observed that all living organisms attempted to perpetuate their kind by means of a variety of reproductive processes, and that species in nature tended to produce many more offspring than necessary to maintain their numbers. Yet, on the other hand, Darwin observed that the actual numbers in terms of population for a particular species remained relatively constant over time. How can this contradiction be reconciled? In fact, the situation is relatively simple and obvious; many of the offspring produced by each generation simply do not survive. One need only go one step further and propose that there is a consistent difference between the offspring that survive and those that do not. A simple illustration may help: Suppose that a particular species of moth lives in an environment where dark individuals are less conspicuous than light ones, and thus less susceptible to attack from their natural predators. The environment acts as a selector, and thereby reduces the contribution of the lighter-colored moths to the next generation; a greater proportion of the lighter moths are caught and killed by predators before the completion of their reproductive life than is true of the darker variants. The darker forms therefore produce more offspring in the next generation than the lighter moths.

Natural Selection and Reproductive Isolation

Thus, the natural circumstances of the environment can be seen to operate in a selective way, reducing in number the poorer-adapted variants of species while increasing the proportion of the better-adapted variants. Darwin called this process *natural selection*. The idea of natural selection enables one to understand in a more profound way how a species can change over a period of time, but it is not immediately obvious how it relates to Darwin's primary concern with the origin of species. To comprehend this relationship one must consider another phenomenon, *reproductive isolation*, a situation in which one group of organisms either cannot or does not interbreed with another. Under normal circumstances reproductive isolation prevails between the members of any two species. Occasionally, one species becomes divided into two or more reproductively isolated subspecies. This might take place for any number of reasons. The separation may be abrupt and immediate—for example, as a result of an earthquake or a torrential rainfall. Such natural disasters as these often result in the subdivision of many of the species living in the affected areas. Or isolation may result from events that take a long time to occur in an environment, such as a drought, or a gradual reduction in the mean annual temperature, or the invasion of an area by a new species. With the appearance of man, many "artificial," or cultural, causes for reproductive isolation came into play. Cultural events affect not only man but other organisms as well (for example, the building of a road or the burning of a field can upset the previous ecological balance and result in reproductive isolation among members of a species formerly able to interbreed). Whatever the cause, it is the results that are important. A group of organisms formerly consisting of one interbreeding unit is divided into at least two such units.

Once a species becomes subdivided into reproductive isolates, natural selection can cause these isolates to become progressively dissimilar. Since no two environments are identical, the differences that distinguish one from another, no matter how subtle, can be expected to be reflected in the adaptive requirements of the organisms that live within them. The final step is a relatively simple one. As the divergence continues, eventually the resulting forms become sufficiently dissimilar to be regarded as separate species. Thus, the description of the way in which one ancestral species can, by means of selection and reproductive isolation, give rise to two new species has answered the original question: How do species originate?

It is difficult to overemphasize the significance and impact of natural selection on the development of biology. The earlier concept—that species and races were essentially unchanging entities—had to be replaced by a view that emphasized continuous change and adaptation, and that regarded contemporary species as the products of a long succession of alterations brought about by natural selection operating on isolated units. In addition to this fundamental change in point of view, a number of more specific consequences also followed, among them the beginning of a deliberate search for fossil ancestors of modern forms, the focusing of attention on the processes of inheritance whereby one generation passes an inborn adaptive potential to the next generation, and the emergence of an entirely new set of interesting problems. These new concepts were not, of course, instantaneously accepted. Many scientists and most laymen rejected the notions of evolution and natural selection, particularly when applied to man. The strongest opposition to "Darwinism" came over the problem of whether or not man had evolved from some lower form.

While the theory of evolution was being developed and debated, anthropology, as a separate, distinct, and self-conscious discipline, began to make its appearance. The evolutionary view was an important part of the early development of scientific anthropology, although more so in cultural than in physical anthropology. There were many writers during the last half of the nineteenth century and in the early part of the twentieth century who applied the processes of evolution to the problem of understanding cultural growth, development, and variation. In physical anthropology the issue of race continued to dominate. Identifying the ways that men differ bio-

Figure 1–3. Charles Darwin (1809–1882). (By permission of the Trustees of the British Museum, Natural History)

Figure 1–4. Gregor Mendel (1822–1884). (Courtesy of the New York Academy of Medicine)

logically, describing these differences, and classifying them by race continued as the major but, for the first time, not the exclusive activity. To resolve the controversy over human evolution required evidence, specifically fossil evidence. Thus the immediate effect of Darwin's work on physical anthropology was to stimulate a deliberate search for fossils of man's ancestors, or, in other words, the differentiation of physical anthropology into heterography *and* paleontology. From this point on, physical anthropology has two histories. We will deal in detail with fossil man in Chapter 6. But what about race? What happened? Did the old view remain completely unchanged? Not completely, but to understand how it changed requires some knowledge of the history of genetics.

GENETICS: A THEORY OF INHERITANCE

One way of regarding natural selection, as Darwin had presented it, was to view it as a mechanism that brought about changes of improved adaptation from one generation to the next. Or, evolution can be defined as a selective accumulation of generational changes. This view suggests one obvious and particularly fruitful way of studying evolutionary change, and that is by determining and analyzing the manner in which one generation passes its characteristics on to the next generation. The modern science of genetics was not known to Darwin, although the work that laid the foundation for it was being done during his lifetime by an Austrian monk, Gregor Mendel. There were, indeed, a number of theories of inheritance available; among them the most prominent were the blending theory of inheritance and—the one most generally accepted by the scientific community of the time—the theory of the inheritance of acquired characteristics. The *blending theory* was essentially a simple, "commonsense" explanation of inheritance, which proposed that offspring were a blend of their parents in their characteristics. There is both evidence to support this view and data that are contrary or that constitute exceptions to it. On the one hand, one is usually able to draw on several instances among his own acquaintances in which the children of a couple tend to be an intermediate "blend" of the parents. On the other hand, there are many exceptions—instances in which a child is like one parent and not like the other, and many cases in which the child is unlike either parent in many characteristics. Although this theory has never been formulated in a systematic way and tested empirically, it is surprisingly common in our society today—to the extent that the multitudinous exceptions are regarded as *throwbacks, atavisms,* or *reversions.* These are all essentially synonymous terms implying that the person in question displays the characteristics of an ancient ancestor. Admittedly, this is no explanation, and the theory has never been taken seriously in modern science. It simply breaks down under the sheer weight of contrary evidence.

The theory of the inheritance of acquired characteristics proposes that the experiences an organism has during its lifetime shape its hereditary material in such a way that the offspring it produces are better able to cope with the same kind of experiences during their lifetime. It is usually associated with J. B. P. A. Lamarck, who did indeed put the theory explicitly in writing, but in fact only slightly modified versions of it had been implicit in the works of many scholars for centuries. This view has been argued for over a hundred years and, based on several recent experiments in molecular biology, is returning to popularity in modified form. The view accepted by Darwin implied that an organism's way of living would cause it to produce offspring better able to lead that way of life. Thus a blacksmith produces sons better able to become blacksmiths. The ancestors of giraffes, for generations stretching their necks to get to the nutritious, succulent leaves at the treetops, gradually produced the giraffe.

One of the most troublesome problems associated with the theory of the inheritance of acquired characteristics stems from the fact that the theory requires a mechanical transfer of the effects of the environment to the genetic material that is passed on from one generation to the next. That is, if the way of life that an individual leads modifies the heritable material, how does this modification take place? This question has never been satisfactorily answered, but one of the most notable attempts to do so was made by Darwin. He proposed the theory of *pangenesis*, which postulates the presence of particles called gemmules in all of the cells of the body which are modified or shaped by the way of life of the organisms. These gemmules then were believed to enter the circulatory system and eventually to combine with other particles present in reproductive cells and modify the nature of these cells accordingly. In effect, what this theory does is to recognize a logical necessity of the theory of the inheritance of acquired characteristics. There is, however, no empirical evidence to support the existence of such gemmules, and the theory of pangenesis has been discarded. For this reason biology has long looked with circumspection upon the theory of the inheritance of acquired characteristics. This is particularly the case in Western Europe and the United States. In recent years it enjoyed popularity in the Soviet Union, though in the past decade this has declined. Ironically, during the same period science has witnessed a growing body of information that points more and more clearly to the conclusion that the life experiences of an organism may indeed modify that organism's genetic material. For example, recent experiments indicate that bacteria deficient in a particular gene will appropriate the gene when it is available in an invading virus. Furthermore, the bacteria-appropriated-virus-gene is apparently capable of being transmitted to the bacterium's daughter cells.

Learning transfer experiments have been more spectacular, though not conclusive from the point of view of genetics. Basically these involve the transfer of brain extracts from animals trained to perform certain tasks to untrained animals, resulting usually in the latter being better able to perform the task. These experiments have been repeated on animals as diverse as flatworms, mice, rats, and fish. The improvement in performance, however, is of short duration, and there is no conclusive evidence that it is genetically transmitted to offspring. Perhaps the only conclusion one may draw is that there is no necessary incompatibility between a theory of the inheritance of acquired characteristics and modern Mendelian genetics.

The theory of inheritance which forms the basis of modern views is the particulate theory, and, as mentioned earlier, the work that led to it was done during Darwin's lifetime but went unnoticed until the beginning of the twentieth century. The *particulate theory* of inheritance proposes that the inherited characteristics of one generation are transmitted to the next by means of particles (eventually called genes) and that these particles are present in pairs in individuals but present singly within sex cells. Thus any individual will receive half of his total number of genes from one parent and half from the other parent.

MENDEL AND THE PARTICULATE THEORY

The experimental work that pointed to the particulate theory is interesting and instructive. It was carried out by Gregor Mendel in the 1860s. His work started simply enough; Mendel kept a vegetable garden, and in it, among other things, he grew some peas. In caring for his plants he observed that the peas differed from one another in several characteristics, such as length and color of the stem, seed-coat color, shape of pod and seed, etc. He decided to investigate generational differences in some of these traits and proceeded to interbreed the plants. In all, he experimented with seven characters, each having but two modes of expression (see Table 1–1).

Table 1–1   Mendel's Initial Crosses and Resulting Hybrids

CHARACTERS	RESULT IN HYBRIDS (F_1 GENERATION)
1. Shape of seed wrinkled × round	all round
2. Endosperm color yellow × green	all yellow
3. Seed-coat color gray × white	all gray
4. Pod shape smooth × constricted	all smooth
5. Pod color green × yellow	all green
6. Position of blossoms axial × terminal	all axial
7. Length of stem long × short	all long

The evidence presented by the hybrid generation was in itself convincing evidence against the blending theory of inheritance, but more important to us is the conclusion Mendel reached concerning the relationship between the two modes of expression for each character. Since one and only one appeared in the hybrids (the F_1 generation), Mendel could distinguish the form that did appear as *dominant* and the one that did not as *recessive*. Had this been the end of his work, Mendel's contribution would have been considered substantial, but he continued his experiments.

Mendel took the hybrids that resulted from the first crossing and interbred them. His results are summarized in Table 1–2.

Such a splendid array of consistency in the results must have astounded Mendel. The appearance of the dominant varieties was no great surprise after the results of the first cross, but the consistent reappearance of the recessive forms could mean only one thing: the quality that determined the recessive character was present even though it was not expressed in the F_1 generation.

Table 1–2   Results of Crosses in the F_1 Generation

F_1 CROSSES	APPROXIMATE RATIOS IN F_2 HYBRIDS
1. round × round	3 round to 1 wrinkled
2. yellow × yellow	3 yellow to 1 green
3. gray × gray	3 gray to 1 white
4. smooth × smooth	3 smooth to 1 constricted
5. green × green	3 green to 1 yellow
6. axial × axial	3 axial to 1 terminal
7. long × long	3 long to 1 short

From these experiments Mendel concluded: 1) the inherited capabilities of one generation are passed on to the next by means of discrete particles that retain their potential effect even though their presence is not indicated by the appearance of the character; 2) that these particles are obtained in pairs, one from each parent, and passed on singly to the next generation. This is called Mendel's first law of inheritance (see Table 1–3).

Table 1–3   Mendel's First Law of Inheritance

First generation "pure" bred crosses (paired units)	Round × wrinkled (RR) (rr)			
Second generation (F_1) paired units inherited singly	Round Rr	Round Rr	Round Rr	Round Rr
Third generation (F_2) paired units inherited singly	Round RR	Round Rr	Round rR	Wrinkled rr

Mendel added another step to his investigation when he decided to examine pairs of characteristics—to cross plants dominant for two traits (for example, round seeds and yellow endosperm) with plants recessive for the same traits (wrinkled and green). In the F_1 generation Mendel observed that all of the hybrids, as expected, were round and yellow, but the interesting question was, What happens to the particles (genes) when the F_1 hybrids are crossed? Do the genes for seed shape and endosperm color stay together from one generation to the next, or do they assort independently of one another? Table 1–4 shows the results. From this experiment he concluded that different hereditary determiners assort independently in the process of inheritance. This is Mendel's second law.

As indicated earlier, even though the evolutionary view focused attention on the hereditary process, the significance of Mendel's work went unrecognized for over

---

Table 1–4   Summary of Mendel's Experiment Using Pairs of Characteristics

---

GENERATION

Parental	Round-Yellow RRYY		×	Wrinkled-Green rryy	
F₁	Round-Yellow RrYy		×	Round-Yellow RrYy	
F₂	9 Round-Yellow RRYY (1) RRYy (2) RrYY (2) RrYy (4)	3 Round-Green RRyy (1) Rryy (2)		3 Wrinkled-Yellow rrYY (1) rrYy (2)	1 Wrinkled-Green rryy (1)

---

thirty years, until 1900, when it was rediscovered. Mendel's work provides the foundation of the study of *genetics*, that aspect of modern science concerned with explaining and understanding how similarities and differences due to hereditary factors arise among individuals. In recent years, genetics has progressed rapidly and has diversified into many subdisciplines, becoming one of the most provocative and exciting areas in modern science. Physical anthropology has drawn heavily from genetics in recent years, particularly from population genetics, a branch of the science concerned with the genetic composition of breeding populations and the factors which cause these compositions to change. Population genetics will be discussed in some detail in Chapter 3.

THE PROBLEM OF VARIABILITY

Natural selection raised the problem of variability; the particulate theory of inheritance solved it in part. Where did variability come from? How was it sustained?

Natural selection could be seen as a formative and creative process that could shape the variation of lines of descent within groups over a period of time in the direction of improved adaptation. Indeed natural selection can be seen as a mechanism that tends to weed out the less-well-adapted range of variation of each generation while favoring the better-adapted. It would seem that a process such as natural selection would eventually lead to uniformity among the members of a particular species. Yet, when one looks around today, after a billion or more years of evolution, an enormous range of variations can be seen, both within and between species. Thus, if we accept the view that living forms reached their present condition by evolution from earlier forms by means of natural selection, then how did such variation arise? Darwin did not know; no one knew. However, Mendel's observations implied an understanding of a related problem: the particulate theory of inheritance clearly implied that, once various genes are present, the generational mechanics specified by the laws of inheritance provided enormous potential for maintaining the variability.* Thus the particulate theory explains two things: 1) the process of biological inheritance, and 2) how variability, once present, can be maintained. Where did the genetic variability come from? The answer to this question is mutation, that is, a change in the material of inheritance. A reasonably clear understanding of this did not come about until several years after Darwin's death.

An appreciation of the significance of mutation depended ultimately on the presence of four other understandings: 1) the evolutionary view that claimed that life changed by modification through natural selection (this was provided by the work of Darwin); 2) the knowledge that heredity in nature was controlled by particles (this was shown in the work of Mendel); 3) the observation that traits controlled by these particles could and did change abruptly from one generation to the next (this was made known by the experiments of a Dutch botanist, Hugo De Vries); and 4) an explanation as to how the particles of heredity could change— an explanation for the occurrence of mutations. It is clear now that several factors can generate new variability; the earliest cause of mutation to be identified was X-radiation.

The first three of these theories were known in 1900, but initially the significance of mutations and their relationships to Mendel's work and to the problem of explaining variation in the context of evolution was not clear. At first it appeared that the discovery of mutations negated the validity of natural selection. That is, if mutations were seen as abrupt changes between one generation and the next, then it appeared that evolution proceeded by these sudden "spontaneous" steps rather than by means of the gradual adaptive changes implicit in natural selection. This is where the work of Mendel was all-important in clarifying the point that there was no contradiction between the two factors. Mendel's work showed how abrupt qualitative changes between generations could occur naturally and regularly and along predictable lines. Thus, Mendel's experiments were enough to account for differences between one generation and the next, but where did *new* variation come from? With a particulate view of the process of heredity, one had only a short step to take to postulate that new variation could come about as a consequence of the alteration of the structure

---

* Two characters combine to form four varieties (see Table 1–4). Each additional character increases the potential varieties by a power of 2. Thus three characters can combine to form 8 varieties $[(2)^3]$, 4 produce 16 $[(2)^4]$, and so forth. Even the simplest organisms have hundreds of genes.

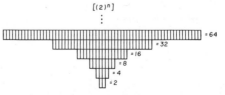

Rapid rate of increase expected under a geometric progression.

of genes, the particles of inheritance. This is, in fact, a reasonable definition of *mutation* in modern genetics—a change in the structure of a gene.

However, a problem is posed as this understanding is reached: What causes the structure of a gene to change? This pushes the problem back; if mutations give rise to new forms of a trait, then what is responsible for mutations? There was no simple answer to this question; it took over twenty-five years after the rediscovery of Mendel's work to obtain the necessary information.

During this time the common fruit fly became an important experimental animal in the study of genetics, and a large amount of information about the genetics of this lowly animal accumulated. One consistent observation on the fruit fly was the regular occurrence of a small proportion of mutant varieties in each generation no matter what the experiment, no matter how stringent the controls. These mutants interested H. J. Muller, who was concerned with the problem of the cause of mutation. He decided to see if he could affect the rate at which these mutant varieties occurred by varying environmental features. With this in mind, he proceeded to subject the fruit flies to a series of environmental changes. He introduced them to varied intensities of light and qualities of motion, to drugs and alcohol; in his words, the flies were "treated with everything except affection from generation to generation." The result was always the same; the next generation showed the same regular but small proportion of mutant varieties. Eventually he experimented with variations in the intensities of X-radiation, and the results were most interesting; the generation of flies produced from the irradiated sample showed a substantial increase in the proportion of mutants. Furthermore, the relationship between the intensity of exposure to X-radiation and the proportion of mutants was highly correlated. That is, the greater the exposure, the more frequently the mutants occurred in the next generation. Thus, at least one answer to the question of the origin of mutations could be given: some were caused by radiation. In retrospect this makes sense, since all living organisms are continually subjected to small but regular doses of radiation. Thus, radiation could be seen not merely as a factor that could increase the ever-present low rate of mutation, it further could be regarded as the cause of that low rate as well.

Since Muller's discovery, a number of other mutagenic agents have been identified; these include specific chemical substances, such as caffeine and phenol, as well as other sources of high-energy radiation. Likewise, a few substances that reduce mutation rates have been identified. In general, the importance of X-radiation as a source of mutation has faded (Crow, 1959) to some degree as more factors have been identified. Though clearly some progress has been made, we remain today largely ignorant of the major causes of mutation, and the situation has become further complicated by the realization that some mutations themselves can influence the rates at which other genes mutate.

NATURAL SELECTION, GENETICS, AND THE NEW PHYSICAL ANTHROPOLOGY

For those pursuing the identification, description, and classification of races, the implications of natural selection and genetics were clear. They lead to the same conclusion: races are continually undergoing change as human beings adapt to the shifting requirements of survival. Thus races may be alike because they have adapted to similar environmental conditions; they may be dissimilar because of different adaptive circumstances. A racial classification is therefore a reflection of a temporary distribution of man's variability. Such a classification has no clear meaning, no obvious implications. As this realization grew, two alternatives emerged; one was simply to abandon the notion of race and get on with other activities. The second alternative was to integrate racial analysis with the implications of selection and genetics. The latter option was by far the more popular. But how was it to be achieved? Simply by using only traits which were not influenced by selection as the bases for racial classifications; these traits became known as nonadaptive traits.

The reasoning is that if selection modifies the expression of genetic variability, then the modified traits cannot be relied upon in identifying and classifying races. But perhaps, not all traits are modified by selection, and if they are not, such nonadaptive traits could be regarded as extremely useful tags in identifying racial affiliation.

The standard body measurements that had been used for a long time were inadequate. Traits such as stature, weight, head length, arm length, etc., are all measures of overall body size, which is readily modified by the environment through diet, infection, and trauma. Thus it was easy to suspect the influence of natural selection. There was, however, a more promising technique among those traditionally used by physical anthropologists; namely, the practice of combining two or more measurements into ratios which, when converted to percentages, are known as indexes. For example the ratio of nasal breadth/nasal length multiplied by 100 is the nasal index; the ratio of head breadth/head length multiplied by 100 is the cephalic index.

Indexes are independent of overall body size; a person with a large head could have the same cephalic index as one with a small head. At first, then, indexes appeared to be ideal for racial analysis since they were believed to be nonadaptive traits. But early in this century Franz Boas (1912) conducted a study on Polish immigrants to the United States which suggested strongly that the cephalic index is, in fact, influenced by the environment. This and subsequent studies served not only to cast doubt on all indexes, but on the whole notion of nonadaptive traits as well.

The traditional concept of race was beginning to show more than merely endearing signs of age. On close inspection of its structure one could see dangerous cracks in the foundation. What was to be done? Plenty. All over the world people were rapidly disappearing. They were dying out because they lacked the strength to withstand either the physical force of colonizing peoples or the diseases they introduced. Likewise many peoples were losing their distinctiveness as a result of interbreeding. In any case, to the physical anthropologist the result was the same; valuable information on man's biological variability was rapidly disappearing and needed to be recorded and preserved at all cost.

Dominated by this urgency, the first few decades of this century consisted of what might be termed salvage physical anthropology. From all over the world living people as well as skeletal remains unearthed by archaeologists were measured with meticulous care, and the results were recorded and published. Cultural anthropologists were doing much the same and for exactly the same reasons. Customs, beliefs, myths, legends, etc., were also dying out rapidly. Both physical and cultural anthropologists were motivated by a philosophy which can be characterized as "collect the data now, think about it later." The result was a rapid accumulation of descriptive information.

Salvage physical anthropology flourished during the 1920s and 1930s. During the period two events took place that were to have far-reaching though decidedly different effects on physical anthropology. One was the beginning of systematic observations on the behavior of man's closest relatives, the *Primates*. This event bears very little importance to the issue of race, so we will simply note its occurrence here and return again to the subject in Chapter 2.

The other event bears directly on race, though it has taken a long time to fully appreciate its significance. It was itself an event that took some time to happen, the gradual realization of the importance of inherited characteristics to the problems of physical anthropology. Interest began to grow as more information accumulated on the blood groups, particularly the ABO blood groups. This is a subject which again we will deal with in more detail later on; our interest at this point is in identifying the early effect on physical anthropology. Gradually the blood groups began to appear as the ideal answer to a prayer for nonadaptive traits. They appeared, in other words, as the perfect bases for answering the long-standing problems of race. Consider their attributes; the blood groups are: 1) constant throughout life, 2) strictly inherited, 3) readily determined, 4) easy to analyze in numerical form, and 5) varied in the rates at which they occur (that is, their frequencies) from one place to another (Boyd, 1950). In addition there was no prejudice attached to different blood types, and they were presumed to be unaffected by selection.

The data on blood groups began to accumulate slowly during the 1920s and 1930s. World War II accelerated the process with the addition of routine blood typing procedures applied to vast numbers of persons from all over the world. By 1950 it was possible to take an overview, to evaluate the contribution of all this information to the problem of race, particularly to classification. William Boyd, an immunochemist at Boston University, published a book (Boyd, 1950) which brought together all of the information on blood groups and a few other inherited traits and attempted to establish a classification of human races. In other words, Boyd, using only traits under strict genetic control, attempted the same task that Blumenbach had tried 150 years earlier. How do their classifications compare? *They are almost identical.* Boyd classified mankind into six races. Five of them were the same continental races that Blumenbach arrived at. The sixth consisted solely of the Basques, separated from the rest of the Europeans because of their extraordinarily high frequency of Rh negative.

After 150 years we can find very little evidence of progress in our understanding of race. The notion could have been abandoned completely on the grounds that it was of negligible use. Indeed, a few physical anthropologists did just that (see Montagu, 1964; Livingston, 1964; Brace, 1964; Kelso, 1967; Hierneaux, 1964), but most did not. Curiously, the most encouraging sign over the past twenty years is a growing confusion on the subject of race. We will deal with the current situation in more detail in Chapter 9.

Before leaving the subject, it should be emphasized that the investigations of the blood groups had more subtle and more profound effect on the current situation in physical anthropology. To understand the change and how it came about consider yourself, for a moment, as a physical anthropologist during the 1930s measuring people and taking blood samples; trying, in other words, to save information which would soon be gone forever. As long as all you did was collect the information, you would have had no special problems. However, as you attempted to analyze and report the information, it would gradually become more clear that measurements and blood types imply different things. Measurements, at least in principle, could be used to compare and evaluate relationships between *individuals* by applying a simple principle—in general the greater the similarity between individuals, the closer their relationship. But it is clear that this principle does not readily apply to blood types. Brothers and sisters as well as parents and children regularly differ in blood types. Whereas unrelated individuals often have identical blood types. However, as blood group data accumulated, it became more clear that a modified principle could be applied to groups of individuals, that is, to *populations*—the greater the similarity between populations, the closer the relationship. Indeed this is the basic principle underlying Boyd's classification.

The change was a fundamental one, for it shifted the focus of attention from the individual to the population as the basic unit of study. In addition, population differences which had formerly been explained as a result of admixture began to be recognized as adaptive differences. At first the change served merely to separate young physical anthropologists from older ones.* Unexpected rewards, however, awaited those who pursued the genetic approach, for very quickly they found a well-developed theory of population genetics that could readily be applied to human populations. The theory had been developed and tested using experimental plant and animal populations. At first physical anthropologists tested the theory out on human populations by examining the same questions raised earlier on the experimental groups. How may the effects of natural selection be measured? How does inbreeding affect the genetic structure of a population? Does population size have any bearing on the way populations evolve? Eventually the theory led to questions specifically dealing with human populations. What does the genetic variability of a population imply about its evolutionary past? About its potential for adapting to future changes? What effects do cultural practices have on the genetics of populations?

The reader can perhaps begin to see that what started as a problem in dealing

---

* The controversy surfaced clearly for the first time in a symposium on the *Origin and Evolution of Man* held in June, 1950, at the Biological Laboratories at Cold Spring Harbor, Long Island. The papers and discussions were published in 1951 as Volume XV of the Symposia on Quantitative Biology.

simultaneously with measurements and blood types developed into a new emphasis, a new strategy. The emphasis shifted from the individual to the population, from problems of racial analysis and the history of peoples to issues of adaptation and population dynamics. The strategy moved from simple description to experimentation and problem-solving. The changes were sufficiently abrupt and striking that the field, since World War II, has often been called the "new physical anthropology" (see Washburn, 1951).

PHYSICAL ANTHROPOLOGY IN THE UNITED STATES

Differences in emphasis, interpretations, and vocabulary often follow political boundaries, but physical anthropology in the United States has become increasingly distinctive over the past fifteen years. Why? Certainly one contributing factor, and probably the most important one, has been the availability of large sums of money from the government for research and for training graduate students. This is, of course, a general trend in the United States and not at all unique to physical anthropology; it took place on a broad scientific front and resulted in some general consequences. Research skills became more highly prized and more heavily rewarded. Graduate education was given more emphasis. And, most important, science was drawn more and more into the service of national goals and priorities.

The traditional concerns of physical anthropology yield only a few products of modest national interest. Most conspicuous among these products are two areas of research that have been of interest to the military for a long time: 1) anthropometry, and 2) stress physiology. Anthropometry, the techniques for measuring human beings, was applied to the design of military clothing and equipment and to the improvement of the efficiency of interaction between man and machinery. This activity has long been called applied physical anthropology.

Stress physiology studies have explored ways that human beings adapt their bodily processes under environmental extremes. The strategic value of this work to the military may be seen from some of the problems that have been approached. For example, questions along the following lines have been asked: What changes do people undergo when brought to live at high altitude? What do they need in adapting to climatic extremes? Are some persons better able to adapt than others?

Apart from these areas research in physical anthropology has not been well supported *except as it might be of importance to some other area of scientific interest*. Thus it is that recent research into human evolution and human heterography has been dominated in the United States by particular interests in genetics, physiology, and other areas of basic medical and dental research. Within anthropology physical anthropology is somewhat unique in this symbiotic role. Archaeological research as an independent activity has been supported substantially by the National Park Service and the National Science Foundation. Ethnology has been supported by several agencies, most notably the National Science Foundation and the National Institute of Mental Health.

In this way anthropologists have responded to national interests. It is too soon to evaluate the effectiveness of the response, but it is possible to see one clear overall consequence on the field—increasing specialization. This implies narrowing interests, objectives, and techniques and more and more refined vocabularies. Specialization strains the connecting bonds between physical and cultural anthropology. Perhaps you will be better able to judge if this is desirable and what the outcome is likely to be after you have read the rest of the book.

MAJOR POINTS IN CHAPTER 1

1. Biology begins with a search for evidence concerning the nature of life.
2. The search began systematically with Linnaeus's classification of the varieties of life.
3. Blumenbach classified the varieties of human beings.
4. Evolutionary interpretations were first intended as solutions to the problem of biological variability.
5. Natural selection was the first factor to be identified which might cause evolutionary change.
6. Mendel formulated the particulate theory of inheritance and the two basic laws of heredity.
7. Mutations generate genetic variability.
8. Physical anthropology draws upon evolutionary theory and genetics to explain man's biological variability.
9. Until recently the history of physical anthropology has been dominated by a racial perspective.

REFERENCES AND SUGGESTIONS FOR ADDITIONAL READING

BARNES, HARRY ELMER
  1965   *An intellectual and cultural history of the Western world.* 3d rev. ed. 3 vols. New York: Dover.
BOAS, FRANZ
  1912   *Changes in bodily form of descendants of immigrants.* (Final report.) New York: Columbia.
BOYD, WILLIAM C.
  1950   *Genetics and the races of man.* Boston: D. C. Heath.
BRACE, C. LORING
  1964   A nonracial approach towards the understanding of human diversity. In *The concept of race,* ed. Ashley Montagu. New York: Free Press.
BROCE, GERALD
  1973   *History of anthropology.* Minneapolis: Burgess.
COMAS, JUAN
  1960   *Manual of physical anthropology.* Rev. ed. Springfield, Ill.: Charles C Thomas.
COUNT, EARL W., ED.
  1950   *This is race: An anthology selected from the international literature on the races of man.* New York: Henry Schuman.
CROW, JAMES F.
  1959   Ionizing radiation and evolution. *Scientific American* 201, September, pp. 138–160.
DARWIN, CHARLES
  1859   *On the origin of species by means of natural selection, or the preservation of favored races in the struggle for life.* London: John Murray.
  1871   *The descent of man.* In *This is race: An anthology selected from the international literature on the races of man,* ed. Earl W. Count, pp. 133–144. New York: Henry Schuman, 1950.
EISELEY, LOREN
  1960   *The firmament of time.* New York: Atheneum.
GREENE, JOHN COLTON
  1959   *The death of Adam: Evolution and its impact on Western thought.* Ames: Iowa State University Press.
HIERNEAUX, JEAN
  1964   The concept of race and the taxonomy of mankind. In *The concept of race,* ed. Ashley Montagu. New York: Free Press.
HOOTON, EARNEST A.
  1946   *Up from the ape.* Rev. ed. New York: Macmillan.
HOWELLS, W. W.
  1965   Some present aspects of physical anthropology. *Annals of the American Academy of Political and Social Science* 357:127–133.
  1970   Recent physical anthropology. *Annals of the American Academy of Political and Social Science* 389:116–126.
HUXLEY, THOMAS H.
  1896   *Man's place in nature.* New York: Appleton.

KELSO, A. J.
    1967   The concept of race. *Improving College and University Teaching* 15:95–97.
    1969   Review of: Science and the concept of race, ed. Margaret Mead, Theodosius
          Dobzhansky, Ethel Tobach, and Robert Light. New York: Columbia. In
          Human Biology 41:145–146.

KUHN, THOMAS S.
    1962   *The structure of scientific revolutions.* Chicago: University of Chicago Press.

LIVINGSTONE, FRANK B.
    1964   Human populations. In *Horizons of anthropology,* ed. Sol Tax. Chicago:
          Aldine.

MAYR, ERNST
    1959   Darwin and the evolutionary theory in biology. In *Evolution and anthropology:
          A centennial appraisal,* pp. 3–12. Anthropological Society of Washington.
    1963   *Animal species and evolution.* Cambridge: Harvard University Press.

MONTAGU, ASHLEY, ED.
    1964   *The concept of race.* New York: Free Press.

MONTAGU, M. F. ASHLEY
    1960   *An introduction to physical anthropology.* 3d ed. Springfield, Ill.: Charles C
          Thomas.

MOORE, RUTH
    1961   *The coil of life.* New York: Alfred A. Knopf.

PENNIMAN, T. K.
    1965   *A hundred years of anthropology.* 3d ed., rev. London: Gerald Duckworth.

STEWART, T. D.
    1959   The effect of Darwin's theory of evolution on physical anthropology. In *Evolu-
          tion and anthropology: A centennial appraisal,* pp. 11–25. Anthropological
          Society of Washington.

STOCKING, GEORGE W., JR.
    1968   *Race, culture, and evolution.* New York: Free Press.

STURTEVANT, A. H.
    1965   *A history of genetics.* New York: Harper and Row.

TROTTER, MILDRED
    1956   Notes on the history of the AAPA. Presidential address to the 25th annual
          meeting of the American Association of Physical Anthropologists. *American
          Journal of Physical Anthropology* (n.s.) 14:350–364.

WASHBURN, S. L.
    1951   The new physical anthropology. *Transactions of the New York Academy of
          Sciences,* ser. 2, vol. 13, pp. 298–304.

WENDT, HERBERT
    1956   *In search of Adam.* Boston: Houghton Mifflin.

WILSON, R. J., ED.
    1967   *Darwinism and the American intellectual: A book of readings.* Homewood, Ill.:
          Dorsey.

2 Man and His Relatives

INTRODUCTION

Introductory courses in physical anthropology usually begin with a unit called "man's place in nature," "man as a member of the animal kingdom," or, here, "man and his relatives." The information presented under these headings generally consists of descriptive statements about the various taxonomic units to which man belongs, and that is the kind of information contained in this chapter. Since man is an animal, it is necessary to discuss, for example, the distinguishing characteristics of the animal kingdom, and, more particularly, since man is a primate, the distinguishing characteristics of the primates.

Why should this material be presented in a course of physical anthropology? One answer to this question is obvious; if you intend to take up the study of man's biological evolution and contemporary variability, you should certainly be informed that man is an animal, and that his closest living relatives are primates. But the information presented herein is intended to provide much more than merely a convincing argument that man is a member of specific taxonomic units. It is intended to provide one category of minimal information which must be mastered for the practice of physical anthropology. What problems, for example, immediately confront a student of human paleontology? He must be able to recognize significant fossil material; to interpret the significance of a discovery as it relates to others; and, on occasion, to reconstruct the significance of the morphology and ecological setting in which the newly discovered animal lived. Without an awareness of the "man's place in nature" material, a person would be unable even to recognize the significance of a fossil discovery. In short, to comprehend and appreciate the significance of fossil discoveries requires an awareness of the range of variability among living forms.

One caution should be mentioned before proceeding to the problems of zoological classification; the listing and discussion of characteristics that distinguish one grouping from another has the effect of making it appear that the groups and their distinctive attributes are fixed, immutable, and eternal. Keep in mind that the groups and their characteristics were brought about by evolutionary processes that operated not merely at some time in the distant past, but which continue to operate in the present and can be expected to give rise to new forms in the future. It is easy to forget the dynamic, formative, and systemic character of the evolutionary process when inspecting some of the minute details it has produced.

ZOOLOGICAL CLASSIFICATION

The most convenient way of presenting and summarizing the total range of variability within living animal groups, and further of showing how man fits into the animal kingdom, is by means of the already well-established system of animal classification. The subdivision of zoology that is directly concerned with the application of this system is known as *systematic* or *taxonomic zoology*. The general outlines and the regulations governing the classification of living things were set forth by Linnaeus two hundred years ago. Both the system and the rules governing its formulation have changed in considerable detail since the time of Linnaeus, but the objective is the same now as it was then: to achieve a systematic classification that accurately reflects the true biological distance between and among the animal groups.

At first the problem may sound reasonably simple. A competent specialist should be able to examine an animal, note its features, and make a decision concerning its classification, just as a chemist might be given some material which he can analyze and determine whether it is gold, copper, zinc, or whatever. However, there are many pitfalls in this apparently straightforward procedure. Animals are classified most often by judging degrees of apparent similarity. Human beings always emphasize vision. There is no a priori reason why animals could not be classified by means of tactile, olfactory, or auditory similarities and differences, but they are not. They are classified largely on the basis of visually perceived similarities and differences. We have already encountered the fundamental regulating principle in zoological classification. In its most general form the principle may be stated as follows: the greater the degree of similarity, the closer the degree of biological relationship. This is another deceptively simple proposition, for some similarities do indeed indicate close common ancestry and thus close biological relationship, but others are merely superficial. Those similarities which indicate close biological relationships are called *homologies*. Homologies can be recognized as detailed structural similarities built upon a basic pattern which presumably characterized the common ancestor. Superficial similarities that might lead one to think that two forms are closely related when in fact they are not are called *analogies*. Thus, the wings of a bat and the wings of a beetle are functionally similar, but structurally dissimilar; they are analogies. However the wings of a bat and the forelimbs and extremities of rodents are functionally dissimilar but structurally similar; they are homologies.

So in deciding relationships among animals, the problem is not as simple as it might appear at first. In addition to distinguishing between homologies and analogies, a classifier must also make judgments about the relative importance of traits. This problem will not be discussed in detail here, since it is basically the specialist's problem, but it can be illustrated by the following question: When classifying a particular animal, is the fact that it has hoofs more important than the fact that it has antlers? Frequently the taxonomist just can't make a judgment on such a problem. This is one of the most frequent sources of disagreement among zoological classifiers.

Another problem area in animal classification is that of determining in how many ways two groups or specimens must differ before they are considered to be different units (for example, species) in the classification. While attempts have been made to eliminate this problem by standardizing procedures, there continues to be an element of personal preference among qualified zoologists. Because of this unavoidable ambiguity, it is possible to recognize two major groups of classifiers: 1) those who regard either few or slight differences between the compared groups as significant (the *splitters*) and 2) those who regard few or slight differences as unimportant (the *lumpers*). Though mankind today is but one species, the catalogue of erect bipedal fossil forms, any one or all of them possibly in man's ancestral line, includes discoveries originally classified into more than a dozen different genera. This is an extreme case of taxonomic splitting, and for a long time was one of the most formidable obstacles in the way of interpreting the fossil evidence of human evolution. Today, as the reader will see in Chapter 6, the situation is much more simple, as the lumpers have displaced the splitters.

The problem of zoological classification, as we have seen, is by no means a simple one on methodological grounds alone. It is, however, further complicated by the fact that the actual evidence available to the classifier is often crude and incomplete. This is particularly true in the case of fossil animals, with very often the only evidence available consisting of little more than a few fragments of bone or possibly a single tooth.

Because of these difficulties particular classifications are often found to be in error and are thus the subject of more or less constant revision. Perhaps the classification of the future will be more stable and less subject to error. If so, this might be a consequence of a relatively recent trend in taxonomy, which is to employ more criteria than simply morphological attributes as bases of a classification. New criteria of classification have been derived from histological, biochemical, and behavioral studies. As applied to the primates, the new approaches have tended to confirm the basic validity of older standard classifications. The fact that these criteria have had little effect on old classifications may be due to the methodological problems associated with interpreting the taxonomic significance of the results, or simply because such studies are, like those based on anatomical characteristics, fundamentally morphological and thus can be expected to reflect the same kind of relationship. A complete classification of the many forms of life might involve the use of as many as twenty-one levels in the taxonomy hierarchy, but only seven of these are in frequent and regular usage. They are:

Kingdom
Phylum
Class
Order
Family
Genus
Species.

MAN'S PLACE IN NATURE

The physical anthropologist is interested in knowing not only in what category man belongs at each taxonomic level, but he is also interested in knowing the membership of the other categories, particularly within those levels that include his closest relatives. In the discussion that follows, the primate order and its subdivisions will be considered in some detail, whereas the higher taxonomic levels will be dealt with very briefly. In this way one may obtain at least a minimal understanding of man's place in nature.

Kingdom: Animalia

This is a major subdivision of life. The traditional way of dividing life is to divide it into two major categories: plants and animals. During recent years biologists have become less satisfied with this simple dichotomy for two main reasons: 1) many living organisms possess characteristics which simply do not qualify them to fit neatly into either the plant or animal kingdom (for example, bacteria and protozoa), and 2) many organisms have attributes characteristic of *both* plants and animals. The dissatisfaction arising out of these difficulties has brought about a number of suggested changes at the kingdom level, but for present purposes the standard division of life into plants and animals will be adequate. Within the animal kingdom there is an enormous range of variation, and thus it is difficult to point to many common distinctive features. There are structural and functional characteristics that distinguish animals from plants, but in general, animals are capable of locomotion, and plants practice photosynthesis. (The process of photosynthesis is the means by which the sun's energy is converted into the energy of life.) However, there are exceptions that vex the classifiers. A few animallike organisms are photosynthetic, and a few plantlike organisms move about. And some plants lack the photosynthetic ability! If one's objective is an orderly classification, then "exceptions" are bothersome. If not, then they might be informative. In this case, for example, the "exceptions" bear upon an argument that comes up occasionally concerning the number of times that life originated. We encountered a similar argument over the origin of races in the last chapter. The issue is the same here: one side argues that life emerged once (monophyletic), the other holds that life originated more than once (polyphyletic). The "exceptions" at the kingdom level are exceptional because varieties overlap in the established categories. This overlapping supports the monophyletic view more than the polyphyletic view though it certainly does not resolve the issue.

Phylum: Chordata

How many different kinds of animals are there? One answer might list and count everything identifiable as animal; that is to say, there are bears, spiders, geese, beetles,

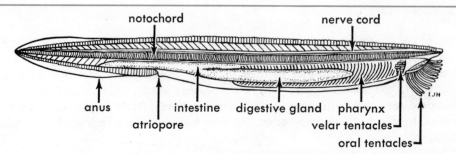

Figure 2–1. *Amphioxus* dissected from the right side. Illustrates position of the notochord. (After P. D. F. Murray)

dogs, deer, oysters, and so on. This obviously is not too helpful; what is called for here is a grouping together of general categories of animals that share some fundamental similarity in organization of their body structures. Animals that share this basic similarity are said to be members of the same phylum. For example, insects and spiders are grouped together in the phylum Arthropoda; clams, oysters, and a variety of other shellfish are in the phylum Mollusca. Man belongs to the phylum Chordata.

The phylum Chordata includes an extraordinarily diverse group of animals all of which have, at least at some time during their life cycle, gill slits and an elastic tubular structure known as a notochord (see Figure 2–1) located along the back (or dorsal) surface. The notochord is the basic feature common to all members of the phylum Chordata. The notochord, in other words, is an homology shared by an otherwise very heterogeneous group of animals. This widely diverse group shares a fundamental similarity in the arrangement of their body structures. In some members the notochord is a lifelong trait. In one subphylum of the Chordata, the vertebrates, it appears during the embryonic stage and is ultimately replaced by a vertebral column, a more complex linear sequence of segments containing a spinal cord.

Class: Mammalia

There are eight classes of vertebrates: 1) the primitive jawless "fish" (Agnatha), 2) the primitive armored fishes (Placodermi), 3) the sharks and their relatives (Chondrichthyes), 4) the bony fishes (Osteichthyes), 5) the amphibians (Amphibia), 6) the reptiles (Reptilia), 7) the birds (Aves), and 8) the class to which man belongs, the mammals (Mammalia). The mammals occupy many different types of environments. Some spend much of their life underground, some fly, some live in the sea; but by far the majority live on land, and these are distributed over practically the entire surface of the earth. As might be expected from the diversity of environments they live in, mammals are highly varied; yet they share in common several characteristics of adaptive significance.

Basically mammals are a distinctive class of chordates because of the characteristics they share that are associated with reproduction and care of the young. All
mammals conceive their young within the uterus of the mother and, after the offspring are born, nourish them by means of mammary glands. Among living mammals
there are three basic variations in this process: 1) some, the Prototheria mammals
(such as the duckbill platypus), like other vertebrates, lay eggs but feed their newborn by means of mammary glands, 2) others, the Metatheria, like the kangaroo and
opossum, bear their young in an immature condition and permit their development
in a pouch, and 3) in the most common group, and the one to which we belong,
the Eutherian mammals, the mothers carry their young within the uterus until an
advanced state of development is reached. This is made possible by the placenta,
which connects the embryo to the wall of the uterus and enables nutrients and
oxygen to get to the offspring and, likewise, provides a means for eliminating waste
products.

Mammals are distinctive in other ways. For example, mammals have hair, are
warm-blooded, have relatively large brains, and display a number of characteristics
in their skeleton that, compared to other vertebrates, appear to be more efficient
simplifications.

Clearly the mammals possess a range of homologies of enormous adaptive significance. The young are developed over a relatively long period of their total life
within the highly protected environment of their mother's uterus. Once they are
born, they are already well along in their developmental process, but even so,
mammals are further protected and allowed to develop more fully before being
confronted by the problems of food-getting and offense and defense by being provided with milk from the mother's mammaries. These attributes, those previously
mentioned, and many others not mentioned enabled the mammals to replace the
reptiles as the dominant vertebrates, a status they achieved about one hundred
million years ago and which they continue to enjoy at the present time. The factor
of dominance is determined largely by two measures: 1) the amount of influence
over other forms of life, and 2) the range of different environmental zones occupied.

Until now, the discussion has been concerned with generalized characteristics
common to mammals and the benefits they provide in meeting the requirements of
survival. In a more specific context, some mammalian characteristics may be seen as
facilitating the survival of man and his culture. The relatively long period of post-
natal care, prolonged even further in man, facilitates the transmission of culture from
one generation to the next by freeing the young from the rigorous requirements of
survival during the period of life when they are able to learn quickly and with
greatest ease. This period of becoming "cultural" is essential not only for the continuity of culture but for development and progress as well.

There are many other ways in which the fact that man is a mammal conditions
the general character of culture. To be specific with regard to the cultural consequences of being a mammal is virtually impossible. However, one can begin to
appreciate the significance of man's mammalian heritage by asking a few strategic
questions such as: Would culture be different if man were cold-blooded? Or if his

young were hatched from eggs? Or if mankind depended upon wind, birds, and insects as the mechanisms of fertilization? Clearly the answer is an emphatic *yes*. However, it would be impossible to know exactly how these factors would modify the details of culture. From these conditions one should be able to see that being a mammal is a prerequisite for man's having culture as we know it.

Table 2–1*   The 32 Orders in the Class Mammalia

ORDERS	FAMILIES			GENERA		
	EXTINCT	LIVING	TOTAL	EXTINCT	LIVING	TOTAL
Monotremata	0	2	2	0	3	3
†Multituberculata	5	0	5	35	0	35
†Triconodonta	1	0	1	8	0	8
†Pantotheria	4	0	4	22	0	22
†Symmetrodonta	2	0	2	5	0	5
Marsupialia	5	8	13	81	57	138
Insectivora	12	8	20	88	71	159
Dermoptera	1	1	2	2	1	3
Chiroptera	2	17	19	16	118	134
Primates	7	11	18	99	59	158
†Tillodontia	1	0	1	4	0	4
†Taeniodonta	1	0	1	7	0	7
Edentata	7	3	10	113	19	132
Pholidota	0	1	1	3	1	4
Lagomorpha	1	2	3	23	10	33
Rodentia	10	30	40	275	344	619
Cetacea	9	9	18	137	35	172
Carnivora	6	9	15	261	114	375
†Condylarthra	6	0	6	42	0	42
†Litopterna	2	0	2	41	0	41
†Notounculata	14	0	14	105	0	105
†Astrapotheria	2	0	2	9	0	9
Tubulidentata	0	1	1	1	1	2
†Pantodonta	3	0	3	9	0	9
†Dinocerata	1	0	1	8	0	8
†Pyrotheria	1	0	1	6	0	6
Proboscidea	5	1	6	22	2	24
†Embrithopoda	1	0	1	1	0	1
Hyracoidea	2	1	3	10	3	13
Sirenia	3	2	5	14	2	16
Perissodactyla	9	3	12	152	6	158
Artiodactyla	16	9	25	333	86	419
Total	139	118	257	1932	932	2864
Percent	54%	46%		67%	33%	

* Reprinted from Simpson's "Formal Classification of Mammalia," *Bulletin of the American Museum of Natural History,* 85 (1945): 35. Courtesy of the American Museum of Natural History.
 † Indicates extinct orders.

The mammals are comparatively recent arrivals on earth, appearing on the evolutionary scene probably no more than two hundred million years ago. At first they were small and inconspicuous when compared with the huge and magnificent dinosaurs that were beginning to dominate the landscape. But the reptiles, particularly the large ones, eventually found survival more and more difficult. Mountains were being built, causing major changes in the earth's topography; areas that were moist and swampy with ample food supply were beginning to dry up, and as they did, the large reptiles were more and more restricted in range and eventually reduced to a degree that doomed them to extinction. In fact, the early mammals may have helped to speed up the process by feeding on their eggs.

As the reptiles underwent the process of mass extinction, they left behind them vast evolutionary possibilities which the mammals began to take advantage of, resulting in rapid diversification within the class Mammalia. This diversification is reflected in the number of mammalian orders. Simpson (1945) classified mammals into thirty-two orders, eighteen of which still have living representatives. Table 2–1 is taken from Simpson and lists the thirty-two orders, indicating the number of extinct and living families and genera known for each. From this, one may see that while there remain approximately as many families today as have become extinct, there are more than twice as many extinct genera known as living ones. Clearly, the information indicates that mammals have been involved in a great expansion, proliferation, and diversification. One product of this evolutionary explosion is the order Primates, the mammalian subdivision to which man belongs.

Order: Primates

The primates are good examples of generalized mammals and are themselves a diversified and evolutionarily successful group. At first sight, most members of the order do not appear to be likely candidates for the dubious honor of being closely related to man: many are small, nocturnal, insectivorous, and almost all live in trees. When they are examined closely, however, they begin to show traits that more clearly indicate an affinity to man. By observing their behavior, we see that they are alert, curious, heavily dependent upon vision, playful, capable of semierect or erect posture, able to use their hands to manipulate objects in their environment, banded together in organized and territorially defined groups, and they appear capable of carrying on some degree of communication with one another. By inspecting their structural traits, we find other similarities: stereoscopic vision, elongated limbs with five digits, complex and large brains, big toes and thumbs that can be placed in opposition to the other digits of the foot or hand, nails instead of claws. No list of traits, however, can be expected to provide anything like a profound appreciation of the many ways in which the primates are distinctive as a group and the ways in which man shares these distinctive features with the rest of the members of the order. One can only list a few of the most important features and emphasize the fact that primates are not highly specialized. They share a large number of traits in common but do not show any particular tendency to specialize in any one, except possibly brain size and intelligence (although this would seem to be more a particular specialization of man and his ancestors rather than a general one for the primates).

Most of the attributes common to the primates stem from either of two factors: 1) the retention of ancient or primitive generalized vertebrate or mammalian characteristics, and 2) the development of an arboreal adaptation. The first set includes a very large number of characters common to but not distinctive of the primates. For example, the structural differentiation of the hands and feet into five digits is in fact not a "primate" trait in the sense that it was developed by them or is unique to them, but is rather a "vertebrate" trait much older than the primate order but which has been retained in that group. Likewise the versatile structure of the limbs, the retention of a functional clavicle in the shoulder, the basic pattern of cusps on the molar teeth are all generalized vertebrate traits shared by the primates with a large number of other vertebrates.

The second set of attributes, those associated with an arboreal adaptation, includes traits distinctive but seldom common to all the primates. We will identify these in some detail in Chapter 5, but for the moment we can illustrate the point by reference to vision. As a result of their adaptation to an arboreal way of life, the primates are said to have developed an emphasis on vision. This is indeed the case, but the expression of the emphasis is highly varied. Some primates have stereoscopic vision, some do not. Some have specialized in night vision, other have not. Some are able to make refined color discrimination, others are not. Clearly, living in the trees raises some common adaptive problems, but there have been differing solutions. The variety is due in part to the fact that as primates have evolved, they have improved their adaptation to tree dwelling, and in part because "living in the trees" is not in itself a homogeneous thing. So an emphasis on vision is a primate characteristic, but the expression of it is variable. Some primates see better than others; some primates see differently from one another. The consequences of poor vision in an arboreal form are obvious: falling out of the trees, injury, and death.*

As a group, then, the primates may be broadly described as generalized, arboreal, and clever. They are broadly distributed throughout the tropical regions of both the New and Old World. The primate order may be subdivided into three suborders (see Table 2–2): Prosimii, Platyrrhinae, and Catarrhinae. The following is a more detailed consideration of the primates and each of these suborders and their subdivisions.

---

* It would seem worthwhile to introduce here a point that is not always emphasized: Monkeys and apes do fall out of trees and, what is more, do it all the time. We are inclined to think that man is the only imperfect animal; while it is human to err, we think of other animals as going about their daily lives in more or less perfect adaptation to their environments. But of course animals err too, and when they do, the consequences are more likely to be fatal. It is perhaps a measure of just how convinced we are of their perfect adaptation to observe the reaction to a monkey or squirrel falling out of a tree. Often the observer will remark that "the little things are human after all."

Table 2–2   Classification of Modern Primates

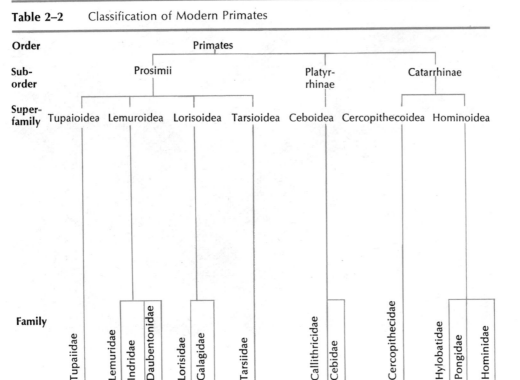

Order	Primates						
Sub-order		Prosimii			Platyr-rhinae		Catarrhinae
Super-family	Tupaioidea	Lemuroidea	Lorisoidea	Tarsioidea	Ceboidea	Cercopithecoidea	Hominoidea
Family	Tupaiidae	Lemuridae / Indridae / Daubentonidae	Lorisidae / Galagidae	Tarsiidae	Callithricidae / Cebidae	Cercopithecidae	Hylobatidae / Pongidae / Hominidae

Prosimians — Monkeys — Apes — Man

PROSIMII.   The prosimians were the first primates and thus represent the earliest stage in the evolution of the primates. Examine Table 2–2. Compare the *Prosimii* with the *Platyrrhinae* and *Catarrhinae*. The prosimians consist of more families and more superfamilies than the other suborders together. This contrast would be even more pronounced if the table included extinct varieties. The implication is obvious: the prosimians are more variable. Thus they are more difficult to characterize as a group. What they share in common is that they are the living descendants of the earliest primate evolutionary experiment, the arboreal adaptation. If there is any-thing that provides this group with biological integrity, it is the fact that all members show, in a lesser or greater degree, the consequences of the early ancestors of the primates taking to life in trees. This is, of course, true of all living primates, but the prosimians provide us with some insight into the earliest ways that this arboreal adaptation was translated into morphological characteristics. To be sure, the living

Figure 2–2. Tree shrew (*Tupaia*). (Courtesy of the Zoological Society of San Diego)

prosimians give us a biased view of this early stage in the evolution of the primates, since they include, on the one hand, only the descendants of the successful groups that continue to survive, while, on the other hand, they do not include representatives of the more progressive ancestors that eventually evolved into higher primate forms. It is clear, then, that the prosimians are of interest to physical anthropology not only because they belong to the same order as man, but furthermore because of the insights they may provide concerning the origin of the primates. We can take a closer look at the prosimians by considering the four superfamilies: Tupaioidea, Lemuroidea, Lorisoidea, and Tarsioidea.

Morphologically the Tupaioidea (tree shrews) of Southeast Asia stand between more typical primates on the one hand and insectivores on the other. Because of this intermediate appearance, zoological taxonomists have disagreed on the classification of the tree shrews; some put them into the Insectivora, others include them with the primates, and one primatologist has concluded that they belong in a separate order all to themselves.

The tree shrews are generally described by such adjectives as quick, alert, small, and arboreal. On first appearance they look like small squirrels, but on closer inspection one can see many distinctive features. Like the primates and unlike the insecti-

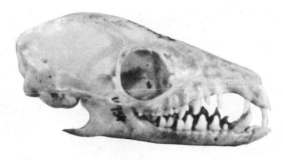

Figure 2–3. Front and side views of a female tree shrew skull (*Tupaia nicobarica surda*). Courtesy of the Smithsonian Institution)

vores, the tree shrews have large eyes, more-fully-developed visual areas of the brain, and less-fully-developed olfactory areas. They have highly mobile fingers and toes that can be used for grasping. And, while their diet is predominantly insectivorous, they will eat fruit, seeds, small mammals, and, if confined together, one another. They differ from other primates in terms of the following characteristics: all their digits have claws; they lack stereoscopic vision; they commonly have multiple births and multiple pairs of mammaries; their lower jaw has three incisors in each quadrant (thus they have a total of six incisors in the lower jaw), wheras the upper jaw has two in each quadrant (total of four).

One subfamily, the Tupainae, are generally diurnal; another, the Ptilocercinae, nocturnal. The Ptilocercinae have bald tails except for a tuft of hair at the very tip. Both subfamilies are indeed adapted to life in the trees, but members of all species spend much of their life on or near the ground. They live in pairs or small groups and build nests for sleeping.

In summary, the tupaioids display a most unusual assortment of traits, some of which ally them with the primates, others with the insectivores, and still others are not common to either order. It is, however, for these very reasons that the Tupaioidea are of interest to the primatologist; there are good reasons to believe that the primates evolved from insectivore ancestors, and thus the tree shrew provides some important indirect information about the kinds of animals that bridged the evolutionary gap between the orders.

The Lemuroidea are confined to Madagascar and the Comoro Islands and consist of three families, Lemuridae, Indridae, and Daubentonidae. The Lemuridae are often referred to as the "true lemurs." Like all lemuroids, they are a combination of familiar primate characteristics and specialized adaptations rarely found in other primates. Among the usual primate features are fingernails (except for the second toe on each foot, which has a claw), opposable great toes and thumbs, enormous eyes, and heavy dependence on vision. Further, the females generally bear but one offspring at a time.

Figure 2–4. A brown lemur (*Lemur fulvus*) of the family Lemuridae. (Courtesy of Oregon Regional Primate Research Center, photo by F. S. Shininger)

Figure 2–5. A ring-tailed lemur (*Lemur catta*) of the family Lemuridae. (Courtesy of Oregon Regional Primate Research Center, photo by F. S. Shininger)

The most peculiar specialization found among the Lemuridae is the distinctive habit of one subfamily, the Cheirogaleinae, to estivate, that is, to sleep throughout the hot season, during which time they obtain sufficient nutriment to survive by drawing upon a massive deposit of fat located near the base of the tail. Most species of the Lemuridae are nocturnal, and all are arboreal. They are primarily vegetarian, but will eat insects and small birds. They show considerable variability in the sizes of their social units, ranging from species whose members lead mostly solitary lives to others organized into troops of up to two dozen individuals. Lemurs spend their lives in small, sharply defined territorial ranges varying in size from about five to fifteen acres. The sense of smell plays a more prominent role in their lives than it does in most other primate groups. Lemurs have several different scent glands which they use to mark themselves and their territories and to display aggression, among other things (Jolly, 1966).

The Indridae display the same generalized primate traits mentioned above in connection with the Lemuridae. Their most distinctive features are: 1) except for the opposable great toe, the other four toes are webbed together, and 2) they have two incisors in each quadrant of the upper jaw and only one in each quadrant of the lower jaw.

The Daubentonidae show a number of specialized traits when compared not only with other families of the Lemuroidea superfamily, but with any other primate

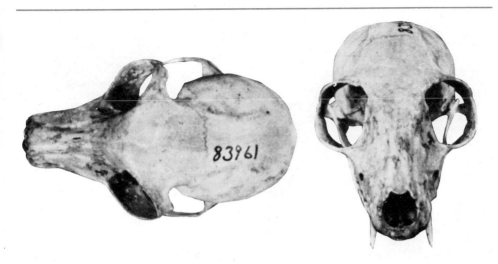

Figure 2–6. Top and front views of a lemur skull (*Lemur ruffifrons*). (Courtesy of the Smithsonian Institution)

group as well. They are commonly called Aye-Ayes, and their most distinctive features include: 1) long, curved, chisellike incisors that look like and function as the incisors of rodents, and 2) except for the great toe all other digits of both the hands and feet have claws. There is only one genus, and all members are nocturnal, arboreal, and often live in pairs.

The Lorisoidea are more broadly distributed than the Lemuroidea. Lorises may be found in South and West Africa and in Southeast Asia and Malaysia. Both families are adapted to a nocturnal, largely solitary, and arboreal way of life in the tropical forests of Africa and Asia. The families contrast sharply in several respects, but most conspicuously in locomotion. The Lorisidae are small, slow-moving animals with enormous eyes and possess a long claw on the second toe of each foot, which is used to impale and extract grubs embedded in bark.

The Galagidae (known also as "bush babies") vary the general lorisoid adaptive theme by possessing a specialized architectural structure on their feet, involving a lengthening of the heel and ankle bones to provide for a hopping mode of progressing through the trees. In this respect they are like the tarsiers.

The Tarsioidea superfamily is represented among living primates by only one genus. The individuals that belong within this group show several peculiar specializations, most of which are related to the hopping mode of progression they share with the Galagidae. The tarsiers have elongated heel and ankle bones and, in addition, small suction pads on the soles of their feet.

If one can ignore the specializations of the tarsier, however, it begins to become obvious that this group of prosimians is somewhat more advanced than the others.

Figure 2–7. A potto (*Perodicticus potto*) of the family Lorisidae. (Courtesy of Oregon Regional Primate Research Center, photo by F. S. Shininger)

Figure 2–8. Front and side views of a skull from the family Lorisidae (the slow loris or *Nycticebus coucang*). (Courtesy of the Smithsonian Institution)

They have a more fully developed visual apparatus which includes not merely large eyes, but an enlarged area of the brain that controls vision and a bony orbit which houses and encloses most of the back of the eye (as in higher primates). This more highly developed vision is accompanied by a corresponding reduction in the brain center that controls the sense of smell. These features are so strikingly advanced in the tarsier that one anatomist claimed that these little prosimians were man's closest living relatives. However, this is certainly not the majority opinion.

Tarsiers may be found in their natural habitats in the Philippines, Borneo, and the Celebes. All are small, arboreal, and nocturnal, and all have very large eyes and are able to rotate their heads 180 degrees. This ability to completely reverse their vision, coupled with their ability to hop as high as six feet in getting from branch to branch, makes them interesting and entertaining to watch, but not much is known about their behavior, as they do not survive well in captivity, their habitats are difficult to get to, and tarsiers are most active at night.

Figure 2–9. A galago or bush baby (*Galago senegalensis*) of the family Galagidae. (Courtesy of Oregon Regional Primate Research Center, photo by F. S. Shininger)

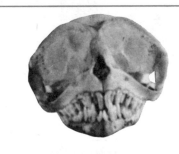

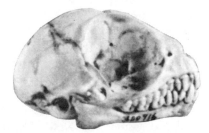

Figure 2–10. A Philippine tarsier (*Tarsius syrichta*) of the family Tarsiidae. (Courtesy of Oregon Regional Primate Research Center, photo by F. S. Shininger)

Figure 2–11. Front and side views of a male tarsier skull (*Tarsius bancanna*). (Courtesy of the Smithsonian Institution)

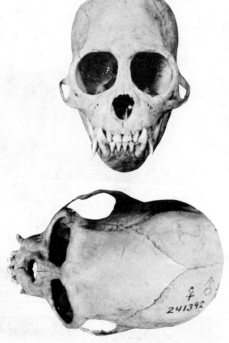

Figure 2–12. Hooded capuchin (*Cebus capucinus*) of the family Cebidae. (Courtesy of the Zoological Society of San Diego)

Figure 2–13. Front and top views of a female capuchin skull (*Cebus albifrons*). (Courtesy of the Smithsonian Institution)

PLATYRRHINAE. This suborder consists entirely of monkeys found exclusively in Central and South America, and is made up of one superfamily and two families. There is no sharp qualitative distinction between the platyrrhines and the prosimians, but there are several differences in degree that, when taken as a whole, serve to distinguish them clearly. It would seem that the New World monkeys display the morphological consequences of the early arboreal adaptation in a more fully developed way than the prosimians do. As pointed out earlier, the living prosimians do not include representatives of their more progressive ancestors, but such illustrations can be found among the living monkeys. The platyrrhines differ from the prosimians in that the platyrrhines are generally larger, more intelligent, and have more highly developed vision. All New World monkeys are arboreal, and all possess greater dexterity than the prosimians in the use of their hands and feet for grasping and manipulating objects. In short, the platyrrhines are more representative of the "typical" primate pattern than are the prosimians.

The family Cebidae includes animals with a wide range of adaptive features.

Figure 2–14. Howler monkey (*Alouatta seniculus*) of the family Cebidae. (Courtesy of the Zoological Society of San Diego)

Some are brachiators, that is, they get from one branch to another by grasping a branch with the hands and swinging their bodies under the branch and leaping to the next one. (The brachiating mode of locomotion is also characteristic of the Hylobatidae and Pongidae, both of which are families of the Catarrhinae.) Some Cebidae have prehensile, or grasping, tails, which they use for grasping, suspending, and balancing.

All but one species of the Cebidae are diurnal, and all have opposable big toes with the thumbs either imperfectly opposable or completely without function.

Included within the family Callithricidae are the marmosets and tamarins, the most aberrant of the platyrrhines. Except for the great toe, all the digits have claws instead of nails, and females commonly bear two or three offspring at one birth. The marmosets and tamarins are small, diurnal, and subsist principally on insects and fruit. It is impossible to know whether the unusual features found among the

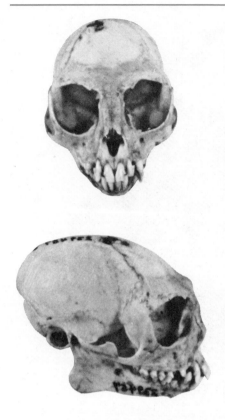

Figure 2–15. Front and side views of skull of a male marmoset (*Mico argentata*) of the family Callithricidae. (Courtesy of the Smithsonian Institution)

Figure 2–16. Cotton-topped tamarin (*Leontocebus spixi*) of the family Callithricidae. (Courtesy of the Zoological Society of San Diego)

Callithricidae are primitive or specialized. Traits are primitive if they represent retentions of old adaptations in more advanced lines. They are specialized when they are recent and represent specific responses to an adaptive problem within one phylogenetic line.

CATARRHINAE. The Catarrhinae are subdivided into two superfamilies: the Cercopithecoidea, or Old World monkeys, and the Hominoidea, including the apes and man. It should be clear from this that the Catarrhinae are more varied than the Platyrrhinae. In beginning our discussion of the Old World forms, it will be more convenient to compare the platyrrhines to the Cercopithecoidea rather than to the catarrhines in general. In this way, the comparison is between New and Old World monkeys rather than between New World monkeys on the one hand and Old World monkeys, apes, and man on the other.

Figure 2–17. Some Old World monkeys. Top: Right, langur; Bottom: Left, gelada baboon; Right, mona guenon. (Courtesy of the Zoological Society of San Diego, photo by Ron Garrison)

The superfamily Cercopithecoidea may be thought of as differing from the prosimians in the same general way that the platyrrhines do. In detail, of course, the platyrrhines differ from the Old World monkeys, the Cercopithecoidea, in many respects. The Platyrrhinae have prehensile, or grasping, tails; the Cercopithecoidea have tails, but they are not prehensile. The New World monkeys have three pre-molars, whereas the Old World monkeys have two. Some New World forms brachiate; no cercopithecoids do. Old World monkeys use all four limbs in getting about from one place to another. Old World monkeys are able to oppose both their thumbs and their great toes with strength and efficiency; the platyrrhines are much

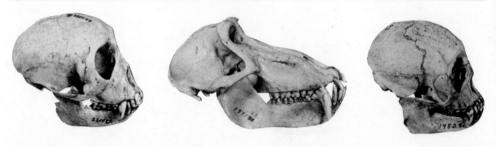

Figure 2–18. Skulls of three Old World monkeys. Left: guenon (*Cercopithecus mona*). Middle: baboon (*Papio comatus*). Both are members of the subfamily Ceropithecinae. Right: langur (*Presbytis rubicundes*) of the subfamily Colobinae. (Courtesy of the Smithsonian Institution)

less able to oppose their thumbs to their fingers and palms than they are their great toe to their other toes and plantar surfaces. Finally, the Old World monkeys show distinctive calloused areas on their buttocks known as ischial callosities, which are not found among the platyrrhines. The function of the ischial callosities is still uncertain, but they appear to be related to the fact that the cercopithecoids sleep in a sitting position in the trees. Any particular Old World monkey will differ in many more ways from any particular New World monkey. The differences listed here are the most conspicuous.

While the cercopithecoids all fall into the family Cercopithecidae, they are divided into two subfamilies, the Cercopithecinae and the Colobinae. The major distinction between these subfamilies is that the cercopithecines have cheek pouches into which they stuff food to be carried away, chewed, and digested in an area which might be safer than where the food is actually found. The Colobinae subsist primarily on leaves, and, instead of cheek pouches, they have a series of stomachs adapted to the peculiar digestive requirements of this kind of food.

Most of the Old World monkeys are arboreal. The exceptions are the baboons and patas monkeys of Africa and the macaques of Asia and a small corner in Northwest Africa. These terrestrial monkeys are interesting for a number of reasons. They are not bound to forest habitats; their distributions range over far greater areas than those of their arboreal relatives; and, like man, their ancestors descended from the trees and adapted to a way of life on the ground. Unlike human beings, however, the terrestrial monkey continues to be skillful at climbing trees. Indeed, some regularly sleep in trees and use them for protection when attacked by predators.

Included also with the Catarrhinae are apes and man, grouped together in the superfamily Hominoidea. The apes are classified into two families: the gibbons and siamangs in the Hylobatidae, and the orangutan, chimpanzee, and gorilla in the Pongidae (see Figure 2–19). As a group, the apes are distinctive primarily because of their adaptation to a brachiating mode of progression in the trees. Like the New World brachiators, they possess longer forelimbs than hind limbs, flattened front to

Figure 2–19. Representatives of the Hominoidea. Top: Left, chimpanzee; Right, lowland gorilla. Bottom: Left, agile gibbon; Right, orangutan. (Courtesy of the Zoological Society of San Diego, photo by Ron Garrison)

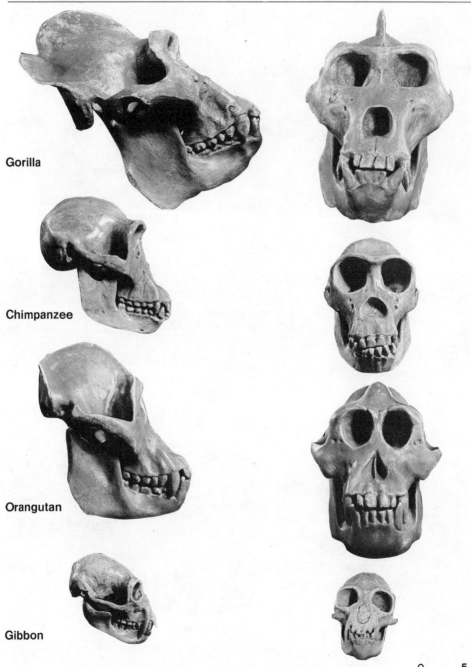

Gorilla

Chimpanzee

Orangutan

Gibbon

Figure 2–20. Side and front views of modern apes' skulls.

0   5 cm

back contours of the chest cavity, and large clavicles (the collarbone which serves in part to keep the shoulder joints to the side). In other respects (those not associated with brachiation) the apes are much more like the Old World cercopithecoids than the platyrrhine brachiators. Indeed, many have maintained that the apes are more closely similar to man than they are to the monkeys, but this is difficult to resolve, since man's physical makeup does not enable us to know with confidence if his ancestors shared a brachiating ancestry in common with the apes. Man has, for example, the well-developed clavicle and flattened thorax of an efficient brachiator, but he lacks the long forearms relative to hind-limb length. Since the evidence is ambiguous, there is room for disagreement, and this is indeed reflected in the question of whether or not man's ancestors passed through a brachiating ancestry. Must the argument be resolved before we can conclude if man's closest living relatives are the apes or the Old World monkeys? Something of a compromise may not only bypass this problem, but may, in fact, be nearer to the truth as well. It is certainly within the realm of possibility that efficient brachiation and its associated anatomical specializations are relatively recent things among the ancestors of the modern great apes. If this is indeed true, then man and the apes could have shared an evolutionary phase during which their common ancestors just were not very good brachiators, and thus lacked the controversial specializations. This would, of course, mean that man is more closely related to the great apes and would further help to explain the discordance between the two groups in the attributes associated with brachiation.

In summary, it is now possible to view the variation within the primate order as a consequence of major adaptive shifts (for example, arboreal way of life, brachiation) followed by proliferation and ramification into the environmental possibilities opened up by these major shifts. Only one major primate group remains for our consideration here, and that is the one we are most interested in knowing about, the one that includes man and his immediate ancestors, all of whom belong to the family Hominidae. Man is a distinctive member of the Hominoidea superfamily by virtue of two major adaptive features: erect posture, with its associated bipedal gait, and, of course, culture.

Erect posture had the effect of distinguishing man morphologically quite sharply from the rest of the primates. In fact, most of the anatomical features in which man is unique are a result of erect posture. (Most of the unique morphological features which distinguish between and among contemporary groups within the human species may be due to cultural factors.) Among the most important features that came about as a consequence of erect posture and ultimately served to distinguish the hominids as a group are the following: large relative brain size, a pelvis adapted to erect posture, an S-shaped vertebral column (see Figure 2–22), and a large number of features of the skull which appear to be principally a consequence of man's dependence on culture.

Culture enables us to understand why the abrupt changes brought about by erect posture did not result in a rapid expansion and a proliferation of species within the Hominidae. Culture provides the means for man to evolve biologically without

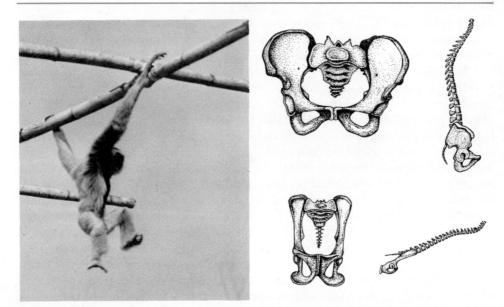

Figure 2–21. White-handed gibbon brachiating. (Courtesy of the Zoological Society of San Diego, photo by Ron Garrison)

Figure 2–22. Comparison of pelvis and spinal column in man and quadrupedal primate (stump-tailed macaque).

splitting into separate species largely because of two features: 1) Culture makes it unnecessary for groups of mankind to adapt to differing environmental requirements by the usually slow process of accumulation of somatic changes which necessarily results in speciation in lower forms. Man could and did adapt by cultural means rather than biological means. 2) Culture offers the basis for communication and cooperation which are unknown and unavailable to other species. As a consequence of these factors, the normally expected proliferation and diversification has not occurred in the Hominidae. Man remains a single species today, and there is good reason to conclude that this has been true ever since he became man; that is, since he became an erect, bipedal, and cultural animal.

Genus: Homo

The genus to which we belong is distinctive among the primates in having erect posture and bipedal locomotion. These traits have characterized four groups: 1) the australopithecines, occasionally referred to as *Homo africanus;* 2) *Homo erectus;* 3) *Homo neanderthalensis;* and 4) *Homo sapiens.* Our knowledge of the first three of these is based entirely on paleontological and archaeological evidence. The nature of this evidence is considered in detail in Part II.

Species: sapiens

Sapiens is the only living species of the genus *Homo;* it includes all mankind. Our species has specialized in relative brain size and intelligence. These are, of course, related to, but should not be confused with, wisdom. The distribution of variation within the species *sapiens* is discussed in Part III.

PRIMATE BEHAVIOR

Throughout the preceding discussion the emphasis has focused almost exclusively on morphological features; that is, groups have been contrasted with others on the basis of having or lacking one or more physical characteristics. This necessarily introduces some distortion, for, as noted earlier, it emphasizes a static and immutable quality in the discussion of taxonomy. In fact, however, the morphologies of organisms are the products of the dynamic interaction between their genetic potentials and the environments in which they occur. Stated in simplified form:

$$\text{Environment} \times \text{Genetic Potential} \rightarrow \text{Morphology}$$

In this way it is possible to see that morphological variability is the product of a continuous process of dynamic interaction.

Turning attention now to behavior, it is perhaps surprising to find that the comments just made about morphology can also be made about behavior. Behavior too is a product of interaction between genetic and environmental factors. Moreover, behavior and morphology interact together so that the relationships might be expressed more simply as follows:

$$\text{Environment} \times \text{Genetic Potential} \underset{\searrow}{\overset{\nearrow}{\rule{2cm}{0.4pt}}} \begin{array}{l} \text{Morphology} \\ \\ \text{Behavior} \end{array}$$

Thus morphology and behavior may be seen as aspects of the same interacting elements, and each may be used to inform us about the ways in which organisms adapt to their environments.

Until recently, the way in which animal behavior was investigated was not conducive to improving our understanding of human evolution and human variation. Investigations were commonly carried out on animals only remotely related to man under controlled laboratory conditions. In recent years, there has been a great increase in the number of studies that have examined the behavior of animals in their natural setting, and nowhere has this increased interest been more pronounced than in the area of primate behavior. Up to ten years ago the picture that anthropologists presented of primate behavior was clear and simple, consisting of the following elements: 1) primates live in socially organized groups that, both within and between species, vary in size and structure; 2) typically a group consists of a dominant male, a group of sexually mature females, their immature offspring, and, as outcasts on the periphery, the other adult males; and 3) behavior among the members of the group is a function largely of sexuality. The dominant male was portrayed as a sultan and the females as his harem; he would guard the females against the advances of the outcast males and thereby protect his exclusive sexual rights, and, as a result, the integration of the group could be maintained.

This view can be traced directly to some observations of primate behavior conducted in the early 1930s. Early field studies on gorillas and chimpanzees established the fact that these animals live in socially organized groups and that the composition of the group varied widely from one locality to another. Carpenter (1934) conducted what has come to be regarded as the pioneer work in systematic observations of primates living in their natural habitat as he studied howler monkeys in Central America. His observations led him to a view of primate behavior and social organization that contrasted sharply with the "typical" view characterized above. Carpenter observed that howler monkeys displayed very little competition for sexual partners, and in general noted that sexuality seemed to play a relatively minor role in their lives.

Carpenter's observations tended to be regarded simply as evidence of the vast difference between New and Old World primates. The typical view of social organization among Old World primates stems from the earlier work of Solly Zuckerman (1932) on baboons. First it should be emphasized that Zuckerman based his conclusions almost exclusively on observations of animals in captivity. Nevertheless, he and many others regarded this as no serious limitation and generalized his conclusions to apply not merely to baboons in nature, but to all Old World primates. His observations led him to put forth the view of primate society summarized above: groups of animals dominated by sexuality and characterized by jealousy and promiscuity. The dominant male, dominant by physical strength, remained in that position until a stronger rival deposed him. Not only did Zuckerman believe this form of social organization to be common to all the Catarrhinae, but since man evolved in the Old World, he felt as well that it represented a stage of social organization through which man's ancestors passed in their evolution.

Zuckerman's views were widely accepted by anthropologists for the next twenty-five to thirty years. E. A. Hooton (1942), in synthesizing the available data on primates, agreed in all essential features with Zuckerman but added, for reasons that are hard to understand, the proposition that the closer one comes to man in the taxonomic classification, the more intelligence and individuality tempered the sexually motivated behavior. As recently as 1959, Sahlins, in surveying much the same material as Hooton did, concluded that sexuality and dominance were the primary bases of primate social organization, but, unlike Hooton, Sahlins failed to see human social organization as a simple outgrowth of the gradual ameliorative effects of increasing intelligence and individuality. Sahlins presented the view that human social organization was a product of cultural factors (particularly economic) that simply do not occur in nonhuman primates.

Field observations on primates in their home territories resumed during the late fifties and early sixties. As an indication of the effort, from 1959 to 1965 extensive field studies were published on howler monkeys (Altmann, 1959), baboons (Washburn and DeVore, 1961; Hall and DeVore, 1965), macaques (Altmann, 1962; Koford, 1963; Simonds, 1965), langurs (Jay, 1963; Ripley, 1964), chimpanzees (Van Lawick-Goodall, 1963; Reynolds, 1963), and the gorilla (Schaller, 1963). In addition there were several less extensive reports on other species; two new journals dealing with primates were started; an international society for the study of primates was formed; and the United States Public Health Service established several primate research centers in various locations throughout the United States.

Of these newer studies, anthropologists were particularly influenced by the work of Washburn and DeVore on baboons, by the studies of Jane Goodall on chimpanzees, and the work of George Schaller on mountain gorillas. While each of these is of interest in its own right, they all led to the same basic conclusion: the behavior of primates is highly variable. In contrast to the stereotype created out of Zuckerman's work, these later studies showed among many other things that: 1) primate social organization differs markedly from one group to another; 2) sexuality is seasonal and but one of several factors that integrate primate society (see also Harlow and Harlow, 1965); and 3) dominant structures vary between species and function in more complex ways than was formerly believed.

The new work demonstrated a point: Primates behave in various ways. To anthropologists the point was interesting but a bit distracting, since they had intended to learn more about human evolution by studying primates. Evolution implies adaptation; adaptation implies pattern; and the more variation, the greater the difficulty of identifying patterns. Perhaps because the original task appeared to become more difficult as information accumulated, research on primates during the late sixties focused more and more on individual behavior, on psychological issues, and particularly on behaviors which seem to foreshadow more typically human ways of doing things. To a few investigators the primates were regarded as simply funny, though hairy, little people.

At present this emphasis is expressed particularly in the studies of chimpanzees trained to communicate with human beings by means of sign language (Gardner and Gardner, 1971; Premack, 1971; Hewes, 1973). Interest in these is very intense, though the long-term significance of the studies remains unclear. To some the sign-language-using chimpanzees appear to underscore the close relationship between man and chimp. To others the same evidence supports an opposite view, that is, how pathetically incompetent chimpanzees are in the business of communication when compared with human beings.

At the same time, however, one can recognize a return of interest to the issues of adaptation and population dynamics within ecological settings, a return, that is, to an interest in pattern (Kummer, 1968; Struhsaker, 1969; Altmann and Altmann, 1970). We are beginning to recognize that variability, far from making the task more difficult, in fact provides a rich source of information for testing hypotheses concerning human evolution (Washburn, 1971; Van Lawick-Goodall, 1971). With more thought, one can anticipate exciting advances in the future.

So what may be said about the primates? They are arboreal. Some are, some are not. They are tropical. Even excluding human beings, some are and some are not. They are gregarious. Some are, some are not. Studies of behavior as well as studies of morphology teach us to be cautious of any statements about the primates in general.

This completes a brief tour through the animal kingdom, which enabled us to obtain only the barest impressions of the differences that prevail between man and his relatives. But the trip has shown some important things; all the groups examined here are unique, yet all are similar in some ways too. Man is a primate, a mammal, a chordate, and an animal. He is unique both in morphology and in having culture. Realizing how man is like and how he differs from other animals is at least a beginning to an understanding of man's place in nature.

MAJOR POINTS IN CHAPTER 2

1. Zoological classification estimates biological relationships among animal varieties by assessing their similarities.
2. In general, the greater the degree of similarity, the closer the biological relationship.
3. Man is an animal, a chordate, a vertebrate, a mammal, a primate, a hominoid, and a hominid.
4. Primates behave in various ways.

REFERENCES AND SUGGESTIONS FOR ADDITIONAL READING

ALTMANN, STUART
   1959   Field observations on a howling monkey society. *Journal of Mammology*
          40:317–330.
   1962   A field study of the socio-biology of rhesus monkeys, *Macaca mulatta. Annals
          of the New York Academy of Sciences* 102:338–435.

ALTMANN, STUART, AND JEANNE ALTMANN
   1970   *Baboon ecology.* Chicago: University of Chicago Press.

CARPENTER, C. RAY
   1934   A field study of the behavior and social relations of howling monkeys. *Com-
          parative Psychology Monographs* 10.
   1940   A field study in Siam of the behavior and social relations of the gibbon
          (*Hylobates lar*). *Comparative Psychology Monographs* 16:1–212.

COON, CARLETON S.
   1962   *The origin of races.* New York: Alfred A. Knopf.

DAY, CLARENCE
   1920   *This simian world.* New York: Alfred A. Knopf.

DEVORE, IRVEN
   1965   *Primate behavior.* New York: Holt, Rinehart, and Winston.

EIMERL, SAREL, AND IRVEN DEVORE
   1965   *The primates.* New York: Time, Inc.

FIEDLER, W.
   1956   Ubersicht über das System der Primates. In *Primatologia*, ed. H. Hofer, A. H.
          Schultz, and D. Stark, 1:1–266. Basel: S. Karger.

GARDNER, BEATRICE, AND R. ALLEN GARDNER
   1971   Two-way communication with an infant chimpanzee. In *Behavior of nonhuman
          primates*, ed. A. Schrier and F. Stollnitz, vol. 4. New York: Academic Press.

HEWES, GORDON W.
   1973   Primate communication and the gestural origin of language. *Current Anthro-
          pology* 14:5–24.

HALL, K. R. L., AND IRVEN DEVORE
   1965   Baboon social behavior. In *Primate behavior*, ed. Irven DeVore. New York:
          Holt, Rinehart, and Winston.

HARLOW, HARRY F., AND MARGARET K. HARLOW
   1965   The affectional systems. In *Behavior of non-human primates*, ed. Allan M.
          Schrier, Harry F. Harlow, and Fred Stollnitz, 2:287–334. New York: Academic
          Press.

HOOTON, EARNEST ALBERT
   1942   *Man's poor relations.* Garden City, N.Y.: Doubleday, Doran.
   1947   *Up from the ape.* Rev. ed. New York: Macmillan.

JAY, PHYLLIS
   1963   The Indian langur monkey (*Presbytis entillus*). In *Primate social behavior*, ed.
          Charles H. Southwick. Princeton, N.J.: Van Nostrand.

JAY, PHYLLIS C., ED.
   1968   *Primates: Studies in adaptation and variability.* New York: Holt, Rinehart, and
          Winston.

JOLLY, ALISON.
   1966   *Lemur behavior*. Chicago: University of Chicago Press.
KOFORD, CARL B.
   1963   Group relations in an island colony of rhesus monkeys. In *Primate social behavior*, ed. Charles H. Southwick, pp. 136–152. Princeton, N.J.: Van Nostrand.
   1965   Population dynamics of rhesus monkeys on Cayo Santiago. In *Primate behavior*, ed. Irven DeVore. New York: Holt, Rinehart, and Winston.
KUMMER, HANS
   1968   *Social organization of Hamadryas baboons*. Chicago: University of Chicago Press.
MAYR, ERNST.
   1963   *Animal species and evolution*. Cambridge: Harvard University Press.
MOODY, PAUL A.
   1962   *Introduction to evolution*. 2d ed. New York: Harper and Row.
MORRIS, DESMOND
   1967   *Primate ethology*. Chicago: Aldine.
NAPIER, J. R., AND P. H. NAPIER.
   1967   *A handbook of living primates: Morphology, ecology, and behavior of non-human primates*. New York: Academic Press.
OXNARD, CHARLES E.
   1968   Primate evolution—a method of investigation. *American Journal of Physical Anthropology* (n.s.) 28:289–301.
   1969   Mathematics, shape, and function: A study in primate anatomy. *American Scientist* 57:75–96.
PREMACK, DAVID
   1971   Language in chimpanzee. *Science* 172:808–822.
QUIATT, DUANE
   1966   Social dynamics of rhesus monkey groups. Ph.D. dissertation, University of Colorado.
REYNOLDS, VERNON
   1963   An outline of the behaviour and social organization of forest-living chimpanzees. *Folia primatologica* 1:95–102.
RIPLEY, SUZANNE
   1964   Intertroop encounters among Ceylon gray langurs. Cited in *Social dynamics of rhesus monkey groups*, by Duane Quiatt. Ph.D. dissertation, University of Colorado, 1966.
SAHLINS, MARSHALL D.
   1959   The social life of monkeys, apes, and primitive man. *Human Biology* 31:54–73.
SCHALLER, GEORGE B.
   1963   *The mountain gorilla: Ecology and behavior*. Chicago: University of Chicago Press.
SIMONDS, PAUL E.
   1965   The bonnet macaque in South India. In *Primate behavior*, ed. Irven DeVore. New York: Holt, Rinehart, and Winston.

SIMPSON, GEORGE GAYLORD

1945 The principles of classification and a classification of mammals. *Bulletin of the American Museum of Natural History* 85:1–350.

1949 *The meaning of evolution: A study of the history of life and of its significance for man.* New Haven: Yale University Press.

1950 Some principles of historical biology bearing on human origins. *Cold Spring Harbor Symposia on Quantitative Biology* 15:55–66.

1961 *Principles of animal taxonomy.* New York: Columbia University Press.

1963 The meaning of taxonomic statements. In *Classification and human evolution*, ed. S. L. Washburn. Viking Fund Publications in Anthropology, no. 37. Chicago: Aldine.

SNYDER, LAURENCE H.

1954 The effects of selection and domestication on man. *Journal of the National Cancer Institute* 15:759–769.

STRUHSAKER, T. T.

1969 Correlates of ecology and social organization among African cercopithecines. *Folia Primatologica* 11:80–118.

VAN LAWICK-GOODALL, JANE

1963 My life among wild chimpanzees. *National Geographic* 124:272–308.

1967 *My friends the wild chimpanzees.* Washington: National Geographic Society.

1971 *In the shadow of man.* Boston: Houghton Mifflin.

WASHBURN, SHERWOOD L.

1971 On the importance of the study of primate behavior for anthropologists. In *Anthropological perspectives on education*, ed. S. Diamond and F. O. Gearing. New York: Basic Books.

WASHBURN, SHERWOOD L., AND IRVEN DEVORE

1961 The social life of baboons. *Scientific American* 204, June, pp. 62–71.

ZUCKERMAN, SOLLY

1932 *Social life of monkeys and apes.* London: Kegan Paul.

3 The Background of Genetics

INTRODUCTION

The most outstanding intellectual achievement in biology since Darwin's time is the demonstration that life is controlled by the same physical and chemical laws that regulate other forms and organizations of matter. The basic view is not a new one, but the experimental evidence supporting it has been accumulated largely within the last twenty years. This work has brought about a new and revolutionary approach in biology, but most particularly in genetics.

Therefore, a consideration of genetics and its bearing on physical anthropology is essential. After all, physical anthropology can expect to advance at least in part as biology advances, and at the present time, genetics is biology's most rapidly advancing area. Yet there are other reasons for turning to genetics, and among the most compelling are the following: 1) Physical anthropology attempts to explain human evolution. Genetics provides a basis for investigating similarities and differences between parent and offspring generations. Indeed, evolution may be defined as the accumulation of genetic changes over generations. 2) Physical anthropology attempts to describe and explain man's biological variation. Genetics has made it possible to employ a distinctive set of traits, inherited ones, in describing and analyzing man's variation, and these may be analyzed in ways that other traits cannot (see Chapter 9). 3) In classifying man's variation, physical anthropologists have relied heavily on racial classifications that basically are pre-Darwinian or nonevolutionary in outlook. Genetics, in the development of its theory of population structure, has laid the foundations for classifying human variation into categories with clearer evolutionary unity and thus with clearer biological meaning than traditional racial classifications imply. In short, physical anthropology can be discussed without a knowledge of genetics, but such discussions are destined to be specialized, trivial, or both.

The field of genetics has diversified rapidly since 1900, and any attempt to cover the field in a complete way would have to give attention to at least the following subdivisions: medical, formal, population, experimental, biochemical, cytological, behavioral, quantitative, developmental, molecular, plant, microbial, serological, and immunological genetics. Several books and countless articles have been written on each of these specialties, and, clearly, it is not desirable, in view of the objectives of this book, to deal with each of them. The discussion here is limited to: 1) *formal genetics* since its conclusions are basic to all the others, 2) enough *molecular* and *biochemical genetics* to illustrate some of the important recent advances, and 3) *population genetics* because of its direct relevance to the problems and traditional interests of physical anthropology. These should serve to sharpen one's understanding of the paleontological record even though it is not at present possible to deal with it directly in genetic terms. Likewise, these discussions should help one to see that heterographic variation is a clue to the dynamics of evolutionary processes, and to appreciate more clearly the present status of physical anthropology and its future probabilities.

DEFINITIONS

Before considering formal genetics in some detail, it will be useful to introduce a few basic terms. A *gene* is the physical structure transmitting hereditary potential from one generation to the next. A *chromosome* is a discrete set of genes arranged in linear order. The space a gene occupies on a chromosome is referred to as a *genetic locus*. As the structure of a gene varies, its hereditary potential varies. Changes in the structure of a gene are *mutations*. Mutations give rise to alternative structures of the same gene; these alternative forms of a gene are *alleles*. Under normal conditions, a person obtains one complete set of genetic loci from his mother and another from his father. Thus, he has a pair of alleles for each locus. One complete set is said to contain the *haploid* number of chromosomes; one complete set of pairs, the *diploid* number. If at any locus a child obtains the same allelic form from his mother as from his father, he is *homozygous* for that gene. If he obtains different alleles he is *heterozygous*. The pair of alleles an individual inherits constitutes his *genotype* for that particular locus. The hereditary potential of the genotype may be modified by environmental factors, and the manner in which the genetic material is expressed in an individual is termed the *phenotype*. Thus identical genotypes can, in contrasting environments, result in differing phenotypes. Likewise, different genotypes can, under many circumstances, result in indistinguishable phenotypes in a similar manner.

The term *frequency* is used commonly throughout this and later chapters. The *frequency* of an event is the number of times it occurs out of the total number of occasions it could have occurred. Thus, if you flip a coin twelve times, and if seven of those flips come up heads, the frequency of the event "heads" is seven out of twelve, a relationship that may be expressed as a fraction (7/12), or a proportion (.58), or a percentage (58 percent).

FORMAL GENETICS

Formal genetics investigates the ways in which genes are transmitted from parents to their offspring. Mendel's laws are the basic components of formal genetics. As discussed in Chapter 1, his experiments led to the conclusions that: 1) inheritance is particulate; 2) the particles, that is, the genes, are present in pairs which separate in the formation of sex cells (first law); and 3) the segregation of one pair of alleles is independent of that of any other pair (second law). In the words of our new vocabulary, alleles segregate, and genes assort independently. Thus Mendel not only discovered what later were called genes, but also two basic laws regulating the manner in which they are passed on from one generation to the next. These remain today as the basic laws of heredity.

Since Mendel's time formal genetics has advanced in three major ways. The field advanced: 1) by establishing the generality of Mendel's laws, 2) by following out the implications of Mendel's laws, and 3) by integrating information obtained as a result of advances in laboratory techniques and equipment.

Generality of Mendel's Laws

This point was established rather quickly after the discovery of Mendel's work in 1900. Essentially the point is that inheritance follows the same predictable patterns in organisms as diverse as primroses, pineapples, porpoises, and people. As always this new information gave rise to a new set of questions: How could genetics be used to improve the quality of domestic animals? To increase the yield of food crops? To advance the practice of medicine? What about the genetics of organisms which reproduce in nonsexual ways? These and many other questions have been pursued vigorously, and each has led to its own discoveries and advances.

Implications of Mendel's Laws

Thus Mendel's laws may be seen as general propositions. They apply to all forms of life, and it has taken a long time to follow out their far-reaching implications.

Specifically, Mendel's laws implied that: 1) the genetic potential for variation between generations is enormous, and 2) the same relationships that hold within a family between parents and their children hold between one generation and the next in a population.

POTENTIAL FOR VARIATION. In our earlier discussion we dealt with the genetic basis for variability between generations. Mendel's first and second laws of heredity imply that the components of an organism's genotype, the genetic loci and the alleles that occupy them, are reshuffled and brought together in new combinations in the process of forming sex cells. As an illustration, consider an individual with the following genotype for two genetic loci:

	Allele 1	Allele 2
Locus 1	*A*	*a*
Locus 2	*B*	*b*

The individual is heterozygous at both loci.

Mendel's second law implies that *A* is as likely to be combined with *B* as with *b* in the formation of sex cells; likewise *a* is as likely to end up with *B* as with *b*. The process is random; the offspring obtains a complete set of genetic loci from each parent. Thus, from the parent in the illustration a child must get either *A* or *a*, and either *B* or *b* (first law), but whether the offspring get *AB*, *Ab*, *aB*, or *ab* is entirely a matter of chance (second law). Table 3–1 shows how two parents, both heterozygous for two loci, are able to generate nine different genotypes.

Table 3–1   Genetic Variability between Generations as Implied by Mendel's Laws: An Illustration

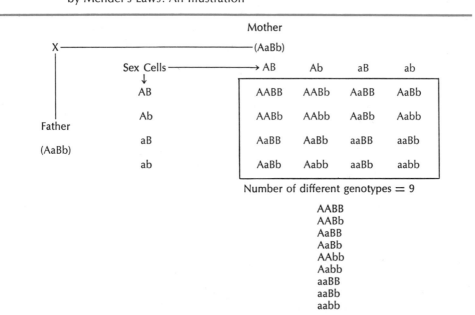

The implication of variability is clear enough, but in point of fact it did not always hold true. Some genes, or more properly some *combinations* of genes, were identified which do not follow Mendel's laws. Exploring these "contradictory" cases led eventually to a modification of the laws to accommodate a major exception, genetic linkage. The genes, as noted earlier, are located on chromosomes, and one chromosome contains many loci. Since chromosomes normally remain intact, genes located together on the same chromosome are transmitted together as a single genetic package. Thus, in the illustration used above, if *A* and *B* were linked together, then *a* and *b*, their alleles, would also be linked together on the homologous chromosome, and the two loci could not assort independently. In this instance a child could receive only *AB* or *ab* from that parent. The effect is to reduce variability. In the event of linkage, two parents heterozygous at two loci could produce only three different genotypes, as shown in Table 3–2. Thus a geneticist who finds two or more loci that do not assort independently has evidence that the loci are linked together on the same chromosome. Thus chromosomes, not genes, assort independently.

Table 3–2   Limitation on Genetic Variability between Generations as Implied by Linkage: An Illustration

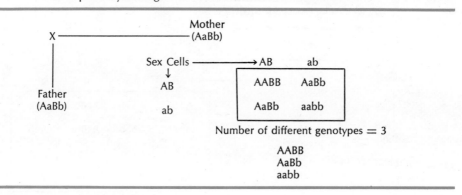

These discoveries led ultimately to chromosome maps that show what loci are linked and the order of their appearance on the chromosome. The latter point, the linear order, can be estimated as a function of another exception, in this case an exception to linkage. Linked loci can and do become separated by a process called *crossover*, wherein two homologous chromosomes exchange segments. Again, if *A* and *B* and *a* and *b* are linked, and crossover should occur between them, the result will be to link together *A* and *b* and *a* and *B*, thus:

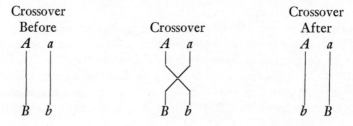

Linear order of the loci may be obtained as an extension of the assumption that *the closer together two linked loci are situated, the less likely they will be separated by crossover;* or, conversely, the farther apart two loci, the more frequent their separation by crossover. Thus the two loci most frequently separated are those at the extreme ends of the chromosome, and having discovered these, it is possible to determine by crossover frequencies the map of the chromosome. Although detailed maps are available on a few organisms, not enough is known about linkage groups and crossover frequencies to be able to construct such a map for man.

FROM FAMILIES TO POPULATIONS. The validity of Mendel's laws also makes it possible to apply probability theory and combinatorial mathematics to genetic problems and to the formulation of genetic theory. This has contributed greatly to the rapid development of the field. To go into this point in detail would involve a long digression. Basically what is meant here is that advances in biological and behavioral sciences are restricted for the most part to inductive methods employing the technology of statistics. One advantage to the inductive approach is that any scientific investigation may begin with a hypothesis that two or more conditions or events are related in specific ways; for example, that the widths of tree rings are directly related to mean annual rainfall. This is a relationship that can be tested by appropriate experimental and analytical procedures, which, in turn, should make it possible to draw either the conclusion that tree-ring width and mean annual rainfall are unrelated, or that they might be related. Inductive methods are, of course, essential in all sectors of science.

However, some relationships simply cannot be tested, some because of deficiencies in the instruments of science, some because the available statistical procedures are inadequate, and, more to the point when studying man, still others because we are unable to apply the appropriate experimental procedures. On occasion, however, it happens that the broad implications and general applicability of a discovery make it possible to advance directly on many investigative fronts at once with great speed. In these instances what is involved is the discovery of a basic or fundamental principle of nature. This is a comparatively rare event in science, but when it occurs, it makes possible the employment of more efficient methods of deduction in predicting the outcomes of specific experiments and in generating new theories to serve as guides for the formulation of new hypotheses. Mendel made this kind of discovery and thereby made possible the rapid formulation of genetic theory that has served to direct much of the work in experimental genetics, which, in turn, produces a confirmation or modification of the theory. (An example of this can be seen in Table 3–3.)

From Mendel's laws alone, if one is able to identify the genotypes of the parents, then one can predict the genotypes and their expected frequencies in the offspring. Moreover, and this is the most important realization, the same relationships that hold within a family between parents and their children hold between one generation and the next in a population. That is, it is possible by a comparatively simple extension

Table 3–3 Implications of Mendel's Laws in the Distribution of Genotypes among Offspring from All Mating Types

PARENTS MATING TYPES			EXPECTED PERCENTAGES OF OFFSPRING GENOTYPES		
♂		♀	AA	Aa	aa
AA	×	AA	100		
AA	×	Aa	50	50	
AA	×	aa		100	
Aa	×	AA	50	50	
Aa	×	Aa	25	50	25
Aa	×	aa		50	50
aa	×	AA		100	
aa	×	Aa		50	50
aa	×	aa			100

of the logic implied in Table 3–3 to construct a more generalized table summarizing the expected proportion of offspring genotypes that arise from a parental population of any determinable genetic structure. To extend the logic in this manner requires making some assumptions, but having made them allows the logical foundation for the branch of genetics known as population genetics (see page 92). At this juncture, the important point is that Table 3–3 can be constructed solely on the basis of Mendel's laws.

TECHNICAL IMPROVEMENTS AND FORMAL GENETICS. Some advances in our understanding of formal genetics have been made largely as the results of technical improvements. Among the most important of these are: 1) meiosis and mitosis, 2) karyotyping, and 3) refinements in our understanding of the concepts of dominance and recessiveness.

Meiosis and Mitosis. The physiological mechanism underlying Mendel's laws is *meiosis*, the process that produces sex cells. As far as genetics is concerned, the most important consequence of meiosis is that it results in cells that contain only one complete set of alleles. Since genes are located on chromosomes, this means that cells produced by meiosis contain only half the chromosome number that other cells have, the haploid number as compared with the diploid number. *Mitosis* is the cellular process that results in two cells identical to one another and to the parent cell that divided to produce them. All have the diploid number of chromosomes. The two processes are simplified in Figure 3–1. In human beings, meiosis produces cells with 23 chromosomes in the nucleus, and mitosis produces cells with 46.

The processes of meiosis and mitosis have been observed in considerable detail and, though continuous, have been subdivided into phases (for example, anaphase, metaphase, etc.) for even more detailed analysis. Since our interest here is more narrow, we will avoid the complex details and direct our attention to the issue of how the processes relate to Mendel's laws. Since only meiosis is significant in this

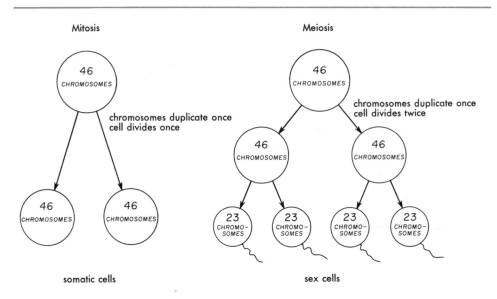

Figure 3–1. Comparison of mitosis and meiosis of male germ cells. Meiosis of female cells differs in detail but not in principle.

regard, we may ignore mitosis. Meiosis begins with the diploid number of chromosomes. In sexually reproducing species the diploid number is always even since it consists of a set of chromosome pairs. One chromosome of each pair is, ultimately, derived from father, the other from mother. Paired chromosomes are called homologous chromosomes, they contain identical genetic loci, but, of course, the loci may be occupied by different alleles. We will illustrate how meiosis relates to Mendel's laws by using a simple case involving only two pairs of chromosomes, C_M derived from mother and C_F the homologous chromosome derived from father, and, in a like manner, the other pair H_M and H_F.

Thus we begin with the diploid number of four chromosomes, two sets of pairs:

$$C_M \quad C_F$$

$$H_M \quad H_F$$

One of the first things to happen in meiosis is that every chromosome duplicates, that is, makes an exact copy of itself. Later in this chapter we will discuss the duplication process; at this point it is important only to realize that the cell now contains *eight* chromosomes, as follows:

$$C_M \quad C_M \qquad C_F \quad C_F$$

$$H_M \quad H_M \qquad H_F \quad H_F$$

Next the cell divides, but in a very precise way so that homologous chromosomes are invariably separated. This is the step which underlies Mendel's first law, the law of segregation. To understand what takes place at this time one must be able to distinguish clearly between what *may* happen and what *can* happen. A cell dividing in this precise way *may* produce four different kinds of daughter cells, but it *can* produce only two. A cell may produce:

C_M C_M	C_M C_M	C_F C_F	C_F C_F
H_M H_M	H_F H_F	H_M H_M	H_F H_F

However, only two cells can be produced when one cell divides and the assortment of chromosomes each obtains is not independent. If one cell receives C_M C_M and H_M H_M, the other must receive C_F C_F and H_F H_F. Likewise if one receives C_M C_M and H_F H_F, the other must combine C_F C_F and H_M H_M. So we have two possibilities:

	Either				Or	

C_M C_M	C_F C_F		C_M C_M	C_F C_F
H_M H_M	H_F H_F		H_F H_F	H_M H_M

Next the cell divides a second time, and again in a very precise way. In this division the duplicate chromosomes segregate. Thus if the first of the two possibilities above is the one that actually happens, then we see four cells, each with the haploid number of chromosomes, as follows:

C_M	C_M	C_F	C_F
H_M	H_M	H_F	H_F

If the second possibility is the one that actually occurs, then four haploid cells result as follows:

C_M	C_M	C_F	C_F
H_F	H_F	H_M	H_M

Whether this or the other set of four sex cells is produced is entirely a matter of chance. Any particular assortment of chromosomes is thus independent of any other. This is the basis of Mendel's second law, the law of independent assortment.

In summary, then, meiosis begins with one diploid cell and concludes with four haploid cells. In between three events occur which make this take place: 1) the chromosomes duplicate; 2) the cell divides and segregates homologous chromosomes; and 3) the resulting cells divide again and segregate the duplicate chromosomes.

Karyotyping. In recent years, largely because of the rapid improvement in laboratory techniques and equipment, it has become possible to study chromosomes in great detail. Figure 3–2 is a photograph of the chromosomes of two human beings.

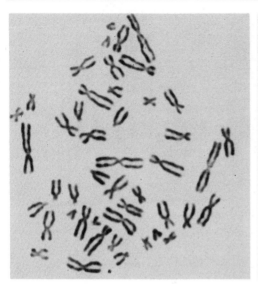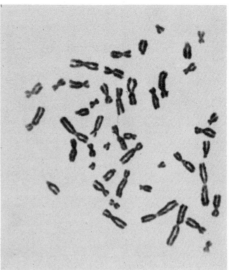

Figure 3–2. Metaphase plate showing the chromosome complement. Left: a normal human male. Right: a normal human female. (Courtesy of David T. Arakaki)

The photograph was taken after the chromosomes had duplicated but before the cell had divided. The chromosomes appear as severals Xs in the photograph. Actually each of these Xs is a chromosome and a duplicate of itself joined together at a location known as the centromere. Man's chromosomes have been classified into the conventional groups on the basis of their size and the position of the centromere. The photograph is an indication of how refined the cytological techniques have become, and it should not be mistaken as a rare one-of-a-kind picture. Such procedures, called karyotyping, are employed more and more frequently as aids in the diagnosis of certain kinds of disease. For example, mongolism, more properly called Down's syndrome, is associated with an extra chromosome in the G group.

During 1971 a new technical breakthrough in staining chromosomes made it clear that it is now possible to identify the pattern of bands along a chromosome. The pattern, moreover, is distinctive for each chromosome. Thus instead of grouping chromosomes it appears now that it is possible to identify specific chromosomes. The advance is an exciting one with potential significance we will realize more fully in this decade. It is a discovery that must lead to a clearer understanding of the structure and function of chromosomes.

In classifying human chromosomes, one encounters a clear and consistant difference between males and females. Figures 3–3 and 3–4 are karyotypes of a normal female and a normal male. The normal male has fifteen chromosomes in the C group; the female has sixteen. The normal male has five chromosomes in the G group; the

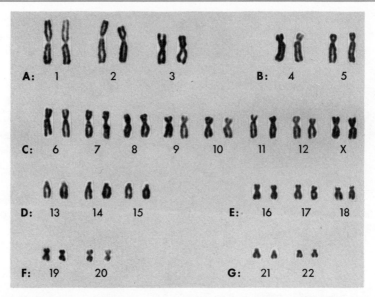

Figure 3–3. Karyotype of a normal human female. (Courtesy of David T. Arakaki)

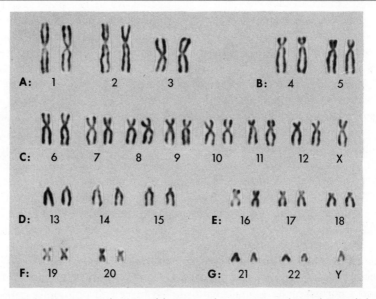

Figure 3–4. Karyotype of a normal human male. (Courtesy of David T. Arakaki)

female has four. Thus both sexes have twenty-three pairs; twenty-two pairs are called autosomal chromosomes, and the pair differentiating males and females, sex chromosomes. The larger sex chromosome is called the X chromosome; females, of course, have two. Males have only one X chromosome and another, in the G group, called the Y chromosome. Thus it is the male that determines the sex of the offspring in man. Females contribute X and only X chromosomes; males contribute X or Y chromosomes.

Because of the way in which sex is determined in man, the traits controlled by genes located on the X and Y chromosomes are more readily recognized than traits inherited on the autosomes. Genes located on the Y chromosome, for example, may be found only in males. In fact, there are no well-documented Y-loci traits in man, and it may be that the entire chromosome functions only in producing the enzymes necessary for the production of male hormone, which, in turn, regulates the development of male sex characteristics.

The X chromosome bears genes that influence a number of characteristics in human beings that have nothing to do with sex. Genes inherited on the X chromosome are, however, called sex-linked genes and include such things as one form of color blindness, hemophilia, an enzyme deficiency in glucose-6-phosphate dehydrogenase, and a blood group gene, the Xg group. Because of their location on the X chromosome, these traits have a distribution that differs between males and females. Homozygous conditions on the sex chromosomes require two alleles in females, one in males (*hemizygous*). Heterozygous conditions cannot occur in males for sex-linked traits. Thus hemophilia, a homozygous condition determined by a rare allele, is much more common in males than females. Normal females who are heterozygous for hemophilia transmit the condition to half of their sons on a statistical basis.

Examination of human chromosomal material during interphase, the so-called resting period of mitosis, reveals another difference between males and females: females have a mass of chromatin material that may be observed to be balled up on the edge of the nucleus (see Figure 3–5). Males do not show this phenomenon. Although the significance of this difference is still a controversial subject, the most widely accepted theory is one proposed by Dr. Mary Lyon (1962) which specifies that in any cell, one and only one X chromosome is active and functional. Some support for this view comes from an investigation of nuclei with abnormal numbers of sex chromosomes. The number of X chromosomes identifiable at metaphase is always one more than the number of sex chromatin bodies identifiable at interphase. Thus an XXY (Klinefelter's syndrome) individual is a male, a sterile one to be sure, and one whose cells show a sex chromatin body during interphase. Likewise XXX females have been identified, and they show two sex chromatin bodies.

Dominant and Recessive. *Dominant* and *recessive* are two terms with long histories of respectable use in genetics. The meanings of the two words are clear enough: dominant alleles are those expressed in both homozygous and heterozygous combinations, and recessive alleles are expressed only when paired together in a homozygote. In recent years, however, the need to use the terms has decreased as

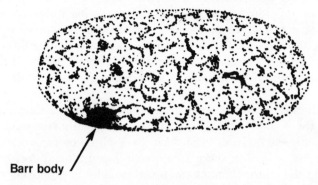

Barr body

Figure 3–5. Sex chromatin mass in a normal human female cell. (Drawing of photograph–photo courtesy of David T. Arakaki)

improved techniques have made it possible to distinguish heterozygotes from homozygotes in many cases where it was formerly impossible to do so. If the genotypes are distinguishable, then it would seem to be unnecessary to continue the dominant-recessive dichotomy. This is not to say that classic examples of dominants and recessives no longer exist; indeed they do, and it may never be possible to detect differences between heterozygotes and homozygotes for these loci. But if recent trends are indicative, we might hope that such distinctions will eventually be made.

Summary of Formal Genetics

The area of formal genetics was established first for the obvious reason that its principles underlie investigations in all other subdivisions. Essentially it specifies the ground rules of gene and chromosome behavior: 1) inheritance is by means of genes; 2) genes are situated on chromosomes; 3) chromosomes are paired in the nuclei of cells, a condition maintained by mitosis; 4) chromosome pairs segregate and assort independently in meiosis. Two such cells, one from a male and one from a female, when joined together re-pair the chromosomes and thereby initiate the development of a new individual.

In this manner formal genetics has established clearly a relationship between genes and traits in the phenotype, thus:

ENVIRONMENT

Gene → Trait

But a clearly established relationship is not the same as a clearly understood one. More questions have been generated by formal genetics than have been answered. Among the most penetrating of these are the following: What is the nature of the gene? How does a gene act to produce a trait in the phenotype? The search initiated by these problems has produced the most exciting and most consequential genetic discoveries of this century. These are the discoveries that have joined genetics, and thereby all of biology, to the well-established laws and highly developed theories of modern physics and chemistry. These developments are new, and their full impact is only now beginning to be felt.

MOLECULAR AND BIOCHEMICAL GENETICS

The Nature of the Gene

If one asks simply the question, What is a gene? there are several acceptable answers. The question of interest here, however, is more particular. It asks: What are the material elements that make up a gene, and how do they fit together? An obvious place to begin to investigate the molecular properties of the gene is within the nucleus of the cell—for two good reasons: 1) this is where the chromosomes are located, and 2) males and females contribute equally to the hereditary composition of their offspring, and equally in nuclear material but unequally in the nonnuclear components of the cell.

In the nucleus, one may find in abundance three kinds of molecules: water, protein, and nucleic acids. Water, as the element of heredity, is, of course, out of the question; its simple structure could not begin to account for the wide variety of gene effects. Nuclear proteins are large and complex molecules consisting of long sequences of amino acids capable of being varied in almost endless ways and were, for this reason, considered for a time as the hereditary material. However, experimental evidence eventually eliminated nuclear proteins from consideration, and, in the process, focused attention on the nucleic acids.

Genetic Transformation

The foundation for the conclusion that the nucleic acid material is the genetic material was laid down in 1928 as the outcome of an experiment demonstrating genetic transformation. The classic transformation experiment involves two strains of *Pneumococcus*, the bacterium that can cause pneumonia. These strains differ in appearance and effect. One, the smooth strain, is encapsulated in a shell composed of sugar molecules joined together to form a polysaccharide. This is the virulent strain. The other, the rough strain, lacks both the polysaccharide capsule and the virulence. The experiment performed by F. Griffith (1928) involved the inoculation of mice with a mixture of living rough and dead smooth *Pneumococcus* bacteria. One might expect little effect on the mice, since the rough strain is not virulent and the smooth strain injected consisted only of dead cells. Surprisingly, however, many of the mice died of pneumonia, and, in addition, examination of the blood of the mice revealed the presence of living smooth as well as living rough bacteria. Some of the rough bacteria had apparently become *transformed* into smooth *Pneumococci*. Moreover, the transformed smooth strain, when allowed to divide and proliferate, produced smooth type daughter cells, indicating clearly that the transformation was a genetic one.

Refinements in techniques eventually made it possible to demonstrate transformation in the test tube, and this, in turn, meant that greater precision and control could be introduced into the experiment. The components could be tried one at a time or in all possible combinations, and, by this means, it was discovered that only a part of the smooth bacteria was required to bring about the transformation. The part required was identified as the nucleic acid, deoxyribonucleic acid, or DNA (see Hershey and Chase, 1952).

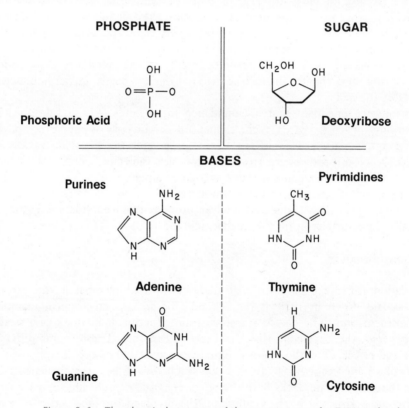

Figure 3–6. The chemical structure of the components of a DNA molecule.

At this point it is possible to answer the question, What is a gene? in a more satisfactory way. A gene is presumably some part of DNA. This raises another obvious question: What is DNA?

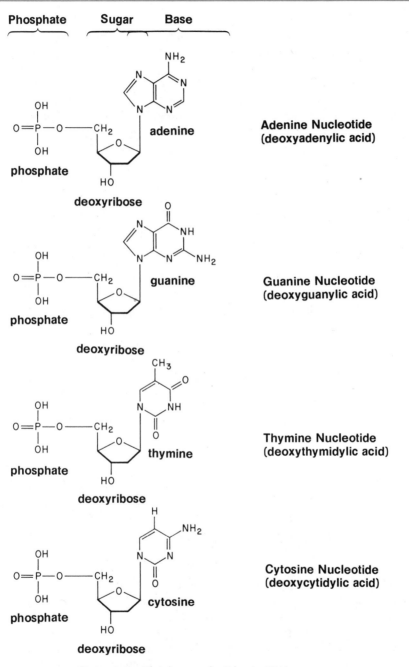

Phosphate	Sugar	Base

Adenine Nucleotide
(deoxyadenylic acid)

phosphate — deoxyribose — adenine

Guanine Nucleotide
(deoxyguanylic acid)

phosphate — deoxyribose — guanine

Thymine Nucleotide
(deoxythymidylic acid)

phosphate — deoxyribose — thymine

Cytosine Nucleotide
(deoxycytidylic acid)

phosphate — deoxyribose — cytosine

Figure 3–7.   The four nucleotides in DNA.

DNA

DNA is made up of carbon, hydrogen, nitrogen, oxygen, and phosphorus. These elements are joined together in various ways to form purine, pyrimidine, deoxyribose, and phosphate molecules. Two kinds of purines, adenine and guanine, and two kinds of pyrimidines, cytosine and thymine, are found in DNA. Phosphorus occurs only in the composition of a phosphate ion that is invariable in its structure and always found to be a part of the DNA substance. Likewise, deoxyribose is always a part of DNA and is the five-carbon sugar that gives the substance its name. The chemical structure of all of these components is illustrated in Figure 3–6. The basic unit that these components join together to form is called a *nucleotide*, which consists of one phosphate group joined to one molecule of deoxyribose, which, in turn, is joined with either one purine or one pyrimidine. Since there are two purines and two pyrimidines, there are then four possible nucleotides, and these are illustrated in Figure 3–7. Nucleotides are themselves joined together in pairs by weak bonds known as hydrogen bonds. In DNA, nucleotide pairs always join together one purine and one pyrimidine; more precisely, the pairs always consist of adenine joined together with thymine, or guanine joined to cytosine. These pairs are illustrated in Figure 3–8. The DNA molecule consists of a long chain of these nucleotide pairs joined together on both sides at the phosphate group. A section of the DNA molecule is illustrated in Figure 3–9.

Most of these advances are recent and have been the result of X-ray diffraction studies and chemical analyses of the composition of DNA which were initiated by the transformation experiments. These different lines of investigation were brought together by J. D. Watson, F. H. C. Crick, and M. H. F. Wilkins, who were awarded a Nobel Prize for their work. In their view, which is the generally accepted view, the DNA molecule is not simply a flat chain of polynucleotide pairs, but rather a doubly coiled helix (see Figure 3–13 on page 86).

This helps to improve our understanding of the composition of DNA, but it does not further an understanding of the nature of the gene. If asked the question, What is a gene? at this point, we would still have to answer that it is some part of DNA. We would indeed be able to say something about DNA, but nothing more about the gene. Is a gene a nucleotide? This is unlikely on logical grounds alone, since there are only four different nucleotides, and genes can reasonably be expected to have considerably greater variation than this provides. For the same reason, a gene is not likely to be equivalent to a nucleotide pair, since, even with reciprocals, there are only four different pairs: adenine and thymine, thymine and adenine, guanine and cytosine, cytosine and guanine. Moreover, the DNA (or some part of it) must be able to duplicate, to allow for the implicit requirements of mitosis and meiosis. Our understanding of the details of these processes has been greatly improved by research into the question of what a gene does, or, more broadly, how a gene functions. We know that a gene can influence the phenotype, but how does it manage to exert its influence?

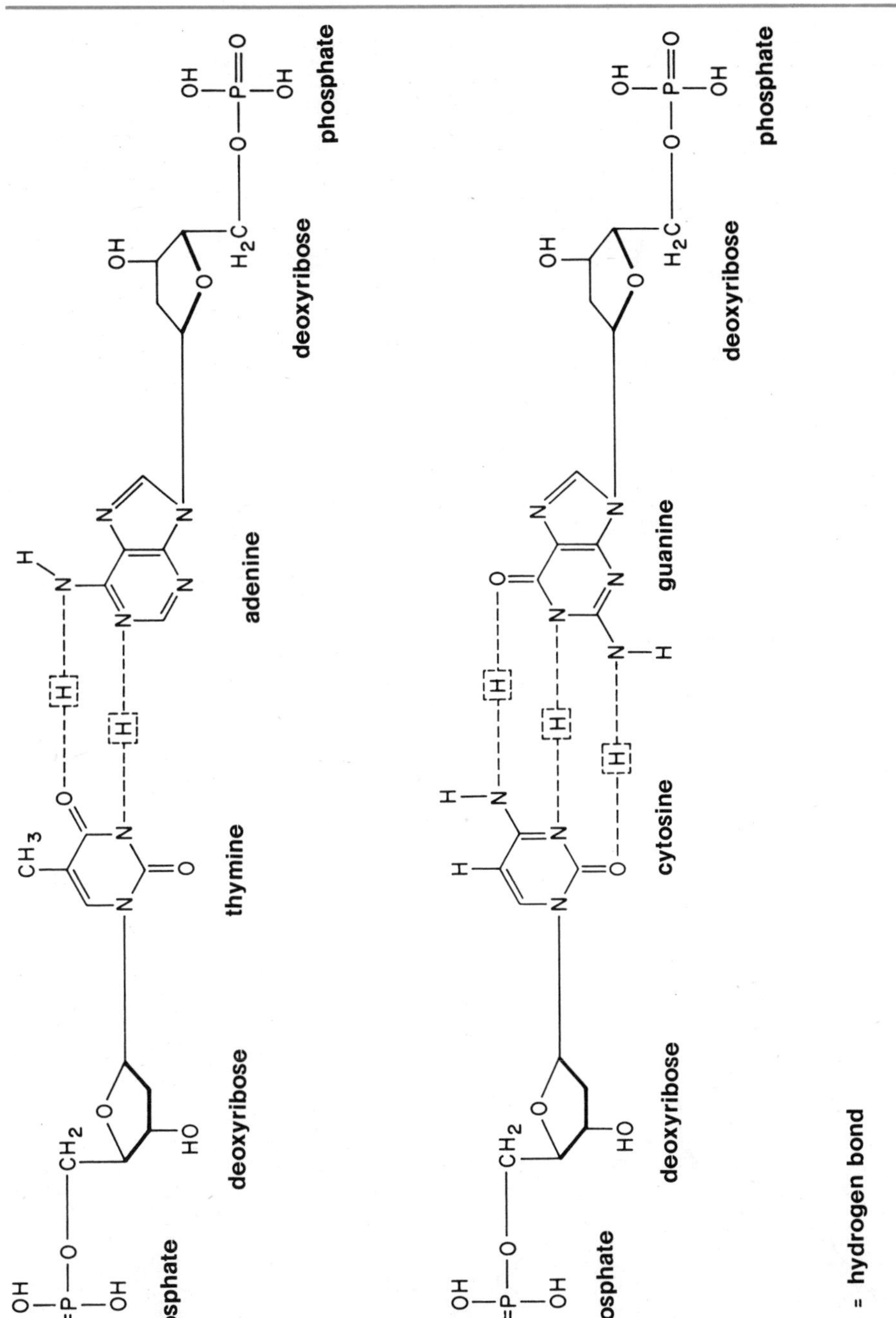

Figure 3–8. Comparison of the two kinds of nucleotide pairs.

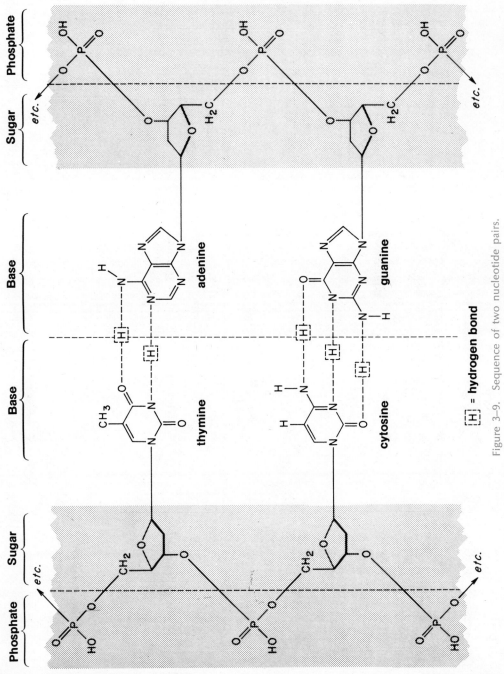

Figure 3-9. Sequence of two nucleotide pairs.

The Function of a Gene

Some of the earliest information about gene function was obtained from studies on human beings. Two hereditary conditions pointing to the same general conclusion about the function of a gene are alcaptonuria and phenylketonuria. These are both rare inherited diseases. The striking symptom of alcaptonuria is that the urine of a person with the disease turns black on exposure to air. This is a consequence of the fact that alcaptonurics have in their urine an unusual substance, homogentisic acid, which normal persons lack. The presence of homogentisic acid in the urine indicates a simple metabolic defect in which affected persons lack the enzyme needed to convert homogentisic acid to acetoacetic acid, the latter a compound commonly found in the urine of normal persons. Thus it would appear that the genetic difference between normal persons and those with alcaptonuria is nothing more than the presence of an enzyme in the former that is absent in the latter.

The condition known as phenylketonuria (PKU) has been given much attention recently and points to a similar flaw. In this case, normal persons possess an enzyme that converts phenylalanine to tyrosine. Persons lacking the enzyme build up excessive amounts of phenylalanine in their bloodstream and excrete in their urine a by-product of phenylalanine known as phenylpyruvic acid. Normal persons do not excrete this substance. In the case of PKU, the associated symptoms are more severe than in that of alcaptonuria. Phenylketonurics are always mentally deficient, and they tend to have light skin color and blond hair. The condition, if detected sufficiently early, can be ameliorated by feeding the affected person a diet low in phenylalanine.

The significant observation in regard to phenylketonuria for the present discussion is that, like alcaptonuria, the inherited condition again corresponds with the absence of a specific enzyme. This is the same conclusion reached in the more completely controlled investigations of one of the organisms responsible for bread mold, *Neurospora*. This organism has several characteristics which make it a particularly useful one for genetic studies, but without going into them we may simply observe that several strains of *Neurospora* have been produced by means of radiation-induced mutations, and many of the strains are unable to complete their normal metabolic activities due to the lack of specific and identifiable enzymes. The work on *Neurospora* indicated too that a one-to-one relationship exists between a gene and an enzyme; or, more broadly, that the life process may be thought of as an orderly steplike sequence of physical-chemical events with each step controlled by a specific enzyme which, in turn, is produced by a particular gene (see Beadle and Tatum, 1941). These indications have subsequently been confirmed on several other organisms, and the conclusion is now widely accepted that genes apparently function by controlling the reactions carried out by living organisms in converting their food resources to the substances required to carry out the life processes. Although it has had to be revised slightly, the accumulation of evidence led to the one-gene-one-enzyme hypothesis, or, in other words, that for every enzyme there is one gene controlling its synthesis.

These experiments provide an empirical basis for answering the question, What is a gene? in a more detailed way than we have been able to do up to now. It is reasonable at this point to say that a gene is some part of DNA that controls the manufacture of a particular enzyme. As before, the definition raises additional questions, and among them the very pertinent one: How does this occur? To understand the answer that is now generally accepted concerning the way that genes make enzymes requires a consideration of an even more basic question: What is an enzyme?

ENZYMES AND OTHER PROTEINS. First of all, an enzyme is a protein. Enzymes function by regulating the sequence and rate of chemical reactions. They are basic to the occurrence of any biological reaction. Enzymes are, however, only one of two kinds of protein. The other kind is called structural protein, which may be found in the structure of cell walls, connective tissue, muscle, hemoglobin, collagen, etc. The differences between enzymes and structural proteins are essentially functional. Structurally they are made up of the same kinds of molecules organized in the same general ways. These structural similarities suggest the broader possibility that genes function to make proteins, and, as the evidence has accumulated, this view has replaced the narrower one-gene-one-enzyme hypothesis. Thus, the broader question of what a protein is should be discussed before returning to the problem of how genes manufacture them.

HEMOGLOBIN. Figure 3–10 is an illustration of a model of the structure of hemoglobin, a structural protein. As the illustration clearly shows, proteins are too complex to be described directly. It is necessary to take them apart and put them back together again before one can have a detailed understanding of their structure. The first impression that one is likely to get on looking at Figure 3–10 is that the surface contour of the molecule is highly twisted and folded back on itself. This particular corrugated form is characteristic of all hemoglobin molecules. Proteins have their own distinctive shapes, which are presumed to be responsible, to a large extent, for the specific properties of the protein. That is to say that in the case of hemoglobin, all normal hemoglobin molecules are believed to have the same surface configurations and thus the same amount and kind of electrical charges on the exposed surfaces, which, in turn, are responsible for the particular physical-chemical properties of hemoglobin.

The pattern of electrical charges present on the surface of the molecule is controlled, however, by more than simply the gross configuration of the structure. Clearly the components that make up the macro-molecule are also involved. On opening up the hemoglobin molecule, it would be possible to note that the surface structure is fixed by molecular linkages that join together the long chains that make up most of the hemoglobin material. On breaking these linkages (and ignoring their composition), however, the hemoglobin molecule may be seen to be made up of four chains—not just one long one, as might be expected. Spectacular refinements which have been made in laboratory procedures in the last few years make it possible to examine the composition of these chains. Applying these procedures and thus looking even more deeply into the structure of hemoglobin, one can see that the

Figure 3–10. Model of a molecule of horse hemoglobin. (From V. M. Ingram, *The Hemoglobins in Genetics and Evolution,* copyright 1963, by permission of Columbia University Press)

four chains are, in fact, two pairs of twin chains, a pair of alpha and a pair of beta chains. Examination of these chains, one at a time, would reveal that each chain is itself twisted helically and that the molecules that make up a chain are amino acids. All amino acids share a common molecular core. There are twenty different kinds of amino acids, and each one adds a distinctive molecular configuration to the common core (see Figure 3–11). Amino acids are joined together by strong bonds known as peptide bonds, and because of this, chains of amino acids are referred to as *polypeptide chains.*

Thus, hemoglobin is made up of two pairs of polypeptide chains. An alpha chain consists of 141 amino acids; a beta chain of 146. Moreover, the sequence is identical in all normal human hemoglobin; it is always as it is shown in Figure 3–12. Hemoglobin is, of course, but one of many kinds of proteins; not all are made up of four polypeptide chains—some have only one chain, others more than four. All proteins, however, are basically constructed of amino acids joined together by peptide bonds. Each chain is itself twisted helically and, finally, folded into a distinctive surface configuration.

It has become clear, in recent years, that genes function directly to regulate the construction of polypeptide chains. How the chains get together to form the larger

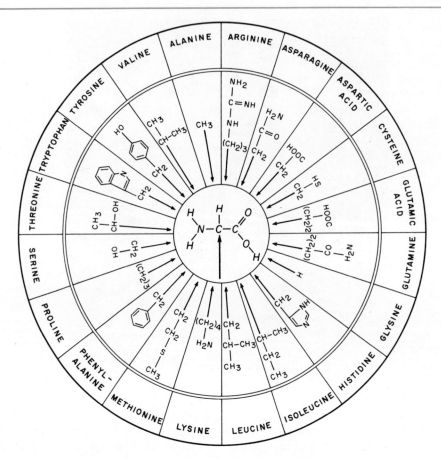

Figure 3–11. Common core to amino acid structure and the distinctive side chain for each amino acid.

macro-molecule remains unclear. It is, however, certain that the earlier one-gene-one-enzyme hypothesis must be generalized not simply to one-gene-one-protein, but even more broadly to one-gene-one-polypeptide chain. This implies a modification of our answer to the question of what a gene is: at this point it is obviously more correct to answer that a gene is some part of DNA that controls the manufacture of a particular polypeptide chain. Thus the relationship established earlier should be modified to:

ENVIRONMENT
Gene → Polypeptide Chain → Trait

This draws our attention to the next problem: How is it that genes make polypeptide chains?

REPLICATION. Genes have two functions: 1) they duplicate themselves, and 2) they regulate the construction of polypeptide chains. As noted earlier, Watson and Crick (1953) proposed the generally accepted theory of the structure of DNA. They also put forth an explanation for the way in which DNA copies itself as required in the normal processes of mitosis and meiosis. They proposed that the complementary strands of a molecule of DNA come apart at their hydrogen bond joints, and each strand then acts as an assembly line for the construction of two DNA molecules identical to one another and to the original sequence of nucleotide pairs. Thus any pair of nucleotides, for example adenine-thymine, separate at the hydrogen bond sites that normally join them together in the intact DNA molecule. On the one strand, adenine will "accept" thymine and only thymine from among the free nucleotides available as metabolic by-products in the nuclear environment; whereas, on the other, the thymine-bearing nucleotide will "accept" only adenine. This highly selective process, continuing the entire length of both sides of a DNA chain, results in two identical DNA chains, as illustrated in Figure 3–13. A number of experiments conducted since the original proposal have tested the validity of this theory, and all have reached conclusions that support this view of DNA replication.

In explaining how DNA controls the construction of a polypeptide chain, the first obstacle is essentially a spatial one; protein synthesis has long been known to occur in the cytoplasm in particles known as ribosomes, whereas DNA is located in the cell nucleus and is walled off from the cytoplasm by the nuclear membrane. The obvious question then is: How is it that the DNA in the nucleus can influence the manufacture of proteins in the cytoplasm?

RNA

Some insight has been obtained into the structure of DNA and the manner in which it replicates itself, but until now no attention has been given in this chapter to the multitude of reactions known to occur outside the nucleus. Since it is known that ribosomes are the sites of protein synthesis, and this is the process under investigation, they would seem to be reasonable places to begin. Ribosomes themselves are made up of two major molecular components: 1) protein, and 2) a polynucleotide chain remarkably similar, but not identical, to DNA. The protein part can be ignored, since it is the synthesis of protein that is the interesting question. The nucleotides of the ribosomal chain consist of components like those in a chain of DNA: a phosphoric acid molecule, a distinctive sugar known as ribose, and one purine or pyrimidine. The purines are identical to those found in DNA: adenine and guanine. The pyrimidines include cytosine, but, instead of thymine, the ribosomal polynucleotide chains contain the pyrimidine uracil. These and other attributes to be considered presently clearly distinguish this polynucleotide chain from DNA, and, drawing largely on the sugar molecule again for its name, this kind of chain is called ribonucleic acid, or RNA. Figure 3–14 compares a thymine nucleotide of DNA with a uracil nucleotide of RNA; note the differences between deoxyribose and ribose, and between thymine and uracil.

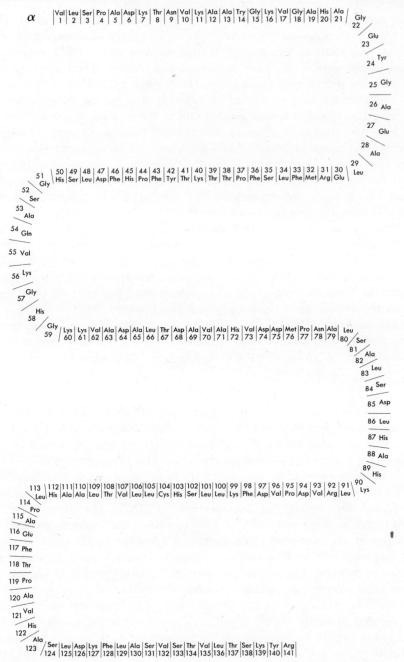

Figure 3–12(A). Sequence of amino acids in the alpha chain of normal hemoglobin.

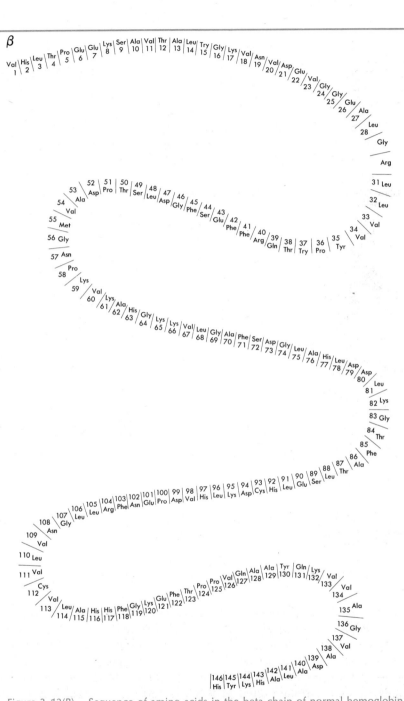

Figure 3–12(B).   Sequence of amino acids in the beta chain of normal hemoglobin.

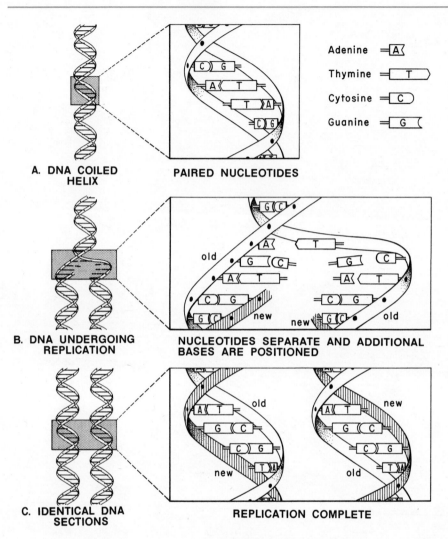

A. DNA COILED HELIX   PAIRED NUCLEOTIDES

Adenine = A
Thymine = T
Cytosine = C
Guanine = G

B. DNA UNDERGOING REPLICATION   NUCLEOTIDES SEPARATE AND ADDITIONAL BASES ARE POSITIONED

C. IDENTICAL DNA SECTIONS   REPLICATION COMPLETE

Figure 3–13. DNA replication.

RNA may be found elsewhere in the cytoplasm. This soluble or transfer RNA (sRNA or tRNA) is identical to ribosomal RNA in its basic components. The soluble RNA consists of short polynucleotide chains with specific functions to be discussed presently. The important observation at this point, however, is the clue provided by yet a third form of RNA that may be found in *both* the nucleus and the cytoplasm. This particular kind of RNA is distinctive in that it is able to pass

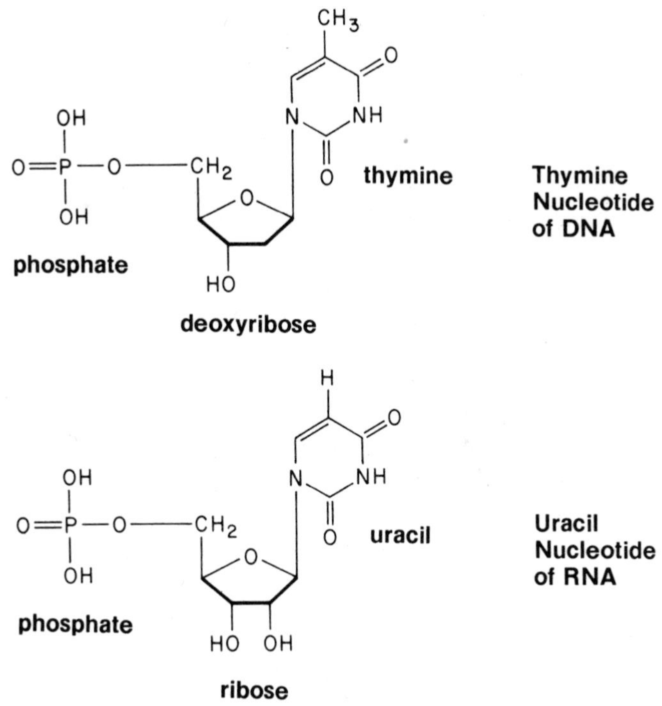

Figure 3–14.   Comparison of a thymine nucleotide of DNA with a uracil nucleotide of RNA.

freely through the nuclear membrane and thus to act as the vehicle by which the genetic information is taken into the cytoplasm. This third kind of RNA is thus referred to as *messenger* RNA.

Together DNA and the three forms of RNA constitute the basic tools the cell employs in making a protein. The entire process is not as yet entirely clear, but the major sequence seems well established. DNA makes messenger RNA in a manner strikingly similar to that it employs in replicating itself. The messenger RNA breaks off in short strands, and each of these may well correspond to a gene, but in any event it should be emphasized that a strand of messenger RNA is the exact comple-ment of the DNA template on which it is formed, just as in DNA replication. The two processes are distinguished by the substitution of ribose for deoxyribose and of uracil for thymine in the synthesis of messenger RNA. Also, unlike DNA, messenger RNA is a single chain of nucleotides. It is not a sequence of paired nucleotides.

These small strands of messenger RNA enter the cytoplasm, where they become the sites of attachment for one or more ribosomes. Ribosomes are generalized in a sense; any ribosome is able to attach to any strand of messenger RNA and carry out its function. Ribosomes act rather like the magnetic head of a tape recorder. They "sense" the nucleotide sequence "pulses" of the messenger RNA and provide the location for their translation into a polypeptide chain. The process of building up a sequence of amino acids requires the resolution of both a selection problem and an activation problem. That is, at the ribosome, the appropriate particular amino acid must be called into position and must be joined to the segment already formed. The selection of appropriate amino acid is made on the basis of the ribosome's "sensing" of the messenger RNA polynucleotide chain, itself a transcription of DNA. The positioning and joining together of the amino acid is taken care of by soluble RNA. There are twenty different kinds of soluble RNA, each constructed so that it is able to attach to one and only one kind of amino acid. Amino acids get into the cytoplasm as the by-product of an organism's food. They enter the cell simply as free amino acids. Any particular kind of soluble RNA attaches to its specific amino acid, and in doing so, the amino acid becomes activated for its role in the biosynthesis of a polypeptide chain and is provided with the energy needed to play this role. The activation process is known in some detail, but will not be considered here.

Thus it is that DNA makes messenger RNA, which enters the cytoplasm. Ribsomes interpret the genetic instructions of the messenger RNA and call for a particular sequence of amino acids attached to activated transfer RNA molecules. The amino acids are set into place and joined together at the ribosome, which moves the entire length of the messenger RNA strand, thereby producing a complete polypeptide chain. The entire process is illustrated in Figure 3–15.

Genetic Code

Reference was made previously to ribosomal RNA acting in a manner similar to that of a tape recorder head sensing the impulses provided by the messenger RNA as transcribed directly from the DNA in the nucleus. In this analogy, it is clear that DNA may be thought of as a set of instructions coded in the sequence of purines and specifying thereby the sequence of amino acids to be joined together to form a polypeptide chain. Looking at it in this way, it then becomes a logical step to inquire into the nature of the code; that is to say, how does DNA code for a particular amino acid? Some progress in solving this problem can be made on logical grounds alone. A coding unit of DNA, that is, a codon, necessarily consists of more than one nucleotide, since there are only four nucleotides, and, obviously, four different things taken one at a time cannot code for twenty different amino acids. Likewise nucleotide pairs are insufficient, since four different things can make only sixteen different pairs. Thus, on logical grounds alone, the minimum number of nucleotides has to be three. However, four different nucleotides can be arranged into sixty-four triplet sequences, and, as noted, there are only twenty amino acids. At this point logic alone cannot advance our understanding much further. We need more information. For example, are some triplet sequences redundant? That is, does more than

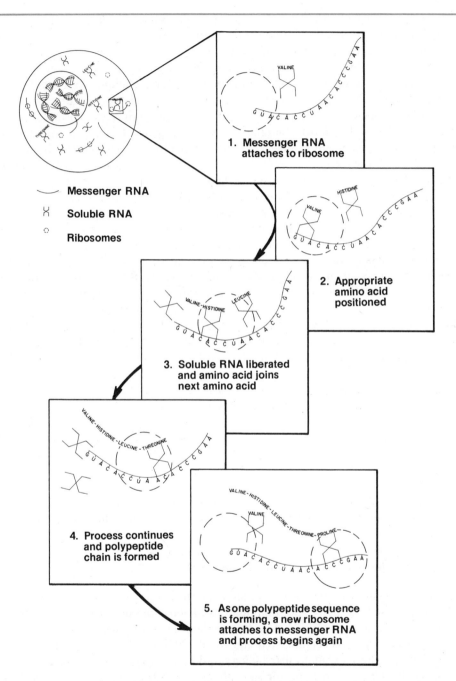

Messenger RNA

Soluble RNA

Ribosomes

1. Messenger RNA attaches to ribosome

2. Appropriate amino acid positioned

3. Soluble RNA liberated and amino acid joins next amino acid

4. Process continues and polypeptide chain is formed

5. As one polypeptide sequence is forming, a new ribosome attaches to messenger RNA and process begins again

Figure 3–15. Steps involved in the synthesis of a polypeptide chain. The illustration shows the positioning of the first five amino acids in the beta chain of human hemoglobin.

one triplet code specify the same amino acid? Are some triplets meaningless? Or does DNA contain codes for other kinds of information? These are questions that can be answered only by experimentation.

The genetic code has been cracked, and the extraordinary work that broke it was made possible largely because of refinements in the techniques of analyzing the contents of living cells outside of the cells. The basic ingredients of these cell-free studies of the genetic code are messenger RNA, transfer RNA, ribosomes, amino acids, and enzymes. These may be obtained by using gentle techniques that destroy cell walls without damaging cellular contents. In a cell-free environment, the normal process of protein synthesis stops very quickly because messenger RNA is rapidly used up and there is no DNA to produce new strands of it. It is, however, possible to synthesize messenger RNA artificially with known purine-pyrimidine sequences, and this synthetic RNA can be introduced into the cell-free medium to act as messenger RNA. The earliest experiment of this kind introduced synthetic messenger RNA consisting entirely of uracil nucleotides; it was found to stimulate the production of a polyphenylalanine chain. Presuming that the genetic code consists of triplet sequences, then, by implication, the messenger RNA codon for phenylalanine is $U - U - U$, and, extending the implications even further, the DNA codon for phenylalanine is $A - A - A$. Subsequently, it has been determined that adding synthetic messenger RNA consisting of adenine nucleotides made only polylysine; that with only guanine produced polyglycine; and, finally, strands of only cytosine nucleotides of RNA, when added to the cell-free medium, resulted in the amino acid polyproline chains.

Eventually messenger RNA was synthesized in various triplet combinations, and today the genetic code is known in detail, as shown in Table 3–4. An examination of the table reveals that the code is redundant; that is, more than one triplet may code for the same amino acid. Likewise it may be seen that two triplets ($U - A - A$ and $U - A - G$) code for no amino acid. These "nonsense" triplets appear to be the genetic equivalent of a period in punctuation. They terminate the synthesis of messenger RNA on the DNA template. At this point, if one were so inclined, he could turn to Table 3–4 and, with a knowledge of the genetic code, infer the precise sequence of purines and pyrimidines in the messenger RNA that makes the beta chain of human hemoglobin.

Summary of Molecular and Biochemical Genetics

This section began with the broad question of the nature of the gene and subsequently considered the more specific questions of what the physical components of the genetic material are. How do they fit together? How do they work? In reviewing the evidence that has accumulated and the conclusions that have been drawn in regard to these questions, molecular biology and biochemistry have yielded answers in such detail that to even hope for such things twenty-five years ago would have been presumptuous. We have touched here only on the highlights and indeed not all

Table 3-4   The Genetic Code

AMINO ACID	MRNA TRIPLET CODE*			AMINO ACID	MRNA TRIPLET CODE*		
	1st	2nd	3rd		1st	2nd	3rd
1. Alanine (Ala)				12. Lysine (Lys)			
	G	C	C		A	A	A
	G	C	U		A	A	G
	G	C	A	13. Methionine (Met)			
	G	C	G		A	U	A
2. Argenine (Arg)					A	U	G
	C	G	C	14. Phenylalanine (Phe)			
	C	G	U		U	U	U
	C	G	A		U	U	C
	C	G	G	15. Proline (Pro)			
	A	G	A		C	C	C
	A	G	G		C	C	U
3. Asparagine (Asp-NH₂)					C	C	A
	A	A	U		C	C	G
	A	A	C	16. Serine (Ser)			
4. Aspartic Acid (Asp)					U	C	C
	G	A	U		U	C	U
	G	A	C		U	C	A
5. Cysteine (Cys)					U	C	G
	U	G	U		A	G	U
	U	G	C		A	G	C
6. Glutamic Acid (Glu)				17. Threonine (Thr)			
	G	A	A		A	C	C
	G	A	G		A	C	U
7. Glutamine (Glu-NH₂)					A	C	A
	C	A	A		A	C	G
	C	A	G	18. Tryptophan (Try)			
8. Glycine (Gly)					U	G	A
	G	G	C		U	G	G
	G	G	U	19. Tyrosine (Tyr)			
	G	G	A		U	A	C
	G	G	G		U	A	U
9. Histidine (His)				20. Valine (Val)			
	C	A	C		G	U	C
	C	A	U		G	U	U
10. Isoleucine (Ileu)					G	U	A
	A	U	C		G	U	G
	A	U	U	no amino acid			
11. Leucine (Leu)					U	A	A
	U	U	A		U	A	G
	U	U	G				
	C	U	U				
	C	U	C				
	C	U	A				
	C	U	G				

* G = Guanine, C = Cytosine, U = Uracil, and A = Adenine.

of them, but a summary of these would now seem to be in order. 1) DNA is the genetic material. 2) DNA consists of a long, helically coiled chain of paired nucleotides. 3) The paired nucleotides separate in the process of DNA replication, and the two surfaces thus exposed serve as templates for the construction of two identical chains, thereby fulfilling the implicit structural requirements of mitosis. 4) DNA specifies the sequence of amino acids in the biosynthesis of polypeptide chains, which, in turn, constitute the primary components of proteins. To accomplish this function, DNA makes messenger RNA, which, when it passes into the cytoplasm, directs the activity of soluble RNA at the cellular sites of protein synthesis, the ribosomes. 5) The specifications of DNA are coded in triplet sequences of nucleotides. The messenger RNA triplet sequences that specify particular amino acids form the genetic code.

A consideration of the elements of formal genetics led to the realization that the laws of heredity apply to all living things. In a like manner, at the molecular and biochemical levels of organization, the life process for all organisms consists of a complicated series of chemical reactions driven and replenished by the available food resources and controlled and directed by enzymes. Not all organisms have been studied, of course, but from those that have, it is becoming increasingly clear that this is true for all, from the simplest to the most complex.

This brief survey of advances in molecular and biochemical genetics should make it clear that whenever a limit is reached in our ability to extend our knowledge further by means of logic, then it becomes essential to obtain new information. In these areas and in formal genetics, the acquisition of new information usually implies experimentation. But physical anthropology has its primary interest in man, and clearly man is not amenable to experimentation. How can the science of genetics be applied to improving our understanding of human evolution and human variation? This is the question of particular interest to physical anthropologists. Or, conversely, how may human beings be studied to inform us further about genetics? This is the question of greatest interest to human geneticists. Population genetics has been the most informative area in both of these problems and thus serves as a common ground of interest for both human genetics and physical anthropology.

POPULATION GENETICS

Experimental and Natural Populations

Families, as we have seen, are ideal units to observe in our effort to learn more about genetics. In experimental genetics a researcher can proceed directly to answer questions by creating artificial families. Thus we know a great deal about the genetics of peas, pineapples, pets, poultry, etc. They are all amenable to genetic experimentation. Man is not (hopefully never will be), and for this reason our knowledge of human genetics has lagged behind. The gap would be greater were it not for the relationship identified previously, that is, families are similar to populations in many respects. This relationship is the basis of population genetics.

Under experimental conditions, the genetic structure, that is, the distribution of genes, genotypes, and mating types, may be controlled. In natural populations, such as human populations, this is information which must be determined. Population genetics is concerned with the determination of the genetic structure of natural populations and the factors that maintain or alter that genetic structure.

Hardy-Weinberg Law of Equilibrium

Fundamental to the genetic investigation of natural populations is the realization that, given certain assumptions, the proportions of genotypes will remain constant from generation to generation. Shortly after the rediscovery of Mendels' work in 1900, a notion began to formulate which carried with it the implication that dominant genes must, over time, become more and more abundant and eventually swamp out of existence their respective recessive alleles. This notion, known as *genophagy*, was erroneous, and was shown to be incorrect in 1908 by two persons working independently, Hardy,* a British mathematician, and Weinberg, a German physician. Their discovery resulted from applying probability rules to aspects of Mendel's laws, and in the process, they formulated what has come to be known as the Hardy-Weinberg law of genetic equilibrium. The law specifies that, contrary to the notion of genophagy, the frequencies of the genes and proportion of genotypes will reach and remain at a stable equilibrium level after one generation of random mating in a population. This may be illustrated by returning to Table 3–3 on page 66. Consider the table to represent an idealized population that just happens to marry in the nine different ways shown in the table. First, it may be seen that among the parents, the alleles A and a occur with equal frequency, and, since there are only two alleles, their frequencies must total unity. Thus, in this case, if p equals the frequency of A, and q equals the frequency of a, then $p = .50$ and $q = .50$ and $p + q = 1$. Or, more generally, to cover all cases, $p =$ the total number of AA persons plus one-half the Aa persons and this total divided by the total number in the sample. Thus:

$$p = \frac{AA + Aa/2}{AA + Aa + aa} \quad \text{and} \quad q = \frac{aa + Aa/2}{AA + Aa + aa}$$

Now according to the implications of genophagy, one would anticipate an increase of dominants (in this case A-bearing genotypes) among their offspring. If, however, each marriage produces four children, then, by Mendel's laws, we would expect the offspring to be distributed as shown in Table 3–5. If one compares the distribution

---

* For an informative exchange on this see the comments of Mr. Udny Yule (1908) and the reply by G. H. Hardy (1908).

of alleles among the parents with that found among the children, it is apparent that the frequencies have not changed; thus for both generations:

$$p = .50$$
$$q = .50$$
$$p + q = 1$$

But what about the genotypes? Among the parents one-third are AA, one-third are Aa, and one-third are aa; whereas among the children, one-quarter are AA, one-half are Aa, and one-quarter are aa. What happens in subsequent generations? Hardy and Weinberg were able to demonstrate that no matter what the original values of p and q, the geneotypes in a randomly-mating population will remain in the ratio of p^2 (AA) to $2pq$ (Aa) to q^2 (aa). Thus, in this instance, if the assumptions required by the Hardy-Weinberg law are applicable, the next generation of genotypes and all subsequent generations can be expected to remain in the proportion of 25 percent AA, 50 percent Aa, and 25 percent aa. For this genetic locus under these conditions the population is said to be in genetic equilibrium.

Table 3–5 Distribution of Offspring Genotypes Assuming Four Offspring per Mating Type

MATING TYPE ♂		MATING TYPE ♀	OFFSPRING GENOTYPES AA	Aa	aa
AA	×	AA	4		
AA	×	Aa	2	2	
AA	×	aa		4	
Aa	×	AA	2	2	
Aa	×	Aa	1	2	1
Aa	×	aa		2	2
aa	×	AA		4	
aa	×	Aa		2	2
aa	×	aa			4
Total			**9**	**18**	**9**

What does the law of genetic equilibrium imply? Basically it implies that genetic information may be looked at in a different way, may be viewed from a perspective which, as noted earlier, has had a profound effect on physical anthropology. Breeding populations have genetic structures consisting of genes, genotypes, and mating types. The law of genetic equilibrium informs us as to how these parts are interrelated and enables us to predict their distributions in future populations. But, one may ask, do the predictions go wrong? Are the structures ever found to be different from what we would expect under genetic equilibrium? Yes, of course; this is what population genetics is all about. What happens, for example, if the population is not mating at random?

Random and Nonrandom Mating

The requirement of random mating has been mentioned as a condition necessary for the equilibrium specified by the Hardy-Weinberg law. This is but one of several factors that are needed to fulfill completely the logical and mathematical requirements of the law. Before presenting a definition of random mating, it might be helpful to provide a few illustrations of nonrandom mating and the consequences on the proportions of genotypes. Consider, for example, a population that permitted only marriages between persons who are alike in some biological aspects. Although less rigidly defined, such a mating system exists in our own society, wherein people of the same race tend to marry. Moreover, even within a race, people tend to marry others like themselves with respect to stature, intelligence, and certain personality characteristics. To illustrate the effect of this kind of nonrandom mating, it will be useful if we remain with the more clearly stated case where alikes and only alikes are allowed to marry, and, furthermore, where "alike" is defined in terms of genotypes. Then we may return to the situation considered in Table 3–5. In a population such as this, mating under the nonrandom system, wherein only persons genotypically alike for this locus are allowed to marry, there could be only three kinds of marriage. Presuming that each type yields four offspring, the expected genotype proportions are shown in Table 3–6.

Table 3–6 Expected Distribution of Offspring Genotypes under Complete Positive Assortative Mating

MATING TYPE		OFFSPRING GENOTYPES		
♂ ♀		AA	Aa	aa
AA × AA		4		
Aa × Aa		1	2	1
aa × aa				4
Total		5	2	5

This form of nonrandom mating is referred to as positive assortative mating, and it may be seen from the table that its effect on the distribution of genotypes in the offspring generation is to increase the proportion of homozygous genotypes, and thus, correspondingly, to decrease the proportion of heterozygotes. Making analogous assumptions, the reverse system of mating, negative assortative mating, wherein persons genotypically alike are forbidden to marry, is illustrated in Table 3–7. Negative assortative mating results in a higher proportion of heterozygotes and thus a lower proportion of homozygotes than would be expected under genetic equilibrium.

The illustrations are extreme as far as human populations are concerned. To the extent that assortative mating occurs in man, it is in the form of a *tendency* for likes to marry or a *tendency* for likes to avoid one another. If, however, these tendencies involve inherited traits, the effect is the same: positive assortative mating distorts equilibrium expectations by increasing the proportion of homozygotes, negative assortative mating by increasing the proportion of heterozygotes.

Table 3–7   Expected Distribution of Offspring Genotypes under Complete Negative Assortative Mating

MATING TYPE ♂	♀	OFFSPRING GENOTYPES AA	Aa	aa
AA × Aa		2	2	
AA × aa			4	
Aa × AA		2	2	
Aa × aa			2	2
aa × AA			4	
aa × Aa			2	2
Total		**4**	**16**	**4**

Another form of nonrandom mating of particular interest to physical anthropologists is inbreeding, wherein biological relatives are more likely to marry one another. In many human societies, the preferred marriage is between cousins, and for this reason there is a substantially higher frequency of marriages between related persons than expected by chance. Since related persons share a much closer common ancestry than unrelated or distantly related persons, they are more frequently alike in genetic characteristics; thus the effect of inbreeding is the same as positive assortative mating: homozygosity increases. Outbreeding, where relatives are forbidden to marry, is similar in effect to negative assortative mating.

Perhaps the phenomenon of random mating is clearer now. It is the lack of any systematic tendency in the mate selection process within a population. A population is mating at random with respect to any particular trait if individuals select mates independently of their having or not having that trait. Any departure from random mating upsets the equilibrium distribution of genotypes specified by the Hardy-Weinberg law; a single generation of random mating will, however, restore the equilibrium. In effect what Hardy and Weinberg showed was that the genetic structure of populations will not change unless some force causes them to change. Thus, in an evolutionary sense, a population at rest will remain at rest. In this way, the natural population may be seen as a unit with evolutionary integration, as a unit with biological significance. This might well have been demonstrable by other means, but the Hardy-Weinberg law yields the logical basis for joining these properties to the laws of formal genetics and thereby enables the further investigation of the genetics of natural groups. From the point of view of physical anthropology, this raises the interesting question of identifying the forces, other than nonrandom mating, that can cause changes in the genetic structures of populations and the exciting prospect of answering such a question by means of the study of human groups. As noted earlier, the entire evolutionary process may be regarded as the accumulation of changes in the genetic structure of populations, and with this as a definition, it is reasonable to refer to the forces that cause these changes as mechanisms of evolution. They occupy a position of central importance in population genetics.

Mechanisms of Evolution

What other factors can bring about changes to the genetic structures of populations? We have already identified two: 1) assortative mating changes the frequencies of genotypes, and, from an earlier discussion, 2) mutations change the physical structures of genes. Together these two kinds of change, that is, changes in form and changes in frequency, are, when looked at over time, the very essence of evolution.

Factors that cause such changes to occur are called mechanisms of evolution. Thus mutation and assortative mating are mechanisms of evolution. Are there others? Yes, natural selection, genetic drift, and gene flow.

NATURAL SELECTION. In Chapter 1, natural selection was identified as the first known mechanism of evolution, described and detailed by Darwin over one hundred years ago. It will be recalled that the view of selection presented by Darwin may be thought of as a continuously fluctuating environmental template, the form of which at any given time determines the outline of variation in living species. Within any species, individuals with attributes that do not fit the contours of the template leave fewer offspring than those that do. The product of this process is a gradual streamlining of the species' variation to conform to the requirements of selection. Thus from the standpoint of selection, the only measure of fitness within a species is the number of offspring produced which, in turn, go on to reproduce subsequent generations.

This is a view that can be understood directly on a population level. It provides an explanation for the origin of species by means of natural selection. It is, however, a view that focuses on broad generational changes, and, as our knowledge of genetics has grown, our understanding of selection has become more refined. The specific question of interest at this point is: How does natural selection affect the genetic structure of populations? Darwin provided a general answer; modern population genetics offers more detail.

Consider again A and a as an illustration. If the following assumptions are made: a) that the population is mating at random for this locus, and b) that at the outset each allele is equally frequent, then we see that:

$$p = .50 \qquad q = .50$$
$$AA(p^2) = .25 \qquad Aa(2pq) = .50 \qquad aa(q^2) = .25$$

In this way the genetic structure of the population is known. Moreover, the frequency of each type of marriage may be determined by a simple application of the probability rule: the rate of occurrence of a compound event is the product of the frequencies of its component events. Since the frequency of AA genotypes is p^2, then in a randomly-mating population the frequency of $AA \times AA$ marriages is $p^2 \times p^2 = p^4$. The frequencies of all possible marriages are shown in Table 3–8.

Table 3–8   Frequencies of Mating Types under Random Mating

MATING TYPE		FREQUENCY UNDER RANDOM MATING		
♂	♀	GENOTYPE FREQUENCIES		MATING TYPE FREQUENCIES
AA × AA		p^2 × p^2	=	p^4
AA × Aa		p^2 × $2pq$	=	$2p^3q$
AA × aa		p^2 × q^2	=	p^2q^2
Aa × AA		$2pq$ × p^2	=	$2p^3q$
Aa × Aa		$2pq$ × $2pq$	=	$4p^2q^2$
Aa × aa		$2pq$ × q^2	=	$2pq^3$
aa × AA		q^2 × p^2	=	p^2q^2
aa × Aa		q^2 × $2pq$	=	$2pq^3$
aa × aa		q^2 × q^2	=	q^4

Natural selection may alter the genetic structure of a population at any level. We will deal primarily with its effect on genotypes. Given the assumptions in our illustration, we can see that, with respect to the distribution of genotypes, natural selection is able to exert its influence in any of four ways, selection against: 1) either homozygote, 2) either homozygote and the heterozygote, 3) both homozygotes, and 4) the heterozygote.

Selection against One Homozygote. Consider now a simple case wherein persons of one homozygous genotype, say *aa*, are sterile; that is to say, so severely selected against that they leave no progeny. Then of the nine possible types of marriages only four produce offspring, or, stated in another way, out of every 100 marriages only 56.25 percent yield offspring (see Table 3–9).

Table 3–9   Mating Types Producing Offspring with Complete Selection against One Homozygote (aa)

MATING TYPE		FREQUENCY	FREQUENCY ASSUMING $p = q = .50$
♂	♀		
AA × AA		p^4	.0625
AA × Aa		$2p^3q$	.1250
Aa × AA		$2p^3q$	.1250
Aa × Aa		$4p^2q^2$	.2500
Total			.5625

If each of the mating types is presumed to be equally productive, then Table 3–10 shows the expected number of offspring by genotypes per 100 matings. The effect is clear: not only is the proportion of *aa* genotypes reduced, but the frequency of the *a* allele is likewise reduced. The value for

$$p = \frac{100(AA) + 50(Aa)}{225} = .67 \text{ and for } q = \frac{25(aa) + 50(Aa)}{225} = 33.$$

Beginning with these changed frequencies and continuing under the same conditions, subsequent generations will continue the trend. The four mating types producing offspring account now for 79.40 percent of all possible matings in the population (see Table 3–11).

Table 3–10 Expected Distribution of Offspring Genotypes per 100 Marriages under Complete Selection against aa Genotype

MATING TYPE ♂ ♀		FREQUENCY	OFFSPRING BY GENOTYPE (ASSUMING 4 CHILDREN PER MARRIAGE)		
			AA	Aa	aa
AA × AA		.0625	25		
AA × Aa		.1250	25	25	
Aa × AA		.1250	25	25	
Aa × Aa		.2500	25	50	25
Total			**100**	**100**	**25**

Table 3–11 Expected Distribution of Mating Types and Offspring Genotypes with $p = .67$, $q = .33$, and Complete Selection against aa Genotype

MATING TYPE ♂ ♀		FREQUENCY		OFFSPRING BY GENOTYPES (ASSUMING 4 CHILDREN PER MARRIAGE)		
				AA	Aa	aa
AA × AA		p^4	2015	80		
AA × Aa		$2p^3q$	.1985	40	40	
Aa × AA		$2p^3q$	.1985	40	40	
Aa × Aa		$4p^2q^2$	.1955	20	40	20
Total			**.7940**	**180**	**120**	**20**

Thus, the number of offspring produced is increased, the proportion of both *aa* and *Aa* individuals reduced, and the gene frequency of *a* is reduced from .33 to .25.

Changes in the frequencies of p and q over the three generations are summarized in Table 3–12.

Table 3–12   Three Generations of Gene Frequencies under
Complete Selection against aa Genotypes

		Generation		
		1 →	2 →	3
p	=	.50	.67	.75
q	=	.50	.33	.25

The trend that will continue for as long as the conditions prevail is established. The genetic structure of the population moves each generation systematically toward: a) a greater proportion of A alleles, and b) increasing AA homozygosity. It should be noted, however, that even with this intensity of selection, the rate at which these events proceed declines with each generation, and, for this reason, it takes many generations of intense selective pressure to eliminate an allele completely (see Figure 3–16). Although it is indeed true that in man some homozygous conditions are eliminated each generation in a manner similar to the illustration, for the vast majority of genetic loci the pressure of selection is apparently more gentle and reflected only through slight differences in the contributions of particular genotypes to the next generation. The effects are at times so subtle that they cannot readily be detected. Under these more common circumstances, the rate of change per generation per genetic locus (that is, evolution) is slower, and it takes many generations to eliminate an allele.

Selection against One Homozygote and the Heterozygote. Only one form of selection produces faster results in altering the genetic structure of a population: selection against an allele in both homozygous and heterozygous genotypes. Under these conditions if selection is complete, then the allele will be eliminated in one generation. In between complete selection against the homozygote and complete selection against both the heterozygote and one homozygote there exists an intermediate selection: complete selection against one genotype and partial selection against the other. For example, complete selection against a homozygote and partial selection against the heterozygote. If selection is complete against, say, *aa* and partial against *Aa*, then the heterozygotes produce fewer offspring than the *AA* homozygotes. Again this would, of course, result in a trend toward increasing the frequencies of the A allele and the AA genotypes (see Figures 3–17 and 3–18). The rate at which this would occur would fall between that brought about by complete selection against only the homozygote on the one hand, and complete selection against the heterozygote and one homozygote on the other.

Selection against Both Homozygotes. Complete selection against *both* homozygotes, or, in other words, selection favoring only heterozygous organisms, has

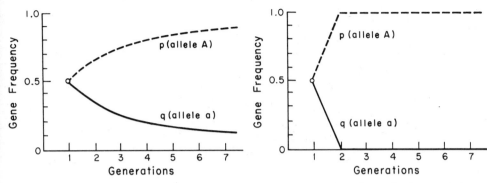

Figure 3–16. Complete selection against one homozygote (aa) with alleles equal in frequency at the onset.

Figure 3–17. Complete selection against one homozygote (aa) and the heterozygote (Aa).

only one significant mating type: $Aa \times Aa$. These conditions produce an equilibrium; no matter what the initial values of p and q in the parental population, once these conditions prevail, the gene frequencies for p and q adjust to .50 in one generation and stay at that level for as long as the conditions continue. Moreover, the genotype frequencies stay at the p^2 (AA), $2pq$ (Aa), and q^2 (aa) levels. There are several interesting implications to this situation, but the point deserving emphasis is that selection can act to maintain the genetic variability of a population. Selection need not always act by eliminating alleles and the genotypes they combine to form; it need not always act, that is, by reducing the genetic variation of a population (see Figure 3–19).

Selection against the Heterozygote. Under complete selection against the heterozygote, four mating types are productive:

$$
\begin{array}{ccc}
\text{♂} & & \text{♀} \\
AA & \times & AA \\
AA & \times & aa \\
aa & \times & AA \\
aa & \times & aa \\
\end{array}
$$

In this instance the effect of selection depends on the values for p and q at the time that selective conditions begin. If p and q are equal, that is, $p = .50$ and $q = .50$, then the genetic structure of the population remains constant and will continue to remain in this equilibrium as long as the conditions remain the same. If, however, p and q are not equal, then complete selection against the heterozygote brings about a steady increase in the allele which is more frequent at the outset and in its homozygous genotype. The rate at which this occurs depends on the initial values of p and q; in general the closer the initial frequencies, the slower the increase in the more frequent allele (see Figure 3–20).

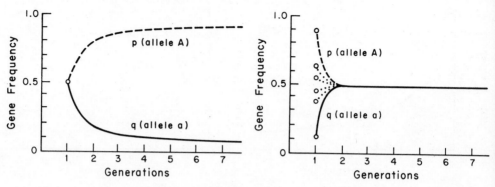

Figure 3–18. Complete selection against one homozygote (aa) and partial selection against the heterozygote (Aa).

Figure 3–19. Complete selection against both homozygotes (AA and aa) with various beginning frequencies for A and a.

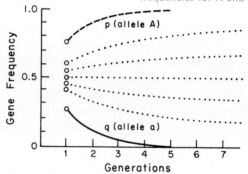

Figure 3–20. Complete selection against the heterozygote (Aa) with various beginning frequencies for A and a.

From these last two illustrations it may be seen that selection is able to bring about effects that may at first glance seem impossible. On the one hand, selection against both homozygotes results in an equilibrium with constant and high frequencies of sterile genotypes every generation. On the other hand, selection against the heterozygote genotype will, if the initial frequencies are unequal, result in the elimination of an allele which otherwise is selectively equivalent to its alternate.

This discussion of selection involves simplification and the omission of many things. Its purpose, however, is to show how selection may operate on the genetic structure of natural populations. The situation very quickly becomes more complex when one goes beyond the simple illustration used here. For example, selection may act directly upon mating types, as in the case of the Rh blood system in man. Rh negative females can conceive Rh positive offspring. In such instances the mother develops antibodies to her offspring's blood. What is the effect of selection here?

If one looks at the offspring, then it is selection against the heterozygote, since Rh negative mothers can conceive only heterozygous Rh positive children. But if one looks at the mother, then selection appears to be acting against one homozygote. We will examine the Rh system in more detail in Chapter 8. We mention it here merely to illustrate that our discussion has been simplified.

As we have seen, natural selection acts by favoring elements and combinations of elements of genetic variability that improve or at least maintain adaptation and by rejecting other elements and combinations. In this activity, it is limited to the available supply of variability. If the supply is not adequate, the population becomes extinct. But where does genetic variability come from? Or, in other words, what source provides natural selection with its raw materials? The answer is genetic mutation, another mechanism of evolution.

MUTATION.* Any change in the structure of a gene is called a mutation. Most mutations are caused by one of the following factors: radiation, chemical analogue substitution, and replication error. Radiation, as noted in Chapter 1, was the first to be identified. By this process the normal bases are transformed by the physical bombardment of their structure with electrons. Electrons, moving at incredible speeds, collide with the purine and pyrimidine molecules and in doing so cause a physical alteration, which, in turn, modifies the effect of the nucleotide in replication and protein synthesis. Chemical analogues are classes of structurally similar molecules. There are many substances similar in their makeup to the bases which are normally a part of DNA. On occasion, instead of the normal purines and pyrimidines, analogues will be drawn into the DNA replication process causing an unstable situation. Substitutions of this kind are believed to be at least partly responsible for cancerous cell growth when they occur during mitosis. If analogue substitution occurs during meiosis, it can, of course, also produce heritable mutations.

Replication errors occur when mistakes are made in the normal pairing of bases in DNA. Adenine and thymine constitute a normal pair, as do guanine and cytosine, but in rare instances a mistake occurs, and thymine, for example, pairs with guanine. Again an unstable situation results. When the DNA with the error replicates itself, the strand containing thymine will, in all likelihood, pair normally with adenine, while the other with guanine pairs normally with cytosine. In this way stable daughter strands of DNA are produced which ·in fact are not identical, and, as illustrated in the genetic code, a change of a single nucleotide is sufficient to produce a change in the gene product. At this point, the major interest in mutations is in understanding how they are able to bring about changes to the genetic structure of a population. In considering this effect, it will be useful to make assumptions similar

---

* This discussion deals solely with the effects of genetic mutation as the source of variability and ignores the variety of chromosome changes (for example, polyploidy, inversions, translocations, etc.) that produce evolutionary novelty. They are omitted so that the discussion may be simplified. Interested readers will find clear discussions of these topics in Crow (1963) and Srb, Owen, and Edgar (1965).

to those made in the discussion of natural selection: the population is very large, mating occurs at random, and mutation is the only evolutionary mechanism at work.

From one standpoint, the effect of mutation on the genetic structure of a population is simple and obvious. If A mutates to a, this is in and of itself a change in the genetic composition of the population. To be sure, if this happens only once in a very large population, the effect is very slight indeed. Yet this slight change, should it be repeated over generations, will, given enough time, lead to the complete replacement of A by a. In this process, mutation is irreversible, that is:

$$A \to a$$

One can see that the effect here is simply a product of the rate at which A mutates to a and the number of generations this process has been at work. But what of the condition in which A mutates to a and a mutates to A? That is:

$$A \rightleftarrows a$$

Clearly, if the rates are equal, that is, if the proportion of A's changing to a's is equal to the proportion of a's changing to A's, the two alleles will tend toward equal frequencies no matter what their original frequencies. For example, if one in ten A's changes to a, and one in ten a's changes to A, the frequency of A and a will eventually be the same, that is, $p = q = .50$. Some alleles are, however, more stable than others, and it is far more common to find that A mutates to a at a rate different from the one at which a mutates to A. At first it might appear that the allele that mutates more rapidly will eventually disappear, but a little reflection will make it clear why this is not the case. Consider, for example, the situation wherein one in every ten A's mutates to a, and one in every five a's mutates to A. No matter what their original frequencies, the alleles will in time reach a stable equilibrium where p = gene frequency of A = .66 and q = gene frequency of a = .33. Under these conditions 6.6 of every 66 A alleles mutate to a (one in ten), and 6.6 of every 33 a alleles mutate to A (one in five). Thus a stable situation is achieved with the proportion of A alleles mutating to a exactly matching the proportion of a alleles mutating to A. The equilibrium depends solely on the rates at which A and a mutate; no matter what the beginning values of p and q, the equilibrium values of $p = .66$ and $q = .33$ will be reached if the rates of mutation are as illustrated, one in ten and one in five.

In sharp contrast to the rates of one in ten and one in five that are employed here to illustrate the effect of mutations on the genetic structure of populations, mutations in nature are very rare events. Most mutation rates in man, for example, fall between one in 10,000 and one in 100,000. Or, in other words, from one in 10,000 to one in 100,000 sex cells will contain a mutant allele for any particular genetic locus. Thus, when considered in the context of a particular genetic locus, mutations are indeed rare. There are, however, thousands of genetic loci in every human sex cell—so many, in fact, that the occurrence of mutations per sex cell is undoubtedly a commonplace event, with most, if not all, carrying several loci with mutant alleles.

Distinguishing between the rate per genetic locus and the rate per sex cell emphasizes the two most important ways that mutations may influence evolution. One we have discussed already, that is, the production of totally new allelic varieties of a gene. Mutation is ultimately the source of all new genetic variation, a role that is impossible to overemphasize in any discussion of evolution. If, however, one takes a broader look, the effect of mutation may be seen in a different way. To see it in this perspective, it will be necessary to consider the following propositions: 1) included in the genetic composition of all natural populations is a regular supply of mutations; 2) the adaptation of a population to its environmental requirements is a fine and delicate balance that may take millions of years to bring about; and 3) mutations are changes, and, under these conditions, it may be seen that any change in this situation is much more likely to disrupt the intricate and delicate adaptation of the population than it is likely to improve it. From this point of view, the mutation process may be seen as a continuous source of pressure against the formation of a "perfect" adaptation in any natural population. This feature of the mutation process has been recognized for over thirty years, and was first identified by Sewall Wright as *mutation pressure*.

MUTATION AND SELECTION. To illustrate their respective properties, it is helpful to isolate mutation and natural selection and deal with each separately. In any natural population, however, the two factors are commonly in operation at the same time, but acting in different directions. Mutations continually replenish and add to the background of variability. Most are detrimental or offer no adaptive value and for this reason are eliminated or kept at very low frequencies as the mutation rates and selection intensities approach equilibrium. Thus in any natural population, selection brings about *adaptation;* mutation provides for *adaptability*. This is the impression one is left with by considering them separately, and it is essentially correct. But when mutation and selection are examined simultaneously, it is possible to obtain an added insight into the evolutionary process of far-reaching significance. For with this background in the two evolutionary mechanisms, it may be seen that any particular inherited locus may be identified as *monomorphic, idiomorphic,* or *polymorphic* (see Morton, 1967).

A monomorphic locus shows a distribution that includes one and only one allele. The locus may be structurally very stable and resist mutation, or selection against all but one genotype may be complete. Thus the entire population is, for that trait, homozygous, and the genetic structure homogeneous. Since no heterogeneity exists, the monomorphic trait is of no interest to the geneticist, for without some variation, the inheritance of a trait cannot be determined.

Idiomorphs are rare alleles, those with frequencies less than 1 percent. Their distribution is distinctive since they may be maintained at low frequencies by mutation alone even though the selective pressure against them may be very intense. Thousands of genetic diseases are controlled by idiomorphs.

Polymorphs are common alleles; the traits they control in the phenotype are called polymorphisms. The ABO blood group system is a familiar illustration of a polymorphism in man. (See Chapter 10 for a discussion of other polymorphisms in man.) Among European-derived Americans, for example, the allele frequencies for the ABO system are approximately as follows:

$$A = .25$$
$$B = .09$$
$$O = .66$$

Polymorphisms are of special interest to physical anthropologists for two reasons: 1) they are, in a sense, unexpected, and 2) the frequencies of polymorphs vary from one locality to another. They are unexpected simply because a separate consideration of mutation and of selection usually leads to the expectation that what really exists in natural populations are monomorphs, idiomorphs, and perhaps polymorphisms on their way to becoming idiomorphisms and monomorphisms. But stable polymorphisms are known to be a common phenomenon (see Chapter 10 for a discussion of some well-known polymorphisms in human populations), and the interesting question this raises for the population geneticist is how they can be maintained. On reflection it will be recalled that three factors already considered can maintain a polymorphism: 1) selection for the heterozygote, 2) nonrandom mating, and 3) reversible mutations. In science, investigation of the unexpected often leads to the most exciting kinds of new understanding.

The fact that the frequencies of polymorphs vary from locality to locality raises the obvious question of what the differences mean. As the reader will recall, one of the main objectives of physical anthropology is to provide explanations for human variation. Obviously we will want to return to polymorphisms again.

Selection and mutation together provide an almost complete picture of the mechanics of evolutionary change. However, other factors which have been identified can change the genetic structure of a population and thereby qualify as mechanisms of evolution.

GENETIC DRIFT. In small populations, special circumstances exist and can produce rapid changes in the genetic structure, changes that may be completely independent of selection and mutation. In the foregoing discussions of selection and mutation, the effect of population size is ignored, and populations are presumed to be large. In general, however, it may be said that the larger the population, the more resistant its genetic structure to changes from accidental or chance causes. Conversely, the smaller the population, the more susceptible it is to change due to chance. Thus in a small population, chance may act as an evolutionary mechanism, and as such it has been identified variously as: 1) Sewall Wright effect (after the man who first drew attention to the mechanism), 2) small-population-size effect (for obvious reasons), and 3) genetic drift, which will be used here.

As an illustration, return again to the A and a alleles, their genotypes, and the mating types formed by them. In earlier discussion, these mating types have been assumed to be equally productive and, moreover, to produce offspring genotypes in exactly the proportions specified by Mendel's laws; thus an $Aa \times Aa$ mating produced one-quarter AA children, one-half Aa, and one-quarter aa. In very large

Table 3–13   Change in Genetic Structure Due to Genetic Drift

MATING TYPE			OFFSPRING PRODUCED		
♂		♀	AA	Aa	aa
AA	×	AA	4		
AA	×	Aa	3	1	
AA	×	aa		4	
Aa	×	AA	2	2	
Aa	×	Aa	1	2	1
Aa	×	aa		2	2
aa	×	AA		4	
aa	×	Aa		2	2
aa	×	aa			4
Total			**10**	**17**	**9**

populations, this is not an unreasonable view, since genetic segregation and fertility accidents in one direction are likely to be balanced by others of equal magnitude in the opposite direction. For example, by chance alone one would expect about four $Aa \times Aa$ matings in a thousand to produce four aa genotypic offspring, but within that same thousand mating types, four others may on chance alone be expected to produce four AA genotypes in their offspring. Moreover, within a mating type, if fertility is not affected by other factors, the mean number of offspring will be the resultant of many individual marriages above and below the mean. The essential point is that in small populations this stability due to size is absent, and the genetic structures of such populations are thus more volatile.

As a specific example consider Table 3–13. In a very large population each of the mating types may occur thousands of times, but we can consider a very small population wherein each occurs only once. This implies that at the outset A and a are equal, or:

$$p = .50$$
$$q = .50$$

To make the illustration as clear as possible, we will assume further that each mating type is equally productive (four children) and that no other evolutionary mechanism is affecting the distribution of the gene in the genetic structure of the population. Now to illustrate genetic drift consider the second mating type, $AA \times Aa$. Normally this mating is one that produces half homozygous and half heterozygous offspring. However, it will by chance produce different proportions on occasion. The proportions shown here (Table 3–13) of three to one can be expected to occur by chance alone in a family of four children in 25 percent of such marriages, so the event is not an exceptionally rare one, but in a small population its effect is reflected in the resulting gene frequencies:

$$p = \frac{10 + 17/2}{36} = .51 \qquad\qquad q = \frac{9 + 17/2}{36} = .49$$

Chance alone is the factor responsible for the changes in genetic structure; the population has "drifted" in its genetic composition, and the drift bears no systematic relationship to the adaptive requirements of the organism. The change is random and controlled entirely by chance.

Genetic drift is a potential panacea for the solution of problems in physical anthropology. When, for example, two or more populations which are believed to be distantly related are found to be similar in gene frequencies, the *similarity* can be explained as due to genetic drift, or, in other words, to chance. The American Indians and Polynesians provide a case in point. These two groups are believed on other grounds to be derived by very different historical routes from common but ancient Asian ancestors. Their ancestry would imply that the Polynesians are more closely related to, say, the Micronesians than they are to the American Indian. Yet in terms of the frequency of the B polymorph in the ABO blood group system, the Polynesians and American Indians are more alike than are the Polynesians and Micronesians. B is rare among both Polynesians and American Indians and somewhat more common among Micronesians. This similarity between the Polynesians and American Indians is usually rejected as a true indication of a closer relationship between them and considered as due to chance, that is, genetic drift.

Conversely, genetic drift may be used to explain *differences* between populations believed on other grounds to be closely related. Thus, the differences between the Micronesians and Polynesians may be explained by genetic drift. Or two communities separated by only a mile or two in the same valley in New Guinea having very different genetic structures may be "explained" by genetic drift.

These may be correct explanations, since the effect of genetic drift is random, but to accept drift as the explanation for discordancies in situations where it cannot be demonstrated with some conclusiveness leads to a complacent acceptance and conformity with "traditional" explanations. Under these conditions, the demonstration of genetic differences or similarities is considered unimportant and uniformative unless it supports a more standard view. Yet, it is certainly possible that these discordant similarities and differences between populations may be the source of exciting new discoveries, either about the populations or about the processes of evolution or both. For this reason, genetic drift might well be considered the least acceptable explanation in doubtful cases.

Since genetic drift is effective only in small populations, it follows that it must have played a more significant role in man's early stages of evolution than it does today. The magnitude of the role is impossible to measure directly, but it is certainly clear that at one time all of man's ancestors lived in exactly the conditions that permit chance factors to operate effectively in bringing about change, that is, in small isolated groups. Moreover, these are the conditions that prevailed throughout the vast majority of time that man has been in existence. Over 95 percent of his past man resided in small inbred groups consisting entirely of familiar persons in familiar surroundings and held together by the strong social bonds of kinship, of family. From an evolutionary viewpoint this situation maximizes the effect of accidental changes in genetic structure between generations and, since the modifications are controlled by chance, serves as well to randomize the differences between such groups. With the introduction of agriculture, and particularly irrigation agriculture, into the stream of cultural evolution, population size and density increased, with sedentary communities emerging as the first step in a trend that today culminates in huge sprawling urban centers. This, however, is recent, and as the conditions worsen, we learn more and more clearly how poorly man's biology is adapted to the stresses of crowding.

POPULATION STRUCTURE, GENE FLOW, AND MIGRATION. Populations, especially human populations, have special properties. Populations expand and contract, collide with one another, subdivide internally, proliferate, colonize, and diversify. Two markedly different analogies come to mind; neither is, by any means, perfect, but perhaps between the two one will be able to get an idea of how population structure can change in unusual ways. Populations are at once like amoebas and like galaxies. Like amoebas, populations get bigger and smaller and proliferate by sending out parts of themselves to form the bases of new colonies. Like galaxies, populations can collide and interact in ways that result in new combinations of old structures. Populations, in other words, have a dynamic all their own. Populations are systems consisting of interrelated and integrated parts; the parts and their relationships constitute population structure.

The genetic structure of a population may be modified as a consequence of changes in the demographic composition of the popoulation itself.

For example, population structure may change as a result of migration. From one point of view, the effect of migration as an evolutionary mechanism is obvious. If a population, characterized by a particular genetic structure, is the recipient of a group of migrants with a different distribution of gene and genotype frequencies, then clearly if they intermarry the resulting generation will have a genetic structure that is different from either parental population. This is a simple model and rarely approximates real situations in human populations. It has, however, been elaborated and developed to the point where it is possible, given the genetic structures of both the original population and the migrants, and the rate of intermarriage, to calculate the genetic effects of the migration on the offspring generation (see Glass and Li, 1954).

A common situation in natural populations is the presence of subpopulations within them. The analysis of this condition requires a different view of population structure. Up to this point, a population has been considered as a homogeneous and undifferentiated unit consisting of individuals that intermarry at random. This latter condition, however, implies that the structure of a population may be internally heterogeneous and highly diversified. That is, a population may consist of many subunits that tend to mate more often within themselves but are nonetheless linked together by regular outmating, the rate of which may vary from one subunit to another. Under these circumstances, no actual migration need take place for the same kind of phenomenon described above to occur and, for this reason, the phenomenon is now generally identified as gene flow instead of migration. Gene flow identifies the source of changes in the genetic structure of populations that arise through the differentiation of a population into integrated subunits.

Some of the more interesting advances in population genetics today center around the problem of population structure. Indeed, the area serves as an intellectual battleground for one of the exciting controversies presently emerging among both human geneticists and physical anthropologists. An example will illustrate the fundamental differences in outlook. Are the several communities existing together in one valley best thought of as so many separate populations (isolates) differentiated by genetic drift, or might it be more appropriate to represent such a situation as a single population consisting of subunits which may vary in genetic structure, thereby contributing to the total variance in the population, and which are linked together by continuous outbreeding? In this situation, the solution depends, obviously, on the empirical circumstances. Anthropologists are accustomed to the isolate model—so accustomed, indeed, that it has determined both the kind of information they have sought and the choice of groups they have studied (see Morton, 1968).

The main point to be emphasized here is that gene flow can and does alter the genetic structures of natural populations, but the magnitude of its effects is difficult to measure without an adequate model of population structure. This point, in turn, serves to demonstrate the related observation that an understanding of gene flow in any population requires a knowledge of population structure, inbreeding, the movements in and out of the population, mating practices, and the effect of other evolutionary mechanisms on the population and its subunits. It is an interesting but complex area in the study of natural populations. We return in Chapter 11 to some speculations on the significance of population structure in the future of physical anthropology.

Population Genetics and Physical Anthropology

These constitute the known factors that can operate to alter the genetic structures of natural populations. It is certainly possible that many more will be identified, but for the time being, these are the only means known to be capable of changing gene, genotype, or mating type frequencies. Nevertheless, one might well wish to know at this point how population genetics is relevant to the problems of physical anthropology. To some, the relevance may be obvious, but to the beginner, it may be useful to consider some illustrations. You will recall that the broad areas of interest to physical anthropology are: 1) the investigation and interpretation of human evolution, and 2) the examination of the causes and significance of the range of man's heterographic variation. How can population genetics be of use in the solution of these problems? Consider first the area of human evolution. In all candor, population genetics has contributed little to the resolution of conflicting interpretations of the fossil record of primate and human evolution, though in Chapter 11 we suggest ways in which it may. However, in detecting changes in the genetic structure of populations in the present, population genetics provides a most powerful background of theory and technique. Suppose, for example, that we wish to know whether a population is undergoing evolutionary change with respect to the Aa locus. Assuming an appropriate model of population structure, an investigator able to obtain a large unbiased sample of nuclear families (both parents and all their natural offspring) near or beyond the completion of their reproductive period can determine whether, in fact, the distribution of offspring genotypes is that expected under Mendel's laws, or whether there are consistent distortions in the expected distribution of genotypes from particular mating types. The existence of such distortions is direct evidence of evolution. The cause of the distortion remains to be determined, but the activity of one or more evolutionary mechanisms is implied. It should be emphasized also that the lack of segregation distortions does not necessarily imply the absence of evolutionary mechanisms. The genetic structure of the population may be undergoing change at the locus at a rate too slow to be detected by a two-generational segregation analysis.

A simple adaptation of this approach can also be used to illustrate a way in which population genetics can be applied to a problem in human heterography, namely, the effects of outcrossing. Outcrossing is often referred to as race mixture, and estimating the effects of such marriages on the resulting offspring has been a problem of long-standing interest in human biology. There are two contradictory views on the subject. There are those who argue that race mixing may lead to harmful effects in the offspring. Others maintain that race mixture may result in more vigorous, more healthy, and more fertile offspring. The evidence is not conclusive for either viewpoint. The one classic study by Davenport and Steggerda (1929) concluded that race mixture is harmful; however, the research was badly designed, vague, and illogical. Those studies supporting heterosis (hybrid vigor) in man (Shapiro, 1929, 1936; Hulse, 1957, etc.) are hampered by an inability to distinguish between heterosis and selective migration. That is, the offspring can on many grounds be demonstrated to be more "vigorous" in outcrossing, but it is not clear whether this is due to some heterotic effect or to the fact that the parents are a hardier group than the average members of their respective source populations. Likewise, some apparent heterosis could be due to environmental factors, since the children are often reared under conditions very different from those of either parent group. Morton, Chung, and Mi (1967) applied principles of population genetics to this traditional problem in physical anthropology and concluded that among the many crosses between distinctive groups in Hawaii there is no apparent effect in either direction.

These may serve to illustrate ways in which population genetics may be of use in solving traditional physical anthropological problems, but, in fact, the most common way of relating the two areas is in the presumed potential of population genetics in the solution of the hoary physical anthropological problems of tracing past migrations and establishing degree of biological relationship among contemporary populations. Population genetics provides a means of characterizing human groups in terms of gene frequencies. As noted earlier, the frequencies of *A* and *a* can be determined directly and simply when all three genotypes are recognizable. Thus:

$$\text{Frequency of } A = p = \frac{\text{No. of } AA \text{ persons} + \frac{1}{2} \text{ No. of } Aa \text{ persons}}{\text{Total } AA, Aa, aa \text{ persons}}$$

$$\text{Frequency of } a = q = \frac{\text{No. of } aa \text{ persons} + \frac{1}{2} \text{ No. of } Aa \text{ persons}}{\text{Total } AA, Aa, aa \text{ persons}}$$

The calculation is slightly more complicated when the locus in question involves more than two alleles, and also when it is not possible to distinguish all the genotypes. Many physical anthropologists and human geneticists have believed that these gene-frequency estimates can be used to disclose migrations that took place in the past and to detect the degree of biological relationship between two or more populations. The assumption underlying both applications is simply that the more similar the frequencies, the closer the relationship. Some aspects of this problem will be taken up again in Chapter 9, but from the earlier discussion it now should be clear that gene-frequency estimates drawn from natural populations are affected by sampling procedures, intensity of inbreeding, population structure, and, of course, by any one or more of the mechanisms of evolution. Contrary to the view that similarity in gene frequencies implies close relationship, the potential influence of these factors makes it impossible to know with any confidence just what any particular gene frequency may imply. Leaving aside this limitation, however, population genetics more than any other subdivision of genetics serves to draw the attention of physical anthropologists to the processes and dynamics of evolutionary change in human populations.

MAJOR POINTS IN CHAPTER 3

1. Genetics offers a means of describing human variation and of explaining it in evolutionary terms.
2. Mendel's laws apply to all forms of life.
3. Variability between generations may be preserved by genetic processes.
4. Genes are segments of DNA.
5. DNA is a long coiled sequence of nucleotides.
6. Genes make enzymes.
7. Enzymes consist of chains of amino acids.
8. Given certain assumptions, the genetic structure of a population is stable from one generation to the next.
9. Populations evolve as their genetic structures change.
10. Natural selection may act to maintain or to eliminate the various components of the genetic structure of populations.
11. Mutations produce new genes, a process which may alter the frequencies of genes.
12. Genetic drift refers to generational changes in genetic structure that are caused by accidental or chance factors.
13. Changes in the demographic structure of a population can produce changes in the genetic structure of a population.

REFERENCES AND SUGGESTIONS FOR ADDITIONAL READING

BEADLE, G. W., AND E. L. TATUM
1941 Genetic control of biochemical reactions in *Neurospora*. *Proceedings of the National Academy of Science* 27:499–506.
BRACE, C. LORING
1963 Structural reduction in evolution. *American Naturalist* 97:39–49.
CAVALLI-SFORZA, L. L., AND W. F. BODMER
1971 *The genetics of human populations.* San Francisco: W. H. Freeman.
CROW, JAMES F.
1963 *Genetics notes.* Minneapolis: Burgess.
CROW, J. F., AND M. KIMURA
1970 *An introduction to population genetics theory.* New York: Harper and Row.
DAVENPORT, C. B., AND M. STEGGERDA
1929 Race crossing in Jamaica. *Carnegie Institution of Washington* 395:454–477.
DOBZHANSKY, THEODOSIUS
1959 Evolution of genes and genes in evolution. *Cold Spring Harbor Symposia on Quantitative Biology* 24:15–30.
DUNN, L. C.
1959 *Heredity and evolution in human populations.* Cambridge: Harvard University Press.
1963 Cross currents in the history of human genetics. In *Papers on human genetics*, ed. Samuel H. Boyer, IV. Englewood Cliffs, N.J.: Prentice-Hall.
GLASS, B., AND C. C. LI.
1954 The dynamics of racial intermixture–an analysis based on the American Negro. *American Journal of Human Genetics* 5:1–20.
GRIFFITH, F.
1928 The significance of pneumococcal types. *Journal of Hygiene* 27:113–159.
HARDY, G. H.
1908 Mendelian proportions in a mixed population. *Science* 28:49–50.
HERSHEY, A. D., AND M. CHASE
1952 Independent functions of viral protein and nucleic acid in growth of bacterio-phage. *Journal of Genetic Physiology* 36:39–56.
HULSE, FREDERICK S.
1957 Exogamie et hétérosis [Exogamy and heterosis]. *Archives Suisses d'Anthropologie Générale* 22:103–125. English translation by the author in *Yearbook of Physical Anthropology* 9:240–257.
LERNER, I. MICHAEL
1968 *Heredity, evolution, and society.* San Francisco: W. H. Freeman.
LYON, MARY F.
1962 Sex chromatin and gene action in the mammalian X-chromosome. *American Journal of Human Genetics* 14:135–148.
MAYR, ERNST
1959 Where are we? *Cold Spring Harbor Symposia on Quantitative Biology* 24:1–14.
MENDEL, GREGOR
1866 Experiments in plant hybridization. *Proceedings of the Natural History Society of Brünn.* English translation–Cambridge: Harvard University Press, 1948.

MORTON, NEWTON E.
> 1967 Genetic studies of northeastern Brazil: Summary and conclusions. *Ciencia e Cultura* 19:14–30.
> 1968 Problems and methods in the genetics of primitive groups. *American Journal of Physical Anthropology* (n.s.) 28:191–202.

MORTON, N. E., C. S. CHUNG, AND M. P. MI.
> 1967 *Genetics of interracial crosses in Hawaii.* Basel: S. Karger.

MORTON, N. E., AND N. YASUDA
> 1962 The genetical structure of human populations. In *Les déplacements humains*, ed. J. Sutter. Paris: Hachette.

SHAPIRO, H. L.
> 1929 Descendants of the mutineers of the Bounty. *Memoirs of the B. P. Bishop Museum.* Honolulu.
> 1936 *Heritage of the Bounty.* New York: Simon and Schuster.

SNYDER, LAURENCE H., AND PAUL R. DAVID
> 1957 *The principles of heredity.* 5th ed. Boston: D. C. Heath.

SRB, ADRIAN M., R. D. OWEN, AND R. S. EDGAR
> 1965 *General genetics.* 2d ed. San Francisco: W. H. Freeman.

STANSFIELD, WILLIAM D.
> 1969 *Schaum's outline of theory and problems of genetics.* New York: McGraw-Hill.

STERN, CURT
> 1960 *Principles of human genetics.* San Francisco: W. H. Freeman.

SUTTON, H. ELDON
> 1965 *An introduction to human genetics.* New York: Holt, Rinehart, and Winston.

WAHLUND, S.
> 1928 Zusammensetzung von populationen und korrelationserscheinungen vom Standpunkt der Vererbundslehre aus betrachtet. *Hereditas* 11:65–106.

WATSON, JAMES D.
> 1965 *Molecular biology of the gene.* New York: W. A. Benjamin.
> 1968 *The double helix.* New York: Atheneum.

WATSON, J. D., AND F. H. C. CRICK
> 1953 Molecular structure of nucleic acids. *Nature* 171:737–738.

WORKMAN, P. L.
> 1969 The analysis of simple genetic polymorphisms. *Human Biology* 41:97–114.

YULE, U.
> 1908 Comments on Mendelism in relation to disease. *Proceedings of the Royal Society of Medicine* 1:164–166.

PART II HUMAN PALEONTOLOGY

THE CONCERN OF THIS BOOK IS WITH MAN, and the focus of this section on human paleontology is on the fossil evidence of human evolution. That evidence is contained within a thin outer layer of the earth's crust. The earth is estimated to be six billion years old, but human evolution has taken place within the last few million years. Most of the material in this section deals with these last few million years, but an effort is made to put the human period into proper perspective by first presenting brief discussions of the earlier parts of the geological record.

Life began over three billion years ago. During this vast period, the earth has undergone enormous changes, some abrupt, some gradual. Land forms changed; ocean levels shifted; mountains were formed, eroded, and formed again; volcanoes erupted; and time and again glaciers swept out from the poles and down from the mountains scarring the earth's crust, depositing and redepositing its surface in unlikely places. All the while, the less dramatic forces of wind and water erosion were constantly changing the earth's surface. These and many other forces placed continual pressure on living species to adapt to the changing environmental circumstances or face the only alternative—to become extinct. Those that survived did so because they were able to adapt, or, put in a different way, had a sufficiently wide range of variability upon which to draw during these changing conditions to survive them. Since the better-adapted members of the species contribute more offspring to the next generation, the effect over time is not simply change, but systematic improvements in the species' adaptation. This is, of course, evolution, and its effects are seen in the staggering array of variation that may be found within the nearly two million species of animals alive today.

It would be both useful and comforting to know the details of the changes that life has undergone over this long time period, but this is impossible, since no record exists on which we might reconstruct the details. There is some direct evidence, however, that enables us to learn something about the general outlines of the record—the evidence of fossils, the artifacts of life. Discovering, describing, and interpreting the significance of the fossil evidence is the province of the science of *paleontology*.

115

4 Paleontology and the Fossil Record of the Primates

FOSSILS: EVIDENCE OF THE PAST

Definition

There is a widespread view that fossils are simply bones that have become mineralized or turned to stone. This is often, but not always, true. A fossil is anything that provides us with direct information about organisms that lived in the past. Thus, in reconstructing the distant past, a fossil may be an imprint, a soil discontinuity caused by a burrowing animal, a seed, a completely preserved form, as well as many other kinds of things. In addition, the human paleontologist has another fossil record to be concerned with over and above that usually confronting a paleontologist—the fossil record of cultural change, or, as it is more commonly called, the archaeological record. An attempt is made in Chapter 6 to integrate the details of these two fossil records, but at this point the discussion will focus on some of the problems associated with the analysis of bones and teeth, the more common paleontological fossils, and with the archaeological record.

Interpretation

Far too often we assume that the facts speak for themselves. For example, it might be held that all the human paleontologist needs to do is to discover relevant fossil material and describe it, and eventually the answers to all significant questions would then be found. This view demonstrates a lack of awareness of some fundamental principles of scientific procedure. How, for example, do we decide that a particular fossil is relevant whereas another is not? Since any bone, or fragment of a bone, can be thought of as possessing an infinity of attributes, how do we develop our description? What observations do we note? What measurements do we record? These sound like impractical objections, but much valuable information has been lost, destroyed, or simply not obtained because of an investigator's naïve presumptions that he could recognize and describe all relevant attributes. Unfortunately, no amount of information or training can provide us with certainty in our judgments about relevance. No one knows what information may be called for in future investigations and analyses. However, some simple general principles can be recognized. In the description of fossil materials, features should be observed and measured: 1) on

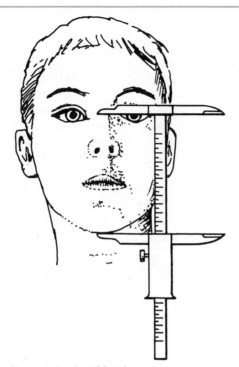

Figure 4–1. Facial height measurement.

the basis of their utility for comparative purposes, and 2) on the basis of their integrity as functional units themselves. The first of these criteria is the less justifiable; in effect what it says is that measurements should be taken because others have taken such measurements. This alone is not a good principle, but following it does make comparing one fossil with another not merely easier, but possible. Employing the second criterion in the choice of measurements and attributes for description is usually more desirable but more difficult to apply, for it involves serious thought and careful judgment. Consider, for example, facial height (see Figure 4–1). What is the functional integrity or significance of this measurement? Is this a measurement of some element of the face that has some physiological, anatomical, genetic, or evolutionary integrity? No. In fact it crosses two major functionally integrated parts of the face: the mouth and the nose. This is not to say that there are no important functional relationships between eating and breathing, but rather from the standpoint of unit integrity it is useful to separate them—just as breathing is functionally related to running, yet it is useful to consider them as separate activities. The evolutionary forces responsible for the size and form of the mouth (food, techniques for preparing and storing food, the use of the mouth as an implement, sources of tooth wear, etc.) are most certainly different from the evolutionary forces responsible for the form and size of the nose (temperature, humidity, altitude, degree of cultural development, etc.). Indeed, it is likely that the factors responsible for the length of the nose may be different from those that determined its width.

So what sense does it make to take facial height as a measurement? Only the sense that follows from tradition—anthropologists have been doing it for many, many years. This is a reason, but not a very good one.

Deciding what units constitute biologically meaningful and functionally integrated features is a task for trained professional specialists. There are ways of arriving at correct decisions, but at least one element appears to be fundamental not only to the solution of this particular problem, but to the problems of interpreting paleontological data in general—a knowledge of the properties of bone and at least a minimal understanding of the processes of fossilization.

BONES AND HOW THEY FOSSILIZE

We are inclined to think of bone as an essentially solid and fixed material that serves as a firm base to hold the other body parts together and provide some structure. We think of bone as stable and as playing an important but passive role in its relationships to the rest of the body, like that of a coat hanger to a coat. Bone is, of course, strong, but it is by no means inactive; the elements that make it up are continually undergoing changes accommodating the requirements of growth and development, responding to regular fluctuations in diet, restoring damaged tissue, and carrying out regular physiological functions, such as the production of red blood cells. These are only a few of the factors known to cause alterations in the structure of bony tissue.

Some of the activity of bone is implicit in its structure, particularly as we view it under the microscope. Figure 4–2 is a microscopic view of a very small area of a thin cross section of one of the larger bones in the body, the femur. You will notice patterns of concentric rings, each surrounding a hole in the center. The concentric rings are called lamellae, and the holes are known as Haversian canals. With the exception of the Haversian canals, the light areas are deposits of minerals, particularly calcium and phosphate, which provide bone with much of its solid structure. The little black areas with extensions are lacunae, in which the bone cells or osteocytes lived in life. The thin branches of the osteocytes come into contact with adjacent osteocytes, and all are ultimately connected with one or more Haversian canals. In this way the bone cells remain in contact with the circulatory system, taking on food and eliminating waste materials, for running through the Haversian canals are blood vessels and nerves. Looking through a longitudinal section (Figure 4–3), it is possible to verify that the Haversian canals run longitudinally through the bone and form complicated network connections with one another. Already bone can be seen to be structurally more complicated than might be concluded by casual inspection. However, one should realize that these osteocytes, lamellae, and Haversian canals are continually undergoing change and replacement. Viewing it thus, one

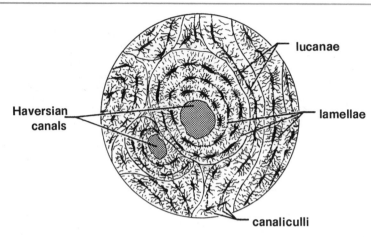

Figure 4–2. Microscopic view of a cross section of a long bone.

can begin to appreciate the structure of bone and the activity continually going on within it. When one adds to this the function of bone as a reservoir for the storage of minerals and as a center for the manufacture of blood cells, he has taken an important first step in realizing the plastic quality of bone. This is really the point to be emphasized—there is nothing fixed or immutable about the form of bone. Within broad limitations set by genetic factors, bone responds to the mechanical and physiological forces that operate on it, and these are largely responsible for both its gross and microscopic form. Thus when one looks at a bone, he is examining the product of forces imposed by the environment on the genetic potential of the individual. This view is fundamental to the appropriate interpretation of fossil bones.

What happens to a bone when it becomes fossilized? Almost everyone has a general appreciation for the process made explicit in the common statement "it becomes petrified," that is, turns to stone. But how does this happen? First it should be emphasized that it does not happen often. Bones must be deposited in just the right circumstances to become fossilized, and not only are the conditions rare, but the likelihood that bones will be discovered is even more rare. Far more often the agencies of decay and erosion cause bones to decompose and disintegrate, leaving no detectable trace. However, rare events do occur; some bones are preserved and discovered, and these constitute the major part of the known fossil record.

The process of fossilization occurs in any of three ways: 1) the replacement of the organic components with minerals, 2) chemical changes in the inorganic components of the original bone, and 3) a combination of these two processes.

Once a bone is deposited and exposed to soil, its original components begin a series of gradual chemical reactions with the materials around it. The organic components such as the osteocytes, nerves, and vascular tissue decompose and disappear rapidly, most often from action by soil bacteria. From time to time water is likely

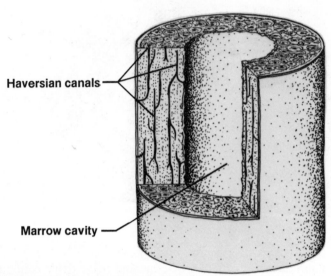

Haversian canals

Marrow cavity

Figure 4–3. Microscopic view of a longitudinal section of a long bone.

to seep through the soil, and, as it does, there is a slow but regular depositing of the minerals contained in the water in the gaps formerly occupied by the organic substances. This process was at one time thought to be the only way in which bones became fossilized, but there are a number of fossil bones now known in which the major changes can be seen in the composition of the inorganic components and in which, for instance, a sizable proportion of the lacunae formerly occupied by osteocytes remain empty. Thus, it is clear that simple substitution of inorganic for organic is by no means the entire explanation. The changes undergone by the inorganic matrix of bone are irregular, varying largely as a function of the elements that are present in the soil. It may be said that these elements enter into a complex of reactions with the bony matrix and with themselves, with the eventual result of changing the entire structure of the original bone. In short, fossilization usually involves the filling up with inorganic materials of all the holes, including the large marrow cavities, the Haversian canals, and the lacunae and canaliculi, and, in addition, involves a series of unspecifiable changes in the structure of the original organic matrix, such changes depending upon the local conditions in which the bone is deposited.

Fossilization of bone can be seen, then, as a long-term process, as indeed it is. It is not a process, however, with a common or constant rate. Thus when one finds a fossil bone, he can conclude only that it is old—not how old it is. Variations in the rates at which the process occurs depend upon such factors as soil composition, bacterial concentrations, and humidity.

One of the striking consequences of the way in which some bones become fossilized is the retention in the fossil of an exact copy of the structure of the original bone right down to the preservation of the microscopic features mentioned earlier. One is often able to see the original Haversian canals and lacunae, as well as the more obvious and expectable features of the bone's gross morphology. This is of more value than simply appealing to one's antiquarian instincts. As mentioned before, the arrangement of the Haversian canals within the shaft of the bone is determined by the mechanical requirements the bone accommodates in the living animal. Thus they provide an unexpected direct clue, not only about the way the bone functioned, but ultimately how the animal behaved. Clearly there is more to be learned from the fossil record than simply the structure of the bones.

DIMENSIONS OF PALEONTOLOGY

Knowing about the structure of bone, the forces responsible for its form, and the factors that cause it to fossilize are all important to the human paleontologist but preliminary to the main business of the field, the description and analysis of the fossil evidence bearing on man's ancestry. Adequate description and analysis in human paleontology depend upon the recovering of correct information for all fossil material in the following dimensions: time, space, and form. The human paleontologist must know for any fossil how old it is (time), where it was discovered (space), what its properties are (form), and how it functioned (inferred from form) before he can obtain an adequate appreciation of its significance. Recovering information in the dimensions of time, space, and form is the essence of paleontological work, and requires the application of methods and specific techniques.

The need to recover temporal information underscores a basic difficulty confronted by paleontologists when compared with other zoological taxonomists. Recall from Chapter 2 how the zoological taxonomist attempts to classify animals by assessing degrees of similarity. Paleontology has the same objective, but, by the nature of the subject matter, deals with forms of life that lived at some time in the past. Thus, using fragmentary information, paleontologists must assess degree of relationship between and among animals that may have lived millions of years ago and, in addition, assess the degree of relationship between these ancient forms of life and contemporary species. This is obviously a formidable task, and it should be clear from this that the recovery of information about the time during which fossils were living is a dimension basic to paleontology.

How do paleontologists estimate the age of a fossil? There are two general ways: 1) by evaluating the properties of the fossil itself, or 2) by inference from the location in which the fossil is discovered. The former method may be illustrated by either the fluorine or the C^{14} dating technique. Consider for a moment the fluorine test. Buried bones are from time to time exposed to the percolation of ground water. The water often contains fluorine picked up from the soil. The bone takes on some of the fluorine from the ground water and incorporates it into its structure as part of the fossilization process. The amount of fluorine a particular fossil has, then, will vary according to the following factors: 1) the amount of fluorine in the soil, 2) the degree of exposure to ground water, and 3) the length of time the bone has been in the ground. For fossils found together in the same location, it is reasonable to assume that the first two factors might be constant. Thus any variation in fluorine content should reflect differences in age. It was this technique that led to the disclosure that Piltdown man was a hoax (see page 213). The jaw and skull fragments had different fluorine contents, and both differed from the fossil remains of other animals found in the same location.

Likewise, the well-known carbon 14 dating technique is based on the observation that C^{14}, which is present in all living materials, begins to disintegrate at a known rate at the time an organism dies, and thus a measure of the amount remaining is an indication of the amount of time that has lapsed since the organism died. The method has too short a range (from 20,000 to 40,000 years) to be of much use to paleontology, but it is well enough known to be a familiar illustration.

The location of a fossil discovery may provide a basis for estimating its age. For example, lava flows can be dated with a high degree of precision by means of the potassium-argon method. Like C^{14}, the K-A technique is based on the knowledge that quantitative changes occur at a known rate. K^{40} disintegrates at a known rate to A^{40}, and in volcanic rock the product is trapped and therefore measurable today. Fossils found near or between vocanic layers can thus be dated by the K-A technique. This has been the most important technique used in dating the fossils discovered in recent years by the late L. S. B. Leakey in East Africa.

From the foregoing it should be clear that the question of the age of a fossil can be answered in either of two different ways. One answer is obvious—the animal lived x many years ago. The techniques available to answer the question in this way are called *absolute* dating techniques; they yield age estimates in terms of years. A second way is to answer: I do not know exactly, but I know that it lived before this fossil and after that one. This is more vague and establishes simply a sequence. The techniques that yield such information are called *relative* dating techniques.

A second dimension of fundamental importance to the paleontologist is that of space—the location of the fossil material. If the paleontologist were interested solely in describing and naming the material he discovered, then the location of a fossil in terms of altitude, longitude, and latitude would simply constitute additional data of use in deciding where the material should be placed in the taxonomic system. The location of the fossil becomes more important as the magnitude of the taxonomic category gets smaller. But the paleontologist, like the modern taxonomist, wishes to know more; he wants to know the significance of differences and similarities and wishes to identify the factors responsible for them. To do this, the paleontologist must confront several unique problems. Explanations for differences and similarities invariably require a knowledge of the ecological setting, and the paleontologist is unable to observe this. Therefore, he depends on reconstruction and inference.

The ecological setting is particularly important to the human paleontologist, for, in understanding the course of human evolution, it is important to know about the opportunities for intermixture or, as indicated earlier, gene flow. This involves knowing what factors may have acted as barriers, or alternatively, what connections may have been open in the past that are closed today. Did man's ancestors, for example, have access to routes between equatorial Africa and Asia that are no longer open? Apparently so. The Sahara was not always the severe barrier to migration that it is today.

In recovering information on location and ecological setting, paleontologists may employ any of a number of excavation techniques. Good field paleontologists pride themselves on "clean excavations." This usually means a carefully worked out plan of excavation, one of several possible choices of systems of locating the site and fossils within it in terms of latitude, longitude, and altitude, and an adequate set of records for preserving as much information as possible. A "clean excavation" also means straight lines and vertical trenches. This may sometimes reflect no more than a compulsive neurosis on the part of the investigator-in-charge, but, more often than not, it implies that attention is being given to details, and in the process of obtaining information about location and setting, much attention must be given to details. Flexibility is also a desirable attribute in any excavation.

Thus it is that the paleontologist finds himself continually concerned with the information provided by a knowledge of where fossils come from. Should you make a discovery and ask a paleontologist to identify it, this will become clearer, for the first question he is likely to ask is: "Where did you find it?"

So far, we have been talking about bones—how they become fossilized, how they are discovered, and, once discovered, what is done with them. Clearly two items of fundamental importance to know about them are their age and location. We now know something minimal about the procedures available for obtaining information on these matters. These constitute two of the three fundamental dimensions of human paleontology, time and space. The third is form. In paleontology, form refers to all the properties of a fossil. The formal properties of a fossil may be viewed in two ways: 1) from the point of view of *structure*, that is, all of the physical features such as length, width, ridges, joint surfaces, tubercles, etc.; and 2) from the point of view of *function*, that is, the way in which the structural components are inter-related, and how they relate to the way of life of the complete organism. In more familiar terms, form is the appearance of the fossil and what its appearance offers in evidence for the way the animal lived. Form is the basic dimension of paleontology, the one to which paleontologists pay the most attention, for it is primarily on the basis of formal properties that judgments are reached on the degrees of relationship among fossils, and between them and living organisms. Such judgments can be reached entirely on the basis of form. For example, it is possible to conclude that a particular fossil is a member of the genus *Homo* and species *sapiens* completely on the basis of structural features and without knowing where the fossil came from or when it lived. The reverse is obviously not possible; without a knowledge of its formal properties it is of little value simply to know where a fossil came from and how old it is.

Measurements and observations are the means we use to translate the form of a fossil into a useful description of the fossil. Paleontologists, in dealing with temporal and spatial factors, confront unusual problems in description because of the nature of the fossil record. These limitations have made it necessary for paleontologists to emphasize the details of structure in their descriptions, since these can be seen directly. In dealing with fossil material, the functional aspect of form can be known only indirectly through inference. For this reason, paleontologists commonly base their interpretations on the one thing they can readily measure and observe—the structure of fossils. This approach is, of course, necessary, and indeed has yielded virtually everything known about the evolutionary histories of modern plants and animals, but it has its dangers, particularly when conclusions are reached on very little evidence. An example will make this clearer. In 1922 a fossil tooth from Nebraska was identified as that of an ape. This was amazing, since no fossil apes had ever been found in the New World, but the tooth was later identified as that of a fossil pig. The lesson to be learned from this is simple: the amount of fossil evidence available influences the reliability of interpretations.

Paleontologists are becoming more and more interested in the functional aspect of form. How do they obtain information on function? There are two general ways: 1) from the functional properties of the structure of the fossil, and 2) from the context in which it lived. In drawing inferences about the functional significance of bone structure, we draw heavily upon the field of compartive anatomy, and particularly it subspecialty, comparative osteology. As we have seen already, the shape of a bone is determined by genetic and evironmental factors. The genetic factors appear to establish initial functional relationships, and environmental factors, such as strain and load, determine much of both the microscopic and gross morphological structure of bone. Thus, it is clear that studies of the microscopic and gross structure of bone should provide us with direct information on the strain and load factors the bone was subjected to in life. Such information provides us with a basis for drawing conclusions about how the particular bone functioned. Again, such studies as these depend on analogies with structures found in living animals. Advances in experimental functional anatomy can be expected to provide broader insight and better understanding of the functional significance of skeletal structure.

Statements and conclusions about function can also be based on observations of the context in which a particular fossil lived. With particular reference to fossil material, the study of functional processes implied by attributes in the context is known as *paleoecology*. Ecological data can provide evidence on such factors as climate, population structure and density, diet, predators, disease, and many other items that bear upon the functional or processual relationships between the species represented by the fossil and the many elements of its environment. Inferences drawn concerning the functional properties of fossil forms, on the basis of ecological data, are probably more subject to error simply because they require assumptions about relationships for which there often is little empirical evidence.

Having located our fossils in time and space, and having extracted all the relevant structural and functional details of their formal properties, what comes next? Fossils are of value as they improve our understanding of evolution. Thus, we use the data provided by human paleontology as a background of empirical information on which are tested hypotheses and theories about the course of man's evolution.

This discussion has been properly formal, but in all honesty somewhat misleading. From the discussion one is led to anticipate that paleontology, though hampered by incomplete evidence, has a straightforward task—locate fossils, analyze them carefully, and the result should be a clear interpretation. In fact paleontologists, especially those who deal with the evidence of man's evolution, disagree all the time and often on basic issues. In some cases the controversies are themselves interesting and help us better to understand the problems presented by the available fossile material. These will be discussed. In other cases issues will be regarded from a point of view which seems to be the most reasonable. The reader should keep in mind that fossil evidence is usually ambiguous, and ambiguity leaves room for different, sometimes even contradictory, interpretations. We turn now to the fossils and some of the theories and insights they have generated.

THEORIES OF THE ORIGIN OF LIFE

A problem of long-standing interest to man is the question of how life originated. This is but one of several possible convenient places to begin; one could begin, for example, with other questions, such as the origin of matter, of the universe, of our galaxy, our solar system, or our planet, but the answers to these questions are either completely unknown or dependent upon theories based on scant evidence. Apart from being of greater immediate importance, the evidence now available on the subject of the origin of life is enough to be scientifically respectable, and, put together in a logical way, makes a fascinating story.

Almost everyone has an answer to the question of how life came into being. This is true not only for members of our own society, but for primitive cultures as well. The question is apparently one that has been of interest to man for a very long time, and, further, one which all groups of men have felt compelled to answer in one way or another. The condition of not knowing the answer appears to be intolerable to man. So there are some feelings of uneasiness that generally accompany the subject, particularly in a scientific context. Apart from this difficulty, the question seems hopeless, since the event, the origin of life, took place so long ago that trying to find any evidence of its occurrence can only be regarded as futile. This is, of course, true; there is no fossil evidence to bring to bear on the problem. There does exist, however, a reasonable scientific argument and enough experimental evidence to support it to make it plausible. That argument and some of the evidence supporting it are presented in what follows.

In general, there are only three possible ways to answer the question of how life originated: 1) life was created from nothing, that is, simply willed into existence by a supernatural force; 2) life arose from preexisting life—say, for example, that life on earth arose from life that reached here from some other planet; or 3) life is a product of nonliving matter.

Creation

The belief that life was made from nothing, that it arose as a product of the will of a supernatural being, is by far the most commonly accepted view of the origin of life. It has a peculiarly comfortable appeal to human beings. Men make things all the time, so when they are confronted with the problem of explaining the existence of something they did not and could not make, it is an easy psychological step to conclude that some power that has *super*natural abilities did the making.

In any event, Creation, as such, is an unacceptable explanation in science, for it requires the invoking of a force *outside* of nature to account for natural events, and this violates the fundamental ground rules of science. Man uses science to explain and better understand his experience by establishing relationships between and among naturalistic phenomena. That is, science attempts to explain nature, or the materialistic world, in terms of itself. When Creation is invoked, it implies something outside of nature, a supreme being, as the cause of the origin of life, and thus is not a scientific explanation. This does not make it good or bad, right or wrong—just outside of science.

We cannot, then, in this context consider the Creation explanation further, except to point out that it is not necessarily incompatible with acceptable scientific views on the origin of life and matter. Life could very well have come from inorganic substances by means of naturalistic and knowable processes and still be regarded as an event in the unfolding of a Creator's plan.

Biogenesis

The view that life arose from preexisting life is, of course, no explanation whatever for the origin of life. It merely postpones the problem. It is perhaps some comfort to say that life on earth arose from life that already existed somewhere else in the cosmos, but to explain it in this way is to provide only an answer to the problem of the origin of life *here on earth*. It does not even attempt to answer the general question of how the first life came into being. At best it is endless. It is like asking how life came about, and being told that it arose from preexisting life, and then asking where the preexisting life came from, and being told that it too came from preexisting life, and on and on.

Apart from the logical difficulties, the notion of life originating elsewhere in the universe is weakened further by the fact that it lacks any solid empirical evidence. To be sure, there is the realm of possibility; that is, life on earth could *possibly* have come from life elsewhere, and it could *possibly* have come to earth by way of a meteor or some celestial vehicle, or it could *possibly* have begun here as the organic garbage left behind by some interplanetary or intergalactic visitors billions of years ago. But there is no evidence for any of these things, and the question of how life originated would still be left unanswered.

Spontaneous Generation

Having rejected Creation as unknowable and biogenesis as irrelevant, it seems that science has no alternative but to conclude that life must have sprung from inorganic matter. But when we begin to look into the situation, we find that this question has come up time and again in the history of science under the name of spontaneous generation. In fact, people believed in spontaneous generation for many hundreds of years, and they had apparently good reasons for believing in it. Anyone could see that flies arose spontaneously from decaying food, or that rats could be made by putting the right things in a damp, dark room for a long enough time. There have been, in fact, published books which contained "recipes" for creating various kinds of animals. By following one recipe you could bring about flies, by following another, rats, snakes, etc. This is spontaneous generation; given the right materials and the appropriate environment, life emerged from the nonliving ingredients.

However much common sense supported this view, experimental evidence did not. Redi, in the seventeenth century, demonstrated that flies did not emerge from putrefying meat if it was placed in a jar covered with gauze, thereby preventing flies from laying their eggs in it. Spallanzoni, in the eighteenth century, showed that boiled broth sealed from the air kept indefinitely and did not develop microorganisms. And Pasteur, in the nineteenth century, refined the experiment of Spallanzoni by designing a special container for the broth which, by means of a curved tube, allowed air to get to the nutrient but trapped the bacteria outside.

All these experiments pointed to exactly the same conclusion: life does not originate from nonliving matter.

It would appear that the problem is perhaps one that science simply cannot handle—one that should be left entirely in the hands of theologians. Creation and biogenesis were rejected, and spontaneous generation was clearly demonstrated as false over one hundred years ago. There is one loophole that can provide a basis for retaining the view of spontaneous generation: all that Pasteur's work, and that of his predecessors, showed was that life does not arise from nonlife *at the present time*. Thus one could still argue that life could have originated some time ago when conditions were different from what they presently are. This is fundamental to the modern scientific interpretation of the origin of life, which views it as the product of a very long series of accumulating events that eventually resulted in life, in a compound able to draw upon substances in its environment and, from them, duplicate itself.

For anyone who knows anything about the chemical makeup of living organisms, this steplike process of gradually accumulating the necessary parts sounds like nonsense, for it is clear that the crucial parts of living organisms are fats, proteins, and carbohydrates. Granted, these are made largely from elements that were known to have been plentiful in one form or another in the early atmosphere of the earth —carbon, oxygen, nitrogen, and hydrogen—but they are extraordinarily large and complicated molecules, and to imagine even the simplest of them arising spontaneously would appear to be out of the question. It would appear to be out of the question, that is, if it were something which had to happen within a relatively restricted time period, or if it had to happen again and again. In fact, we are considering an event which could well have taken over a billion years to happen, an event that needed to occur only once as far as our central problem, the origin of life, is concerned. Furthermore, the taking of each step may well have increased the likelihood that the next step would be taken, so we might well be talking about a chainlike sequence, the outcome of which becomes more and more likely as each new link is added.* Until recently this theory was supported almost exclusively by experimental evidence alone, but recently was given further support by the discovery of amino acids in the Murchison meteorite.

Cannot one argue, however, that this is only in the realm of possibility, as in the case of biogenesis? Is it not true that all that is being offered here is simply something that could *possibly* have occurred? In one sense, yes, but in the very same sense we would have to argue that all we have ever learned from scientific exploration was nothing more than simply possible. Science cannot prove anything; it strives to solve problems by establishing relationships between and among things and events. Appropriate scientific procedures and availability of empirical information enable investigators to determine probabilities between things and events. This science can do, and it is what has been done here. The evidence for the view that life originated gradually and sequentially, as proposed here, is by no means conclusive. No one has proved that this is the way it happened, and no one ever will. But the conclusions are supported by empirical evidence of processes that are known to occur in inorganic substances today, and thus by the orderly formulation of hypotheses, testing them against the data, and the correct application of the rules of logic, we have put probability on the side of this view. Someone who wishes to challenge the view will have to do so by showing: 1) the reasoning is invalid, 2) there is empirical evidence that contradicts it, or 3) another explanation has a higher probability of being correct.

Without arguing the issue further, one thing can be agreed upon: life did occur. Once it came into existence, natural selection and mutation must have begun to

---

* For a detailed and readable account of this view see Wald, 1955.

operate immediately, bringing about a very slow process of adaptation and differentiation and eventually readaptation and redifferentiation, and on and on.

At first, this process must have occurred wholly within the sea, and the first living organisms must have been very simple. Perhaps, were it possible to observe the circumstances, even now it might be impossible to distinguish between living and nonliving substances. It is likely that these simple life substances subsisted on the simpler organic molecules, themselves the end products of a very long accumulative process. The natural breakdown of organic materials by organisms is a process known as fermentation, and, at first, it must have been a very slow process indeed, taking up perhaps one-half of the total amount of time that has lapsed since life began and leaving virtually no clear evidence of its existence. It was, however, a process that had to end, for even though it progressed slowly, it went on more rapidly than the rate at which organic molecules accumulated. Thus the food supply, upon which the fermentation process depended, decreased inversely as life expanded. It was one of the waste products of fermentation—carbon dioxide—that, together with water and chlorophyll, provided a new way for living systems to obtain energy —the process of photosynthesis. Photosynthesis enables plants to obtain the energy necessary for carrying out the life process directly from the sun and to convert this energy into a form usable in the manufacture of their own cells. Part of the process involves extracting hydrogen from water and thereby liberating free oxygen as an unused waste product. Thus, as plants evolved, at first in the sea and later on land, an increasing amount of free oxygen entered the earth's atmosphere and ultimately permitted animals to live on land.

THE FOSSIL RECORD OF MAJOR EVENTS
UP TO THE ORIGIN OF THE PRIMATES

The Precambrian

The origin of life, photosynthesis, and oxygen respiration are clearly events of enormous importance to understanding the evolution of life. Yet none of these momentous events is clearly recorded in the paleontological record. Our understanding of how they originated is inferential and indirect, based on recent experimental evidence. By the time organisms began to leave a clear and reasonably continuous record of their existence, they had already differentiated into plants and animals, many with complex and specialized parts, implying a long but largely unknown evolutionary past. The fossil record of approximately one-half billion years is simply the relatively small visible part of a process that began over three billion years ago. Paleontologists refer to the "submerged" part of the record as the Proterozoic and Archaeozoic eras, or the Precambrian (See Table 4–1). Some of the best evidence of what happened during the Precambrian comes from the vast expanses of exposed rock that make up the Canadian and Baltic shields. These have been exposed through normal erosion by

Table 4–1   Sequence of Geological Eras, Periods, Epochs

ERA	PERIOD	EPOCH	TIME (approximate beginning in millions of years ago)*
CENOZOIC	Quaternary	Pleistocene	2
		Pliocene	12
	Tertiary	Miocene	28
		Oligocene	40
		Eocene	60
		Paleocene	75
MESOZOIC	Cretaceous		145
	Jurassic		170
	Triassic		200
PALEOZOIC	Permian		225
	Carboniferous		280
	Devonian		335
	Silurian		375
	Ordovician		435
	Cambrian		520
	Precambrian		3000

* Except for the Pleistocene, these dates are from Stirton (1959).

wind and water, and through the more abrupt effects of repeated glaciations that have swept out from the north, scarring the earth's surface, jarring loose the top layers, and redepositing them farther south. From geological evidence, it appears that the features of the earth were much the same during the Precambrian times as they are now. There were mountains, rivers, lakes, and oceans and regular fluctuations in temperature, including glaciations on all continents. The important difference between then and now is the extreme rarity of evidence of life throughout this vast expanse of time. The oldest fossil is a bacterium, or very much like one. The discovery came from rocks in South Africa dated at over 3.3 billion years ago. This corresponds with the estimated dates of two other events, the origin of photosynthesis and end of the event that magnetized the moon. Perhaps all three events are related. Clearly, life originated during the Precambrian, developed slowly, and, by the close of the era, began to leave occasional lasting signs of its existence.

Until recently Precambrian fossils were very scarce indeeed and consisted for the most part of traces of very simple organisms such as algae and fungi. Most of these fossils come from deposits in the Canadian shield estimated to be over two billion years old. For a time the evidence created a peculiar problem since it contrasted so sharply with the next epoch, the Paleozoic, which begins with a rich record of many different kinds of highly complex organisms. However, more recent discoveries from the Ediacara Hills in Australia have added considerably to our knowledge of the Precambrian and at the same time helped resolve the problem. The Australian deposits reveal that during the Precambrian there lived an astounding variety of life forms including highly evolved forms of jellyfish, corals, and worms (Glaessner, 1961).

As these and other investigations have continued in recent years, the Precambrian has become less and less a mystery. There are now good indications of not only the algae and fungi, but of other plants and, more important for present purposes, of animals as well. By the close of the Precambrian, there is evidence of coelenterates (today including the corals and jellyfish), crustaceans (lobsters, crabs, shrimp), porifera (sponges), and trilobites (no living representatives).

So much for the dark ages of the origin and early evolution of life. The fossil record becomes more abundant as it continues into the Paleozoic.

The Paleozoic

In dividing the geological record into epochs, periods, and eras, it should be stated that these are largely arbitrary divisions in a long and continuous sequence.

However, there are good geological reasons for distinguishing between the close of the Precambrian and the beginning of the Paleozoic. Events occurred which can be said to have divided one from the other. These geological events are known as revolutions, even though they were drawn out over millions of years, and their general features have been divided into three stages, as follows: 1) a period of intense volcanic activity, usually along the edges of large continental land masses; 2) a period of mountain-building and extreme fluctuations in temperature variation; and 3) the long, slow processes of erosion, weathering down the uplifted surfaces, and the consequent effects on sea levels and coastlines. The causes of these revolutions are not well known, and the problem is not one that needs to be examined here. What is important is that the Paleozoic began during one of these revolutions. The eras, periods, and epochs that followed were also initiated by geological changes, generally of less magnitude than revolutions, but of sufficient consequence to bring about the relatively clear stratigraphic discontinuities of the paleontological record.

At the outset of the Paleozoic, the contours of the continents as we know them were very different. Nevertheless, the major continental land masses were recognizable. The actual boundaries during this stage are not well known for any part of the world, but are better known around Europe and North America than anywhere else. As indicated in Figure 4–4, the continents were covered in part by inland waterways. These were a product of the Charnian revolution and are of greatest importance in appreciating the first significant event in the evolution of life that occurred during the Paleozoic—the filling up of these seaways with a vast array of marine plants and animals and the eventual rise to dominance of many forms of invertebrates. The variation of life forms was so great that, even from the earlier phases of the Paleozoic, it appears that there is fossil evidence of organisms representing all plant and animal phyla. The distinctive feature about these life forms to keep in mind is the fact that during the earlier stages of the Paleozoic all forms were marine.

Beginning in the Cambrian and indeed throughout most of the Paleozoic, the invertebrates remained dominant. By the time the Palezoic drew to a close, however, some important advances had taken place in the evolution of life. Plants had invaded the earth's land surfaces, and true fishes, amphibians, reptiles, and ancestral mammals had become established. These terrestrial plants and animals appeared as the inland seaways gradually disappeared and as the troughs they occupied began to fill up. Some of the plants and animals whose ancestors were exclusively aquatic adapted first to a transitional and eventually to a completely terrestrial way of life.

The Paleozoic lasted over 300 million years, which, though it staggers the imagination, is small when compared with the vast period of time in the Precambrian. Mountain-building, volcanic eruptions, glaciations, earthquakes, wind and water erosion, and the activity of living organisms all acted to bring about alterations in the earth's environment. Changing environmental conditions provided continual and often ruthless challenges to living forms to adapt or die out. The possible responses to these stimuli at any one time were limited by the range of life's variations. However, as adaptation followed adaptation, the range of variation increased, providing for new adaptive possibilities. The record of these changes is preserved, in part, in the fossil record, testifying clearly to the succession of events beginning with the Cambrian plants and invertebrates, followed by the appearance of simple vertebrates, true fishes, amphibians, reptiles, and mammallike reptiles, or perhaps true mammals, as the era draws to a close.

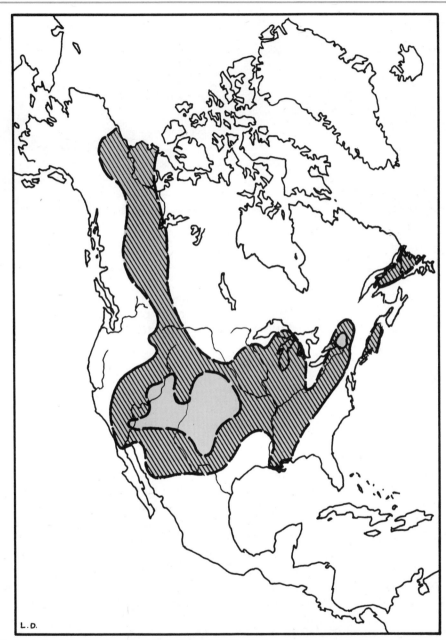

Figure 4–4.   Inland waterways (shaded areas) in North America during late Cambrian times. (After R. A. Stirton)

Figure 4–5. *Brontosaurus*, a giant amphibious dinosaur. (Courtesy of the American Museum of Natural History)

The Paleozoic came to a close about 200 million years ago with a period of geological upheaval, often referred to as the Permian-Triassic crisis. This marked the beginning of the Mesozoic, the era during which the reptiles emerged as the dominant forms of life.

The Mesozoic

In the evolutionary record of the reptiles, the Mesozoic is an era of extremes. This is best noted in the appearance of the dinosaurs. Their origin may be found in the curious, small, terrestrial reptiles of Triassic times (see Table 4–1), some of which had developed a new way of getting around—bipedal locomotion—walking on the two hind limbs. This group of reptiles is known as thecodonts. This modification, so important in man's evolution, liberated the forelimbs from locomotion. How these were put to use provides the basis for most of the fundamental differences between and among the thecodont descendants. Some retained a bipedal gait and reached enormous size, as in *Tyrannosaurus*, probably the most fearsome carnivore ever to walk on land. Others, like *Brontosaurus*, grew to lengths of eighty feet and developed bulks weighing over forty tons, supporting their bulk on all four limbs in swampy areas and shallow lakes. Unlike *Tyrannosaurus*, *Brontosaurus* was a herbivore (see Figures 4–5 and 4–6). Although often pictured together, they were separated by about 50 million years.

Still other descendants of the thecodonts developed wings which allowed them to glide from heights, but probably not to fly as we usually think of flight. The Mesozoic was indeed the age of reptiles, and as far as most of them were concerned, including the dinosaurs, it spanned their beginning and their ending. There was an abrupt extinction of many groups before the Cenozoic began. One factor that

Figure 4–6. *Tyrannosaurus* (left) and *Triceratops,* two terrestrial dinosaurs. (Courtesy of the American Museum of Natural History)

undoubtedly contributed to extinction of the dinosaurs was the selective pressure and competition they faced with the emergence of the mammals. To be sure, the mammals of the Mesozoic were no match for brutish dinosaurs, but they might well have had a taste for reptile eggs, and, under the right circumstances, this could be a most effective selective pressure. In addition, the mammals began to develop an attribute that the reptiles lacked conspicuously—intelligence. Many of the large dinosaurs had brains smaller than the human fist. However, before concluding that this made them inferior, recall that dinosaurs, as a group, lived hundreds of times longer than man seems likely to live.

The mammals, though small and unobtrusive, were clearly present in Mesozoic times. In the fossil record, the evidence for their existence consists of skeletal and dental remains that possess many mammalian features, but these are of secondary adaptive importance when compared with such characteristics as warm-bloodedness, internal development of the young in the mother's uterus, and the feeding of off-spring by means of mammary glands. The fossil record fails to provide much direct evidence bearing on the acquisition of these features. An interesting suggestion has been offered that the enlarged "fin" on the backs of some Mesozoic reptiles was a device providing for internal temperature regulation. On skeletal evidence the modern monotremes are very much like reptiles. Perhaps they represent the kind of adaptation that characterizes the earliest mammals. If so, then perhaps, like the modern monotremes, the earliest mammals may have hatched their young from eggs and then fed them from mammary glands. Apart from these considerations, however, what we know about the Mesozoic mammals is based on very little skeletal evidence.

Among the most interesting animals of the Mesozoic is a group known as the Pantotheria. These are mammals that appear about midway through the Mesozoic and retain a number of reptile characteristics. The Pantotheria are a diverse group;

some were probably carnivorous, others herbivorous, and still others were insectivorous. This latter group, the insect-eating Pantotherian mammals, probably gave rise to the earliest placental mammals. It is possible that these early placental insectivores gave rise to most of the modern placental mammals. This is a conventional view, but one which is based on very little fossil evidence (Simons, 1972).

Another event during the Mesozoic had far-reaching consequences in modifying the earth's environments—the origin of flowering plants, the angiosperms. Plants had been adapted to living on land since Silurian times. The appearance of flowering plants is of more than passing importance to one interested in the origin of the primates. The angiosperms produce seeds, flowers, and fruits. Thus, while plants abounded on land prior to the Mesozoic, their variety was limited to mosses, ferns, horsetails, conifers, etc. The spread of the angiosperms beginning in the Jurassic provided new adaptive possibilities in the evolution of animals. Insects, for example, were clearly affected. Likewise, mammalian evolution was affected by these changes. Some mammals adapted to grasslands and to forests while retaining a terrestrial way of life. Others adapted to living in the many new kinds of trees, that is, to an arboreal way of life. It was this arboreal adaptation in the evolution of the early mammals that eventually led to the origin of the primates.

The appearance of flowering plants also played an important role in the evolution of another group of vertebrates that made its first appearance during the Mesozoic, the birds. Like the mammals, birds arose from reptile ancestors, and in most fundamental features they closely resemble the reptiles. They differ in two important and related ways: 1) they are warm-blooded, a feature they share with mammals, and 2) they have feathers. Accounting for the origin of feathers is a guessing game at best. Embryologically, feathers developed in much the same way as scales in reptiles, but it is not known what selective factors operated to differentiate the birds, as a group, from their reptile ancestors. In any case, it appears that feathers functioned as heat insulation, reducing heat loss due to continuous and rapid activity, thereby providing the birds with a means of regulating their internal body temperatures. Only secondarily, it would appear from the fossil evidence, and only after modifications occurred in the structure of forelimbs, did the ancestors of the modern birds become successful and eventually graceful flyers.

The events of the Mesozoic were of great importance in the eventual appearance of true primates. If all the events were known—their time, place, and duration—it would be possible to thread them together into clearly outlined deterministic relationships. But only a few of the events are known, and these in a general way. There are enough, however, to provide us with important clues. In summary, the most important features of the Mesozoic times were: 1) *Reptiles were dominant.* They were highly varied and reached extremes in size, and most became extinct by the close of the Mesozoic. 2) *Flowering plants appeared*, bringing about decided and far-reaching changes in the composition of many of the earth's environments. Many new adaptive possibilities were thereby made available. 3) *Birds appeared* and proliferated rapidly with their descendants diversifying and occupying several different adaptive niches. 4) *Mammals appeared for the first time.* Among the earliest placentals were the small insectivores, some descendants of which took to living in the trees. It is the evolution of these that we will continue to follow.

The Mesozoic ended in another great geological upheaval, of which the Rocky Mountains are a magnificent remnant. At the beginning of the Cenozoic, the flora and fauna of the earth appeared much like those of today, with one conspicuous exception: there were no mammals that looked much like today's. Horses, camels, hippopotami, lions, squirrels, mice, dogs, sheep, goats, moneys, apes, and men had not yet evolved. But they were evolving, and the way in which they evolved is recorded in the fossil record of the Cenozoic. Since our interest is with man, we will proceed to consider the earliest members of man's order, the primates.

MAJOR POINTS IN CHAPTER 4

1. Paleontologists interpret the significance of fossils from a knowledge of their appearance, behavior, and when and where they lived.
2. Organic molecules arose as products of the chemical evolution of inorganic molecules.
3. Life emerged from the chemical evolution of organic molecules.
4. Life began in Precambrian times.
5. By the close of the Paleozoic, life had diversified into an enormous variety of plants and animals.
6. Placental mammals began during the Mesozoic.

REFERENCES AND SUGGESTIONS FOR ADDITIONAL READING

COLBERT, EDWIN H.
 1955 *Evolution of the vertebrates.* New York: John Wiley and Sons.
DE BEER, GAVIN
 1964 *Atlas of evolution.* London: Thomas Nelson and Sons.
EISELEY, LOREN
 1946 *The immense journey.* New York: Random House.
GAFFRON, HANS
 1960 *The origin of life.* In *The evolution of life: Its origin, history, and future.* Vol. 1 of *Evolution after Darwin,* ed. Sol Tax, pp. 39–84. Chicago: University of Chicago Press.
GLAESSNER, MARTIN F.
 1961 Pre-Cambrian animals. *Scientific American* 204, March, pp. 72–78.
GREGORY, W. K.
 1951 *Evolution emerging.* 2 vols. New York: Macmillan.
JEPSEN, GLENN L., ERNST MAYR, AND GEORGE GAYLORD SIMPSON
 1949 *Genetics, paleontology, and evolution.* Princeton: Princeton University Press.

MOODY, PAUL A.
1962   *Introduction to evolution.* 2d ed. New York: Harper and Row.
MURRAY, P. D. F.
1936   *Bones.* London: Cambridge University Press.
OPARIN, A. I.
1957   *Origin of life on the earth.* 3d ed. New York: Academic Press.
ROMER, ALFRED S.
1941   *Man and the vertebrates.* 3d ed. Chicago: University of Chicago Press.
1966   *Vertebrate paleontology.* 3d ed. Chicago: University of Chicago Press.
SIMONS, ELWYN L.
1967   Unraveling the age of earth and man. *Natural History*, February, pp. 53–59.
1972   *Primate evolution: An introduction to man's place in nature.* New York: Macmillan.
SIMPSON, GEORGE GAYLORD
1949   *The meaning of evolution: A study of the history of life and of its significance for man.* New Haven: Yale University Press.
1960   The history of life. In *The evolution of life: Its origin, history, and future.* Vol. 1 of *Evolution after Darwin*, ed. Sol Tax, pp. 117–180. Chicago: University of Chicago Press.
STIRTON, R. A.
1959   *Time, life, and man: The fossil record.* New York: John Wiley and Sons.
TAX, SOL, ED.
1960   *The evolution of life: Its origin, history, and future.* Vol. 1 of *Evolution after Darwin.* Chicago: University of Chicago Press.
WALD, GEORGE
1955   The origin of life. In *The physics and chemistry of life*, pp. 3–26. A Scientific American Book. New York: Simon and Schuster.
WELLER, J. MARVIN
1969   *The course of evolution.* New York: McGraw-Hill.
ZEUNER, F. E.
1952   *Dating the past: An introduction to geochronology.* 3d rev. ed. London: Methuen.

THE MODERN PRIMATES

Until now, the direction taken in our presentation of the origin and evolution of life has been to move from the past toward the present. However, now that our attention is to be focused on the primates, it will be of use to recall the information presented in Chapter 2 on contemporary members of the order, and to point out some of the factors peculiar to the problem of interpreting the evidence of primate paleontology.

First of all, it should be emphasized that there is a great deal of evidence that bears directly on primate evolution. Very little of the evidence, however, is fossil evidence. Most of it comes from living primates, for included among them are representatives of every major evolutionary stage through which the order has passed. The primates are unique among mammals in this respect, having, as they do, living representatives of the insectivore-to-primate transition (tree shrews), of the early arboreal adaptation (prosimians), of the later, more successful, arboreal offshoots of the prosimian radiation (the New and Old World monkeys), of the brachiation adaptation (the apes), and finally of the erect-bipedal-cultural stage and its phases. In its most general outline, this is the story of primate evolution, but it is the very existence of this chainlike ordering of living forms that serves to confound interpretations of the fossil record. In popular discussions it causes confusion, for it leads to the impression that man is descended from the apes, which, in turn, are descended from the monkeys, etc. This is, of course, plain nonsense. That the modern species of primates were not ancestral to man is supported best by the fact that they are living species. They are current products of evolutionary pathways that did *not* lead to man but rather to their present adaptive niches. That this confusion continues to be common is probably due to the simple way in which the "evolutionary controversy" is often presented as a choice between special creation and believing that man is descended from monkeys. Claiming that man's ancestors passed through a prosimian or a monkey stage in their evolutionary history is not at all the same as saying that tarsiers, baboons, or gorillas are in our ancestral line. In the same way, saying that the Australian aborigines present a stage in the evolution of culture is not the same as saying that their culture is ancestral to modern culture.

Figure 5–1 illustrates the problem we confront in this chapter. The living primates are arranged in a line of increasing similarity to man. This arrangement repre-

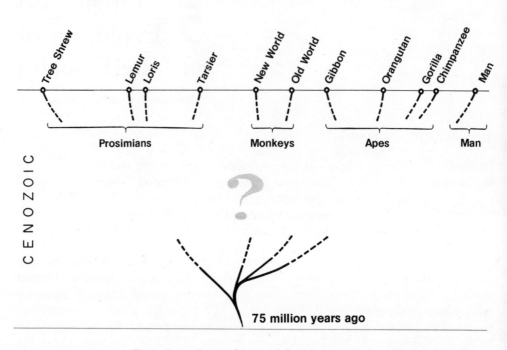

Figure 5–1.   Terminal array of the Primate order.

sents what paleontologists call a *terminal array*, a range of related varieties produced by a succession of evolutionary events. We know that the array has been produced within the last 75 million years, that is, within the Cenozoic. Thus we have several end points, the terminal array, and a point of origin millions of years ago. The problem we confront is determining how the original primates evolved into the variety of forms in the terminal array.

The logical possibilities are almost endless, but, again, logic by itself is not enough. We need evidence; we need fossils to serve as markers to help us determine the multitude of pathways our primate ancestors followed during the course of their 75-million-year journey. In general the fossil evidence supports the prosimian-monkey-ape-man sequence. The fossils are not abundant in any line, since primates have generally lived in tropical regions where conditions allowing fossilization are rare, and, further, because they are more intelligent, they may have avoided getting into circumstances in which duller animals became trapped and fossilized. And wherever there are gaps in the evidence, there is ambiguity and room for disagreement; concordance is rare among primate paleontologists. The following discussion is a continuation of the evolutionary events leading up to modern man, focusing now on the patterns of primate evolution and the available evidence.

INSECTIVORE ORIGINS OF THE PRIMATES

That the primates evolved from insectivore ancestors has already been discussed. The order Insectivora may have been the earliest group of placental mammals to persist. The order has a long and reasonably complete fossil record going back approximately 130 million years. The only other living mammalian order with comparable antiquity is the order Carnivora, and there is no clear record of which of the two was the earlier.

In any case, the Insectivora evolved very rapidly as the Mesozoic was drawing to a close. In addition to providing the ancestral basis for the primates, they also gave rise to the rodents, the lagomorphs (rabbits and hares), and an order that has since become extinct known as the Multituberculata. The insectivores and their early descendants were all small animals with small brains. For example, many had skulls that took up less volume than man's little finger. All were insectivorous, as implied by the name of the order. Beyond these simple features shared in common, most of the known information concerning their differences is drawn from evidence of their dentition, since teeth are by far the most common fossils.

The dentition of the insectivores is often highly specialized, evolving as it has in response to the unusual selective requirements of obtaining and eating insects as the major, or possibly sole, source of food. The degree of specialization is reflected in the arrangement of the teeth, their differentiation into types such as molars and incisors, and particularly in the form of the incisors themselves. Some lines developed incisors for chiseling, others for snipping or gnawing, and, in the case of the rodents, incisors that continued to grow throughout the animal's lifetime.

Provided with the fundamental advantages of mammalian characteristics, and confronted with very little serious competition in their environment, the early insectivores evolved very rapidly, as indicated by the record of fossil teeth. Eventually the ancestral insectivores generated their own most serious competitors, as they gave rise to the rodents, multituberculates, and primates, and as a result they declined, perpetuating themselves in a few specialized lines such as the present-day hedgehogs and shrews.

The transition from insectivore to primate is not clearly documented in the fossil record. As noted earlier, the only evidence available for speculating about this phase is from the modern *Tupaia*, the tree shrews. It will be recalled that the tree shrews are, in most important respects, primates, but they have retained many features characteristic of the insectivores. Their diet is largely insectivorous, and they depend heavily on their sense of smell, as implied by their long snouts and the large olfactory areas in the brain, in comparison with other primates. Thus, it seems reasonable to view them as illustrative of the insectivore-primate transition, but it would be better if there were fossil evidence to reinforce this assumption. As it is, no fossil material has ever been conclusively identified as tupaioid. Two forms have been suggested (*Adapisorex* from the Eocene and *Anagale* from the Oligocene) as fossil tupaioids, but the status of each has been questioned.

The important features of the emergence and evolution of the early pre-primate insectivores can be summarized briefly as follows: 1) They are possibly the oldest placental mammalian order. 2) They evolved and diversified rapidly during the latter part of the Mesozoic, and, by early Cenozoic times, had given rise to three more mammalian orders, the rodents, the multituberculates, and the primates. 3) The subsequent evolution of the insectivores is characterized by a decline in their diversity and habitat range. 4) While the fossil record of insectivore evolution is reasonably good in some lines, the transition from insectivore to primate is not documented by fossils. The basis of knowledge about the transition is by inference from living forms. 5) There is sufficient reason to suspect, however, that the major factor which served to distinguish the primates as a separate order was an arboreal adaptation. The adjustment made by the early primates to living in the trees is by far the most important event in the evolution of the primates, and there is a reasonable amount of direct fossil evidence bearing on the early stages of the evolution of the prosimians, which were the first primates to show the effects of this adaptation.

ARBOREAL ADAPTATION

Evolutionary Consequences

Enumerating the consequences of an arboreal way of life on the early insectivores that eventually evolved into prosimians is very nearly the same thing as listing the distinctive characteristics of the primate order, for, fundamentally, members of the order are like one another and unlike other mammalian orders because of the changes required for success in the trees. One could probably find evidence for the evolutionary effects of the arboreal adaptation in any and all aspects of primate features. The most significant and far-reaching consequences, however, were those affecting the limbs, the senses, and the brain. Further discussion of each of these should help to make more clear the enormous significance of the arboreal adaptation on the primates.

THE LIMBS. That the primates are an unspecialized order of mammals has already been emphasized. Taking this view enables one to discern something fundamentally unique about the pattern of primate evolution, and that is the retention of generalized adaptations that may often be found in very ancient ancestral forms. Thus, when we find the primates adjusting to new circumstances, as the early prosimians did in adjusting to their life in the trees, we expect and find that they are not developing a variety of new and specialized traits, but rather that they are rearranging very old adaptive characteristics. This feature of primate evolution may be seen in the consequences of an arboreal adaptation of the limbs and the hands and feet, particularly when contrasted with other terrestrial mammalian orders. The presence of five digits on each of the hands and feet, the structural and functional differentiation of the fore- and hind limbs, and the functional versatility of movement of the limbs, hands, and feet are all attributes that may be found in reptiles and amphibians and might best be regarded as primitive terrestrial vertebrate characteristics. More recently, terrestrial mammals have specialized, with some reducing the number of digits, minimizing the differences between the fore- and hind limbs, and limiting much of the free range of movement in the limbs and extremities. In doing so, these terrestrial mammals have improved particularly in their speed ranges.

Thus, when one reads that as the primates took to the trees, the forelimbs and hind limbs became differentiated, it should be clear that this is not a brand-new characteristic, but rather a relative statement implying simply that the differentiation was carried somewhat further in the primates than it had been in their ancestors. The forelimbs, and particularly the hands, became much more actively involved in grasping, balancing, and directing the progress of the early primates as they moved through the trees. Too, the hind limbs and feet were active in grasping, balancing, and directing, but, more fundamentally, they provided structural support and strength for the animals' movements in the trees. In a very real sense the arboreal adaptation as expressed structurally in the limbs is reflected functionally in locomotion. As they adapted the ancient vertebrate characteristics to the particular requirements of living in trees, the primates very early displayed a variety of locomotor patterns. Some are comparatively simple adaptations of the terrestrial quadrupedalism of their ancestors. One is more spectacular, the vertical clinging and leaping form of locomotion (Napier and Walker, 1967) which may be seen today in some prosimians such as tarsiers, bushbabies, and sifakas. These animals make remarkable leaps in going from branch to branch; they often feed while clinging to the underside of a branch and hop from place to place while on the ground.

Understanding the background of generalized vertebrate characteristics, the altered functional requirements imposed by the arboreal environments, and the way in which natural selection operates makes it possible to understand in a more profound way the simple statement that as the primates took to the trees, their forelimbs and hands became structurally and functionally differentiated from their hind limbs and feet.

This differentiation was ultimately of great importance to man's origin and evolution, as will be seen in the next chapter. Even in the early stage of primate evolution, it resulted in an improved capacity to pick up, examine, and manipulate objects. The selective refinement of the ability to explore and manipulate objects in the environment can provide some assistance in our understanding of another feature of primate evolution—the development of nails as opposed to claws. Fingernails and toenails are specializations within the primates that require some special explanation. Unfortunately, there is no cogent standard argument which can be readily supported by the facts of the fossil record and contemporary primate variation. As an educated guess, Le Gros Clark (1960) suggests that the development of the nail in primates is probably associated with a relative advantage in solving problems of locomotion, since nails permit greater dexterity and greater tactile sense.

OLFACTORY LOBE

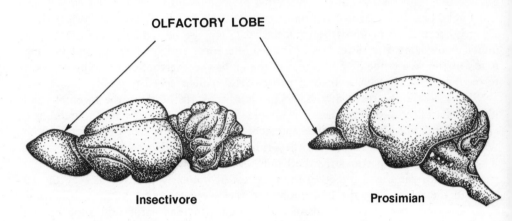

Insectivore   Prosimian

Figure 5–2. Comparison of the side views of an insectivore (*Cententes*) brain with a prosimian (*Tarsius*) brain. The insectivore brain has been increased by two-thirds to make the comparison clearer. Note the greater development in the olfactory bulb in the insectivore brain. (After W. E. Le Gros Clark)

Taking to the trees, then, may be seen as an event that initiated important modifications in both the morphology of the limbs and in the overall behavior patterns of the early primates.

THE SENSES.   Insectivores depend primarily on the sense of smell to inform them about the features of their environment that are important to them. The evidence for this is clear and unambiguous; they have long noses with complicated and delicate internal structures that function to refine their smell discriminations. They have *rhinaria*, areas of moist skin surrounding the tip of the nose, that help to locate the direction of odors. And, finally, the olfactory areas of their brains are much more fully developed than the areas controlling the other senses. In the modern as well as the early prosimians, the sense of smell continues to be important, but less so in relation to the other senses when compared with insectivores. The olfactory area of the brain is large (see Figure 5–2); the snout in most is long and its internal structure complicated; and some retain the rhinaria to the present time.

While the olfactory sense is obviously important to both the insectivore and the prosimian, the other senses, particularly vision, are much more fully represented in the cortical areas of the prosimians. Thus, there are good structural reasons for concluding that a change in emphasis took place in the insectivore-primate transition, and there are good functional reasons for concluding that this change took place because of the requirements imposed by an arboreal adaptation. The functional basis for the increasing importance of vision is obvious—for an animal the size of even the small prosimians to move rapidly from branch to branch requires a knowledge not only that another branch is there and its direction, but also a knowledge of exactly how far away it is. In this situation stereoscopic vision is necessary to permit depth perception.

One of the most striking features in the appearance of the modern lemurs and tarsiers is the large size of their eyes. This development is apparently due not simply to the increasing importance of vision in the emergence of the primates, but to the fact that these modern prosimians are nocturnal. It might be tempting to conclude from this that all the early primates were nocturnal, but this would not appear likely since the photoreceptors, which are required for effective daylight vision, were certainly present in earlier forms. It would seem, then, that night vision among the primates is a secondary adaptation which, like fingernails, developed in primate evolution sometime after the order became distinct. Furthermore, it apparently took place twice, once in the line leading to the modern prosimians and again in the line leading to *Aotes*, a nocturnal New World monkey. Apart from these, all the modern primates have both rod (dark) and cone (light) photoreceptors on their retinas. In fact, beyond the prosimian level there are very few differences in the structure of the eyes of monkeys, apes, and men. Yet the evidence is clear that man's vision is much better than that of the others, which indicates that the improvements are related more to overall improvements in the areas of the brain that control vision and not to structural changes in the eye.

The evidence for the changes that might have taken place in the other special senses in response to an arboreal adaptation is not as abundant nor as easy to deal with as in the cases of vision and olfaction. With regard to the sense of touch, it should be noted that prosimians have well-developed tactile hairs, and in this feature they are like many other mammals and not like the higher primates. As we have noted already in connection with the development of finger- and toenails, the efficient arborealists developed sensitive feeler or digital pads and in the process lost the tactile hairs. Thus, again, an arboreal adaptation can be seen as the basis for modifying the sense discriminations among the primates.

There is even less to say about the senses of hearing and taste. Apart from the external ear, very little work has been done on the comparative anatomy of primate hearing apparatuses. The external ear does not vary a great deal from group to group, and, where variations occur, they seem often to be due to temperature regulation more than to differences in hearing discriminations. Again, however, there is an absolute and relative increase in the areas of the brain that control hearing, and from this, one might tentatively conclude that the sense has undergone improvements, but it is not something that can easily be related to the consequences of an arboreal adaptation.

When the early primatelike insectivores took to the trees, the successful ones, at least, underwent some changes in their dietary habits. Structurally this fact is implicit in the record of dental modifications. Functionally this implies increased variety in food sources. This is supported by studies of prosimians today, which, in their natural habitats, regularly eat insects, fruits and leaves, and occasionally meat (Jolly, 1972). Primates, it seems, have been omnivores for a long time. This may imply

Table 5–1   Summary of Important Tertiary Discoveries of Fossil Primates

NAME	LOCATION	TIME	MATERIALS DISCOVERED
Plesiadapis	Europe, North America	Paleocene	One almost complete skull and an incomplete skeleton (Europe), several teeth and jaw fragments and an incomplete skeleton (North America).
Notharctus	North America	Eocene	Skulls, teeth, postcranial bones, and an almost complete skeleton.
Smilodectes	North America	Eocene	Several skulls and several postcranial bones.
Protoadapis	Europe	Eocene	Fragmentary mandibles.
Adapis	Europe	Eocene	Several skulls and teeth.
Necrolemur	Europe	Eocene	Several skulls and limb bones.
Parapithecus	North Africa	Oligocene	Lower jaw; though other fragments have been discovered, they are not described. Before 1960, misinterpretations were common due to the absence of the middle portion of the jawbone, which went unrecognized until then. Probably the earliest Old World monkey.
Apidium	Egypt	Oligocene	Originally a few fragments; additional material, including some juveniles, discovered recently. Perhaps a close relative of Parapithecus.
Propliopithecus	Egypt	Oligocene	Lower jaw and teeth. Small gibbonlike form that may be ancestral to gibbons, apes, and man.
Aegyptopithecus	Egypt	Oligocene	Five partial lower jaws and an almost complete skull. Possibly the oldest hominid.
Limnopithecus	East Africa	Miocene	Represented by several fragmentary remains, including limb bones. Perhaps more correctly included with Pliopithecus.
Proconsul	East Africa	Miocene	Considerable remains, including limb bones, a skeleton of a hand, and an almost complete skull. Probably an African member of the Dryopithecus group.
Dryopithecus	Europe, Asia, Africa	Miocene to Pliocene	Known mostly from a large inventory of jaws and teeth.
Mesopithecus	Europe, East Africa	Miocene to Pliocene	Abundant remains particularly from Greece.
Pliopithecus	Europe	Miocene to Pliocene	Several discoveries assigned to this genus including an almost complete skull. In the gibbon phylogeny.
Sugrivapithecus, Bramapithecus, Sivapithecus, Paleosimia	Africa, Europe, Asia (mostly India)	Miocene to Pliocene	Several fragmentary upper and lower jaws and isolated teeth. Probably all of these should be included with either Dryopithecus or Ramapithecus.
Kenyapithecus	Africa	Miocene to Pliocene	Upper jaw fragments with one lower tooth. Possibly an African variety of Ramapithecus.

Table 5–1   (Continued)

NAME	LOCATION	TIME	MATERIALS DISCOVERED
Oreopithecus	Europe	Miocene to Pliocene	Abundance of remains including an almost complete skeleton.
Ramapithecus	Originally from India. Now believed to have had wide distribution over Old World.	Miocene to Pliocene	Originally, one fragment of an upper jaw; a few other jaws and teeth have been assigned to this genus. Possibly the oldest hominid.
Gigantopithecus	India, China	Pliocene	Very large teeth and jaws of an ape that is now extinct.

something about modifications to the sense of taste, but if it does, these implications are not at all clear.

THE BRAIN.   In addition to the changes in the senses, the earliest primates were subjected to selection for improved motor dexterity. These two factors are, of course, controlled by the brain; thus, improvements to them would seem to call for improvements in those areas of the brain that control them, and this is exactly what appears to have happened. Figure 5–2 illustrates the comparison of an insectivore and prosimian brain. Motor dexterity and the senses are controlled in areas of the outer covering of the brain, the neopallium. The center controlling olfaction is comparatively smaller in prosimians; the centers controlling vision are very much larger. This is even more obvious in higher primates.

The important implication here is simply that the brain underwent substantial changes as the early prosimians adapted to a life in the trees. Furthermore, these changes led to an overall improvement in the structure of primate brains over those of other mammals. Even the lowliest primates are alert, intelligent animals. This is an adaptive investment that has continually reaped dividends in primate evolution. Hopefully for man, intelligence will continue to hold its own in the ruthless, competitive marketplace of evolution.

Fossil Evidence: Paleocene and Eocene

The earliest stages in primate evolution are better documented by fossils than are many of the later periods. (For a summary of the most important fossil primates consult Table 5–1.) From the Paleocene and Eocene epochs, there are fossil representatives of over sixty genera, which have been grouped into eight families. The best candidate for the oldest primate fossil is a tooth discovered in Montana deposits of late Cretaceous to early Paleocene age. The tooth is contemporary with some of

Figure 5–3.   Purgatorius tooth. (Drawing of photograph—photo courtesy of A. W. Compton)

the last surviving dinosaurs. The tooth has been classified as within the genus *Purgatorius,* which is known from several teeth found in more recent Paleocene deposits. Because of its age, *Purgatorius* is of great interest to primate paleontologists. However, from Paleocene and Eocene deposits there are fossil representatives of over sixty genera, classified into as many as eight families, and some of these are known in much greater detail than *Purgatorius.* From the Paleocene, one of the most interesting and best-known forms is *Plesiadapis,* whose remains have been found in both North America and Europe. *Plesiadapis* had a specialized set of teeth. Its incisors were adapted for chiseling. Moreover, *Plesiadapis* had claws, and not nails, on its toes and fingers. Thus, it would appear that this is not a likely candidate for the ancestral line leading to higher primates. *Plesiadapis* does, however, represent one of the lines that lay along the transitional pathway from insectivore to primate, or, in other words, it represents a morphological translation of the early effects of an arboreal adaptation on the primates.

Whereas the Paleocene was of short duration, lasting approximately 15 million years, the Eocene continued for about 20 million years. Middle Eocene fossils found in North America, Europe, and Asia resemble in considerable detail some modern prosimians, particularly the lemurs. These include *Notharctus, Smilodectes, Protoadapis,* and *Adapis.* One form, *Necrolemur,* known from skull fragments, teeth, and partial remains of the postcranial skeleton, is similar in many details to modern tarsiers (Simons, 1972, pp. 162–163).

One clear impression of primate origins emerges from an inspection of the fossil record of Paleocene and Eocene deposits—the earliest primates were an extraordinarily diverse group of animals. The evidence is clear from *structure* as reflected in the numerous taxonomic categories created to accommodate the morphological variation. *Functional* variability is implicit in locomotor and dietary adaptations. In locomotion

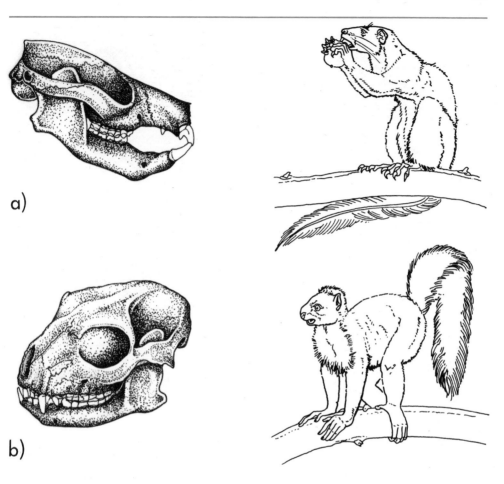

Figure 5–4.   Comparison of: a) the Paleocene *Plesiadapis* with b) the Eocene *Smilodectes*. (Adapted from "Early Relatives of Man," by E. L. Simons. Copyright © 1964 by Scientific American, Inc. All rights reserved.)

the variety represented among the earliest primates extends from vertical clinging and leaping to different kinds of quadrupedalism. From the point of view of diet, the dentitions suggest that a wide range of food sources were drawn upon from very early in primate evolution.

Finally, the range of variability of early primates is attested to by their *distribution* and their *abundance*. They have been found in New and Old World deposits and in some locations account for as much as 20 percent of the fauna (Barth, 1950). The earliest primates as a group were considerably more variable, more widely distributed, and more common than the living prosimians.

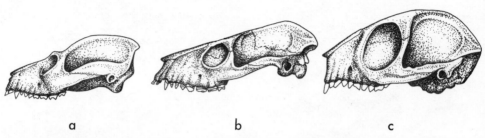

a   b   c

Figure 5–5.   Lateral view of the skulls of: a) *Adapis parisiensis*, b) *Notharctus osborni*, and c) *Necro-lemur*. (After W. E. Le Gros Clark)

This rapid and extensive diversification of the early primates clearly implies that they enjoyed a kind of adaptive luxuriance during Paleocene and Eocene times. Gradually circumstances changed, and as they did, the requirements for survival intensified. Some varieties died out. Some of those that did were simply unable to cope with the requirements of the new environments; others could not compete successfully with the rodents and lagomorphs. Some varieties stabilized in their adaptations reaching the forms which may be observed today among living prosimians. Most important, however, is the fact that the changing circumstances also generated higher primates, that is, bigger and smarter primates with a rich increase in their behavioral versatility. The monkeys, the first of the higher primates to appear, take up the arboreal adaptation where the early prosimians left off.

Fossil Evidence: Oligocene

Perhaps the most interesting feature of the early record of primate evolution is that in spite of the abundance of fossils, it is impossible to relate the evidence clearly either to the origin of higher primates or to the evolution of the modern prosimians. From Oligocene times on, the fossil record of the evolution of the prosimians is very sparse. No doubt this is due partly to the fact that the prosimians themselves became more scarce.

The details of the evolutionary background of the New World monkeys, the Platyrrhinae, would doubtless be informative and interesting, but unfortunately we know very little about them. Furthermore, no higher evolutionary stage of primates emerged in the New World. Thus, it is an area of less importance to the understanding of human evolution. For these reasons their evolution and fossil record are ignored by anthropologists.

In many ways the catarrhine monkeys are simply advanced prosimians. The trends in primate evolution initiated by the arboreal adaptation and represented by the prosimians are more obviously represented in the Old World monkeys. The monkeys, better than any other group, represent the generalized primate adaptation. Insofar as they embody in a more efficient way the effects of an arboreal adaptation, it follows that a listing of primate characteristics is a listing of monkey characteristics, much more so than characteristics for prosimians, apes, and man. Clearly, the fossil documentation of the emergence of the Old World monkeys could provide key insights into the general evolutionary picture of the primates, but, in fact, this record simply does not exist. Oligocene deposits from Egypt have yielded remains of two genera, *Apidium* and *Parapithecus*, which may represent the earliest catarrhines. The interpretation of *Parapithecus*, known originally only from one lower jaw, has been confused by the fact that it appeared to have only two incisors instead of four, as in other primates. For this reason, some authorities felt that *Parapithecus* might not even have been a primate. A recent reinvestigation of the original discovery, however, in the light of the many new finds of Simons' expeditions makes it appear that *Parapithecus* did indeed have four incisors, and may well be the oldest Old World monkey. The confusion appears to have come about as a result of the disintegration of the front part of the jaw at the time it was discovered.

Though the status of *Parapithecus* appears to be cleared up by the additional discoveries, we still know very little about the early evolution of the Old World monkeys. The only Oligocene deposits to yield remains of higher primates in the Old World have been those in Egypt. The next monkeys we have knowledge of are from the Miocene of East Africa (*Victoriapithecus*) and the Pliocene of Europe (*Mesopithecus*). These appear to represent an ancestral stage in the evolution of the Colobinae, the modern arboreal monkeys that subsist on leaves.

The Oligocene Egyptian deposits are of interest for yet another reason: they have also produced the oldest apes, *Propliopithecus*, *Aeolopithecus*, and *Aegyptopithecus*. *Propliopithecus* has long been considered the earliest ancestor of the gibbons and siamangs. Simons (1963) had suggested that *Propliopithecus* may be more generalized in some of its features (for example, small size and short face) than had been recognized and thus might represent an ancestor common to all the hominoids. More recently, however, Simons (1972, p. 214) has set aside this suggestion because of "a dramatic increase in our understanding of the basic functioning of the hominid dental mechanism" (see Figure 5–7).

Aeolopithecus is the name of an Oligocene ape jaw similar in many details to the jaws of modern gibbons. Thus it appears that the line leading to the gibbons and siamangs had become clearly distinct in the Oligocene irrespective of the interpretation of *Propliopithecus*.

From 1906 to 1964 *Aegyptopithecus* was known solely from one jaw. Several additional discoveries, including a remarkably complete skull (Figure 5–8), have been made since then. These new discoveries have generated a great deal of interest and in the process suggested a position of great importance for *Aegyptopithecus* in the evolution of the higher primates. These discoveries strongly suggest that *Aegyptopithecus* may lie along the beginning of the ancestral line leading to the

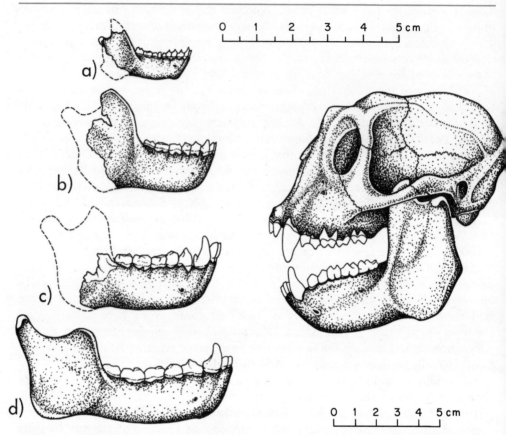

Figure 5–6. The mandibles of: a) *Parapithecus,* b) *Propliopithecus,* c) *Pliopithecus,* and d) modern gibbon. (After W. E. Le Gros Clark)

Figure 5–7. Skull of a Pliocene monkey, *Mesopithecus pentelicus.* (After W. E. Le Gros Clark)

Great Apes and man. The differentiation of that line into those leading, on the one hand, to the apes and, on the other, to man may have taken place close to the time of *Aegyptopithecus,* for in the next period there are some indications of fossil apes similar to those of today.

This draws our attention forcibly to the Miocene, but before considering the fossils from the next period, a brief summary of the Oligocene appears to be in order. If the Paleocene and Eocene can be called epochs of diversification, then the Oligocene may be called an epoch of progress in primate evolution. The progress is represented in the first appearance of three major groups of higher primates, the monkeys, the gibbons, and the possible common ancestor of the Great Apes and man. Yet we know very little about the relationships among the Oligocene higher primates, since all of the Old World discoveries have come from a single location.

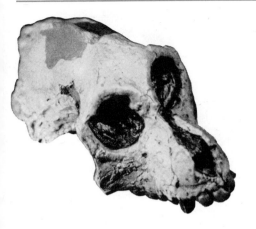 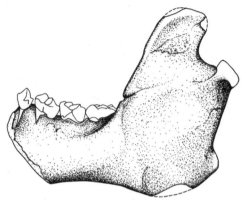

Figure 5–8. Remarkably complete skull of *Aegyptopithecus* discovered in Egypt in 1967 and first reported by E. L. Simons in early 1968. *Aegyptopithecus* is Oligocene in date and interpreted by some as the oldest hominid. (Photo of cast by J. H. McCullough)

Figure 5–9. Lateral view of the left lower jaw of *Aegyptopithecus zeuxis*. (After E. L. Simons)

Fossil Evidence: Miocene

There are a few Miocene fossils which appear to be in the evolutionary lines leading up to the prosimians and monkeys. We will ignore these and direct our attention to the remains of immediate importance to the evolution of the Great Apes and the hominids.

First we may note some additional fossils connecting the Oligocene forms and the modern gibbons. These Miocene forms are known as *Limnopithecus* and *Pliopithecus*. The remains of *Limnopithecus* include parts of the postcranial skeleton, including the limbs. If one were to classify the animal on the basis of the limb proportions and features, it is likely that *Limnopithecus* would be included with the cercopithecoids. The limbs lack the expected specializations associated with the brachiation adaptation of the modern gibbons. *Pliopithecus* is also a fossil member of the gibbon-siamang group. It is Miocene to Pliocene in date and is known from remains found in Europe. Actually, *Pliopithecus* and *Limnopithecus* are very similar, and it may be that they should be regarded as members of the same genus. As a group, they fit rather well into a sequence of the evolution of the gibbons, which begins with the affinities being apparent in the morphology of the teeth and is then characterized by modifications in the limbs brought about, undoubtedly, by the brachiating adaptation.

The fossil evidence of large apes from the Miocene is abundant and clear; the interpretations of the evidence are also abundant but by no means clear. A first

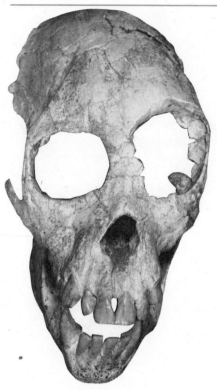

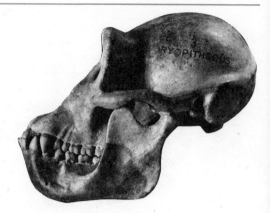

Figure 5–11. Side view of a *Dryopithecus* skull. (Courtesy of the American Museum of Natural History)

|||||||||||||||||||||||||||||||||||||||||||||||||||||||||||||||||||||||||||||||||||
MILLIMETER

Figure 5–10. *Proconsul* skull. (By permission of the Trustees of the British Museum, Natural History)

problem of interpretation emerges over the comparatively simple issue of what to call the Miocene apes. The first discoveries were made in Europe and were called *Dryopithecus*. Subsequent discoveries from Africa were identified as *Proconsul*, and from Asia variously as *Sugrivapithecus, Sivapithecus, Bramapithecus, Paleosimia*, and *Ramapithecus*.

A second confusion arises from the disagreement among paleontologists over the taxonomic status of the Miocene fossils. Are they apes? Did they brachiate? Are they monkeys? Are they, perhaps, hominids? This is an understandable uncertainty. The early ancestors of the modern apes and man would, of course, retain many characteristics of their ancestors, while at the same time displaying features which ultimately distinguished their descendants.

These problems cannot be solved to everyone's satisfaction. The issues, however, can be simplified first by adopting the increasingly acceptable convention of calling all the Miocene apes dryopithecines and, second, by providing a special place for *Ramapithecus* for reasons to be discussed below.

The Miocene apes, the dryopithecines, are distributed throughout the Old World. They are a highly variable group in their morphology. The forms from Europe and

Asia are known almost exclusively from jaws and teeth. Their dentition is remarkably similar to that of the modern apes, and in the size of their molars they are more similar to modern apes than they are to the African dryopithecines. The African varieties have smaller molars than those found among contemporary apes.

The African dryopithecines are known from far more complete remains which include skulls and limb bones. As may be seen in Figures 5–10 and 5–11, they are themselves a diverse group of primates, some of which, by Miocene times, had become very similar to modern apes (compare Figure 5–11 with Figure 2–20). Evidence inferable from limb bones suggests that the dryopithecines ranged in size from that of a small chimpanzee to that of a large gorilla. The proportions of the limb bones are more like those of modern monkeys and of modern man than they are of the living apes. Thus it is clear that at this time the dryopithecines were not specialized brachiators. These features developed more recently in the lines leading to the chimpanzee, gorilla, and orangutan and may never have developed extensively in the line leading to man.

Until recently, the hominids were presumed to be very recent arrivals with an antiquity estimated at somewhere between 1 and 2 million years. That they might be much older was indicated first in a reconsideration of a group of fossils known from India which had been interpreted as recent pongids. Identified first as separate genera, four are named after Hindu gods, *Sugrivapithecus*, *Ramapithecus*, *Bramapithecus*, and *Sivapithecus*, and the fifth is known as *Paleosimia*. These have been known since 1935 and until recently occupied a questionable position of secondary importance as evidence bearing on the evolution of the apes. This appears to be due to the fact that they were at first thought to be Pleistocene in date, and thus too late to be of much interest, but it now appears that some at least go back to late Miocene or early Pliocene. This has brought about a reconsideration of the fossils, which has brought to light two major changes in the interpretation. First, it has become clear that *Sugrivapithecus*, *Sivapithecus*, and *Paleosimia* are dryopithecines, very similar to their European and African contemporary relatives. Second, a reconstruction of the upper jaw of *Ramapithecus* has resulted in the startling conclusion that it is a hominid and not a pongid. The similarities are, of course, based on the jaw and teeth (see Figure 5–12), specifically the form of the palate and the dimensions of the teeth (one of which, the canine, was reconstructed on the basis of the size of its socket), and it is this that is hard to accept. It is one thing to say that *Ramapithecus* is more like man, but the essential distinction between the pongids and hominids is the fact that the latter are bipedal with erect posture, and this cannot be concluded with confidence from evidence of the jaw and teeth. *Bramapithecus* may belong to the same group as *Ramapithecus*.

Further support for the Miocene antiquity of the hominids has come from Africa. *Kenyapithecus wickeri*, recovered in East Africa by L. S. B. Leakey in 1962, is strikingly similar to *Ramapithecus* and of comparable age. In further support of the hominid status of *Kenyapithecus wickeri*, Leakey offered evidence (1968) that the Miocene form may have been using bone tools. This remains highly conjectural. However, if *Kenyapithecus wickeri* turns out simply to be an African representative

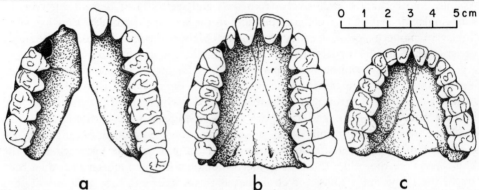

0 1 2 3 4 5 cm

a   **b**   **c**

Figure 5–12. Comparison of the upper jaw of: a) *Ramapithecus,* b) orangutan, and c) man. In each comparison the jaws have been made the same size. *Ramapithecus* is clearly more like man than he is like the orangutan. (Adapted from "Early Relatives of Man," by E. L. Simons. Copyright © 1964 by Scientific American, Inc. All rights reserved.)

of *Ramapithecus*, then it appears that, in addition to the monkeys, three major groups of higher primates had differentiated by the close of the Miocene. First, the gibbon line continues from Oligocene beginnings through the Miocene, as represented by *Limnopithecus* and *Pliopithecus*. Second, the ancestors of the gorilla, chimpanzee, and orangutan may be recognized as a broadly distributed diversified group of apes known as the dryopithecines. Third, the line leading to man may have become distinct by the Miocene, and, if so, then it appears that it, too, was broadly distributed from its beginnings. Two genera have been proposed to designate these earliest hominids, *Ramapithecus* and *Kenyapithecus*. Because they are very similar and because *Ramapithecus* was named first, it appears likely that the two will be merged, and *Ramapithecus* will be the name of these contenders for the title of earliest hominids.

When did the hominids separate off as a distinct lineage? Again we may offer the most common answer in science: it all depends. In this instance it depends on which timepiece you choose to believe. The choice is important since the estimates range from 2 million to 35 million years ago.

Actually there are two main reasons for the difference. Which timepiece, that is, which dating technique, one chooses is a subject we will discuss presently, but it is not the sole reason. Another factor is an old issue, the one which has focused on whether or not there were brachiators in our ancestry.

The ability to get through the trees by means of swinging by the forelimbs under the branches is called *brachiation*. The apes are distinctive as a group among the Old World primates primarily because of the attributes they have acquired in the evolutionary process of becoming efficient brachiators. As previously discussed, it would appear that the arboreal adaptation was the first major event in primate evolution, producing, as it did, the prosimians and the monkeys. Brachiation is another major event. As an adaptive response, it resulted in the morphological features distinctive of the apes, and some changes in the ways that brachiators related to and functioned in their environments can be inferred from this adaptation.

The consequences of brachiation have been reported by Virginia Avis (1962). She has carefully and thoughtfully explained the importance of brachiation and its significance in man's evolutionary past. The question she raises as to whether or not man's ancestors brachiated has long been warmly debated in physical anthropology (see Straus, 1949). Attempts to answer the question usually have resulted in simple lists of the pros and cons. On the pro-brachiator side of the issue is the fact that man and the apes have similar conformation of the thorax, well-developed clavicles, and a variety of skeletal and muscular features that appear to be the result of a brachiating ancestry. On the other side are the proportions of the limbs, a well-developed and strong thumb, and another list of skeletal and muscular features that appear to be too generalized to have continued through the filter of a brachiating ancestry. The question is clearly fundamental to the timing of the separation of the hominids and pongids. Since brachiation is a specialized development in the lineage leading to the apes, then the pro-brachiators are accommodated by a more recent date, and vice versa.

Since the evidence both of fossils and from comparative anatomy appears to allow either alternative, it seems that the question cannot be answered. Some headway can be made, however, if the problem is approached in a modified way. Is it essential, for example, that brachiation necessarily implies a highly specialized animal? Or, in another way, was the brachiation adaptation necessarily a limiting one, or, as Avis claims, could it at one time have expanded the adaptive possibilities of the ancestral forms that gave rise to apes and perhaps man? Is it a reasonable likelihood that modern apes represent extremes in their adaptations that arose from an ancestry of less efficient, less specialized, perhaps more clumsy brachiators? If one admits the possibility of these alternatives then the original controversy loses some of its meaning. It allows for the view that man and the great apes share a common ancestry beyond the monkey stage of primate evolution. The common ancestor would presumably be a brachiator, but not a very good one, and thus lacking many of the modern apes' specializations.

Younger physical anthropologists tend to accept this modified view and are thus less involved in the brachiation controversy than their elders were twenty years ago. The dating of the separation continues, however, to be a problem; today the differences focus more directly on the second issue, the accuracy of dating techniques.

There are two contending approaches, the molecular (or biochemical) and the geological. The molecular approach yields the more recent dates for the divergence. The technique is too complex to detail here (see Sarich, 1971). In general terms, the molecular technique arrives at dating estimates by comparing nearly identical substances common to all the living hominoids. Thus, for example, albumin is a protein that may be found with slight variations in the sera of all of the hominoids. Sarich, the main proponent of the molecular technique, identifies the differences as the result of mutations which occur and become established at a known rate. Thus the number of differences in the structure of albumin between two living species may be used to estimate how long it has been since they shared a common ancestor. Sarich currently estimates that the African pongids and hominids diverged about four million years ago (Sarich, 1971, p. 70). Accepting this estimate implies that man's ancestors were at one time specialized brachiators and casts serious doubts on the hominid status of *Ramapithecus*.

The geological technique for estimating age is less rigorous, more traditional. Simons opposes the molecular-based estimates mostly on the grounds that they are simply incompatible with the fossil evidence. To Simons the fossils and the geological strata in which they are found imply a separation that may be greater than 35 million years between the modern pongids and man (Simons, 1969, p. 326).

In fact there is much more to the issue than merely the problem of dating. On the one hand, molecular biologists, accustomed to dealing with the materials of genes, see evolution as the steady accumulation of alterations in the genes themselves. As they view them, molecular changes need not result from the systematic effects of natural selection. Paleontologists, on the other hand, are accustomed to viewing fossils in the context of adaptation, to interpreting changes in the fossil record as the expression of natural selection. One may recognize this disagreement as a modern version of a very old controversy which continues without resolution.

Thus we continue in doubt concerning the relationships among the Miocene fossils and, more important, between them and us. Two kinds of new fossil discoveries could help to settle the argument: either additional discoveries of *Ramapithecus*, or Pliocene remains connecting the Miocene higher primates with those of the Pleistocene.

Fossil Evidence: Pliocene

The Miocene yields evidence of various monkeys, apes, and perhaps of the earliest hominids. Many of the monkeys and apes are similar in their appearance to their modern descendants. From this we might expect Pliocene deposits to present a record of animals intermediate in their appearance between the Miocene and modern apes and monkeys. If, however, that is our expectation, then the Pliocene is an epoch of surprises.

To begin with there is very little evidence of continuity from the Miocene. To be sure there are a few discoveries of large dryopithecines from early Pliocene deposits in Asia Minor. But apart from these and some recent discoveries of late Pliocene hominids, the Pliocene presents no clear connections between Miocene and Pleistocene higher primates. This is undoubtedly due in part to the changing climatic conditions. Beginning in the Miocene one can observe a gradual recession of the extensive warm weather forests from northern latitudes. As temperatures gradually cooled, these were replaced by grasslands and open savannahs. These were adapted

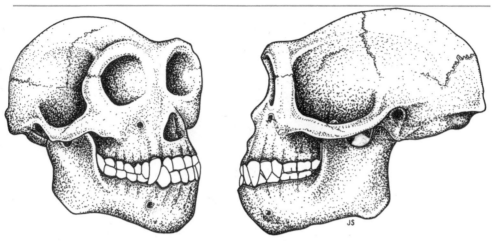

Figure 5–13.   Reconstructed skull of the August 2, 1958, discovery of *Oreopithecus*. (After J. Hürzeler)

to by grazing animals, rodents, and carnivores among the mammals. Apparently the ancestors of today's primates were being slowly moved closer together in a band narrowing toward the equator. This would make the discontinuity in northern latitudes less mysterious.

The only reasonably well-documented fossil Pliocene primate from Europe is an extraordinary animal named *Oreopithecus*, which has been the subject of widely differing interpretations. It has been regarded by various authorities at different times as an Old World monkey, an ape, a transitional form between the monkeys and apes, and a transitional form between the apes and man, and recently it has been said to be of Miocene and not Pliocene age (Simons, 1972). It was first described in 1872, and, until 1958, all that was known about the form was based on fragmentary jawbones and teeth. In 1958, a most remarkable discovery was made in Italy of approximately fifty individuals of oreopithecine remains, including an almost complete skeleton of one individual. These remains have been dated as early Pliocene. The abundant remains seem largely to justify the earlier confusion, for in the rest of the skeleton may be found a surprising amalgamation of monkey, ape, and hominid traits. So far it would appear that the remains have done little more to clarify the phylogenetic and taxonomic position of *Oreopithecus* than to remove from contention the view that it was an ancestral catarrhine. The question now focuses more directly on the issue of whether it should be classified with the Hominidae or Pongidae or if it should be assigned to a separate family. William L. Straus, Jr. (1963), has made an extensive analysis of the *Oreopithecus* material and concludes that: "There is no valid reason for regarding [*Oreopithecus*] as belonging to the family Pongidae. Hence it must either be classified as a member of the family Hominidae or placed in a family of its own, the Oreopithecidae. . . . I am at present

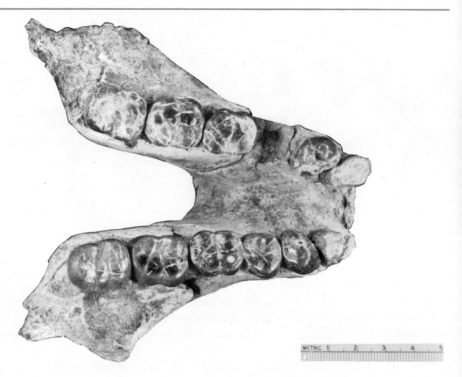

Figure 5–14.   Jaw of *Gigantopithecus,* a giant ape form that apparently became extinct. Its remains are known from China and India. This jaw from India was reported in the summer of 1968 by E. L. Simons. (Courtesy of E. L. Simons)

inclined to classify *Oreopithecus* as a primitive, aberrant member of the Hominidae." It is difficult to appreciate the basis for Dr. Straus's conclusion without some sophistication in comparative anatomy. However, it should be emphasized that his choice is essentially a matter of taste, and another competent investigator could easily conclude that *Oreopithecus* belongs in a separate family of its own. The ambiguity over its correct classification is probably due, in part, to the lack of other fossil forms from the same general time period.

Some of the earlier dryopithecines apparently gave rise to some very large descendants, as evidenced by the large collection of teeth and a few jaws known from the Pliocene of China and India. These have been placed in the genus *Gigantopithecus*. Evidence for the existence of *Gigantopithecus* was obtained first in 1935 by G. H. R. von Königswald. At the time von Königswald was investigating some exciting discoveries of Pleistocene hominids near Peking. He learned that the Chinese use fossil teeth for medicinal purposes. Well, so to speak, so do paleontologists. A trip to the drugstore turned up a few very large primate teeth; he called them

Gigantopithecus. The manner in which the discovery was made left most of the interesting questions unanswered. How old were the teeth? Where did they come from? Do very large teeth necessarily imply a very large animal?

Beginning in the late 1950s, Chinese paleontologists uncovered hundreds of additional remains of *Gigantopithecus.* These were almost all teeth, but there were also a few jaws. In 1968 an almost complete *Gigantopithecus* jaw was discovered in India. All of the *Gigantopithecus* remains have come from middle-to-late Pliocene deposits. Apparently *Gigantopithecus* is an Asian descendant of the dryopithecines, a very large one which seems to have become extinct by early Pleistocene times.

Are there hominids of Pliocene age? A few years ago the answer to that would have had to be a cautious "probably yes." Today we may be much more confident. The change is due to the evidence obtained by an extensive paleontological investigation of the Omo basin in Ethiopia. The investigation has involved scientists from all over the world, and, for our purposes, its most interesting discoveries have been the remains of hominid forms of Pliocene age which heretofore had been well known only from the early Pleistocene. The Omo basin hominids have come from deposits which have been dated by means of the Potassium-Argon technique as from 1.9 to 3.75 million years old (Brown and Lajoie, 1971).

Additional support for Pliocene hominids comes in the form of an almost complete skull and some long bones from Pliocene deposits near Lake Rudolf in Kenya. These remarkable remains were made public in November, 1972, by Richard Leakey (see also R. Leakey, et al., 1971, 1972). We can expect these new discoveries to revive old controversies, but one issue that appears to be settled is the presence of erect, bipedal hominids in late Pliocene deposits.

From the late Miocene to late Pliocene we confront what must have been a most important chapter in primate evolution, but in many ways we know less about it than we do of earlier periods. The forces that drove man's ancestors out of the trees must have been gathering, but exactly what these were remains a subject of speculation with little data available.

PROBLEMS IN INTERPRETING PRIMATE EVOLUTION

In surveying the evidence bearing on primate evolution, one cannot help but realize that much of our understanding of the course of events is based on very little fossil evidence. Most of the better conclusions are reached by imposing the facts of modern primate variability onto the fossil record, rather than by the seemingly more logical process of interpreting the modern from the evidence of the fossils. Thus it is that we learn about the past from the present, rather than the other way around.

When one hears of interpretations of the phylogeny of the primates, it would be well for him to keep the following in mind: 1) The early periods in the Paleocene and particularly the Eocene are comparatively well known, being represented by many fossils of prosimians, divided into at least five families. 2) From Eocene times onward, the primates clearly underwent many important modifications; this much is clear from the comparatively sparse fossil evidence. How, where, and when these modifications took place are not questions that can be answered in most cases.

Certainly we need more fossils to increase our knowledge and to increase our confidence in our conclusions. However, it may be that even more important information is needed. What might be more important is a reevaluation of some fundamental issues, the answers to which have been presumed and unquestioned too long. For example, what are fossils able to tell us about phylogeny? About the significant evolutionary events in a particular line? Can we with reason expect to reconstruct phylogeny with a more complete fossil record, or is this too much to expect? If, again, we draw a parallel with artifacts and cultural evolution, the problem may become more clear. It is only under the most extraordinary circumstances that an archaeologist is able to make developmental connections between the artifacts of a particular site and the history of a contemporary group. Artifacts provide one basis for drawing inferences about the way in which culture has progressed along its many lines, and the general outlines of the picture are becoming more and more clear and more and more consistent with the facts of present-day cultural variation.

Similarly, it might improve our overall understanding if fossils were thought of in this way, that is, as a basis for general statements about the way in which primates have evolved. No one, of course, claims that a particular fossil is ancestral to a particular modern form, but the step from a particular fossil to the presumption that it represents a population that may have been ancestral to a modern form is not a great one.

As others have noted, evolution is a two-faceted phenomenon (see Sahlins and Service, 1960, or Dobzhansky, 1962). One aspect of evolution is adaptive. Forms diversify and radiate into niches, and progress is relative to their success in meeting the requirements of the adaptive problems. Sahlins and Service call this aspect *specific evolution* and contrast it with *general evolution,* which results in the production of higher forms and where progress can be measured absolutely in terms of overall *adaptive capability*. They were writing particularly about cultural evolution, but clearly there is a parallel in biological evolution. Archaeological artifacts are used mostly to provide information about general evolution, and only rarely about specific evolution. Perhaps the limitations of the archaeologist are the same as for the primate paleontologist.

Finally, primate paleontology may have to rediscover evolution. While it is appealing to anyone with a sense of history to attempt to reconstruct the details of the phylogenetic record to try to answer the particular questions of which forms are related and in what ways, these are likely to be problems that will be with us forever. It would seem that it is the very process of evolution that makes that approach a practical impossibility. As living organisms adapt to their environments, they do so by continuing to diverge, converge, specialize, and generalize; in the process, they cover up the very tracks some would hope to follow in reconstructing phylogenetic histories. It is, however, this dynamic process of continual change that is recorded in the fossil record, and in retrospect it is this very thing that paleontology set out to study.

MAJOR POINTS IN CHAPTER 5

1. Primates are believed to be descendants of insectivore mammals.
2. The earliest primates were prosimians.
3. The early prosimians were diverse, widespread, and abundant.
4. Monkeys and small apes first appear in Oligocene deposits.
5. Large apes and possibly hominids appear first in the Miocene.
6. Though the origin of the hominids is uncertain, they are present in deposits of Pliocene age.

REFERENCES AND SUGGESTIONS FOR ADDITIONAL READING

AVIS, VIRGINIA
 1962 Brachiation: The crucial issue for man's ancestry. *Southwestern Journal of Anthropology* 18:119–148.

BARTH, FREDRIK
 1950 On the relationships of early primates. *American Journal of Physical Anthropology* (n.s.) 8:139–149.

BROWN, F. H., AND K. R. LAJOIE
 1971 Radiometric age determinations on Pliocene/Pleistocene formations in the lower Omo basin, Ethiopia. *Nature* 229:483–485.

CLARK, W. E. LE GROS
 1957 *History of the primates.* Phoenix Books. Chicago: University of Chicago Press.
 1960 *The antecedents of man.* Chicago: University of Chicago Press.

DOBZHANSKY, THEODOSIUS
 1962 *Mankind evolving.* New Haven: Yale University Press.

EIMERL, SAREL, AND IRVEN DEVORE
 1965 *The primates.* New York: Time, Inc.

GREGORY, W. K.
 1922 *The origin and evolution of human dentition.* Baltimore: Williams and Wilkins.

HOOTON, EARNEST ALBERT
 1947 *Up from the ape.* Rev. ed. New York: Macmillan.

JOLLY, ALISON
 1972 *The evolution of primate behavior.* New York: Macmillan.

LEAKEY, L. S. B.
 1968 Bone smashing by late Miocene hominidae. *Nature* 218:528–530.

LEAKEY, R. E. F., J. M. MUNGAI, AND A. C. WALKER
 1971 New australopithecines from east Rudolf, Kenya. *American Journal of Physical Anthropology* 35:175–186.
 1972 New australopithecines from east Rudolf, Kenya (II). *American Journal of Physical Anthropology* 36:235–252.

McKENNA, MALCOLM C.
 1963 New evidence against tupaioid affinities of the mammalian family Anagalidae. *American Museum Novitates* 2158:1–16.

NAPIER, J. R., AND A. C. WALKER
 1967 Vertical clinging and leaping: A newly recognized category of locomotor behavior of primates. *Folia Primatologia* 7:204–219.

PATTERSON, BRYAN
 1954 The geologic history of non-hominid primates in the Old World. *Human Biology* 26:191–209.

PILBEAM, D. R., AND E. L. SIMONS
 1965 Some problems of hominid classification. *American Scientist* 53:237–259.

SAHLINS, MARSHALL D., AND ELMAN R. SERVICE, EDS.
 1960 *Evolution and culture.* Ann Arbor: University of Michigan Press.

SARICH, VINCENT
  1971 A molecular approach to the question of human origins. In *Background for man: Readings in physical anthropology*, ed. Phyllis Dolhinow and Vincent Sarich. Boston: Little, Brown.

SIMONS, ELWYN L.
  1960 New fossil primates: A review of the past decade. *American Scientist* 48:179–192.
  1963 Some fallacies in the study of hominid phylogeny. *Science* 141:879–889.
  1965 New fossil apes from Egypt and the initial differentiation of Hominoidea. *Nature* 205:135–139.
  1969 The origin and radiation of the primates. *Annals of the New York Academy of Sciences* 167:319–331.
  1972 *Primate evolution: An introduction to man's place in nature.* New York: Macmillan.

SIMPSON, GEORGE GAYLORD
  1940 Studies on the earliest primates. *Bulletin of the American Museum of Natural History* 77:185–212.

STRAUS, WILLIAM L., JR.
  1949 The riddle of man's ancestry. *Quarterly Review of Biology* 24:200–223.
  1963 The classification of *Oreopithecus*. In *Classification and human evolution*, ed. S. L. Washburn, pp. 146–177. Viking Fund Publications in Anthropology, no. 37. Chicago: Aldine.

WASHBURN, SHERWOOD L.
  1951 The analysis of primate evolution with particular reference to the origin of man. *Cold Spring Harbor Symposia on Quantitative Biology* 15:67–78.
  1967 Perspectives and prospects. Paper presented to Wenner-Gren Supper Conference on Primate Studies. April 27.

6 Origin and Evolution of Man

INTRODUCTION

Uniqueness of the Record

In evaluating the evidence of primate or mammalian evolution, paleontologists depend very heavily on the comparative anatomy of living forms as a crucial source of supplementary information. In the effort to understand the details of human evolution, the comparative anatomy of contemporary groups of modern men is of no value. Man is a single, highly varied species, and, unlike the evolutionary stages reflected in the major groups of living primates, the so-called races of man do not represent phases in the evolution of man. Each is the end product of an evolutionary pattern characterized by intersecting phylogenies which has continually folded in upon itself. This pattern of evolution has provided for growth, diversification, and expansion within the species without resulting in the formation of new species. Thus, it would seem that the human paleontologist is limited to the strict details of the formal properties of fossils and, when available, the temporal coordinates. Time becomes particularly important, since the entire course of human evolution took place within a few million years. This implies that our scope of interest is to be focused on considerably smaller evolutionary units and processes when compared with the sweeping panorama taken in viewing the evolution of life and the evolution of the primates. It is one thing to conclude with some confidence that the Paleozoic reptiles included the ancestors of today's birds and mammals, but quite another to claim that an early Pleistocene fossil discovery is (or is not) a member of a species or population that ultimately gave rise to modern man.

These cautions are intended to remind the reader at the outset that when attention is directed at human evolution specifically, the scope implied is a very limited one indeed. The human paleontologist focuses on the evolution of one species that lived over 90 percent of its existence in some of the world's most inaccessible areas —an evolution which took place virtually overnight, geologically speaking.

These are useful cautions to keep in mind, but one should realize as well that the difficulties brought about by limiting the scope are made up for by the rather abundant fossil record of hominids and by the even more abundant archaeological record of culture. Even when the many sites yielding remains of modern man are

166

excluded, say within the last 20,000 years, there are still over one hundred fossil-man sites and thousands of archaeological sites. It would, of course, be ideal if the sites were known equally well from all stages over the last few million years, but in fact most are known from the last 70,000 years.

As both the archaeological and paleontological records become more complete, and as man's understanding of the interrelationships between the biological and cultural factors improves, it will probably become less and less desirable to separate the two fossil records for consideration. As matters stand now, however, it is difficult or impossible to know what one implies concerning the other, that is, what archaeological remains may imply about the biological status of the hominids that made the objects, or vice versa. It is, however, becoming increasingly clear that man's biological variation is one expression of a complex of interdependent and interrelated factors that includes culture as well as the animate and inanimate aspects of the broader environment. All factors must be considered as a collective totality if we are to understand comprehensively the ways in which man and his ancestors have adapted, survived, developed, and thrived. Both theory and technique are at present too poorly developed to achieve this ideal objective. However, in what follows, an attempt is made to present not only the fossil evidence, but the relevant archaeological, paleontological, and, on occasion, geological and climatological information as well.

The Pleistocene

The Pleistocene began approximately two million years ago. On four separate occasions within that time, much of the Northern Hemisphere was covered with massive continental glaciers. There are several theories that attempt to explain the cause of the glaciers, but at present it is not possible to decide definitely on the correct one. Whatever the cause, it is clear that ice sheets gradually expanded outward from mountaintop elevations and southward from polar latitudes. On each occasion the process of expansion continued for thousands of years and then stopped; the climate moderated; the ice sheets receded; and the scenery returned to a condition much like that of today in the same areas. Indeed, most specialists claim that we are now in an interglacial period.

The onset of any particular interglacial is never easy to recognize, undoubtedly begins at different absolute times in different parts of the world, and is a particularly difficult or impossible dating criterion to apply to fossil remains from the Southern Hemisphere. As evidence for dating, the effects of the glaciations are not limited simply to the areas covered by ice, but interpreting the evidence in the southern latitudes is an area of uncertainty and confusion. Until the last few years, it was widely held that the glacial-interglacial sequences of the north corresponded to alternating wet-dry periods in the south. This would have made relating events in the two hemispheres a straightforward problem if it were true, but there is evidence for only two such sequences of wet-dry periods, and these are not widely spread throughout the Southern Hemisphere. Furthermore, if and how they relate to the Pleistocene glaciers is not at all clear. What appeared to be a promising and simple relationship turns out to be much more complex and of questionable value, forcing geochronologists to use other techniques yielding more reliable, but often disappointingly limited, estimates of age.

The Archaeological Record

From time to time it will be useful in the discussion of the fossil evidence of human evolution to refer to the archaeological materials in association with the fossil skeletal material. The archaeological record is a reasonably continuous one beginning over one million years ago. It will be useful to digress briefly and consider the general outline of this record.

The sequence of glaciers implies something about the environmental challenges our ancestors were required to meet, and the archaeological record tells us something about how they met the challenges. The sequence of cultural remains from the Old World has been classified into two major stages, the Paleolithic and the Neolithic. The Paleolithic (Old Stone Age) begins with the origin of culture and ends with the origin of agriculture. Agriculture began between 10,000 and 15,000 years ago, and, since man had reached his modern form by that time, attention will be given here only to the Paleolithic (see Table 6–1).

There are five basic types of stone implements from the Paleolithic: pebble, chopper-chopping, core, flake, and blade tools. Later in this chapter an attempt is made to integrate the fossil record of human evolution with the archaeological record; so at this point these tool types are discussed only briefly.

Pebble tools are the oldest type of stone implement. They were made by the simple process of striking two rocks together until a sharp edge was obtained. They are known from several locations throughout Africa, where they are identified as the Oldowan industry. Core-tool traditions have been discovered in Europe, the Near East, southern Asia, and Africa. Core tools are made by shaping a large piece of stone (the core) by striking off smaller pieces (flakes) from all sides. Core tools are known also as hand axes, and improvements in the techniques of the manufacture provide the bases for distinguishing stages in development of the archaeological record. In Europe, the sequence is from Chellean through Acheulean; in Africa it is identified as the Chelles-Acheulean sequence.

Flake tools are smaller than core tools, more diversified in form, and more specialized in function. They are found together with hand axes in Europe, Africa, and parts of Asia. In northern latitudes, there is a well-established sequence of flake-tool industries that lacks core tools. This is identified as the Clactonian-Levalloisian sequence. The presence of two distinctive traditions in Europe during Lower Paleolithic times has been interpreted by some as evidence for the existence of two groups of human beings. This is unlikely; it is possible that the flake-tool assemblages represent simply a cold-weather tool kit, whereas the hand-axe assemblages represent

Table 6–1   Old World Paleolithic Sequences

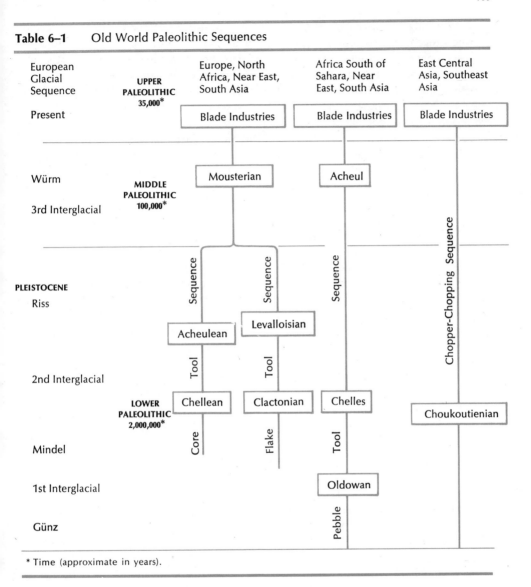

European Glacial Sequence	UPPER PALEOLITHIC 35,000*	Europe, North Africa, Near East, South Asia	Africa South of Sahara, Near East, South Asia	East Central Asia, Southeast Asia
Present		Blade Industries	Blade Industries	Blade Industries
Würm	MIDDLE PALEOLITHIC 100,000*	Mousterian	Acheul	
3rd Interglacial				Chopper-Chopping Sequence
PLEISTOCENE Riss		Sequence Sequence	Sequence	
		Acheulean Levalloisian		
2nd Interglacial		Tool Tool		
	LOWER PALEOLITHIC 2,000,000*	Chellean Clactonian	Chelles	Choukoutienian
Mindel		Core Flake	Tool	
1st Interglacial			Oldowan	
Günz			Pebble	

* Time (approximate in years).

implements used mainly during warmer times of the year. Coalescence of the core-
and flake-tool traditions in Europe represents the beginning of the Middle Paleolithic,
which is identified with the Mousterian industry.

The chopper-chopping tools are similar, on the one hand, to pebble tools, in that
they are rather crudely made, but this may be due simply to the fact that the stone

used in making chopper-chopping tools is difficult or impossible to shape accurately. On the other hand, the chopper-chopping tradition is similar to the core- and flake-tool sequences to the west, in that the implements were used in similar ways, and in both areas the traditions lasted throughout most of the Paleolithic.

Blade tools are well-made implements that may be found throughout the Old World. Their appearance signifies the beginning of the Upper Paleolithic, and they are found with anatomically modern man.

The archaeological record of man in the New World extends back only to about 20,000 to 30,000 years ago. This indicates that when man first reached America, the Upper Paleolithic blade tools had already become established throughout most of the temperate zones in the Old World.

THE ORIGIN OF THE HOMINIDS

The origin of the hominids is obscure. There are no archaeological remains; they appear later. There are only a few fossils, and their status is uncertain, as we noted in the discussion of *Ramapithecus*. The geological evidence of dating conflicts to a great extent with biochemical indications. The available evidence is indirect, and for this reason we must proceed with unusual caution.

First, the basic issue should be clear. What, exactly, are we asking when we raise the question of the origin of the hominids? In fact, the issue implies three direct questions: 1) When did the hominids begin? 2) Where did the hominids begin? and 3) What are the circumstances which brought about the beginning of the hominids? The first two can be answered directly; there is disagreement over when the hominids began, as we know from the earlier discussion of the dating of *Ramapithecus*. Since Africa has yielded most of the earliest hominid remains, we may wish to assume that hominids began there. But before dealing with the third problem it may be helpful to recognize that we have yet another question to answer, one which we might otherwise take for granted, that is, what is a hominid?

Science provides us with a simple, straightforward, but useless answer: A hominid is any member of the family *Hominidae* of the order *Primates*. What is needed, of course, is something more—an answer, that is, which would make it possible for us to identify a hominid when we encounter one. That, too, is a simple problem, for human beings are hominids; in fact they are the only living hominids. Thus, as we look at the terminal array of primates, the hominids are readily identifiable and distinguishable from all the rest. The hominids stand erect, walk on their two hind legs and feet, have small canine teeth set in a jaw with a distinctive shape, are able to mate continually, bear young which are dependent for a long time on parental care for survival, have large brains, and, as time passes, depend more and more heavily on culture to provide the means for survival.

Figure 6–1 compares a hominid skull with that of a pongid, specifically a chimpanzee. In the first comparison, the frontal view, there are, as you would expect, some striking differences. The chimp has large brow ridges above its eye orbits, a

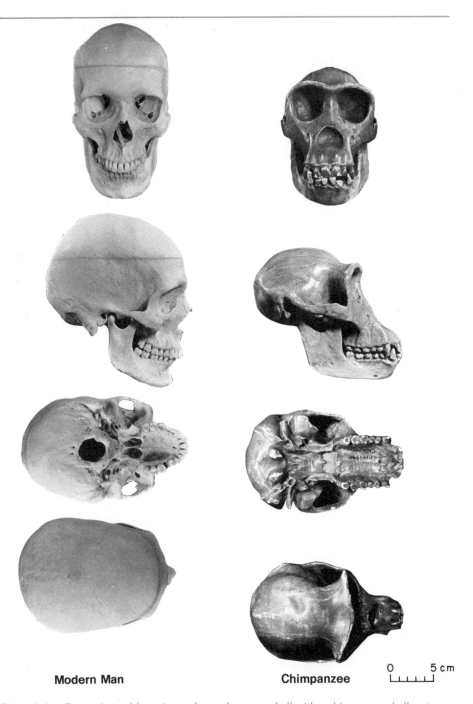

Modern Man   **Chimpanzee**   0   5 cm

Figure 6–1.   Comparison of four views of a modern man skull with a chimpanzee skull cast.

broad and massive appearance to the face, projecting canines fixed in a dental arch that is more angular than that of man. If you look at the top of the skull in this view, two slight bony ridges may be seen to course along the sides of the skull. These serve as areas for the attachment of some of the muscles that move the jaw. No such ridges may be seen in the modern man; instead the skull of man shows a smaller and narrower face with a distinct forehead and a smooth, rounded contour to the top of the skull. It lacks the projecting canines and, in general, conveys a less rugged appearance.

From the side, the most striking feature distinguishing the two is the size of the brain case. In man it is very large and continuous with the front of the skull, and in the chimp it is rather a second area of the skull, attached as it is to the back side of the face. Looking down on the chimp's skull, one can see that it is more obviously separated in this view by the deep grooves running under the zygomatic arches (cheekbones) and behind the supraorbital ridges. Returning to the profile again, we may note the large mastoid processes in man, the differences in the chin contours, and the presence of another ridge of bone, the occipital crest, which, like the sagittal crest, serves as an area of muscle attachment, in this instance for the muscles that move the neck. In three dimensions we would again note the coarser, more rugged surfaces on the chimp as compared with man.

Looked at from below and without the lower jaw attached, the most striking features are the shape of the dental arch and the location of the foramen magnum, the large hole through which the spinal cord passes. Unlike the angular contour of the ape, the dental arch in man is open and rounded. The position of the foramen magnum implies erect posture in man, situated, as it is, well underneath the base of the skull and closer to the center gravity of the skull. In the chimp it is located well behind the skull's center of gravity.

Looked at as a totality, the two skulls may be seen as structures that served different functions in the organisms' adaptive requirements. Apart from its common service as the entrance for food and the housing of the olfactory, auditory, and visual sense receptors, the skull of the chimp is equipped with a face and with teeth that are built to pierce, crush, and tear. This is implicit in the projecting snout (prognathism), the long and pointed canines, the massive jaw, and the sagittal and occipital crests, attesting to the massive muscles that drive the movements of the jaw and neck. Clearly, the chimp's facial region may be effectively used for defensive as well as subsistence purposes. With this in mind, the comparison with man is difficult to make, for the striking distinction is the size of the brain case. This is the skull of a thinking animal, of a form that uses its brain to accomplish the objectives for which the chimp is equipped with sharp teeth and massive muscles.

Among contemporary groups of men there is tremendous variation. Figure 6–2 illustrates some of the variation in skull form, but the main features are common throughout—large brain, presence of a forehead, large mastoids, chin, smooth surfaces, and lack of sagittal and occipital crests.

Today the earth is covered with hominids; a few million years ago there were hardly any. As we will see, there are vast differences between us and the earliest

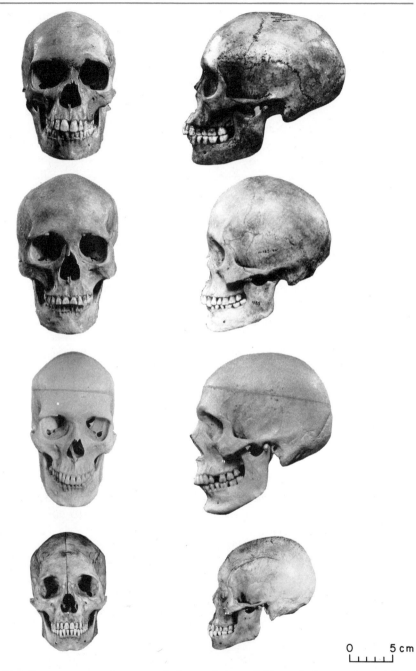

Figure 6–2. Variations among modern man skull morphology. (African photos courtesy of G. K. Neumann)

hominids, but we share one fundamental adaptive feature in common—erect posture and, associated with it, bipedal locomotion. The origin of the hominids is the origin of these adaptations. This relationship makes it possible to alter one of the primary questions asked above; what conditions caused the ancestors of the hominids to adopt erect posture and bipedal locomotion? No one knows all of the circumstances, but one factor is certain to have been a most important cause—moving from a primarily arboreal to a primarily terrestrial way of life.

What caused the transition? Again no one knows for certain. Perhaps the proto-hominids *were driven out* of the trees by animals, possibly even primates, better adapted to an arboreal way of life than they were. Perhaps our ancestors were more purposive and, seeing the advantages, *chose* to come down from the trees. If this were the case, we would, however, expect to find rationality well developed among contemporary hominids.

A third proposal is more appealing, for it takes more into consideration and thus explains more. This view sees coming out of the trees as the result of an adaptive effort to stay in the trees. There is no contradition here, though there appears to be one. Basically this interprets the event as a conservative phenomenon, one which could easily have taken place under either of two conditions. Our ancestors may have resided in a dense forest which was being thinned gradually by the invasion of grasslands, or they may have attempted to expand their range into the transitional zones between forests and more open grasslands. Fossil evidence of early hominids is generally found under such ecological conditions. In either case our ancestors would have been required to cover increasing terrestrial expanses to remain arboreal. In this way a radical evolutionary event may be seen as the result of essentially conservative adaptations.*

Whatever the causes, coming down from the trees was a necessary event in bringing about the origin of the hominids; necessary, but not sufficient to account for their distinctiveness. Other primates are terrestrial, but none are habitually bipedal, and none possess fully erect posture. Perhaps selection favored some obvious advantages. Erect posture frees the hands from continuous involvement in locomotion and makes possible their employment in manipulating objects, in making tools, in carrying food, and in the aggressive activities of fighting and protecting. In the same way bipedal locomotion enabled the protohominids to cover wider territorial ranges, albeit more slowly.

These are speculative suggestions, but one observation is clear—the change, though initially perhaps conservative, proved to be of enormous adaptive potential. The adaptations of erect posture and bipedal locomotion immediately placed a very high survival value on such aspects of intelligence as guile, cunning, cleverness, and memory. These may be recognized as a legacy the earliest hominids could draw

---

* This is a loose description of a general evolutionary process recognized in other situations first by A. S. Romer. Stated in general terms it is sometimes called Romer's rule.

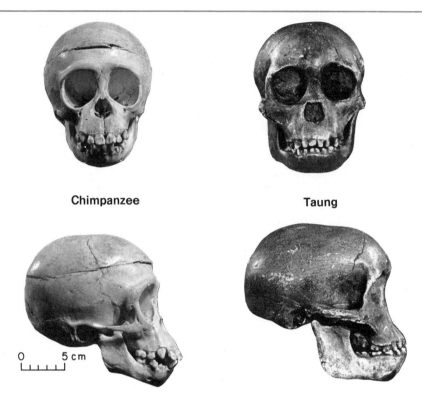

Chimpanzee   **Taung**

0   5 cm

Figure 6–3.   Comparison of an infant chimpanzee skull with Taung child skull cast.

upon as inheritance from their earlier ancestors in primate evolution. These are assets the primates had been storing up from the time of their earliest appearance. The hominids apparently put them to work at once, for the earliest fossil representatives in the hominid line (again excluding *Ramapithecus*) show them to be small, gracile, relatively large-brained, and highly varied primates known collectively as the australopithecines and formally as the genus *Australopithecus.* In some respects the genus is like modern apes, but in the essential hominid characteristics of erect posture and bipedal locomotion they are like us.

AUSTRALOPITHECUS

In 1924 the first of a continuing series of fossil hominid discoveries was made about eighty miles north of Kimberley, South Africa. The original discovery consisted of the fragmentary remains of the skull of an infant about five to seven years of age. It was brought to the attention of the energetic and imaginative young anatomist Raymond A. Dart, who judged it to be the remains of a type of hominid hitherto unknown, and thus a form that could be the "missing link." He called it *Australo-pithecus africanus*, which means, roughly, South African ape-man. These were the remains of a very ancient animal, perhaps early Pleistocene in date, which, if indeed it was a hominid, could be of great importance to our understanding of the origin of the hominids. Yet on superficial examination this significance was not easy to see. The skull looked very much like an infant chimpanzee's (see Figure 6–3). Apart from the truly extraordinary fact that the skull had broken open and that, as a result of this, a cast of about one-half of the animal's brain became fossilized, it might have gone unnoticed. Dart, and eventually Robert Broom, were convinced that it was an infant hominid and not an infant chimp. They pointed out that, when compared with a chimpanzee, the *Australopithecus* child had a large brain for its age, that if it were a pongid, it should have begun to show some signs of the crests and ridges so characteristic of adults, and, more importantly, that the teeth were in many ways more like man's than like those of chimpanzees and gorillas. While the original discovery created considerable interest and concern, it was impossible to conclude anything definite about its significance. The discovery of one individual is not convincing. New discoveries of *Australopithecus* were made in 1936 and, except for a gap during World War II, have continued to occur ever since. The remains have been recovered from sites in Africa, the Near East, Asia, and Java. Figure 6–4 shows a comparison of an australopithecine with modern man. In the facial view, the impression is immediately conveyed that *Australopithecus* is clearly apelike in its appearance. Yet, one can, on careful inspection, see a combination of manlike and apelike traits. The comparatively small brain falls within the range of modern apes and well outside the ranges of modern man. The supraorbital ridges are well developed; the forehead is low-lying and slopes back abruptly from the brow ridges; and the snout projects forward, putting the incisors well out in front of the rest of the face. On some forms there is an occipital crest, small in comparison with that of modern apes, but, on the whole, the back of the head, including the poorly developed contour of the mastoids, is more like that of a chimpanzee than like man.

From the bottom, the australopithecine tooth row may be seen to be more sharply angled than modern man's. The foramen magnum is situated well underneath the skull as in modern man, indicating that *Australopithecus* walked completely erect. This extraordinary assemblage of traits has caused some experts to refer to the australopithecines as ape men or as man apes, depending on which aspects they wish to emphasize.

Almost all of the australopithecine fossil material has been discovered in South or East Africa. The two localities have yielded different kinds of evidence which at first appeared to be contradictory but which is gradually being recognized as complementary. The South African material was discovered first. The fossils have come from five sites (see Table 6–2 and Figure 6–5): Taung, which has produced only the original discovery of the child's skull; Makapansgat, like Taung, the site of a former cave located about 180 miles north of Johannesburg; and three more cave sites within a few miles' radius of one another, Sterkfontein, Kromdraii, and Swartkrans.

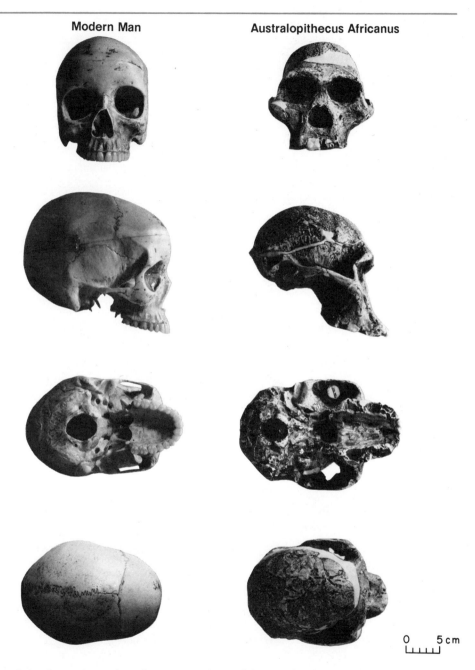

Figure 6–4. Comparison of modern man and an adult australopithecine. The australopithecine pictured is a cast of a specimen sometimes referred to as Sterkfontein 5 or "Ms. Ples."

Table 6-2   Sites Yielding Evidence of *Australopithecus*

	LOCATION	DATE FOUND	COMMENT
1.	**South Africa** Taung	1924	Almost complete skull and mandible of a child. This was the original discovery that some felt was a fossil chimp.
	Sterkfontein	1936-1957	Site yielding an abundance of skull fragments, teeth, mandibles, and postcranial bones. Among the most interesting remains are an almost complete skull and pelvis. The material was originally identified as *Plesianthropus transvaalensis*.
	Swartkrans	1948-1952	Apart from the *Homo erectus* remains, this site has produced several fragments of skulls, jaws, teeth, and postcranial bones. Original designation: *Paranthropus robustus*.
	Kromdraii	1938-1941	Compared with Swartkrans fewer and less complete remains but also identified as *Paranthropus robustus*.
	Makapansgat	1947-1962	An almost complete skull, fragments of others, of mandibles, teeth, and postcranial bones, including pelvic fragments. Originally called *Australopithecus prometheus* (it was mistakenly thought that there was evidence for the controlled use of fire). The remains here are recognized as similar to those from Taung and Sterkfontein.
2.	**East Africa** Olduvai	1959-present	According to Leakey (1965) these deposits indicate the coexistence of three hominids in early Pleistocene times: *Australopithecus* (originally *Zinjanthropus*), *Homo erectus,* and *Homo habilis.* Le Gros Clark (1967), among others, feels that *Homo habilis* and *Zinjanthropus* are both australopithecines.
	Lake Natron	1964	An almost complete mandible found about fifty miles from Olduvai Gorge.
	Lake Eyasi	1938	Three teeth and a fragment of an upper jaw.
	Lothagam	1967	Australopithecine mandible estimated to be 5.5 million years old.
	Omo Basin, Ethiopia	1968	Three complete mandibles (two without teeth), one partial jaw with two teeth, and several dozen isolated teeth. Some teeth are at least 3.5 million years old.
	East Rudolf	1968-present	Sixteen australopithecine fossils including crania, facial bones, jaws, and long bones. Discovered by R. E. F. Leakey and co-workers.
		1972	Large-brained hominid (approximately 850 cc.) of uncertain affinities estimated at 2.5 to 3 million years old.
3.	**Chad** Koro Toro	1960	The skull fragments here were identified by their discoverer as *Australopithecus,* but he and others now suggest that the remains may be more like those of *Homo erectus.*
4.	**Israel** Ubeidiya	1959	Fragments of two skulls and a tooth.
5.	**Java** Sangiran	1939-1953	Three mandibles and some teeth of alleged australopithecine affinity.

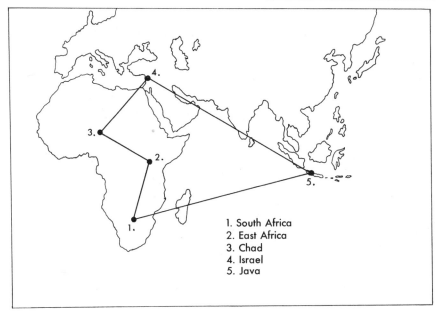

Figure 6–5.   Geographic distribution of *Australopithecus*.

1. South Africa
2. East Africa
3. Chad
4. Israel
5. Java

Except for the Taung child, all of the remains have been recovered from unstratified cave deposits, but it is not entirely clear from these hominid remains whether or not *Australopithecus* was himself a resident of the caves. At any rate, the deposits are mixed up, and the fact that they were cut out during quarrying excavations and subsequently investigated makes it impossible to arrange the material in any satisfactory sequence. The only sequence suggested by association with climatic and faunal changes separates the five sites into two phases: 1) an early phase represented by the remains from Taung, Sterkfontein, and Makapansgat; and 2) a later phase, which includes the Swartkrans and Kromdraii sites. This division has some morphological justification in the fact that smaller variants of *Australopithecus* have been found in the early-phase sites, and the larger variants in the later-phase caves. The morphological differences between the large and small variants are substantial (Greene, 1973) and localized, which would seem to provide the necessary basis for distinguishing these as two separate species: 1) *Australopithecus africanus*, the smaller, apparently earlier form; and 2) *Australopithecus robustus*, the larger and later variant.

When one looks exclusively at the fossil evidence from the South African sites, the picture is indeed puzzling. Prior to 1959 this is where all of the material had been discovered. The sites present different kinds of evidence which are not easy to interpret since there is simply no modern-day analogue to the way of life of *Australopithecus*. For this reason it may be best simply to enumerate some of the most important pieces in the puzzle.

1) All the remains have come from caves or fissures. These have filled up in whole or in part, and some have been tourist attractions for many years before they were known to contain evidence of *Australopithecus*. The Taung location has been completely destroyed by limestone quarrying operations.

2) The manner in which the deposits might have accumulated in the caves makes it impossible to be certain that remains found together are of forms that lived at or near the same time. In spite of this difficulty, most investigators presume a rough contemporaneity for the fauna within a cave but are reluctant to extend this presumption to the other sites in any precise way. •

3) Collectively, the remains within these deposits include an extraordinary abundance of the bones of a small extinct variety of antelope and of a small extinct species of baboon, together with a variety of other mammalian forms.

4) The abundance of baboons and antelopes raises the question of how they got there; neither is a cave dweller by choice. A number of explanations have been offered, but the one most consistent with the evidence is the explanation that *Australopithecus* brought them there. The support for this view is largely circumstantial but, taken as a totality, is moderately convincing. The vast majority of baboon skulls show evidence of having been killed by a blow on the head with the traditional blunt instrument, and of having had the skulls subsequently bashed open. This is decidedly not the way that carnivores kill their prey, but more distinctly the way that tool-using primates might. The antelope's long bones show signs of having been split open. Hyenas split bones to get at the marrow, but in the process usually leave distinctive tooth markings; such markings are lacking. *Australopithecus* may have been after the same thing with his hands or perhaps assisted by an implement. And, finally, there is an amount of peripheral "evidence" that conforms only in the sense that it permits the hypothesis that the australopithecines brought the animals into the caves; the baboons and antelopes are small enough, and it is not the kind of assemblage that carnivores (such as the scavenging hyenas), observed under natural conditions, leave behind in their lairs today. Furthermore, modern apes and some monkeys occasionally eat meat as part of their natural diet, thereby implying that the dietary precedent necessary for the australopithecines to have been able to eat meat is a trait that had been established among the primates for a long time. While it is clearly possible that the cave deposits in South Africa may have been laid down in a very different manner, the bulk of the evidence would seem to favor the conclusion that the australopithecines could have been and probably were responsible for bringing in most of the skeletal remains.

5) No good evidence exists to suggest a reliable conclusion concerning the manner in which the animals may have been killed. One reasonable view is that *Australopithecus* was a part-time scavenger, that is, that many of the animals were either killed by large carnivores or died as a result of other natural factors, and *Australopithecus* took what was left back to the caves for perhaps a more protected eating place and a locality in which he might share his food with other australopithecines. There is, of course, no evidence of sharing, but had he done so, *Australo-*

pithecus would have had an easier time adapting, and thus surviving. In all, the sharing behavior might have bestowed as much survival potential at the australopithecine level of adaptation as erect posture and perhaps language, but such reasoning is clearly not direct evidence that it existed.

Scavenging is probably not a good way to describe the manner in which *Australopithecus* obtained his food. It implies that he lurked in the shadows waiting for a carnivore to kill a large animal and to eat his fill, and after the carnivore wandered off to rest, then *Australopithecus* moved in to take what was left. This is a common way for hyenas to obtain their food. Again the evidence is not direct, but since most modern primates, including modern man, depend heavily on plant food sources, it seems logical to conclude that *Australopithecus* did too. A view of *Australopithecus* as an animal that moved over large territories seeking food of any kind wherever it was available seems almost certainly to be closer to the real situation than the view suggested by calling him a scavenger. Perhaps it would be better to think of *Australopithecus* as an omnivore that was engaged in more or less full-time food collecting, whether from plant or animal sources.

6) Two opposing but not entirely contradictory views exist on the issue of whether or not *Australopithecus* lived in the caves as a regular tenant. They exist because it is clear, on the one hand, that he must have been on the move constantly to obtain food and therefore could not have lived in any one location as a permanent resident. On the other hand, it is clear that, if they brought the animals into the caves, then the australopithecines must have occupied the caves regularly to build up such an enormous quantity of bones. Both views could be true simultaneously if *Australopithecus*, at a time when animals were available, retired to the caves as protected areas in which to eat, whereas when he was not eating animal food, no such precautions were taken.

Professor Raymond Dart has proposed an interesting theory which, if it represents what in fact was happening, would have an important bearing on the way that *Australopithecus* lived and particularly on how he may have dispatched the animals and used the cave. He proposes to account for the large number of bones, particularly the antelope bones, by stating that they were used as implements—in other words, that the skeletal remains are, in fact, the implements that *Australopithecus* used to kill and cut up more animals. Thus, it would be at once an archaeological and a paleontological assemblage. Since archaeological assemblages are named, he calls this large assemblage of bones, horn cores, and teeth the Osteodontokeratic (bones, teeth, horn) culture. It is an interesting theory, but an impossible one to demonstrate conclusively as true or false with present evidence.

7) Careful studies have been carried out on the climatic conditions prevalent at the time the caves were used, but these have not produced much new information because of the problems already discussed with regard to temporal and distributional factors. These have resulted in the observations that Taung appears to have been occupied during hot, dry, desertlike conditions; the other areas are better watered. During much of the time the caves were frequented by the australopithecines, the

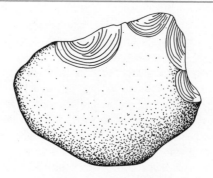

Figure 6–6.   Kafuan or Olduwan pebble tool.

climatic conditions do not appear to have been markedly different from those prevailing there today.

8) Irrespective of the validity of the Osteodontokeratic theory, australopithecines have been found in association with stone tools of the earliest of the pebble tool traditions, the Oldowan or pre-Chelles-Acheul. The assemblages consist of crude hand-axe-like pebble tools and crudely made flake implements (Figure 6–6). Earlier objections that *Australopithecus* was too dull to have made the implements seem to have been overcome by the recent evidence that chimpanzees are toolmakers, and if they are able to do as well as alleged, then the accomplishments of the australopithecines are more reasonable to expect. The Oldowan is the earliest known stone tool assemblage, and it is the first stage in a continuous development that goes through the Chelles-Acheul, Clactonian-Levalloisian, Mousterian, etc., sequence.

From South African materials, answers to the most interesting questions concerning the australopithecines would have to run as follows: Did they make tools? Yes. Were they hunters? No, not in any usual meaning of that word. Did they eat meat? Yes. When did they live? The evidence from South Africa is inconclusive. Were they ancestral to us? This requires separate consideration of the two australopithecine species. In 1959, when the only evidence was that from South Africa, there was a growing suspicion that *africanus* gave rise to two evolutionary descendants—*robustus*, who died out leaving no modern descendants, and the earliest members of the genus *Homo*, who, of course, evolved eventually into modern man. This remains today as a widely accepted view, but the new material from East Africa has given us some new perspectives to consider; specifically, it leads us to suspect that variability among the early hominids may be vastly greater than was heretofore believed.

Almost all of the East African australopithecine fossils have been discovered by one or another member of the remarkable Leakey family. The first discovery, made by Mary Leakey in 1959, consisted of an almost complete skull of a large hominid, which her husband, the late Louis Leakey, thought to be the remains of a completely new genus. He named the specimen *Zinjanthropus boisei* (see Figure 6–7). Subse-

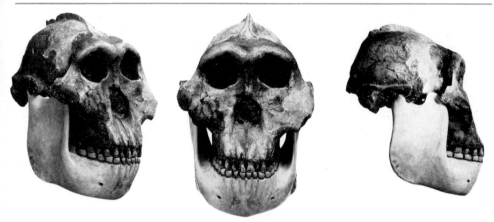

Figure 6–7. Three views of a *Zinjanthropus* skull cast. (Reconstruction by Phillip V. Tobias and R. Clarke, photo by R. Campbell and A. R. Hughes)

quently, it was renamed *Australopithecus boisei* (Tobias, 1967), yet, even so, most authorities regard it as merely the East African variety of *Australopithecus robustus*.

The discovery attracted a lot of attention partly because of its location and appearance but primarily because of its age. Volcanic rock near the discovery was dated at 1.75 million years old by means of the potassium-argon technique. Up until then, most authorities presumed that the Pleistocene had not lasted more than one million years, and that it was within this period that the hominid phase of primate evolution took place. Here, however, was evidence of an erect bipedal hominid roaming around East Africa about 750,000 years earlier. The consequences of the age estimate were perhaps predictable; many authorities flatly denied the validity of the discovery. Others claimed contradictory evidence was available, but most quietly accepted the new estimates and revised their view of the Pleistocene accordingly. In fact, the effect was in some ways welcome, since the many major events known only by relative age and formerly sandwiched within one million years could now justifiably be spread out over two.

Adjusting to the revised estimates of antiquity proved to be temporary. Subsequent discoveries from other East African localities (the Omo River basin in Ethiopia and along the shores of Lake Rudolf in Kenya) have shown that both *africanus* and *robustus* existed together as long as four to five million years ago. Additionally, Richard Leakey, just two months after his father's death, announced the discovery of a hominid much more modern in appearance than either australopithecine. The discovery was made at Lake Rudolf and consisted of an essentially modern femur and a skull with brain capacity estimated at approximately 850 cc. The remains add evidence in support of the view that modern man's ancestors were contemporaries and not descendants of the australopithecines. The estimated age for these ancient bones is from 2.5 to 3 million years ago.

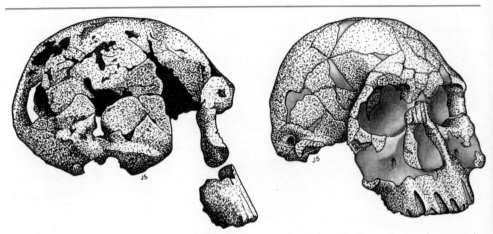

Figure 6–8.   Large-brained hominid discovered in late 1972 by Richard Leakey and named tentatively as "1470 Man." The form is estimated to be 2.8 million years old. The left figure is drawn from a photograph in the November 12, 1972, edition of the *New York Times*. The right figure is redrawn from a figure in the June 1973 issue of the *National Geographic*. (Courtesy of the National Geographic Society)

The recent discoveries have helped to clarify two issues. First, it is clear that the *africanus* and *robustus* varieties were contemporaries and not ancestor-descendant species as many have suspected. Perhaps, as some have argued (Brace, 1967), they may represent merely differences within a single species, though their differences appear to be far too great for such a view to be acceptable (Greene, 1973). In any event they appear clearly to have lived at the same time. A second issue to be clarified by the recent discoveries is that the australopithecines go back further into time than had been indicated previously. Fairly abundant remains from East Africa place them back at least four million years ago, and one tooth found in Ngorora, Kenya, has been estimated to be nine million years old.

As they have helped to clarify some issues, however, the recent discoveries have also added fuel to a long-standing controversy over the place of *Australopithecus* in our ancestry. Louis Leakey argued for years that *Australopithecus* could not be ancestral to *Homo* because the two genera were contemporaries a long time ago. His first evidence for the great antiquity of the genus *Homo* was unearthed in the 1930s and consisted solely of the Kanam mandible. More recently he had pointed to several remains from Olduvai Gorge which were more modern in aspect and which he called *Homo habilis*. The recent discovery by Richard Leakey adds considerable support to his father's views.

Some authorities (for example, Le Gros Clark, 1967) have failed to see the distinctiveness of *Homo habilis* and instead have regarded the remains as within the range of variation one could expect in the *Australopithecus* genus. If this view is correct, then *Australopithecus* is probably in our ancestry; if Leakey's interpretation

Table 6–3   Locations Yielding Evidence of *Homo erectus*

LOCATION	DATE FOUND	COMMENT
1. Java	1890–1891	Original discoveries of skull fragment and femur. Originally designated as *Pithecanthropus erectus.*
	1936	Incomplete skull of an infant. Originally designated *Homo modjokertensis.*
	1937–1939	Three incomplete skulls found about forty miles from original 1890 discovery. Also identified as *Pithecanthropus.*
2. China	1927–1937	Several fragments of fourteen skulls and eleven mandibles. All were designated earlier as representative of *Sinanthropus pekinensis.*
	1963–1964	Mandible and skull fragments. Referred to as Lantian man.
3. Germany	1907	A mandible, also called Heidelberg jaw and *Homo heidelbergensis.*
4. Algeria	1954–1956	Fragments of three mandibles which have been designated *Atlanthropus mauritanicus.*
5. Morocco	1954	From Sidi Abderrahman, a fragmentary mandible.
6. South Africa	1949	Some jaw fragments, teeth, and two bones of the postcranial skeleton. Designated originally as *Telanthropus capensis.*
7. Tanzania	1960	Skull fragments referred to as Chellean man.
	1964	Identified by Leakey as "George," a skull reconstructed from many small fragments.

is correct, then *Australopithecus* is an interesting episode in the evolution of the hominids, but not on the line leading to modern man. For the time being, we will have to be satisfied with not knowing for certain.

HOMO ERECTUS

The next recognizably distinctive hominids include a variety of forms variously known as Java man, *Pithecanthropus, Sinanthropus,* Peking man, *Atlanthropus,* Chellean man, *Homo heidelbergensis,* and *Homo erectus* (see Table 6–3). We will classify them all together and refer to them by the last designation, *Homo erectus.* The earliest indication of *Homo erectus* was a discovery made in Java in 1890 by Eugène Dubois. This, as it turned out, was the first of several discoveries of *Homo erectus* to be made in Java, the earliest ones by Dubois, later ones, beginning in 1936, by von Königswald, and most recently between 1960 and 1966 by Sartono and Jacob. Additional material of the same general morphology has been discovered in several other locations in the Old World. In spite of the fact that several locations have produced important indications of *Homo erectus,* the total fossil material available is not particularly suitable for reconstruction and the recovery of useful comparative formal characteristics. In many parts of the world, for example, the only

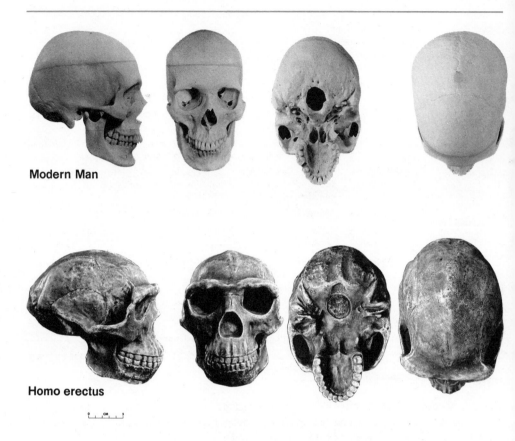

Modern Man

Homo erectus

Figure 6–9.   Comparison of four views of a modern man skull with a *Homo erectus* skull cast.

available remains consist of jawbones, whereas in Java a large section of the facial skeleton has never been recovered. Nevertheless, putting together mostly what is known from Java with material subsequently discovered in China, we can make some general statements concerning *Homo erectus* in comparison with modern man (see Figure 6–9).

From the front, the contours of the face in *Homo erectus* are angular, as are those of the eye orbits. The forehead barely rises above the supraorbital ridges and slopes back, converging with the parietals, which themselves form an angle that, while clearly not a sagittal crest, is the suggestion of something similar to one. One may also notice from a frontal view that the greatest breadth of the skull is lower down and, as may be noted from the top, farther back on the *Homo erectus* skull than it is in modern man.

From the side, the face can be seen to project farther forward than in modern man, and the relatively small brain is evident, as are the more fully developed brow ridges. The occiput shows a rugged surface and a sharply angled contour, and the mastoids are not well developed.

From below, there are few striking differences between *Homo erectus* and modern man apart from gross size. The foramen magnum is well under the base of the skull, and the teeth are set in a dental arch like that of modern man and unlike the rectangular contour of modern apes. The cranial capacity of *Homo erectus* ranges between 900 cc. and 1100 cc., whereas the average for modern man is approximately 1400 cc. to 1500 cc. If, as would seem likely, *Homo erectus* is ancestral to modern man, then clearly the most significant evolutionary forces acting since *Homo erectus* times were those involved in increasing both the absolute and relative size of the brain.

Again, one should keep constantly in mind that terms such as *modern man*, *Australopithecus*, and *Homo erectus* are simply labels for widely varying hominids. As a demonstration, one needs to go no further than daily experience to know just how widely divergent can be the variation that is included in the category of modern man. Just look around you. There is no reason to presume that morphological variation among the earlier hominids was any less. Indeed, there is some evidence to the contrary, but since conclusive evidence on the total range of variation in these earlier forms is lacking, the issue cannot be resolved.

Two variants of *Homo erectus* are readily identifiable and distinguishable, one represented by the Javanese discoveries and the other by a series of discoveries that began to be made by Davidson Black near Peking, China, in 1927, and subsequently by von Königswald. Front and side views of each (Figure 6–10) demonstrate that the Chinese discoveries consist of individuals somewhat less brutish and apelike in their features than the Javanese remains. That is, each has essentially the same assemblage of distinctive traits setting them apart from modern man, but they are more marked in the Javanese material. Peking man has smaller supraorbital ridges, slightly more of a chin and forehead, less prognathism, a slightly less marked gabling effect to his skull vault, and a moderately larger brain than Java man.

Recently, in 1963 and 1964, a lower jaw and skullcap were discovered in China in the Lantian district southwest of Peking. Although the evidence is meager, it appears that morphologically the Lantian fragments are more similar to the Javanese *Homo erectus* discoveries than the material from nearby Peking. There is evidence, likewise, that the Lantian discovery is older than those from Peking. In general *Homo erectus* is distributed throughout the Old World (see Figure 6–11). *Australopithecus* is essentially tropical; *Homo erectus* lived in both tropical and temperate areas.

Absolute dating estimates of *Homo erectus* made on materials from Africa, Java, and Europe all place him in time at between one-half and one million years ago. Unfortunately, the early discoveries from China were lost during an attempt to remove them to the United States at the outset of World War II, and thus they

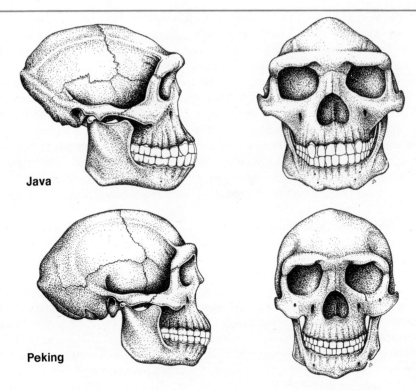

Figure 6–10. Comparison of two varieties of *Homo erectus*.

have not been evaluated in light of recent advances in geochronology. Subsequent work from the same deposits was begun in 1949 and to date has yielded a humerus and tibia that are said to be like those of modern man, and five teeth and a jawbone that are similar to the earlier Peking man material. Recent absolute dating estimates of the geological layer (Trinil) in Java that contained almost all of the *Homo erectus* remains have yielded dates of approximately 500,000 years ago, which is consistent with earlier estimates.

Thus it is relatively simple and straightforward to estimate the time that *Homo erectus* was present, but very difficult to estimate his duration. About the only satisfactory estimate amounts to presuming that the 500,000 year estimate is at or near the mean, and from this to conclude that *Homo erectus* was on the scene during second (Mindel-Riss) interglacial times. The only evidence of duration—and it remains highly tentative—is the dating of the two *Homo erectus* forms from Leakey's excavations in Olduvai Gorge, one from near the bottom of Bed II ("George") and one from near the top (L.L.K.).* The volcanic rock that forms the bottom of Bed II has

* *George* and *L.L.K.* are the names for the skulls and other bones.

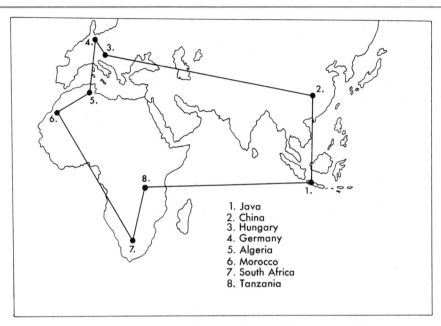

1. Java
2. China
3. Hungary
4. Germany
5. Algeria
6. Morocco
7. South Africa
8. Tanzania

Figure 6–11. Geographic distribution of *Homo erectus*.

been dated at one million years old, the top at 490,000 years old. There is no reason to question the dating estimates here, but it is not clear as yet whether the two fossil discoveries actually are properly classified as members of the *Homo erectus* grouping. Presuming this to be true, however, the earlier estimates of 500,000 years would seem to date *Homo erectus* toward the end of his existence as an identifiable morphological unit and place his origin back to first interglacial or even earlier times. The East African dates are encouraging for a number of reasons, but most important among them is the fact that they provide us with a dimension that until now has been lacking in the interpretation of *Homo erectus*, the dimension of time depth.

While the fossil-producing locations are unequal in their content, it would appear that *Homo erectus* definitely preferred but was not restricted to warm climates. This is true in the case of European and Asian remains as well as those from Africa. Consider as evidence the fossil animals found with him in China; *Homo erectus* shared his habitat with tigers, elephants, rhinoceroses, ostriches, camels, and hyenas. In North Africa, the list is similar but includes also a giant baboon similar to forms previously known only from the earliest part of the Pleistocene from East and South Africa. The situation in East Africa is becoming more clear. The details differ from earlier reports, but the essential feature of the fauna is clear; it too seems to indicate a warm, moist climate.

The original discovery of the Java *Homo erectus* was made in a location which undoubtedly is not where the forms had died. The site is on the Solo River in a deposit which had been accumulated earlier by water action, and thus almost everything in it had been moved, shuffled, and removed again. This makes it impossible to be very confident of context information, but what there is of it is in general very similar to the better-known African and Asian assemblages, including hippopotami, elephants, and fossil monkeys and apes. The remains from the lower levels are likewise similar to the faunal assemblage from the Peking discoveries, including lions, tigers, hyenas, rhinoceroses, and hippopotami.

If one tried to make specific comparisons of fauna from one site to another, the resulting picture would probably be confusing. Undoubtedly many of the species were different and thus would show differing adaptive capabilities, and further, since few good absolute dates are known from outside East Africa, the comparisons would be made between faunal groupings that lived at various times and with varying durations. Nevertheless, there is evidence from the Chinese and European discoveries suggesting that *Homo erectus* was able to live in cold climatic conditions. From Peking, in addition to the remains of tigers, elephants, and camels, also discovered in the same deposits were fossilized remains of varieties of wolves, dogs, foxes, bears, horses, bison, and buffalo. The situation would doubtless be clearer if the deposits were stratified, but they are not; they are mixed up somewhat, having been extracted from what used to be caves, a fact that will be of importance to us again presently. Perhaps this peculiar assemblage reflects the faunal succession in an area once warm, moist, and densely vegetated, gradually changing to a colder, more typically temperate climate.

The evidence from Heidelberg suggests something similar to that from Peking. The European fauna was, of course, very different in earlier Pleistocene times, as evidenced by the different fossil species of elephants and rhinoceroses, as well as others not found at all in the China deposits, such as species of dogs, bison, horses, beavers, etc., found in association with *Homo erectus* from Heidelberg.

No doubt there is room for much speculation based on faunal evidence, and, in fact, we have already indulged in some by referring to some animals as warm-, others as cold-climate animals. It is certainly possible that earlier forms differed in their adaptive capacities from their modern counterparts, and thus one should be cautious in inferring such things from fossil remains. In careful terms, a summary of the faunal remains found together with *Homo erectus* could read as follows: in the North Temperate Zone, *Homo erectus* remains are found in association with remains of animals that today include both cold- and warm-adapted varieties. In today's tropical areas, *Homo erectus* remains are found in association with animals that today have only warm-adapted descendants.

Turning to the archaeological evidence, progress in reaching generalizations about *Homo erectus* is hampered by the fact that not all sites yielding fossil bones have produced cultural artifacts. Nevertheless, the avilable evidence is interesting and informative and is sufficient to allow some tentative generalized inferences. In Java, the fossil remains of *Homo erectus* have never been found in direct association with archaeological remains. The earliest evidence of archaeological material to be discovered in Java is an assemblage of crudely made flake and chopper-chopping tools that has been called the Patjitanian industry. Almost all of the materials discovered so far and assignable to the Patjitanian were recovered from a single large site of uncertain age in central Java. It is probable—but circumstances of their location at the time of discovery make it impossible to know for certain—that they are from the Trinil stratum that yielded the remains of Java man. However, if this is true, they are found higher up and not at all clearly associated with the *Homo erectus* remains. Recall, however, that the fossil bones had been redeposited, and thus their original position likewise is not clearly known.

Apart from the associated fauna and the limited inferences it allows, there is little more to be extracted from the information provided by context from Java, perhaps largely because it was not discovered in its original context. Since the evidence is ambiguous, no conclusions are possible, but more reliable guidelines may be obtained by turning to other areas where richer sources of data exist.

In the recovery of the *Homo erectus* material from China, an abundance of archaeological remains was also discovered. The discoveries were made just outside of Choukoutien, a small village situated about twenty-five miles outside of Peking. The fossils were found within fissures in a massive limestone deposit that was being quarried at the time. Over the years, the fissures had filled up with debris either blown in by the wind or brought in by various animals frequenting the caves. *Homo erectus* was one of the animals that made use of the cave, and from the evidence of what he left behind, apparently used it for a long time.

The composition of the fossil material discovered is itself interesting and suggestive. There is a surprising disparity between the large number of skull fragments and the relatively few fragments of the postcranial skeleton. Furthermore, four of the five skulls appear to have been bashed in at the bases. This is interesting, and these two facts taken together have led others to speculate that this might imply that the Chinese *Homo erectus* remains were of individuals who were killed, probably outside the cave, their heads cut off, skulls bashed in, brains removed, and the fragmented bony remains tossed to the back of the cave. These speculations generate even more remote ones. Since it was probably other members of his species that did the deed, then here is a basis for concluding that *Homo erectus* was a cannibal. And, since cannibalism is rarely practiced outside a ceremonial context among contemporary primitive people, its existence may imply ceremonialism, and ceremonialism implies culture. Therefore *Homo erectus* had culture. That is a lot of speculation to emerge from so little empirical information. And, if the existence of culture is the crucial problem, it would seem completely unnecessary, since there is good evidence that he not only made tools but also knew how to make and use fire. The assemblage of artifacts is known as the Choukoutienian.

The Choukoutienian is an early assemblage of implements in the chopper-chopping developmental sequence found throughout eastern Asia. (Figure 6–12 illustrates some differences between choppers and chopping tools.)

That *Homo erectus* knew how to use and control fire is unquestioned. The evidence includes fireplaces found at several locations within the cave deposits, and many of the fossil bones of the other animals that apparently were brought in by

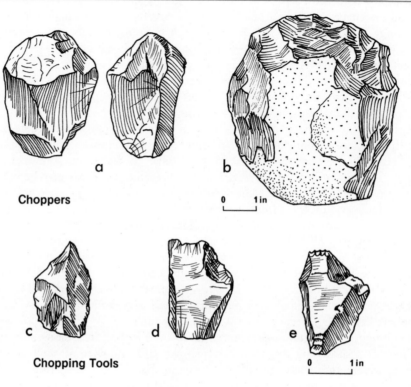

Choppers

0   1 in

Chopping Tools

0   1 in

Figure 6–12.   Comparison of choppers with chopping tools. (After K. P. Oakley)

Homo erectus have been burned and charred. From this it would seem reasonable to conclude that he ate meat, perhaps a lot of it, that he may have "cooked" it in some way, and thus that fire was important as a processing technique as well as a source of warmth. By extension of this reasoning, it would seem reasonable also to conclude that some, if not most, of the Choukoutienian implements must have been used to cut meat and scrape hides.

This is, however, only a small part of the story. *Homo erectus* was confronted with the problems of getting animals as well as preparing them. Hunting animals, particularly as large and fast as many of those found within the caves, requires either an elaborate technology or a more modest technology combined with a doggedness and determination such as that found among some contemporary primitive hunters such as the Australian aborigines and the Bushmen of the Kalahari Desert. These contemporary populations have, however, a technology which, although simple and meager, is far advanced over that of *Homo erectus*. Thus one cannot help but hesitate in labeling him, and presumably other members of his species, as efficient hunters. They could, for example, have been primarily dependent on the gathering of plant foods, while still obtaining a modest amount of meat from the remains left behind after a carnivore kill and from small, comparatively slow game they killed themselves. In short, the fact that *Homo erectus* is found within deposits which also include remains of animals he probably brought in does not necessarily imply that he was a hunter in the usual sense of that word. The artifacts found in the same deposits support the view that he was a meat-eater, but not that he was an efficient hunter of large game. Other implements made from more perishable materials such as wood could have been used, but these would not have been preserved. There are some who claim that markings on some of the deer antlers found in these deposits indicate their use as tools. Nevertheless, it seems unlikely that implements made from any materials sufficiently sophisticated in their design to enable *Homo erectus* to be an efficient hunter of the animals whose remains he is found with would be associated with such a crude assemblage of stone tools. Alternatively, he may have depended on communal hunting procedures wherein game animals are stampeded over cliffs or driven into traps where they can be readily killed, cut up, and then perhaps taken off to the caves for consumption. These methods usually call for the cooperative efforts of several individuals and result in irregular periods of abundance in animal food. This is a relatively common hunting technique among recent primitive people.

One final point of interest about Choukoutien deposits yielding remains of *Homo erectus* is the observation that this location has served as a habitation site for hominids for a very long time. The deposits are about 160 feet deep, and artifacts and fossil bones are scattered throughout. Both the fauna and the Choukoutienian archaeological material remain decidedly stable from bottom to top, a fact which would seem to imply that *Homo erectus* lived there for a long time. It would be helpful if there were some reliable indications of the duration of his occupation in these caves, but this is not known. Of unusual interest also is the fact that evidence has been obtained from the same locality of modern man living in more recent times with an assemblage of implements that combines chopper-chopping tools with very well-made objects that, in Europe, are found in the Upper Paleolithic industries. This is known as the Upper Cave industry, and, as the name would seem to imply, it has been found in a cave at the top of the same limestone deposits that farther down yielded *Homo erectus* and the Choukoutienian industry. The Upper Cave remains include four crania of modern-man morphology that in all likelihood are representative of the recent ancestors of the modern Asians from the area. There is a gap between the lower and upper caves—one large enough that some can still claim with justification that there is no proof of an ancestral relationship between the residents of the two levels. If one holds this view, it then becomes awkward to account for the continuity that would seem to be indicated by the presence of the same kind of chopper-chopping tools in both locations.

In summary, as indicated by the Peking remains, *Homo erectus:* 1) lived in caves, 2) had fire, 3) ate meat, 4) used chopper-chopping tools, and 5) continued his adaptation over a long time.

In Europe, as already noted, the evidence for *Homo erectus* is meager. In 1965, a discovery was made of an occipital bone in Hungary that at first was assigned to the *Homo erectus* category, but which has recently been referred to as a Neanderthal. This was at Vétesszöllös, a site that earlier had yielded chopper-chopping tools. As yet, it has not been described in detail, but, if the initial interpretation turns out to be correct, it is of interest simply because outside Asia most of the *Homo erectus* material recovered has been the remains of jaws and teeth. Thus, the basis of our comparison here is the Heidelberg jaw. This jaw was found in association with wild pigs, deer, elephants, woolly rhinoceroses, horses, bison, saber-toothed tigers, lions, wildcats, beaver, and elk. On the whole, this would seem to represent a heterogeneous fauna and thus imply a heterogeneous environment. The dating of the jaw has never been very clear. It was found at a depth of over eighty feet from the surface. On the basis of the associated fauna, the climatic circumstances appear to be temperate interglacial in a well-watered area with temperature fluctuations extending to greater average extremes in the succession of the seasons.

No archaeological material was found with the Heidelberg man, but there is no doubt that tools were being made at the time, whenever that may have been, and there is little doubt that *Homo erectus* made them. For over two hundred years, Europe has been producing indications of the existence of some people who occupied the Continent a long time ago and made sometimes crude, sometimes splendid stone tools, and who lived a way of life very different from that of today. The evidence has consisted almost entirely of stone implements. Apart from the controversial Swanscombe and Fontechevade fragments, little is known about the men who made the artifacts. As noted earlier, the Mousterian was the outgrowth of what has been interpreted as two separate tool traditions: 1) the hand-axe sequence which consists of sites containing both core and flake tools and is known as the Chelles-Acheul tradition, and 2) the flake-tool sequence made up of sites exclusively containing flake tools and called the Clactonian-Levalloisian tradition. The usual way of illustrating the relationship between these two is shown in Figure 6–19 on page 208. From this it can be seen that the Clactonian-Levalloisian and the Chelles-Acheul traditions are two separate and distinct traditions. The Clactonian began first, but, after the Chelles-Acheul began, the two were found over the same temporal and spatial distributions. It is becoming increasingly awkward to maintain this view, and the fact that very few skeletal remains have been discovered in these locations has made the problem more difficult to resolve. It now appears at least possible, if not probable, that the two sequences may in fact be aspects of one another, the hand-axe sequence reflecting a warm-weather subsistence adaptation and the flake tools a cold-weather adaptation.

Since 1961 archaeological excavations in Spain have added to our understanding of how *Homo erectus* lived. The sites, near Torralba and Ambrona, have not produced human skeletal remains, but there is good reason to believe that they were occupied by *Homo erectus*. The locations differ from the caves of Choukoutien in that they are out in the open and spread out over a sizable area. Large numbers of core and flake tools have been recovered in these recent excavations. These add further evidence in support of the speculations just discussed. Furthermore the sites in Spain add considerably to the evidence that *Homo erectus* used fire to stampede large mammal herds. This overkill technique, while not especially elegant, once again makes it clear that *Homo erectus* was a meat eater.

Most important for our present interest is the observation that apparently the core- and flake-tool traditions were already under way in Europe by the time that *Homo erectus* was living, and, while it is not by any means certain, it would not be surprising to learn that the European *Homo erectus* populations had adapted to their fluctuating environment, containing an abundance of game, in much the same way as the Asian populations, as illustrated by the Peking remains. If, as discussed earlier, the chopping tools served functions similar to the hand axes, then the Asian and European sequences may be seen as similar adaptations to similar environmental conditions, and thus, by extension, the European *Homo erectus* hominids were leading lives similar to those of their Asian counterparts in Peking. One final fragment of information bearing on this is the fact that some of the animal bones in the deposits again appear to have been broken, as in Peking. This is, of course, speculative. A recitation of the simple factual material concerning the Heidelberg jaw would read as follows: 1) The jaw was found at a depth of eighty feet from the surface near the village of Mauer in central Germany in 1907. 2) No archaeological evidence was recovered in the site. 3) Its age is uncertain, but the associated fauna indicates interglacial conditions, and, at that depth, it may be first interglacial. 4) Archaeological sequences in Europe go back that far and even farther. 5) It is not clear if the jaw belonged to a person who belonged to the species that made the tools, but, if it did, it may be that the European populations of that time were adapted to their environments in ways similar to those known in more detail from Peking.

Four, or possibly five, sites have yielded *Homo erectus* remains in Africa, two in North Africa, two in East Africa, and one uncertain form from South Africa. This is very little to go by, but it is sufficient to indicate that the range of *Homo erectus* is much broader than was believed a few years ago, when it was presumed that he was restricted to South and East Asia. Affinities between the Heidelberg jaw and the Asian discoveries had been noted, but it was not until the last few years, as indications of the range of *Homo erectus* became clearer, that he has been included within the group. In North Africa, the two sites that have produced the skeletal remains are at Ternifine in Algeria and Sidi Abderrahman in Morocco. The remains consist mostly of jaws and teeth, but include one fragmentary parietal, comparable parts of which are similar to the Heidelberg jaw and the Asian representatives of *Homo erectus*. Of particular interest is the Ternifine site, which is that of a Pleistocene lake bed that existed at a time when the climate was apparently more moist than at present. The mammalian remains consisted of fossil elephants, rhinoceroses, zebras, giraffes, antelopes, lions, hyenas, very large baboons, saber-toothed tigers, and wild boars. This fauna indicates warm temperatures in a well-watered open savannah, an area which could include reasonably rich plant food resources as well as an abundance of large game. Today's baboons forage over areas that probably include many of the same features.

The archaeological material found in association with the fauna at Ternifine includes rather crudely made hand axes and an assortment of large flake tools. This industry is the same as that which in other areas is identified as the early stage of the Chelles-Acheul sequence and, if our earlier reasoning is correct, implies a versatile, largely unspecialized dietary adaptation that included animal and plant sources with proportional variations depending on availability, which, in turn, was probably controlled by seasonal variation in temperature and water resources.

A secondary but less complete indication of *Homo erectus* in North Africa comes from the Sidi Abderrahman site in Morocco. The fossil material consists of a jaw and some teeth found in association with faunal and archaeological materials similar to those at Ternifine.

Judging largely on the basis of the fauna, the North African remains appear to have been of individuals living toward the close of the European first interglacial or, as some would call it, early Middle Pleistocene. For the evidence from East Africa, we turn once again to the extraordinarily rich deposits of Olduvai Gorge in Tanzania.

To obtain some appreciation for the indications of *Homo erectus* in this part of the world, it will be necessary to digress briefly and consider some of the important aspects of the geology of Olduvai Gorge. The gorge consists of a deep cut in the present surface plain which has exposed a series of geological beds in layer-cake order. These have produced an extraordinary series of fossils including the earliest known fully erect bipedal hominid and, in addition, a continuous sequence of cultural remains beginning with the oldest known stone tools and progressing through the Chelles-Acheul sequence of core and flake tools which continues in this part of the world up to relatively recent times. Figure 6–13 is a schematic illustration of the arrangement of the Olduvai Gorge geological beds. The *Homo erectus* fossils have come from Bed II. The lowest levels of Bed II have been dated at slightly older than one million years, and there are indications that the Bed II–Bed III juncture is datable at approximately one-half million years ago. Apart from the geological contrasts in the deposits distinguishing Beds I and II, Bed II includes indications that the climate was undergoing a substantial change at the time it was being deposited. On both faunal and geological evidence, there are good reasons for concluding that the area was much drier during the time Bed II was laid down than during Bed I times. There are, as well, indications of a change in the composition of the mammalian fauna that took place not at the outset, but *after* Bed II had already begun to be deposited. This change marks the appearance of an essentially modern group of mammals as replacements for the earlier fauna, known as the Villafranchian fauna, that extends well back into early Pleistocene, perhaps even Pliocene, times throughout many parts of the Old World. This is an interesting group of mammals whose appearance serves as a dating benchmark for the onset of the Pleistocene. The Villafranchian fauna is associated with warm weather in well-watered areas. It extends into Bed II in Olduvai Gorge, but is displaced during a phase when the area was drier—apparently not parched, but dry. At the top of Bed II, it appears from the evidence of river channels that the area was becoming humid once again.

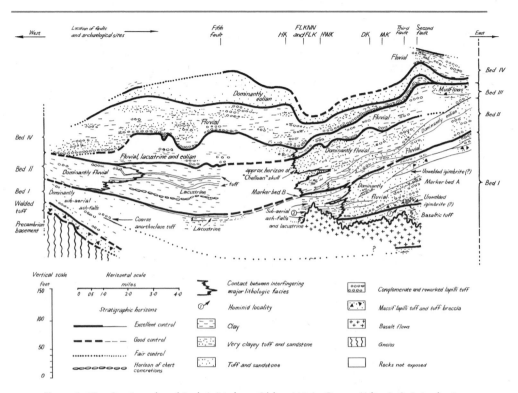

Figure 6–13. Stratigraphy of Beds I–IV along Olduvai Main Gorge. (After L. S. B. Leakey)

The faunal assemblage displacing the Villafranchian in Bed II is similar in many ways to that found in association with the North African remains at Ternifine. The indications suggest again an open savannah type of terrain where a hominid would find himself once again in an area of considerable diversity in both plant and animal food resources. The faunal succession between the earlier and later stages of Bed II is accompanied by a change in the archaeological remains too. During the later stage, the first hand axes known from this area appear, and they are representative of the earliest phases of the Chelles-Acheulean core- and flake-tool traditions in East Africa. The remains of *Homo erectus* have been found in the later phase of the Bed II sequence, that is, in the same deposits that contain the savannah fauna and the early hand-axe archaeological remains. The discovery was made in 1960, at a point about twenty feet from the top of Bed II in an area where the entire bed is about eighty feet thick. The fragments recovered lack the face and jaw, but include the forehead, supraorbital ridges, and occipital crest. Measurements and observations made on these remains demonstrate their similarity to both Asian and European remains of *Homo erectus*. The discovery has been dated at 490,000 years old. One other discovery from the lower part of Bed II has been reported recently; the discovery, referred to by Leakey as "George," consisted of many small fragments and thus required a painstaking reconstruction, so that as yet no adequate description of the material has been made available. According to Leakey, it is the remains of a *Homo erectus* individual. If this is indeed true, then the African variants of *Homo erectus* go back in time to about one million years ago, since this discovery was made at very nearly the bottom of Bed II. This discovery may provide *Homo erectus* with "time depth" that heretofore has been hard to document except on morphological grounds.

The East African remains are too few to provide a basis for firm conclusions, but they tend to present a picture of *Homo erectus* that is consistent with the others considered so far, not only from the standpoint of morphology, but in more general adaptive terms as well.

The only other candidate for *Homo erectus* in Africa is from a South African site, Swartkrans, which has produced remains of australopithecines as well. This is the discovery which for many years has been known as *Telanthropus*. The material assigned to this group includes two incomplete lower jaws, a fragment of an upper jaw that may have belonged with one of the two mandibles, and a few other fragments. These are similar to the Peking and Heidelberg jaws and teeth, and, on morphological grounds, it would seem consistent and appropriate to include this South African material within *Homo erectus*. There is, however, very little to go on, as was the case with the other African and European discoveries, particularly at Ternifine, Sidi Abderrahman, and Heidelberg. Furthermore, the deposits in which the Swartkrans material was discovered were such that it was impossible to estimate their age confidently or to ascertain details of their faunal and archaeological contexts. It would seem that all that might be inferred from the Swartkrans site is that *Homo erectus* may have resided there.

The unevenness of the information available from the various parts of the Old World makes it difficult to summarize the general characteristics of *Homo erectus*, but some tentative generalizations can be reached. 1) He was distributed throughout the Old World. 2) Available dating estimates place him in time from about one-half to one million years ago. 3) He made tools. These differ in form between the African-European (Chelles-Acheul) and the Asian (chopper-chopping) *Homo erectus* associations, but it seems likely that both traditions served similar subsistence functions. Each would seem to be a generalized assemblage consistent with subsistence patterns that include both animal and plant food sources. 4) His appearance in the fossil record seems to be associated with a change in the mammalian fauna, and the newer fauna usually includes indications of a moderately warm, moist climate in open (as opposed to densely forested) terrain. 5) We know that he was in control of fire, and further that fire seems to have been used for food preparation and in hunting large game. 6) Likewise, *Homo erectus* occupied caves near Peking, and the South African material was from what was once a cave too, but the others are from open sites. A fair guess of the habitations of *Homo erectus* might be that he frequented caves where they were available, but probably not as a permanent resident.

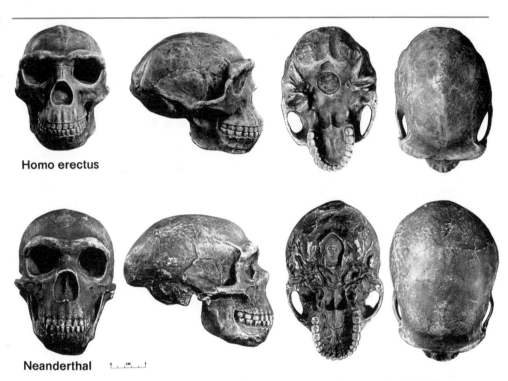

Homo erectus

Neanderthal

Figure 6–14. Comparison of four views of a *Homo erectus* with a Neanderthal skull cast.

Seasonal or even daily fluctuations in the available plant and animal food sources must have kept *Homo erectus* on the move. Large kills of many animals at one time, such as were possible by driving a herd over a cliff, might have provided occasional periods of abundance, as would seasonal variation in plant foods. Apart from these periods, the factor that determined much of the way of life of *Homo erectus* must have been his continual search for food.

NEANDERTHAL MAN

Figure 6–14 compares a skull of *Homo erectus* with one of the Neanderthal varieties. The most striking difference is in brain size. Previously, in speculating on the origin of the hominids, the suggestion was made that selection for intelligence must have begun to intensify at the time our ancestors came down from the trees. To the degree that brain size reflects intelligence, it appears that the intensity of natural selection increased as brain size increased. From *Australopithecus* to *Homo erectus*,

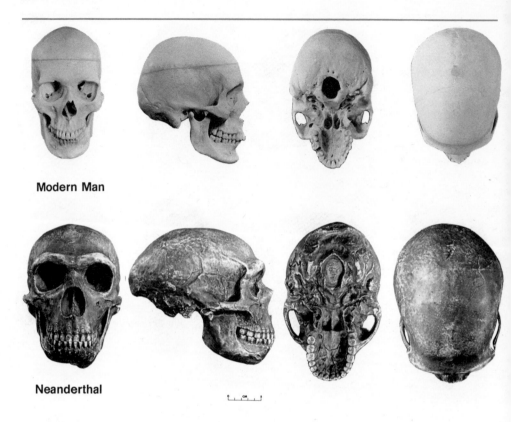

Modern Man

Neanderthal

Figure 6–15. Comparison of four views of a modern man skull with a Neanderthal skull cast.

assuming the former to be ancestral to the latter, average brain size increased by approximately 50 percent over a three- to four-million-year period. From *Homo erectus* to Neanderthal man there is an increase of approximately 60 percent over a period of a few hundred thousand years. Thus the major morphological difference between *Homo erectus* and Neanderthal man is brain size; the difference is substantial and apparently did not take long to develop.

Figure 6–15 illustrates a Neanderthal skull in comparison with modern man. From the frontal view, Neanderthal impresses one with its massive face, large eye orbits, rather low-lying forehead, and the lowered position of the skull's greatest breadth. Yet it lacks the crest and large projecting canine teeth that give so much distinction to the fierce appearance of the chimpanzee. From the side, one again notices the sloping forehead and chin, the large supraorbital ridge, and the somewhat more sharply angled contour to the back of the skull. But what is most striking about the profile view is the size of the brain. Neanderthal brain size is comparable to that of modern man; in fact, on the average, the Neanderthal brain may be slightly larger.

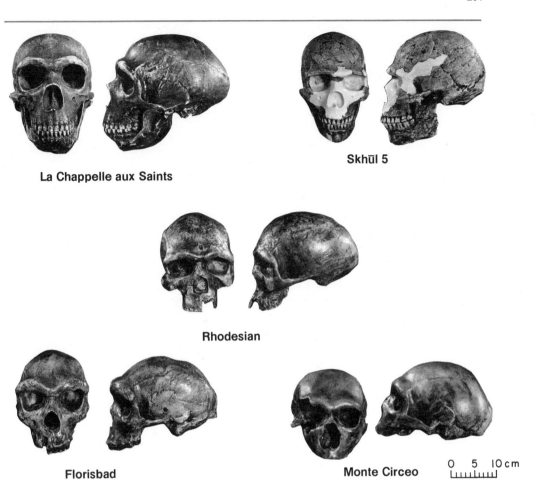

Figure 6–16. Variations in morphology among Neanderthal skulls.

Looked at from below, the differences between the Neanderthal and modern man are slight and difficult to discern. A closer inspection than is possible in an illustration would bring to light some differences in the size of the teeth, and, in larger samples, average differences in location and size of cusp pattern are also detectable.

As in the case of modern man, there is substantial variation within the category Neanderthal (see Figure 6–16). This is not at all surprising in view of the fact that Neanderthal remains have been found over a broad range in the Old World, including sites in Europe, North, South, and East Africa, the Near East, Russia, China, and Java (see Figure 6–17).* This distribution clearly indicates that Neanderthal

---

* Many investigators prefer to use the term *Neanderthal* to refer exclusively to the European discoveries.

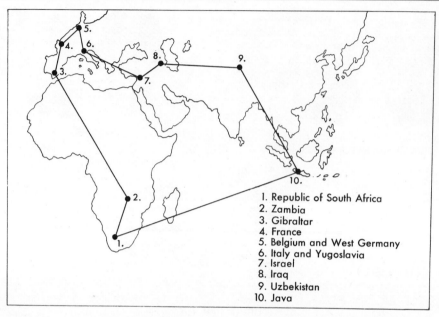

Figure 6–17. Distributional range of Neanderthals.

was able to adapt to a wide range of environmental contrasts, including, for the first time in the evolution of the hominids, extremely cold climatic conditions.

If one includes only the remains with well-established absolute dates from among the many Neanderthal discoveries, the period within which it lived is rather sharply defined as between 110,000 and 35,000 years ago (see Oakley, 1964). This is a period which, in the Northen Hemisphere, began during the warmest phase of the third (Riss-Würm) interglacial and ended during the early major advance of the Würm glaciation.

As mentioned earlier, the most effective way of extending our information about fossil forms is by means of inferences drawn from the material itself and, more particularly, from the relationship between the material and the context in which it is found. Until recently, it was a relatively simple matter to talk about the "way of life" of Neanderthal. Everyone "knew" that this was the hominid that lived around the Mediterranean toward the close of the Pleistocene, that made a characteristic inventory of implements known as the Mousterian industry (see Figure 6–18), and, since he lived during glacial times, his distinctive morphological features must have been due to the cold climate. During the last few years, it has become more and more obvious that such a view of Neanderthal is not correct. A new view is only now beginning to emerge, based on the following propositions: 1) The Mousterian industry is internally more diversified and complex than it was formerly thought to

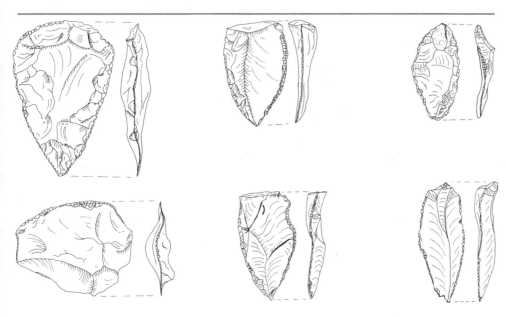

Figure 6–18.   Mousterian assemblage of stone implements. (After Frederick Wulsin)

be. 2) Likewise, the Neanderthal physical type is more heterogeneous than presumed, consisting of several presumably local, but recognizable, variants on the same morphological theme. 3) The distribution of the Mousterian industry is considerably more restricted than the distribution of Neanderthal variants. 4) Explaining "the Neanderthal physical type" as a product of an adaptation to cold climate is not only inadequate, but completely illogical. 5) Recognizing their broader distribution in space, the existence of variants through both space and time reopens the possibility that the form we have been calling Neanderthal man may be no more than the name for a stage through which our ancestors passed. 6) Perhaps not every Neanderthal population gave rise to modern man.

Clearly, then, the problem of extracting inferences from the contexts in which Neanderthal remains are found is not the straightforward one that it used to be. Mention should also be made here concerning two extreme points of view which have prevailed for a long time, each of which, in its own way, inevitably introduces distortion in any effort to draw inferences about either the Mousterian cultural assemblage or Neanderthal man. These are: 1) the very common presumption that Neanderthal must have hunted mammals similar to those that live in cold climates today, and 2) that Neanderthal's needs must always be thought of as having to be met in a cold climate.

These cautions should suffice as warning that we may not get very far in an attempt to draw broad generalizations about Neanderthal from contextual information, but keeping them in mind, it may be useful to subdivide Neanderthal's environment into two parts, the natural and the cultural, and to examine them briefly to see what more there is to conclude about Neanderthal man.

Two main factors should be kept clearly in view when considering Neanderthal man's natural environment. 1) It consisted, in the temperate latitudes, of sharp seasonal contrasts during a year, and over a longer period was affected in both hemispheres by shifting of the earth's climatic zones; and 2) the present-day mammalian fauna is regarded by paleontologists as an impoverished one, many species having become extinct during the last 10,000 years. In other words, one should not presume that everything was very much as it is now, only colder. From the distributional and temporal evidence we have already presented, we know that Neanderthal man lived under three major climatic conditions—temperate interglacial, temperate glacial, and subtropical to possibly tropical climates in Asia and Africa (see Table 6–4). Availability of food sources differed markedly in each zone, and this fact alone must have forced the inhabitants of each zone to adapt their ways of life accordingly, or to face inevitable extinction. Most certainly, plant food was more readily available (and present in substantial abundance) in the tropics, subtropics, and, for much of the year at least, in the temperate zone during the third interglacial than it ever was under the conditions in the fourth (Würm) glaciation in the north temperate latitudes. It is tempting, therefore, to conclude from this observation that, while the Neanderthalers of glacial conditions were hunters, the others were predominantly plant food gatherers. This may indeed be correct, but it would be a conclusion unjustified by the evidence. All that we can reasonably string together from the above is: 1) some Neanderthal peoples were living around glaciers; 2) edible plant life was scarce; and 3) large mammals were abundant. Therefore, the glacial Neanderthal people were hunters.

To say that the other Neanderthal groups were therefore not hunters, however, would not be justified. It is likely that the interglacial residents of the temperate zone were of necessity part-time hunters for the winter months, and thus could be expected to show greater contrast in their adaptations to the environment. The tropical and subtropical Neanderthalers could not be expected to show the same degree and kind of contrast due to climatic factors, simply because their environments lacked the sharp seasonal contrasts of winter and summer. What effect the northern glaciers had on the climatic conditions south of the equator is not clear. It may be that the corresponding change was reflected more in the decreasing amount of annual rainfall (from wet to dry) than in the decreasing average temperatures.

Undoubtedly other factors in the natural environment played important roles in the life of Neanderthal man—abundance and availability of marine resources, wind velocities, tides, currents, and many more. We have been able to consider only two (availability of land food sources and changing climatic conditions) that must have had an immediate effect on Neanderthal man's way of life, since they bear so directly on the basic survival requirements of nutrition and shelter. How, if at all, are these conditions of the natural environment related to the formal properties of Neanderthal

Table 6–4   Some Fossil Discoveries of Neanderthal Varieties

NAME	LOCATION	HEAD LENGTH IN MM.	HEAD BREADTH IN MM.	DATE* BEFORE PRESENT	CULTURAL ASSOCIATION
Neanderthal	Germany	201	147	35,000–70,000	?
Spy I	Belgium	200	146	35,000–70,000	Mousterian
Spy II	Belgium	198	150	35,000–70,000	Mousterian
La Chapelle	France	208	156	35,000–45,000	Mousterian
La Ferrassie	France	209	158	>35,000	Mousterian
La Quina	France	203	138	35,000–55,000	Mousterian
Gibraltar	Gibraltar	190	148	35,000–70,000	Levallois-Mousterian
Monte Circeo	Italy	204	156	35,000–70,000	Pontinian (Micro-Mousterian)
Shanidar	Iraq	207†	155–158†	60,000–96,000	East Mousterian
Skhūl and Tabun	Israel	192‡	144‡	35,000–70,000	Levallois-Mousterian
Saccopastore	Italy	181	142	60,000	?
Krapina	Yugoslavia	178	149	?	Mousterian
Teshik-Tash (child)	Uzbekistan	185	144	?	Mousterian
Rhodesian	Zambia	208	144	35,000–70,000	——
Saldanha	Republic of South Africa	200	144	40,000	Fauresmith
Solo I	Java	196	148	?	Ngandongian
Solo V	Java	220	147	?	Ngandongian
Solo VI	Java	192	144	?	Ngandongian
Solo IX	Java	201	150	?	Ngandongian
Solo X	Java	203	155	?	Ngandongian
Solo XI	Java	200	144	?	Ngandongian

* These dates have been compiled from Oakley (1964).

† These figures were kindly provided by Dr. T. D. Stewart, senior physical anthropologist at the Smithsonian Institution. Dr. Stewart emphasizes that the overall dimensions have been distorted because of slight warping of the skull vault.

‡ These measurements were obtained on the most complete skull (Skhūl V).

man? For a very long time, two major "kinds" of Neanderthal have been recognized in the temperate latitudes, corresponding to two of the three climatic zones already discussed: 1) a temperate interglacial variant, variously called a pre-Würm, interglacial, and progressive form, with less distinctive Neanderthal features and thus with an appearance more like that of modern man than other "more typical" Neanderthal variants; and 2) a temperate glacial variety long regarded as the "typical" Neanderthal and characterized by having all the distinctive Neanderthal features in their most fully developed form. Thus, the earlier forms look more like human beings of today than the later forms, a somewhat surprising situation that led to uncertainties in assessing interrelationships between Neanderthal man and modern man.

In addition to these two, a third variety is now recognized from the tropical and subtropical regions of the Old World, combining distinctive Neanderthal features with characteristics more commonly associated with modern man in ways which cannot properly be called intermediate, but rather different from both northern Neanderthals and modern man. There are considerably fewer remains that fall into this category, but on the basis of what is known, it appears that they were living in the south from about 70,000 to 30,000 years ago, thus overlapping in time the two northern Neanderthal groups.

The contextual information provided by factors in the natural environment in relationship to the distribution of Neanderthal remains tends to support some modest and tentative but important conclusions: 1) Three variants of Neanderthal are recognizable—an interglacial, a glacial, and a tropical form. 2) Each one lived in an area which contrasted with the other two in climatic conditions and available food supply. 3) Only among the glacial Neanderthalers is it possible to conclude with confidence that hunting was the primary basis of subsistence. 4) In the interglacial and tropical areas, it seems likely that plant food constituted a more important part of the diet.

Cultural evidence provides more contextual detail and allows us to conclude more about how the various Neanderthalers lived. Until recently, it was easy to present the information about the culture of Neanderthal man. It was simply the assemblage of artifacts that has been known as the Mousterian. Accompanying this simple view were several misleading assumptions that together made up an unfortunately distorted stereotype of Neanderthal as a hairy, stoop-shouldered, long-armed, bull-necked ape of a man, staring stupidly off into the golden future, walking with a bent-knee shuffle, and usually dragging his wife along by the hair. Other views, based on only a tiny bit more information, pictured the same kind of stereotype dwelling in a cave and wearing skin clothing. We do not know how hairy Neanderthal was, nor if he was bull-necked, nor how he may have transported his wife; but we do know he was not stoop-shouldered, not particularly long-armed, and he did not walk with his knees bent. He did live in caves and rock shelters (at least some Neanderthalers did for part of their lives), and he almost certainly wore skin clothing, but beyond that the picture becomes hazy. It will be helpful to deal with each Neanderthal group separately.

The glacial Neanderthalers are the ones that have been thought of as "typical" and have for a long time been known as the manufacturers of a characteristic assemblage of stone tools collectively referred to as the Mousterian industry. In recent years, however, it has become increasingly clear that the Mousterian is a label for several different assemblages of artifacts. Fundamentally, the Mousterian is characterized by side scrapers (*racloirs*), knifelike flake tools, and points that may or may not have been hafted, and thus may or may not have been spear points. Beyond this common core of implements, Mousterian sites vary in terms of the proportions in which these implements occur, and also with respect to whether they are found in deposits containing bifacial core tools, the so-called hand axes. Single caves have been discovered with stratified sites showing these contrasting assemblages of Mousterian implements overlying one another.

At our present stage of understanding, it is impossible to know what, if any, significance the proportional differences of flake tools imply concerning how glacial Neanderthal man lived. Perhaps the dichotomy of Mousterian into assemblages with hand axes and those without may be more readily significant; the two kinds of sites are found in different localities. The hand-axe Mousterian sites are along the coast of Europe, and the assemblages lacking hand axes are situated farther inland on rivercourses and at higher elevations. Also, each tends to be concentrated in time, the non-hand-axe assemblages being more frequently associated with the glacial Neanderthal than the ones with hand axes. This is not intended to imply that the glacial Neanderthalers did not have or use hand axes, but rather that the "typical Mousterian" tools were much more common.

The temperate interglacial Mousterians are difficult to characterize archaeologically. The Riss-Würm interglacial is a period of great complexity in its archaeological content, particularly in the north. Older archaeological traditions, such as the Acheulean hand-axe and Clactonian-Levalloisian flake-tool assemblage (see Figure 6–19), some with very broad distributions, are replaced by the Mousterian. As a result there are "hybrid" industries particularly early in the interglacial followed by a period in which both hand-axe Mousterian and "typical" Mousterian are found together, often in alternate layers of the same cave deposits. These two coexisting Mousterian traditions are gradually replaced by a predominance of the "typical" (that is, without hand axes) Mousterian during the early advance of the last glaciation, but the hand-axe Mousterian is not completely obliterated until the entire Mousterian complex is replaced by the blade-tool industries (Figure 6–20) of more recent times.

The temperate-zone Neanderthalers are known also to have buried their dead— at least some of their dead—and to have placed implements in the grave. This practice is found commonly among contemporary people, and seems to imply rather clearly the belief in a life after death, and thus belief in a spirit and supernatural world.

The tropical variant of Neanderthal has been found in association with archaeological assemblages known as Fauresmith in Africa (Figure 6–21) and the Ngandongian in Asia, the latter being a local variant of a more broadly distributed industry, the Sangiran.

In Africa, south of the Sahara, the Paleolithic sequence preceding the Fauresmith is similar to the European sequence. On both continents, there was a long and well-established sequence of Acheulean hand-axe assemblages. In general, this part of Africa lacked the Clactonian-Levalloisian flake-tool sequence as a distinct and separate development, as it occurs in the north, where the flake-core tool traditions were replaced by the variants of the Mousterian during Riss-Würm interglacial times. In Africa, the Acheulean developmental sequence, at what appears to be very nearly the same time, is replaced in the densely forested regions of central Africa by the Sangoan industry (Figure 6–22) consisting of picks, cleavers, and crude hand axes. Although no good fossil evidence exists concerning the morphology of the peoples that made the Sangoan, it appears clear that it is in fact a forest adaptation

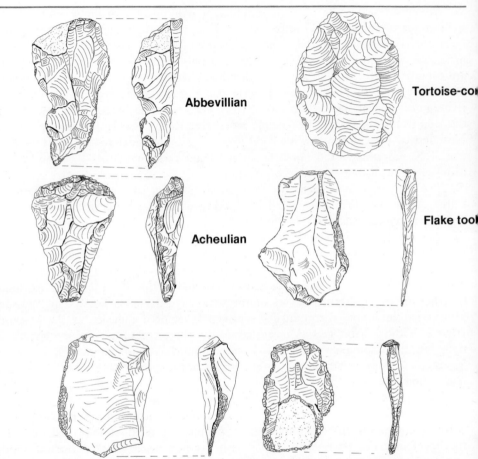

Figure 6–19. Top Left: Paleolithic hand axes. Top Right: Levalloisian tools. Bottom: Clactonian flake tools.

assembly existing contemporaneously with the Fauresmith, which is distributed in the more arid, open areas, grasslands, uplands, and the savannahs of South and East Africa. Fauresmith assemblages include hand axes which are distinctive in being small, often heart-shaped, and usually made from shale, a type of rock with distinctive fracturing qualities that are reflected in the steplike appearance of the hand-axe edges. If, as would seem reasonable, Fauresmith and Sangoan were made by the same species of hominid, then, in Africa, Neanderthal was distributed throughout the continent, having adapted to both open country and forested environments, for there exists good evidence of association between the Saldanha tropical Neanderthaloid and the Fauresmith archaeological assemblage. What is perhaps of even greater interest here is the fact that the ancestral sequence between tropical Neanderthals and

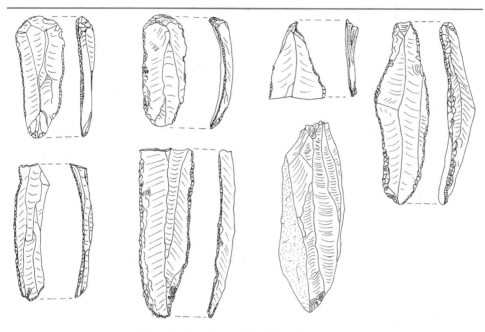

Figure 6–20. Upper Paleolithic blade tools.

modern inhabitants of the areas seems to be more readily accepted by human paleontologists, although in fact the actual evidence is no better than it is in Europe.

From Asia there is less evidence, and the background is quite different. Unlike Africa and Europe, the archaeological sequence throughout much of Asia does not contain the hand-axe sequences until recently. In some areas they do not appear until nearly the end of the European and African Paleolithic. Instead, there is the long period of development in the chopper-chopping tools. Although the name, chopper-chopping tools, may not seem to imply it, there are differences detectable between chopper tools on the one hand and chopping tools on the other. Choppers are usually made by taking a flattened, somewhat large pebble such as you might find along a stream bed or rocky beach, and then, depending on its size, either knocking off a piece at one side and then taking off smaller flakes to sharpen the exposed surface, or proceeding directly to sharpen one edge by knocking off small pieces. It is in many ways a scraper, but made by a core technique rather than a flake technique. The chopper has only one surface on which the flakes are removed, making it suitable as a tool for scraping hides, branches, or whatever. The chopping tool is generally larger and characteristically has both of its surfaces worked, producing a sharp, usually undulating, edge that is useful as a cutting and slicing implement; and since it is larger and heavier, it can also be thought of as serviceable in many of the same contexts as hand axes. Choppers and chopping tools are essentially core tools.

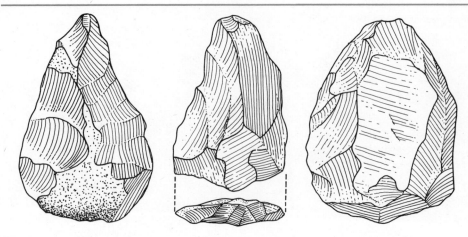

Figure 6–21. Fauresmith implements. (After Sonia Cole)

They constitute a developmental sequence of their own, broadly spread in space throughout eastern Asia, and deeply rooted in time, extending back at least as far as one-half million years.

The chopper-chopping tools may have been used by some Neanderthalers, but, in all likelihood, if they were, it would have been by one of the temperate variants. Figure 6–23 indicates the distribution of the chopper-chopping tools at the close of the Pleistocene. Indeed, recent fossil evidence from China indicates that Neanderthal man was living in Asia at the time, but as yet the evidence is either too fragmentary, the date unknown, or the associations with climatic and faunal evidence are too

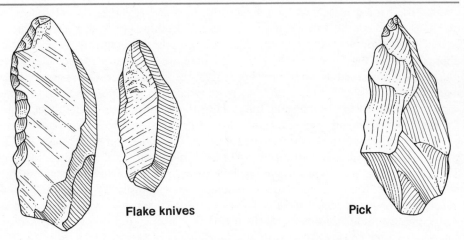

Flake knives **Pick**

Figure 6–22. Sangoan implements. (After Sonia Cole)

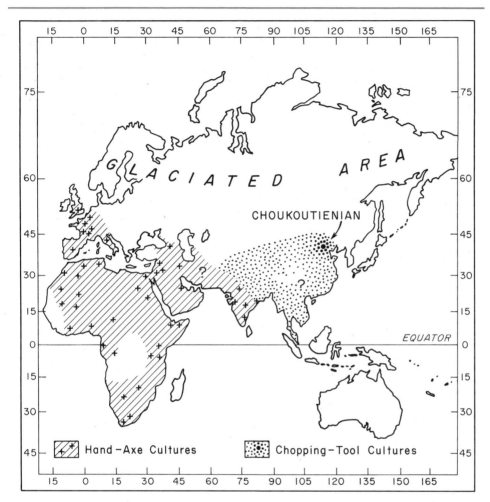

Figure 6–23. Distribution of chopper-chopping tools compared with the core-flake assemblages. (After H. L. Movius)

uncertain to be able to know if there is a distinguishable sequence of interglacial variants as in temperate zones farther west.

Our best evidence for Neanderthal man in tropical Asia was discovered in the Solo River valley in central Java and consists of the remains of several individuals. This Asian form of the tropical Neanderthal is morphologically very similar to the African and appears in an archaeological context of a rather poorly defined flake-tool industry consisting of points, scrapers, rounded stones possibly used as bolas stones, together with antlers that show some indication of having been put to use as pickaxes. This assemblage, known as the Ngandongian, was found in a deposit containing the remains of several forms of mammals now extinct in Java, but probably meat never was as abundant and important as a food basis as in temperate-zone glacial times. Apart from the meagerness of the archaeological and faunal record, one additional difficulty arises from the fact that the skeletal remains are only indirectly associated with the implements, both having been found in the same layer and in the same general area, but not in direct association.

Combining all lines of evidence converging on Neanderthal, some general inferences seem reasonable in summarizing the material considered so far. 1) Neanderthal is the broad name given to various hominid forms that lived in the Old World from at least as early as third interglacial and to at least as recently as fourth glaciation times. 2) Three variants of the broad category are detectable—glacial temperate, interglacial temperate, and tropical to subtropical. 3) These variants made a variety of implements, some assemblages appearing essentially *de novo* with Neanderthal man, such as the Mousterian, which appears to be a cold-climate hunting industry, others being continuations of old traditions begun much earlier. 4) No evidence for deliberate shelter habitation exists outside the temperate zone; within that zone Neanderthal man occupied rock shelters and caves, sometimes apparently for long enough periods to be considered at least semisedentary, a condition presumably made possible by the abundant game or perhaps demanded by the cold weather. 5) Some, and perhaps all, buried their dead and, to the degree that this implies it, believed in an afterlife.

By way of general summary, it should be emphasized that Neanderthal is highly varied, broadly distributed, and deeply rooted in time. He adapted to several environments, manufactured a variety of implements, and thus, presumably, lived in different cultural contexts.

Is Neanderthal man an ancestor of ours? No one knows for certain, though different opinions are often stated as if everyone knew for certain. The source of disagreement consists of the modern man fossils alleged to be geologically older than Neanderthal man. Table 6–5 lists most of this evidence. At first, the evidence appears to be impressive, but careful reevaluation of the material during the last twenty years has caused some drastic revision.

No one takes the first five discoveries as serious contenders in the fossil record, and few if any consider Kanam as representative of early Pleistocene modern man. It is hard to understand why the discovery at Denise attracted as much interest as it did. Several authorities during the latter part of the nineteenth century and the first two decades of this century studied and restudied this material, and all concluded that it was perhaps early Pleistocene. What is remarkable, however, is that this conclusion was repeatedly reached even though the material is only partly fossilized and there is some evidence that it might have been a deliberate burial.

Moulin-Quinon seems to have been a fraud. Boucher de Perthes had done a great deal of important archaeological work in France. Indeed, he is responsible more than anyone else for providing the earliest cultural evidence through archaeological remains that man had lived in Europe in early Pleistocene times. He wanted very badly to discover fossil skeletal evidence of the men that were making the stone tools he had been discovering, and apparently someone deliberately provided him with

Table 6–5   Fossils Used as Evidence for Modern Man's Great Antiquity

NAME	DISCOVERY	MATERIALS DISCOVERED	STATUS AT PRESENT
1. Denise	1844 France	Several skull fragments.	Discounted.
2. Moulin-Quinon	1863 France	Mandible.	Some evidence that this may have been a deliberate fraud. Discounted.
3. Bury St. Edmunds	1882 England	Skull fragment.	Discounted (see text).
4. Galley Hill	1888 England	Skull and parts of post-cranial skeleton.	Regarded as recent burial.
5. Piltdown	1912 England	Skull and jaw fragments.	Deliberate hoax.
6. Mt. Carmel	1929–1934 Israel	Remains of several individuals.	In dispute (see text).
7. Kanam	1932 Kenya	Mandible.	Dating uncertain, relationships uncertain.
8. Swanscombe	1935, 1936, 1955 England	Two parietals and one occipital.	In dispute. Tendency to include with temperate third interglacial Neanderthals (see text).
9. Fontechevade	1947 France	Two parietals and two frontals.	In dispute.

the evidence by burying it and making him think he had discovered it.

Three of the British discoveries, Bury St. Edmunds, Galley Hill, and Piltdown, have been removed largely through the persistent efforts of Kenneth Oakley and his collaborators. All three had been suspected by some experts as being more recent, and all were found to be recent by fluorine analysis.

The Bury St. Edmunds skull fragment may have been given greater significance than it deserved when it was discovered in 1882 in Suffolk. At that time fossils, and particularly human fossils, were scarce, and their importance was easily overemphasized. Looking back, it is clear that the remains were virtually useless for scientific purposes. The Bury St. Edmunds remains were found in association with an Acheulean archaeological assemblage; these are cultural remains that go back to second interglacial (Mindel-Riss) times. Considering these two facts is not, however, sufficient evidence of great antiquity. The discovery site was not examined by a competent geologist or paleontologist; the association of the bones with the Acheulean remains is not certain; the date of the Acheulean remains at this site has not been established (and the Acheulean lasted through the Pleistocene in some parts of the world); and, finally, the skeletal fragment is badly broken.

The story of Piltdown is widely known. It consisted of fragments of an ape jaw, an ape canine, and large fragments of the parietals, the occipital, and the nasal bone of a modern man. These had been stained and filed so that on reconstruction they could be made to fit together, forming the most peculiar anatomical assembly of modern-man-modern-ape characteristics ever known. Reinvestigation in 1950 and again in 1953 revealed it to be a deliberate hoax—made, buried, and probably discovered with the purpose of confounding the experts.

Reinvestigation of the Galley Hill site brought to light the evidence that this discovery, originally estimated as early Pleistocene in date, was in fact a recent burial probably no more than a few thousand years old.

The Kanam and Kanjera discoveries, reported in 1932 by L. S. B. Leakey, consisted of a fragmentary jaw (Kanam) and the fragmentary remains of the skulls of three individuals (Kanjera). The Kanjera materials do not differ from modern man. The Kanam jaw has a pathological growth on the chin region which obscures somewhat its morphological significance and relationships. Leakey claimed early Pleistocene antiquity for Kanam, but an attempt to reexamine the location for geological factors bearing on the antiquity of these remains was frustrated when the original site could not be definitely located. Leakey continued to hold to the view that Kanam was early modern man and claimed to have additional fossil evidence to support his conviction. This additional material is part of the extremely interesting material he and his associates discovered in Olduvai Gorge in East Africa.

The evidence for the great antiquity of modern man, so abundant up to 1940, has declined, or in fact if one ignores the East African material for the time being, has disappeared. There remains, however, the consideration of the Swanscombe, Fontechevade, and Mt. Carmel discoveries.

Swanscombe, as you will note from the table, consists of only three bones. Remarkably, they fit together reasonably well, even though they were discovered over a twenty-year period. The interpretation of this material has been based almost entirely on a careful investigation of the first two discoveries by a special committee established in the 1930s to study the Swanscombe remains. The committee reported (Clark, et al., 1938) that except for the unusual thickness of the bones, they did not differ in any important respect from those of modern man. They likewise affirmed that Swanscombe was second interglacial. Thus, here was evidence of modern man between the Mindel and Riss glaciations. Since then, a reinvestigation (Ovey, 1964) of the fossil material and the site has directed attention to the similarities between Swanscombe and some Riss-Würm interglacial fossil hominids. This has tended to emphasize the significance of Swanscombe as evidence for the great antiquity of modern man, but it continues to be a problem, since repeated investigations have continued to reaffirm its date as Mindel-Riss interglacial.

The Fontechevade discovery was made in 1947 in France in the province of Charenté. The fossil skeletal material consists of a few bones from the tops of the skulls of two individuals; no facial bones have been found. In form, the skulls are like those of Swanscombe. The interesting thing about this discovery is the fact that the remains were found beneath archaeological materials associated elsewhere with Neanderthal. Thus it appears that the more modern form precedes Neanderthal and thereby excludes Neanderthal from our ancestry. The remains are, however, fragmentary, and the interpretation has been questioned (Brace, 1964).

A similar issue was raised as a result of the Mt. Carmel discoveries in Israel. These were made in two caves, Tabun and Skhūl, between 1929 and 1934. Between them the caves yielded an extraordinary amount of fossil material. An almost complete skeleton, a lower jaw, and a few other postcranial fragments were discovered in Tabun, and Skhūl yielded the remains of ten individuals, some represented by almost complete skeletal remains, others by a few fragments.

Though the material is highly varied in form, it is basically like several other Neanderthal discoveries. The variability, however, has been bothersome, since some of the individuals show characteristics remarkably like modern man, and to those who maintain that Neanderthal man could not be in our ancestry, this is somewhat embarrassing. The remains were found together in association with the same kind of archaeological material, and apparently the two caves were occupied at the same or nearly the same time. From this it appears that the remains represent a variety of the Neanderthal hominid.

The evidence for the great antiquity of the present type of man is not very conclusive, or perhaps it might be better to say, is not as convincing now as it was thirty years ago. It is, however, a crucial question for the study of human evolution.

In my opinion Neanderthal man represents a stage in our ancestry. Moreover, I believe that *Homo erectus* is ancestral to Neanderthal and descended from *Australopithecus*. I base my opinion mostly on the archaeological record which may be seen as a continuous development from pebble tools to space laboratories. New discoveries may eventually settle the issue.

MAJOR POINTS IN CHAPTER 6

1. In tracing the evolution of man, there are two sources of evidence to consider: the archaeological and paleontological records.
2. The distinctive morphological features of the hominids are erect posture and bipedal locomotion.
3. The origin of the hominids is not known with certainty.
4. *Australopithecus* is the earliest readily recognizable hominid genus.
5. The *Australopithecus* genus is morphologically diverse, distributed throughout the tropics of the Old World, and lived for over five million years.
6. *Homo erectus* is the earliest species of our genus. Members of the species have been found in both temperate and tropical zones in the Old World from a time period lasting at least one-half million years.
7. Neanderthal man is the name of a highly varied group of fossils which probably represent the earliest members of our species.

REFERENCES AND SUGGESTIONS FOR ADDITIONAL READING

BOULE, M., AND H. V. VALLOIS
  1957 *Fossil men.* Translated by Michael Bullock. New York: Dryden Press.
BRACE, C. LORING
  1964 The fate of the "classic" Neanderthals: A consideration of hominid catastrophism. *Current Anthropology* 5:3–43.
  1967 *The stages of human evolution.* Englewood Cliffs, N.J.: Prentice-Hall.
BRACE, C. LORING, AND M. F. ASHLEY MONTAGU
  1965 *Man's evolution: An introduction to physical anthropology.* New York: Macmillan.
BROOM, R., AND G. W. H. SCHEPERS
  1946 *The South African fossil ape-men: The australopithecinae.* Transvaal Museum Memoir no. 2. Pretoria, South Africa: Transvaal Museum.
BUETTNER-JANUSCH, JOHN
  1966 *Origins of man: Physical anthropology.* New York: John Wiley and Sons.
CLARK, W. E. LE GROS
  1964 *The fossil evidence for human evolution.* 2d rev. ed. Chicago: University of Chicago Press.
  1967 *Man-apes or ape-men?: The story of discoveries in Africa.* New York: Holt, Rinehart, and Winston.
CLARK, W. E. LE GROS, ET AL.
  1938 Report of the Swanscombe committee. *Journal of the Royal Anthropological Institute* 68:17–98.
COMAS, JUAN
  1960 *Manual of physical anthropology.* Rev. and enl. English ed. Springfield, Ill.: Charles C Thomas.
COON, CARLETON S.
  1962 *The origin of races.* New York: Alfred A. Knopf.
DART, RAYMOND A.
  1925 *Australopithecus africanus:* the man-ape of South Africa. *Nature* 115:195–199.
  1957 The Makapansgat australopithecine Osteodontokeratic culture. In *Proceedings of the Third Pan-African Congress on Prehistory,* pp. 161–171.
DART, R. A., AND D. CRAIG
  1959 *Adventures with the missing link.* New York: Harper.
DAY, MICHAEL H.
  1965 *Guide to fossil man: A handbook of human paleontology.* London: Cassell.
DUBOIS, EUGENE
  1894 Pithecanthropus erectus, *eine menschenähnliche Übergansform aus Java.* Batavia: Landesdruckerei.
EMILIANI, CESARE
  1968 The Pleistocene epoch and the evolution of man. *Current Anthropology* 9:27–47.
GREENE, D. L.
  1973 Gorilla dental sexual dimorphism and early hominid taxonomy. In *Primate craniofacial biology,* ed. M. R. Zingeser. Vol. 3, IVth International Primatology Congress Symposia. Proceedings. Basel: S. Karger.

HARRISON, RICHARD J., AND W. MONTAGNA
  1969 *Man.* New York: Appleton-Century-Crofts.
HEMMER, H.
  1969 A new view of the evolution of man. *Current Anthropology* 10:179–180.
HOOTON, EARNEST ALBERT
  1947 *Up from the ape.* Rev. ed. New York: Macmillan.
HOWELL, F. CLARK
  1959 The Villafranchian and human origins. *Science* 130:831–844.
  1960 European and Northwest African Middle Pleistocene hominids. *Current Anthropology* 1:195–232.
HOWELL, F. CLARK, AND THE EDITORS OF LIFE
  1965 *Early man.* New York: Time, Inc.
HOWELLS, WILLIAM W.
  1966 *Homo erectus. Scientific American* 215, November, pp. 46–53.
KENYON, KATHLEEN M.
  1957 *Beginning in archaeology.* Rev. ed. New York: F. A. Praeger.
KROEBER, A. L.
  1948 *Anthropology: Race, language, culture, psychology, prehistory.* Rev. ed. New York: Harcourt, Brace, and World.
LAUGHLIN, W. S., AND R. H. OSBORNE, EDS.
  1967 *Human variation and origins: Readings from* Scientific American. San Francisco: W. H. Freeman.
LEAKEY, L. S. B.
  1965 *Olduvai Gorge, 1951–1961* (vol. 1). London: Cambridge University Press.
LEAKEY, R. E. F., J. M. MUNGAI, AND A. C. WALKER
  1971 New australopithecines from east Rudolf, Kenya. *American Journal of Physical Anthropology* 35:175–186.
  1972 New australopithecines from east Rudolf, Kenya (II). *American Journal of Physical Anthropology* 36:235–252.
MAYR, ERNST
  1950 Taxonomic categories in fossil hominids. *Cold Spring Harbor Symposia on Quantitative Biology* 15:109–118.
MONTAGU, M. F. ASHLEY
  1960 *An introduction to physical anthropology.* 3d ed. Springfield, Ill.: Charles C Thomas.
OAKLEY, KENNETH P.
  1964 *Frameworks for dating fossil man.* Chicago: Aldine.
OVEY, C. D., ED.
  1964 The Swanscombe skull. Royal Anthropological Institute, *Occasional Papers,* no. 20.
SIMONS, ELWYN L.
  1963 Some fallacies in the study of hominid phylogeny. *Science* 141:879–889.
SPAULDING, ALBERT C.
  1960 The dimensions of archaeology. In *Essays in the science of culture in honor of Leslie A. White,* ed. G. E. Dole and R. L. Carneiro. New York: Thomas Y. Crowell.

TAX, SOL, ED.

1960 *The evolution of man: Man, culture, and society.* Vol. 2 of *Evolution after Darwin.* Chicago: University of Chicago Press.

TOBIAS, PHILIP V.

1967 *Olduvai Gorge* (vol. 2): *The cranium and maxillary dentition of* Australopithecus (Zinjanthropus) boisei. London: Cambridge University Press.

WASHBURN, SHERWOOD L.

1960 Tools and human evolution. *Scientific American* 203, September, pp. 62–75.

PART III HUMAN HETEROGRAPHY

HUMAN BEINGS ARE ALIKE; HUMAN BEINGS ARE NOT ALIKE. Both propositions are correct. Human heterography* attempts to describe, to explain, and to interpret the significance of the ways in which we are alike and dissimilar in our biological features. In physical anthropology very little attention has been given to similarities; for this reason the discussion focuses on human variability.

A comparison of the basic units and fundamental divisions of human heterography with human paleontology reveals some unexpected similarities. The primary units of description in human paleontology are the fossils, or, more precisely, the traits that are used to compare them to one another. Explanation of paleontological material requires more than just information on the formal variations of the traits; it calls for the recovery of data on time, space, and context as well. Except for spatial factors, these latter dimensions tend to be ignored in most discussions of contemporary human variation, but they are nevertheless important factors bearing on the ways in which we view, and the manner in which we interpret, the facts of man's variation. To be sure, formal variations and their distributions are of primary importance, but the other dimensions are relevant, and notice of their significance should be taken when considering the various ways in which human heterographic variations have been viewed and grouped.

The primary dimension of interest to both paleontology and heterography is that of form. Much more data on formal variation are available for heterographic analysis, and this offers a more solid empirical basis for the testing of hypotheses and the formulation of generalizations or theories. Details of function, context, and distribution can, for example, be observed directly. This abundance of information might lead one to suspect that heterographic analyses must be considerably advanced over those in paleontology; that is, theories should be more fully developed, and there should be substantially more agreement on basic issues, concepts, and principles. Yet, what one actually finds is an almost complete lack of theory, and, in place of agreement, a sea of confusion. This situation has come about because: 1) the study of

---

* According to the *American Heritage Dictionary of the English Language* (1969), this word has two prior meanings. The word is used to designate inconsistent or unconventional spelling. It is inconceivable that its use here would ever be confused with its prior uses.

human variation is inextricably woven together with the concept and study of race; 2) race is an ambiguous concept, and thinking on the subject often begins with incorrect assumptions which can only lead to error, however logical the route; and 3) even scientists approach the subject with strong emotional and moral commitments, with the result that disorder and lack of direction occur in place of ordered, systematic, and dispassionate analyses. The situation does not come about because of a lack of data or a lack of interest; there is perhaps too much of both. The crucial need at the moment is to recognize how ignorant and confused we are of the processes reflected by the facts of human variation.

Ideally, we might find that the study of human variation would be served best if we were able to approach it with no preconceptions, no idea of how variable mankind is, no idea of how the variation is distributed, and no idea of what the variation and its distribution imply. For example, we "know" that skin color ranges from very dark to very light, that dark skin color is African, or, if we have looked more carefully, equatorial, and that light skin color is temperate in its distribution. Moreover, we "know" that, for the most part, dark skin color is associated with prognathism, kinky hair, thick lips, and broad noses, whereas light skin is found in association with contrasting characteristics. We "know" that these traits identify races, and we think, with confidence, that common membership within a race implies a close historical connection between peoples and a shared phylogenetic past. These are common beliefs and, of course, there are many others, most of them held with such conviction that they are considered obvious or self-evident. For this reason, it is probably unrealistic to ask that the beliefs be suspended. It would be, for example, like asking many seventeenth-century New Englanders to question their attitudes and beliefs about witches. For the present, however—and this may be too much—it would be helpful if one could at least question the belief that these races are fixed, eternal, and real things. If they are anything at all, races are fundamentally clusters of characteristics brought together through normal evolutionary processes. The individual traits have emerged at different times as the products of different evolutionary factors operating at varying intensities. Moreover, these processes of evolution are continually changing, forcing traits that exist now to change in form and frequency. From the standpoint of evolution, a race, if it is anything, is a transitory thing, and what it implies about its members, the traits that distinguish it from others, and its relationship to other races is not at all clear. It may indeed be that it implies nothing about these things. But these are problems that will be taken up in Chapter 9.

To obviate some of the difficulties inherent in most discussions of human variation, the basic material on human heterography is presented in as objective a manner as possible. The data are presented neither to justify a particular classification nor to support one point of view. The discussion is centered first on traits of unknown inheritance which have been used extensively by physical anthropologists to describe man's variation, and then secondly on traits of known inheritance. In both instances some consideration is given to the range of variation in the trait's expression and how this is distributed. In the case of traits of known inheritance, attention is also given the matter of how the trait is inherited. The discussion is primarily descriptive, but along the way some attention is given to explanations that have been proposed. Chapter 9 considers the final step in attempting to derive significance from the range and distribution of human variation.

Before beginning the discussion of specific ways in which human beings vary, it should be emphasized that perhaps the most extraordinary thing about the human species is how alike all of its members are. Consider that man's distribution is global and that he occupies many sharply contrasting environments, and it is possible to appreciate more clearly the extraordinary fact that man is one species only. No other animal even approximates a rival to man in this respect. Man extends his adaptive range primarily by nongenetic means (by culture), and in this way he has been able to retain biological homogeneity while adapting to ecological heterogeneity.

In the past few chapters, attention has been given to filling in some background and reviewing the highlights of the fossil record of human evolution and how it has been interpreted. In the next three chapters the general area of human variation, or, as identified earlier, human heterography, will be the center of interest.

REFERENCES AND SUGGESTIONS FOR ADDITIONAL READING

Coon, Carleton S., with Edward E. Hunt, Jr.
  1965 *The living races of man.* New York: Alfred A. Knopf.
Count, Earl W., ed.
  1950 *This is race: An anthology selected from the international literature on the races of man.* New York: Henry Schuman.
Downs, James F., and H. K. Bleibtreu
  1969 *Human variation: An introduction to physical anthropology.* Beverly Hills, Calif.: Glencoe Press.
Garn, Stanley M.
  1971 *Human races.* 3d ed. Springfield, Ill.: Charles C Thomas.
Kelso, A. J.
  1967 The concept of race. *Improving College and University Teaching* 15:95–97.
Livingstone, Frank B.
  1962 On the non-existence of human races (with comment by Theodosius Dobzhansky). *Current Anthropology* 3:279–281.
Mead, Margaret, Theodosius Dobzhansky, Ethel Tobach, and Robert Light, eds.
  1968 *Science and the concept of race.* New York: Columbia University Press.
Montagu, Ashley, ed.
  1964 *The concept of race.* New York: Free Press.

7 Human Heterography and Morphological Variation: Traits of Unknown Inheritance

INTRODUCTION

A literal interpretation of the title of this chapter might lead one to believe that it will not deal with inherited characteristics, but will examine the ways in which human groups vary. Since man varies in an infinite number of ways, obviously it is impossible to treat the subject comprehensively; a choice must be made at the outset on the kinds of traits to be considered. Basing our decision largely on tradition, and thereby including the ways in which physical anthropologists usually describe human variation, some illustrations of each of the following kinds of characteristics will be considered: physical, physiological, and developmental; a very brief comment on psychological characteristics will conclude the chapter.

PHYSICAL CHARACTERISTICS

Since human groups vary widely in their physical characteristics, a further choice must be made at this point on the traits that are to be considered. Attention will be given to the following measurements, indexes, and observations: 1) stature and weight; 2) head breadth, head length, and cephalic index; 3) nose length, nose breadth, and nasal index; 4) skin color; 5) hair form; and 6) distinctive morphological characteristics of restricted distribution. The discussion of the first three is based largely on a statistical analysis of the anthropometric data on approximately three hundred samples of adult non-European males reported in Biasutti (1959). The data on European populations have been drawn from Martin and Saller (1955–1966). This represents a deliberate attempt to report anthropometric data in a form similar to that used for genetic characteristics in the next chapter. The discussion on the rest of the traits is less detailed.

Before beginning a discussion of the traits, it may be useful to distinguish measurements, indexes, and observations. A *measurement* represents numerically the expression of a trait in terms of an independent scale of fixed intervals. Thus, stature, weight, head length and breadth, and nose length and breadth can be measured, that is, expressed numerically in terms of independent scales (inches, pounds, centimeters,

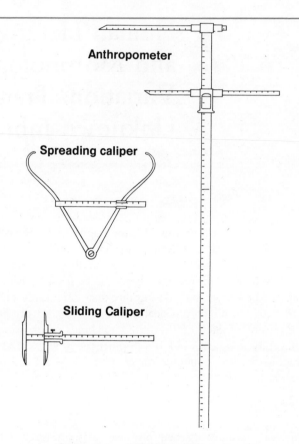

Anthropometer

Spreading caliper

Sliding Caliper

Figure 7–1.   Anthropometric equipment.

etc.). Measured—or, as they are more commonly called, quantitatively variable—traits provide some of the most interesting questions in human heterography, but investigation of them has been hampered by the absence of information about how they are inherited. There are no proved, well-documented, readily accepted hypotheses on the mode of inheritance of quantitative traits in man. There exists a general theory which has been applied with some success to the hereditary variations of quantitative traits in some lower organisms. For the most part, it presumes that such traits are controlled by several loci occupied by genes with equal and additive effects. The theory is interesting and its applications fascinating, but it must remain a theory until it can be related in a clearer way to the better-established theory of gene action. Genes act to produce polypeptide chains, and, so far as we know, that is all that genes do; how this fits in with the theory of the inheritance of quantitative traits is not at all certain at the present time. Relating these concepts may be the next outstanding advance in the science of genetics. (Figure 7–1 shows some of the instruments used to measure man's physical characteristics.)

Indexes express numerically the proportional relationships between two or more measurements. The cephalic index, for example, expresses as a percentage the relationship between head length and head breadth, and the nasal index expresses the proportional relationship between nose length and nose breadth. Indexes are useful in describing human variation, in that they express relative differences. All measurements reflect gross body size; indexes do not. A person with a large head can have the same cephalic index as one with a small head, if head length and head breadth are in the same proportions.

Observations record qualitative variation; thus any particular observation is classified into a category. For example, observations of variation in hair form are usually classified into one of the following categories: straight, low wave, wavy, curly, tightly curled, kinky, and peppercorn. This is an elaborate illustration; commonly a trait will be noted simply as present or absent. The distinction between measurements and observations is due, at least in part, to the status of the techniques of measurement. Skin color, for example, has for many years been presented in the form of observational data. Now, with the development of reflectometers, it may be measured in terms of light reflectance units. Thus, what today may be regarded as a characteristic of several qualities may, as our measurement skills improve, be measurable in quantitative terms tomorrow. The primary purpose of scientific instruments is to assist the investigator in quantifying his experience.

Stature and Weight

Average variation in height in normal males ranges from 140 cm. to 185 cm. The geographical distribution of this variation is by no means random. Table 7–1 shows how this variation is distributed throughout the major areas of the world.

Table 7–1   Mean Stature and Standard Deviation by Major Areas of the World*

AREA	MEAN STATURE CM.	STANDARD DEVIATION CM.	NUMBER OF SAMPLES
1. Africa	164.9	7.24	115
2. Asia	163.0	4.13	74
3. Europe	167.2	3.00	149
4. Oceania	167.3	5.24	26
5. American Indians	163.7	5.79	55

* The mean is, of course, the average, and the values given here have been arrived at after weighting for sample size. Thus a sample of ten persons contributes one-tenth what a sample of one hundred does in calculating the mean. The standard deviation is a figure that provides information about variability in the population; the larger the standard deviation, the greater the variability. Except for Europe, these data have been compiled from Biasutti (1959) and weighted for sample size. The figures for Europe have been estimated from a graph of data obtained from Martin and Saller (1955–1966).

In Europe, the second-tallest average stature is combined with a comparatively small range of variability. The way in which the variation is distributed in Europe is clearly not random, but also it fails to follow any clear and simple pattern. Both the tallest and the shortest average statures occur in the north: the shortest Europeans are the Lapps of northern Sweden, Norway, and Finland; the tallest Europeans are the non-Lapp populations of these same countries. In the central areas, intermediate-to-tall statures may be found, whereas in the south, average statures do not vary much from the mean for the Continent.

In Asia the distribution is again a complex one and is characterized by a wider range of variation as well as the lowest overall mean. An inspection of the distribution reveals no clear north-south gradient in stature; the shortest Asian populations are found at both extremes (see Table 7–2). The significant feature of the distribution is that from west to east stature shows a gradual decline. The correlation† between longitude and stature (−.51) for these populations is highly significant.

Table 7–2   Mean Stature Among Asian Populations*

AREA	MEAN STATURE CM.	STANDARD DEVIATION CM.	NUMBER OF SAMPLES
1. Malay Peninsula and Archipelago	155.62	3.92	16
2. North Asia	158.82	2.32	14
3. Vedda	159.35	2.26	4
4. Southeast Asia	160.32	3.10	17
5. India, Castes	162.67	2.13	3
6. Far East	162.97	1.98	8
7. Central Asia	164.30	2.14	9
8. India, Various Locations	164.45	3.53	13
9. Iran, Armenia, Assyria	165.28	2.51	11
10. Asia Minor	167.26	1.80	9

* These data have been compiled from Biasutti (1959) and weighted for sample size.

The tallest and the shortest human populations in Africa reside within a zone marked approximately by the equator and 10° north latitude. Although it may appear from Table 7–3 that the Bushmen are the shortest Africans, in fact the Pygmies scattered throughout the northern Bantu peoples of central equatorial

---

† Correlation coefficients range from −1 to +1. Negative correlations imply that as one variable (stature, for example) increases, the other decreases. Positive correlation coefficients imply that as one thing increases, so does another. Values at or near zero mean that one variable changes independently of changes in the other. Actually another judgment needs to be made in evaluating a correlation coefficient. However, understanding this is beyond the scope of this book. For those interested, the coefficients have been tested for significance and the results taken into account in the discussion.

Africa fall considerably under the average Bushman stature with mean values commonly below 150 cm. Adjusting for this clustering of extremes near the equator and looking at the entire continent, there is a significant correlation (.22) between stature and latitude. Thus, average stature increases as one moves either north or south from the equator. An inspection of the distribution reveals that the rate at which this occurs is more rapid to the north.

Table 7–3   Mean Stature Among African Populations*

AREA	MEAN STATURE CM.	STANDARD DEVIATION CM.	NUMBER OF SAMPLES
1. South Africa (Bushmen, Hottentots)	157.93	2.81	4
2. Northern Bantu (Equatorial)	161.95	7.40	42
3. Madagascar and Indian Ocean	164.55	1.94	4
4. North Africa	166.64	3.90	14
5. East Africa	168.17	2.70	26
6. Sahara	168.64	3.21	9
7. Central Bantu	168.75	2.35	11
8. West Africa	169.07	3.65	30
9. East Sudan	173.76	5.85	14

* These data have been compiled from Biasutti (1959) and weighted for sample size.

The data from Oceania are fragmentary (see Table 7–4), but they suggest that, in contrast to the distribution in Asia, there is among Pacific populations an *increase* in average stature from west to east. The correlation between stature and longitude in these Pacific groups is .54. The tallest peoples are the Samoans, Tahitians, Hawaiians, and Marquesans of the eastern Pacific, and the shortest are the Pygmy groups of New Guinea in the west. Moreover, there is a correlation between stature and latitude (.57) in Oceania, indicating that as distance (north or south) from the equator increases, average stature likewise increases.

Table 7–4   Mean Stature Among Pacific Populations†

AREA	MEAN STATURE CM.	STANDARD DEVIATION CM.	NUMBER OF SAMPLES
1. New Guinea and Melanesia	156.69	6.83	8
2. Australia	168.45	2.24	8
3. Polynesia and Micronesia	169.41	3.70	11

† These data have been compiled from Biasutti (1959) and weighted for sample size.

Although, once again, the data are not too extensive among the Indians of North and South America, a correlation between stature and latitude appears (.52) like that found in the Pacific populations. With the conspicuous exception of the Eskimos, who are similar in stature to other circumpolar peoples, populations of shorter American Indians cluster around the equator within a zone roughly 20° wide from 10° north to 10° south latitude (see Table 7–5). Outside of this zone average statures increase to maximum values in both the north and south temperate latitudes.

Discounting for the moment the complex European situation (and it will be necessary to do this regularly), it is clear from the above that the distribution of stature over each of the major habitation zones is distinctive. In Asia, stature is correlated with longitude; in Africa and North and South America with latitude; and in the Pacific with both longitude and latitude. Apart from this, one other general observation appears justified: equatorial zones include extremes in average stature.

Table 7–5   Mean Stature Among American Indian Populations*

AREA	MEAN STATURE CM.	STANDARD DEVIATION CM.	NUMBER OF SAMPLES
1. Central America	159.06	4.15	10
2. Andes	159.50	6.52	4
3. Eskimo	162.80	3.04	4
4. Amazon Basin	163.39	4.45	17
5. Patagonia and Tierra del Fuego	163.93	8.38	7
6. Northwest Coast	163.99	3.57	10
7. Plains and Prairie (North America)	167.50	2.88	4
8. Southwest United States	168.87	3.80	3
9. Eastern United States	171.45	1.06	4

*These data have been compiled from Biasutti (1959) and, with the exception of the Eastern United States, where a raw mean and standard deviation are used, are weighted for sample size.

Stature is a complex trait, the resultant of a variety of environmental forces acting upon an underlying genetic structure. To what extent is stature inherited? That is, to what extent is it determined by genes? If one asks this question in reference to any particular individual, there is no way to answer it, since we know neither how many alleles nor how many loci are involved. However, some progress can be made if one asks the question in a different way: How much of the variation in stature that is found in a population is due to genetic factors? One can obtain some estimate of this by comparing correlations in stature between identical and fraternal twins. The higher the correlation between pairs of identical twins, the greater the contribution the genetic component makes in determining the variation. Such comparisons yield heritability estimates and are expressed numerically as the coefficient of heritability.*

Identical twins are highly correlated for stature, thereby indicating that the genetic component plays a major role in determining stature variation. Osborne and De George (1959) report a heritability coefficient of .79 for males and .92 for females. Shields (1962), reporting only for females, calculates an h value of .89, and in their classic study, Newman, Freeman, and Holzinger (1937) calculate a value of .81 on a total sample including males and females. Why it is that values differ between the sexes (if indeed they do) is not clear, but it is clear that genetic factors are responsible for much of the variation in stature.

Weight, in contrast to stature, has a low heritability (.05 for males, .42 for females [Osborne and De George, 1959], .57 for females [Shields, 1962], .775 for a pooled sample [Newman, Freeman, and Holzinger, 1937]). Although the variability in heritability coefficients between the sexes and among the samples is not readily explainable, it is clear that the environment plays a larger role in determining the variation of weight than it does in the case of stature. Mainly because of this, weight has never been particularly useful to physical anthropologists, since it is difficult to know what differences in weight signify.

If both weight and stature are considered together and attention is given to the distribution of total body form, it has been presumed for a long time that a lean, linear body conformation is characteristically tropical, whereas a more rotund, corpulent form becomes more common as distance from the equator increases. If this were an accurate way to characterize the distribution of body form in man, then human beings would represent a special case of a more general regularity in the distribution of body forms among mammals. Bergmann's rule (1847) notes that in mammals the larger animals within a particular species could generally be found in the colder regions of the species' range. If one interprets this to mean simply stature, then obviously it does not apply to human populations. To take such a view would be inappropriate, since stature measures body size in but one dimension. What Bergmann was describing was the relationship between body volume and surface area, which appears to reflect efficiency of heat regulation. A low surface area to high volume proportion is efficient in retaining heat; the reverse, high surface area to low body volume proportion, is efficient in dissipating heat.

Allen's rule (1877) refers more specifically to the relationship between temperature and the size of extremities and appendages. It specifies that in the colder regions of a species' distribution the parts of the body most conspicuously susceptible to

---

* Where r_1 is the correlation coefficient for identical twins and r_F is the correlation coefficient for fraternal twins, then:

$$h = \frac{r_1 - r_F}{1 - r_F}$$

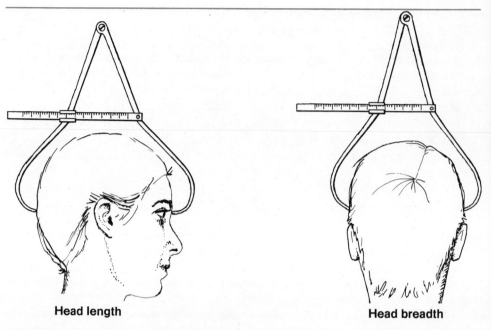

Head length   **Head breadth**

Figure 7–2. Measurement of head length and head breadth. Regarding head length, Hooton (1947) mentions that some observers prefer to work from the left side, holding the caliper horizontally. "However," he continues, "there is some advantage in holding the caliper vertically so that its hinge is above the subject's head and the horizontal scale falls in the sagittal or median front-to-back line of the head." In measuring head breadth, Hooton (ibid.) notes that the operator stands behind the seated subject, and that the caliper can be held either horizontally with the hinge toward the observer or vertically with the hinge above the head of the subject. (Courtesy of G. W. Hewes)

frostbite (noses, ears, fingers, toes) tend to be shorter than they are in members of the species situated in warmer areas. By considering both Bergmann's and Allen's rules, it is readily deduced that the cold-adapted varients of a species would tend to be rounded and globular with relatively slight interruptions to their contours made by the extremities and appendages. Those found in the warmer zones would be expected to be more linear and to have more pronounced irregularities to their contours. These rules are simplifications and overly generalized. Nevertheless they tend to be reasonably correct descriptions of the ways in which body form is commonly distributed among mammals, particularly large ones. In man the situation is complicated by culture, and the available data on body form are more impressionistic than quantitative. In one study Newman and Munro (1955), reporting on a large sample of soldiers, suggest that the regularities specified in Bergmann's rule may be found in the distribution of American males.

In recent years, investigators have become more interested in measuring the components of body weight. For example, fat calipers have been developed to measure total body fat, and X-ray photography has been used to measure the contribution that bone weight makes to total body weight and volume. These and other refinements have so far been applied to only a few human populations, but they illustrate how anthropometry is being adapted to current problems.

Head Length, Head Breadth, and Cephalic Index

If our skulls were perfectly spherical, variation in head form and head size could be expressed in one diameter, but, of course, this is not the case. To describe head form completely would require an infinite number of measurements, but one can obtain a crude overall estimate from just two: head length and head breadth (see Figure 7–2). Each could be taken up separately, but more commonly they are considered together and expressed in the form of the cephalic index, thus:

$$\text{Cephalic index} = \frac{\text{head breadth}}{\text{head length}} \times 100.$$

A low cephalic index implies a narrow head, whereas a broad head is expressed as a large cephalic index. Human population averages vary from 70 percent to 90 percent. Table 7–6 summarizes the distribution of cephalic indexes by major habitation areas of the world.

Table 7–6 Mean Cephalic Indexes and Standard Deviations By Major Areas of the World*

AREA	MEAN PERCENT	STANDARD DEVIATION PERCENT	NUMBER OF SAMPLES
1. Africa	76.17	2.33	115
2. Asia	80.32	4.38	74
3. Europe	81.60	3.00	49
4. Oceania	78.76	3.92	26
5. New World	80.58	2.85	57

* Figures in the table have been compiled from data contained in Biasutti (1959) and Martin and Saller (1955–1966). Mean and standard deviation for Europe have been estimated from a plot of the data; the others have been calculated and weighted for sample size.

Africans have simultaneously the narrowest heads and least variation (see Table 7–7). There are two notable characteristics of the distribution of cephalic indexes in Africa: 1) a gradual decline in average values from west to east within the continent, and 2) a striking negative correlation (−.51) with stature, or, put more simply, taller Africans have narrower heads. This is an observation made on an impressionistic basis by several investigators, some of whom have assumed that it is true for all human beings; but, as we will see presently, in the Pacific and in the New World there is no indication of this. Indeed, there is a suggestion that the reverse might be the case: taller peoples in these areas may have broader heads.

Table 7–7   Mean Cephalic Indexes Among African Populations*

AREA	MEAN PERCENT	STANDARD DEVIATION PERCENT	NUMBER OF SAMPLES
1. Central Bantu	74.14	1.96	11
2. East Sudan	74.66	2.67	14
3. Sahara	74.73	1.59	9
4. East Africa	74.90	1.24	26
5. South Africa (Bushmen, Hottentots)	75.10	1.39	4
6. North Africa	75.96	2.15	15
7. West Africa	76.22	2.09	30
8. Northern Bantu	77.21	1.90	41
9. Madagascar and Indian Ocean	78.75	2.08	4

* These data have been compiled from Biasutti (1959) and weighted for sample size.

The distribution of cephalic indexes in Asia is like that of Africa in one respect and unlike it in another (see Table 7–8). In Asia, as in Africa, there is a negative correlation between stature and cephalic index (−.24). Likewise there is a gradient from west to east, but, in contrast to Africa, the correlation between longitude and cephalic index in Asia is positive (.24). Thus there is a tendency for cephalic indexes to increase as one goes from the Middle East to the Far East. Although, again, the distributional pattern in Europe is extremely complex, there is some indication that the west-to-east trend is the same as in Asia. This is not to say, however, that the gradient is continuous from Atlantic to Pacific, for it is clearly bimodal; some of the people with the broadest heads in the Old World reside in central and eastern Europe.

In the Pacific islands, an east-to-west increase in cephalic index may be observed. The narrow-headed Pacific populations are in the east, the broad-headed in the west, and the intermediate ones in the middle (see Table 7–9). The correlation coefficient between longitude and the cephalic indexes of the twenty-seven populations included in the analysis is .34. In this respect, Oceania is like Asia and unlike Africa, and in another respect it is unlike both: the negative correlation between stature and cephalic index does not exist in the Pacific. In fact, there is a suggestion that with more information one might confirm a significant positive correlation between them.

The American Indians have the second-highest average cephalic indexes, and among them there are no significant large-scale distributional regularities (see Table 7–10). The Eskimos have the narrowest heads among indigenous Americans, and the Andeans have the broadest. The Eskimos combine narrow skulls with broad faces,

Table 7–8   Mean Cephalic Indexes Among Asian Populations*

AREA	MEAN PERCENT	STANDARD DEVIATION PERCENT	NUMBER OF SAMPLES
1. Vedda	75.65	7.16	4
2. India, Various Locations	76.49	2.94	13
3. India, Castes	77.33	1.27	3
4. Asia Minor	79.87	4.68	9
5. Iran, Armenia, Assyria	80.22	5.29	11
6. Malay Peninsula and Archipelago	80.83	2.75	16
7. Southeast Asia	80.94	3.28	17
8. Far East	81.06	1.72	8
9. Northern Asia	81.26	2.64	14
10. Central Asia	82.49	3.69	9

* These data have been compiled from Biasutti (1959) and weighted for sample size.

Table 7–9   Mean Cephalic Indexes Among Pacific Populations†

AREA	MEAN PERCENT	STANDARD DEVIATION PERCENT	NUMBER OF SAMPLES
1. Australia	72.66	1.49	8
2. New Guinea and Melanesia	77.74	3.49	8
3. Polynesia	80.66	2.93	11

† These data have been compiled from Biasutti (1959) and weighted for sample size.

Table 7–10   Mean Cephalic Indexes Among American Indian Populations‡

AREA	MEAN PERCENT	STANDARD DEVIATION PERCENT	NUMBER OF SAMPLES
1. Eskimo	78.08	1.00	4
2. Patagonia and Tierra del Fuego	79.10	3.17	7
3. Eastern Woodlands	79.65	.65	4
4. Amazon Basin	80.14	1.73	17
5. Central America	81.10	3.67	10
6. Southwest United States	81.30	3.48	3
7. Plains and Prairie	81.35	2.67	4
8. Northwest Coast	83.20	3.85	10
9. Andes	84.08	4.27	4

‡ These data have been compiled from Biasutti (1959) and weighted for sample size.

and in this respect are like some Asian populations. These features provide them with a decidedly distinctive head form as compared with other native American populations. The American Indians are like the peoples of the Pacific with respect to the correlation between stature and cephalic index; they, too, show a weak positive correlation (.11) between them.

Table 7–11 shows the various heritability coefficients that have been calculated on identical-twin samples for the cephalic index. The coefficients are similar to those obtained for stature (see discussion beginning on page 228) and support the conclusion that the majority of variations in cephalic index is due to genetic factors.

Table 7–11   Heritability Coefficients for Cephalic Index

SEX	H	SOURCE
Males	.90	Osborne and De George (1959)
Females	.70	Osborne and De George (1959)
Males and Females	.75	Newman, Freeman, and Holzinger (1937)

Nose Length, Nose Breadth, and Nasal Index

Often lurking behind the more pristine reasons for classifying mankind into races is the desire to scale groups of human beings; that is, to locate them on an imaginary ape-to-advanced-modern-man scale. The procedure behind this is simple: the larger the number of traits like the modern ape, the lower the position on the scale. The population with the highest number is therefore the most apelike, and the one with the fewest is the most advanced. The outcome is, of course, entirely manageable, and thus the exercise is meaningless, and even if one were "objective" and chose for comparison traits selected at "random" and "independent" of one another, it is not at all clear what the results would mean. Suppose, for example, that it could be demonstrated that you are more like a mouse than I am. What could be reasonably inferred from that "fact"? Nothing, of course. In any case, nose form has been extensively used in descriptions and classifications of human variation, not merely because it distinguishes some groups from others, but further because some forms are much more "apelike" than others. In fact, the forms of the nose found in man are substantially different from those found in the apes. As E. A. Hooton (1947) put it: "To have a nose like an ape, you would have to be one."

Classifying nose forms has been done in four ways: 1) from a profile view (Figure 7–3), 2) from underneath (Figure 7–4), 3) from the front, and 4) by calculation of the nasal index, thus:

$$\text{Nasal Index} = \frac{\text{nasal breadth}}{\text{nasal length}} \times 100.$$

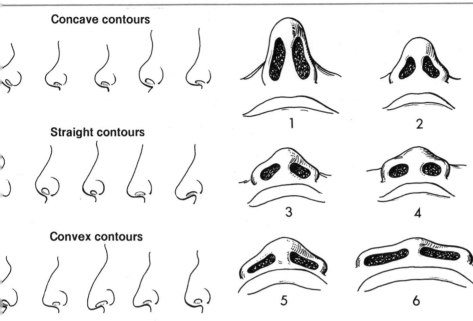

Figure 7–3. Variations in nasal profiles. (After R. Martin and Karl Saller)

Figure 7–4. Variations in nasal flatness. (After R. Martin and Karl Saller)

Most commonly, the classification involves a simultaneous judgment concerning the length and breadth of the nose, two continuously variable traits that may well reflect two distinctive adaptations. It is possible on the basis of the distribution of these features that the length of the nose is mainly controlled by selective factors imposed by variations in temperature, whereas the breadth is controlled more by the forces imposed by variations in humidity. The details here may be argued, but if the principle is sound, that is, if nose length is largely independent of nose breadth in terms of the selective agencies impinging upon them, this would be a suitable reason for distinguishing them as separate traits. Since, however, the data on the measurements are not as often reported as nasal index, we will have to violate our own cautions and examine the distribution of the index as though it were a single trait.

The nasal index expresses nasal breadth numerically as a percentage of nasal length. Martin and Saller (1955–1966) report the range of variation among human beings as from 40 percent to 147 percent, i.e., from individuals whose nose breadth is less than half their nose length to persons with noses which are almost half again as broad as they are long. Mean variation among human populations ranges from 60 to 110 percent (see Table 7–12).

How does nose form vary over the face of the earth, and how does its variation compare with the distributions of stature and cephalic index? Consider Africa, which

Table 7–12   Mean Nasal Indexes and Standard Deviations by Major Areas of the World*

AREA	MEAN PERCENT	STANDARD DEVIATION PERCENT	NUMBER OF SAMPLES
1. Africa	84.67	13.88	115
2. Asia	71.85	9.09	74
3. Europe	66.00	2.00	20
4. Oceania	82.77	9.82	26
5. New World	74.78	6.35	57

* Figures for this table have been compiled from data contained in Biasutti (1959) and Martin and Saller (1955–1966). The mean and standard deviation for Europe have been estimated from a plot of the data; the others have been calculated and weighted for sample size.

has: 1) the largest average nasal index, and 2) the greatest range of variability. This is the reverse of the situation with cephalic index, where Africa had the lowest average and the least variability. In Table 7–13 one can see that once again the Bushmen and Hottentots of the Kalahari Desert come out at one extreme, but, as noted in the instance of stature, it should again be emphasized that the Pygmies, included within the northern Bantu group, commonly have mean nasal indexes over 100 percent. Since these large values occur at the equator, it is of interest to determine whether there is any consistent pattern in the distribution of values to the north and south, and in fact there is a striking negative correlation (−.64) between latitude and mean nasal index in Africa. A negative correlation with latitude implies that as one moves away from the equator, mean nasal index declines. It appears from an

Table 7–13   Mean Nasal Indexes Among African Populations†

AREA	MEAN PERCENT	STANDARD DEVIATION PERCENT	NUMBER OF SAMPLES
1. North Africa	70.29	4.32	14
2. East Africa	74.27	8.72	26
3. Sahara	75.17	7.72	9
4. East Sudan	88.04	3.65	8
5. Central Bantu	93.84	4.61	11
6. West Africa	95.21	6.81	18
7. Northern Bantu	95.53	7.81	27
8. South Africa (Bushmen, Hottentots)	103.93	3.85	3

† These data have been compiled from Biasutti (1959) and weighted for sample size.

inspection of the data that the values decline more rapidly to the north. The pattern is the opposite of that observed in the distribution of stature, and this is reflected in a significant negative correlation between nasal index and stature (−.36).

Looking at the distribution from the standpoint of longitude, there is a tendency for average nasal indexes to decrease at any particular latitude from west to east. This means that whereas the mean values of nasal index differ from north to south at any point along that continuum, the smaller averages can be expected in the east. This pattern is the same as the one observed in the distribution of cephalic indexes in Africa, and thus it is not surprising to find a positive correlation (.13) between nasal and cephalic indexes.

Europeans have the narrowest noses and display the least variability of any of the major areas. If Europe is regarded as a part of the Euro-Asian continent, then the low average nasal indexes of Europeans may be seen as the western extreme of a marked west-to-east increase in average nasal index among Euro-Asians (see Table 7–14 for more detail). Thus, in contrast to Africa, where the larger values are in the west, the large Euro-Asian nasal indexes are in the east. Stature may be thought of similarly, with the Europeans representing the western extremes of a continuous west-to-east decline. From this it follows that for the Euro-Asian area, stature increases as nasal index decreases. This is expressed in the results of a correlation analysis conducted on the Asian populations which yielded a striking negative correlation between stature and nasal index (−.75). Thus, if you enter Asia from eastern Europe and travel eastward to the Pacific, you will likely observe on the way that the residents become shorter, and their noses become broader.

As noted earlier in the discussion of cephalic index, there is in Asia a gradual increase in mean cephalic index from west to east, just as there is in mean nasal index. This positive correlation (.13) implies that in Asia, populations with broad heads tend to have broad noses.

Table 7–14   Mean Nasal Indexes Among Asian Populations*

AREA	MEAN PERCENT	STANDARD DEVIATION PERCENT	NUMBER OF SAMPLES
1. Asia Minor	61.54	4.40	9
2. Iran, Armenia, Assyria	63.66	2.97	11
3. Central Asia	69.21	7.15	9
4. India, Various Locations	74.18	6.30	12
5. Far East	74.75	1.85	2
6. Northern Asia	78.90	3.77	8
7. Southeast Asia	82.80	5.21	3
8. Malay Peninsula and Archipelago	84.44	6.60	13
9. India, Vedda	85.52	5.55	4

* These data have been compiled from Biasutti (1959) and weighted for sample size.

Table 7–15   Mean Nasal Indexes Among Pacific Populations*

AREA	MEAN PERCENT	STANDARD DEVIATION PERCENT	NUMBER OF SAMPLES
1. Australia	99.58	4.23	8
2. New Guinea and Melanesia	85.26	6.62	7
3. Micronesia and Polynesia	79.08	3.58	11

* These data have been compiled from Biasutti (1959) and weighted for sample size.

    The striking characteristic of the distribution of nasal index in the Pacific is the fact that it is bimodal; that is, there are two decidedly different distributions, one in Australia and one among the rest of the island populations. The Australian aborigines have nasal indexes similar to those found among African Pygmy and Bushman populations (see Table 7–15).

    When the two distributions are separated, too few populations remain in each group to enable one confidently to draw conclusions through statistical procedures. However, it would appear that among the non-Australian populations, nasal index increases from west to east as cephalic index does, and in this regard the distributions parallel those in Asia.

    Although the picture remains unclear in Oceania and complicated in Europe, it appears that for the rest of the world, nasal index and stature are negatively correlated. This observation is confirmed in the distribution of nasal indexes among the Indians of North and South America (see Table 7–16).

Table 7–16   Mean Nasal Indexes Among American Indian Populations†

AREA	MEAN PERCENT	STANDARD DEVIATION PERCENT	NUMBER OF SAMPLES
1. Eskimo	68.45	3.16	4
2. Andean	69.98	2.11	4
3. Plains and Prairie	71.98	2.01	4
4. Patagonia and Tierra del Fuego	72.80	3.33	7
5. Northwest Coast	78.85	6.33	10
6. Southwest United States	79.45	2.45	2
7. Central America	81.06	3.02	9
8. Amazon	81.44	4.97	16

† These data have been compiled from Biasutti (1959) and weighted for sample size.

The correlation coefficient between stature and nasal index obtained on the data reported here is −.50. Stature among the American Indians, it will be recalled, increases as the distance from the equator increases; nasal indexes are largest among American Indians living near the equator, and they decline as distance from the equator increases. The correlation coefficient expressing this distribution pattern is the one between nasal index and latitude, which for the populations included here is −.32. This is the same relationship noted in the distribution of nasal index by latitude in Africa. Also paralleling the Africa distribution, it appears once again that at any particular latitude in the New World, the larger nasal indexes are to be found in the west.

The most conspicuous exception to the north-south distribution among the American Indians is the low average nasal index reported from the Andean populations living near the equator. Since these are people living at high altitudes, and thus subject to cold temperatures, it suggests the likelihood that their narrow noses are of some adaptive advantage in cold, low-oxygen, dry climates.

The distribution of nasal indexes among American Indians is not significantly correlated with the distribution of cephalic indexes; the two vary independently of each other.

One further point on the subject of nose form deserves consideration before turning to skin color, and that is the ecological rule known as Thompson's rule. Thompson's rule refers to nose breadth and notes that in cold climates noses tend to be narrow, whereas in hot climates they tend to be broad. The underlying explanation usually provided to account for the distribution of nasal breadth is the function of the nose in regulating the temperature of the external air before it reaches the lungs. It is based on the simple impression that the narrower the nose, the warmer the air that reaches the lungs, while broader noses have less effect on the temperature of inspired air. This rule is consistent with the distribution of nasal index in Africa and in the New World, but not particularly consistent with the pattern in Asia, where longitude appears to have substantially more influence on nasal index than latitude.

Skin Color

Among normal persons, variation in skin color is due largely to differences in the amount of melanin in the skin. Melanin is a large and complex pigment molecule formed by specialized cells, melanocytes, located beneath the superficial layers of the skin. The melanocytes produce the dark-brown-to-black melanin in the form of granules which are excreted into the intracellular spaces in the deep and outer layers of skin. There is no substantial difference between dark- and light-skinned persons in the number of melanocytes, but there is a great difference in the density of melanin granules.

Until recently physical anthropologists have been forced to *judge* skin color variation instead of *measuring* it, but in the past decade instruments that measure light reflectance (reflectometers) have begun to be used. Reflectometers allow for greater precision, comparability, and objectivity. However, at present there are comparatively few reports of data obtained using the reflectometer. In discussing variations in skin color, it continues to be necessary to rely upon the subjective and qualitative data that have accumulated over hundreds of years.

The distribution of skin color can be summarized best by means of a map (see Figure 7–5). A casual inspection of the map reveals nothing startling. Dark skin color is tropical, and depigmentation increases as distance from the equator increases. On closer inspection one could note complexities in the distribution, but since the data on which the map is based are imprecise, it is of little value to consider these in detail. A discussion of the complexities would focus on the exceptional areas, i.e., tropical areas inhabited by light-skinned peoples. The exceptions are usually understandable on cultural grounds. As Hulse (1955) has pointed out, many of the irregularities in the distribution appear to be due to the relatively recent expansion of agricultural people into new areas.

The distribution of skin color in man is a special case of an ecological regularity called Gloger's rule. Originally Gloger's rule was formulated to point out distributional regularities observed in the pigmentation of feathers and furs. The rule stated that the darkly pigmented varieties within a species are found in the warm and humid parts of the species' range.

Is it obvious why pigmentation decreases as distance from the equator increases? Not at all. In one way the distribution is the opposite of what one might "obviously" expect. In hot, humid areas one might expect light skin color, since it reflects rather than absorbs heat as dark skin color does. Two proposals are presently in competition to explain the distribution of skin pigmentation in man. One notes that pigmentation increases as solar ultraviolet radiation increases and concludes from this that skin color is essentially a protective shield against the harmful effects of radiation. The equator is exposed to the greatest solar ultraviolet radiation, for the simple reason that there is most daylight there, and the sun is more directly overhead than in any other part of the earth. This proposal has been around for a long time but has failed to gain general acceptance, mainly because it fails to explain the distribution. To be sure, the intensity of solar radiation decreases as distance from the equator increases, but the intensity of exposure to the radiation does not necessarily decrease. The thick overgrowth that prevails throughout much of the equatorial tropics provides a kind of protective umbrella, so that the actual amount of radiation reaching the ground is less in many areas of the tropics than it is in Denver, Colorado.

The other proposal says that pigmentation acts as an adjustment mechanism in the production of vitamin D. This, too, is not a new idea, but interest in it has been revitalized recently by an article written by W. F. Loomis (1967), a biochemist at Brandeis University. Vitamin D is known as the sunshine vitamin; what this means is that solar radiation activates the synthesis of the vitamin in the skin. Once synthesized, the vitamin diffuses throughout the circulatory system and functions in the

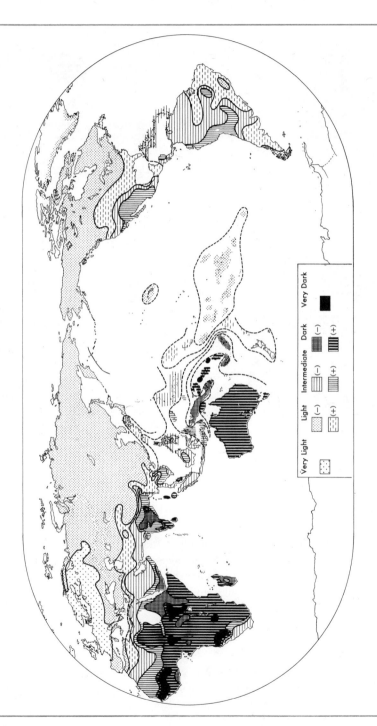

Figure 7–5. Distribution of skin color. (From Renato Biasutti, *Le Razze e I Popoli Della Terra*, courtesy UTET)

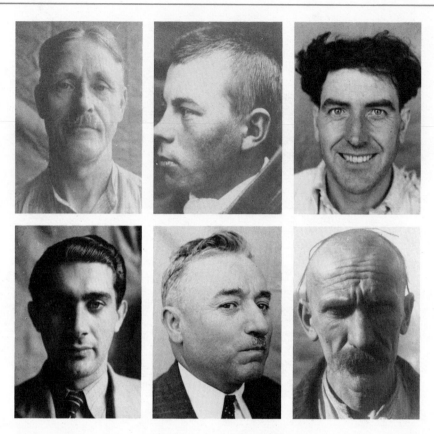

Figure 7–6. Europeans. Top: Left, Swede; Center, Lapp; Right, Irishman. Bottom: Left, Basque; Center, Magyar; Right, Albanian. (Courtesy of Carleton S. Coon)

absorption of calcium and in the deposition of the inorganic matrix in bone. Vitamin D is an unusual vitamin in that too much of it as well as too little can result in death. Heavy pigmentation, according to this view, filters out a large percentage of the activating radiation and thereby inhibits the overproduction of vitamin D. Light skin facilitates the synthesis of the vitamin and thus assures that minimum quantities are produced in areas where exposure to the sun is considerably reduced. Skin color from this point of view is seen as essentially a regulating device that makes it possible for human beings living at different latitudes to obtain a constant amount of vitamin D.

How is skin color inherited? No one knows. On this issue, there is general agreement on only two points: the inheritance of skin color 1) is complex, and 2) involves more than one genetic locus.

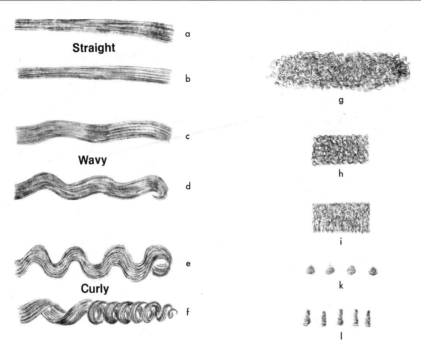

Figure 7–7. Variations in hair form. (Redrawn from an illustration in Rudolf Martin and Karl Saller, *Lehrbuch der Anthropologie,* by permission of Gustav Fischer Verlag)

Hair Form

Hair form has been used frequently in standard racial classifications, since the various forms of the hair correspond in their distribution to the common notion of race, going back to the time of Blumenbach. If one were to classify man's variation on the basis of hair form alone, one would end up with classes very much like the old fivefold classification. In many respects the distribution of hair form corresponds better to this kind of classification than does skin color. Like all of the "racial" characteristics, however, hair form displays considerable variation within and between the areas where one form may predominate.

Hair form varies from straight to tightly wound spirals with intermediate forms of low wave, wavy, deep wave, and kinky. These are illustrated in Figure 7–7. Variations in hair form tend to be associated with variations in the thickness of the individual hair strands. Among dark-haired people, the thickest cross sections occur among people with very little or no wave, and the thinnest are found among those with tightly spiraled hair. Very little is known of the evolutionary significance of hair form. About the only theory presently available to account for the variations states that hair form provides a kind of general protection to the brain against damage

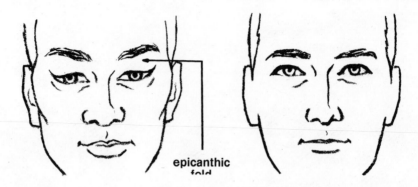

epicanthic
fold

Figure 7–8.   Comparison of eyes having the epicanthic fold with eyes lacking that trait.

through trauma and through the effects of radiation. Perhaps this is true, but, if so, the work of demonstrating its validity remains to be done.

Morphological Traits of Restricted Distribution

The list of observed physical characteristics could be extended indefinitely. Indeed, only a meager sample of facial and skull traits has been mentioned to provide an introductory familiarity with the distribution of heterographic variability and the kinds of problems that have confronted physical anthropologists in their efforts to describe man's morphological variation. Before considering the physiological aspects of heterography, some mention should be made of a few characteristics that are clearly distinctive, but with restricted distributions. The traits to be considered briefly here are the epicanthic eye fold, shovel-shaped incisors, and steatopygia. The first two traits range predominantly among Asian and American Indian populations. Steatopygia is African, or, more specifically, South African.

EPICANTHIC FOLD.   The epicanthic fold is one of several factors contributing to the characteristic appearance of the mongoloid eye. In extreme form it consists of a fold of skin that, when the eye is open, comes down over and runs on a line with the edge of the upper eyelid (see Figure 7–8). Together with a depressed nasal bridge, wide and projecting cheekbones, and deposits of fatty tissue overlying the cheekbones, the epicanthic fold is responsible for the slant-eyed appearance of the mongoloid eye. It is commonly found among infants from all over the world and, among adults, more commonly found among females than males, and particularly, of course, among people of Asian origin (see Figure 7–9).

SHOVEL-SHAPED INCISORS.   Shovel-shaped incisors (Figure 7–10) have a distribution among contemporary human beings similar to that of the epicanthic fold. It is known, however, as a trait with a broader distribution in fossil-man times, having been found commonly among European and African fossils as well as Asian remains.

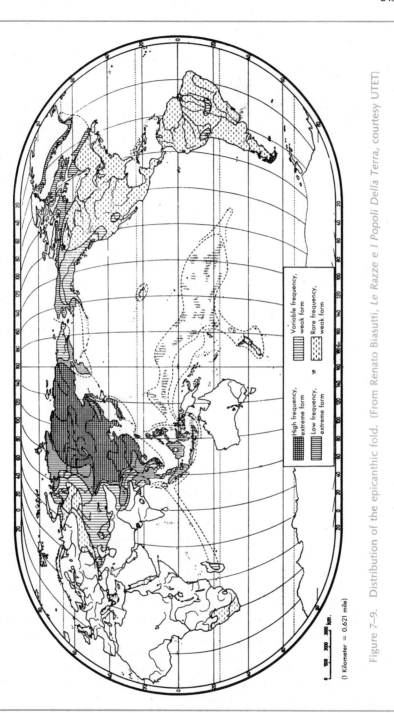

Figure 7–9. Distribution of the epicanthic fold. (From Renato Biasutti, *Le Razze e I Popoli Della Terra*, courtesy UTET)

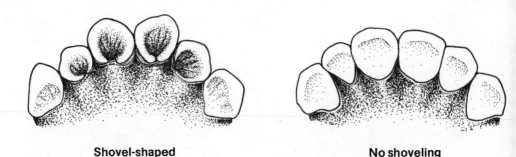

Shovel-shaped **No shoveling**

Figure 7–10. Comparison of shovel-shaped incisors with incisors lacking that trait.

The folding inward of the incisor teeth increases their chewing surfaces without increasing their breadth in relation to the size of the dental arcade. To the extent that increased chewing surfaces is in itself functionally desirable and improves the durability of the teeth, the adaptive value of shovel-shaped incisors is not too difficult to see. The problem, however, comes up in trying to account for its distribution today. Why is it retained in some modern populations and not in others? Brace (1963) puts forth structural reduction as the explanation, reasoning that in those parts of the world where the functions of the incisor teeth are displaced by other factors (food preparation techniques, sharp cutting tools) the genes that determine their structure become free to vary in their composition. The most probable consequence, he reasons, is a structural reduction in the form of the incisors. In distributional terms, there is some support for this. Shovel-shaped incisors are less frequent among the descendants of those people who have solved, by cultural means, the problems that incisors usually solve biologically and who have done so for the longest period of time. Among the modern populations with high frequencies of the trait and whose histories and cultural adaptations are known to be grossly diversified, the pattern is not at all clear.

Anthropology has had a long and time-honored tradition of noting and doting on the unusual, the weird, the bizarre. Perhaps it was felt that unusual things needed to be emphasized, but unfortunately, because they are unusual, little effort to do anything more than report their discovery and perhaps estimate their frequency has ever been done. To the early European observer such traits as epicanthic folds and shovel-shaped incisors fell into this category. An attempt was made by Virginia Carbonell (1963) to deal with shovel-shaped incisors in a comprehensive way. Her efforts were frustrated by the lack of standards and the absence of simple correlative data that would have made the older studies so much more useful (for example, the absence of family studies). Her paper illustrates the underlying complexities of an attribute thought to be a single trait and shows the distributional details of shoveling in modern and fossil-man populations.

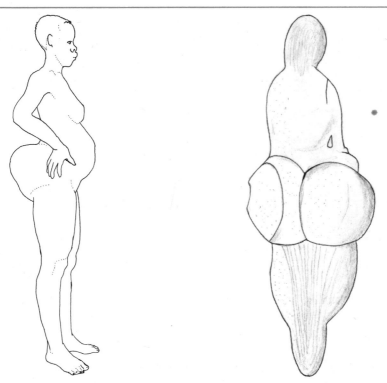

Figure 7–11. Steatopygous female Bushman of southern Africa.

Figure 7–12. Ancient steatopygous figurine, drawn from a photograph of "Venus" of Lespugue.

STEATOPYGIA. Steatopygia is another of the biological curios that usually manage to get into discussions of racial variation. The trait consists of an extraordinary enlargement of the upper thighs and buttocks due to the accumulation and localization of fat in these regions of the body. Today it is generally thought of as a feature distinguishing the Hottentots of South Africa. It is particularly developed in Hottentot females (see Figure 7–11). There are some reasons for believing that during Upper Paleolithic times in Europe steatopygia may have been a relatively common attribute. The evidence for this is the discovery of figurines (Figure 7–12) which have clear indications of the trait. It could, of course, be merely the artistic stylization of the form, or perhaps simply representative of generalized obesity, which in the closing days of the glaciation of Europe might have been regarded as a desirable attribute in females.

Nothing is known concerning the significance nor the inheritance of steatopygia. It represents an instance of another ecological regularity called Rensch's rule, which notes that in mammals, the members of a species adapted to hot climatic conditions have localized deposits of fat. This fails, of course, to explain the significance of steatopygia; it merely notes that when peculiar localized accumulations of fat occur in mammals, they tend to occur in hot climates. The Hottentots live in South Africa and raise cattle as their principal means of subsistence. They are similar and almost certainly closely related to their desert hunting and gathering neighbors, the Bushmen.

The discussion of heterographic variation has become progressively more general as it has passed from metrical to observational to uncommon traits. From this point on, the discussion will deal with physiological, developmental, and, briefly, psychological characteristics, and, at present, there simply is not an extensive body of data on the range of human variation in any of these areas; so the discussion will continue to be at a general level.

PHYSIOLOGICAL CHARACTERISTICS

As we have seen, human populations differ from one another in terms of measureable *things* such as stature, cephalic index, steatopygia, etc. They differ also, as we are about to see, in terms of *processes*, such as may be identified in examining differences in physiology, growth, and behavior. Thus at this point the discussion not only shifts from one topic to another, but the perspective changes as well. The focus continues to be the distribution of human variation, but we shift from things to processes.

By now the change is a familiar one, one taken earlier in the discussion of paleontology and archaeology, the change from *structural* to *functional* differences. In fact the distinction between structure and function is not as sharp as it may appear. For example, stature is considered as a measurement of structure, yet on reflection it is clear that stature is the functional result of many processes. However, it is useful to regard stature as a thing rather than as a measure of process in most, but not all, cases, as will become clear presently in the discussion of growth.

Distinguishing between structure and function opens up an entirely different way of viewing human variability. We know already that Eskimos and Europeans are different in their appearance (that is, structure); now we wish to see if they react (that is, function) differently. For an obvious example, do Eskimos and Europeans react differently to extreme cold? Or, do residents of tropical forests accommodate to the stresses of high temperature and high humidity in the same way as people who live at high altitudes? Do rice cultivators adjust to protein deficiency in the same manner as reindeer herders?

To answer questions of this kind requires a comparison of reactions. Typically these reactions are obtained by measuring physiological, developmental, and behavioral processes. Since physical anthropologists have been more involved with physiological reactions, we will consider them first.

Do human populations differ in their physiological reactions to various kinds of stress? Yes. Furthermore the differences are not especially surprising. In general, people who live in the tropics are better able to adapt to the stresses of the tropics than people who live elsewhere. The same could be said for arctic peoples, for peoples living at high altitudes, etc. From this we may conclude straightaway that human populations who regularly live under conditions of physiological stress more readily adapt to that stress than other populations. Does that close the case? Yes, if that were the only issue. However, as always, the resolution of one issue gives rise to other problems. Adaptations, as we have learned, may come about as the result of the activity of evolutionary mechanisms on evolving units. What, then, does the adaptive variability imply?

Selection continually scans the variability presented by mutation, rejecting most of it, but on occasion favoring a variant and thus causing it to become more and more common over time. Size, structure, mating patterns, and movements in and out of the population may act to cause lasting evolutionary consequences too, but selection and mutation would seem to be more continuous and systematic, thus over the long range more forceful. There is, however, another kind of adaptation with which we are all familiar: the adaptations we each make to the daily variations occurring in our environments. Our body temperatures remain extraordinarily constant in environments that vary widely in humidity and temperature. Our cells receive abundant oxygen to carry out their functions over a broad range of altitude variation. The ability of our systems to adapt to changing environmental conditions is known as *physiological plasticity*, and it is a phenomenon that can be found to occur under many more circumstances than simply variations in temperature, moisture, and altitude. We are continually responding in physiological ways to internal and external stimuli such as fear, crowding, and dietary imbalances, as well as to the usual activities required of us daily, such as walking, talking, and even resting.

Thus adaptations to stress may reflect either the *adaptability* provided by physiological plasticity or the *adaptation* produced over time by evolutionary mechanisms acting on the genetic structures of populations. Because the differences may be produced in either of two ways, the significance of the adaptations is at one level obvious and at another not at all clear. It is obvious that plasticity makes survival possible; otherwise we would all have to live in impossibly constant environmental conditions. What is not clear is the cause or causes of the different qualities of physiological plasticity. Is a native of the Congo jungle able to adjust more efficiently to extremes of heat and humidity than, say, a native of North English, Iowa, because he was born there and grew up there, or because, through selection among his ancestors over a long time, he has come to have some special genetic capacities? The resolution is not to be made here, and we will not take even a middle-of-the-road view that "it's probably some of each," for there is as little evidence for that view as for either extreme. It is clear, however, that before deciding on this issue, we should have some awareness of the work that has been done.

Until recently most research on physiological adaptations has attempted to identify the effects of environmental extremes in altitude, temperature, and humidity. This work continues and is, in fact, expanding, but in addition during the last ten years there has been an enormous increase of interest in the physiological effects of culturally produced stresses such as air and water pollution, crowding, noise pollution, etc. We may first review the effects of altitude and temperature, the evidence on these subjects being more extensive, and then consider the subject of cultural stress.

Altitude Stress

The biological processes that are common to our species are tuned primarily to work well in tropical and subtropical environments. Yet, primarily by means provided by culture, human beings do very well indeed outside the tropics. High-altitude environments offer perhaps the most continuously stressful conditions for man: low temperatures, high radiation levels, excessive dryness, and, most important, reduced oxygen pressure. In technologically advanced societies adaptation to these circumstances may be achieved wholly by cultural means, as we know very dramatically from space flights and more routinely from commercial air travel.

For many populations, however, there is no technological way to "adjust cabin temperature and pressure" for their comfort. Some people, for example in the Himalayas of South Asia and the Andes of South America, live out their lives in communities over ten thousand feet above sea level. These populations are distinctive in a number of ways, and most of their distinctiveness appears to be related to the availability of oxygen. In body build they possess very large barrel-shaped chests which accommodate lung volumes approximately 10 percent larger in capacity than found among people living at lower elevations. High-altitude residents have more blood, approximately 30 percent more than people at sea level. The difference in blood volume is due primarily to the greater amount of red blood cells in the high-altitude populations.

These features appear to be directly related to the low oxygen pressure. Larger lung volumes accommodate more air, and more red blood cells imply more efficient transport of oxygen and carbon dioxide. In recent years attention has been drawn more and more to three other distinctive aspects of the physiologies of high-altitude residents; they have: 1) very low rates of diseases of the heart and vascular system, 2) a higher death rate among the newborn, and 3) a slower rate of maturation, that is, they reach full maturity later in life. These characteristics are undoubtedly related to altitude stress, but exactly how is not clear. Better understanding may come soon, as investigators from all over the world have joined together in an International Biological Program. One of the major objectives of the program is the intensive investigation of high-altitude adaptation in man. Though the IBP is only a few years old, results are beginning to appear, and we can expect significant advances in the near future.

Do the high-altitude characteristic features reflect genetic adaptation or physiological adaptability? No one knows for certain; the evidence is inconclusive. Persons raised at sea level, when moved to high altitudes, experience a number of symptoms which together are referred to as anoxia. Typically anoxia begins with a headache and fatigue accompanied by shortness of breath. These symptoms may be followed by vomiting; the hands and feet become blue, and in extreme cases a person goes unconscious and dies. If anoxia were common, then one would surely conclude that the high-altitude differences are genetic. However, if the sea level resident makes his ascent gradually, the symptoms of anoxia may be very mild or even completely unnoticeable. Thus if one takes his time, his physiology adjusts; his blood volume and his lung capacity increase. These differences then may reflect plasticity at least in part. The problem remains.

Most of our knowledge of the effects of altitude come from studies conducted at extreme elevations. The few studies that have been carried out at intermediate altitudes indicate that the effects are directly correlated; thus people living at five thousand feet differ from those living at sea level in the same way but to a less marked degree than people who live at, say, fifteen thousand feet. Thus the possibility exists of systematic variation among populations which are correlated with altitude instead of latitude and longitude. By implication, two or more distantly related populations may be alike in some respects simply because they live under similar conditions of altitude stress.

Temperature Stress

Mammals are warm-blooded.
Man is a mammal.
Therefore, man is warm-blooded.

A syllogism with a conclusion we all accept. We accept it so readily that perhaps we fail to realize how delicately sensitive we are to temperature changes and how much our bodily processes are continuously involved in adjusting to the changes. A large part of the energy we use is expended simply in the regulation of body temperature. The control is complex; it involves the integration of the central nervous system with the endocrine glands, the respiratory system, the sweat glands, and the digestive and circulatory systems.

Our interest is, fortunately, simple. The problem of concern continues to be the question of whether human beings vary in their ability to respond to temperature stress. As already indicated, the answer is yes, and apparently the variation is systematic—people who reside in temperature extremes adjust more readily to the extremes than people who do not. The generalization is based on several lines of evidence.

Apart from casual observations (and on the subject of adaptation to environmental extremes, there are many of these), evidence on man's physiological adaptations has emerged from two sources: 1) distributional studies showing correlations between anthropometric characteristics and selected ecological variables such as temperature and humidity; and 2) experimental studies on human subjects selected because of their somatic characteristics and observed for the limits of their variability (tolerance) under varying, but usually extreme, environmental conditions. Distributional studies tend to be concerned with more interesting problems but provide much less convincing results. For example, D. F. Roberts (1953) has demonstrated a high negative correlation between mean body weight and mean annual temperature by going through the available figures on each variable from around the world. As is the case with the correlations reported above between anthropometric traits and longitude and latitude, it is difficult to conclude what the significance of such a correlation may be. Does it mean that some systematic evolutionary pressures have been applied to human populations living in hot climates to weed out those individuals with the genetic determiners to become heavy (or, conversely, pressures on populations living in cold climates to reduce the thinner variants)? Does it mean that temperature variations affect the quality of metabolism, causing fat to be stored in colder climates more efficiently than in the tropics? Does it mean that the persons living in warm climates have less to eat, or, perhaps, simply eat less? There are at present no clear and unambiguous answers to these questions. As Roberts points out, much more work is necessary; body weight is often not reported in anthropometric surveys; mean annual temperature is a crude estimate at best of the thermal variations the peoples of the world are subjected to; and reasonably comparable nutritional surveys are almost entirely lacking. Assuming that the work gets done, and eventually it will, this would seem to be potentially a most productive way to investigate man's adaptive characteristics. The approach makes no assumptions about racial clusters.

Experimental studies on physiological variations in man are usually made to determine if races are the same or different in their abilities to tolerate and in the ways they adjust to environmental stress. Thus, the experimental work begins by presuming that, if physiological plasticity varies in man, the variation should be maximized in interracial comparisons.

Stanley Garn (1971) lists eleven investigations of this kind; ten of them include European or American subjects as a basis for comparison. The one that fails to include Euro-American subjects makes no comparison. Studies comparing the reactions of African and European-derived populations in general support the view that people with recent tropical or subtropical ancestry are more tolerant of the stresses of high temperature and high humidity. Other comparisons investigating cold habitat groups such as the Eskimo and Australian aborigines support the converse. These studies of temperature stress suggest the following: 1) mankind in general is better adapted biologically to heat stress than to cold stress; 2) though it may be that some populations are better adapted biologically to cold stress than others, man's major adaptation to cold is cultural.

Many studies of physiological changes under temperature stress illustrate clearly the limitations of beginning with a racial approach. For example, studies comparing reactions of Negroes and Caucasians to extreme temperatures tend of necessity to support the view that any differences noted must necessarily be real, that is, genetic, biological, racial differences. Would the differences in heat regulation and sweat loss noted between blacks and whites subjected to variable conditions of moisture in hot climates be greater than differences between males and females, between young and old, between tall and short, between Democrats and Republicans? We don't know.

Figure 7–13. Asians. Top: Left, Tamil; Center, Rajput; Right, Kalmuck. Middle: Left, Vedda; Center, Ainu; Right, Japanese. Bottom: Left, Tungus; Center, Formosan; Right, Andaman Islander. (Courtesy of Carleton S. Coon)

Are the differences characteristic, say, of tropical as compared to temperate populations? We don't know. Are the differences due to plasticity or to real genetic differences? We don't know, although Baker argues forcefully for genetic causation in both temperature (1958) and altitude stress (cited in Garn, 1971).

The point to be emphasized here is that when studies begin with racial comparisons, they are already limited to conclusions about racial differences, conclusions that may or may not be justified. Chapter 9 deals with the significance of heterographic variability in man in more detail. Studies of physiological reactions between races, however, illustrate well the peculiar limitations of the racial approach to understanding human variability.

Before concluding this brief consideration of physiological characteristics, some special attention should be given to nutrition. Physiological traits are considered not only because they constitute an additional basis for describing human variation, but also because, in some ways, they provide a means for explaining variation as well. If, for example, two groups are compared and found to have significantly different chest circumferences and further found to contrast in the altitudes of their environments, the known relationship between high altitude and large chest circumferences may explain the contrast. Such relationships probably occur very commonly in connection with nutritional factors. Two populations may differ significantly in all their body dimensions not because they are adapted differently nor because their relationship is remote, but simply because they eat differently, either in quantity or quality of food. Thus, the effect of nutritional variation is important in interpreting relationships between and among human populations, but, in fact, is often neglected due to lack of information or to the complexity it introduces into an analysis. For example, there are clear indications of metabolic differences between groups of men. Eskimos not only eat more fat, but their physiological systems break it up, store it, and use it in ways that differ from Caucasians. Some groups live on daily diets with compositions that, with the same energy output, would be starvation diets for others. Since it is clear that overall body size is affected by the quality and quantity of food, then it follows that two or more populations may be *alike* because of either similar food sources or differential physiological utilization of different food sources. Likewise, it is possible for two or more populations to *differ* in some respects from one another either because of different food sources or differential physiological utilization of the same food sources. Clearly, in attempts to describe and explain man's heterographic variation, it is important to know not only what foods people eat, but how they are digested, stored, utilized, and what effects they have on the phenotype. This is a large order, and, for practical purposes, it will probably continue to be necessary, usually, to deal with heterographic variation under the assumption either that nutritional variations have no relevant effects or that their effects on man's variations can be recognized and taken into consideration. This will undoubtedly prove too simple, but even considering their limitations, these assumptions accommodate only food-source variation and, to some extent, physiological variation in the metabolic processes. What specific effects foods have on the phenotype are essentially unknown;

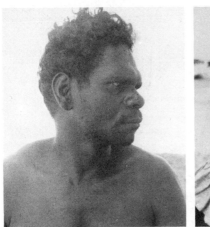

Figure 7–14.   Oceania: Left, Tiwi; Right, Micronesian. (Tiwi courtesy of Carleton S. Coon)

some general impressions have begun to accumulate in studies of growth and development. Birth weight, for example, would seem to be more a reflection of environmental factors (such as the mother's health, nutrition, parity, and twinning) than of the genotype of the child. Furthermore, the striking trend in increasing stature observed in European and American communities over the last one hundred years seems to be due mostly to dietary improvements.

Cultural Stress

Man adapts to his environments primarily by cultural means. As technology has advanced, culture has provided more effective means of adaptation. Thus yesterday we built a fire when we were cold; today we simply turn up the thermostat. The things of culture, in other words, have become more efficient in their control over our surroundings. Though today these observations are obvious, we have become generally aware (that is, even Congressmen know) of this relationship between man and culture only recently.

Our appreciation of culture has been accompanied by the realization that the relationship is by no means perfect. The things of culture can produce enormous food surpluses, yet starvation continues and in some places worsens. The technologies of transportation and communication are awesome indeed, yet as by-products we find our streets are jammed, the air we breathe is polluted, and one of our most common complaints is that we are unable to communicate. Conception can take place without intercourse and vice versa, yet infant mortality remains high, population density increases, and illegitimacy becomes more common. Drugs and medicine relieve pain and cure illnesses that a few decades ago were grotesquely painful killers, yet hospitals are overcrowded, and every year an increasing part of our income goes to medical care, and the drugs themselves have become more common sources of pain and death.

Clearly, as culture evolves, it generates its own adaptive problems for human beings. Culture stress produces a unique problem, for the means we have used to adapt are the very factors which produce the stress.

How does cultural stress affect human physiology? We do not know a great deal about this, but what has been learned confirms our suspicion that the effects are harmful. For example, we learned quickly that overcrowding, air pollution, and noise pollution produce harmful physiological and psychological consequences. In the early sixties it was shown that laboratory rats subjected to crowded conditions displayed higher mortality and decreased fertility. In 1972 the same results were suggested in a study conducted on persons living in Chicago. With regard to air pollution the relationship between oxidants in the atmosphere and respiratory diseases is well documented on human beings. Noise pollution has been investigated more by psychologists than physiologists, yet it has been shown that increasing noise levels permanently damage hearing, interfere with sleep, cause constriction of the blood vessels, and stimulate pituitary and adrenal gland secretions.

Human beings, thus, adapt to cultural stress. Are some people better able to adapt than others? If so, how do the differences arise? What are the long-term physiological effects of adapting to cultural stress? No one knows the answers to these questions. Because of their obvious importance, however, we may expect a marked increase in related studies in the immediate future. Physical anthropologists, particularly those with an understanding of culture, may be in a strategic position to contribute substantially to our understanding of the effects of cultural stress.

DEVELOPMENTAL CHARACTERISTICS

Growth is a process, the result again of interaction among a number of physiological systems, such as the endocrine, metabolic, muscular, and skeletal systems. The study of growth is itself a highly diversified enterprise, containing within it several specializations. It is, perhaps, more accurate today to think of growth studies as a part of a rather new branch of science known as developmental biology, which includes such apparently diverse areas as reproductive and perinatal biology, developmental genetics, developmental psychology, and gerontology. The major thread of consistency that holds these areas together is a common interest in the interaction through time of genetic and environmental factors in producing the form and behavior (the phenotype) of the individual. This is an objective which, at present, seems idealistic and perhaps unrealistic, but there are several good reasons for being hopeful. Investigations in developmental genetics are beginning to provide some understanding of gene action and how the activity of genes is correlated with morphological changes in the structure of chromosomes. Developmental embryology has, in the last few years, made discoveries that have brought about a reevaluation of the older views of fertilization and implantation. Pharmacology is more and more concerned with the effects of drugs on the normal processes of growth.

Though growth and development are often considered together, there is a fundamental difference between them. Growth necessarily implies an increase in size; development does not. Thus growth is readily measurable by conventional means. Development, however, we may think of as passing through a sequence of regular stages such as in the familiar one of infancy-childhood-adolescence-maturity-postmaturity-senescence. Growth and development are highly correlated through the first three stages, yet exceptional cases make it clear that the two processes are independent; some persons grow in a normal way but remain developmentally retarded; others develop normally but fail to grow.

Physical anthropologists have dealt extensively with growth and almost not at all with development. Our attention here, therefore, will focus on the question of variations in growth among human populations. Do human groups vary with respect to growth? Yes, and in every possible way. Populations regularly differ in size, in the rate and velocity of growth, and in the time at which developmental events occur. This conclusion appears to be firm though based on only a modest number of comparative growth studies. Such studies are unusually difficult to conduct under field conditions since they involve either longitudinal or cross-sectional sampling. Longitudinal studies measure the same persons at regular intervals throughout their lives and are obviously impractical for use with primitive populations. An investigator would need either to remain with the group for several years or to return at regular intervals to locate and identify the members of his sample. Neither is impossible, but both are impractical.

Cross-sectional studies can be done over a short period of time, since they involve sampling several persons of different ages and making inferences about growth regularies. For example, a cross-sectional study might proceed by measuring all the five-year-olds, six-year-olds, and seven-year-olds in a school. A growth curve could then be plotted for the ages from five to seven. This approach would be more practical than a longitudinal study in primitive populations, but, in addition to limitations inherent in all longitudinal studies, would be handicapped in most cases by the inability to determine age with precision.

Thus the information available on variation in growth is fragmentary. That is limitation enough, but the situation is made even more difficult because the data are usually reported in racial terms. We find (see Garn, 1971), for example, that: 1) prior to birth the bones of the leg grow most rapidly in Negroes, slower in Caucasians, and slowest in Japanese, 2) bone density is highest among Negroes, lowest among Asians; 3) supernumerary skull bones (Wormian bones) and shovel-shaped incisors occur most commonly among Asians and American Indians; and 4) Australian aborigines have the largest teeth, the Lapps the smallest.

These will serve as illustrations. From them one should be able to conclude that the situation with regard to growth is similar to the one encountered with physiological characteristics. The racial strategies in both cases set severe restrictions on how we may learn about human variation. To say that the long bones of Negroes grow more rapidly during the prenatal period than they do in other races is simply to make a declarative statement about African and African-derived blacks. The statement may be correct or may serve to obscure the fact that the trait may, for example, be characteristic of people adapted to tropical conditions. The value of such research is not obvious, for the information it yields is ambiguous, and it explains absolutely nothing.

In summary the status of growth studies in physical anthropology may be described as sparse and chaotic. Yet even so the following points appear to be well accepted: 1) Individuals differ considerably in such features as the rate and velocity of growth and in the time at which developmental events occur. 2) These individual variations may cluster together with other racial characteristics, but the details are not at all clear. 3) To what degree the variations are due to genetic, and thus evolutionary, differences or to environmental agencies is not known. 4) The most striking result of growth studies has been the indication that, no matter how much variation there may be in the ways of accomplishing growth, the overall growth pattern is similar for all groups of human beings and, indeed, between man and the rest of the primates when obvious and appropriate corrections are applied.

PSYCHOLOGICAL CHARACTERISTICS

Psychologists attempt to explain many aspects of human behavior. For example, they deal with learning, temperament, intelligence, mental illness, perception, motor skills, group behavior, etc. So we might anticipate an abundance of information on human variation in each of these areas. In fact there is very little comparative information on any of these factors with one very conspicuous exception—intelligence. There is a superabundance of commentary, observation, and data on the subject of racial differences in intelligence.

Race and intelligence apparently hold a broad appeal. The subject appears regularly in popular books and magazines as well as in scientific publications. Persons with the most varied backgrounds make authoritative pronouncements on the subject. In the past few years alone one can find widely circulated and influential treatments of the subject by businessmen, politicians, Nobel prize-winning physicists, clergymen, psychologists, historians, anatomists, sociologists, geneticists, and, of course, anthropologists.* With so many experts from such diverse backgrounds handling the situation already, one enters the matter with some apprehensiveness.

---

* For a sample of such writings, the interested reader could consult *Environment, Heredity, and Intelligence* (1969), a compilation of articles from the *Harvard Educational Review*, or *Science and the Concept of Race* (1968), a collection of papers presented at the 1966 annual meetings of the American Academy of Sciences in New York. See also Scarr-Salapatek (1971), Eysenck (1971), Shockley (1969), and Putnam (1967). For complete references consult the bibliography at the end of the chapter.

In dealing with this subject the temptation is almost irresistible to enter it on one or another side of an argument. That could be a trap in itself, so keep in mind that the present discussion centers on the question: Do human populations differ with regard to psychological factors? Yes indeed. Everyone is in agreement on this. The controversy arises again over the explanation for the variation and particularly with respect to intelligence. Some maintain that psychological differences are the consequences of learning in different cultural circumstances. This is similar to physiological plasticity, except, of course, it refers to psychological factors. Human beings are psychologically malleable, and culture does the shaping. Thus, according to this view, if one wishes to understand psychological differences, one should look for the cultural determinants.

Others regard psychological differences as reflections of genetic differences. This is a fairly common view, particularly among some whites, on the issue of racial differences in intelligence. They proceed to reach their main conclusion by means of the following argument:

Differences in intelligence are due either to cultural or genetic factors.
Differences persist when cultural factors are held constant.
Therefore, differences in intelligence are due to genetic factors.

Those who reject the conclusion do so because the cultural factors, they maintain, are never held constant. Perhaps the popularity of this view is due partly to its simple implication—if some peoples are dumber than others, then it is easy to understand why some peoples have achieved less than others. Thus it appears to explain in very simple terms many differences between populations. Yet, of course, the view is circular. Why is it that some people achieve more than others? Because, they say, these people are genetically endowed with more intelligence. But how, you may ask, do we know they are genetically superior in intelligence? By their achievements, of course. Once again we are returned to the original question.

A third view appears as a reconciliation between this modern version of the old nature-nurture argument. The view, stated simply, is that psychological differences are due to interaction between cultural and genetic factors. This is a strategy scientists have learned from politicians—controversy may be resolved by compromise. Perhaps.

Perhaps the entire issue is nonsense. Perhaps asking if one race is more intelligent than another is like asking if Democrats are fatter than women. The question is simply nonsense. Psychological differences may be distributed in ways similar to the variations noted in physiological and developmental traits; that is, they may be distributed in ways that have nothing whatever to do with race. We return to this subject in Chapter 9.

Clearly this is a troublesome topic. The strength of beliefs on the subject, many of them contradictory, tends to be inversely proportional to the amount of evidence in support of them. This is not a situation in which there can be a dispassionate discussion of the evidence, for two good reasons: 1) people are not dispassionate about racial differences in psychological traits, and 2) there is no unambiguous evidence to bring to bear on the subject. The only correct statement one is able to make about the distribution of psychological variation is to say that, indeed, it does occur (perhaps one might state the situation more precisely by saying that persons get different scores on psychological tests), but how the variations are associated with other attributes is not known. Furthermore, the significance and source of variation in psychological characteristics are not known. To continue the discussion further would be analogous to taking an unmarked trail to an unknown destination—an intellectual random walk.

MAJOR POINTS IN CHAPTER 7

1. Heterography assesses the extent and the significance of man's biological variability.
2. Human biological variability may be assessed in terms of structural and functional traits.
3. Traits considered in this chapter share two things in common: 1) we do not know precisely how any of them are inherited, and 2) they are commonly regarded as racial characteristics.
4. Though in any particular location variations of these traits may cluster together, their overall distributions are independent.
5. Independent distributions may imply separate causes.

REFERENCES AND SUGGESTIONS FOR ADDITIONAL READING

ALLEN, J. A.
1877 The influence of physical conditions in the genesis of species. *Radical Review* 1:108–140.

ANONYMOUS
1969 *Environment, heredity, and intelligence.* Reprint Series no. 2. *Harvard Educational Review.* Cambridge, Mass.

BAKER, PAUL T.
1958 The biological adaptation of man to hot deserts. *American Naturalist* 92:337–357.

BAKER, PAUL T., AND J. S. WEINER, EDS.
1966 *The biology of human adaptability.* London: Oxford University Press.

BARNICOT, N. A.
1957 Human pigmentation. *Man* 144:1–7.

BERGMANN, C.
1847 Uber die Verhältnisse der Wärmeökonomie der Thiere zu ihrer Grösse. *Göttingen Studien* 3.5:95–708.

BIASUTTI, RENATO
1959 *Le razze e l popoli della terra.* 2d ed. 4 vols. Torino: UTET.

BIELICKI, TADEUSZ, AND Z. WELON
1964 The operation of natural selection on human head form in an East European population. *Homo* 15:22–30.

BRACE, C. LORING
1963 Structural reduction in evolution. *American Naturalist* 97:39–49.

BRUES, ALICE
1959 The spearman and the archer—an essay on selection in body build. *American Anthropologist* 61:457–469.

CARBONELL, VIRGINIA M.
1963 Variations in the frequency of shovel-shaped incisors in different populations. In *Dental anthropology*, ed. D. R. Brothwell, pp. 211–234. New York: Macmillan.

EYSENCK, H. J.
1971 *The I Q argument.* New York: Library Press.

GARN, STANLEY M.
1965 *Human races.* 2d ed. Springfield, Ill.: Charles C Thomas.
1971 *Human races.* 3d ed. Springfield, Ill.: Charles C Thomas.

GARN, STANLEY M., ED.
1960 *Readings on race.* Springfield, Ill.: Charles C Thomas.

HARRISON, G. A., J. S. WEINER, J. M. TANNER, AND N. A. BARNICOT
1964 *Human biology: An introduction to human evolution, variation, and growth.* New York: Oxford University Press.

HOOTON, EARNEST ALBERT
1947 *Up from the ape.* Rev. ed. New York: Macmillan.

HULSE, FREDERICK S.
1955 Technological advance and major racial stocks. *Human Biology* 27:184–192.

LOOMIS, W. F.
  1967 Skin pigment regulation of vitamin-D biosynthesis in man. *Science* 157:501–506.
MARTIN, RUDOLF, AND KARL SALLER
  1955–1966 *Lehrbuch der Anthropologie.* 3d ed. 4 vols. Stuttgart: Gustav Fischer Verlag.
MEAD, MARGARET, T. DOBZHANSKY, E. TOBACH, AND R. LIGHT, EDS.
  1968 *Science and the concept of race.* New York: Columbia University Press.
NEWMAN, HORATIO H., F. N. FREEMAN, AND K. J. HOLZINGER
  1937 *Twins: A study of heredity and environment.* Chicago: University of Chicago Press.
NEWMAN, MARSHALL T.
  1961 Biological adaptation of man to his environment: Heat, cold, altitude, and nutrition. *Annals of the New York Academy of Sciences* 91:617–633.
  1962 Evolutionary changes in body size and head form in American Indians. *American Anthropologist* 64:237–257.
NEWMAN, RUSSELL W., AND ELLA H. MUNRO
  1955 The relation of climate and body size in U.S. males. *American Journal of Physical Anthropology* (n.s.) 13:1–17.
OSBORNE, RICHARD H., AND FRANCES V. DE GEORGE
  1959 *Genetic basis of morphological variation: An evaluation and application of the twin study method.* Cambridge: Harvard University Press.
PARNELL, R. W.
  1965 Human size, shape, and composition. In *Human body composition: Approaches and applications,* ed. Josef Brozek. Symposia of the Society for the Study of Human Biology 7:61–72.
PUTNAM, C.
  1967 *Race and reality: A search for solutions.* Washington, D.C.: Public Affairs Press.
ROBERTS, D. F.
  1953 Body weight, race, and climate. *American Journal of Physical Anthropology* (n.s.) 11:533–558.
  1960 Effects of race and climate on human growth as exemplified by studies on African children. In *Human growth,* ed. J. M. Tanner, pp. 59–72. New York: Pergamon Press.
SCARR-SALAPATEK, S.
  1971 Race, social class, and IQ. *Science* 174:1285–1295.
SHIELDS, JAMES
  1962 *Monozygotic twins.* London: Oxford University Press.
SHOCKLEY, W.
  1969 Offset analysis description of racial differences. Abstract. *Proceedings, National Academy of Sciences* 64:1432.
WENT, F. W.
  1968 The size of man. *American Scientist* 56:400–413.

8 Human Heterography and Morphological Variation: Traits of Known Inheritance

INTRODUCTION

One conclusion that seems clearly to be supported by the distributional evidence of man's morphological variation is that traits tend to be found in clusters of association rather than randomly distributed over the surface of the earth. On reflection, this is not surprising, since groups of people living within an area can be expected to display their common evolutionary background in the form of similar adaptations which, translated into morphology, imply similar anatomical, physiological, and developmental characteristics. If this is a reasonable expectation, then it would seem logical to anticipate not only that genetic characteristics would tend to cluster together, but also, to the extent that they reflect common evolutionary episodes, that they should be found in association with clusters of morphological traits as well. This raises an interesting question: Are genetic characteristics of any more value in solving the traditional problems of physical anthropology than measurements and observations on morphological traits? The simple observation, for example, that human beings have various blood types, while it may have important clinical implications, is in principle no different from the well-established fact that men have various forms of hair, various skin colors, etc. Furthermore, to the extent that physical anthropology concerns itself solely with purely historical problems (for example, Are the Hopi more closely related to the Zuni than to the Santa Clara Pueblos?), inherited traits are probably of no greater value to it than the usual anthropometric measurements and observations. In the past twenty years, however, physical anthropology has become increasingly involved with problems of evolutionary process and the dynamics of adaptation, and in these, inherited characteristics have properties that make them much more useful than the traits of unknown inheritance (see Tinsman, 1971). The advantages are in some ways obvious, but will in any event be easier to comprehend after some background details are presented. The best-known (and thus most interesting) inherited characteristics in man are the blood groups and the hemoglobins, and these will be discussed in some detail, to be followed by a brief discussion of other traits of known inheritance in man.

THE BLOOD GROUPS

If you prepare a slide of your blood and look at it under a microscope, you will find no basis whatever for distinguishing between it and that of any other normal person's blood. The components are all there: red cells in large numbers and considerably fewer white cells, all supported by a relatively clear liquid medium called plasma. If the blood is allowed to clot, the plasma loses some of its components (those needed to form the clot), and the remaining liquid medium is then referred to as serum. Furthermore, if you examined the functions of the clotted elements, you would find no basis for distinguishing one person's blood from another's. The red cells transport oxygen from the lungs to the tissues and carry away carbon dioxide as a waste product. The white cells provide one major physiological defense against infection, and the plasma functions in bringing nourishment to the cells of the body, in removing the waste products of metabolism, in clotting the cells on injury, and, in a different fashion than the white cells, in resisting the effects of infection.

Suppose, however, that you mixed a drop of your blood with a drop of some-one else's—what would happen? Nothing from the above would lead you to suspect that anything would occur, but it is likely that clumps of cells would form islands in the solution, as illustrated in Figure 8–1. This is agglutination; the cells would have, by some means, become attached to one another, and if you were given this blood in a transfusion, the result could very well be fatal. Clearly, the conclusion based only on microscopic observation and functional analysis is incorrect—one person's blood is not the same as another's.

From this evidence, one might be tempted to believe that every person's blood is unique, which would imply that any person's blood would agglutinate the blood of everyone else. In fact, however, the correct interpretation requires more information. What causes the agglutination? If you take out the cells and mix them together, do you observe agglutination? Does the serum or plasma from one person agglutinate the cells of another? If so, would the reverse always be true?

These are the problems that confronted Karl Landsteiner when he recorded a series of observations inquiring into the same problems, for which he eventually won the Nobel Prize. His discovery (1900) consisted of the following observations: 1) the serum of some individuals will agglutinate the cells of others; 2) the reactions are not always reciprocal; and 3) these observations have clear implications for medical practice. Thus, Landsteiner made it clear that not all bloods were the same, nor were they all different; rather, there are types of blood. He had discovered the ABO types.

The discovery of the blood types implied the presence of: 1) compositional differences (known as antigens) in the red cells and 2) substances in the serum called antibodies, which distinguish particular antigens from others in a very specific way, causing the agglutination of the cells. This antigen-antibody phenomenon is very widespread as a physiological defense mechanism against the effects of exposure to foreign proteins. It is, for example, this mechanism that protects us against bacterial

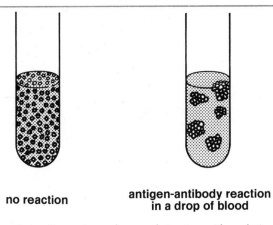

no reaction　　　　**antigen-antibody reaction
in a drop of blood**

Figure 8–1.　Comparison of nonagglutination with agglutination.

infections. Infectious microorganisms also introduce foreign substances (antigens) which stimulate the production of antibodies that attack the antigens and thereby the microorganisms themselves.

The ABO blood groups discovered by Landsteiner have come to be known in detail, and as more has been learned about the system, it has become evident that it has characteristics which make it unique. Since the time of Landsteiner's discovery, a number of other blood group systems have been discovered, and, with a few exceptions, these are all controlled by genetic loci that segregate independently. The red blood cell is indeed a complicated thing having several different antigenic properties.

The medical implications of different blood types have been obvious since Landsteiner's original discovery, but the anthropological implications became evident only gradually as it was learned that these types (or, more particularly, the genes responsible for them) occurred with varying frequencies in different populations. This implied that they might be useful to anthropologists in classifying races and in solving a multitude of specific historical problems. In addition, and unlike the usual anthropometric measurements, the blood groups are traits that can be determined with precision (a person is either type A or he is not) by relatively simple procedures. Also, they have other assets of anthropological significance: 1) they are constant throughout an individual's lifetime; 2) no one has any preconceived prejudices about them, as they do about other morphological traits; and 3) at the outset at least, they appeared to be totally uninfluenced by selection. These properties imply enormous anthropological potential.

ABO Blood Groups

Every person's red blood cells can be typed into one, and only one, of the following four types: A, B, O, and AB. These were the groups that Landsteiner discovered in

1900. Implications and ramifications of the discovery continue to be investigated today; yet, basically, the original observations were quite simple. There are two antigens, A and B, and two antibodies, anti-A and anti-B, and they are combined as indicated in Table 8–1.

Table 8–1 Antigen-Antibody Combinations in the ABO Blood Types

TYPE	ANTIGEN* A	B	ANTIBODIES ANTI-A	ANTI-B
A	+	−	−	+
B	−	+	+	−
O	−	−	+	+
AB	+	+	−	−

* + means present; − means absent.

Thus, when a sample is classified as blood type A, it means the following: 1) the cells have the A antigen and do not have B; and 2) the serum contains anti-B antibodies and lacks anti-A. Type B is the reverse of type A; type O blood has neither antigen and both antibodies; and type AB the reverse, both antigens and neither antibody.

How does a person become blood type A, as opposed, say, to blood type O? This is completely under genetic control; that is, one is blood type A because he has inherited certain genes from his parents. But in what way, one may ask, does this come about? Or, how many different kinds of genetic determiners are involved in producing four types? It will be useful for overall understanding to digress here for a moment to consider the problem this represents. Our illustration will be the ABO blood groups, but the problem is common to all inherited traits. Consider for a moment a few possibilities: 1) *two alleles*. This cannot be the correct number, since,

Table 8–2 Implications of Competing Hypotheses on the Inheritance of the ABO Blood Types

HYPOTHESIS #1 THREE ALLELES, ONE LOCUS				HYPOTHESIS #2 TWO ALLELES, TWO LOCI				
Parent Sex →	A	B	O	Parent Sex →	AB	A'B	AB'	A'B'
Cells ↓	Offspring Genotypes			Cells ↓	Offspring Genotypes			
A	AA	AB	AO	AB	AABB	AA'BB	AABB'	AA'BB'
B	AB	BB	BO	A'B	AA'BB	A'A'BB	AA'BB'	A'A'BB'
O	AO	BO	OO	AB'	AABB'	AA'BB'	AAB'B'	AA'B'B'
				A'B'	AA'BB'	A'A'BB'	AA'B'B'	A'A'B'B'

no matter how hard one might try, it is not possible to combine two things into more than three different pairs, AA, AB, BB, and the problem here involves the inheritance of four types. Thus, it is logical to conclude that more than two determiners are involved, but, without additional knowledge, it is not possible to tell if the ABO blood types are controlled either by: 2) *three alleles*, that is, three *different* determiners acting in pairs, or 3) *two separate genetic loci*, each with a pair of alleles. Table 8–2 illustrates the difference between these alternatives; neither is immediately encouraging, since with three alleles there are six *different* possibilities, whereas with two loci there are nine, and our problem is to account for four and only four. The answer seems clearly to be dominance, but it is still not clear in which of the alternatives. Suppose, for example, that A is dominant over A', and B over B'; this will produce four blood types, as follows:

$$AB = AABB,\ AABB',\ AA'BB,\ AA'BB'$$
$$A = AAB'B',\ AA'B'B'$$
$$B = A'A'BB,\ A'A'BB'$$
$$O = A'A'B'B'$$

That fulfills the requirements, but, then, so will three alleles when A and B are co-dominant and both are dominant to O, as follows:

$$AB = AB$$
$$A = AA,\ AO$$
$$B = BB,\ BO$$
$$O = OO$$

How can the correct possibility be determined? Only by empirical test. For example, in the first case, involving two pairs of alleles, it is possible for parents both of whom are AB to have an O child in the mating AA'BB' × AA'BB'; likewise O offspring could result from AB × A or AB × B marriages. The other model implies that whenever at least one of the parents is AB, the mating cannot produce an O child. On inspection of family blood groups it was discovered that AB parents never produced O children; thus the three-allele explanation is consistent with both logical and empirical demands. It tells us how the ABO blood groups are inherited.

The details of our knowledge of the ABO blood groups continue to expand rapidly. Some of the new information is of interest only to the specialist, but some has anthropological significance, and among the most important discoveries are the following: 1) There is a water-soluble form of the A and B antigens which can be detected in the saliva of some individuals, and this trait is itself under genetic control. This trait, known as the secretor factor, will be discussed in more detail later. 2) The antigenic substances are extraordinarily complex molecules known as mucopolysaccharides. 3) These substances, or others very much like them, are present in the composition of many plants. 4) Some diseases are more commonly found among persons of one blood type than they are in other blood types. Well-documented associations are summarized in Table 8–3. 5) ABO incompatibility can affect a couple's reproductive abilities, as can the better-known Rh incompatibility. 6) The A and B antigens have been found in monkeys and apes (Wiener and Moor-Jankowski, 1963).

Table 8–3   Well-Established ABO Blood Group-Disease Associations

BLOOD GROUP	DISEASE
A	Stomach Cancer
B	Pernicious Anemia
O	Ulcers, Gastric and Duodenal

These touch on some of the more striking things that have been learned about the ABO blood groups, and while they are perhaps intriguing on their own merits, the problem remains of dealing with the question of why physical anthropologists find the ABO blood groups particularly interesting—for many reasons over and above the general ones discussed earlier in connection with all blood groups. The ABO blood groups were the first to be discovered, and information on their frequencies in populations accumulated so rapidly that their distribution remains much better known than the distribution of any of the other blood types. Earlier they were of interest to scholars wishing to construct racial classifications, who presumed them to be unaffected by the environment and thus ideal racial tags. Ironically, perhaps, it is precisely because they appear now to be surprisingly sensitive to environmental influences that the ABO blood groups are a particularly informative genetic system in studies of evolution in contemporary populations. Their frequencies vary in puzzling ways that virtually cry out for explanation. Consider first the A allele. The highest frequencies of A are found among two widely separated groups, the Blackfoot Indians of the northern plains in North America and the Lapps of northern Scandinavia. High frequencies of A are also found among the aboriginal inhabitants of southern Australia and the peoples of Polynesia. It is low in frequency or entirely absent among Central and South American Indians. For most of the world, however, A gene frequencies range between .10 and .35.

The B allele is highest in central Asia with frequencies from .30 to .35. It is virtually absent, however, among American Indians and Australian aborigines. Its absence among American Indians has always posed a difficult problem for those wishing to use the ABO blood groups as indicators of racial affiliation, since on morphological and archaeological grounds it is clear that the American Indians are the descendants of migrants from Asia. Thus the morphological and archaeological evidence is not supported by this sharp discrepancy in the frequency of the B allele. The usual explanation given for this is genetic drift, implying that the gene frequencies of the early migrants were changed as a result of chance factors. Thus it is merely an accident that modern Indians do not reflect their degree of relationship to. the modern Asians in this regard. This is a convenient explanation, but, in fact, little if any evidence exists to support it. The two groups could, for example, be closely related phylogenetically and yet, in recent generations, be affected differently by selective agencies. In this instance, their differences could provide a first clue in the solution of the problem of what environmental factors influence the frequencies of the ABO alleles. This is an interesting problem, and there is as yet no answer to it. Surprisingly, there are very few hypotheses attempting to explain it.

Among the rest of the world's populations the B allele ranges between .05 and .25. The frequencies of O, of course, are known when the frequencies of A and B are given.

What do these distributions mean to the anthropologist? The patterns do not correspond closely to any of the anthropometric distributions considered in the previous chapter. What do the variations in frequency imply about the histories of modern groups? Do they offer any new insights into the patterns and dynamics of human evolution? Are they informative on the question of whether or not man is continuing to undergo evolutionary change? These constitute some of the core problems facing physical anthropologists today, as they confront the task of inte-grating and interpreting the vastly diversified ways in which human beings differ.

Perhaps these remarks about the ABO blood groups will underscore the differ-ences between traits of known inheritance and those in which this information is lacking. From the point of view of classifying man's heterographic variation, the two kinds of traits are essentially of equal value, and in their taxonomic use they share the same deficiencies. However, from the standpoint of evolutionary dynamics, inherited traits appear to hold enormously greater potential. The most exciting part of this is the fact that this potential is only now beginning to be realized. Only now are the really interesting questions about the sources of man's variation beginning to be asked with some reasonable expectation of obtaining answers. Simply because we know more about them, the ABO blood groups are likely to receive the greatest amount of attention at the outset, but there is, of course, much more.

MN Blood Groups

The next blood types to be discovered were those of the MN system. These, too, were discovered by Landsteiner, together with his collaborator, Philip Levine, in 1927. This system was discovered as a result of some clever reasoning and the appli-cation of some elegant techniques. The reasoning proceeded from a hypothesis, which had been repeatedly demonstrated as correct in other contexts, that if you inject a protein substance (in this case red blood cells) into an animal, the animal usually develops antibodies to that substance. That is, if given an injection of type B cells, an organism might well form anti-B antibodies, and if these are removed from his serum and still agglutinated some B cells, then one possible reason for this would be that the animal had developed antibodies to an antigen not formerly identified. This is essentially how the MN blood groups were discovered. Landsteiner and Levine (1927) injected immunized rabbits with different ABO blood types and, after a time, obtained samples of the rabbits' blood, from which they drew off the serum. The expected antibodies (anti-A and anti-B) were removed by a technique known as absorption, and the serum was then tested against a variety of human cells. It was discovered by this process that individuals could be classified into three groups on the basis of their reaction to the rabbit sera: 1) those that reacted only to one type of antiserum (designated anti-M), 2) those reacting only with another type (designated anti-N), and 3) those reacting with both. The results are stated in Table 8–4.

Table 8–4   Reactions of Human Cells to Rabbit Antisera

THE MN BLOOD GROUPS

	ANTIBODIES*	
TYPE	ANTI-M	ANTI-N
1. M	+	−
2. N	−	+
3. MN	+	+

* + means agglutination.

Shortly after their discovery, the fact that these were inherited was established by investigation of families. The way they are inherited is entirely consistent with the model of two co-dominant alleles. Thus, unlike the situation in the ABO system, only three genotypes are possible, and, since the alleles are not dominant to one another, there is a complete one-to-one correspondence between phenotype and genotype, thus:

$$\begin{array}{ccc} \text{Phenotype} & & \text{Genotype} \\ \text{M} & \longleftrightarrow & \text{MM} \\ \text{N} & \longleftrightarrow & \text{NN} \\ \text{MN} & \longleftrightarrow & \text{MN} \end{array}$$

The MN system contrasts with the ABO system also in that human beings normally do not have antibodies to the MN antigens. Thus, the system lacks the medical implications for blood transfusions that the ABO types have. The MN locus is closely linked to one controlling the expression of another blood group antigen, the S locus. The significance of this linkage association is, of course, important in a number of ways to human geneticists confronted with the problem of interpreting the occurrence of the two traits in families, but for present purposes it is probably enough to point out that the most important implication has to do with the ways in which genes segregate and recombine before being transmitted from parents to offspring. Loci linked together on the same chromosome remain combined and thus are transmitted together. Loci located on separate chromosomes are transmitted independently to recombine in random associations in the offspring, and this is what is meant by independent segregation. Since one is either S-positive or S-negative, the two loci may be combined to form one blood group system with six phenotypes, as follows:

MS	Ms
MNS	MNs
NS	Ns

The S locus illustrates the very common mode of inheritance involving a pair of alleles, one of which is dominant over the other. Thus, while there are three genotypes (SS, Ss, ss), there are only two phenotypes, S-positive (SS, Ss) and S-negative (ss).

The highest gene frequencies of M, ranging from .75 to .90, may be found in American Indian populations. Lower frequencies, but still well above .50 (approximately .60–.70), characterize most of continental Asia with, in general, the frequencies increasing westward from the Pacific coast and dropping off at the Euro-Asian frontier. In Europe and Africa there is less variation, with the frequencies clustering around .50. The lowest frequencies of M are found among the Papuan peoples of New Guinea, aboriginal Australians, and Micronesians. The frequencies of M, of course, imply those of N; thus, the distribution of N is the reciprocal of that for M.

S is highest among Europeans, where it reaches a high of approximately .45. Very few reports exist on the distribution of S in central Asia. However, the frequencies for India are similar to those of Europe. American Indians likewise have not been tested extensively, but they appear to be similar to the Africans, with both showing frequencies from .10 to .30. As in the case of M, the lowest frequencies of S are found in aboriginal Australia, New Guinea, and Micronesia.

One further interesting feature of the MNS chromosome is the additional linkages with two antigens known as Hunter and Henshaw. Both are commonly found in African populations and rarely or never found in others.

The puzzling distribution of the MNS alleles, the recognizability of homozygous and heterozygous genotypes, and their linkage associations make these blood group systems interesting. As more is learned about their relationships to one another and about their distributions over the world, they have the potential to rival the ABO blood groups in the information they provide on the subject of human evolution and in improving our understanding of man's heterographic variation.

P Blood Groups

In the same studies that resulted in the discovery of the MN system, Landsteiner and Levine also discovered the P groups. The antibody was produced by immunizing rabbits, and it reacted with 78 percent of all human red cells in a way that crosscut the MN and ABO phenotypes, indicating a totally independent blood group system. At first it appeared to be a system inherited in a simple and straightforward way, controlled by a pair of alleles, with P dominant to p. Dominant homozygotes showed strong reactions, heterozygotes weaker ones. The weak reaction complicated the technical procedures to a degree that made it difficult to use this locus in describing differences between populations, for it was found that apparent differences were often due to mistakes in typing the weak P-positive reactions. This fact, taken together with the additional one that relatively few populations have been tested for the P antigen, makes it impossible to characterize its worldwide distribution with any confidence. Enough is known, however, to say that its frequency does vary considerably, and thus the system should become of more importance to anthropological problems as more information becomes available.

The Rh System

The Rh system is interesting for three different reasons: 1) the precise way in which it is inherited remains an unresolved problem forming the basis of two competing theories; 2) pregnant Rh-negative females develop antibodies that can destroy the red blood cells of their unborn offspring; and 3) the Rh alleles show wide variation in their frequencies in samples drawn from populations all over the world. There are many other aspects necessary to obtain a reasonably complete understanding of the system and its history, but these will serve to direct attention to the features of greatest importance to physical anthropology.

Again it was Karl Landsteiner, collaborating on this occasion with A. S. Wiener, who in 1940 reported the initial discovery of an Rh antigen. They observed that rabbits immunized with red blood cells from rhesus monkeys developed an antibody that agglutinated the red blood cells of 85 percent of a sample of New Yorkers and failed to react with the cells of 15 percent. The experiment itself seems improbable and puzzling. Why inject rabbits with monkey blood cells and then test the rabbits' serum on the cells of human beings? However, one should recall that the M, N, and P factors had been discovered by immunizing rabbits with human cells. Moreover, Landsteiner and Wiener were deliberately trying to learn as much as possible about human blood groups. Furthermore, the reasoning behind the experiment becomes clearer in view of the observation that no additional systems had been disclosed in continued investigations of rabbit serum immunized with human cells. Why not inject cells from another animal, perhaps a taxonomic neighbor of man, and see what happens? Rhesus monkeys had been used regularly in medical research and thus provided convenient subjects, and it is, of course, from them that the Rh factor got its name. However improbable the experiment might seem, the consequences were far-reaching indeed, and it is this kind of response to an educated hunch that raises brilliant scientists above the level of run-of-the-mill scientists.

Initially, the antigen discovered by Landsteiner and Wiener appeared to be under

Table 8–5   The D Factor in the Rh System*

| | ANTIBODIES | |
TYPE	ANTI-D	ANTI-d
DD	+	—
Dd	+	+
dd	—	—(?)

* + means a positive antigen-antibody reaction.

the control of a single genetic locus that could be occupied by one or another of a pair of alleles with the positive condition dominant to the negative, and, in a sense, this remains a correct interpretation. Today, when we speak of a person as Rh positive or Rh negative, it is this antigen-antibody reaction that we are referring to, and the positive reaction is understood as dominant to the negative. However, two discoveries have greatly affected our views of this subject: 1) the demonstration that Rh incompatibilities between mother and offspring can and often do produce serious defects in the newborn child (It was this clear medical implication that stimulated an intensive investigation of the Rh system. The details of this discovery will be discussed presently.), and 2) the discovery of five additional antigen-antibody relationships that, taken together with the first one, make up the totality of the Rh blood group system.

To understand the inheritance of the Rh system requires an understanding of these newer antigens and antibodies and how they are interrelated. To try to follow the historical development of this system involves a heavy commitment to a discussion of serological techniques, for many of the new antibodies were discovered as the consequences of applying some ingenious laboratory procedures which, while they are interesting in themselves, are nevertheless remote from the point of view of our objectives. So it seems reasonable to begin by giving the name of the original antigen discovered by Landsteiner and Wiener—it is called the D factor. Thus, positive reactions are genotypically DD or Dd, and negative results dd. One of the newer antibodies agglutinates the red blood cells of persons with the d factor,* and thus this system may be seen as similar to the MN blood types in the sense that all three genotypes are distinguishable, as shown in Table 8–5.

Another pair of antibodies and their antigens, designated as C and c, has also been identified, and for the moment these can be considered completely separately

---

* This bends the facts a bit. Anti-d was first reported in 1946. There are good reasons now for questioning the correctness of the results. In fact, there never has been a satisfactory demonstration of this antiserum, although, largely because of the symmetry of the rest of the system, many investigators believe that it exists. It has not been conclusively identified as yet.

Table 8–6   The C Factor in the Rh System*

TYPE	ANTIBODIES	
	ANTI-C	ANTI-c
CC	+	—
cc	+	+
Cc	—	+

* + means a positive antigen-antibody reaction.

from the Dd antigens. The Cc system also consists of three phenotypes, and these imply the underlying genotypes, so that its reactions can be characterized as in Table 8–6.

If there were no more to it than the Cc and Dd systems, it would be simple and straightforward; but, in the inspection of data obtained on families, it became clear that the Cc and Dd loci did not segregate; that is, the two loci are not independent, but rather are closely linked to one another. This, too, is similar to the MN system with the addition of the Ss locus closely linked together with it. The Rh system, however, is characterized by yet a third locus, Ee, closely linked together with the Cc, Dd loci. The Ee antigen-antibody relationships are analogous to the Cc, Dd loci (see Table 8–7) and, again, linked together with them. The five additional antibodies are thus accounted for: d, C, c, E, and e. With the original D it is possible to identify all eight different kinds of arrangements as shown in Table 8–8. Thus, everyone's complete genotype for the Rh system is a pair (one chromosome from each parent) of these eight possible arrangements.

Consider for a moment the genetic implications of loci closely linked together on the same chromosome. Linked loci can be separated by a process known as crossover (see Chapter 3), wherein paired chromosomes exchange parts of themselves and thus break up former linkage associations. The likelihood that a linkage association

Table 8–7   The E Factor in the Rh System†

TYPE	ANTIBODIES	
	ANTI-E	ANTI-e
EE	+	—
Ee	+	+
ee	—	+

† + means a positive antigen-antibody reaction.

Table 8–8   Antigen-Antibody Reactions in the Rh System*

TYPE	ANTIBODIES					
	ANTI-C	ANTI-D	ANTI-E	ANTI-c	ANTI-d	ANTI-e
CDE	+	+	+	−	−	−
CDe	+	+	−	−	−	+
CdE	+	−	+	−	+	−
Cde	+	−	−	−	+	+
cDE	−	+	+	+	−	−
cDe	−	+	−	+	−	+
cdE	−	−	+	+	+	−
cde	−	−	−	+	+	+

* + means a positive antigen-antibody reaction.

between one locus and another will be destroyed by crossing over is proportional to the distance between them; the greater the distance, the more likely the crossover. Thus, loci linked on opposite extremes of a chromosome are more likely to be separated by crossover than two loci adjacent to one another. How close together are the Cc, Dd, Ee loci? Apparently, very close. No case of their linkage being rearranged by crossing over has ever been conclusively proven. This in itself is interesting. If they are so close together that they never cross over, how is it that they can be called three separate loci? Is it not possible that the various reactions are the expressions of a single locus that can be occupied by any one of eight alternative alleles? Yes, indeed it is. These two alternatives have been the core of a long and heated controversy over the inheritance of the Rh system. The model employing three closely linked loci was proposed by R. A. Fisher and R. R. Race in 1948. The single-locus-multiple-allele model was put forth in 1949 by A. S. Wiener, Landsteiner's collaborator in the original experiments. Instead of chromosomes, Wiener's theory postulates eight alleles controlling the expression of eight antigens (agglutinogens in Wiener's vocabulary) and their reaction patterns with six antisera. Table 8–9 compares the essential features of each view. For our purposes the models are

Table 8–9   Comparison of Rh Nomenclatures

THREE CLOSELY LINKED LOCI	SINGLE LOCUS—MULTIPLE ALLELES
FISHER—RACE	A. S. WIENER
CDE	Rh_z
CDe	Rh_1
CdE	rh_y
Cde	rh'
cDE	Rh_2
cDe	Rh_0
cdE	rh''
cde	rh

equivalent. Each provides a logically consistent way of accounting for the empirical information known about the system. It is not, at this time, possible to choose one theory over the other on solid empirical grounds.

Today, most people are aware in a vague sort of way that the Rh blood types can be a source of difficulty in bearing normal children. Women particularly have become sensitive to the fact that if they are Rh negative they might well face the prospect of bearing moribund offspring. This general awareness arose as one consequence of the Landsteiner-Wiener discovery and another reported a year earlier by Levine and Stetson. As already noted, Landsteiner and Wiener (1940) discovered anti-D. Levine and Stetson (1939) noted that a woman who had delivered a stillborn child had an unusual antibody in her serum, and they proposed that it had been developed in response to an antigen introduced into her bloodstream by her developing child. The unusual antibody and anti-D were found to be identical, and further investigation established that children born with a disease known as *erythroblastosis fetalis* were the D-positive offspring of D-negative mothers and D-positive fathers. What Levine and Stetson had proposed for a particular case turned out to be of general validity.

Most commonly the incompatibilities arise as a consequence of the following conditions: 1) mother is D-negative (one could also say Rh negative); 2) father and child are D-positive; 3) the child's D antigen gets into the mother's bloodstream and causes the reaction any foreign protein would—it stimulates anti-D antibodies; and 4) the antibodies contact the child's blood cells and destroy them. If the antibodies are few in number, as usually is the case in first pregnancies, often no effect may be seen in the child, or it may cause a mild anemia. Subsequent D-positive pregnancies are likely to increase the number of antibodies in the mother's bloodstream and thereby increase the severity of the condition in the offspring.

As mentioned, this is the most common way in which Rh incompatibility results in erythroblastosis fetalis, and the reason for this will become clearer presently in the discussion of the frequencies of the eight chromosomes. However, it is not the only way in which it can occur. The incompatible possibilities and the genotypes that can produce them are listed in Table 8–10.

This makes it appear that Rh incompatibility must be a common event, but in fact it is not as frequent as might be assumed, because antibodies, for reasons not at all well understood, often do not develop under circumstances where they might be expected to, and, in addition, chromosome frequencies are by no means equally distributed. In fact, four chromosomes (CDe, cDE, cDe, cde) make up over 95 percent of the eight possible types, and these four show striking and interesting patterns of variation over the world.

The CDe chromosome is the most common. It has a very high frequency in the Pacific islands, reaching as high as 90 percent in some populations. Europeans, North Africans, and Southwest Asians are alike in having high frequencies of CDe, but their frequencies are substantially lower than those in the Pacific, falling more between 40 percent and 60 percent, with the Chinese, Japanese, Korean, and South-

Table 8–10   Maternal-Child Incompatibilities in the Rh System

GENOTYPES		
MOTHER	CHILD	ANTIBODY PRODUCED
ee	Ee	Anti-E
cc	Cc	Anti-C
dd	Dd	Anti-D
EE	Ee	Anti-e
CC	Cc	Anti-c
DD	Dd	(Anti-d)*

* The status of anti-d remains uncertain.

east Asian population frequencies even higher, but generally lower than those in the Pacific. American Indians have been found to have more variation in their frequencies, from approximately 30 percent to 70 percent, thus including the normal range of European variation and overlapping the northern to southwestern Orientals. Africans south of the Sahara have the lowest CDe frequencies in the world; the chromosome is entirely absent from some African populations and rarely exceeds 15 percent.

The European, North African, and Southwest Asian populations are remarkably homogeneous in the frequencies of their Rh chromosomes. In addition to sharing similar CDe frequencies, the populations in these areas are alike in having the highest cde chromosome frequencies of from 25 percent to 50 percent. Sub-Saharan Africans and the rest of the Asian peoples have lower frequencies of cde, the Africans with a range from approximately 5 percent to 25 percent, the Asians from zero to 10 percent. The cde chromosome is absent in the Pacific and among American Indians.

The cDe chromosome is common only in sub-Saharan Africa, where it regularly accounts for from 30 percent to 60 percent of the Rh chromosomes. It ranges from zero to 10 percent everywhere else. This is similar to the situation of the cDE chromosome, which is very common among American Indians (approximately 25 percent to 60 percent) and rare (zero to 20 percent) in all other groups. Table 8–11 provides a summary of the distributions of the common chromosomes in major parts of the world.

Even from this brief summary, it should be clear that a great amount of information is known about the Rh system. We know a great deal about how it is inherited, even if it cannot be conclusively shown that it is controlled by one or three loci. Its relationship to erythroblastosis has been well documented and has become widely known among educated persons. Even though it was discovered forty years later than the ABO blood groups, we know nearly as much about its global distribution as we do about that of the ABO blood groups. Yet, on reflection, it becomes evident that we are completely without well-documented answers to some of the most interesting, exciting, and basic questions regarding the system. For example, if three loci

Table 8–11   Summary of the Distribution of Common Rh Chromosomes

CHROMO-SOME	NORTH AFRICA, EUROPE, SOUTH-WEST ASIA	SUB-SAHARAN AFRICA	SOUTHEAST ASIA: CHINA, JAPAN, KOREA	PACIFIC	AMERICAN INDIAN
CDe	high frequencies	lowest frequencies	marked variation; very high frequencies	highest frequencies in the world; not greatly varied, all high	marked variation; high frequencies
cDE	low frequencies	lowest frequencies	low frequencies	low to moderate frequencies	marked variation; highest frequencies
cDe	very low frequencies	marked variation; highest frequencies	very low frequencies	very low frequencies	very low frequencies
cde	highest frequencies	low to moderate frequencies	very low frequencies	absent	absent

control the inheritance of the system, why is it that they have come to be so close to one another on the same chromosome? Or, on the other hand, if only one locus is involved, what, if any, is the special significance of several alleles? What factors account for the variations in the frequencies of the four common chromosomes? What is the relationship between the common combinations and the rare ones? And, most importantly, why is it that the cde chromosome, for which Rh-incompatible mothers are most frequently homozygous, is as common as it is in some populations of the world? Is it not reasonable to expect that if homozygous cde mothers have a greater likelihood of bearing defective offspring than mothers of any other type, the cde chromosome should be rare? Yet we have found it to be as high as 40 to 50 percent in some European populations and as high as 30 to 35 percent in some Asian populations. This raises a very interesting point which will be discussed presently.

Other Blood Group Systems

Since 1940, several other blood group systems have been discovered. As a group, these give the appearance of being of great potential value to the physical anthropologist, since in virtually every instance the alleles involved appear to vary sharply in their frequencies in different parts of the world. At this point, however, we are able to speak confidently only concerning their potential value, largely because, in most instances, only a comparatively small number of populations have been sampled. Moreover, in every case the inheritance of these systems was at first thought to be simple and straightforward, but subsequent discoveries have created much confusion.

The confusion is only now beginning to be clarified, and we will have to wait until the antisera become more generally available to know with confidence the geography of these systems.

Reference is made here to the following systems: Lutheran, Lewis, Kell, Duffy, Kidd, and Diego. The Kell system is in many ways similar to the Rh system in that multiple alleles (at least four) are involved, and these are compatible with either a single-locus-multiple-allele model or a pair of closely linked loci that can be occupied by either of two pairs of alleles. The Lutheran, Lewis, Duffy, and Kidd loci have had remarkably similar histories. The first antigen-antibody reaction in each system to be discovered was followed by the discovery of its complementary antibody, and at this point the genetic determination appeared to be simple—two alleles determining three genotypes, which, in turn, produced three recognizable phenotypes. Each system was then shown to have a fourth phenotype, which was negative for the earlier two antigens. Thus, like the ABO blood groups, each has four phenotypes. The phenotype similarity is not, however, a basis for concluding that the inheritance of these four systems is like that of the ABO system. In the case of the Lewis system, for example, it appears now that this locus involves only two alleles, whose genotypic expression is modified by a totally independent genetic determiner, the secretor locus, which is discussed below.

The Diego system is new, and it may be that its inheritance will be further elucidated by discoveries similar to those that have taken place in the Lutheran, Lewis, Duffy, and Kidd groups. The attention of anthropologists has been directed rapidly to Diego because very early it became clear that it showed sharp variations between races. Diego positives are common among some American Indian groups and among the few populations tested from Southwest Asia, China, Japan, and Korea.

In 1962, the first report appeared of a sex-linked locus controlling the appearance of a blood group antigen. This is the Xg locus, and, at present, it is of primary interest to geneticists in learning more about the X chromosome and the arrangement of genes on it, and in testing genetic hypotheses on the role of the sex chromosomes. Its value to anthropological problems is uncertain.

These few remarks do not begin to do justice to the complexities of these systems. However, detailing these complexities would not, at this point in our knowledge of the systems, advance our general appreciation of the elements of physical anthropology.

SECRETOR

There are two forms of antigens in the ABO system: 1) an alcohol-soluble form that is found on the surface of the red blood cells, and 2) a water-soluble form which may be found in the tissues, saliva, and other body fluids of only some individuals. Except in very rare instances, all human beings have the alcohol-soluble antigens, but not everyone has the water-soluble form of the antigens. Moreover, whether or not a person has the ABO water-soluble antigens is genetically determined. Those who do are known as *secretors;* those who do not are *nonsecretors.* The secretor locus segregates independently of the ABO locus and can be occupied by either of a pair of alleles, Se or se. Secretors are either SeSe or Sese, and nonsecretors are all sese.

The existence of ABO antigens outside of the red blood cells had been recognized as early as 1910, and the manner in which the trait is inherited was worked out in 1932. The frequencies of Se and se were found to vary from place to place in no clear pattern, but apart from this, the trait was regarded for many years as little more than a genetic oddity.

Lewis antigens may also be found in a water-soluble form in saliva and other fluids, but their appearance in, say, saliva seemed to be completely independent of the secretor and ABO loci, since only some secretors have Lewis antigens in their saliva, whereas some nonsecretors do too. However, Grubb (1948) observed that the Lewis antigens, if any were present at all, were different in nonsecretors from those found in secretors. Specifically, nonsecretors had Le (a+, b−), and secretors Le (a−, b+). Recall that: 1) the ABO locus is independent of the secretor locus; 2) the secretor locus nevertheless determines whether or not the ABO substance is converted to a water-soluble form; 3) the secretor and Lewis loci are independent of each other, as both are of the ABO locus; and 4) the secretor and Lewis loci appear to interact in some way in their effect on the phenotype. To explain the relationships among these elements, Grubb proposed a theory which, at the time, seemed improbable and complex. However, subsequent work has demonstrated his view to be not only sound, but simplifying as well. In brief, the elements contained in his theory are as follows: 1) Everyone inherits the ability to produce a generalized polysaccharide known as a precursor substance. 2) The Lewis system involves only two alleles (Le^+ or Le^-). 3) Lewis positive genotypes (Le^+Le^+ or Le^+Le^-) convert the precursor substance to Le^a. The Lewis negative (Le^-Le^-) genotype does not modify it at all. 4) Secretors convert the precursor substance to the water-soluble ABO antigens and the Le^a to Le^b. The details of this are less important than the general realization that secretor and Lewis loci well illustrate an understanding that is becoming increasingly clear in genetics today: inherited traits can no longer be thought of as distinct and separate entities, to be taken up and analyzed one at a time, but rather as the products of interaction among the loci as well as between the genetic elements and the environment. To the physical anthropologist interested in the dynamics of human evolution this may mean that, for example, a simultaneous consideration of allelic frequency variations in the ABO, Lewis, and secretor loci will be more informative than a consideration of each one separately.

Inherited variations in the antigenic properties of the red blood cells in man have received much attention in physical anthropology for reasons which should by now be clear. It is, moreover, likely that they will continue to be of importance, although probably as applied to new and different problems, for many years to come. This emphasis tends to obscure the fact that the red blood cell antigens are but one of several classes of antigen systems that are known to exist in man and to show frequency variations in different populations. The white blood cells, for example, display antigen differences that make it possible to divide them into blood types. Likewise, there are interesting genetic variants of proteins that occur normally in human serum. Research into these areas is comparatively new and is likely to produce many insights in the future. At present, however, what we have learned about these traits tends to confirm rather than to add to the basic understandings provided by the red blood cell types. All are alike in the following features: 1) the various types are inherited; 2) the frequencies of the alleles controlling them vary among human populations; and 3) the causes for the frequency differences are largely unknown.

There is another class of inherited traits in man that deserves particular attention, for it does add to our fundamental knowledge of human heterography—the hereditary variations of hemoglobin.

HEMOGLOBIN

In Chaper 3, hemoglobin served as an illustration of the way in which the genetic material, DNA, is translated into the construction of a protein. In that context, there was no particular reason to call attention to the fact that different kinds of hemoglobin have been discovered, although it will be helpful to do so here. Before proceeding to investigate these variations, it will be useful to recall the following basic facts about hemoglobin: 1) hemoglobin is found within the red blood cells and functions to carry oxygen to cells throughout the body and to carry away carbon dioxide; 2) the hemoglobin molecule consists of four long chains of amino acids, or, more precisely, of two pairs of identical chains, two α and two β; and 3) the sequences of amino acids in both the alpha and beta chains are known. At the molecular level, it is clear that considerably more detail is known about hemoglobin than about the polysaccharides responsible for blood group factors. The functions of blood groups are not known, and, while a substantial beginning has already been made in this field, we know comparatively little about the structure of the blood group substances.

Hemoglobin variations can come about in three ways: 1) alterations in the normal sequence of amino acids in either α or β chains; 2) molecular modifications of the structure of hemes, the iron-bearing structures located in the interstices of hemoglobin which serve as sites for the attachment of oxygen; and 3) quantitative differences in the production of α and β chains. A change of any one of these is almost always harmful to the organism, varying in severity from mild anemias to fatal diseases. We shall largely ignore the quantitative differences and those arising as a result of structural modifications to heme and concentrate on changes in amino acid sequences of the alpha and beta chains. More particularly, our discussion will

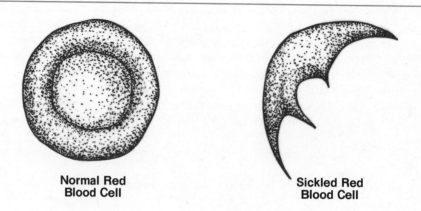

**Normal Red
Blood Cell**

**Sickled Red
Blood Cell**

Figure 8–2.   Comparison of a normal red blood cell with a sickle-shaped red blood cell.

focus on an unusually interesting disease, sickle-cell anemia, which is a condition resulting from an alteration in the normal amino acid sequence of the beta chain.

Sickle-cell Anemia

Sickle-cell anemia has been recognized for a long time as a disease with high frequencies in parts of equatorial Africa, the Mediterranean, India, and southern Asia. It may also be found in derived populations, such as some groups of American blacks, but is virtually absent everywhere else. It is a hemolytic anemia, that is, one characterized by the presence of free hemoglobin in the plasma. This is an abnormal condition, but not in itself sufficiently distinctive to distinguish sickle-cell anemia from other anemic conditions. Associated with this condition, however, is a most distinctive trait; the red blood cells of persons with sickle-cell anemia have a very characteristic shape. Figure 8–2 compares normal red blood cells with those from a patient suffering from sickle-cell anemia. The unusual shape is reminiscent of the form of the blade of a sickle, hence the name. The cells often become distorted and rupture, thereby emptying their contents, mostly hemoglobin, into the plasma. Thus the number of functional cells is reduced, but even more important is the fact that even the intact cells are unable to carry out efficiently their function of transporting oxygen and carbon dioxide, and, as a consequence, the victim almost always dies before he reaches maturity.

Analysis of the parents, brothers, and sisters of persons suffering from sickle-cell anemia resulted in two important observations: the disease is inherited, and there are three (rather than two) ways of classifying people with regard to this disease: 1) those with normal cells; 2) those with sickle cells; and 3) those whose cells are normal in shape in their bloodstream but fan out into sickle shapes when placed in a reduced-oxygen environment. These three were shown to be the phenotypic expressions of the three genotypes expected in a trait controlled by a pair of alleles. Thus:

Homozygous normal	$Hb^A Hb^A$	no sickling
Heterozygous	$Hb^A Hb^s$	sickling in reduced-oxygen environment
Homozygous sickle cells	$Hb^s Hb^s$	sickling in bloodstream

However, another discovery, reported in 1949, resulted in a much wider interest in the disease and particularly in hemoglobin. The discovery, made by Linus Pauling and his co-workers, was that persons suffering from sickle-cell anemia had a different kind of hemoglobin from that of normal persons, and, furthermore, even though their red blood cells were normal in their bloodstreams, the heterozygotes had both normal and sickle-cell hemoglobin. In the years that followed, the molecular structure of hemoglobin was worked out in detail, and it became evident that sickle-cell hemoglobin (Hb^s) differed from normal hemoglobin in but one amino acid in the sequence of 146 that make up the beta chain. Homozygous individuals lack the ability to produce any normal beta chain sequences and, as a consequence, usually die during the first decade of life. Heterozygotes produce normal beta chains in equal proportions to the abnormal chains, and physiologically this is apparently sufficient to enable them to lead normal and healthy lives.

A curious sidelight to the sickle-cell anemia story is the fact that heterozygous individuals are highly resistant to malaria, a protozoan disease which has a high incidence in areas in which sickle-cell anemia is most common. Heterozygotes therefore have a substantial survival advantage over completely normal persons in malarial areas, and a hereditary disease that might otherwise slowly disappear is perpetuated.

Since 1949, over fifty other abnormal hemoglobins have been discovered. Clearly hemoglobin and its various abnormalities are, like the blood groups, extraordinarily interesting. On the one hand, we know much more about the molecular structure of hemoglobin than we do of the blood group substances. Perhaps this is due in part to the fact that, in spite of there being a large number of amino acids in a protein, they can be joined together by only one kind of bond, the peptide bond. There are comparatively few basic sugars that go into the makeup of the blood group polysaccharides, but they may be joined together in an almost endless variety of ways. On the other hand, a good deal more is known about the distribution of variation in the blood groups, and it is this fact particularly that makes the blood groups of greater value at the present time to anthropological problems.

Whatever the differences and whatever the advantages, the striking feature about both the blood groups and the hemoglobins is that we are only now at the threshold of understanding their significance and implications. As more is learned about the molecular structure and the geographical variation of the various forms of inherited traits as separate entities, more is also learned about interaction between and among them. This simplifies their interrelationships and thereby lays the foundation for the formulation of new and more profound questions about their evolutionary, historical, and ecological significance.

OTHER TRAITS

With the discovery of inherited variations in the structure of the hemoglobin molecule and the exciting consequences of the discovery, it is easy to understand why it was that other proteins soon began to be investigated in similar ways. Of those that show considerable variation, the most thoroughly investigated have been the proteins normally found in serum. Among the serum proteins, haptoglobin is perhaps the best known in terms of its geographic variation, and for this reason may serve as an illustration.

Haptoglobin

Haptoglobin is a protein that combines with free hemoglobin and prevents its passage into the kidneys, where it could cause damage to the tissues. Three common kinds of haptoglobin have been identified on the basis of differences detected in the electrical charges on the surface of the molecules. These have been shown to be the expression of a pair of alleles in the usual three possible combinations:*

$$Hp^1 \ Hp^1$$
$$Hp^1 \ Hp^2$$
$$Hp^2 \ Hp^2$$

Haptoglobin allelic frequencies vary considerably in an interesting way. Table 8–12 indicates that high frequencies of Hp^1 tend to cluster along the equator in both Africa and South America. From about 15 degrees north the frequencies of Hp^1 are intermediate, ranging from approximately .20 to .45, with exceptions on the high side noted among the Eskimo and Apache and on the low side among the Asian Indians. The Bushmen of South Africa and some Australian aborigines have very low frequencies.

The significance of the variation is not known, and the interpretation is further complicated by the fact that, in some populations, a small proportion of otherwise normal individuals has been reported to lack haptoglobin entirely (Hp^0). Curiously, the highest frequencies of this phenomenon (ahaptoglobinemia) are associated with the highest frequencies of Hp^1.

---

* Subsequent investigations have disclosed rarer variations which are ignored here.

Table 8–12* Distribution of Haptoglobins in Various Populations
(Hp⁰ individuals were subtracted from the total population before computation of Hp')

POPULATION	N	Hp^1	Hp^0
Caucasian:			
United States White			
Ann Arbor	68	.43	0
Seattle	350	.38	.003
Canadian	49	.46	0
British	180	.43	.005
British	218	.39	.03
Australian White	100	.43†	0
Australian White	323	.38	.003
Swedish	160	.41	0
Swedish	220	.44	0
Norwegian	1000	.36	0
Danish	2046	.40	0
Finnish	891	.36	.002
Swedish Lapps	329	.32	.02
Greenlanders	74	.30	0
Bavarians	273	.46	0
Swiss	920	.40	0
French	406	.40	0
Italian			
Berra	120	.41	.01
Cologna	208	.35	0
Naples	93	.34	0
Sardinia	147	.37	0
Sicily	107	.40	0
Spanish Basques	107	.37	.01
Iranian	34	.25	0
Indian	74	.18	0
Indian	33	.17	0
Indian	219	.09	.02
Venezuelans ("hybrid")	208	.55	0
Mongolian:			
Orientals (Seattle, mostly Japanese)	242	.25	0
Japanese	349	.24	.01
Japanese	488	.27	
Japanese (United States)	23	.30	0
Malays	236	.24	.01
Chinese	167	.28	.01

* From H. E. Sutton et al., "Distribution of Haptoglobin, Transferrin, and Hemoglobin Types among Indians of Southern Mexico and Guatemala," *American Journal of Human Genetics*, 12 (1960): 342–343. Reprinted by permission. Readers interested in the original sources of the above information should consult the article.

† Based on paper electrophoresis only.

Table continues on page 286.

Table 8–12—*Continued*

POPULATION	N	Hp¹	Hp⁰
Mongolians—*Continued:*			
Alaskan:			
Eskimo	167	.33	.005
Eskimo	418	.30	0
Anaktuvuk	57	.52	.04
North Athabascan	202	.42	.01
Tlingit	82	.44	.02
Apaches	98	.59	0
Central American			
Non-Maya	170	.57	.01
Maya (less Lacandon)	414	.59	0
Lacandon	31	.93	.10
Peruvian Indians	173	.73	0
Oceanic:			
Borneo	22	.50	0
Micronesian (Marshall Islands)	52	.58	0
Tongans	200	.60	0
Negroid:			
American Negro			
Ann Arbor	43	.59	.10
Seattle	760	.54	.04
California	51	.61	.02
Nigeria:			
Yoruba	99	.87	.32
Yoruba	30	.72	.23
Habe	120	.60	.27
Fulani	111	.76	.37
Liberia, Ivory Coast	614	.72	
Gambia	157	.70	.40
Ibo	70	.49	.48
Congo			
Metropolitan	186	.60	.05
Nonmetropolitan	468	.57	.21
Pygmy	125	.40	.31
Cape Colored	88	.47	0
Hottentot	59	.51	0
Zulu	116	.53	.03
South African (Xhosa and Msutu)	315	.55	.05
Bushmen	113	.29	.02
Australian Aborigines			
Central Australia	100	.63†	0
North Queensland	123	.46†	0
Western Desert	133	.17	.01

† Based on paper electrophoresis only.

Taster

There exists a group of substances that some persons identify as having a bitter taste, whereas others find them tasteless. This phenomenon has been recognized since 1931. Whether or not one is able to taste the substances is determined genetically by a pair of alleles (T, t), as follows:

TT taster
Tt taster
tt nontaster

The heterozygote is indistinguishable from the TT homozygote; thus T is said to be dominant over t.

The geographic distribution of the alleles shows no correlation with gross climatic categories. High and low frequencies are found in the tropics, the temperate latitudes, and in the circumpolar region (see Table 8–13). In attempting to provide some explanation for this distribution, most investigations have proceeded from the observation that the substances (usually either phenylthiocarbamide—PTC—or phenylthiourea—PTO—are used) which distinguish tasters from nontasters are all known to suppress activity of the thyroid gland. Tasters could be expected to have some advantage over nontasters in resisting nodular goiter by rejecting these bitter-tasting thyroid activity suppressors. Indeed, it has been demonstrated (Azevêdo, Krieger, Mi, and Morton, 1965) that nontasters are more commonly victims of nodular goiter than would be expected by chance.

The demonstrated relationship between taster status, thyroid function, and goiter is informative but fails to account, in any comprehensive way, for the geographic variations in allelic frequencies. The suggestion has been made that the taster locus might be associated with variations in body size. The reasoning behind this is simple: nontasters ingest thyroid-suppressing foods more commonly than tasters; the thyroid gland controls growth rates; therefore, the nontasters might be expected to be smaller than tasters. Only one preliminary study of the empirical basis for this has been undertaken (Johnston, Hertzog, and Malina, 1966), and, while its results are interesting and supportive, its design is awkward, and the conclusions are tentative.

INHERITED DISEASES

Even one with only a vague awareness of genetics is likely to feel that something is missing on completing a section dealing with inherited traits in man that deals exclusively with blood types, hemoglobin varieties, serum proteins, and a few other factors. What of the many other disorders known to be inherited in man, such as hemophilia, phenylketonuria, albinism, etc.? To be sure, there are many such traits of known inheritance. These are the rare, usually pathological traits that constitute

Table 8–13* The Incidence of Nontasters of Phenylthiocarbamide and Related Compounds in Different Populations

POPULATION	NUMBER TESTED	PERCENT NONTASTERS†
English	440	31.5
United States White	3643	(29.8)
Danes	314	31.8
Norwegians	266	30.5
Finns	202	29.2
Spaniards, Northeastern	306	24.8
Basques, Spain	98	(25.0)
Lapps, Norwegian and Swedish	140	6.9
Africans, mostly West African	74	2.7
Chinese (in London)	66	10.6
Chinese (in Malaya)	50	2.0
Japanese	295	7.1
Formosan "Natives"	1756	(1.8)
Malays	50	15.6
Tamils in Malaya	50	27.2
Bombay Indians	200	(42.5)
Ramah Navahoes	264	(2.0)
Cree and Beaver Indians, Northern Alberta	489	(2.0)
Eskimos, Labrador	130	(41)
Eskimos, Northern Alaska	68	25.8
Negritos, Malaya	50	18
Aborigines (Senoi), Malaya	50	4
Arabs, Assiut		(18)
Bantu, Kenya	208	3.8
Arabs, Kenya	63	25.4
Indians, Brazil	163	1.2
Welsh	203	17.24
Portuguese	454	24.0

* From A. C. Allison and B. S. Blumberg, "Ability to Taste Phenylthiocarbamide among Alaskan Eskimos and Other Populations," *Human Biology*, 31 (1959): 355. Reprinted by permission of Wayne State University Press. Readers interested in the original sources and testing procedures should consult the article.

† Parentheses indicate studies in which techniques other than selection were used.

the major area of interest in the subdivision of genetics called medical genetics. Physical anthropology is less concerned with these traits simply because they are very rare in frequency whenever they occur and, for this reason, are uninformative in assessing degrees of relationship among modern populations. The genes responsible for these rare conditions are maintained by mutation, and the frequency of a particular condition appears to be a result of both the mutation rate and the degree of inbreeding, and no good reason exists that would lead one to believe that these variables reflect the degree of relationship. Since research on these rare inherited pathologies requires the development of mathematical models for the calculation of mutation rates and inbreeding coefficients, these pathologies have been given a great deal of attention in population genetics as well as in medical genetics.

The primary objective of this and the preceding chapter is to summarize man's heterographic variation, emphasizing, on the one hand, a selected group of traits of unknown inheritance and, on the other, some of the better-known characteristics for which the mechanisms of inheritance are known. In discussing the latter, it has been necessary to deal with a large number of details concerning the genetic aspects of the traits, and in doing so a more comprehensive understanding should result. It is now time to reconsider the distributions of both categories of traits to determine as well as possible whether the traits cluster together. If they do, are similar clusters indicators of racial affiliation or common adaptation, or do the traits vary in their distributions in a crazy-quilt pattern with little or no indication of overall distributional regularities suggesting underlying common adaptations or close common descent? In short, what, if anything, does the present-day spatial distribution of man's formal variations imply about his past? This is the main question considered in the next chapter.

MAJOR POINTS IN CHAPTER 8

1. Human biological variability may be measured in terms of traits whose precise mode of inheritance is known.

2. Traits of known inheritance, and particularly those with common variations, offer some distinctive advantages in dealing with problems of interest to physical anthropology.

3. This chapter summarizes the extent of variation in the best-known of these characteristics.

4. The overall distributions of traits of known inheritance appear to be largely independent of one another.

REFERENCES AND SUGGESTIONS FOR ADDITIONAL READING

ALLISON, A. C.

1954 Protection afforded by sickle-cell trait against subtertian malarial infection. *British Medical Journal* 1:290–294.

1955 Aspects of polymorphism in man. *Cold Spring Harbor Symposia on Quantitative Biology* 20:239–255.

1964 Polymorphism and natural selection in human populations. *Cold Spring Harbor Symposia on Quantitative Biology* 29:137–149.

ALLISON, A. C., AND B. S. BLUMBERG

1959 Ability to taste phenylthiocarbamide among Alaskan Eskimos and other populations. *Human Biology* 31:352–359.

AZEVÊDO, E., H. KRIEGER, M. P. MI, AND N. E. MORTON

1965 PTC taste sensitivity and endemic goiter in Brazil. *American Journal of Human Genetics* 17:87–90.

BEARN, ALEXANDER G., AND W. CAREY PARKER

1965 *Genetics and evolution in three human serum proteins.* Birth Defects Original Articles Series, vol. 1. New York: National Foundation–March of Dimes.

BRUES, ALICE M.

1963 Stochastic tests of selection in the ABO blood groups. *American Journal of Physical Anthropology* (n.s.) 21:287–299.

COON, CARLETON S., WITH EDWARD E. HUNT, JR.

1965 *The living races of man.* New York: Alfred A. Knopf.

GARN, STANLEY M.

1965 *Human races.* 2d ed. Springfield, Ill.: Charles C Thomas.

GRUBB, R.

1948 Correlation between Lewis blood group and secretor character in man. *Nature* 162:933.

JOHNSTON, FRANCIS E., KEITH P. HERTZOG, AND ROBERT M. MALINA

1966 Phenylthiocarbamide taste sensitivity and its relationship to growth variation. *American Journal of Physical Anthropology* (n.s.) 24:253–255.

KELSO, A. J.

1962 Dietary differences: A possible selective mechanism in ABO blood group frequencies. *Southwestern Lore* 28:48–56.

KELSO, A. J., AND GEORGE ARMELAGOS

1963 Nutritional factors as selective agencies in the determination of ABO blood group frequencies. *Southwestern Lore* 29:44–48.

LANDSTEINER, K.

1900 Zur Kenntnis der Antifermentativen, Lytischen, und Agglutinierenden werkungen des Blutserums und der Lymphe. *Zentralblatt für Bakteriologie, Parasitenkunde, Infektionskrankheiten, und Hygiene* 27:357.

LANDSTEINER, K., AND P. LEVINE

1927 A new agglutinable factor differentiating individual human bloods. *Proceedings of the Society for Experimental Biology* 24:600.

LANDSTEINER, K., AND A. S. WIENER

1940   An agglutinable factor in human blood recognized by immune sera for rhesus blood. *Proceedings of the Society for Experimental Biology* 43:223.

LEVINE, P., AND R. E. STETSON

1939   An unusual case of intragroup agglutination. *Journal of the American Medical Association* 113:126–127.

LIVINGSTONE, FRANK B.

1958   Anthropological implications of sickle cell gene distribution in West Africa. *American Anthropologist* 60:533–562.

1960   Natural selection, disease, and ongoing human evolution, as illustrated by the ABO blood groups. *Human Biology* 32:17–27.

MANN, J. D., A. CAHAN, A. G. GELB, N. FISHER, J. HAMPER, P. TIPPETT, R. SANGER, AND R. R. RACE

1962   A sex-linked blood group. *Lancet* 1:8.

MOURANT, ARTHUR E.

1954   *The distribution of the human blood groups.* Springfield, Ill.: Charles C Thomas.

MOURANT, A. E., C. KOPEC, AND K. DOMANIEWSKA-SOBCZAK

1958   *The ABO blood groups.* Springfield, Ill.: Charles C Thomas.

OTTEN, CHARLOTTE M.

1967   On pestilence, diet, natural selection, and the distribution of microbial and human blood group antigens and antibodies. *Current Anthropology* 8:209–226.

PAULING, LINUS, HARVEY A. ITANO, S. J. SINGER, AND IBERT C. WELLS

1949   Sickle cell anemia, a molecular disease. *Science* 110:543–548.

RACE, R. R.

1948   The Rh genotypes and Fisher's theory. *Blood* 3, suppl. 2:27–42.

RACE, R. R., AND R. SANGER

1962   *Blood groups in man.* 4th ed. Oxford: Blackwell.

SUTTON, H. E., G. A. MATSON, A. R. ROBINSON, AND R. W. KOUCKY

1960   Distribution of haptoglobin, transferrin, and hemoglobin types among Indians of southern Mexico and Guatemala. *American Journal of Human Genetics* 12:338–347.

TINSMAN, JAMES H., JR.

1971   The human blood groups: Frequency differences by age and sex. Doctoral dissertation, University of Colorado.

WIENER, A. S., EVE B. GORDON, AND LILLIAN HANDMAN

1949   Heredity of the Rh blood types. *American Journal of Human Genetics* 1:127–140.

WIENER, ALEXANDER S., AND J. MOOR-JANKOWSKI

1963   Blood groups in anthropoid apes and baboons. *Science* 142:67–69.

9 Implications of Human Heterography

INTRODUCTION

If physical anthropology were concerned solely with describing man's variation, its future could be expected to be simply the expansion and refinement of the information presented in the last two chapters. The future would be secure, for as new traits were discovered or as more was learned about old ones, specialists would continue to have the task of determining the range and location of their variation. But, of course, physical anthropology is interested in much more, specifically, in what the variation implies. The question of interest at this point, then, is: How is it possible to learn from the facts of variation? The answer necessarily depends on what one is interested in learning more about (for example, evolutionary history or taxonomy). Progress along either line will, however, first require that the facts of variation be organized in some useful way; that is, a classification is called for, since (no matter how often one hears the contrary) facts simply do not speak for themselves.

The first step, then, in learning more about human variability is to classify it. In this chapter three different kinds of classifications of human heterographic variation are discussed: 1) typological, 2) populational, and 3) clinal. Many other kinds are logically possible, but these three are in common use today. Indeed, much of the confusion that exists today could be obviated if those involved could be made to realize that any type of classification may improve our understanding, and that no one classification is *the* correct one. The particular way of grouping human variation that one may select should be governed exclusively by the kind of understanding one hopes to obtain from the distribution of variation.

Any classification, then, should serve a purpose, and at the present time there are three fundamental biological reasons for constructing a classification of man's heterographic variation: 1) to identify clusters of attributes; 2) to reflect common phylogenetic histories, or, in other words, close biological relationship; and 3) to delineate integrated evolutionary units. When a taxonomist classifies a group of organisms into a species and species into higher categories, these purposes are satisfied simultaneously. However, when a classification is devised for specific subgroupings, there is no reason to conclude that a scheme satisfying the requirements of one necessarily satisfies the requirements of the others. Failure to realize this has been a basic source of confusion and controversy.

292

In addition to the biological purposes, economic competition among distinguishable groups of human beings provides sociological reasons for classifying man's heterographic variation. The biological basis of such classifications is often incidental and accidental, or, on occasion, entirely lacking, as in the classification that divides people into groups on the basis of political boundaries or linguistic distinctions. When the biological component appears more readily identifiable, as, for example, in the distinction between white and colored in the United States, it turns out, on closer inspection, to be arbitrary, accidental, and incidental to the more obvious sociological purpose. Many illustrations of the arbitrary character of such a classification could be used. A simple one is the observation that several years ago, in many parts of the country, persons regularly identified and treated as Negroes found that if they wore a fez, they would often be identified as Near Eastern and thereby be able to participate more fully in activities that otherwise would not be available to them.

To say that the biological component is arbitrary and incidental to the purpose of a sociological classification is not, however, to claim that the units identified are arbitrary and incidental. They are social realities that have provided a basis for suspicion, hatred, segregation, suffering, degradation, violence, and even death. Nor does it mean that such a classification has no significant biological implications; indeed it has. The subject is generally thought to be the academic property of sociology and will not be explored here in any detail. Instead, the types of classifications commonly used in physical anthropology will be discussed here, with illustrations using the traits discussed in Chapters 7 and 8 whenever possible.

TYPOLOGICAL CLASSIFICATIONS

A typological classification divides human beings into geographical groups on the basis of the regular occurrence together of distinctive heterographic traits. This definition makes it appear a relatively simple and straightforward problem to obtain a complete typological classification. Apparently all that is involved is investigating man's formal variation, deciding on where traits tend to occur together, and drawing a boundary line around the area. Yet there are a number of implications not made explicit in the definition in the interest of keeping it general and clear. First, since the classes include human beings in particular geographical areas, it is clear that both spatial and formal factors are involved in the classification. Space is, however, a function of the range over which the morphological traits occur together, and therefore the limits of the geographical area depend on the kind and, to some extent, the number of traits considered to be distinctive. Secondly, even though it is not stated, there is an implicit element of time generally involved in typological classifications, amounting to something very much like what the ethnologists call the ethnographic present. In cultural anthropology, an analogous typological classification divides the totality of cultural variation into culture areas (see Figure 9–1). Culture areas pro-

Figure 9–1.   Culture area map of North and Central American indigenous peoples. (After A. L. Kroeber)

vide a means of summarizing and identifying the fundamentally similar cultural features of, say, the Plains Indians and of distinguishing these from those features distinctive of another area, such as the Arctic Eskimo. By using the notion of the ethnographic present, cultural anthropologists make it clear that culture areas are temporary and, furthermore, come together at different times and hold together for different durations. To use the Plains Indians of North America as an example, they developed their distinctive features, flourished, and died out all within the nineteenth century. The Arctic Eskimo, on the other hand, has been adapted to his environmental requirements in ways that extend back over one thousand years or more and which may still be seen today. So the ethnographic present refers to a relative point in time. It usually corresponds closely to the time when the particular area begins to be regularly affected by the spread of Western civilization.

Typological classifications imply a heterographic present, that is, the period prior to the massive migrations of people into, or even out of, the particular area under consideration. For most parts of the world, the ethnographic and heterographic presents will correspond closely, since both are usually due to the same technological and economic factors. They differ only in that the ethnographic present refers to assemblages of cultural traits, and the heterographic present to assemblages of morphological traits. Whatever the time period selected, it should be kept clearly in mind that it is representative itself of but one instant in man's phylogeny that was preceded by a long, complex, but essentially unknown history that must have involved extensive migrations, countless adaptations and readaptations, and continual fluctuations in population size, density, and structure, all occurring within a perpetually changing environment. The decision to deal with a heterographic present is one of convenience; it makes easier the task of describing contemporary human variation and constructing a typological classification.

This leads to another part of the definition that is not entirely clear— *distinctive heterographic traits*. Distinctive is perhaps clear enough; it restricts attention to variable traits that occur together and thus may serve as a basis for distinguishing one area from another. For example, hearts, lungs, stomachs, and intestines are traits that occur together, but they always do so and thus fail to distinguish one group from another. If these attributes varied from one area to another, they could be regarded as distinctive, and in fact they may indeed show some consistent variation, but, at present, this is difficult and impractical to demonstrate. There remains, however, an infinite number of characteristics that distinguish groups from one another. In principle, these include both traits of known and unknown inheritance, although the use of traits of known inheritance is more recent. In fact, typological classifications most commonly use a rather small number of visually perceptible, readily observable, somatic characteristics, such as skin color, stature, hair form, nose form, limb proportions, etc. However, there is no valid reason for not using blood groups, serum proteins, taster, secretor, etc., in typological classifications. Indeed there is no logical reason for excluding tactile, olfactory, auditory, or even gustatorial distinctions, but they are not made and probably will not be, since we are primates, and, as everyone knows, primates rely very heavily on vision.

A practical question to raise at this point is: Into how many groups does a typological classification divide mankind? The answer is perhaps by now obvious—it all depends. Ideally, perhaps, the number of groups should depend solely on the distribution of heterographic variation. If attribute clusters were tightly restricted and clearly distinctive within a well-defined area, there would be little or no problem. In practice, however, human variation is distributed in such a way that the range of variation within a typological unit is greater than the variation distinguishing one unit from another. Thus the number of groups is not a simple function of the distribution of traits; it depends as well on: 1) the number and, to some extent, the kinds of traits employed in the classification, and 2) the degree of refinement used in evaluating "distinctiveness." The first of these can be readily illustrated. Consider, for example, a typological classification based solely on one trait, dark skin color. A typological classification using this trait alone would require placing together in the same group peoples from Africa, Asia, Indonesia, and parts of Oceania. Add to dark skin color another attribute, say a broad nose, and the group would include fewer people within each area. If kinky hair is then considered, the group of dark-skinned, broad-nosed, kinky-haired people will include some Africans and the Negritos of New Guinea and the Philippines. Tall stature as a characteristic will provide a basis for eliminating the Negritos from other dark-skinned, broad-nosed, kinky-haired people. Thus, by using a minimum of four traits, it is possible to identify a cluster of traits concentrated in parts of Africa south of the Sahara. Certainly, many persons included within this region are not dark-skinned; some have narrow noses, others wavy hair, and in some areas there are whole populations of quite short people. Yet, recognizing these exceptions—even recognizing them to be common—does not invalidate a broad generalization intended only to summarize some of the major features of variation that tend to cluster together in this part of the world. A more adequate description would include more traits. The effect of adding more traits is to increase the general background of information on the inhabitants of the area as well as increase the number of individuals that are "exceptions" for one or more traits. In fact, if one were to describe any of the heterographic areas of the world in terms of from ten to fifteen distinctive features, it is likely that few, if any, persons within the area would possess all the traits.

The degree of refinement used in evaluating distinctiveness is likewise of crucial importance in determining the number of groups in a typological classification. A crude scale, for example, may distinguish only between, say, tropical and nontropical peoples, or, as is done more commonly, between the major continental groupings of mankind. A more refined scale might distinguish within the tropical group those living at high altitudes from all others, or, within the European continental division, between Mediterraneans and Scandinavians. Even more refined restrictions on distinctiveness can, of course, be imposed, and, clearly, as this is done, the number of groups increases. Stanley Garn (1965) has recognized this effect and attempted

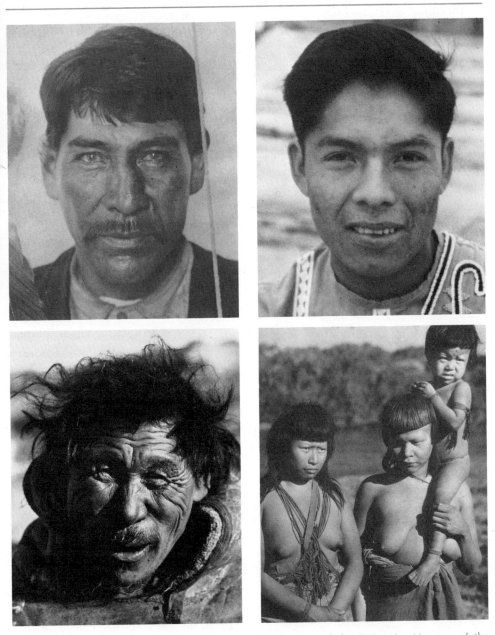

Figure 9–2. American Indians. Top left, Iroquois (Courtesy of the University Museum of the University of Pennsylvania). Top right, Choctaw (Courtesy of Carleton S. Coon). Bottom left, Eskimo (Courtesy of the National Film Board of Canada, photo by G. Gely). Bottom right, Bororo Indians of South America (Courtesy of the University Museum of the University of Pennsylvania).

to formalize levels of distinctiveness into groups he calls geographical races, local races, and micro races. These are in the order of crude to refined in evaluating distinctiveness.

If the construction of a typological classification rests so heavily on these external factors that the number of groups identified is almost arbitrary, then one may reasonably inquire as to the value of a typological classification. This problem can be considered in the context of the purposes of a heterographic classification, which (as discussed earlier) are to: 1) group together clusters of attributes, 2) reflect biological relationship, and 3) identify integrated evolutionary units. Does a typological classification fulfill one or more of these functions? A typological classification fulfills one and only one of these functions: it groups together clusters of attributes. The clusterings may in some instances be due to a common phylogenetic history, and thus may reflect biological relationship, but whether or not they are is a problem to be solved, not a solution implicit in the classification. The problem may be stated simply: Is the fact that two or more populations share a number of characteristics in common evidence of close biological relationship? The answer is—perhaps, but not necessarily. Similarities between two or more populations may be due to other factors. For example, two groups that are not closely related in their evolutionary histories may be similar because each has adapted to common environmental requirements. This phenomenon, known as *convergence*, would seem to be at least partly responsible for some of the similarities between the South African Bushmen and the aborigines of Australia. Furthermore, as has been noted earlier, human beings have a reserve of adaptive potential that permits them to adjust to environmental changes. This *physiological plasticity* may be responsible for the clustering together of characteristics. Thus it is, for example, that persons living at high altitudes share a variety of characteristics in common that do not imply close relationship. Finally, *chance factors* may act to produce similarities; such factors appear to have been responsible for producing some of the similarities between Polynesians and American Indians.

One might also consider the problem of whether or not groups delineated by a typological classification constitute evolutionary units. That is, do they correspond to integrated units of evolutionary change, to groups that are undergoing common selective pressures distinguishable from those affecting other parts of the world? The answer to these fundamental questions of evolutionary integrity is—not necessarily. For example, the area designated as Africa south of the Sahara and described as inhabited by dark-skinned, broad-nosed, kinky-haired, tall (as opposed to Pygmy) people contains many identifiable groups experiencing sharply contrasting ecologies, competing for different resources, and thus subjected to different evolutionary forces. One may feel that Africans south of the Sahara are distinct as an evolutionary unit from, say, the Asians north and east of India, since they contrast in the inventory of traits clustering in each. There is no question that these differences exist, but their existence alone does not imply some present-day evolutionary integrity. The clusterings may be due to the fact that each group has descended from separate and

Figure 9–3. Africans. Top: Left, Tunisian (Courtesy of J. H. McCullough); Center, Bedouin (Courtesy of William M. Shanklin); Right, Hausa. Bottom: Left, Batonga; Center, Bushman; Right, Zulu (Courtesy of Carleton S. Coon)

contrasting breeding units. Thus, the ancestral populations may have been integrated units that diverged and ramified into several descendant units, each one continuing to display features that attest to their common origin in the past, but modified by the processes that caused the diversification and by the subsequent evolutionary factors imposed on the populations adapting to new ecological requirements. In any event, it should be clear that a typological classification results in groups that are not logically equivalent to integrated evolutionary units. Whether any particular group is empirically equivalent is a problem to be solved through empirical investigation.

From this discussion, it may be seen that typological classifications are useful devices in summarizing the complex distributions of man's heterographic variation. They may be useful in suggesting hypotheses concerning possible relationships between attribute clusters and the environments in which they are located, and in offering convenient units for instructors to use in presenting the material on man's heterographic variation.

Traditional racial classifications are, of course, typological classifications, but an effort has been made deliberately to avoid these until this point, for racial classifications have usually implied much more about the units classified than typological ones. As we have noted, typological classifications attempt to reflect nothing more than the ways in which human variation is distributed at some point in time, whereas racial classifications tend also to imply phylogenetic relationships and evolutionary integrity. This is unwarranted, and failure to separate these various implications has been a basic source of misunderstanding and confusion in the dialogue on race in the professional journals. The situation is analogous to that of a cultural anthropologist drawing the conclusion from a culture area classification that, since the societies grouped together in an area are similar in many traits, they must therefore be derived from the same cultural antecedents. For example, all the societies within the Plains culture area would be presumed to have emerged from a common cultural source. Likewise, if culture areas were the logical equivalent of races, then, by implication, the groups within an area would be presumed to form an integrated unit of cultural evolution.

Typological classifications divide mankind into units, the composition of which is determined largely by the distribution of heterographic variation. The size of the units can, however, vary, depending on the number of characteristics and how refined the classifier chooses to be in regarding one unit as distinct from another. The essential value of such a classification is to provide information which can facilitate communication and an empirical background to the formulation and testing of specific hypotheses. Investigators with specific hypotheses may wish to classify segments of the variation in different ways that are necessary to the resolution of particular problems. Thus, typological classifications can result in groups and areas of varying sizes and compositions. It is not a question of which one is the most nearly correct, but rather which is most useful, and that is determined by the specific purposes the classifier has in mind.

But what of the other purposes for constructing classifications of human variation? Is it possible, for example, to divide mankind into units with evolutionary integrity? Such a system could be very useful in adding to our understanding of evolutionary processes affecting man at the present time, and indeed might imply biological relationship as well, thereby fulfilling the requirements for classifying human biological variation. Physical anthropologists have recognized the deficiencies of racial classification and have attempted to resolve them in a variety of ways. Some, as we have seen, have proposed a hierarchical arrangement of races (geographical races, microgeographical races, local races, etc.); some have discarded the term *race* entirely; some say that races do not exist (they really mean that the group brought together for descriptive purposes does not correspond to an evolutionary unit); and some continue to be confused. But the most common reaction among professionals has been to draw upon the theory of population genetics that contends that breeding populations qualify as minimal integrated units of evolutionary change.

POPULATIONAL CLASSIFICATIONS

Recall the discussion of population genetics presented in Chapter 3. From this it may be seen that a division of mankind into breeding populations apparently bypasses the problem of *discovering* evolutionary units as implications of a racial classification by *specifying* what these units are. A breeding population is the basic unit of evolutionary change—the unit that, regulated by the Hardy-Weinberg law, tends toward equilibrium in the composition of its genetic structure—the unit whose structure changes in response to the action of the mechanisms of evolution.

The population as a unit of classification has been increasing in popularity among physical anthropologists and human geneticists during the last twenty years. It has, in fact, served as a kind of basic distinction between the approaches of the younger generation and the "typological" approach characteristic of their teachers. Prior to this time, classification of human variation had been based solely on traits of unknown inheritance and was found repeatedly to lack the conclusive evidence required to reconstruct the myriad of events through which the "types" had passed. The first effect that genetics had on the problem of reconstructing racial histories was simply the addition of inherited traits, such as the blood groups, to the others with the expectation that the inherited traits might produce more definite bases for reconstructing racial histories. Since then two things have become clear: 1) traits of known inheritance are no more informative in solving the problem of racial history than others; 2) they are, however, of much greater value than other attributes in learning further about the processes of evolution, but traditional typological classifications are of no use in realizing this potential. If, as implied in the Hardy-Weinberg law, evolution is change in the genetic structure from one generation to the next, then the logical unit of evolutionary analysis is a reproductive unit, a group of individuals that mate and produce a subsequent generation, or, in other words, a breeding population. It will be recalled that for the equilibrium specified by the Hardy-Weinberg law to be attained, the following conditions within the population are necessary: 1) it must be large; 2) individuals must mate randomly with respect to the alleles involved; and 3) the locus should not be affected by the mechanisms of evolution. These formed a basic core of problems which population geneticists have continued to be concerned with right up to the present. That is, they have wanted to know what happens when populations are small, when the locus is controlling a feature that influences the choice of a mate. What are the consequences of inbreeding? How can selection or mutation alter the equilibrium? General answers to these questions must be made deductively by means of the techniques of mathematics, since human populations rarely, if ever, satisfy these conditions, and experimental populations are too artificial to extend results obtained on them to all populations.

The mathematics was simple and crude by comparison with more advanced sciences, but the results were compelling and dramatic. It would seem that the urge to try them out on real populations was perhaps overwhelming, and, as we have already seen, the result was a rapid accumulation of gene-frequency data. The effect of these advances on the subject of human variation was to focus attention on breeding populations as biologically and evolutionarily integrated units and to describe them in terms of their gene frequencies. Yet, as implied earlier in the chapter, substantial confusion resulted. Races, for example, were defined variously as synonymous with a breeding population (a race is a breeding population), or as groups of breeding populations (a race is a group of breeding populations with the same gene frequencies), or as nonexistent superstitions (there are no races, just breeding populations). Clearly, the population, and particularly the breeding population, has passed from the abstract unit existing under ideal conditions suitable only for mathematical or experimental manipulation to a real, finite, and discoverable thing. That substantial confusion existed on this issue is implicit in the fact that gene frequencies have been obtained on such strikingly heterogeneous "breeding populations" as Spaniards, Negroes, Americans, Russian mothers, Ethiopians, Sea Dyaks, and Blackfoot Indians. The effect on physical anthropology has been basic, extensive, and permanent. The entire focus of attention and the fundamental reason for studying human variation has shifted from an almost exclusive concern with racial history to an almost exclusive concern with human evolution. Correspondingly, the traditional traits used to characterize typological units, traits such as stature, skin color, and hair form, are becoming more and more confined to the elucidation of specific problems in which their use is immediately applicable. Blood groups and other inherited characteristics are, however, used more and more by physical anthropologists to characterize man's general heterographic variation.

Some authorities have attempted to integrate the typological and populational approaches, but up to now their efforts have been little more than verbal, and the effect has probably been to create more confusion. For example, races have been defined as breeding populations differing in their gene frequencies. On closer inspection, this definition raises some serious difficulties in practical situations. Does it mean, for example, that two populations with the same gene frequency for one locus are to be included in the same race? If so, then absurd results follow: the Ainu of Japan belong to the same "race" as the Berbers of northwestern Africa if only MN frequencies are considered. One group of Berbers sampled would, however, be in a race apart from another. Does the definition mean, on the other hand, that populations with many of their genetic loci occupied by alleles in the same frequencies are to be considered groups within the same race? But no two populations have an identical array of gene frequencies; so empirically there would be as many races as populations. Moreover, the units usually specified by the term *race* are not equivalent to the units specified by a populational classification. To fail to recognize that typological and populational classifications are fundamentally different is to add to an already confusing situation.

What are the distinctive characteristics of a populational classification of human variation? First the units of classification are necessarily *groups* of individuals. In a typological classification, it is possible in principle to classify individuals without knowing where they reside. That is, if one is familiar with the criteria on which a classification is based, he should be able to classify any individual into one and only one of the classes. To be sure, mistakes will occur, for, as we have already noted, exceptions within an area are common. In a population classification, however, it is not possible to assign an individual to a class by inspection of his features. Even though a complete knowledge of his inherited characteristics may be available, it would not be possible to do so. (He might have a trait, however, that is very rare and known to occur only in a very restricted area, and this could provide a basis for concluding that he belonged to a particular population. This foreknowledge would, however, be rare.)

An individual may be assigned to a populational class only by identification of the marriage or breeding group to which he belongs. This implies the second distinctive characteristic of a populational classification: the boundaries between one class and another are fixed by mating practices. It will be recalled that in a typological classification the boundaries between the classes are fixed essentially by the actual distribution of the traits. Classifiers using the same criteria can arrive at larger or smaller units depending on their bias, but nonetheless the limits of the classes remain a function of the distribution of traits. In a populational classification, traits serve simply as the basis of description; that is, differences and similarities between breeding populations may be noted by comparing the traits that occur within them. For example, a particular group of persons, all of whom select their mates from within the group, can be identified as a breeding population. Now such a class can be compared to another on structural grounds alone and without reference to physical differences between the membership; that is, they can be compared on the basis of such things as population size, age and sex distributions, whether or not internal subdivisions exist, etc. Likewise, the classes can be compared in terms of physical differences and similarities found among the persons identified (on other grounds) as belonging to one or the other breeeding population. Ideally, in a typological classification, the procedure is reversed; after inspecting the distribution of traits, the classifier identifies clusters, and these serve to distinguish between classes. Finally, descriptions of breeding populations are presented almost exclusively in terms of gene frequencies. There is no reason for excluding the traditional measurements and observations of physical anthropology as bases for describing breeding populations, but they are rarely included.

In summary, then, a populational classification is distinctive in the following ways: 1) the units classified are of necessity *groups* of individuals; 2) one group is distinguished from another on the basis of breeding isolation; and 3) the classes are usually described in terms of the frequencies of genes. By contrast, in a typological classification: 1) individuals are the basic units of classification; 2) one class is distinguished from another largely on the basis of differences in the distribution of heterographic variation; and 3) the classes are usually described in terms of traits of unknown inheritance. So much for the formal differences between these two kinds of classifications. Two practical questions remain for consideration in this discussion of populational classifications: How many breeding populations are there? And to what extent do populational units satisfy the reasons for constructing a classification of man's heterographic variation?

How many breeding populations are there within the human species today? If mankind were neatly divided into isolated breeding populations, the answer to this question would be readily ascertainable. As it is, however, the actual fabric of human mating behavior today is made up of such a complicated and continually changing weave that not only is a simple count impossible, but even an estimate is a deception. It is at this point that attention is readily drawn to some of the basic problems associated with applying a populational approach to heterographic variation in man. For example, is Denver, Colorado, properly identified as a breeding population? An inspection of the situation in Denver or in any urban center would reveal that the parents have been drawn from all over the world, and that, as they mature, their offspring marry persons from all over the world. Thus, in one sense, Denver is but one part of an "isolate" that is worldwide. But, one may argue, there is a clear tendency for Denverites to marry other Denverites, and this tendency diminishes as distance from Denver increases. In arguing this way, one might conclude that for practical purposes it can be considered as a breeding population. Indeed Sewall Wright (1943) over twenty years ago presented a model (the isolation by distance model) for "isolating" such populations by statistical means. But the very same inspection of the actual marriage practices would reveal that Denver can be internally subdivided into many reproductive units. Whites tend to marry whites, blacks to marry blacks, and even within these social divisions smaller groups with imagined or real common economic and ethnic backgrounds tend to choose marriage partners from within the group. Thus, in another sense, Denver is the location of several breeding populations. Additionally, as if the problem of trying to deal with these difficulties by the standard means were not enough, the situation is made more complex when primitive societies are considered. Are the Bushmen of South Africa an isolate? Are they part of a larger reproductive unit? Are they divisible into several such units? As in the case of Denver, the answer to each of these questions is probably yes, although the composition and structure of each population are very different. Again, one can find a comparable problem in cultural anthropology, and that is the question of deciding on the limits of a society. Does Denver constitute a social system? Is it part of a larger whole that is integrated socially? Are there several systems within the geographical limits of the city? As above, the answer to each of these questions is yes.

Considering the specific question of how many breeding populations there are raises some doubts about the validity of applying the populational classification to the human species, but before any general conclusion is reached, some attention should be given to the question of the value of a poulational classification: 1) in identifying clusters of heterographic attributes, and 2) in delineating evolutionarily integrated units.

If the objective of a heterographic classification is simply to discover types, that is, to locate clusters of distinctive traits, then a populational classification is wholly inappropriate and inefficient as a typological classification. As noted previously, the process by which an investigator identifies a breeding population is the antithesis of the process involved in arriving at a typological class (usually called a race). The attributes in a populational classification are the means by which breeding populations are described and compared. Thus it is that, except for unusual situations, all breeding populations have the same characteristics—the same blood groups, the same serum proteins, etc. They differ from one another in the frequencies of the alleles controlling these traits. In a typological classification, the traits and their distributions are the primary factors used to identify a class.

It is indeed possible that frequencies of two or more alleles vary in systematic ways from one population to the next. Thus it may be shown that frequencies cluster together as in the case of the S and M alleles in Australia, Micronesia, and New Guinea. These associations would seem more likely to be forthcoming from a third way of ordering heterographic data, by the clinal approach, which is becoming more popular in physical anthropology, and which is discussed in the next section.

As far as "delineating evolutionary units" is concerned, the breeding population as a unit of study meets every logical requirement. It is, by definition, a reproductive or generational unit, and, again by definition, any change in the genetic structure of the unit is an evolutionary change. The problem associated with the use of the breeding population as a basis for improving our understanding of the significance of heterographic variation in man is not, however, a logical one; it is a practical one. Today human beings live in groups that rarely, if ever, even remotely approximate the requirements of any breeding-population model. In most cases this discrepancy between the real situation and the theoretical model has simply been ignored, and investigators have presumed the limits of a breeding population rather than determined them. From these "isolates," painstakingly chosen random samples of persons have been tested and the results reported in gene frequencies. One may well ask what such frequencies imply. Suppose, for example, that random samples of equal size are selected from two communities, and each is tested for several traits of known inheritance. On the basis of these determinations, gene frequencies are calculated and the results tabulated. It is not obvious what these frequencies imply. Many factors can affect any gene-frequency estimate; among the most important are the following: 1) *Sampling error.* One sample may include more relatives, thereby increasing the likelihood that the same alleles will be counted more than once. 2) *Population structure.* One population may be subdivided into several more or less isolated reproductive units, whereas another may not. The error inherent in any estimate may be greatly different in these two situations. 3) *Mating practices*. In Chapter 3, the effects of various forms of nonrandom mating on the genetic structure of a population were demonstrated. Since nonrandom mating affects the distribution of genotypes, and since gene frequencies are calculated from genotype frequencies, it should be clear that different mating practices can affect gene-frequency estimates. This would be particularly the case in gene-frequency estimates for traits in which a heterozygote is indistinguishable from a homozygote. 4) *Evolutionary mechanisms*. Two or more populations may be the same or different in their array of gene frequencies because of the action of one or more of the mechanisms of evolution. How these exert their influence was also dealt with in Chapter 3.

Since any one or all of these things can influence any gene-frequency estimate, then any array of frequencies is not a reliable indication of the degree of relationship between the two populations. As stated above, with all these contingencies it is not at all clear what these frequencies imply.

In summary, a populational classification is inefficient as a means of identifying attribute clusters, impractical to apply to processual problems in human heterography, and inappropriate as a basis for assessing degrees of relationship between and among subspecific groupings in man. This view is by no means a generally accepted one among physical anthropologists today, and that, more than any other, is the reason for dealing so laboriously with the issue here. Physical anthropologists continue to take random samples and report gene frequencies as though the units were equivalent and the meaning of the figures were obvious. While this effort has resulted in very little progress in solving the usual problems approached by investigations of human variation, it has yielded a considerable quantity of gross and unrefined descriptive information on the distribution of genes throughout the world. These data, together with those already available on phenotypic traits of unknown inheritance, form the basis for the clinal approach, another method of dealing with human variation, and one which orders the variations in still another way.

CLINAL CLASSIFICATIONS

Breeding populations and the races of a typological classification are in reality transitory, continually changing units that provide vague and fleeting glimpses of history and evolutionary processes. In any particular classification, however, they must be dealt with as finite, and, with the limitations discussed above, are able thereby to add to our general knowledge of how traits and the genes that control them vary in form and frequency. A different kind of classification is possible if attention is focused on the distribution of individual traits and gene frequencies. A particular trait, whether its inheritance is known or unknown, may be thought of as infinite in its possible expressions, but if, as we know already, the real variation is limited at any one point in time, then the distribution of identical forms can be grouped together into zones and separated from other areas by boundaries that are determined by the ranges over which a particular trait may be found to have a common expression. The delimited zones are called *clines*.

The theoretical background necessary for dealing with clines and relating them to evolutionary theory is still in a crude state. If the initial assumptions prove to be correct, such classifications hold out new possibilities for understanding the evolutionary fine structure of traits and their variations. The assumptions are simple and stem from evolutionary theory and the more special axioms of population genetics. In simplified form, a clinal analysis assumes that: 1) traits vary; 2) systematic variations in the traits are due to systematic forces; 3) the systematic forces may be due either to an evolutionary mechanism, such as selection or migration, or to other factors, such as physiological plasticity; 4) the two kinds of systematic forces are, in principle, separable; and 5) trait distributions offer an alternative way of relating the facts of heterographic variation to the theory of evolution.

The clinal approach has a familiar ring to anthropologists. For many years, cultural anthropologists sought to obtain detailed lists of trait distributions for the purpose of studying diffusion and ultimately for reconstructing the histories of particular peoples. It is today generally recognized that trait distributions only accidentally provide useful information for historical reconstruction. There does seem to be considerable potential insight to be gained by attempting to learn about evolutionary process in the biological sphere, and there are indications that cultural anthropologists are studying processes of adaptation and evolution just as the biologist wishes to do.

The theoretical foundation for the interpretation and analysis of clines is only now beginning to be formulated. To appreciate the value of such an approach requires the development of analytical models very different from those presently available for the study of finite populations. The work needs to be done.

Table 9–1   Comparison of Three Ways of Grouping Heterographic Variation

TYPE OF CLASSIFICATION	CRITERIA	RESULTING UNITS
Typological	Trait clusters	Races and other "types"
Populational	Mating systems	Breeding populations
Clinal	Individual trait distributions	Clines

SUMMARY

A comparison of typological, populational, and clinal classifications may clarify their differences. Table 9–1 presents a summary of the essential features of each. The trait clusters of typological units can and do crosscut the reproductive boundaries of mating systems. Likewise clines may vary independently of races and breeding populations.

THE CONCEPT OF RACE

In the last few chapters the subject of race has surfaced several times. We turn now to a direct discussion of race as we conclude consideration of the implications of human biological variation.

Scientific concern over race is more than two hundred years old. When the work began, the issue appeared to be simple. Everyone agreed on the meaning of the term. Everyone agreed that mankind was made up of races. Everyone agreed on what was to be done—the determination of the exact number of races and the ways in which each differed from the others. Everyone agreed that the work would take a long time and consume a great deal of effort.

The time has passed and the effort has been spent. What does science have to say on the subject of race today? Fortunately we have a ready answer. In 1966 the American Association for the Advancement of Science sponsored a symposium on "Science and the Concept of Race." The symposium was published in a book by that title (1968) edited by Margaret Mead, Theodosius Dobzhansky, Ethel Tobach, and Robert Light.* The book was explicitly "intended as an inventory of what science has to say on the subject of race," and as an effort which might "help to dispel the evil myths that persist about race." Yet what one finds within the book is one contradiction after another on even the most basic issues. For example:

1. Is race a valid concept in biology?
On page 59 we read "From a biological viewpoint the term race has become so encumbered with superfluous and contradictory meanings, erroneous concepts, and emotional reactions that it has almost completely lost its utility."

Whereas on the same issue we read on page 108 "The concept of race on the biological level is understandable and logically defensible on every ground . . . ."

2. Is it appropriate to describe race differences in terms of averages?
". . . if we ever mention mean differences between population groups which are labelled as races, let us realize that to compare them in terms of mean values is not merely misleading but actually quite pernicious" (from pages 104–105).

The title of one full paper (pages 113–121) in the symposium is, however, "The need to investigate average biological differences among racial groups."

3. Can we learn about human racial differences by studying other animals?

---

* The discussion of the book is the substance of a review of it which I wrote for *Human Biology* (vol. 41, 1969). I acknowledge with gratitude the permission of the publisher to use the materials here.

On page 60 we learn that the answer is no: "From a strict scientific viewpoint, the human species is genetically unique, and one cannot apply any conclusion derived from another species directly to our own."

Yet one then wonders why an entire article (pages 16–25) reports on the results of an investigation of the behavior of *different colored chicks*.

4. What is the status of current research on race?
On this we find our two main editors in basic disagreement. Margaret Mead has this to say (page 5): "A field in which no new research is being reported goes dead; both students and laymen feel that old knowledge couched in an out-of-date vocabulary must somehow be wrong and is at best unchallenging and uninteresting . . . . The absence of fresh research on race can be attributed in part to political events of the last thirty years."

Theodosius Dobzhansky (page 78) obviously does not see things in the same way: "Some people have claimed that nothing new has been discovered for a long time about races in general. I hope that this symposium will show how far off the mark is this claim."

We seem to have lost a lot of ground in the last two hundred years. Clearly the concept of race is of negligible value in science. The racial approach is a deceptive strategy for collecting information on human variation, and the concept of race explains nothing at all.

Drawing upon our discussion of heterographic variation in man we may see that geographical areas can be characterized by the presence within them of clusters of traits, and the people included therein may be said to be members of the same race. However, if a race is delineated in this way, one should keep in mind that similarities within such races may be due to: 1) close common ancestry, 2) similar adaptive responses to common evolutionary forces, or, in some cases, 3) the direct influence of the environment on the inhabitants. In almost every case, it is impossible with present information to know the sources of the observed similarities, and it may never be possible to do so. The mechanisms of evolution and of physiological plasticity operating over time with changing ecological conditions act to cover up the phylogenetic tracks that might otherwise indicate the relationships between and among the groups included within such races. Evolutionary integrity, and thus biological meaning, is not a characteristic of such races. Furthermore, the traits that cluster together have, when taken individually, much broader distributional ranges continuing well outside the area. Dark skin color may well cluster together with broad noses and kinky hair in Africa south of the Sahara, but it continues as a trait within a broad belt along both sides of the equator. Its distribution crosscuts and varies independently of many other racial characters, suggesting that to the extent that these traits are due to evolutionary mechanisms, they are the consequences of separate factors operating at varying intensities over variable durations. Thus, such classifications not only fail to imply phylogenetic relationships among the groups that make them up, but may serve to *obscure* the adaptive (or nonadaptive) significance of the traits on which they are based as well.

Why, then, is it that these descriptive geographic "races" are considered at all? Because, even with the above limitations, they continue to be useful. They identify trait clusters within continuous geographic areas among groups of people who have been isolated in varying degrees for unknown periods of time. They are useful for two main purposes: in providing a broad range of background information on the distributions of human variation, and also as a basis for determining the effects that might be due to long-term geographical isolation. As may be seen from the preceding discussion, these "races" are not self-evident, natural units; they are merely useful and convenient ways of dividing up human variation. Any "natural" or "real" qualities they might have remain to be demonstrated.

The entire subject is confusing, but the confusion is itself a healthy sign that scientific usage of the word *race* and the concept to which it refers is changing from the old, standard, "typical" view into new ways of regarding human variation that appear to have greater scientific potential. The term *race* is ambiguous; the units to which it has been applied are not at all equivalent, and they have been established to achieve different objectives. In attempting to increase our understanding of human variation, the result has been confusing and unproductive.

The purpose of this discussion is unusual in that it is not primarily intended to inform the reader, nor to provide him with new information on the subject of race. There is, rather, an opposite objective that is being sought—to take away the comfortable feeling that most people in our society have when they use the term *race*. They know what they mean, and, further, there is something "out there" that corresponds to what they mean. If you started to read this chapter with a knowledge of what race is, and you are no longer sure of that knowledge, then the discussion has served a useful purpose. Consider, if you will, how your answers to the following questions might now be different: How many races are there? When did each begin? Is it harmful for two persons of different races to marry? Are the Jews a race? In all likelihood, if you try these questions out on others, you will find that the only persons with ready answers are those who have not thought very much about the subject.

MAJOR POINTS IN CHAPTER 9

1. Classifications of human biological variability may help us to understand better the significance of the variability.

2. Three heterographic classifications are common: typological, populational, and clinal.

3. In attempting to understand the significance of man's biological variabil-

ity, much of the work of physical anthropologists has been done from the perspective of a typological classification, namely a racial classification.

4. Racial classifications have been of negligible value in furthering our understanding of man's variation.

5. Scientific statements on the subject of race are confusing and contradictory.

REFERENCES AND SUGGESTIONS FOR ADDITIONAL READING

BRACE, C. LORING
  1964 A nonracial approach towards the understanding of human diversity. In *The concept of race*, ed. Ashley Montagu. New York: Free Press.
COON, CARLETON S.
  1962 *The origin of races*. New York: Alfred A. Knopf.
COON, CARLETON S., WITH EDWARD E. HUNT, JR.
  1965 *The living races of man*. New York: Alfred A. Knopf.
COON, CARLETON S., STANLEY M. GARN, AND JOSEPH B. BIRDSELL
  1950 *Races: A study of the problems of race formation in man*. Springfield, Ill.: Charles C Thomas.
DOBZHANSKY, THEODOSIUS
  1962 *Mankind evolving*. New Haven: Yale University Press.
GARN, STANLEY M.
  1965 *Human races*. 2d ed. Springfield, Ill.: Charles C Thomas.
HULSE, FREDERICK S.
  1955 Technological advance and major racial stocks. *Human Biology* 27:184–192.
  1962 Race as an evolutionary episode. *American Anthropologist* 64:929–945.
KELSO, A. J.
  1967 The concept of race. *Improving College and University Teaching* 15:95–97.
  1969 Review of *Science and the concept of race*, ed. Margaret Mead, Theodosius Dobzhansky, Ethel Tobach, and Robert Light. In *Human Biology* 41.
KROEBER, A. L.
  1948 *Anthropology: Race, language, culture, psychology, prehistory*. Rev ed. New York: Harcourt, Brace, and World.
LIVINGSTONE, FRANK B.
  1964 Human populations. In *Horizons of anthropology*, ed. Sol Tax. Chicago: Aldine.
MEAD, MARGARET, THEODOSIUS DOBZHANSKY, ETHEL TOBACH, AND ROBERT LIGHT
  1968 *Science and the concept of race*. New York: Columbia University Press.
MONTAGU, ASHLEY, ED.
  1964 *The concept of race*. New York: Free Press.
MORTON, N. E., AND N. YASUDA
  1962 The genetical structure of human populations. In *Les déplacements humains*, ed. J. Sutter. Paris: Hachette.
WASHBURN, SHERWOOD L.
  1944 Thinking about race. *Science Education* 28:65–76.
  1963 The study of race. *American Anthropologist* 65:521–531.
WRIGHT, S.
  1943 Isolation by distance. *Genetics* 28:114–138.

10 Natural Selection in Modern Human Populations

THE PROBLEM

Is man continuing to undergo evolutionary changes today? If in 1940 one had gathered together into one room all the specialists in human biology and asked them this question, about half would have answered yes, and about half would either have answered no or maintained that the answer is not known. If one had asked why it was that they disagreed, he would have found that those scientists who had answered in the affirmative would have emphasized that man is an animal and subject to the same laws as all other life forms, that paleontology has produced solid evidence for the existence of trends that continue right on up to the present, and that one can readily demonstrate the presence of adaptive characteristics among contemporary populations. Those persons answering otherwise would have argued that, while it is certainly true that man is an animal, he has culture which functions as a protective screen providing him with an extrasomatic means of adapting to his environment and thereby the means of escaping the ruthless screening process of evolution that continually confronts all other animals and plants. They would have pointed to the many apparent nonadaptive traits that may be found in man, and would have concluded their stand with the disclaimer that trends and adaptive traits do not conclusively prove the existence of evolution in human populations today. If one were to bring together specialists in human biology today, those answering the question with a confident *yes* would be an overwhelming majority.

To understand what caused the change, it will be helpful to consider each of the arguments presented above and determine what, if anything, has happened to alter its forcefulness today. Before turning to these arguments, two points should be discussed. First, even though the question is often asked in reference to the operation of evolution, it is almost always understood to refer specifically to natural selection. One can readily point to the occurrence of mutations and migration in today's populations and readily admit that genetic drift, even though its role may be considerably less significant today, must have been an important force in the recent past. So the question under consideration is really: Is natural selection operative in human populations today? The arguments offered above by both sides refer specifically to natural selection.

Second, one must consider a preliminary problem that has to be resolved before any progress can be made on the main question. Consider the question of what kind of evidence constitutes proof that evolution is operating in human populations today. It is here that the reader should recall the material from Chapter 3 on population genetics. Evolution alters the genetic structure of populations, and thus any such change is an evolutionary change. If one can demonstrate that the genetic composition of a population changes from one generation to the next, he has perforce provided reasonably conclusive proof for the operation of evolution. Becoming more precise and providing a convincing case that such a change is due specifically to natural selection is more difficult. Evolutionary changes due to the action of natural selection must be systematic, that is, not due to chance, and must be reflected through differential reproduction. Some people, or, more precisely, some combinations of genotypes, must contribute disproportionately to the number of viable offspring in the next generation.

SOURCES OF EVIDENCE

These are the basic criteria that may be used to evaluate the evidence bearing on both the general question of the continuation of evolution and the more specific one of the operation of natural selection in the human species today. Consider now the ways in which the question has been argued on both sides.

Logic

If the only basis for a decision were logic, then the issue would be irreconcilable, since conclusions supporting both points of view can be arrived at by valid arguments. In support of the stand that man is presently undergoing evolutionary change, one might begin with the proposition that evolutionary processes are detectable throughout the universe, and conclude from this that they must therefore be affecting the human species. If matter is divided into three levels of organization—inorganic, organic, and extrasomatic—evolution may be seen in operation at each level. On the inorganic level, it is becoming more and more comprehensible to speak of the evolution of matter and of the universe. At the organic level it is, of course, commonplace to accept evolution, and at the extrasomatic, or cultural, level of organization an evolutionary perspective is essential to the understanding of the different forms of cultural variation. Or, heading toward the same conclusion, it could be pointed out that man is a highly variable, highly mobile species occupying an enormous range of adaptive zones. All of these are features that one would expect to find as ideal grist for the mill of natural selection.

There is nothing particularly wrong with these arguments. They reason, in effect, that since evolution is all around man, and since man has all the characteristics for the effective operation of natural selection, therefore he is indeed undergoing evolutionary change by means of natural selection. One could argue just as reasonably that in man's case it is culture that makes the critical difference—that as culture has evolved, the effectiveness of natural selection has been reduced to nothing. Evidence in support of this position may be obtained from two sources: 1) the many diseases and defective conditions that survive in modern society imply that as man and culture evolve, the effect of selection is reduced; and 2) the wide range of man's variation may be offered as evidence for the ineffectiveness of natural selection. In recent years, this view has lost some of its forcefulness as it has become more evident that, while culture may indeed alter the effectiveness of natural selection, it may as well generate new adaptive requirements of its own. The following quotation from White (1959) is submitted as an illustration of how all-pervasive culture is in man's life:

> The purpose of culture is to serve the needs of man. These needs may be divided into two categories: (1) those that can be served only by exploiting the resources of the external world; and (2) those that can be served by drawing upon the resources of the human organism only. Man needs food and materials of many kinds for clothing, utensils, ornaments, etc.; these must be obtained, of course, from the external world. But man has inner, psychic, social, and 'spiritual' needs that can be fed and nourished without drawing upon the external world at all. Man needs courage, comfort, consolation, confidence, companionship, a feeling of consequence in the scheme of things that life is worthwhile, and some assurance of success. It is the business of culture to serve these needs of the 'spirit' as well as the needs of the body.
>
> Life is continued only by effort. Pain, suffering, lonesomeness, fear, frustration, and boredom dog man's steps at almost every turn. He requires companionship, courage, inspiration, hope, comfort, reassurance, and consolation to enable him to continue the struggle of life. Cultural devices serve man here. Mythologies flatter, encourage, and reassure him. By means of magic and ritual he can capture the illusion of power and control over things and events: he can 'control' the weather, cure disease, foresee the future, increase his food supply, overcome his enemies. Various devices relate him to the spirit world so that he may enjoy the blessings and avoid the wrath of the gods. Cosmologies give him answers to all fundamental questions, of life and death and the nature of all things. Thus culture gives man a sense of power and of confidence. It assures him that life is worth living and gives him the courage to endure it. It comforts and sustains him when he meets defeat or frustration. It provides him with companions, divine as well as human. It attacks boredom and manages at times to make life pleasurably exciting and of fine flavor. In short, culture gives man the illusion of importance, omnipotence, and omniscience. These inner spiritual—or *intraorganismal*—needs of man are of course as real as those for food, shelter, and defense; in fact, they might be felt even more keenly. And these needs must be served if man is to succeed in the struggle of life.*

As culture evolves, the means of satisfying these needs change. Culture elements com-

---

* From *The Evolution of Culture*, by Leslie A. White. Copyright, 1959, by the McGraw-Hill Book Company. Reprinted by permission of McGraw-Hill Book Company.

bine in ways that generate new adaptive challenges to mankind. Again the argument sounds reasonable, and sufficiently so to forestall acceptance of the conclusion that man is not at present undergoing evolutionary change. But at this point, something more than a logical argument is required. The problem requires more information; specifically, it requires data to answer the significant and fundamental question: Do these culturally induced situations create a systematic selective pressure on the genetic structures of one or more subdivisions of the human species? What other sources of evidence are available that might have a bearing on this issue?

Trends

One category of evidence frequently used in support of the stand that man is continuing to undergo evolutionary change is the existence of trends extending back over a long part of the paleontological record as well as others with much more recent origins. The basis of their applicability in the present problem is simple and perhaps obvious; changes, presumed to be evolutionary changes, begun in the past and continuing up to the present must still be going on and probably will continue into the future. Most commonly cited as illustrations of evolutionary trends are: 1) *Brachycephalization of modern man*. Once anatomically-modern man is clearly established as the only hominid form on earth, there begins a trend from narrow-headed to broad-headed that may be found, wherever the paleontological evidence is abundant, throughout both the New and the Old World. 2) *Reduction in the size of third molars (wisdom teeth)*. One of the contrasts between modern man and the fossil hominids that preceded him is that modern man has smaller teeth. Thus it would appear that reduction in tooth size is a general trend in man's phylogeny. More particularly, however, there are some indications that since man obtained his modern anatomical form, the last two molars, and, of these, particularly the last, or third, molar, have been greatly reduced in size. Indeed, many human beings today completely lack third molars. This lack of a third molar is itself occasionally claimed as a trend. As time passes, the proportion of persons without third molars increases, but the paleontological evidence to support this contention is meager and ambiguous. 3) *Increasing stature*. The belief that mankind has been getting taller over the last several thousand years is very widespread indeed, but, as it turns out on closer examination, probably not true. E. A. Hooton (1947) has discussed the bases for this belief as follows:

> There are two tales respecting alleged increases in stature during historical times that are always being dinned into the ears of anthropologists. One is that of the tourist who attempts to seat himself in one of the seats in the Colosseum where the sporting populace of the ancient Romans used to be entertained by watching lions lunching upon obstinate Christians. This tourist invariably reports that the seats are scarcely large enough to accommodate a single modern buttock. My reply to this is: firstly, that Italians are still small people, used to living in cramped quarters; secondly, that one has only to arrive late at a football game to

discover that modern builders of concrete stadia are none too liberal in allotting space where pinched posteriors mean extra dollars. The seat of the latecomer has to be discovered by a process of long division, and he then has to be driven into it like a wedge.

The other tale, involving a supposition that our forebears were smaller men, is also purveyed by tourists who gape at empty suits of armor and simply cannot understand how a normal-sized man could be fitted into one. To these, I would point out that a metal suit standing alone in the middle of the floor is necessarily somewhat telescoped and does not attain the altitude of the person it was supposed to fit. Again I would suggest that these extant suits may have survived because they were outgrown by their owners, like the dress suits of our youth. Odd sizes are generally numerous in bargain basements. And, finally, our own ancestors may have been big even in those days, but perhaps they were churls and thralls and varlets and knaves who could not afford or did not rate suits of mail.*

To be sure, the average stature of adults has increased dramatically in European and American populations over the past fifty years. There are conflicting opinions among experts concerning the causes of this trend, and, at present, there is no way to resolve the conflict. A scientific conservative could claim that, as far as it provides evidence for the effect of selection in human populations today, resolving the conflict is immaterial. Even if it were shown to be the result of selection, who knows if it is continuing at the present time?

The last illustration of evolutionary trends is: 4) *Gerontomorphism to paedomorphism.* Consider for a moment the distinctive differences in appearance between very old (gerontomorphic) persons and infants (paedomorphic). A number of investigators have pointed out that in course of human evolution, the phenotypic differences between the two extremes are diminishing, as paedomorphic traits become more and more commonly characteristic of adults. At first, this trend seems simply to be a curious oddity. Why, as time passes, should youthful characteristics be retained more and more commonly among adult human beings? However, if this is indeed an evolutionary trend, then it implies that selection opposes early maturation in favor of the retention of youthful characteristics into later years. As pointed out by Sir Gavin De Beer, in his interesting book *Embryos and Ancestors* (1958), this can provide a means by which phylogenetic lines involving species with highly specialized features in the adults can give rise to more generalized descendant lines. Even so, the interesting questions remain unanswered; assuming the trend is indeed a real one, what factors are responsible for it? Why does selection operate to increase paedomorphism in man? Does culture have anything to do with this trend?

These are a few of the many trends that have been cited as evidence to support the position that man continues to be modified by selective pressures. Taken as a

---

* From *Up from the Ape,* by Earnest Albert Hooton. Copyright, 1947, by the Macmillan Company. Reprinted by permission of the Macmillan Company.

whole, they do indeed point to that conclusion, but a skeptic would see that the evidence they provide is inconclusive and equivocal. The existence of temporal trends may imply the action of natural selection, but these trends are not proof of such action. To what extent, for example, might the changes in the dentition be influenced in nongenetic ways by cultural factors such as improved cutting tools, cooking techniques, grinding implements, and, more recently, industrial food processing, canning, and artificial water fluoridation? Moreover, even granting that these trends result from selection, the development of trends through the past does not *prove* that they are continuing today. Recall that the proof demanded is a demonstration of a systematic change in the genetic structure of a population. Paleontological evidence clearly demonstrates the existence of systematic changes, but it fails to show conclusively that they are due to selective forces that continue to operate.

Adaptive Characteristics

Another source of evidence for continuing evolution is the existence of adaptive characteristics among contemporary groups of human beings. To illustrate, adaptive characteristics might include the following: 1) the morphological features which enable Eskimos to adapt more readily to extreme cold than other groups; 2) traits found among tropical peoples that provide for more efficient heat dissipation than found in nontropical groups; or 3) the distinctive attributes possessed by peoples living at high altitudes that physiologically compensate for the lower concentration of oxygen in the atmosphere.

One can argue, for example, that many of the differences between groups adapted to contrasting environments and those that are not are the results of selective factors. If one accepts this proposition and recognizes that the relevant environmental conditions still prevail, then it is a small logical step to conclude that the fact of adaptive characteristics is proof of the continuing action of natural selection. But should we accept the initial proposition? Perhaps we should, but if we do, we do so partly on faith, for the only basis on which we can 'accept the stand that adaptive characteristics are the result of selective factors is by presuming that we know that the differences are not due to physiological plasticity, which, as indicated in Chapter 7, is simply not justified.

In the earlier discussion, trends were regarded as systematic changes over time, and the evidence for them was, thus, paleontological. Analogously, adaptive traits may be thought of as systematic variation through space, and the evidence for them is heterographic. As the temperature gets cooler, the elevation higher, and the atmosphere more humid, there is often a systematic increase in the frequencies of the relevant adaptive characteristics. As in the case of trends, adaptive traits may in fact be due to the continuation of selective agencies, but they do not prove the existence of such agencies, since any one or all of them might be due to plasticity.

As Stanley Garn (1957) has said:

. . . it is one thing to prove either logically or experimentally that a given trait may be beneficial, and another thing to demonstrate survival value. Given a sun-lamp and a timer one can easily show that the Negro is slower to reach erythema and subsequent discomfort. Given a tank of cold water and a thermocouple it is no trick to show that Eskimo skin temperatures remain higher and that peripheral blood flow is twice that of whites (Brown, Hatcher, and Page, 1953). But to clinch the argument, selective survival must be demonstrated; the possessors must be differentially represented in the next generation.

Trends and adaptive traits, then, provide suggestive but equivocal evidence on the issue.

Inherited Traits and Disease Susceptibility

Trends and adaptive characteristics constituted the only source of evidence thirty years ago, and this makes more clear why it was that specialists were divided on the issue of man's continued susceptibility to the effects of selection. Two lines of investigation have been taken up since then, and each has added support to the stand that selection continues to affect human populations. One of these is the increasing number of demonstrations of systematic associations between inherited traits and diseases, such as those noted in Table 8–3 on page 268. What do these associations mean? An association between blood type A and stomach cancer simply means that there is a higher percentage of blood type A persons among stomach cancer patients than there is in the total population. How might this be interpreted? One obvious way to view these associations is to interpret them as direct evidence of the action of natural selection. That is to say, one might reason that if persons who are blood type A are more likely to die from stomach cancer than persons who are some other blood type, then blood type A must be selected against. Again recall, however, that while such a view may be reasonable enough, it is not the kind of evidence we have demanded; it does not of itself provide proof that a change in the genetic structure of the population is under way. For example, stomach cancer is a disease that characteristically has a late onset, and people who die from it usually have completed their reproductive periods. And since, as we have seen, selection may act only through differential reproduction, it is entirely possible that such an association may have no effect whatever on the genetic structure of the resulting generation. To prove the point that blood type A is at a selective disadavantage, one would have to show that type A parents contribute proportionately fewer type A offspring to the next generation, and this has not yet been shown, nor has the comparable demonstration been made for any of the associations. In any attempt to analyze the effects of selection among human beings today, there are two interesting problems to be resolved. First of all, one must, of course, solve the problem of whether or not selection is active. Then secondly, if it is, what factors in the environment are responsible for the action? In demonstrating associations between diseases and inherited traits, it is the second problem that is at issue, but what needs to be done is to solve the first.

Polymorphisms

The situation regarding inherited traits is, like trends and adaptive traits, strongly suggestive of the action of selection. It differs as a source of evidence in that the associations provide a better opportunity to show the action of selection, but as yet that proof is lacking. The best evidence has come from the separate but related study of genetic polymorphisms, sets of alleles with frequencies more common than idiomorphs. Traits of this kind have been known for a long time and include, for example, all of the traits of known inheritance discussed in Chapter 8.

The common logical view of selection implies that it acts largely by reducing variation; that is, in any particular environment the prevailing conditions will create, for any particular gene, a favorable situation for one allele, and thereby greatly reduce in frequency or eliminate completely its alternates. Polymorphisms seem at first to contradict this; their existence proves that two or more alleles can be and often are found together in the same population, and, moreover, they can be in very high frequencies. Now the question of interest is, how is this possible? If selection acts continually to favor one allele or one genotype, then is it not odd that polymorphisms are so common? One solution to the problem could be that all alleles presently identified as polymorphs are simply caught in the evolutionary act of becoming idiomorphs or monomorphs. These unstable systems are known as *transient polymorphisms*. If this were the case, then the existence of polymorphisms, far from offering contradictory evidence, would provide ideal illustrations of the classical view. But such is not the case; in man there are many polymophisms that show no indication whatever of being transient. On the contrary, they appear to be completely stable. These are known as *balanced polymorphisms*, and they do, at first, create some problems.

How is it that the existence of balanced polymorphisms in human populations may be used as evidence in support of the view that man is continuing to undergo evolutionary change? In fact, not all of those that are known have offered such evidence, but one in particular has—the hemoglobin polymorphism. In particular, the best-documented instance is the situation involving Hb^s, the abnormal hemoglobin allele that in homozygous form results in sickle-cell anemia.

The distribution of Hb^s reveals one of the most intriguing problems ever to come up in the study of human evolution. As indicated in Chapter 8, persons who are homozygous for the Hb^s allele fail to produce any normal hemoglobin and usually die from the resulting anemia before they reach maturity. Genetically, the condition is lethal—homozygotes leave no offspring. Under the classical evolutionary view, the normal expectation from conditions like this would be to find the allele, wherever it occurs, in very low frequencies. Yet in some African populations, the Hb^s allele reaches frequencies as high as .40. That is to say that 40 percent of all the genes responsible for producing the beta chains of hemoglobin in these populations produce an abnormal chain which in homozygotes is lethal. How is it possible for an allele with such obviously harmful effects to be present in such high frequencies?

In Chapter 3, attention was given to the means by which the genetic structure of a population may be changed by the mechanisms of evolution. Are there any means by which an allele with extremely harmful effects can be maintained at high frequencies? Indeed there is at least one way that could fit this situation—selection favoring the heterozygote. Recall that one of the unusual features of this particular form of selection was that by this means selection could act to maintain variation, or, as we might wish to say at this point, to generate and maintain a balanced polymorphism.

So much for the logical possibility. What, if any, empirical evidence exists in the case of sickle-cell anemia? In the case of Hb^s, the answer is reasonably well known: heterozygous individuals enjoy a selective advantage over homozygous normals in that the heterozygotes resist malaria more effectively than persons with completely normal hemoglobin. This relationship was first suggested by the concordance between the distribution of sickle-cell anemia and the distribution of malaria and was subsequently confirmed in an experiment by A. C. Allison (1954).

Thus, the Hb^s allele with lethal effects on homozygotes reaches and is maintained at high frequencies in malarial areas by providing heterozygotes with a survival (thus reproductive) advantage over the normal Hb^A homozygotes, thereby assuring the retention of Hb^s in high frequency. The demonstration of this relationship implied that as the likelihood of contracting malaria increased, the frequency of the Hb^s allele should likewise increase, and Frank B. Livingstone (1958) showed that this is indeed the case. The particularly elegant feature about Livingstone's article is that in it he integrates the distributions of sickle-cell anemia with the intensity of malaria by bringing to bear linguistic, archaeological, and ethnographic detail. In doing so, he illustrates how physical anthropology is able to bridge the gap between the strictly biological and strictly cultural realms of man's variation.

The confirmation of the relationship between malaria and Hb^s provides a sharp insight into the way in which man has adapted genetically to his environment and has resulted in a reevaluation of the distribution of other inherited traits in an effort to relate them to diseases and other selective agencies in their environments. Malaria, for example, appears to be at least partly responsible for the distribution of the inherited conditions thalassemia and glucose-6-phosphate dehydrogenase deficiency, although the evidence bearing on the relationships is less conclusive than in the case of Hb^s. Thalassemia is a general term for several hereditary anemias resulting from a deficiency of a particular kind of hemoglobin chain. Glucose-6-phosphate dehydrogenase (G6PD) is a red cell enzyme inherited as a sex-linked trait. The red blood cells of persons deficient in this enzyme will break open when such persons are given certain drugs (primaquine, sulfonamides) or, curiously, when they inhale the pollen from, or eat, the fava bean. In other respects, the cells of these deficient individuals are normal. Both traits are distributed over the same region as Hb^s and are rare or absent outside this area. Although the picture is as yet unclear, perhaps Hb^s, thalassemia, and G6PD may represent phenotypic interaction similar to that discussed earlier for independently segregating blood group loci.

SEGREGATION ANALYSIS

The very existence of balanced polymorphisms has been enough to convince almost all human biologists that man is still very much an object of natural selection's action. But even evidence of polymorphism is not completely conclusive. No one has yet demonstrated unequivocally that in areas where malaria is common, sickle-cell heterozygotes do in fact possess some systematic advantage with respect to reproduction over the homozygous normal individual.

The critical experiments are yet to be carried out. The design of such an experiment is comparatively simple and, as pointed out earlier, involves the acquisition of genetic data on nuclear families; that is, on both parents and the offspring they produce together. If data on a sufficiently large sample of nuclear families can be obtained, then the distribution of genotypes among the offspring can be compared with the distribution predicted by Mendel's laws, and any systematic differences between the observed and expected distributions can be noted. Is one particular mating type more fertile than any other? Do marriages, for example, where both parents are heterozygous produce one-quarter AA, one-half Aa, and one-quarter aa genotypes in the children? Or is there some systematic tendency for one genotype to be more frequent than expected? This analytical approach, known broadly as segregation analysis, has rarely been applied to human populations. N. E. Morton and his co-workers (1966) collected data on a large number of nuclear families in Brazil. The most surprising feature about the results of segregation analysis on this Brazilian data is the fact that Morton found very few differences between the observed distribution of genotypes and that expected under Mendel's laws. That is to say, for almost all of the genetic loci tested, the various mating types were, in fact, producing the expected proportions of genotypes among their children. On the one hand, this may be deceiving; natural selection may be acting too gently or too subtly to be detected by segregation analysis. On the other hand, it could very well mean what it appears to mean; the traits may be selectively neutral and thus represent instances of the equilibrium specified by the Hardy-Weinberg law. If this latter interpretation is correct, it raises once again the problem of nonadaptive traits. At one time selectively neutral, or nonadaptive, traits were taken for granted as self-evident facts of life. More recently the opposite view has been considered as self-evident: there are in reality no selectively neutral traits. Morton's data indicate that perhaps it would be best to forgo any definite decision until more information is available.

CONCLUSION

All sources of evidence considered point toward the same conclusion: human populations continue to be under the influence of natural selection. To reject this conclusion or even to remain uncommitted on the issue would be unnecessarily conservative.

The problem is, in general, resolved. However, in every particular case where the action of natural selection can be shown, there remains a secondary problem: What elements of the environment cause selection to act the way that it does? Except for sickle-cell anemia and a few other malaria-dependent polymorphisms where this secondary question was first resolved, virtually nothing is known on this question. As our knowledge improves, there are more and more reasons to believe that the significant environmental factors responsible for directing natural selection in human populations are cultural factors. In contrast to the view that culture shields man from selection, this implies that cultural elements impose unique selective requirements on man. If this is correct, then man's biological future might best be predicted by a knowledge of cultural events.

MAJOR POINTS IN CHAPTER 10

1. There is a widespread view that culture protects human beings from the effects of natural selection.
2. Until recently the sources of evidence bearing on the question were inconclusive.
3. The more recent evidence of polymorphisms, and particularly that presented by sickle-cell anemia, has convinced specialists that human populations continue to be influenced by natural selection.
4. Segregation analysis offers an effective technique for assessing the effect of selection on human polymorphisms.
5. As culture evolves, it generates its own adaptive problems.

REFERENCES AND SUGGESTIONS FOR ADDITIONAL READING

ALLISON, A. C.
    1954 Protection afforded by sickle-cell trait against subtertian malarial infection. *British Medical Journal* 1:290–294.

BIELICKI, TADEUSZ, AND Z. WELON
    1964 The operation of natural selection of human head form in an East European population. *Homo* 15:22–30.

BROWN, G. M., J. D. HATCHER, AND J. PAGE
    1953 Temperature and blood flow in the forearm of the Eskimo. *Journal of Applied Psychology* 5:410–420.

CHAMLA, MARIE-CLAUDE
    1964 L'Accroissement de la stature en France de 1880 à 1960: Comparaison avec les pays d'Europe occidentale [The increase in stature in France from 1880 to 1960: A comparison with the countries of western Europe]. *Bulletin Société Anthropologie de Paris* 6.201–278. English translation by John Robert Kane in *Yearbook of Physical Anthropology* 12:146–183.

DE BEER, GAVIN
    1958 *Embryos and ancestors.* 3d ed. London: Oxford University Press.

DOBZHANSKY, THEODOSIUS
    1960 The present evolution of man. *Scientific American* 203, September, pp. 206–217.

GARN, STANLEY M.
    1957 Race and evolution. *American Anthropologist* 59:218–224.

HOOTON, EARNEST ALBERT
    1947 *Up from the ape.* Rev. ed. New York: Macmillan.

LIVINGSTONE, FRANK B.
    1958 Anthropological implications of sickle cell gene distribution in West Africa. *American Anthropologist* 60:533–562.

MEDAWAR, P. B.
    1960 *The future of man.* London: Methuen.

MORTON, N. E., H. KRIEGER, AND M. P. MI
    1966 Natural selection on polymorphisms in northeastern Brazil. *American Journal of Human Genetics* 18:153–171.

MULLER, HERMAN J.
    1965 Means and aims in human genetic betterment. In *The control of human heredity and evolution,* ed. T. M. Sonnenborn. New York: Macmillan.

SIMPSON, GEORGE GAYLORD
    1950 Some problems of historical biology bearing on human origins. *Cold Spring Harbor Symposia on Quantitative Biology* 15:55–66.

WHITE, LESLIE A.
    1959 *The evolution of culture.* New York: McGraw-Hill.

11 Epilogue

INTRODUCTION

FROM TIME TO TIME I HAVE STATED THAT the main task of physical anthropology is to explain man's biological variation. Yet the survey we have made gives us something less; it provides us with an inventory of information, a host of facts about man's variation. Clearly we must have knowledge of the extent of human variation today and as it was in the past, but the task of explaining it remains largely in the future.

Thanks to the work of our predecessors, we have many data already at hand that will need to be supplemented and explained. No longer is it possible to justify doing anthropometric, genetic, or paleontological surveys simply because they are there to be done. Increasingly we recognize the need to confront the enormous problem that has been there all along, that of understanding, of interpreting the meaning of the data. This is the problem that will shape the future of physical anthropology.

As we focus on the problem of explanation, we may appreciate more deeply the potential of physical anthropology. Such potential is already recognized by distinguished specialists in other fields (for example, Handler, 1970, or Puck, 1971). Our understanding will advance as the data, the problems, and the perspectives of physical anthropology coalesce with those of other fields.

In what follows an attempt is made to specify a few areas which I believe will suggest some useful understandings. It is probable that the most significant advances will come as physical anthropology converges with cultural anthropology, nutrition, and endocrinology. We can discuss some possibilities for each of these scientific mergers.

PHYSICAL ANTHROPOLOGY AND CULTURAL ANTHROPOLOGY

One obvious truth which has been a part of the catechism of anthropology for decades is that physical anthropology is somehow more basic, perhaps even more scientific, than cultural anthropology. A corollary expression of this simple verity is the assumption that as we learn more about man's biology, we may expect ultimately to learn more about culture. Thus when students in anthropology (usually those interested in culture) ask why they are required to study physical anthropology, they are told by professors (usually those interested in physical) that by doing so they will appreciate more fully the biological parameters to human behavior. Many students are satisfied with this answer, perhaps because it is so familiar. It is but a sophisticated version of the same answer we are so often given to the question Why?—because it is good for you. Perhaps so, but I suspect in this case the reverse may also be correct; cultural anthropology is good for physical anthropology! Understanding of human biological variation will follow more as a consequence of physical anthropologists' knowing about culture than the reverse.

How might this be illustrated? As noted earlier, one of the main problems presented by the facts of human variation is the problem of polymorphisms. Much effort has been spent in trying to explain specific polymorphisms, usually as consequences of selection favoring heterozygous genotypes. Apart from sickle-cell anemia and a few other malaria-dependent polymorphisms, this effort has not been fruitful. Perhaps a knowledge of culture might be helpful.

We have extensive information from the study of contemporary preliterate peoples and from the archaeological record. From this information we may infer with confidence that our early ancestors lived in small, largely isolated populations, dispersed broadly over the tropics and subtropics of the Old World. As time passed, man and culture grew more efficient in their capacities to exploit the resources of nature. This improved efficiency had a number of conspicuous consequences: 1) the overall density of our species increased, 2) the number of populations increased, 3) the isolation of populations began eventually to break down as competitive contact among them grew more frequent, and 4) human populations spread into the temperate and eventually northern Arctic zones of the Old World.

Anthropologists are, of course, aware of all this and are in general agreement on the consequences. These observations are merely a simplified version of the Paleolithic. If we compared the distribution of human populations in early Paleolithic times (over 1 million years ago) with the late Paleolithic (approximately 20,000 years ago), the contrast would look something like that in Figure 11–1.

What is responsible for this change? We know one more important thing about the process: it accelerates. Cultural evolution started slowly and has been picking up speed ever since. Today the small, isolated populations our ancestors lived in are almost completely extinct. They have been replaced by villages, towns, cities, and enormous urban centers. Why? Clearly culture is evolving much faster than human beings are evolving biologically. Clearly a knowledge of culture is imperative to understand the process fully.

But our concern is with polymorphisms. How do we put the facts of man's cultural evolution to work in helping us better to understand human polymorphisms? First we need to recall some population genetics. Small populations we know are

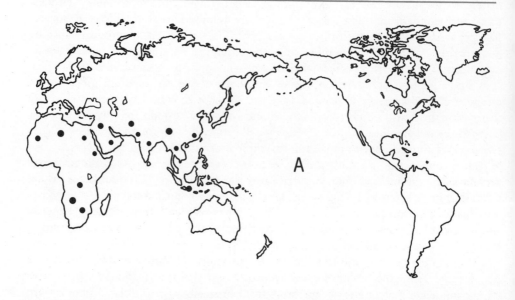

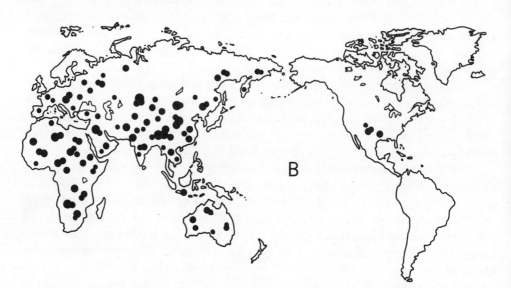

Figure 11–1. Schematic comparison of the distribution of human populations at the beginning and at the close of the Paleolithic.

Figure 11-2. Early Paleolithic. Small, largely isolated populations are readily susceptible to the randomizing effects of drift and the homogenizing effects of inbreeding.

very susceptible to the effects of genetic drift and inbreeding. Both of these are factors which serve to reduce genetic variability within populations. Ancestral human populations throughout the Paleolithic were ideal structures to respond to the genetic and evolutionary effects of drift and high levels of inbreeding. Both mechanisms lead to the fixity of alleles, but the alleles that become fixed are entirely a matter of chance. With respect to any particular genetic locus the implications are clear enough, variability *within* populations is reduced, whereas differences *between* populations are randomized. The situation for the early Paleolithic is illustrated in Figure 11–2. Homozygotes are common, but the alleles involved are randomized.

However, as culture evolved and as populations grew larger and more numerous, the isolation between populations gradually broke down. Thus by the close of the Paleolithic the situation was probably reasonably close to that illustrated in Figure 11–3. By comparing Figure 11–2 with Figure 11–3 we can begin to see the effects of cultural evolution on the distribution of human genetic variability. As isolation breaks down, populations begin to collide and coalesce, and as they do, heterozygosis reappears. In this way populations become more variable internally, and the differences between populations become less sharp.

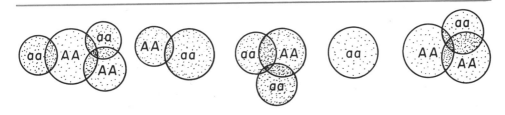

Figure 11–3. Late Paleolithic. Contact between populations became more common as the number of populations increased. Heterozygosis is restored, though homozygosis remains common.

Today there are very few isolated human populations. Most of us live within units of great size and complexity. Figure 11–4 provides a general, simplified illustration. One feature emerges clearly as we compare the illustrations—the cultural evolutionary trends set in motion during the Paleolithic are reflected in the distribution of genetic variability today.

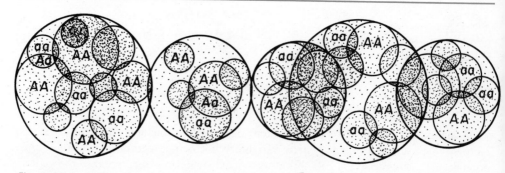

Figure 11–4. Today. Populations today are enormous in size and are complex amalgamations of subpopulations. Neighborhoods, ethnic groups, races, and religious groups, for example, tend to intermarry, but their isolation is far from complete. The result is the production of polymorphisms.

In this light, polymorphisms may be made to appear less enigmatic. Polymorphisms may be the expected results of the dramatic changes which have taken place in population size and structure.

This is a specific illustration which relates cultural evolution to polymorphisms. If the relationship is correct, it may have much broader implications. Indeed the relationship may eventually be stated in terms of a biocultural theory as follows: *As culture evolves, the biological variability within human populations increases.* If the theory is correct, it may help us greatly to understand the significance of the distribution of human biological variation. Indeed, it may help to open up a new way of seeing questions concerning such variation. The data needed to test the relationship are available in the numerous descriptive reports which have accumulated over the past several decades.

If the theory holds, it may be stated as a biocultural law. Scientists, particularly social scientists, rarely discuss laws. So I hesitate to pursue this discussion much further. Yet, on reflection, it is clear that the same processes that may have generated increasing variability within human populations have served also to reduce or minimize the differences between them. Isolation and inbreeding give rise to abrupt differences between populations. As we have noted, the variability *within* such populations may be expected to increase as these factors decline in intensity. For the very same reasons, however, the sharp differences *between* them decline. Again it may eventually be possible to formulate this second relationship in terms of a law as follows: *As culture evolves, the biological variability between human populations declines.*

These relationships have not as yet been tested. They are presented here to illustrate the direction that physical anthropology may take in its effort to explain human biological variability. Clearly, much is to be gained by considering simultaneously the interrelationships between culture and man's biology.

PHYSICAL ANTHROPOLOGY AND THE STUDY OF NUTRITION

Dietary differences cause phenotypic differences between human populations. This statement is widely accepted, though it is based almost entirely on indirect evidence. The argument leading to the conclusion may be summarized briefly as follows:

1) Within our society nutritional differences between social classes result in phenotypic differences between them.

2) Human populations often differ in the same phenotypic respects as social classes differ.

3) Therefore dietary differences are believed to be the cause of phenotypic differences between human populations.

The argument is reasonable in the sense that it extends like causes to like effects and in that it is based on clear and reasonably unambiguous evidence. In recent years accumulated evidence from other societies, much of it crude, has tended to support the conclusion that nutritional differences have enormous influence on phenotypes. From these studies it is clear, for example, that inadequate nutrition early in life can lend to such consequences as: 1) increased infant mortality (see Harrison et al., 1964, pp. 503–504), 2) learning disabilities and lowered IQ (see Cott, 1972; Winick and Rosso, 1969), 3) reduced overall body size (see Harrison et al., 1964, pp. 434–436), 4) abnormal difficulties in childbearing (see Read, 1970; Jelliffe, 1970), and 5) increased susceptibility to disease (see Scrimshaw, Taylor, and Gordon, 1968).

Is it not thus reasonable to suspect that a multitude of the differences we may note among human populations are due to diet? Earlier we discussed variations which appear clearly to reflect such environmental variables as temperature, altitude, and cultural stress. In contrast, nutritional anthropology has been largely neglected. Perhaps the neglect is the result of our ready acceptance of the view that when a people function well in their environments they must perforce be adequately fed. We readily accept this view, for example, in our own society, though there is much evidence against it. The detrimental effects of inadequate nutrition may extend far into the future. Gradually we are realizing that minimum requirements are themselves variable from person to person and place to place. Our attention thus is being drawn more forcibly to the effects of nutritional stress. For these reasons we may expect nutritional anthropology to become increasingly important in understanding man's biological variation.

ENDOCRINOLOGY AND PHYSICAL ANTHROPOLOGY

For a long time physical anthropologists have been curious about the biological bases of behavioral differences. The roots of this interest go back at least two hundred years and may be found in the writings of some of the early racial typologists. Most of them approached their work with the presumption that races behaved differently because they were biologically different. More recently a similar interest developed in studies of body typology, more commonly known as constitutional analysis. This approach was based on the assumption that an individual's body type controlled, at least in part, his behavior. Elaborate classifications of body types have been worked out, together with sets of behavioral specifications for each type (see Sheldon, 1963). Racial and body typologies are different in detail, but they are similar in that each presumes that human beings behave differently because their biological compositions are different.

While this kind of biological determinism has lost popularity among anthropologists, some geneticists, particularly behavioral geneticists, continue to pursue this course (see Spuhler, 1967). Anthropologists are more inclined to presume that human beings behave in different ways because they have been exposed to different cultural experiences. Though this appears to be a fundamental difference in outlook, most investigators reconcile it by accepting both points of view. Human behavior, they say, is the result of both influences, the product of interaction between genetic and cultural factors. You may recall that this approach was illustrated in an earlier discussion in Chapter 2.

A related area into which physical anthropologists have moved with much vigor is that of primate behavior. Here the issue is clearer because the determining effect of biology is more conspicuous and more generally agreed upon. Studies of behavior in nonhuman primates have accumulated rapidly in the last fifteen years in large measure because they were expected to provide a better understanding of the connection between biology and behavior. They have indeed taught us a great deal about both, but have so far failed to reveal much about the relationships between them.

The connection between biology and behavioral variation may result from the rapidly growing knowledge of hormones. Briefly, hormones are chemical substances secreted by the endocrine glands. In structure they are large and complex molecules; some are proteins, some are steroids, and some are complex hybrid molecules that join together protein and steroid parts. Hormones function as regulators, causing physiological processes to begin, sustaining them, and causing them to cease, in a manner similar to the action of enzymes. However, as we have seen, enzymes are made within cells and function to regulate their chemical activities. Hormones are manufactured in specialized organs and function to regulate activities *between* cells. One of the unsolved mysteries of physiology is how hormones exercise their control over cellular activity. Interest in the issue has intensified in recent years as a consequence of the remarkable discovery that hormones are also activated by nerve cell secretions, the neurohormones.

The connection between hormones and behavior has been taken for granted for decades, though the basis for the relationship has never been especially clear. Insulin levels, for example, rise and fall in response to dietary changes, surges of adrenalin as we encounter stress situations, and thyroid hormones fluctuate in response to the requirements of growth and development. The discovery of neurohormones provides an intriguing connecting link between the central nervous system and the endocrine system, a link which may lead ultimately to a better understanding of the way in which our daily experiences (as sensed and interpreted by the nervous system) can modify our internal bodily processes (as regulated by the endocrine system).

Endocrinologists and neurobiologists will find these areas fertile for research for some years to come. We can expect that the long-range effect of these advances on physical anthropology will be indirect as specialists outside of our main area of interest identify new hormones and new glands, and as their structures are outlined, their functions are assessed, and as numerous quite different kinds of problems are solved. Physical anthropology, as we have noted earlier, will grow as a result of advances in biology in general, and especially in response to new developments in neurobiology and endocrinology.

The discovery of hormone polymorphisms is a possibility that would have great significance for physical anthropology. Is it not reasonable to expect that particular hormone structures may vary and that such variations may have common frequencies in human populations? If such a discovery is made, we may inquire whether such variations are related in any systematic way to behavioral differences.

Until now much of the research effort on hormones has been stimulated by the pressing need to identify safer, more acceptable solutions to the problem of birth control. As the issue becomes less urgent, we may expect the research effort to shift. Genetics is likely to offer some appealing alternative research possibilities.

CONCLUSION

Our expectations for the future of physical anthropology are high. We have passed well beyond the stage of simply describing variation; increasingly we are demanding to know what the variations mean. This in itself is a significant change. As we come to the end of this survey, our most important conclusion may be that we are on the threshold of changes and advances that will profoundly influence our understanding of man's biological variation. It is time to begin.

REFERENCES AND SUGGESTIONS FOR ADDITIONAL READING

Cott, Allan
  1972 Megavitamins: The orthomolecular approach to behavioral disorders and learn-
         ing disabilities. *Academic Therapy* 7:245–258.
Handler, Philip
  1970 *Biology and the future of man.* New York: Oxford.
Harrison, G. A., J. S. Weiner, J. M. Tanner, and N. A. Barnicot
  1964 *Human biology.* New York: Oxford.
Jelliffe, Derek B.
  1970 Evaluation of nutrition-related village-improvement programmes. In *Malnu-
         trition is a problem of ecology,* ed. P. György and O. L. Kline. New York:
         S. Karger.
Puck, Theodore T.
  1971 *What can the new biology offer man?* Paper broadcast on Voice of America.
         In press.
Read, Merrill S.
  1970 Nutrition and ecology: Crossroads for research. In *Malnutrition is a problem
         of ecology,* ed. P. György and O. L. Kline. New York: S. Karger.
Scrimshaw, Nevin S., Carl E. Taylor, and John E. Gordon
  1968 *Interactions of nutrition and infection.* Monograph Series, 57. Geneva: World
         Health Organization.
Sheldon, William H.
  1963 *The varieties of human physique: An introduction to constitutional psychology.*
         New York: Hafner.
Spuhler, James N.
  1967 *Genetic diversity and human behavior.* Chicago: Aldine.
Winick, Myron, and Pedro Rosso
  1969 The effect of severe early malnutrition on cellular growth of the human brain.
         Pediatric Research 3:181–184.

GLOSSARY

Adaptability: Among evolving units (populations, species), the capacity to make successful adjustments to environmental changes.

Adaptation: The adjustment made by an evolving unit (population, species) to a particular set of environmental requirements.

Aegyptopithecus: A late Oligocene primate form from the Fayum deposits in Egypt. The fossil evidence consists of five lower jaws and an almost complete skull.

Agglutination: The process of forming clumps of red blood cells. A consequence of antigen-antibody incompatibility.

Agnatha: A class of vertebrates to which the primitive jawless fishes belong.

Alcaptonuria: A hereditary disease of human beings caused by the absence or malfunction of an enzyme. The urine of affected individuals turns black on exposure to air.

Allele: An alternate form of a gene. For example, A^1 and A^2 designate alleles of gene A.

Allen's rule: Notes that in the colder regions of a mammalian species' range, the parts of the body most susceptible to frostbite tend to be shorter than they are in members of the same species situated in warmer areas.

Alpha chain: A particular sequence of amino acids linked together by peptide bonds and forming one of two kinds of polypeptide chains found as part of hemoglobin. The other kind of chain is called the beta chain. In any molecule of hemoglobin the alpha and beta chains occur in pairs.

Amphibia: A class of vertebrates transitional in their adaptation. Characteristically Amphibia occur both on land and in water, but ultimately depend on water as a medium for laying their eggs.

Analogies: Similarities among organisms that result from similar functions. Analogies imply similar adaptations, but not close biological relationship.

Angiosperms: The flowering plants.

Animalia: The kingdom of living organisms to which man belongs.

Antibody: A protein substance formed in the plasma as a defense mechanism against attack by a foreign protein.

Antigen: Protein substance that stimulates the production of antibodies.

Apidium: An early Oligocene primate from the Fayum deposits in Egypt. See *Parapithecus.*

Arboreal: Adapted to living in trees.

Archaeology: A subdivision of cultural anthropology which investigates the forms of cultural variability along the dimension of time.

Archaeozoic: The first era of paleontological time. Begins with the origin of life (about three billion years ago) and ends rather vaguely with the appearance of many-celled organisms.

Australopithecus africanus: The smaller and apparently earlier variety of the *Australopithecus* genus. Possibly representative of the ancestor of *Homo erectus.*

Australopithecus robustus: The larger, more recent variety of the *Australopithecus* genus. Status in man's evolution is in dispute. Some authorities maintain that *Australopithecus robustus* became extinct, others that he is transitional between *Australopithecus africanus* and *Homo erectus.*

Aves: The class of vertebrates to which birds belong.

Bergmann's rule: States that among mammals, the larger animals within a species tend to be found in the colder regions of the species' range.

Beta chain: See **Alpha chain.**

Biochemical genetics: A subdivision of genetics that deals with the influence of heredity on metabolism.

Biogenesis: In accounting for the origin of life, the view that maintains that life on earth is the product of preexisting life.

Blade tools: One of five basic kinds of stone implements from the Paleolithic. Blade tools are usually well-made flake implements, usually elongated with both edges sharpened. Blade tools are characteristic of the Upper Paleolithic.

Brachiation: A form of locomotion. The ability to get from one location to another by means of swinging by the forelimbs.

Brontosaurus: A herbivorous dinosaur form which lived during the Mesozoic and grew to lengths up to eighty feet and developed bulks weighing forty tons.

Cambrian: The first period of the Paleozoic era, beginning approximately one-half billion years ago.

Carbon 14 (C^{14}) dating technique: A method used in estimating the age of a fossil. The proportion of C^{14} to C^{12} begins to decline at a known rate at the time an organism dies, and thus a measure of the proportion is an indication of the amount of time that has elapsed.

Carboniferous: A period of the Paleozoic that began approximately 280 million years ago. Divided by some geochronologists into two periods: the Mississippian and the Pennsylvanian.

Catarrhinae: A suborder of the order Primates. Includes the Old World monkeys, apes, and man.

Ceboidea: Taxonomic designation for the only superfamily in the Platyrrhinae suborder of the Primates order. It consists of two families, Callithricidae and Cebidae.

Cenozoic: The geological era in which we are now living. It began approximately 75 million years ago.

Cephalic index: A numerical expression of head form:

$$\text{Cephalic index} = \frac{\text{head breadth}}{\text{head length}} \times 100.$$

Cercopithecoidea: One of two superfamilies of the suborder Catarrhinae. It consists of the Old World monkeys.

Chelles-Acheul tradition: An Old World archaeological sequence of paleolithic core-tool implements. The distinctive feature of sites included in the sequence is the presence of hand axes.

Chondrichthyes: A class of vertebrates to which the sharks and their relatives belong.

Chopper-chopping tools: One of five basic kinds of stone implements from the Paleolithic. Chopper-chopping tools are rather crudely made and have been found in eastern Asia.

Chordata: A phylum of the animal kingdom that includes a diverse group of forms, all of which have at some time during their life cycle a notochord, gill slits, and a dorsal tubular nerve cord.

Choukoutienian industry: The chopper-chopping tool assemblage found in association with the Chinese *Homo erectus.*

Chromosome: The structure in the cell nucleus which contains a discrete set of genes arranged in linear order.

Clactonian-Levalloisian tradition: An Old World archaeological sequence of Paleolithic flake tools.

Class: A major taxonomic category ranking above the order and below the phylum.

Clinal classification: A classification of the varieties of a heterographic trait based on systematic variation of the trait geographically.

Clines: Systematic changes in the distribution of a trait. The word is also used to designate the zones in which similar or identical forms or frequencies occur.

Core tools: One of five basic kinds of stone implements from the Paleolithic. Core tools have been found over a broad area of the Old World. They are large implements, also known as hand axes, made by striking pieces from a rock until it has the desired shape.

Cretaceous: The most recent period of the Mesozoic era, beginning approximately 145 million years ago.

Crossover: A process which separates linked genetic loci by the exchange of segments between homologous chromosomes.

Cross-sectional sampling: A technique used in studies of growth involving the selection of several persons at each of several age groups, therefore drawing inferences about growth regularities.

Culture: The primary means by which man adapts to requirements of the environment.

Deoxyribonucleic acid (DNA): The hereditary material of genes; a doubly coiled helix consisting of a chain of nucleotide pairs.

Devonian: The fourth period of the Paleozoic era, beginning approximately 335 million years ago.

Diploid number: One complete set of pairs of chromosomes. In man the diploid number is 46 chromosomes.

Down's syndrome: A genetic disease associated with the occurrence of an extra chromosome. Also called mongolism.

Dryopithecus: Genus of Miocene apes known from a large number of fossils found throughout the Old World.

Empiricism: The philosophical view that correct knowledge about nature can be obtained only through correct reasoning and by testing the results of reasoning against experience.

Eocene: The second epoch of the Tertiary period, beginning approximately 60 million years ago and lasting approximately 20 million years. In the primates there is considerable evidence of the proliferation and diversification of the prosimians during this epoch.

Epicanthic fold: A skin fold on the eyelid that, when the eye is open, comes down over and runs on a line with the edge of the upper eyelid.

Eutheria: The subgrouping of mammals to which man belongs; Eutherian mammals are distinguished by the fact that mothers carry their young within the uterus until an advanced state of development is reached.

Family: A taxonomic category ranking above genus and below order.

Fauresmith: Stone tool assemblage from South Africa consisting of small hand axes and flake implements. Associated with the tropical variant of Neanderthal.

Flake tools: One of five basic kinds of stone implements from the Paleolithic. Flake tools are small stone implements made by striking flakes off a larger stone (core). Techniques of manufacture vary from a crude trial-and-error procedure to the careful and deliberate shaping of a flake on the core and its removal in a single blow.

Fluorine dating technique: A method used to assess the relative ages of two or more fossils from the same deposits which involves the measurement of the amounts of fluorine they contain.

Formal genetics: A subdivision of genetics that deals with determining the precise modes of inheritance of traits.

Frequency: The number of times an event occurs out of the total number of occasions it could have occurred. Can be expressed as a fraction (e.g., 50/100), a proportion (.50), or a percentage (50 percent).

Gene: The physical structure in the cell nucleus which transmits hereditary potential from one generation to the next.

Genetic code: The messenger RNA triplet sequences that specify particular amino acid units in the synthesis of a polypeptide chain.

Genetic drift: Change in the genetic structure of a population caused by chance factors. Also known as the Sewall Wright effect.

Genetic linkage: Genetic loci situated on the same chromosome. Linked loci are transmitted together as a unit.

Genotype: For any individual, the complete set of allelic pairs he inherits from his parents. For any locus, the particular pair of alleles that has been inherited.

Genus: A taxonomic category ranking above species and below family.

Gloger's rule: Darkly pigmented varieties within a species are found in the warmer, more humid parts of the species' range.

Günz: The earliest of four glacial periods in Europe occurring in the Pleistocene.

Haploid number: One complete set of chromosomes; as distinct from one complete set of pairs (diploid number). In man, the haploid number of chromosomes is 23.

Haptoglobin: A protein found in serum that is believed to combine with hemoglobin and prevent its passage through the kidneys.

Hardy–Weinberg law of genetic equilibrium: Gene and genotype frequencies will reach and remain at a stable equilibrium after one generation of random mating in a large population that is not being affected by the mechanisms of evolution.

Haversian canals: The longitudinal channels in the matrix of bone through which pass blood vessels and nerves.

Hemoglobin: A protein normally present within red blood cells which carries oxygen to the cells of the body and carries away carbon dioxide.

Heterography: The description and investigation of biological variation among living populations.

Heterozygous: Possessing, in the genotype, two different allelic forms of a gene.

Hominoidea: One of two superfamilies of the suborder Catarrhinae. It consists of three families—Hylobatidae, Pongidae, and Hominidae—composed of the apes and man.

Homo erectus: The genus and species designation used to identify the Middle Pleistocene hominids that appear to precede Neanderthal man and to follow the australopithecines.

Homologies: Detailed structural similarities built upon a basic morphological pattern and which therefore indicate close relationship among the forms that share them.

Homo sapiens: The genus and species designating modern man.

Homozygous: Possessing in the genotype the same allelic forms of a gene.

Idiomorph: A rare allele, i.e., one whose frequency is less than 2 percent.

Interphase: A stage in the life cycle of a cell that begins when the cell is formed and lasts until it begins to divide. This has been called the "resting phase," but it is becoming clearer that considerable activity is going on during interphase.

Ischial callosities: Distinctive calloused areas on the buttocks of Old World primates. May be an adaptation to sleeping sitting up in trees.

Jurassic: The second period of the Mesozoic era. The Jurassic began approximately 170 million years ago.

Karyotype: A classification of chromosome pairs according to number and form.

Kingdom: A taxonomic category; the primary subdivision of living forms.

Klinefelter's syndrome: In males, the assemblage of moderately developed female traits together with sterility. The syndrome is associated with an abnormal karyotype containing two X chromosomes together with one Y.

Lamellae: In bone, the concentric deposits of minerals, particularly calcium and phosphorus.

Lemuroidea: One of the four superfamilies of the suborder Prosimii of the order Primates; consists of three families: the Lemuridae, Indridae, and Daubentonidae.

Locus: The position a gene occupies on a chromosome.

Longitudinal sampling: In growth studies, the ascertainment of information on the same individuals at intervals throughout their lifetime.

Lorisoidea: One of four superfamilies of the suborder Prosimii; consists of two families, the Lorisidae and Galagidae.

Lumpers: One of two categories (see also **Splitters**) into which taxonomists may themselves be classified. This group tends to regard differences as less important and thus lumps together the forms displaying these differences.

Mammalia: The class of vertebrates which includes man.

Meiosis: The cellular process that produces sex cells, i.e., cells with the haploid number of chromosomes.

Meiotic drive: The production by heterozygotes of unequal proportions of homologous chromosomes. Also known as prezygotic selection.

Mendel's first law of inheritance: Specifies that whereas an individual has a pair of alleles determining his genotype for all loci, he transmits only one member of each pair to his offspring. Also known as the law of genetic segregation.

Mendel's second law of inheritance: Specifies that genetic loci assort independently in the process of inheritance. Also known as the law of independent assortment.

Mesopithecus: Fossil primate form represented by several remains from the Miocene and Pliocene of Europe and East Africa that may be an ancestral stage in the evolution of the Colobinae.

Mesozoic: A geological era also called the Age of Reptiles. It began approximately 200 million years ago and ended approximately 75 million years ago.

Messenger RNA (ribonucleic acid): A nucleic acid that may be found in both the nucleus and the cytoplasm. It is made by the DNA and plays a fundamental part in protein synthesis.

Metatheria: A subgrouping of mammals distinguished by the fact that the females bear their young in an immature condition and provide for their continued development in pouches. Also called pouched mammals.

Mindel: The second of the four Alpine glaciations during the Pleistocene.

Miocene: The fourth epoch of the Tertiary period. The Miocene began approximately 28 million years ago and lasted for approximately 16 million years. During this epoch it appears that the hominoids become differentiated into pongids and hominids.

Mississippian: See **Carboniferous.**

Mitosis: The process that produces body cells, i.e., cells with the diploid number of chromosomes.

Molecular genetics: A subdivision of genetics that deals with the structure of the materials of inheritance.

Monogenesis: The view that all the races of man share a single origin.

Monomorph: Any allele with a frequency higher than 99.9 percent.

Mousterian industry: A Middle Paleolithic assemblage of archaeological materials including scrapers, flake tools, and, in some instances, hand axes. The Mousterian is commonly found in association with the temperate Neanderthals.

Mutation: A change in the structure of a gene.

Nasal index: A numerical expression of nose form:

$$\text{Nasal index} = \frac{\text{nasal breadth}}{\text{nasal length}} \times 100.$$

Natural selection: The mechanism of evolution proposed and documented by Darwin which implies that the environment imposes requirements on a species which can be met effectively by only some members of the species, which thus are the ones who survive and produce the subsequent generation.

Neanderthal man: A highly varied, late Pleistocene, Old World hominid that may be in modern man's ancestry.

Neurospora: An organism responsible for some types of bread mold and used for some of the basic investigations in biochemical genetics.

New World monkeys: The Platyrrhinae.

Nonrandom mating: Any departure from random mating in a population. May be a tendency for likes to mate (positive assortative mating), for likes to avoid one another as mates (negative assortative mating), or a tendency for biological relatives to mate (inbreeding).

Nonsecretor: One who lacks the ABO substances in water-soluble form in his body fluids. The nonsecretor trait is homozygous recessive.

Nontaster: An individual who is unable to taste certain substances, such as phenylthiocarbamide (PTC), which to others (tasters) has a vividly bitter taste. The nontaster is homozygous (recessive) for the locus determining this trait.

Notochord: An elastic tubular structure situated along the dorsal surface. It is present at some time during the life cycle of all members of the phylum Chordata.

Nucleotide: The basic molecular unit of nucleic acids; it consists of a sugar molecule, a phosphate group, and a base of purine or pyrimidine.

Occipital crest: A ridge of bone running transversely across the lower part of the back of the skull. It serves as an area of muscle attachment for many of the muscles that move the neck.

Oldowan industry: The oldest known assemblage of Paleolithic implements. The Oldowan is a pebble-tool assemblage from Africa.

Olduvai Gorge: Location in Tanzania, East Africa, which has produced an extraordinary amount of paleontological and archaeological evidence bearing on man's origin and evolution.

Old World monkeys: A designation commonly used in place of Cercopithecoidea, the proper taxonomic term.

Oligocene: The third epoch of the Tertiary period. The Oligocene began approximately 40 million years ago and lasted for approximately 12 million years. During this epoch the higher primates (monkeys and apes) make their first appearance in the paleontological record of the Old World.

Order: A taxonomic category ranking above family and below class.

Ordovician: The second period of the Paleozoic era, estimated to have begun approximately 435 million years ago.

Osteichthyes: One of the classes of vertebrates—the fishes with bony skeletons.

Osteocytes: Cells imbedded in the matrix of bone.

Paleocene: The earliest epoch of the Tertiary period. Probably the epoch in which the primates first became clearly distinct as an order of mammals. It began approximately 75 million years ago and lasted approximately 15 million years.

Paleontology: A subdivision of biology that concerns itself with the ancestral forms of modern organisms. Its primary source of data is fossils.

Paleozoic: The geological era lasting from approximately 520 million years ago to about 200 million years ago, in which may be found the first abundant fossil record of the evolution of life.

Pangenesis: A defunct theory proposed by Darwin to accommodate some logical implications of the theory of the inheritance of acquired characteristics. Pangenesis postulates the presence in all body cells of gemmules, which are modified by the way of life an organism leads, and which can then alter the individual's hereditary potential.

Pantotheria: Jurassic reptilelike mammals which, by the close of the Mesozoic, gave rise to the marsupial and placental mammals.

Parapithecus: An early Oligocene primate from the Fayum deposits in Egypt. The evidence consists mostly of a fragmentary jaw, and its significance has been in dispute for some time. The most common interpretation regards

Parapithecus (together with *Apidium*) as the earliest known Old World monkey.

Pebble tools: One of five basic kinds of stone implements from the Paleolithic. Pebble tools are the earliest Paleolithic implements and were made by the simple process of striking two rocks together until a sharp edge was obtained.

Pennsylvanian: See **Carboniferous.**

Permian: The final period of the Paleozoic era; it began approximately 225 million years ago.

Phenotype: In reference to an individual, the sum total of the effects of interaction between that individual's genotype and the environment. Thus an individual's phenotype is what we call vaguely his appearance and includes his morphology and behavior.

Phenylketonuria (PKU): An inherited disease that results in mental deficiencies. It is the result of the absence of a single enzyme.

Photosynthesis: The process by which green plants utilize the sun's energy for their own life processes.

Phylum: A taxonomic category that serves as the major subdivision of the kingdom category; thus it ranks above the class and below the kingdom.

Physiological plasticity: The ability of organisms to adapt during their lifetimes to changing environmental conditions.

Piltdown: The name of a peculiar assemblage of supposedly ape and modern man skull remains from England that was shown to be a deliberate fraud.

Placodermi: One of eight classes of the vertebrates—the archaic jawed fishes.

Platyrrhinae: A suborder of the primates consisting entirely of New World monkeys.

Pleistocene: The most recent epoch of the Cenozoic era. The Pleistocene began over 2 million years ago and contains within it the paleontological and archaeological record of man's evolution.

Plesiadapis: The only primate fossil known from both the New and the Old World. A Paleocene form transitional in its morphology between insectivore and primate characteristics.

Pliocene: The fifth epoch of the Tertiary period, beginning approximately 12 million years ago and lasting approximately 10 million years.

Polygenesis: The view that maintained that the races of man had separate origins.

Polymorphism: A trait controlled by two or more common alleles.

Populational classification: A system used by physical anthropologists and human geneticists which is designed to divide human groups into breeding isolates.

Population genetics: A subdivision of genetics that deals with the determination of the genetic structure of natural populations and the factors that maintain or alter that structure.

Potassium-argon (K-A) dating technique: A rate-quantity dating technique. K^{40} disintegrates to A^{40} at a known rate. In volcanic rock the Argon is trapped as it is formed; thus by measuring the ratio of K^{40} to A^{40} one may estimate the age of the volcanic rock.

Primates: An order of the class Mammalia; the order to which man, the apes, the monkeys, and the prosimians belong.

Proconsul: An African Miocene primate group known from several fragmentary fossil remains displaying considerable variability. It is perhaps more accurate to consider *Proconsul* as the African variety of *Dryopithecus*.

Propliopithecus: Generic name given to a lower jaw and some teeth from Oligocene deposits in Egypt. There is disagreement over the taxonomic status of this form within the order Primates.

Prosimii: A suborder of the order Primates. Members of this suborder were the first of the primates to appear.

Proterozoic: The geological era between the Archaeozoic and the Paleozoic. The paleontological record from the Proterozoic is sparse, but the presence of highly developed life forms within it is clearly indicated from the Ediacara Hills in Australia.

Prototheria: A subgrouping within the class Mammalia. These mammals lay eggs, but, like other mammals, feed their newborn by means of mammary glands.

Quaternary: The later period of the Cenozoic era, beginning approximately 2 million years ago.

Ramapithecus: The earliest known hominid. The fossil material consists of fragmentary fossil jaws and teeth that have been dated at from late Miocene to early Pliocene. *Ramapithecus* remains are known from India and Africa.

Random mating: System of mating within a population wherein any individual has an equal probability of mating with any other individual in the population.

Rationalism: The view that truth about nature can be reached by means of correct reasoning alone.

Rensch's rule: Specifies that, in mammals, the members of a species adapted to hot climatic conditions have localized deposits of fat.

Replication: The process of copying or duplicating; the process by which DNA copies itself.

Reproductive isolation: A situation in which one group of organisms cannot or does not interbreed with another group.

Reptilia: A class of vertebrates. The reptiles of modern and ancient times.

Rh factor: A red blood cell antigen that, when it is present in an unborn child, can stimulate the production of antibodies to itself in the plasma of mothers that lack it, with serious consequences to the child.

Ribonucleic acid (RNA): A nucleic acid similar in structure to DNA, but differing from DNA in three basic ways: RNA 1) contains a distinctive sugar; 2) lacks the base thymine and has uracil, which DNA lacks; and 3) consists of a polynucleotide chain—not a pair of chains, as in DNA. RNA functions in the cell to make proteins.

Riss: The third of four Alpine glaciations during the Pleistocene.

Sagittal crest: A bony ridge running from front to back along the top of the skull. It serves as an area for the attachment of the muscles that move the jaw.

Sangoan: An archaeological assemblage from forested regions of central Africa consisting of picks, cleavers, and crude hand axes.

Secretor: One who has ABO antigens in water-soluble form in his body fluids. Whether or not a person is a secretor is genetically determined.

Sewall Wright effect: See **Genetic drift.**

Sex chromatin body: A mass of chromatin material that may be found in the nuclei of female mammalian cells. The belief is common that this body is an inactive X chromosome.

Sex chromosomes: The pair of chromosomes genetically differentiating males and females. In man and many other animals the female has two X chromosomes; the male has one X and one Y chromosome.

Shovel-shaped incisors: Our front teeth are called incisors. In some instances these fold backward at the sides and thereby increase the size of the chewing surface without increasing the width of the tooth. Such teeth are called shovel-shaped incisors.

Sickle-cell anemia: A hereditary disease caused by an abnormality in the sequence of amino acids in the beta chain of hemoglobin. Individuals unable to make normal beta chains (homozygotes for the trait) have grossly distorted red blood cells and commonly die before maturity.

Silurian: The third period of the Paleozoic era, beginning approximately 375 million years ago.

Soluble or transfer RNA (sRNA or tRNA): Short, twisted strands of RNA present in the cytoplasm that activate and position amino acids in the process of protein synthesis.

Species: A taxonomic category ranking below the genus and commonly identified (for bisexually reproducing organisms) as the total group of organisms capable of interbreeding and producing fertile offspring.

Splitters: One of two categories (see also **Lumpers**) into which taxonomists may themselves be classified. Splitters tend to regard small differences as of greater taxonomic significance and thus split similar forms into distinct taxonomic categories.

Spontaneous generation: The view that life arose from nonliving matter.

Steatopygia: A trait characterized by an extraordinary accumulation of fat on the buttocks.

Swanscombe: The name given to three skull bones from Mindel-Riss interglacial times. The bones are like those of modern man and suggest that modern man's antiquity is very great.

Tarsioidea: One of the four superfamilies of the suborder Prosimii, represented today by only one living family and genus, the tarsiers.

Taster: An individual able to taste certain substances such as phenylthiocarbamide (PTC) which others (see **Nontaster**) are unable to taste. The trait is inherited, and the allele determining taster status is dominant to that determining nontaster; thus the taster may be homozygous or heterozygous.

Tertiary: The earlier period of the Cenozoic era, beginning approximately 75 million years ago.

Thecodonts: Small, terrestrial reptiles of Triassic times.

Thompson's rule: Refers to nose breadth and states that in cold climates, noses tend to be narrow, whereas in hot climates they tend to be broad.

Triassic: The earliest period of the Mesozoic era. It began approximately 200 million years ago.

Trilobite: A widely diverse group of invertebrates common throughout the fossil record of the Paleozoic.

Tupaioidea: One of four superfamilies of the suborder Prosimii. The tupaiids display an assemblage of primate and insectivore traits, and, indeed, some taxonomists place them in the order Insectivora.

Typological classification: A classification of variability that divides human beings into groups on the basis of the regular occurrence together of distinctive heterographic traits.

Tyrannosaurus: Enormous carnivorous Mesozoic reptile. This dinosaur was bipedal and is believed to be a descendant of the early Mesozoic thecodonts.

Uniformitarianism: The belief that geological phenomena of the past are the result of processes that are observable today.

Villafranchian: The Old World mammalian faunal assemblage used in some areas as a means of identifying the beginning of the Pleistocene.

Würm: The most recent of the four Pleistocene Alpine glaciations.

Zinjanthropus: Name assigned by L. S. B. Leakey to a skull discovered in 1958 in East Africa. It has subsequently been recognized as a member of the already established genus *Australopithecus*.

INDEX